# THE ILLUSTRATED HISTORY OF
# CATHOLICISM
## & THE CATHOLIC SAINTS

# THE ILLUSTRATED HISTORY OF
# CATHOLICISM
# & THE CATHOLIC SAINTS

A COMPREHENSIVE ACCOUNT OF THE HISTORY, PHILOSOPHY AND PRACTICE
OF CATHOLIC CHRISTIANITY AND A GUIDE TO THE MOST SIGNIFICANT SAINTS

CONSULTANT: REVEREND RONALD CREIGHTON-JOBE • TESSA PAUL

MARY FRANCES BUDZIK • MICHAEL KERRIGAN • CHARLES PHILLIPS

LORENZ BOOKS

This edition is published by Lorenz Books,
an imprint of Anness Publishing Ltd,
Blaby Road, Wigston, Leicestershire LE18 4SE

Email: info@anness.com

Web: www.lorenzbooks.com; www.annesspublishing.com

Anness Publishing has a new picture agency outlet for images for
publishing, promotions or advertising. Please visit our website

Publisher: Joanna Lorenz
Editorial Director: Helen Sudell
Editor: Elizabeth Young
Production Controller: Wendy Lawson

Produced for Anness Publishing by Toucan Books:
Managing Director: Ellen Dupont
Editor: Theresa Bebbington
Project Manager: Hannah Bowen
Designer: Elizabeth Healey
Picture Researcher: Marian Pullen
Proofreader: Marion Dent
Cartography by Cosmographics, UK

Previously published in two separate volumes, *The Illustrated Encyclopedia
of Catholicism* and *The Illustrated World Encyclopedia of Saints*

*Front cover shows, clockwise from left:* St. John the Baptist by Leonardo da
Vinci; lighting prayer candles; Pope Benedict XVI; bible and rosary;
Detail of Saint Joseph of Arimathea from Pieta by Raphael; Virgin and
Child by Sassoferrato; The Last Supper by Leonardo da Vinci; Detail of
Saint Bernardino and Saint Catherine of Siena by Carlo Crivelli.
*Endpaper shows:* St Benedict of Nursia prays with his monks, fresco by
Giovanni-Antonio Bazzi.

# CONTENTS

# INTRODUCTION

With its spiritual, cultural and historical heritage, spanning more than 2000 years, the Catholic religion has a great influence across the globe and has a special place in the hearts and minds of millions. Saints are an integral part of Catholicism. They are recognized all over world, and the Catholic church is responsible for investigating and confirming their status.

This book provides a detailed historical insight into the world of Catholicism and sainthood, featuring a visual directory of more than 500 saints. It discusses the doctrine and practices, unravels the myths, looks at how places became holy sites, the significance of relics and the purpose of pilgrimage.

*Below* This demographic map illustrates the percentage of the Roman Catholic population around the world today.

*Above* Moses and Elijah look on as St Apollinare tends his flock. Ravenna's first bishop was buried in the 6th-century basilica that contains this painting.

Catholicism is the oldest and the largest of the Christian churches, and has become one of the world's largest religions. More than half of the world's Christians take their leadership from the pope in Rome. The number of Catholics in the world stands at around 1.16 billion people – 17.4 per cent (about one-sixth) of the planet's population. (Islam, if all its branches are taken together, just tops that total; none of the other creeds comes close.) One of the world's biggest and most formidably organized institutions, the Catholic Church can call on around 136,000 priests and 750,000 nuns, along with a multitude of loyal lay supporters. It is too important a force to be ignored, and is capable of exerting an influence on public policy and international affairs. Its religious teachings have shaped many millions of lives.

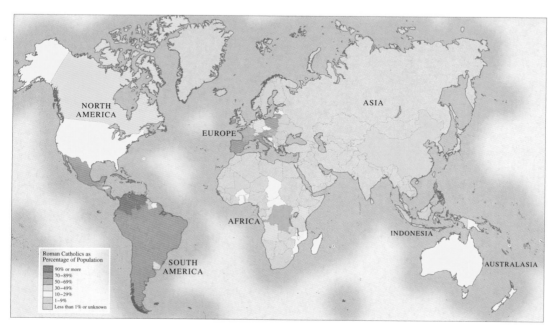

Roman Catholics as Percentage of Population
- 90% or more
- 70–89%
- 50–69%
- 30–49%
- 10–29%
- 1–9%
- Less than 1% or unknown

NORTH AMERICA

ASIA

EUROPE

AFRICA

INDONESIA

SOUTH AMERICA

AUSTRALASIA

## HEAVEN AND EARTH

The Catholic Church would be nothing if it were only an earthly institution – "My kingship is not of this world," its founder Jesus stated (John 18: 36). Looking beyond this life to the hereafter, the Church views humankind's existence in an eternal perspective: the living and departed come together in the Communion of Saints. As this book sets out to demonstrate, Catholicism offers its followers an account of God's Creation, of life and death – along with the possibility of salvation for devout Catholics, with everlasting joy in heaven.

## AN EVENTFUL HISTORY

Divided into five chapters, the first chapter of this book, Catholic History, shows how eventful and exciting the story of the Church has been – and sometimes how complex, even contradictory. Catholicism's truths might be eternal, yet they took many centuries to articulate. Although Catholicism's inspirations might be divine, many of its practitioners have been all too human.

At key turning points in its history, the Church was able to grow in strength even through suffering and struggle; however, at other moments, it persecuted those who stood against it. An inspiration to creativity, Catholicism has played a central role in the Western artistic tradition, if at times it has arguably been too involved in acquiring these splendours. The papacy has provided vital leadership, yet an absolute authority it was endowed with by Christ himself has not always been wielded as conscientiously as it should have been.

*Right* St Peter's Basilica, in the Vatican within Rome, Italy, is both the historic centre of an ancient Catholic Church and at the heart of the modern world. Catholicism continues to flourish amid changing times.

## DIVINE DOCTRINES

The second chapter of the book, Catholic Doctrine, looks at the various teachings that constitute the Catholic faith. It considers beliefs about the eternal truths of existence as well as those that goven the everyday dilemmas of social and personal morality. From the Trinity and transubstantiation to the status of the Scriptures and the significance of the saints, the complete range of the Church's teachings are examined here. Among the questions explored are: What is sin? What does Christ's redemption mean? How are we to understand the concepts of salvation and damnation?

## LIVING THE FAITH

The third chapter of the book, Practising Catholicism, shows how these doctrines find expression in the everyday life of the Church: its institutions, its rituals and its celebrations and festivities. The structures of the Church are also examined, from the Vatican down to parish level, and the functions of its different offices are explained. The varieties of religious life are looked at: the contemplative, the charitable and the missionary vocations; the duties performed by the different sorts of priests and nuns; and the vows such men and women take, along with the reasoning behind them.

The seven sacraments – baptism, confirmation, holy communion, confession, marriage, holy orders and the annointing of the sick – are at the heart and soul of the Catholic church. Each is described in detail, with its rituals and what they mean. These seven sacraments mark out the landmark moments in the life of the believer, from birth to death: the development of reason, full communion with God and, of course, the partnership of marriage – which is a sacred state in the Catholic scheme. The Church has attracted both great admiration and much controversy for its stance on a number of issues of sexual morality and medical ethics.

*Right* St Paraskeva
(Byzantine icon,
15th century).

*Centre* Archangel
Michael, the divine
messenger of God
(Demetrius
Matthiosi, 20th
century).

*Left* St Menas,
a Roman soldier
martyred in
Egypt c. AD 300.
Miracles were
attributed to him
and his grave is
believed to have
curative powers
(Palestinian icon,
17th century).

## THE IMPORTANCE OF SAINTS

During the long and complex history of Christianity, sainthood has been invested with a great many different meanings. There are, however, many characteristics of sainthood that are agreed upon. Whether a saint devotes their life to God, or demonstrates holiness in secular life, they must be a person of great faith and religious devotion. A saint can be born in grace, or be a reformed character, but whatever path their life has traced, they must show certain characteristics that make them "heroic", such as piety, fortitude, humility and courage.

Saints, having been awarded a privileged place in heaven, are thought to be close to God and are able to function as intermediaries between the human and the divine. This combines with the human achievements of the saints to make them exemplars of virtue that the faithful can turn to in times of need.

The importance of saints for people, professions and countries is seen in the adoption of "patron" saints by these groups. Aspects of sainthood are also examined, such as miracles, martyrdom and relics, and describes the diverse ways in which the qualities of sainthood have changed and manifested over time.

The response of believers to the company of saints is described and the official attitudes of both the Roman Catholic and the Orthodox Churches are examined. However, the focus here is on Roman Catholic saints and feast days, because the complex subject of Orthodox saints deserves its own study.

Modern readers may dismiss the extravagant legends of the early saints as untrue, but the number of new saints that have been created may also surprise those outside the Roman Catholic Church. Even the sceptical must applaud the shining example of devotion and sacrifice made by the recently canonized.

The range of people who have achieved sainthood is fascinating, for this special company does not recognize wealth, social status or professional achievement, and thus the canon includes peasants, merchants and kings.

*Above* Mosaic of martyrs in the Basilica Sant'Appolinare Nuovo, Ravenna, Italy (5th and 6th centuries).

## WHAT MAKES A SAINT?

The fourth chapter of the book, Sainthood, explores the importance of saints in the Roman Catholic Church and charts the progression of sainthood from the early Church to modern times. This chapter looks at what it means to be a saint, what individuals and groups have achieved or endured to be conferred this title and honour, and what characteristics single out an individual as deserving of sainthood. This section will clearly set out answers to all of these questions, and present accurate explanations about the mysterious company of saints while largely avoiding the distraction of complex theological debates.

## DIRECTORY OF SAINTS

The final section tells the story of sainthood through the biographies of selected saints. The saints are listed in chronological order, from the Apostles and early Christian martyrs through to 20th-century saints. This is interspersed with essays on special groups who have been accorded saintly status, such as the Holy Family, Patron Saints and martyrs, taken to represent much larger groups whose tragic sacrifices have left no trace in the historical record.

The life and work of each saint is described. There are dozens of well-known and much-loved saints such as St Teresa of Avila, St Francis of Assisi and St Christopher, but entries also include 1st-century martyrs and the fascinating stories of the African saints of the 19th century. Beautiful photographs and fine-art paintings throughout show how these saints have been represented in art.

The Gazetteer of Other Saints deals briefly with a number of more obscure, but interesting saints. It features brief accounts of saints who have not been included in the main directory but nevertheless deserve to be mentioned.

The study of saints is fraught with great difficulty; many saints have been forgotten over time, while thousands of names are obscure or entirely absent from the historical record. There are more than 4,000 saints in the Roman Catholic canon and the selection made here is not intended to be complete or exclusive. Instead, the intent of this work is to bring an understanding of the Church's theology, teachings, and achievements, and to also show that while all saints share a devotion to God, each one has their own talent, personality, and their own story of struggle.

*Right The Virgin in Prayer (Sassoferrato, c.1645-50) shows Mary, the blessed virgin, who is a univeral symbol of purity and motherhood.*

## ABOUT THIS BOOK

Catholicism is a complex creed and the Church a vast and venerable institution, and the purpose of this book is to offer a comprehensive account of the history, philosophy and practice of Catholic Christianity with a visual directory to the most significant and much-loved saints. Illustrated with over 1000 images, including magnificent churches, relics and paintings of saints, this expert guide will inform readers interested in discovering more about Catholicism and the lives and struggles of the Catholic saints.

# TIMELINE

THE CATHOLIC CHURCH HAS A LONG HISTORY. THE TIMELINE BELOW LISTS SOME OF THE MAJOR EVENTS THAT HAVE AFFECTED IT.

## 1ST CENTURY BC
- Romans conquer Judaea, 63 BC.
- Herod the Great begins renovations on the Temple of Jerusalem, c.19 BC.

## 1ST CENTURY AD
- *Anno Domini* – by tradition, the year of Christ's birth.
- Saul witnesses the martyrdom of St Stephen, c.AD 35.
- Council of Jerusalem convened by St Peter, the first pope, c.AD 50.
- Nero launches the first persecution of Rome's Christians in AD 64.

## 2ND CENTURY
- Monumental shrine erected around St Peter's tomb in Rome, c.150.

## 3RD CENTURY
- Persecution of Valerian, 253-60.

## 4TH CENTURY
- Diocletian's "Great Persecution", 303–11.
- Emperor Constantine converts to Christianity in 312.
- Constantine calls the Council of Nicaea in 325.
- Proclamation of the Nicene Creed, 381.
- St Jerome begins work on his Latin "Vulgate" Bible, 382.

## 5TH CENTURY
- St Augustine starts writing his great work, *The City of God*.
- Leo the Great centralizes power in the papacy, 440–61.

## 6TH CENTURY
- St Benedict of Nursia establishes his monastic rule.

*Above Detail from a fresco showing Pope Gregory the Great (540–604), from Vezzolano, Italy.*

- Reforming papacy of Gregory the Great begins in 590.

## 7TH CENTURY
- Muhammad begins receiving his revelations of Islam in 610.
- Arab armies occupy Jerusalem in 638.

## 8TH CENTURY
- The Church is given temporal authority over Rome and its environs under the "Donation of Pepin", 754.

## 9TH CENTURY
- The legendary "Pope Joan" supposedly succeeds to the papacy in 853.

## 10TH CENTURY
- The reformist abbey of Cluny is founded in eastern France, 910.

## 11TH CENTURY
- The Cistercian order tries to take monasticism back to its first Benedictine principles.
- The Eastern Orthodox Church formally parts company with Rome, 1054.
- Urban II calls the First Crusade in 1095. Jerusalem is taken four years later.

*Above Worshippers gather outside the entrance to the Church of the Holy Sepulchre, Jerusalem, Israel.*

## 12TH CENTURY
- The beginning of the Gothic movement in religious architecture.
- The Second Crusade of 1145 breaks down in chaos.
- The Third Lateran Council begins in 1179.
- Saladin recaptures Jerusalem for the Muslims in 1187. The Third Crusade that follows is a failure.
- Peter Waldo denounces the wealth of the Church from 1177.

## 13TH CENTURY
- The forces of the Fourth Crusade (1202–4) sack Christian Constantinople.
- Innocent III proclaims the Albigensian Crusade against the heretical Cathars in 1208.
- St Francis of Assisi begins his ministry in 1209.
- Thomas Aquinas writes the *Summa Theologica*, 1266–74.

## 14TH CENTURY
- Clement V transfers the papacy to Avignon in France, 1309.
- Gregory XI makes Rome the centre of papal power again in 1377 – but rival popes continue in opposition in Avignon after his death in 1378.

## 15TH CENTURY
- The Council of Pisa (1408) fails to resolve the Western Schism. A solution is found in 1417.
- Czech heretic Jan Hus is burnt at the stake in 1415.
- The Spanish Inquisition is at its height, encouraged by the "Catholic Monarchs", Ferdinand and Isabella.
- The Reconquista is complete, with the expulsion of the Moors from Granada in 1492. That same year Columbus starts opening up an empire for Spain in the Americas.

## 16TH CENTURY
- The reconstruction of St Peter's Basilica, Rome, begins in 1505.
- Martin Luther nails his "95 Theses" to the door of the cathedral in Wittenberg, Germany.
- Clement VII is taken prisoner by German forces during the Sack of Rome, 1527.
- The Ottoman Siege of Vienna is successfully repulsed in 1529.
- Henry VIII announces that he and his successors will henceforth be heads of the Church of England, 1534.
- Ignatius Loyola founds the Society of Jesus in 1534.

- Copernicus' theories are published after his death in 1543.
- St Francis Xavier undertakes his mission to the East, 1542–52.
- The Council of Trent gets under way in 1545. Church leaders resist the Reformation.
- Turkish naval power is defeated by the Christian fleet at the Battle of Lepanto, 1571.

## 17TH CENTURY
- Galileo is forced to recant his claims for Copernican astronomy.
- A Congregation for the Evangelization of Peoples is founded to co-ordinate missionary endeavours, 1622.
- The Thirty Years' War ends in 1648, with Europe divided along religious lines.

## 18TH CENTURY
- Denis Diderot and friends begin work on their secularizing *Encyclopédie* in 1750.
- Revolution convulses France from 1789.

## 19TH CENTURY
- Pius IX denounces modern liberalism in his *Syllabus of Errors*, 1864. Papal infallibility will be proclaimed six years later.

- The "White Fathers" are at work evangelizing in Africa, from 1868.
- Papal rule in the city of Rome is brought to an end in 1871.
- Leo XIII throws the Church's weight behind the cause of workers' rights in *Rerum Novarum*, written in 1891.

## 20TH CENTURY
- The Lateran Treaty of 1929 sees the Church enter into partnership with Mussolini's Fascist state.
- A Concordat is signed with Nazi Germany in 1933.
- Pius XI condemns anti-semitic violence in Germany, 1937.
- John XXIII calls the Second Vatican Council in 1962.
- Liberation theology takes root in Latin America from the 1960s. Its followers play a leading role in the Nicaraguan Revolution of the 1980s.
- Pope John Paul II is elected by an enclave in 1978.

## 21ST CENTURY
- Protestant Pentecostalism is on the rise in Latin America.
- Pope John Paul II makes the first papal visit to Israel, in 2000. That same year he becomes the first pope to pray in a Muslim mosque.

*Above* The striking Gothic façade of the 14th-century Duomo di Milano, or Milan Cathedral.

*Above* An 18th-century Peruvian painting of St Francis Xavier. He is the patron saint of all missions.

*Above* John Paul II (served 1978–2005), an influential pope, was the second longest-serving pope to rule in Rome.

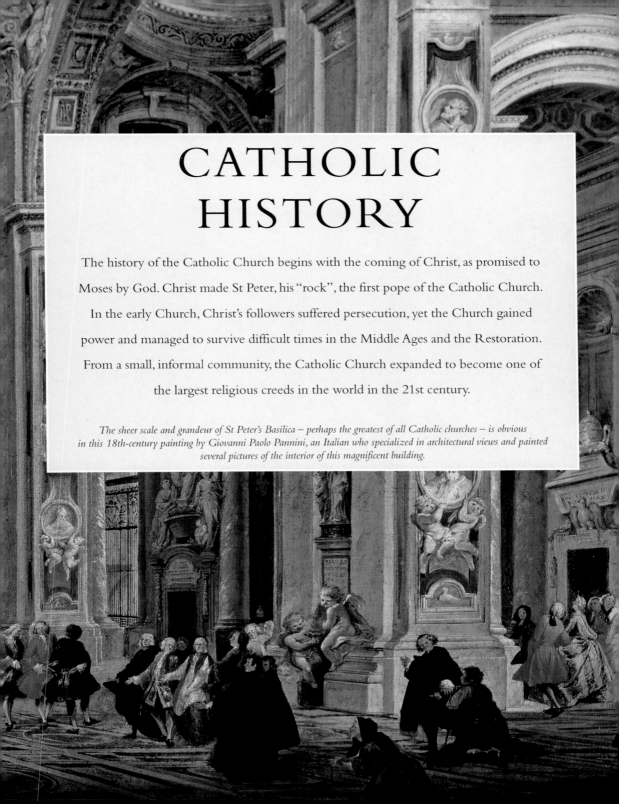

# CATHOLIC HISTORY

The history of the Catholic Church begins with the coming of Christ, as promised to
Moses by God. Christ made St Peter, his "rock", the first pope of the Catholic Church.
In the early Church, Christ's followers suffered persecution, yet the Church gained
power and managed to survive difficult times in the Middle Ages and the Restoration.
From a small, informal community, the Catholic Church expanded to become one of
the largest religious creeds in the world in the 21st century.

*The sheer scale and grandeur of St Peter's Basilica – perhaps the greatest of all Catholic churches – is obvious
in this 18th-century painting by Giovanni Paolo Pannini, an Italian who specialized in architectural views and painted
several pictures of the interior of this magnificent building.*

# THE EARLY CHURCH

The gospels tell an inspirational story. "The word became flesh," says John's Gospel, "he lived among us and we saw his glory." The coming of Christ was the fulfilment of a promise. His remarkable life and death, and above all his Resurrection, made good God's undertaking to both Moses and Abraham. It realized the predictions of the prophets and renewed humanity's hope.

However, inspiration was not enough: as Christ incarnated the word of God, so his message had to be embodied in the institutions and practices of a living, working Church. Catholicism's structures evolved slowly, sometimes painfully, over centuries. Tried in the fire of persecution and torn by dissension – and, ultimately, division – the Church faced many difficulties as it developed. Christian theology was still comparatively new and unexplored, and it had to be systematized by learned scholars.

There were also the difficulties that come with success. The bigger and more secure Catholicism became as a worldwide institution, the greater the political pressures. The emergence of the papacy as a seat of spiritual authority and political power was a temptation as well as a triumph for the Church. Even so, as the 1st millennium came to an end, the faith was the dominant spiritual and cultural force across much of Europe. Catholicism had come a long way in its first thousand years.

*Above The Greek letters Iota (for Iesu, or "Jesus"), Chi (for Christos, or "Christ") and Theta (for Theou, or "Saviour") spell Ichthus, Greek for "fish". The fish, as seen in this 4th-century Italian mosaic, became a Christian emblem.*

*Left In this 1485 painting The Life of Mary by the Master of Aachen, the old priest Simeon blesses the baby Jesus on his presentation in the Temple.*

# IN THE DAYS OF KING HEROD

THE COUNTRY IN WHICH THE CHRISTIAN STORY STARTED WAS A
TERRITORY OF THE ROMAN EMPIRE, ALTHOUGH THE ROMANS
WERE JUST THE LATEST IN A LONG SUCCESSION OF INVADERS.

*Above A Bedouin tends his flock in
the rocky Judaean Desert, just as
Jewish shepherds would have done
2,000 years ago.*

Jesus' birthplace, Bethlelem, and the surrounding regions have an ancient history. Christ was born among the Jews, who saw themselves as the "Chosen People" of Jehovah. However the "Holy Land" that was so important to the Jews was one of the less significant corners of the world at the beginning of the first millenium.

Judaea and Israel, its neighbour to the north, had been brought together under King David from c.1007 BC. The state he created, with its capital in Jerusalem, had come to prominence under his son, Solomon, in the 10th century BC. Though known for his legendary wisdom, Solomon had in reality all but ruined his kingdom; the construction of his celebrated Temple had bankrupted the state. Eventually, the country disintegrated and was conquered by the Assyrians in 841 BC.

## UNDER OCCUPATION

The Jews never accepted their subject status, despite being subjugated for centuries, first under the rule of the Assyrians, then the Babylonians. In the 6th century BC, leading Jews were taken from their country to the imperial capital in what is known as the "Babylonian Captivity", but this failed to break their spirit of resistance.

Persian power proved more benign: after conquering Babylon in 539, Cyrus the Great of Persia let the exiles return to Israel. (He even ordered the reconstruction of the Temple, which had been sacked by Babylon's King Nebuchadnezzar after a Jewish uprising in 587 BC.) The Persians, however, were swept aside by the eastward march of Alexander the Great, who came with his Greek army in 332 BC. After Alexander's death, his vast empire was fought over by his surviving generals. Along with much of the Middle East, Israel fell to Seleucus, a boyhood friend and comrade-at-arms of Alexander. His descendants reigned after him, in what is known as the Seleucid line.

## A TASTE OF FREEDOM

Attempts by the Seleucid ruler Antiochus IV to suppress the religious rituals of the Jews sparked a revolt in 167 BC. Simon

---

### HEROD..."THE GREAT"?

Herod's honorific title, "the Great", strikes modern Christians as strange, given his client-king status – and the part he played in the Gospel account of Jesus' birth. The Magi, wise men who had journeyed from the east by following a star to where they had been told a new king of the Jews would be born, went to Herod and sought his assistance in finding the infant. He was horrified to hear of a rival's birth. However, he begged his visitors to tell him when they found the boy, so that he, too, could pay him homage. Warned by an angel not to tell Herod anything, the Magi instead returned home by another route, whereupon the enraged king had all the infant boys in Israel – the "Holy Innocents" – massacred. This is a cruel and ignominious role in the Christian Scriptures, but

Jewish tradition and mainstream history have judged Herod more kindly. He is called "Herod the Great" on account of his reconstruction of the Temple.

*Below A 14th-century Italian mosaic shows King Herod enjoying a lavish banquet.*

*Above Herod lives in Jewish memory as the rebuilder of the Temple, shown here in a 19th-century painting by James Jacques Tissot (1836–1902).*

Maccabaeus' Hasmonean Dynasty took power and Jewish sovereignty was restored. Jewish rule lasted until 63 BC, when the country was conquered once again – this time by the Roman general Pompey. He let the Hasmoneans stay in office, but as client-kings of what was now named Judaea. They reigned at the beck and call of the Roman emperors, but in return their subjects could still find some comfort in the fact that their country was a kingdom, rather than a mere province.

That the Jews were allowed this degree of autonomy indicates the strength of their identity – however, it also reflects the comparative irrelevance of a people living on the margins. The main centres of wealth and civilization in the ancient world were to the east in Mesopotamia (modern–day Iraq) and Persia, and to the west in the Mediterranean. Palestine was peripheral to both these spheres. Regardless, as insignificant as they were, the Jews had been allowed considerable freedom to live and worship God in the way they had for generations. This freedom was a dangerous thing: many Jews were in no way reconciled to their subjection and were eager to shake off the Roman yoke.

KING OF THE JEWS

For the moment, Rome was firmly in charge and King Herod was the Empire's servant. He had been appointed by the Romans as King of Judaea in 37 BC and was given the title "King of the Jews". In return for his loyalty, Herod won certain privileges for the Jews, and the Romans made no objections to his request when, in 19 BC, he renovated the Temple.

*Above "No foreigners shall enter…" reads the tablet King Herod placed in the Temple. Christ, by contrast, was to reach out to all people.*

# AND IT CAME TO PASS...

THE JEWS HAD BEEN EXPECTING A MIGHTY KING AS A SAVIOUR, BUT INSTEAD CHRIST WAS BORN IN A LOWLY STABLE IN BETHLEHEM. COULD THIS REALLY BE THE MESSIAH THEY HAD BEEN WAITING FOR?

*Above The Messiah was expected to renew the reign of King David, writer of the Psalms, shown in this c.1500 painting by the Master of Riofrio.*

Jewish scriptural tradition had long foreseen the coming of a "Messiah" – whom the Book of Daniel (9:24) referred to as the "anointed one" or "prince". "The people who lived in darkness have seen a great light," prophesied Isaiah (9:2–9). As a king descended from the House of David, it was believed that the Messiah would introduce an eternal era of justice and peace.

Most Jews expected a king to come in glory, but there were Old Testament writers with another vision. Zachary's Messiah (9:9) was envisaged as "lowly, and riding on a donkey". In a chapter of Isaiah (53:3–6), there is a foreshadowing of how the Christian servant-saviour was received: "despised, and rejected by men... he was wounded for our transgressions...and with his stripes we are healed."

## A VISIT FROM AN ANGEL

"Behold, a virgin shall conceive," promises Isaiah (7:14), "and bear a son, and shall call his name Immanuel." That prophecy found fulfilment in the gospel account (Luke, Chapter 1) in which the archangel Gabriel announced to the astonished Virgin Mary the miraculous part she had been appointed to play as the Messiah's mother. The angel's words were later to form the first line of the prayer that is still repeated daily by many Catholics: "Hail Mary, full of grace, the Lord is with thee."

The angel also told Mary that her much older relative Elizabeth was pregnant, despite years of childlessness, so the Blessed Virgin went to see her in the "Visitation". Elizabeth greeted Mary with the words that became the second line of the Hail Mary: "Blessed art thou amongst women, and blessed is the fruit of thy womb."

## THE ANGELUS

Although the custom has fallen victim to the mounting pressures of modern life, for centuries, throughout the Catholic world, the rhythm of the day was set by the sound of the angelus bell. Three sets of three slow, solemn strokes rang out at 6 a.m., 12 noon and 6 p.m. as a signal to the faithful to stop whatever they were doing to meditate on the Annunciation and what it meant. The call-and-response devotion that followed re-enacted the abrupt arrival of the angel in the Virgin Mary's presence and Christ's conception by the power of the Holy Spirit.

*Below "Behold the handmaid of the lord...", begins the Latin inscription beneath this Annunciation by the Italian painter Filippo Lippi, c.1440.*

Mary's reply ("Behold the handmaid of the Lord...Be it done to me according to thy word") is also recollected in the angelus, as are John's words (1:14) on the Incarnation of Our Lord ("And the word was made flesh, and dwelt amongst us").

## THE NATIVITY

Mary, though a virgin, was betrothed to Joseph, whose occupation as a carpenter has made him the patron saint of working men. However, the Gospels of Matthew and Luke are at pains to make the point that he is also a descendant of the House of David: as his son, then, Christ is from Israel's royal line. Yet his is anything but a kingly birth.

At the time when Mary was due to deliver her child, she and her husband were in Bethlehem. The Romans were conducting a census in Judaea and all families had been ordered to go to the ancestral home of the father to be counted. There was no room for them at the inn, so Mary had to give birth in a stable and lay her baby in a manger.

The baby was attended, not by great Jewish dignitaries, but by shepherds from the surrounding hillsides. Although the Magi, "kings" or "wise men", had come to honour the newborn, they were outsiders, summoned from afar. The manner of Jesus' arrival

*Above The most momentous of events, Christ's Nativity in the stable was painted by Hans Leonhard Schaufelein in the 16th century.*

in the world anticipates his later remark (Matthew 13:58) that "a prophet is not without honour except in his own country". By the same token, the coming of the Magi may be seen as a signal that Christ will ultimately find most of his followers abroad.

*Below The Holy Family fled to Egypt when they learned that Herod had ordered the slaughter of all male babies, as shown here in this late 15th-century manuscript.*

### ANNO DOMINI

The "Year of the Lord" – from the Latin *anno domini* (which is commonly abbreviated to AD) – has been taken as a chronological starting point in western tradition. Supposedly, it was the year in which Christ was born. But was it really? Luke's account has the holy family travelling to Bethlehem to take part in a census ordered by the Romans. This could only refer to the survey conducted by Quirinius, Rome's governor in Syria, which is known to have taken place in AD 6–7. However, Matthew implies an earlier date, and some scholars believe that the Nativity might have taken place in 8 BC.

# "YOU ARE MY SON, THE BELOVED..."

JESUS GREW UP QUIETLY IN NAZARETH, A LITTLE TOWN IN GALILEE. NO ONE GUESSED THAT THE BOY THEY SAW HELPING OUT IN HIS FATHER'S WORKSHOP WAS ACTUALLY THE MORTAL SON OF GOD.

Christ may have been born, but "Christianity" was as yet unheard of, and Jesus was raised by his parents in the traditions of Judaism. Like any other Jewish baby boy, he was circumcised at eight days old and, on the 40th day after his birth, Jesus' mother took him to the Jewish Temple for his presentation. Tradition demanded not only that the mother herself should be ritually "purified" after giving birth but that the baby should be formally presented. Jewish law decreed that the Temple had the right to claim any

*Below Simeon, an elderly priest, sees the Messiah during his presentation in this 15th-century painting by Giovanni Bellini.*

firstborn boy for the priesthood, unless he was redeemed with a token payment.

## SEEING SALVATION

The Gospel of Luke (2:29–31) describes how Simeon, an old priest who had prayed to God to let him live long enough to see the Messiah, finally saw the infant saviour during his presentation and realized that God had answered his prayers. "Now master you are letting your servant go in peace," he said in gratitude, "for my eyes have seen the salvation which you have made ready in the sight of the nations." The child was destined to be the deliverance of his people, though he would also face great opposition from

*Above The adolescent Jesus is shown astonishing the elders of the Temple with his knowledge in this early 19th-century Russian icon.*

them and others. Simeon also warned Mary, "a sword will pierce your soul, too" (2:35).

## A SPECIAL BAPTISM

At 12 years old, Jesus disappeared during a pilgrimage his family was making to Jerusalem. His frantic mother found him in the Temple talking to the elders. These experienced scholars were in raptures at his knowledge and insight.

*Above Jesus is determined to be purified through baptism, like any sinner, in this early 14th-century painting entitled* The Baptism of Christ *by Giotto.*

### THE INFANCY GOSPELS

The gospels say little about Jesus' boyhood, so perhaps it is inevitable that popular folklore has made up the shortfall. Among the many Apocrypha (purported scriptural writings of dubious origin) produced in the early centuries after Christ's death and Resurrection were what is known as the Infancy Gospels. These offer more details on Jesus' boyhood, but they view him like a fairytale hero with "magical" powers. Some of his supposed deeds, indeed, could hardly be seen as Christ-like. In one story, for instance, he reacted to an insult by cursing the boy who delivered it so he died; then when the boy's parents complained, Jesus blinded them.

The boy – a little impatiently – dismissed his mother's reproaches: "Why were you looking for me?" he asked (Luke 2:49). "Did you not know that I must be in my father's house?" Though his parents did not understand what their son was saying, this is a clear indication that Jesus' own mind was already on his heavenly kingdom and his earthly mission.

The gospels agree that it was not until many years later, when Jesus was about 30 years of age, that he left home and made his way into the desert beside the River Jordan. There he found John – Elizabeth's son and his relative. Known as John the Baptist, he had already embarked on his own sacred ministry, living simply in the wilderness and preaching to the people, calling on them to change their lives. He baptized the repentant and prophesied the coming of a saviour.

When Jesus appeared, John pointed him out as the one who was to come. John was perplexed

*Right Christ is tempted by the devil in the desert, shown here in this c.1225 stained-glass scene in Troyes Cathedral, in France.*

when the man he regarded as the Messiah asked to be baptized like any sinner, but Jesus was adamant, and John agreed. As Christ arose from the water, the heavens parted and the Holy Spirit descended in the form of a dove. A voice rang out, saying "You are my Son, the Beloved; my favour rests on you" (Mark 1:11).

### THE TEMPTATION
After his baptism, Matthew tells us, Jesus went into the wilderness alone to fast and pray in preparation for the task that awaited him. He spent 40 days and 40 nights in the desert, with his solitude being interrupted only by the devil, who had come to test his resolve.

Satan appeared three times to tempt Jesus. First he offered Jesus all the kingdoms of the world if he would bow down and worship Satan. Then he challenged Jesus to turn stones into bread to satisfy his hunger. Finally, Satan took Jesus to the highest point on the Temple and dared him to jump off (the angels will make sure you are not hurt, he said). Christ refused to rise to these provocations. Dismayed, the devil left and angels arrived with bread to ease Jesus' hunger.

# "BLESSED ARE THE POOR IN SPIRIT"

IT IS UNCLEAR WHETHER CHRIST'S MINISTRY LASTED FOR WEEKS OR YEARS. EITHER WAY, HE HAD TIME TO PERFORM MIRACLES AND PROCLAIM THE MOST REMARKABLE MESSAGE EVER HEARD.

Jesus first performed a miracle at his mother's urging during the Wedding Feast at Cana. Supplies were running low, so he turned jars of ordinary water into wine. Once his ministry got under way in earnest, Jesus cast out demons and healed the sick – and, in the case of Lazarus, he even gave life back to the dead.

From a modern perspective, the early miracles appear to have established Christ's credentials as the Messiah. Certainly, when the apostles saw him walking across the waters of the Sea of Galilee toward their boat, they were left in no doubt of his divinity (but Peter's own faith faltered as he attempted to walk out to meet his Lord).

## A DIVINITY KEPT SECRET

Jesus himself did not necessarily want his divinity known to others. At a number of points, in the Gospel of Mark especially, he urged his hearers to keep what is called the "Messianic Secret". Even when his apostles witnessed him standing on a high mountain in the episode known as the "Transfiguration", blazing forth in all his godly radiance, they were urged to not tell others what they had witnessed.

After one of his first miracles, the healing of a leper (Mark 1), Christ gave the man strict orders that he should tell no one of his cure. However, in his exhilaration, the man ignored this injunction and told everyone he met what Jesus had done for him. Crowds came from far and wide to see this marvellous miracle worker. Some came in hopes of being cured themselves; some to witness miracles or to hear what this new prophet had to say.

## THE BEATITUDES

Christ's teachings have their single, most sustained exposition in the extraordinary episode known as the Sermon on the Mount – although on which particular mount the discourse was delivered is unclear. Wherever it occurred, it was during this sermon that Jesus formulated the Beatitudes (literally, Blessednesses), as is recorded in Matthew 5:3–12:

*Left Jesus is surrounded by his followers as he gives his Sermon on the Mount. He is standing in this painting by James Jacques Tissot, but traditionally Jesus is shown sitting – rabbis often sat while teaching.*

*Above Christ cures a blind man in this warm and intimate scene by an 11th-century Italian artist.*

- *How blessed are the poor in spirit; the kingdom of heaven is theirs.*
- *Blessed are the gentle; they shall have the earth as inheritance…*
- *Blessed are the merciful; they shall have mercy shown them…*
- *Blessed are the peacemakers; they shall be recognized as children of God…*

These blessings gave encouragement to his listeners. However, there were many other components to this thought-provoking sermon, including the Lord's Prayer and what are considered by many people to be the central tenets of Christianity. The convention is that Jesus' life and death created a "new covenant" between God and humankind. This was a merciful reaching out, a second chance for the fallen descendants of Adam and Eve.

This interpretation is true enough, but at the same time, for all the generosity and love it represented, the "deal" Jesus offered was extremely exacting. Those who followed his way, he warned, could expect to endure abuse and persecution. Harder than the insults and violent treatment they were to expect, would be the duty they would have to respond to their oppressors with friendship and forgiveness: rather than retaliate if anyone hit them, they must offer them the other cheek (Matthew 5:39). They should love their enemies, do good to those who wish them harm, and treat others as they would hope to be treated themselves.

NOT ONLY FOR THE JUST
Jesus found his first followers when, walking by the Sea of Galilee, he met the fishermen Simon (whom Jesus promptly renamed Peter) and his friend Andrew, along with two brothers, James and John. Other "apostles" followed: 12 in all, including Philip, Bartholomew and Thomas. None was rich or learned; they represented the working poor rather than the priestly elite. Matthew, a tax collector, was a member of a despised class. But Christ had come to call sinners, he said. His later friendship with Mary Magdalene, the repentant prostitute, underlined his concern that his redemption was for all, not just the traditionally pious.

*Right Jesus dismisses the disapproving stares of his pious companions as Mary Magdalene prostrates herself at his feet in this 16th-century painting attributed to the French School.*

### TEACHING TALES

Arriving as he did to bring God's Word to the poor and uneducated, Christ made his message as vivid as he possibly could. Rather than setting out an abstract code of instructions, he expressed his teachings in strikingly human terms. He spoke of the Sower whose seed fell largely on stony ground; the Samaritan who remembered his charitable duty when his "betters" forgot theirs; and the Prodigal Son, welcomed home from his wanderings by his joyful father. Such parables demonstrated, more strongly than any commandments could, what it might mean to follow in the way of Christ.

*Right Christ's parable of fishermen making an abundant catch but only keeping the best fish is recalled in this c.1530 illustration for medieval readers.*

# THE WAY OF THE CROSS

CHRIST MAY HAVE COME TO BRING HUMANITY EVERLASTING LIFE, BUT FIRST HE HAD TO SUFFER AND DIE. THE AGONIES OF HIS CRUCIFIXION WERE THE PRICE HE PAID FOR MAN'S REDEMPTION.

The climax of Christ's ministry occurred when he made his triumphal entrance into Jerusalem. He did not do so in a chariot or on a noble stallion but mounted on a donkey. This is kingship in the humble spirit of the Beatitudes. The huge crowd cheered the Messiah through the streets, scattering palm leaves before him as he went. The crowd cried out the words of Psalm 118, "Hosanna! Blessed is he who is coming in the name of the Lord!"

However, he received a decidedly cooler welcome from his country's religious establishment. The Christ who had come to call sinners had already alienated both the learned scribes and the self-consciously pious Pharisees. Their devotion, he said, was to the letter of the law, while his was to its spirit. In Jerusalem, it became clear just how radical a reformer he was prepared to be. He was even willing to violate the peace of the Temple, driving out the moneychangers from its sacred precincts. For Jesus, they had turned the house of God into a den of thieves.

*Above Christ's entry into Jerusalem, with palm leaves spread before him, has been captured in this 15th-century fresco by an unknown artist.*

### THE LAST SUPPER

Jesus had journeyed to the capital to join the celebrations for the Passover feast. As a good Jew, he wanted to take the traditional supper of lamb and unleavened bread with his apostles, but he gave the occasion a new and very special slant. Breaking the bread, he gave it to his friends, telling them solemnly, "This is my body". He offered them wine, telling them to drink it and saying, "This is my blood". What was to be his "Last Supper" with his apostles thus became a foreshadowing of the sacrifice he was so soon to be making on Calvary, and, of course, the Catholic sacrament of the Eucharist.

When the meal was over, Jesus and his apostles withdrew to the Garden of Gethsemane to pray in seclusion. Jesus felt all-too-human fear and panicked at the thought of what he was about to face. Men sent by the Sanhedrin – the sacred judges of the Jews – arrived to arrest him, away from the public eye. He was pointed out by his own apostle Judas, who betrayed him for 30 pieces of silver.

### ON TRIAL

Jesus' captors accused him of blasphemy, although the evidence against him proved exasperatingly slight, until he told them that he was Christ, the son of God. His guilt established to their own satisfaction, the judges handed

*Below Jesus feared death, as any mortal would. In the* Agony in the Garden, *painted by Giovanni Bellini c.1465, he prays for help.*

*Above The Crucifixion, and the sign of the Cross, became emblematic of Catholicism. This 13th-century Italian painted cross was an object of devotion.*

him over to the Roman governor Pontius Pilate, claiming that he had been scheming against the state. Pilate was unconvinced, but the clamour of the Sanhedrin and their supporters was so great that in the end he called for water and literally "washed his hands" of the problem. Christ's accusers could have their way, he said.

## THE EXECUTION

Jesus was scourged at a pillar before being made to carry a heavy timber cross to his place of execution. He was mocked and spat upon as he made his slow, painful way through the streets of Jerusalem. Outside the city, on Mount Calvary, he was placed on the Cross, attached to it by nails through his hands and feet, and set up on the hilltop between two condemned thieves. "Father forgive them; they do not know what they are doing," he said of those who tormented him. Only after hours of agony did he die. On that day, a Friday, darkness fell upon the earth, which was convulsed by tremors; the curtain that screened the holiest part of the Temple ripped down the middle.

*Above Judas betrayed Jesus with the sign of love, a kiss, as captured in this 14th-century Spanish painting by the Master of Rubio.*

*Below Jesus staggering under the weight of his heavy Cross is depicted in this sumptuously carved, c. 1460 wooden altarpiece from Antwerp.*

### PASCHAL PAST

The feast of Passover dates back to the deliverance of the Jews from Egyptian enslavement, as told in the Old Testament's Book of Exodus. God had sent nine plagues to afflict the Egyptians, but they still refused to let Moses and his people go. At last God sent an angel down to kill the firstborn of every family. So no Jews should be punished, Moses was instructed that each Israelite household should kill a lamb and mark their doorpost with its blood.

Christ was going to his own death, sacrificing himself to atone for all of humanity's sins. Where the Jehovah of the Old Testament had meted out punishment to the Egyptians for their wickedness, now the "lamb of God" was going to take on the sins of all the world. His death and Resurrection marked the beginning of a "new covenant" in which justice would be tempered with mercy and in which sins might be forgiven.

# HE HAS RISEN

CHRIST'S DEATH WAS THE ULTIMATE EXPRESSION OF LOVE, BUT IT WAS HIS RESURRECTION THAT GAVE IT MEANING. STRIVING HUMANITY HAD A WAY BACK TO GOD, A CHANCE AT LIFE IN HEAVEN.

Numbed by shock and stunned by disbelief, Jesus' friends took him down from the Cross, and his mother cradled him in her arms for the last time. One of his followers, Joseph of Arimathea, had a burial chamber already prepared for himself in a cave nearby. He got Pontius Pilate's permission to lay Christ to rest inside.

With that done, fear for their own physical safety being the least of their problems, Jesus' followers

*Below Christ appears to two travellers on the road to Emmaus in this 15th-century fresco from the Church of the Trinity, Piedmont, Italy.*

turned to despair. What were they to do? Where were they to go? They had been left emotionally and spiritually bereft by the death of their saviour, the one who had promised them eternal life. The darkness that still enveloped the earth matched their complete disorientation and their utter gloom.

## AN EMPTY TOMB

But life had to go on, and part of life is the ritual responsibility of the living to the dead. So on Sunday morning, Mary Magdalene and "the other Mary", mother of the apostle James the Less, made their way to the tomb. (The gospels

*Above Christ cuts an awe-inspiring figure as he floats triumphantly above his open tomb in* The Resurrection of Christ, *painted c.1502 by Raphael.*

differ, but Mark's Gospel mentions a third woman, another friend and follower, Salome.) There, they found that the stone protecting the entrance had been rolled aside. In the doorway, an angel greeted them, informing them that they had made a wasted journey: "He is not here, for he has risen, as he said he would."

In Matthew's account, as the astonished women ran to tell their friends the news, they met Jesus himself nearby. He asked them to tell the disciples to meet him in Galilee. Just hours later, two disciples walking along the road to Emmaus joined a stranger and went to an inn to eat with him. Only when this "stranger" blessed the bread before handing it to them did they realize who he was.

## THE ASCENSION

The risen Christ then revealed himself to a number of disciples at various points, although these tended to be fleeting encounters. The apostles themselves were frightened and demoralized, and

*Above* The apostles gaze up as Jesus is borne aloft on a cloud by angels in this 12th-century Spanish stone relief.

## THE GOSPELS AND THE GRAIL

Joseph of Arimathea is referred to in the gospels for the part he played in the burial of Christ, where he had a limited role in the event. However, he was given a more important role in a later legend. The tradition, most recently popularized by Dan Brown's novel *The Da Vinci Code,* has him carrying Christianity to Britain, along with the Holy Grail. This sacred vessel (widely assumed to be a chalice, although some sources see it as a serving dish) is said to have been used by Christ at the Last Supper. It is a colourful story, but no more than that. The earliest accounts of Christianity in Britain make no mention of Joseph of Arimathea, and it is not until the 9th century that we hear of his involvement. As for the Holy Grail narrative, that is even later in its origins, first appearing in French romances of the 12th century.

Thomas was at first reluctant to believe that the sightings had even taken place. Finally, 40 days after the Resurrection, Jesus appeared before them in a room where they were all gathered. He urged them to carry his message to all the nations of the world. He told them not to fear: the Holy Spirit would protect them. He also said they would be able to pick up serpents and not be harmed, and they would have the power to cast out demons and heal the sick.

What happened next is unclear because the gospels differ on the details. However, there is agreement among the gospel writers that Jesus ascended to heaven: "a cloud took him from their sight", says the Acts of the Apostles (1:9).

## PENTECOST

Left behind again, the apostles withdrew with Mary, the mother of Jesus, and other supporters to an "upper room" – the same one in which the Last Supper was celebrated. For the next few days they prayed together until, on the Jewish feast of Pentecost, the house was suddenly filled with a roaring noise, "as of a violent wind". Tongues of fire came to rest above their heads as the Holy Spirit descended upon them. With this inspiration, they ventured out into the streets to start spreading the word. Miraculously, those who listened, no matter what country they came from, could hear them speaking in their own native language.

*Below* Mary takes pride of place among the apostles in this representation of Pentecost, painted in Florence by Jacopo Orcagna (active 1368–98).

# THE DISCIPLES

"COME AFTER ME," CHRIST HAD TOLD THE FISHERMEN BESIDE THE
SEA OF GALILEE, "AND I WILL MAKE YOU IN TO FISHERS OF MEN."
HIS WORDS CAME TO PASS IN THE EARLY DAYS OF THE CHURCH.

Pentecost is a day of inspiration, marking the day of the descent of the Holy Spirit on the apostles. The disciples' joy was all but intoxicating – although cynics claim that they had, indeed, been drinking. Yet their euphoria, born of the Holy Spirit, is only heightened when they find ordinary people in the streets receptive to the message of Christ. As predicted by Jesus, these disciples became the "fishers of men". On that first day alone, the Acts of the Apostles assures us (2:41) some 3,000 converts were made, and more were recruited daily in the weeks that

*Below Jesus sends his followers to "make disciples of all nations" in a 20th-century stained-glass window by Gabriel Loire.*

followed. Christianity, it seems, was gathering momentum. This was a mass movement, no longer a community – but a Church.

## A NEW WAY OF LIFE

At the time, the disciples' religion was more fervent than thoughtful; Christian doctrine and ritual were works in progress. However, one thing is clear: at this stage the Christians were still emphatically Jewish. At the heart of their ritual, we are told (Acts 2:46), were their daily visits to the Temple together; afterwards, they adjourned to the homes of the community members for the "breaking of bread". This appeared to be both a eucharistic ritual and an act of sharing. The same verse tells us that they "shared their food gladly

*Above The apostles were soon finding many ordinary people willing to convert to Christianity, as shown in this late 15th-century illumination by Jean Poyet.*

and generously". We are told, too, that they sold their possessions and divided up the proceeds so that everybody had what they needed. It is said that they were "looked up to by everyone", and were joined by a steady stream of new recruits.

Like Jesus before them, the apostles worked miracles, but they were careful that the glory went to God, not themselves. They fell foul of the Sanhedrin (the sacred judges of the Jews, who did not believe in resurrection), but they had no grounds on which to condemn them – nor could they explain how the Christians cured the sick and lame.

## A FAITH FOR ALL

These Christians were indeed still scrupulous in their Jewish observance, worshipping regularly and maintaining all the dietary laws. However, that was soon to change. St Peter had a dream in which God instructed him that from now on no animal or bird should be deemed "unclean" (Acts 10:10–15). Additionally, there was news that an angel had appeared to a Roman centurion, Cornelius, and this persuaded Peter that God wanted Christianity to be open to all, regardless of nationality.

For hundreds of years, the Jews had prided themselves on being God's "chosen people", so what Peter was saying was a complete departure. As he was addressing Cornelius and his Roman friends

*Above St Peter continued the ministry of his departed Lord. In this Italian fresco, by Masolino da Panicale, he raises Tabitha from the dead.*

and relatives, the Holy Spirit descended upon them – just as it had earlier on the disciples at Pentecost. Peter's Jewish companions were shocked, but their leader, unruffled, explained that this was a sign that "God has no favourites" (Acts 10:34).

The historical record shows that this principle was ratified at the Council of Jerusalem, held around AD 50 under Peter's guidance. The Council also agreed

that gentiles (non-Jews) could be baptized without circumcision. This was the start of the divergence of Christianity and Judaism. So, too, was St Peter's transfer of his ministry from Jerusalem to Antioch in Syria (modern-day Turkey), and later to Rome, where he was to take his message to the centre of the ancient world.

## A CHRISTIAN CAPITAL

Antioch, or Antakya, now in modern-day Turkey, is not an attractive place to visit. It is a noisy, congested city. However, behind this façade hides a historic and spiritual centre of extraordinary importance. The beautiful buildings may have been swept away, but the legacy of this past has endured in the people, in its small but active Christian community. Today, Antakya's Christians are in an often uncomfortable position: they are caught between the aggressive secularism of the Turkish state and the Islamic devotion of the majority of the population. Yet, they feel strengthened by their sense of 2,000 years of continuous Christian worship here. Under its old name, Antioch, this was a major metropolis. More than that, for a crucial period in the 1st and 2nd centuries, it was the capital of Christianity. St Peter himself is said to have made it his headquarters, and by the 3rd century, according to St John Chrysostom, there were 100,000 Christians in the city.

*Left St Peter preaches in a street that has the distinct look of 15th-century Florence. The painting is from the* Linaiuoli Triptych *by Fra Angelico (c.1387–1455).*

# St Paul the Convert

SAUL STARTED OUT AS AN IMPLACABLE PERSECUTOR OF THE NEW
RELIGION, BUT REBORN AS PAUL HE BECAME A TIRELESS EVANGELIST.
HE PLAYED AN IMPORTANT ROLE IN BUILDING THE EARLY CHURCH.

Saul was born in Tarsus, in what is now the south of Turkey. In the 2nd century BC, this country had been conquered by the Romans. Tarsus had been given an unusual amount of say over its own affairs, and Saul's well-born Jewish family had been granted citizenship. This set Saul apart from the Jews of his time and made him doubly suspicious of Christ's followers, who were a potential threat to Judaism and the Roman Empire.

According to the Acts of the Apostles (Chapters 7–8), Saul first came into contact with Christianity as a witness to the martyrdom of St Stephen, who was stoned in Jerusalem around AD 35. Saul appeared as a mere bystander: those about to kill the

*Below Paul preaches Christ's message in Luca di Tommè's 14th-century representation. The disciple believed the gospels should be spread to all people.*

young man placed their cloaks at his feet for safe keeping. The man from Tarsus did not remain detached for long. Oddly enough, it does not seem to have been either Stephen's proclamations of Christian faith or his criticisms of the Jews that upset Saul. What got his attention was the serenity with which the first martyr met his death and the magnanimity with which he asked God to forgive his killers.

Saul, in anything but magnanimous mood, hurled himself into the task of hunting down and destroying the rest of Stephen's fellow Christians. It was with the aim of rounding up the Christian community in the Syrian city that Saul was on the road to Damascus.

## THE LIGHT OF GOD
As he travelled, a dazzling light appeared. Felled by its force, Saul pitched forward, falling on the

*Above Saul was stopped on the road to Damascus, as seen in this 19th-century stained-glass window from Lincoln Cathedral, England. His conversion greatly influenced the course of Christianity.*

stony road. "Saul, Saul, why are you persecuting me?" thundered God from the sky. Saul, in his shock, lay cowering and helpless. "Who are you, Lord?" he said. "I am Jesus, whom you are persecuting," came the reply. This was a revelation for Saul, and his conversion on the road to Damascus was to be a defining moment for Christianity. Saul had never set eyes on the living Christ, yet, as Paul, he did much to shape the development of Christ's Church.

## SIGHT RESTORED
Having been blinded by the light, Saul was taken on to Damascus by his companions. A disciple named Ananias was told in a dream to go to the house where Saul was staying and restore his sight. Having heard what type of man Saul was, Ananias questioned this instruction. To his amazement, the Lord told him that Saul had to be cured because he was central for his plans for his Christian Church.

The restoration of Saul's sight was of course a symbolic as well as a physical cure: he had been morally blind before but was now enlightened. He became as eager a proselytizer as he had been a persecutor, dedicating his life to the spreading of the gospels.

## THE LETTERS OF THE LAW

Paul covered thousands of miles in the course of his ministry. He took his duty to the gentiles very seriously. Never satisfied with simply making converts, he kept in touch with the communities he had come to know in a series of letters. Part personal greetings, part sermons, part theological arguments with himself, the Epistles were to be incorporated into the Christian Scriptures. Paul's opinions, as set down in his Epistles, had an incalculable influence not only on his various congregations around the ancient world but on the way Christianity was to develop in modern times.

*Right A page of Paul's Epistles can be seen in this detail from a 1473 polyptych (a many-panelled altarpiece) in Ascoli Piceno's Sant' Emidio Cathedral, Italy.*

APOSTLE TO THE GENTILES

The Holy Spirit, we are told (Acts:13), specifically chose Saul for the task of taking the divine word to the gentiles, or non-Jews. It is no surprise, then, that he changed his name to the Roman "Paul" during his first mission to Cyprus, Greece and Asia Minor – or that he took sides with Peter in discussions at the Council of Jerusalem, which were to open the new religion to non-Jews. In subsequent missions, Paul criss-crossed the eastern Mediterranean and Middle East regions, making new converts and revisiting existing Christian communities.

Arrested in Jerusalem, allegedly for bringing gentiles into the Temple in defiance of Jewish law, Paul was accused of blasphemy – just like Christ had been before him. However, because of his background, Paul could appeal to his rights as a Roman citizen, which meant that he was eventually transported to Rome for trial there. His arrival coincided with the first major persecution of the Christians in AD 64. He died a martyr, though the exact date and circumstances are unknown.

*Right Masaccio's 15th-century painting of St Paul shows the disciple armed with the sword of the fighter (and the martyr) and the Bible.*

# A FAITH IN FEAR

"BLESSED ARE YOU WHEN PEOPLE ABUSE YOU AND PERSECUTE YOU," CHRIST SAID. HIS FOLLOWERS WERE TO FIND OUT WHAT THAT FELT LIKE AS THEY BRAVED TORTURE FOR THE SAKE OF THEIR BELIEFS.

Toward the end of AD 64, Nero, Emperor of Rome, launched the first "Great Persecution". In these early days of Christianity, its disciples could pose no conceivable threat. By this time, the numbers in their community in the capital could have been only in the low hundreds at the most.

However, Nero had an agenda. He was widely blamed for the Great Fire of Rome, which had swept through the city that year.

There were reports that the emperor's own household slaves had been seen intentionally setting the fire so that Nero could advance his redevelopment plans for parts of the city centre. As things turned out, the conflagration gutted 10 of the capital's 14 districts. Under the circumstances, Nero was only too eager to have someone else to blame, and the Christian community made the perfect scapegoat.

*Above* *A man is attacked by wild beasts in the arena in this 2nd-century mosaic from North Africa.*

### CRUEL DEATHS

On his orders, Christians were taken prisoner by the score. Some were tossed on to fires – alive – thrown to savage dogs to be torn apart or, notoriously, cast into the arena to be killed by wild animals as a public spectacle. Others were crucified, a common form of execution at the time, but also a sneer at the way the Christians' Messiah had been killed. Peter, who had arrived in Rome at the start of Nero's Great Persecution, was one of those crucified in Rome during this period. One tradition has it that he was hung upside down, at his own request, presumably because it would be presumptuous to be executed in the same manner as his saviour.

### PROLONGED REPRESSION

In many places and for long periods, Christians were tolerated. Yet, sometimes, persecution came not

*Left* *St Peter is often depicted being crucified upside down, such as in this 16th-century French manuscript.*

from the state but from the general public. Christians were harassed – even physically attacked – by their pagan neighbours. Sometimes there were also more serious and sustained outbreaks of mob violence against Christians, with or without the connivance of the authorities.

As is generally the way with such things, hostility increased at times of political uncertainty or economic crisis. There were significant crackdowns during the reigns of Domitian, Trajan, Septimius Severus and Decius. Many priests and bishops were martyred in the reign of Valerian (253–60), including St Laurence, reputedly burnt on an iron grill.

In fairness, part of the problem was the Romans' incomprehension of what was motivating the Christians to resist. As far as they were concerned, they had given the Christians every chance to

*Left St Sebastian, who was martyred in 287, is shown gazing stoically heavenward as arrows pierce his body in this 1480 painting by Mantegna.*

Many others were killed during the eight years of the Great Persecution, but some modern scholars are sceptical about claims by contemporary sources that 10,000 martyrs were crucified on the first day of Diocletian's crackdown. Yet even the conservative estimates are in agreement that thousands were martyred and many thousands more had suffered harassment and torture. Again, the persecution appears to have been prompted by an economic crisis brought on by Diocletian's financial mismanagement. The emperor was also a religious conservative, concerned at what he saw as the abandonment of the traditional Roman gods in favour of new faiths, such as Christianity.

## THE EMPEROR AND THE ANTICHRIST

After being driven underground by Nero's persecution, the Christians communicated using a code based on what was known as "gematria". This was a type of numerological theory that attributed mystical properties to different numbers and saw significance in their relations to the letters of the Hebrew alphabet. Some scholars have studied all the infinite subtleties of gematria for many years, but at its crudest level it can be used to make a straightforward cipher. For Nero, the figures came to 666: the "Number of the Beast" in the Book of Revelation. Many early Christians did, indeed, see this Roman ruler as the model for the "Antichrist".

save themselves by abjuring their religion. They simply could not understand that this new creed could be worth dying for.

### ANOTHER PERSECUTION

In 303, Emperor Diocletian issued his "Edict Against the Christians", ordering that churches should be demolished and Christians enslaved. This would have been bad enough even if it had not been the signal for the start of another Great Persecution. Again, Christians were given a chance to save themselves by offering sacrifices to the pagan gods. Some were intimidated into compliance. Some sources say (though others deny this) that even the pope of the day, Marcellinus, had been persuaded to burn incense before Roman idols. However the pope repented his weakness, reasserted his Christian faith and died a martyr some time in 304.

*Above The grisly manner of St Catherine's execution in Alexandria around 305 has clearly caught the imagination of this late medieval painter, whose work appeared in the 1280 History of Four Saints.*

# New Life among the Dead: The Catacombs

Beneath Rome, men, women and children came together in secret worship. They found a sanctuary in the domain of the dead, where they had buried their loved ones.

In the face of persecution in the world above for their adherence to the creed of Christ, early Roman Christians ventured deep into the earth to the homes of the dead to give their thanks and praise to the living God.

## A PRACTICAL SOLUTION

The catacombs were first and foremost a place to bury the dead, but for the Christians, and perhaps others, they became a place of refuge in times of persecution. As many as 40 of these underground burial complexes existed around the periphery of Rome; construction had begun in pre-Christian times. The pagan Romans, while

*Below Ancient skulls seem to survey the scene in a chamber at the heart of Rome's San Callisto catacombs.*

revering the dead and making offerings at their graves, had also viewed them with fear and banished them beyond the city limits. Burial grounds had sprung up along the main routes out of town. Many people were cremated and their ashes stored in special columbaria ("dovecots"), so-called because the regular niches in which the urns were placed in their hundreds resembled the pigeonholes in which the birds nested in the dovecots of the day.

With pressure growing on space around the city, these facilities were tucked discreetly away underground. More subterranean complexes were built in Christian times, and these had to be more spacious. Burial had replaced cremation for the Christian faithful, who looked forward to

*Above The catacombs were primarily a way of warehousing the dead: floor-to-ceiling niches line this passage.*

the resurrection of the body. Fortunately, the soft and porous "tuff" (volcanic ash) on which much of Rome is founded made excavation easy, and these underground cemeteries quickly grew.

## SAN CALLISTO

Rome's biggest catacombs, the San Callisto, are named after an early pope, St Callistus (although

*Above* Inside the Roman church of San Callisto, the "Crypt of the Popes" houses the relics of Church leaders from the 3rd and 4th centuries.

Areas in the catacombs were crudely customized as churches, and frescoes were painted showing what appear to be eucharistic scenes. The fish often crops up as a symbol — not just because Christ and his apostles had been fishermen but because the letters of the Greek word *Ichthus* ("fish") spelled out the secret slogan *Iesu Christos Theou* (or "Jesus Christ Saviour"). Old Testament scenes are represented as well, such as Moses striking the rock and sending water gushing forth and Jonah being swallowed by the whale.

San Callisto's "Gallery of the Sacraments" has some fascinating paintings. There are more in the San Domitilla catacombs, where key saints of the 4th century were laid to rest in an underground basilica. One side room has a ceiling adorned with a 3rd-century fresco of the Good Shepherd; in nearby niches and passages are paintings of Jesus, his apostles and the Magi.

he was actually one of the few 3rd-century pontiffs not to have been buried in its rectangular "Crypt of the Popes"). They were rediscovered in 1849 by the Italian Giovanni Battista de Rossi, and while more than 20km (12½ miles) of tunnels and chambers have been mapped, there are large areas of labyrinthine passages that have yet to be explored. Tunnels were often created one on top of another, in up to four separate layers.

## SACRED AND SECRET
For decades at a time the Christians had been left alone, and during these settled periods the catacombs appear to have been nothing more than burial places. It was only natural, though, that during periods of official crackdowns, when worshipping in public basilicas or homes was too hazardous, families that had grown used to visiting these underground passages to honour and pray for their dead thought of seeking a sanctuary here. The tombs of martyrs put to death in the persecutions became sacred sites in themselves, and their fellow Christians would visit them later to gather for worship and prayers.

Even in times of toleration, then, the catacombs were a powerful focus for Christian faith. And then, of course, there was the symbolic resonance: the sense of life and affirmation flourishing in the midst of death. It is inconceivable that this could have been lost on the men and women of the early Church.

## MODERN INSPIRATION
Today we can marvel at the courage of these early Christians and see their story as exemplifying hope. The vanquishing of death, the triumph of new life — even in the grave itself — Christianity can hold out no greater promise to the believer. Hence, perhaps, the continuing hold the catacombs exercise over the imagination of the faithful.

*Above* Abraham prepares to sacrifice Isaac, his son, in this fresco. The catacombs hold some of the earliest Christian art.

# THE CHURCH OF ROME

INCREASINGLY, CHRISTIANITY WAS EASING AWAY FROM ITS JEWISH ROOTS. ROME, THE CENTRE OF THE 1ST-CENTURY WORLD, WAS THE NATURAL HEADQUARTERS FOR THIS NEW RELIGION.

*Above Rome is revealed to St Augustine as the "City of God", as shown here in a 15th-century French manuscript.*

Why, despite its Middle Eastern origins, did this new religion become known as the "Roman" Catholic Church? To some extent, the development might seem accidental. The scene of so many martyrdoms had acquired strong emotional and spiritual associations for the early Christians. As early as the 2nd century – long before the age of persecutions had run its course – men and women were making pilgrimages to the tombs of St Peter and St Paul.

### WORLD CAPITAL

There were other reasons that were also important. Rome was the capital of a vast empire: to all intents and purposes the centre of the world. Important decisions were all made there, and Rome ruled in many subject nations. The city was the centre of a web of well-made roads and busy shipping lanes.

*Below Tertullian was a pagan who converted to Christianity c.AD 197. His writings covered many issues in the theological field, providing a picture of religious life and beliefs in his time.*

These advantages would not always have been of interest to the Church, of course. To begin with, Christianity had been influenced by Judaism. In fact, debate had raged over whether gentiles should be baptized at all, and many had been resistant to this change. However, Peter and Paul had prevailed with their literal interpretation of Christ's words, "Go…and make disciples of all nations" (Matthew 28:19).

### LATIN TAKES OVER

Significant, too, was the decision of Tertullian, the Church's leading thinker, to write his works in Latin, the Roman language. Until now, there had been two languages of Christianity: Hebrew, the tongue of the Jews, and Greek, the language of the Seleucid kingdom and the Middle East. The word "Christ" came from the Greek *Christos* ("the Anointed"). Tertullian's decision in *c.*AD 200 made clear the ambition of the Church to reach out beyond its territories of origin to the rest of the known world.

### CONSTANTINE'S CROSS

In 312, the Church found an unexpected supporter in Emperor Constantine I. At noon, in the hours before an important battle with a rival for imperial power, Constantine the Great had been praying to the sun – as Sol Invictus, the supreme deity of his religion. Suddenly, he and his army were astonished to see the blazing face of the sun overlain by the figure of the cross. The unmistakable symbolism was spelled out by an inscription written across the face of the heavens: *in hoc signo vinces* ("in this sign prevail").

Constantine's conversion at the Battle of Milvian Bridge and his patronage gave the Church a welcome boost. With the threat of persecution lifted, its members could meet and worship openly; its clergy could conduct its affairs in public. What had been – necessarily – a low-profile faith, with its adherents meeting quietly, was able to establish a presence in the world. Constantine advanced this process, endowing the Church with resources and working hard to build up its institutions. It was he who called the Council of Nicaea in 325, where important doctrinal questions were debated and resolved. While some felt that Constantine's patronage made Catholicism too "official", it

THE CHURCH OF ROME

allowed access to the structures of the imperial establishment that helped the Church to grow.

Constantine's Christianity was what the Church had needed at a tricky time. Even if the emperor himself was at times less than wholehearted in his commitment to his new faith, his mother St Helena ensured that he stayed loyal to its cause. Having converted following her son's example, she became his religious guide.

## THE NEW CAPITAL

At the same time, Constantine took steps that were to lead to one of the saddest developments in the Church's history: he transferred the empire's capital to Byzantium, or Constantinople as he called it. In the centuries that followed, the city on the Bosporus became the real centre of the "Roman" world, while Rome itself sank into stagnation and decline. In time it was to recover, but by then the Eastern Church had broken away and Christ's followers were divided.

*Above Constantine I is depicted in this 16th-century fresco with his mother, St Helena, the traditional finder of the relics of the "True Cross". She ensured her son never wavered in his beliefs.*

*Below In this 13th-century fresco, Pope Sylvester I baptizes Constantine – a breakthrough for the Church. In fact, the emperor postponed this sacrament until his deathbed.*

## A DOUBTFUL DONATION

Constantine gave Christianity his generous backing, building (among numerous other things) the original Basilica of St Peter's in Rome. However, the one thing the Roman does not appear to have given the Church is the rumoured "Donation of Constantine", in which he supposedly gave Pope Sylvester I and his successors temporal authority over Rome and many of its possessions in Europe and North Africa. Most of these realms fell to a variety of invaders and other rulers, but the popes held on to power in parts of central Italy into modern times. Even today, the Vatican remains a sovereign nation, its status sanctioned by custom, if not by legal title. In fact, the "Donation of Constantine" was revealed as a forgery in the 15th century. It is believed to have been created in the 8th century.

*Below A colossal head of Emperor Constantine from the Roman Forum. It was once the topmost part of a 4th-century full-length statue.*

# THE FIRST POPES

THE INSTITUTION OF THE PAPACY BEGAN WITH CHRIST'S COMMISSION TO PETER, "I WILL GIVE YOU THE KEYS OF THE KINGDOM OF HEAVEN: WHATEVER YOU BIND ON EARTH WILL BE BOUND IN HEAVEN..."

The papacy started to take shape as an institution over time, but the first pope was Peter. His name had been Simon, but Christ gave him a new name to go with his new and crucial role. "You are Peter," he says (Matthew 16:18), punning on the Greek word *petros*, or "stone", "and on this rock I will build my community." The Church over which he presided would be proof against the powers of Satan, Jesus promised, and its leader would have complete spiritual authority on Earth.

## CHRIST'S SUCCESSORS

The "apostolic succession" is key to Catholicism's claims to be the one true Church of God. According to this theory, authority has been transmitted via an unbroken line of pontiffs from Christ and Peter down to the present day.

*Below Christ hands the keys of heaven to Peter, who becomes the first pope, as depicted by Pietro Perugino in this 15th-century fresco.*

That authority is embodied in the office of the pope, who has as his emblem the crossed keys that recall the "keys of heaven" that Christ promised to Peter.

In its early days, of course, the Church was small and less structured, so to be its bishop would not have been a great honour in worldly terms. Christianity was often – due to Roman persecution – a furtive faith, forced to operate underground or on the run. There was no point in its bishops attracting attention to themselves, and they did not need to. Peter had no palace, no Vatican. Even so, his pre-eminence as "Prince of the Apostles" was acknowledged by Christ's followers. He was the Saviour's anointed successor here on earth, and no Christian would have dreamt of questioning his command.

## A CHANGING CHURCH

In the Edict of Milan (313), the Roman state recognized the legitimacy of the Church. Larger and

*Above The keys of heaven have been incorporated in Pope Leo X's coat-of-arms, which were carved in this Roman stone relief of 1513–20.*

no longer persecuted, the Church had become a very different kind of institution. Leadership in what was now a big and international organization became not just a spiritual challenge but also an administrative one. Maintaining doctrinal discipline was proving to be more difficult as well. Individual teachers started striking out in their own directions and, by the end of the 4th century, theological anarchy was threatening the integrity of the Church.

This, moreover, occurred at a time when Rome was in steep decline, beset by both barbarian invasions and by instability that came from within. The centre of political power had shifted to the East, where Constantinople was booming as the capital of a more Asian-orientated "Roman" state. Rome had become a backwater in its own empire. All the indications were that, as the Western Empire declined, the Church was going to go down with it. It seemed that its brief history was going to end in oblivion.

## A POWERFUL PAPACY

Pope Leo I, the Great, was influential in the development of the Church. His approach was far from subtle. He was unashamedly tough in his response to opposition. Democracy was a luxury he felt the Church could not afford. He was confronted with an organization that was in disarray, so he exercised dictatorial powers and centralized all power and doctrinal authority in himself. He formulated the view that the pope was heir to the powers of Peter, as stated in Matthew 16:18. Earlier generations of Christians had looked up to their popes, had valued the apostolic succession and had read and been inspired by Jesus' words to Peter, but they had not necessarily thought of the popes as heirs to Peter. Through these actions Leo the Great helped to strengthen the Church.

*Below When Pope Fabian was elected in 236, the Church was a large organization. In this depiction of his coronation by an artist of the 15th-century Spanish School, a dove (symbolic of the Holy Spirit) is perched on his head.*

### A PERSUASIVE POPE

Leo the Great may have been a masterful pontiff, however he was not a tyrant. He could compel people by his kindness, and won people over with his warmth. That he had a gift for getting his own way could hardly be denied: however, this was, after all, the man who managed to talk Attila the Hun out of attacking Rome. Their meeting, in 452, came after the Asiatic warlord and his army had invaded Italy and were poised to sweep down and sack the capital. Despairing of defending their city against such a ferocious enemy, the military and civic leaders of Rome approached the Pope to ask for his help. Taking two officials with him, Leo went to meet Attila and ask for peace. The latter "was so impressed with the presence of the high priest," wrote one chronicler of the day, "that he ordered his army to give up warfare and, after he had promised peace, he disappeared beyond the Danube".

*Below Leo the Great saved Rome from attack by Attila's forces when he met the Hunnish leader in 452. This c.1860 woodcut was inspired by a fresco in Munich.*

# THE CHURCH FATHERS

MANY SCHOLARS HAVE HELPED IN DEVELOPING THE DOCTRINAL
DETAILS OF CATHOLICISM – BUT FOUR IN PARTICULAR STAND OUT
AS THE "DOCTORS" OF THE EARLY CHURCH.

The Church owes an immeasurable debt to the great "doctors", or teachers, of the early Middle Ages, who helped shape not just its rituals but its faith. Clear though they were in essence, Christ's teachings had implications that had to be explored and examined, principles to be drawn out and systematized. The Church existed in the real world: Christians looked to it not just for inspiration

*Below Gregory, Ambrose, Jerome and Augustine: the four Church Fathers attend the Virgin and Child in this 15th-century altarpiece.*

but also for explanations, for moral guidance and for help in dealing with their doubts and fears. At first, it was ill equipped for this task. Its theology was undeveloped, and its institutional structures were limited.

AN UNBAPTIZED BISHOP
Just how disorganized it was is clear from the fact that, when the Bishop of Milan died in 374, his successor, Ambrose, had not been baptized or ordained as a priest, and he had not received any serious schooling in theology. Yet Ambrose understood the need for

*Above St Jerome had reputedly taken the thorn from a lame lion's paw, hence the cat with which he is traditionally shown, as here in this 15-century painting by an unknown Swiss artist.*

## THE CONFESSOR

Today, St Augustine is best known for his autobiography, *The Confessions* (397) and for his youthful cry, "Lord make me chaste, but not yet!" However, in his eagerness to underline the fact that humanity was, from the beginning of existence, in a "fallen" state, he belaboured himself about offences that far predated this. As a boy, he lamented he had stolen fruit that he did not need; even as a baby, he believed that he had cried deliberately to unsettle the adults around him. This is a strange book in some ways, yet Augustine's self-examination is today admired far beyond the Church for its striking insights into what we would call psychology.

*Right* The Devil holding up the Book of Vices to St Augustine *is the title of this work by Michael Pacher (c.1435–98). St Augustine saw evil and its temptations as a constant threat.*

theological rigour. His first move on his appointment was to give his possessions to the poor; his second was to embark on a programme of self-education. It was a spiritual and intellectual journey in which – thanks to the books he wrote – his fellow Christians were able to accompany him. Ambrose's courage was exemplary (his refusal to be bullied by Emperor Theodosius set the standard for subsequent pontiffs); so too was his piety. He was influential in his emphasis on the role of Mary, the Blessed Virgin.

### LATIN WORDSMITHS

Ambrose benefited from his ease with the Greek sources in which much theological writing until that time had been set down. Writing in Latin, Ambrose can be seen as part of that same process of westernization that Tertullian had begun two centuries before. Jerome continued the process with his translation of the Bible into Latin, which he began in 382. Jerome was a Dalmatian-born

*Right At "St Gregory's Mass", the Saviour appeared with his wounds bleeding and poured his blood into the chalice of the pope, as depicted in this c.1490 illumination.*

scholar who worked from Greek editions because it was recognized that the finest scholarship was to be found in that language. At the same time, the Church was starting to define itself as Western. Greek, since Alexander's day, had been the language not just of Greece itself but of Asia, the home – in the Church's eyes – of heresy.

### FIGHTER FOR ORTHODOXY

St Augustine of Hippo refuted two powerful heresies. As a young man, he held Manichaean views. These views were a product of Persian tradition that pitted the powers of light and virtue against darkness and sin. Manichaeism had exerted a strong influence over Christianity in the East. Augustine rejected this phase of his development, just as he did the dissolute lifestyle of his youth, and became a staunch defender of Western orthodoxy.

Augustine also defended the Roman Christians against the comforting creed of the Pelagians. Pelagius, a 4th-century monk, had argued that humanity had not irrevocably fallen in the Garden of Eden, so had no need of Christ's redemption. Individuals could choose to be good themselves, unaided. It was Augustine who helped to formulate the doctrine of original sin.

### A GREAT REFORMER

Gregory I, the Great, was elected pontiff in 590. His reforms were tireless and far-reaching. From the celibacy of the clergy to the idea of the remission of time in Purgatory for acts of public and private penance, they touched just about every area of religious life. The clamour for his canonization had begun in his own lifetime, though critics claimed he had practically bankrupted the Church with his charitable giving.

# A CHURCH DIVIDED

"ROME HAS SPOKEN, THE CASE IS CLOSED" ARE STRONG WORDS ATTRIBUTED TO ST AUGUSTINE. THE CHURCH'S INSISTENCE ON ORTHODOXY CAME ABOUT AFTER A LACK OF DOCTRINAL DISCIPLINE.

Rome was the centre of the world in the 1st century AD, but the power and control of this empire didn't last. The Dark Ages, from *c*.500 to the 11th century, were not as black as some popular histories claim, but it was an era in which the Church struggled. The Roman Empire was under relentless attack from invaders, and Rome itself was imploding politically, so the survival not just of the state but also of a civilization

was at stake – as was the Church. Yet, at a time when Christian unity was all-important, rivalry threatened to tear the faith apart.

## A CITY UNDER SIEGE

Augustine saw the danger. Rome had just been sacked by the Visigoths when, in the latter part of 410, he started writing *The City of God*. Many Romans believed the fall of their capital had been a judgement of the gods on its

*Above The Church, a fortress, is defended against heresy and sin in this illumination from a 15th-century French manuscript.*

toleration of the Christian religion. However, Augustine's vision was of the city of Rome and the Church as parallel states, beset by barbarism and paganism respectively. Hence the impassioned urgency with which he strove to secure the spiritual integrity of his Church.

## DIFFERENCES OF OPINION

Augustine thought the heretics were the enemies within. There was no shortage of them at this time, and they were often powerful. The adherents of Arianism followed the teaching of Arius, an Egyptian monk who had claimed that Christ, though saintly, was not divine. St Ambrose had led the fight against this heresy as Bishop of Milan in the 4th century, but it flourished and was believed in by many within Europe's ruling class. This heresy was halted when Emperor Theodosius I spoke out against it at the Constantinople Conference of 381. That year's

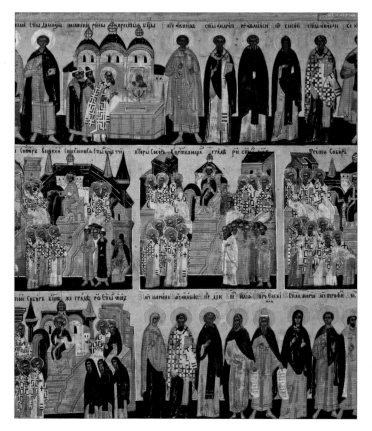

*Left A series of Nicaean Councils in the 1st millennium allowed important doctrinal issues to be thrashed out. It is represented in this Russian calendar dating from the mid-18th century.*

revised Nicene Creed (*see below*) clearly rejected Arianism's claims. Yet its influence persisted in out-lying regions of the West.

The 5th century brought the Nestorian Schism. An Archbishop of Constantinople, Nestorius asserted that Christ as God and Christ as man were not two dif-ferent aspects of the same being but two distinct persons. This heresy was taken up in the East, leading to the breaking away of what became known as the Assyrian Church. Monophysitism, by contrast, held that Christ had only one aspect, the divine. Its supporters were fiercely at odds with the Nestorians in the East.

## OUT OF IRELAND

Augustine's fears for the Church under barbarian attack were by no means exaggerated. Within a cen-tury of the Sack of Rome, Christianity had been almost wiped out throughout western Europe. Only in the remotest reaches of Ireland's Atlantic coast were Christianity and its culture holding out. However, in the 6th and 7th centuries, missionaries from these far-flung monasteries fanned out across western and central Europe (even Italy), rein-troducing the Church of Christ.

## THE EAST–WEST SCHISM

With its own bustling capital at Constantinople, the centre of a thriving empire, the Church in the East was flourishing, and it was increasingly going its own way. Cultural and linguistic differences caused the two halves of the old Roman Empire to diverge: the West was European and Latin; the East Asiatic and Greek. The West was in apparently terminal crisis, while the fortunes of the East were buoyant, so the eastern patriarchs saw no reason to bow before the popes. They owed allegiance to

*Left Heretical books are consigned to the fire in this illustration from a manuscript of the 9th century.*

the Byzantine emperors, who had the right of appointing them. Their loyalty to the pontiff took second place. The authority of Rome was recognized formally, but deference was offered more grudgingly as time went on.

In 1054, Rome placed a papal bull denouncing the patriarch, Michael Kerullarios, upon the altar of Constantinople's great basilica, Hagia Sophia. Kerullarios responded in kind. Pope and patriarch had excommunicated one another – expelled each other from their Church community. The East–West Schism was under way, and the "Orthodox" Church of the East often existed separately from the Catholic Church.

### THE NICENE CREED

We believe in one God,
the Father, the Almighty,
maker of heaven and earth,
of all that is, seen and unseen.

We believe in one Lord,
  Jesus Christ,
the only Son of God,
eternally begotten of the Father,
God from God, Light from Light,
true God from true God,
begotten, not made,
of one Being with the Father.
Through him all things were
  made.
For us men and for our salvation,
he came down from heaven:
by the power of the Holy Spirit
he became incarnate of the Virgin
  Mary,
and became man.
For our sake he was crucified
  under Pontius Pilate;
he suffered death and was buried.
On the third day he rose again

in accordance with the Scriptures;
he ascended into heaven
and is seated at the right hand of
  the Father.
He will come again in glory
to judge the living and the dead,
and his kingdom will have no end.

We believe in the Holy Spirit,
the Lord, the giver of life,
who proceeds from the Father and
  the Son.
With the Father and the Son he
  is worshipped and glorified.
He has spoken through the
  Prophets.
We believe in one holy Catholic
  and apostolic Church.
We acknowledge one baptism for
the forgiveness of sins.
We look for the resurrection of
  the dead,
and the life of the world to come.

Amen.

# THE MIDDLE AGES

The Church's second millennium could hardly have begun with a less auspicious start, split by the East–West Schism. What was really striking, though, was the easy assurance with which Catholicism shook off what should have been a catastrophic blow.

So-called in retrospect because it came between the classical period (Greece and Rome) and the Renaissance, the *medium aevum*, or Middle Ages, marked a breakthrough for the Church. Quite simply, in the West at least, there was no higher human institution: its teachings shaped the way men and women thought. The Church led the reconstruction of the West in the chaotic centuries that followed the fall of the Roman Empire in the 5th century, forming its institutions and culture and influencing architecture, music, literature and every area of learning. Catholicism had left its mark on all of these. The people saw the Church as the source of all their spiritual and moral laws, and rulers looked to it for their legitimacy.

Even so, there would be challenges. As early as the 7th century, Islam had emerged from Arabia. By the 11th century, the rapid expansion of its empire was seen as so great a threat to the West that a series of Crusades were mounted against the Muslims. Yet the existence of such a threat also gave Christendom an enemy against which it could define itself, and the Church continued to go from strength to strength.

*Above Christ looks down from heaven as a choir of monks sings a hymn in this illumination from a c. 1300 manuscript of an English psalter.*

*Left St Bridget of Sweden issues the rule for the Brigettine Order (Giovannantonio di Francesco Sogliani, 1522). Monasticism flourished in Europe during the Middle Ages.*

# MEDIEVAL CATHOLICISM

THE MIDDLE AGES IN EUROPE WAS A HIGH POINT FOR THE CHURCH:
EVERY ASPECT OF LIFE – FROM HOW PEOPLE FELT TO HOW THEY WERE
GOVERNED – WAS SHAPED BY CATHOLICISM.

As the main religion throughout Europe, the sect that had hidden itself away in the catacombs was no more. No monarchy could match its pervasive power. Kings consulted closely with its prelates and its pope, and ordinary men and women looked to their priests with all the deference due to God's representatives on Earth. Its teaching set the tone – morally, intellectually and culturally. Its monasteries were repositories of learning, driving forces in literature and science, and its cathedrals displayed the latest and the best in art and architecture.

## FEUDALISM AND FAITH

The Church's power and authority were not just awesome, they were integral to the way in which medieval Europe viewed the world. In the Middle Ages, along with the idea of "faith" went that of "fealty" (from the Latin *fidelitas*, or "faithfulness"). It defined the bond of obedience and loyalty the man had to his overlord. Just as the serf owed fealty to his lord, who in turn acknowledged the overlordship of his king, so the Christian obeyed his or her priest, who was directed by the religious hierarchy.

Medieval Europeans implicitly believed that God had created an orderly cosmos and everything in the universe had its place. It was the responsibility of those entrusted with power, both spiritual and temporal, to ensure that order prevailed here on Earth. The power of the Church and State were thus regarded as two sides of the same coin. Despite their differences – there were disputes between popes and kings – it would

*Above* This 12th-century golden orb, emblematic of the world, surmounted by a jewelled cross, was part of the crown jewels of imperial Germany.

never have occurred to a king to question the divine authority of the pope or his hierarchy any more than it would have occurred to the Church to undermine the power of the king. It was in neither's interest to jeopardize that principle of order on which the entire worldview of the Middle Ages rested.

## POWER AND WEALTH

In truth, the Church wielded a great deal of power over secular affairs as well, and few temporal rulers dared defy its will. None would have dreamt of taxing its wealthy monasteries. Whether in a spirit of piety or in fear for their fate in the afterlife, wealthy magnates bequeathed lavish gifts in land and treasures to their local religious foundations.

*Left* Serfs who worked the land used the crop to pay their tithe to the aristocracy and the Church, as seen in this late 15th-century French illustration from The Playfair Book of Hours.

Meanwhile, year in and year out, poor peasants and craftsmen had to pay a "tithe" (one-tenth) of their income to the Church. Although priests at village level lived pretty much as modestly as their parishioners, things were different further up the hierarchy. In time, the ethics of this would come to be questioned, but, in the meantime, senior churchmen often lived like lords.

## THE ARTS AND LEARNING

At the same time that these senior church members wined and dined stupendously, they also bestowed their patronage freely. As a result of their conspicuous consumption,

art lovers today can appreciate what are considered the greatest masterpieces of Western art. Giotto, Cimabué and countless anonymous artists worked under the auspices of the Church. Church buildings were often also filled with the exquisite work of master woodcarvers and sculptors, whose works brought the stories of the Bible to the illiterate.

Education and learning were to all intents and purposes the monopoly of the Church – and this, too, would eventually become a source of friction. For the moment, though, intellectual discussion and debate all took place within the terms of reference established by

the great Catholic teachers of the day. Pre-eminent among these was Thomas Aquinas, born in Sicily *c.*1225. His *Summa Theologica* (1266–74) was literally a "theological summary", setting out in a single vast and coherent plan all the Church's teachings about God, the universe and the place of man within it. Aquinas' work is valued in its own right by philosophers today, but it was also an important conduit for earlier thought: the ideas of Aristotle, of Arabic thinkers such as Ibn Rushd (Averroës) and Ibn Sina (Avicenna), and of Jewish doctors such as Maimonides all found their way into Western tradition through his work.

*Above With Plato and Aristotle on either side, St Thomas Aquinas is shown with the Arab philosopher Averroës in the foreground in this 15th-century painting by Benozzo di Lese Gozzoli.*

### DANTE

Born in Florence *c.*1265, Dante Alighieri has been revered in modern times as the poet who envisioned hell. His *Inferno* is indeed awe-inspiring, striking in its dreadful beauty but also in the sympathy it shows for the sufferings of the damned. Yet Dante would have been surprised to see it abstracted from his *Commedia* ("Comedy") as a whole.

Hell's torments could make no sense for him except as aspects of a universal order. His *Inferno*, like his *Purgatorio* and his *Paradiso*, is founded in the love of God. He can weep for the sinner while still giving thanks for the overall scheme.

***Below*** *Dante enlightens the citizens of Florence with his vision of the universe in this 1465 painting.*

# THE CRUSADES

SOON AFTER ISLAM AROSE IN THE EAST, VICTORIOUS ARAB ARMIES
SPREAD THEIR FAITH TO THE VERY DOORS OF ROME. FOR NEARLY
500 YEARS, CHRISTIANS FOUGHT BACK IN A SERIES OF CRUSADES.

Roughly at about the same time that
Catholicism had established itself as
the dominant religion in Europe,
Islam was on the rise in the East. This
new expansionist religion posed a
threat to Catholic authority, and the
Church felt urgent pressure to try to
stop its growth.

## THE RISE OF ISLAM

The prophet Muhammad's mission to
spread his Islamic religion began about
610. Arab armies carried his message
to both the East and the West. By 638,
less than three decades later, these
armies were occupying Jerusalem.

Spilling across North Africa, the
forces of Islam crossed the Straits
of Gibraltar into Spain in the early
8th century. By 720 they were
pushing into France, though they had

been turned back at Tours in 732.
Christian rulers in northern Spain
had embarked on a long-term
Reconquista, or "reconquest", but
the south of the peninsula seemed
securely established as al-Andalus, a
Muslim kingdom. With the borders
of the Islamic world expanding at an
incredible speed, Christendom was
in fear for its survival.

## A CALL TO ARMS

In November 1095, Pope Urban II
gave an electrifying speech at the
Council of Clermont. The armies of
Islam stood on the very doorstep
of Christian Europe, he warned.
His words were recorded by the
chronicler Fulcher of Chartres, and
he finished his speech with a
desperate appeal:

*Above Pope Urban II proclaims the
First Crusade during the Council of
Clermont in 1095 in this illustration
from Jean Fouquet's* Les Grandes
Chroniques de France, *c.1460.*

*For this reason I beg and urge you –
no, not I, but God Himself begs and
implores you, as the messengers of
Christ, the poor and the wealthy, to
rush and drive away this mob from
your brothers' territories, and to bring
swift assistance to those who also
worship Christ.*

*Below The crusaders travelled to the
Middle East by both land and sea.*

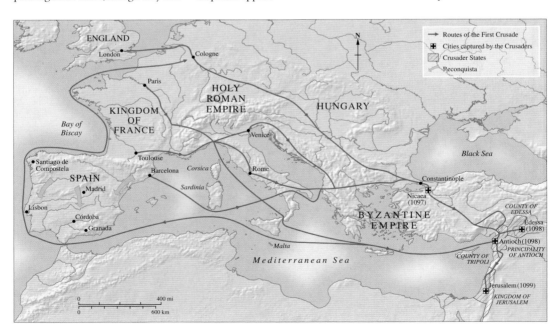

*Right* *Crusaders storm Constantinople –*
*a Christian city – in this 16th-century*
*painting of the Fourth Crusade by the*
*Italian painter Jacopo Tintoretto.*

In response to Pope Urban II's plea, a mass mobilization took place across Europe, involving not just knights and soldiers but also ordinary men and women – and children. Thousands were inspired by what they saw as their sacred duty. Others were drawn for secular reasons: the prospect of plunder or the promise of adventure.

## TO JERUSALEM!

The Crusade had a difficult start. The army that arrived in Constantinople – ready to march through Anatolia (modern-day Turkey) and on to the Holy Land – was big, but it was poorly equipped. Of the 100,000 crusaders, only 40,000 survived the journey over the mountains to Antioch. It then took a seven-month siege to take the Syrian city. Afterward, the crusaders pushed on to Jerusalem. Amid ferocious fighting, the city fell on 13 July 1099, and thousands of its inhabitants were massacred.

## CONTINUED CRUSADES

Jerusalem was soon under threat again from the resurgent "Saracens", as the Christians called the Arab forces. A Second Crusade occurred in 1147 but ended in an undignified rout. In 1187, the Kurdish leader Salah al-Din al-Ayyubi, or "Saladin", recaptured Jerusalem. The English king, Richard I, the Lionheart, and

other Christian kings mounted a Third Crusade in 1189, but they fought in vain.

The Fourth Crusade (1202–4) was short of funds, so the crusaders sacked Constantinople, massacring thousands. This was followed by another tragedy: in 1212, thousands of young French and Germans enlisted in the Children's Crusade, but before they reached the Holy Land they starved or were sold into slavery in North Africa.

The Fifth Crusade (1217–21) approached Jerusalem from the south but proved no more successful

than its predecessors. In 1228, Holy Roman Emperor Frederick II negotiated Jerusalem's return diplomatically, but it fell into Muslim hands again. Two further crusades were mounted in 1248 and 1270: both were catastrophic failures.

Retaking Jerusalem was out of the question after the Ottoman Turks took Byzantium in 1453, but the struggle against Islam went on. In Spain, the Reconquista was coming to a conclusion, which came with the capture of Granada in 1492. In 1529, the Ottomans besieged Vienna, but were finally repulsed. The West's decisive victory came at sea, at the Battle of Lepanto (1571). Christendom had been locked in conflict with Islam for five centuries. The struggle had been very costly in terms of lives and money, but it had done much to shape the Church.

*Left* *Even now an intimidating sight,*
*the 12th-century fortress of Krak des*
*Chevaliers in Syria was built by crusaders.*

# MONASTICISM

THE MONASTERIES WERE IMPORTANT CULTURAL AND ECONOMIC
CENTRES THAT HELPED SET THE TONE OF MEDIEVAL LIFE. THEY
BROUGHT MEN TOGETHER IN COMMUNITIES OF WORK AND PRAYER.

From the beginning, Christians had met in informal communities, with sharing and co-operation being fundamental to their faith. For a beleaguered, sometimes persecuted, minority, the community provided comfort. However, as time went on, organized communities of Christians were established, often living far away from the distractions and temptations of society at large. St Benedict of Nursia (c.480–543) founded at least 12 such communities in the early 6th century.

## THE RULE OF ST BENEDICT

One community in particular – the Benedictines, established about 430 at Monte Cassino, south of Rome – was to have enduring importance. This was where St Benedict first formulated his "Benedictine Rule", a regime prescribing set times for collective worship, private prayer and study. It also allowed time for daily stints of manual work, which Benedict saw as an important way of suppressing personal pride and of giving praise to God. The Rule also

*Above The great pioneer of the monastic movement St Benedict of Nursia delivers the Rules of the Order to St Maurus in this 1129 illumination, produced at the Monastery of St Gilles, Nîmes.*

put clear structures in place. One monk was to be elected "abbot" by his companions; he was to be in charge, though he had to consult with his community on key decisions and was not exempted from the general routines of work and prayer. With 73 points in all, the Rule gave detailed instructions about everything from forms of worship to food and clothing – it stipulated a lifestyle that was simple, but not punitively harsh.

## MONASTIC LIFE

The Rule of St Benedict soon became the basis for an extensive network of monasteries across medieval Europe. Young men flocked to join these communities. They flung themselves into the monastic life in all its aspects, not just prayer and contemplation but also study and work. As beacons of learning, these monasteries soon commanded the respect of the wider communities in which they were based.

Run as they were by a well-motivated and educated workforce, their farms and market gardens thrived. So did their other economic ventures: some monks brewed beer

*Left Monks work in the fields, as depicted by Breu the Elder (c.1475–1537) on this panel from an Austrian altarpiece.*

St Benedict's, young men flocked to join the community. They were drawn by the possibility of a purer, more wholly dedicated religious life. Cluny subsequently became a major monastic centre.

Monasteries elsewhere begged the new community to send out teachers to instruct them in the new rule. The Cluniac Reform quickly spread throughout western Europe. Even where the Cluniac Rule was not explicitly adopted, its influence was felt. Its effects filtered beyond the monasteries and into the wider Church. Catholicism's conscience had been awakened, and individual believers, clergy and institutions all set about reforming themselves and the way they lived.

However, Cluny was a victim of its own success. It became so powerful and influential that some began to feel that it had become too worldly in its turn. In 1098, St Robert of Molesme and St Stephen Harding founded the Cistercian Order — so-called because it was established at the Abbey of Cîteaux. It too set out to restore the Benedictine Rule as originally ordained, and it did so with considerable success. From 1113, under the leadership of St Bernard of Clairvaux, it became an important force for monastic reform.

or other drinks while others prepared medicines from herbs they had grown themselves. The monasteries rapidly became important centres of industry and trade – and their abbots used their influence on local rulers.

## MONASTICISM REINVENTED

But soon some people were asking whether this success had not come at too high a price. Were the monasteries losing their way, becoming too "worldly" in their concerns? In 910, William the Pious, the Duke of

*Above The Cistercian Abbey of Sénanque, located in southern France, was founded in the mid-12th century.*

Aquitaine, founded a new community at Cluny, in eastern France. His idea was that its members would return to the founding principles of monasticism, as originally set down in the Benedictine Rule. William had read the mood of the times and his call for a new kind of monasticism had struck a chord. Though, if anything, the code at Cluny was even stricter than

### MONASTIC MYSTICISM

If the idea of community is as old as Christianity itself, so too is that of solitary contemplation. Christ's sojourn in the desert was emulated by a long tradition of hermits. Others wandered inward, deeper and deeper into their own minds, to find a peaceful place in which they could commune with God.

Some mystics, such as Julian of Norwich and Mechtilde of Magdebourg, can be seen as a kind of counterbalance to the monastic movement, pursuing the same aims as these religious communities but using contrary methods. The less these mystics attended to the world, they felt, the closer they could draw to God. In blindness to the world and its concerns, they could glimpse the truth that really mattered. Enlightenment, wrote one mystic, was to be found in a "Cloud of Unknowing".

*Right Mother Julian of Norwich was one of the great mystics of the Middle Ages. She is depicted in this 20th-century statue in Norwich Cathedral, England.*

# SHRINES AND RELICS

TANGIBLE TESTAMENTS TO HEROIC LOVE AND SACRIFICE, HOLY SHRINES AND SACRED RELICS HAVE REMINDED BELIEVERS THROUGHOUT HISTORY WHAT THEIR FAITH IS ALL ABOUT.

A shrine is considered a sacred place, usually one that has been specially blessed by the presence of a holy person, who carried out an important act, or who lived, died or was buried there. A relic is an item once associated with a saintly personage, anything from a fragment of bone to a scrap of shroud, or a possession of some sort. Catholics believe that shrines and relics have been sanctified by their associations to these holy people, so shrines have often become places of pilgrimage, while holy relics have become objects of veneration.

Even Catholics today find it hard to imagine the transporting spiritual excitement their medieval forebears experienced in the presence of holy shrines and sacred relics. Though the Catholic Church continues to encourage the veneration of genuine relics, this is often misunderstood outside the Church. There is discomfort with it among modern believers, and Catholics are still sensitive to any suggestion of superstition.

## OPEN TO ABUSE

During the Middle Ages, there was undoubtedly an element of the grotesque in the cult of certain relics, and, indisputably, there was at times an air of opportunistic showmanship about their presentation. Much of their fascination for the faithful may well have been as much about vulgar curiosity as about faith.

At the time, businesses linked to the pilgrimages were thriving, and the possession of holy relics did not merely

*Above St Veronica wiped Christ's face as he carried his cross to Calvary. Miraculously, an imprint of Jesus' face was left on the cloth, as shown in this 15th-century painting by Hans Memling.*

confer prestige, it could also bring (sometimes spectacular) earning potential. Pride of place in Venice's St Mark's Basilica was the tomb of the apostle – the Venetians had actually stolen St Mark's remains from their original resting place in Alexandria. In England, Canterbury was quick to cash in on the martyrdom of St Thomas, with entrepreneurially minded priests selling what was purported to be vials of his blood and scraps of his clothing.

## A VALID TRADITION

So many churches had parts of the True Cross or the bones of various saints that not all of them could have been genuine. Yet even if not all relics were what they claimed to be, over the centuries millions of Catholics have derived great comfort and inspiration from them. Relics were of value not least as a subject for meditation. A visitor to St Thomas à Becket's tomb in Canterbury could wonder at the courage of one who

*Below The cloth said to have been worn by Our Lady at the birth of Christ has been kept at Chartres Cathedral, France, since AD 876. The cathedral is a popular site of pilgrimage.*

*Above Reputed to be the last resting place of the apostle St James the Great, Santiago de Compostela is an important place of pilgrimage.*

had stood up to his own king for what he knew was right. German visitors to the shrine of St Sebaldus in Nuremberg could reflect on what his early mission to Rome and preaching in Nuremburg had meant for their country. Several successive German emperors visited the shrine to pay him homage.

## CONTACT WITH THE SAINTS

There is no doubt that the sense of being able to touch the saintly was part of the reason behind making a pilgrimage. Accordingly, a certain amount of tension arose between the instinct to present sacred relics in what would be appropriate magnificence and the pilgrims' desire for up-close contact. As monuments for these relics grew in size and splendour, they were built with open cavities, or "squeezing places", left in the tomb surround so the faithful could feel they were getting as close as possible to the source of grace.

## DISTRUST FROM OTHERS

This need for contact would eventually be viewed by non-Catholics as somewhat grotesque. Protestant reformers, like many other modern intellectuals, distrusted Catholicism's instinct for the concrete – what can be seen and touched – an instinct revealed in everything from crucifixes and rosaries to statues and stained-glass windows. To them, the desire to touch a fragment of the "True Cross" or a visit to a saint's tomb could be compared to the time when Jesus told St Thomas to put his fingers in his wounds (John 20:25–9) before the doubting man would finally believe in his Resurrection.

In the 18th century, the philosophers of pre-revolutionary France had denounced Catholicism as a conspiracy to prop up corrupt institutions. Voltaire was one of these philosophers, and among his anti-religious comments was a sneer about the veneration of Christ's foreskin and the Virgin's milk, designed to humiliate Catholics.

For believers, though, the desire for contact with Christ and his saints was not rooted in weakness of faith. Contact was made for love, like that of the woman who touched the hem of Jesus' garment (Luke 8:40–8).

*Below Sacred shrines, such as the one in this 15th-century painting by the Master of San Sebastian, have sometimes been linked to miraculous healings, making them popular pilgrimage sites for the lame and the sick in search of succour.*

### MIRRORS REFLECTING THE RELICS

In Aachen, Germany, in 1440, so many pilgrims flocked to see an exhibition of sacred relics that there was little prospect of anybody actually touching the reliquaries. The most the pilgrim could hope for was glimpses of these sacred treasures through the crush of the crowd. This situation led to the selling of metal-framed "pilgrim mirrors". These mirrors were designed to be clipped to the cap. They supposedly allowed the radiance emitted by the sacred relics to be captured, which the pilgrims could even take home to share with their family and friends.

# PILGRIMAGE

EVERY YEAR, ALONG EUROPE'S HIGHWAYS, TRAVELLERS MADE THEIR WAY, SINGLY OR IN GROUPS, CRISS-CROSSING THE CONTINENT TO SEEK OUT THE MOST SACRED SHRINES OF THE CATHOLIC FAITH.

The idea of the medieval pilgrimage is still well known today to students of literature, thanks to Geoffrey Chaucer's *The Canterbury Tales*. This 14th-century poem tells the story of a group of pilgrims from different walks of life, who travel from London to Canterbury in England. There they intend to offer their devotions at the tomb of St Thomas à Becket, who lies buried in the cathedral where he met his martyr's death. Like many Christians in the Middle Ages, Chaucer's pilgrims hoped to acquire grace in the eyes of God by the commitment they were showing in making a sacred journey.

## AN OLD TRADITION

By this time, the tradition of pilgrimage, or spiritual journey, was already an old one. Since the 2nd century, believers had been travelling to Jerusalem to visit the scenes of their Saviour's ministry and sufferings and to think about what they meant in their own lives. The pilgrimage is by no means a uniquely Christian custom. By the 5th century BC, Buddhists had been trekking to the birthplace of their teacher, the Buddha, at Kapilavastu, Nepal.

Pilgrimage became embedded in the traditions of Catholicism. It was a gesture, a declaration of spiritual intent. Forsaking family, friends and everyday routines, the Catholic set out on what he or she hoped would be a new direction. The pilgrimage itself was just the start, but it could be a profoundly significant start. Removed from the rhythms of daily work and home life, the pilgrim could reflect on that life and how it might be led better. Arriving at the holy place itself, the pilgrim might meditate on the religious drama that had taken place there, or on the life of the saint whose mortal remains had sanctified the spot.

*Above* The Clerk of Oxenford, *one of Chaucer's fictional pilgrims, is shown in* The Canterbury Tales *(1400–10).*

Some made their pilgrimages in hopes of saving a sick relative, or to help secure their salvation in the life beyond. Others were motivated by piety, a desire to perfect themselves; still others went as penitential pilgrims. They might have made their own decision to make a pilgrimage in expiation of some great wrong they had done. Or they might have been ordered by a court to make the journey, or else face a far harsher

## HOUSES OF HOSPITALITY

With thousands of pilgrims on the move, often travelling long distances, a considerable infrastructure was needed to feed, accommodate and protect them. It had to cope with such normal activities as treating their ailments, shoeing their horses and even mending their clothes. Every bit as important in its own time as the tourist industry is to travellers today, the pilgrimage acted as a powerful economic engine. Rather than the desire for leisure, however, it was harnessing Christian piety and spreading prosperity far and wide.

In Jerusalem, and on the great pilgrimage routes such as the road to Santiago de Compostela, monasteries and other religious houses created special hospices, where the pilgrims could stay overnight in safety. These hospices were not like today's hospices, used as places for the sick. The original hospices took their name from the Latin word *hospes*, or "host", which is the root of our modern word "hospitality".

*Right* A hospice (hostel) for pilgrims, one of many established across medieval Europe, is shown in this 15th-century illustration from Antoine de la Sale's Les Cent Nouvelles Nouvelles.

punishment. There were also those who were actuated by less pious motives: a yen for travel or adventure or simply a desire for change.

## SACRED PLACES

The Holy Land, though the ultimate place of pilgrimage, was beyond most people's reach, geographically, financially, and often politically, given that Jerusalem was so long in Muslim hands. Even when it was not, Muslim pirates from Turkey and from North Africa's Barbary Coast preyed on Christian shipping, leaving no alternative to a long, costly and hazardous overland journey through the Balkans. Rome, as both the centre of the Church and with its shrine of St Peter, was another

*Below A 17th-century French map shows the main pilgrimage routes to Santiago de Compostela in Spain.*

popular place of pilgrimage. However, pilgrims from northern Europe had to find their way over the Alps on foot to get there, and many could not make their way across this treacherous mountain range.

There were less hazardous destinations, such as St Andrews in Scotland, reputedly the apostle's final resting place. In Galicia, Spain, the cathedral at Santiago de Compostela was supposed to house the remains of the apostle St James the Great. Another popular site in Spain was Zaragoza, where Our Lady had appeared atop a pillar before St James. Walsingham in Norfolk, England, had been the site of a different Marian apparition (appearance of Mary) in 1061, and it became an important place of pilgrimage.

*Left A pilgrim badge was worn to show that a person had made a particular pilgrimage. This pewter badge of St Thomas à Becket was worn by a person who had travelled to Canterbury Cathedral.*

## SAFETY IN NUMBERS

Even short journeys could be hazardous, and pilgrims often felt obliged to travel in groups in order to avoid attack by brigands. According to an often-practised procedure, pilgrims gathered in their local town centre to receive a blessing from their priest before setting out on their journey together. On longer trips, these groups might join others, forming great congregations hundreds, sometimes thousands, strong.

# GOTHIC GLORY

BUILT TO CELEBRATE THE GLORY OF GOD AND AS HOUSES OF WORSHIP, EUROPE'S IMPRESSIVE GOTHIC CATHEDRALS ARE SPECTACULAR MONUMENTS TO AN AGE OF FAITH.

Imagine how a medieval peasant might have felt on seeing a great cathedral such as Chartres for the first time. Dumbstruck with amazement as far across the fields on the horizon, shimmering slightly in the haze of the August heat, the gigantic structure appeared to be rising out of the ground. They had heard of Chartres' new cathedral, of course – how its spire seemed to soar to heaven, how the clear lines of its solid stone structure dissolved into a riot of statuary figures as you approached. As for its vast interior, its wood carvings and statues bathed in the otherworldly light of a hundred stained-glass windows: that was a promise of paradise on earth. Even so, nothing had prepared them for their first actual experience of one of the great Gothic architectural monuments of the medieval age.

## THE GOTHIC STYLE
Similar to most artistic movements, Renaissance architecture sought to better its predecessors. The term "gothic" was employed pejoratively by the Italian architects of the Renaissance to describe the architecture of the Middle Ages, which they had mistakenly attributed to the Germanic tribes known as the Goths. These tribes had sacked Rome in the 5th century AD, and thus had earned a

*Above Built mainly in the 13th century, Chartres Cathedral in France is one of the great masterpieces of Gothic architecture (its second spire, on the left, was added on top of a previous tower in the 1500s).*

reputation for barbarism. They were seen as the destroyers of classical civilization, which the Renaissance had set out to reinstate. But although the term "Gothic Style" is still in use, it no longer has a negative connotation, and the medieval period is now generally seen as a golden age of European architecture. In fact, the Gothic style enjoyed a major revival in the 19th century.

## REACHING FOR THE SKY
One striking feature of the Gothic style was its thrilling emphasis on verticality. However, for all its aesthetic and symbolic resonances, the style was reliant on advances in engineering. The old Romanesque churches had been held up by the massive masonry of their walls, their rounded arches suitable for only small windows. Now pointed arches distributed the weight, replacing a great deal of outward thrust with downward thrust. This allowed constructions to be taller, and walls and columns to be more slender. The liberal use of pointed pinnacles and spires underlined the accent on the vertical, which made even the grandest Romanesque monuments look squat and stubby.

Since the walls no longer had to bear such a load, they could afford to be less solid and could be fitted with huge, decorative windows filled with stained glass. Chartres Cathedral has more than a hundred of these. All kinds of biblical scenes were presented, creating a stunning pictorial scripture

*Above Stained glass, such as this one from a window in Chartres Cathedral showing Noah and his ark, gave the illiterate vivid access to the Bible stories.*

for the illiterate. No longer dark and gloomy, the inside of the Gothic church could be turned over to the best artists and craftsmen to express themselves in paint and metalwork, carved wood and stone: they created saints' statues and fonts, elaborately ornate wooden pulpits, pews and choir screens.

To go to church in such a setting was to be bombarded with sensory impressions. In many ways it was an experience of wonder and delight. Given the enthusiasm with which medieval artists represented devils and hell's torments, it might also be an experience of fear – but it would always be an experience to be remembered. Demons bedecked the outside, too, with waterspouts turned into hideously decorative gargoyles. Chartres' exterior offers a crash course in medieval culture. Along with religious scenes, the door surrounds are lined with figures of famous kings and queens, prophets and even philosophers.

## COLLECTIVE EFFORTS

The creators of these stunning works were content to remain anonymous, though at the same time it is clear that they were given an astonishingly free hand in determining the design of their works. Where in a modern building the sense of unified, overall design is all-important, Gothic churches seem somehow to have grown organically.

All things considered, this should not be surprising. Such vast and ambitious edifices were beyond the capacity of any one man to construct or even oversee. These churches took years, decades, to build – longer than an artisan's working life – so it was not realistic to expect any continuity of craftsmanship, and generations of workers were involved in their construction. Skilled builders, masons, joiners, woodcarvers and glaziers accordingly went from place to place through the cities of Europe. On any given project, within rough parameters, they would have free rein in producing their work.

It was haphazard, but it worked. The great Gothic churches were essentially communal projects. Apart from that of praising God, and impressing and educating the public, their main purpose was to announce the wealth and prestige of the communities that built them. In that, they were triumphantly successful.

*Right Satan stokes the fire, while demons plunge the souls of the damned into a cauldron in this 12th-century relief from England's York Minster Cathedral.*

*Below The Last Supper is represented in beaten gold in this stunning 11th-century relief from Aachen, Germany.*

# RENAISSANCE & REFORMATION

The Renaissance was the age of undisputed Catholic supremacy in Europe, but it ended in dissension and strife. Outside the Church, the conventional view of modern historians has been of a papacy growing in corruption as it grew in power, with its hierarchy becoming increasingly remote from the people – even from parish priests. Although there is truth in this narrative, it tells no more than half the story of a great institution struggling to negotiate a time of extraordinary upheaval. Social, political, economic and intellectual life – all these were being transformed during this period. Great epidemics had ravaged the communities of Europe; the printing press was democratizing learning; Columbus' voyage had opened the door to the New World.

Martin Luther's stand at Wittenberg in 1517 was one reaction and the creed of Calvin another. In England, King Henry VIII's refusal to obey the pope marked a severing of the old accord between Church and State. However, there were changes within the Church, too. These had been gathering momentum for centuries, but they gained new impetus in the growing ferment.

The Reformation was a period of trauma for the Church, and in several countries it found itself driven back underground. All of Europe suffered from the wars the crisis brought, with martyrs on both sides. At the same time, in forcing a far-reaching process of reappraisal and renewal upon the Church, the Reformation also became a moment of rebirth.

*Above* The prophet Daniel as depicted on the Sistine Chapel ceiling, painted by the Italian artist Michelangelo, 1508–12.

*Left* Religion was the inspiration for much of the greatest Renaissance art, as in this early 15th-century painting, The Resurrection of Christ, by Mariotto di Cristofano.

# RIVAL POPES

DURING PART OF THE EARLY RENAISSANCE, THE ROMAN CATHOLIC CHURCH WAS BASED IN FRANCE. THERE WAS A SHORT-TERM PAPACY IN AVIGNON AND MUCH CONFLICT WITHIN THE CHURCH.

The Church was not only a religious institution but was also an extremely powerful and prominent social organization. Inevitably, it was involved in political affairs. As the Middle Ages concluded and the Renaissance began, the Church was finding its independence increasingly difficult to maintain, with secular rulers seeking to harness its influence to their own ends.

## POPES AND POLITICS

The 13th century had already seen the supposedly transcendent authority of the papacy called into question by the growing interference of kings and aristocratic clans. Pope Nicholas IV had created added difficulties for the papacy when he

*Below* Built by Benedict XII and enlarged by Clement VI, the Palais des Papes in Avignon, France, was the home of a papacy in exile.

bought the support of the Colonnas – an important Roman family – by granting them favours, and when he agreed to crown the French Prince Charles of Anjou, making him King of Naples and Sicily in 1289. The family was in no mood to surrender its special status under Nicholas' successor, Celestine V. In deference to King Charles, he had established his papal court at Naples. However, Celestine was ignominiously out of his depth and abdicated just five months after his election in 1294, making way for the more formidable Boniface VIII, who moved the papacy back to Rome.

Boniface could not be frightened into submission by Charles – or by the French ascendancy he represented – but his confrontational manner served only to precipitate a crisis. From the first, Boniface had both the King of Naples and Sicily and the Colonna family against him.

*Above* Pope Boniface VIII is illustrated drafting canonical law in this 14th-century manuscript from the Decrees of Boniface VIII.

Years of harassment culminated in an assassination attempt in 1303. Although Boniface survived the attempt, he died of natural causes only a few weeks later.

## THE AVIGNON PAPACY

Boniface's successor, Benedict XI, was pulled one way and then the other by Charles and the Colonnas. The French won after Benedict's death with the election of Clement V, who as Bertrand de Got had been the Archbishop of Bordeaux.

Clement had never visited Rome, and four years into his reign, in 1309, he transferred the seat of papal power to Avignon, in southern France. This was just one of the most obvious of Clement's concessions to King Philip IV. A host of new French cardinals were created in an intiative urged by Philip, and Clement outlawed the Order of the Knights Templar in 1307 throughout Europe. Their immense wealth in France was confiscated by the king.

## POPE AND "ANTIPOPE"

It almost seemed the move to Avignon had done the papacy good: it was growing in institutional splendour and in wealth. However, behind the scenes, the French crown was wielding unprecedented power. After Clement's death in 1314, six successive popes reigned from Avignon. The arrangement worked – but at a considerable cost to the Church's autonomy.

The transfer to France had left the Church in Italy in a rebellious mood; Rome was bereft, its purpose of so many centuries gone. There was unease in the wider Catholic Church as well. Queen Bridget of Sweden joined St Catherine of Siena in lobbying for a return. In 1376, Pope Gregory XI removed his court from Avignon to Rome. But the rejoicing was cut short by his death just a few months later.

The French had not finished with the papacy – their possession, as they now saw it. When an Italian, Urban VI, was named as pope in Rome in 1378, the French created their own "pope", Clement VII. In the decades that followed, four "antipopes" were elected as French counters to the popes of Rome. Called to arbitrate in the dispute, the Council of Pisa (1408) made matters worse: for a time the Church boasted not two popes but three, because the French cardinals could not agree among themselves. Finally, in 1417 Pope Martin V (a member of the Colonna family) received the recognition of the entire Catholic Church, with the papacy back in Rome.

*Above In* Roma La Veuve, *an Italian manuscript produced in the Renaissance, the allegorical "Widow of Rome" is illustrated mourning her bereavement after the departure of the papacy, shown outside the city walls.*

### THE WESTERN SCHISM

So-called to differentiate it from the earlier separation, which had seen the Orthodox Church established in 1054, the Western Schism had consequences far beyond the papal courts. Secular rulers had to decide which side to acknowledge: the Roman pontiff or the French-backed Avignon pope. Because both papal courts appointed their own bishops, the lower clergy and the people were left confused – and spiritually adrift. Each side had excommunicated the other's supporters, so ordinary people had no way of knowing whether the sacraments their priests were administering were valid; whether their marriages, or their loved ones' funerals, were acceptable to God.

*Right Clement VII, the first "antipope" of the Western Schism, was enthroned at Avignon in 1378, shown here in the* Chroniques de France ou de St Denis.

# INDULGENCES

THE PAPACY HAD INITIALLY INTRODUCED INDULGENCES TO MEET A
SPIRITUAL NEED. THESE REMISSIONS GAVE MILLIONS OF CATHOLICS
THE HOPE TO STRIVE FOR THEIR SALVATION.

The Catholic Church is generally seen as being dogmatic in its teachings. It is easy to forget, then, that for much of the first millennium, its teachings in several areas were to some extent a work-in-progress in the development of doctrine. One issue that had from early on caused concern among Christians and their clergy was that they felt perilously poised between salvation and damnation. Surely, theologians reasoned, there must be a middle ground for those whose lives had been virtuous, though flawed?

## PURIFYING THE SOUL

By the 5th century AD teachers were talking of a place of temporary chastisement, in which the soul would be purged or purified by the fire, but from which it would eventually be released into heaven, for eternity. The idea had been taken up and developed by Pope Gregory the Great in the 6th century. He had proposed that prayerful observance or good works in this life might lead to "indulgence".

An indulgence gives a period of remission to the sufferings of the soul in Purgatory after death, granted in return for some act of commitment – a pilgrimage, a programme of prayer, for example. It was a radical step, but it re-energized Christianity, giving ordinary men and women new grounds for hope. Few could hope to be saints in the hereafter, but anyone free of mortal sin could strive to do better in their daily lives, to throw themselves into their regimes of prayer and charitable works. The other great thing about the system was that, since people could earn "indulgence" not just for themselves but for their departed loved ones, it fostered a sense of solidarity between the living and the dead.

## THE PLENARY INDULGENCE

As time went on, what had been an inspirational idea became a fully articulated system, with periods of indulgence established for certain observances or acts. In particularly special circumstances, a "plenary indulgence" might be granted, with a complete remission of temporal punishment for sin. If the receiver died in that moment, his or her soul could avoid going to Purgatory.

So far, this was nothing exceptional: the system may have seemed mechanistic, but it gave people a

*Above Michael the archangel weighs souls, separating out the saved from the damned in this c.1450* Last Judgement, *painted by Rogier van der Weyden.*

spiritual incentive to which they could respond. However, at the same time, it was open to abuse: the temptation was always there for the Church to harness it to meet its worldly ends. When Pope Boniface VIII proclaimed a jubilee year for 1300, for example, he promised a plenary indulgence to those who made the pilgrimage to Jerusalem that year. Two million people heeded his call. The suspicion that he was putting on a show of strength for his political enemies in Rome must be set against the wider benefit his jubilee did in reinvigorating the whole Church.

*Left The good are lofted heavenward by flights of angels, while the wicked are carried down into hell in a burning river in Jean Colombe's 14th-century painting.*

## A FINANCIAL TRANSACTION

More problematic was the financial note, which may have been innocent to start with but became corrupt over time. It began with the payment of fees for masses offered for the souls of the dead, another way of gaining them remission. The token sums paid were a welcome supplement to the incomes of poor parish priests. However, the practice spread as the Church first relied on the contributions it gained in this way and then exploited its people's piety. The poor were bullied into paying for prayers, the wealthy bribed with offers of an easy afterlife. Soon high prelates and great religious houses were growing rich on the proceeds.

The perception spread that indulgences existed not for the sake of fallen humanity but for the Church's monetary enrichment. However, this was not always the case. When Jesus gave Peter his papal power, he gave him the keys of heaven; he also promised him that the "powers of death" would not prevail against his Church. Purgatory wasn't mentioned, but by giving his pope authority to "bind" and "loose" the laws of earth and heaven, he gave him, and the popes who followed him, the right to ordain these things as he decided through God's grace.

*Above A bull of Julius II, issued in 1505, announces the indulgences that had been conferred on a group of wealthy benefactors.*

### SALVATION FOR SALE

In 1245, when England's King Henry III set out to rebuild Westminster Abbey, the venture won Pope Innocent IV's approval. More than this, it won his promise that any individual who made a contribution of money to this reconstruction would receive 20 days' indulgence from the sufferings of Purgatory. This was a clear cash transaction, even if it was for a good cause. By the 14th century, indulgences were being openly bought and sold. In Chaucer's *The Canterbury Tales*, the Pardoner carried a sheaf of printed "pardons" in his saddlebag. In 1344, Clement VIII issued 200 plenary indulgences in England alone, which were "earned" entirely by financial endowments to the papacy.

*Below England's King Henry III is shown with Westminster Abbey, which he rebuilt, in this c. 1253 illustration from* History of the English.

# THE FRANCISCAN REVOLUTION

ST FRANCIS IS AMONG THE MOST BELOVED OF SAINTS. TO HIS SPIRITUAL
ARDOUR AND LOVE OF NATURE, HE ALLIED A TACTFUL RADICALISM THAT
WAS TO HAVE A FAR-REACHING IMPACT ON THE CHURCH.

***Above** Christ officiates as St Francis
takes Lady Poverty as his bride, depicted
in this 13th–14th century allegorical
scene by Giotto.*

Francesco di Pietro di Bernardone
(*c.*1181–1226) was one of Assisi's
most fashionable young men, known
for his love of all things French. He
was devoted to music, poetry, fashion
and flirtation. However, he also had
a more serious side. In the 1200s,
when he was a young man in his
twenties, a series of spiritual crises
caused him to question his worldly
preoccupations. He left behind his
old pursuits and his old friends to
care for lepers. The romantic enthusiasm of old was evident in the way
he hurled himself into this new life,
though now the mistress of his heart,
he said, was "Lady Poverty".

## BEGGARS IN CHRIST

This was a huge transformation, but
the change in Francis was by no means
done. In 1209, he was in a church in
Assisi when a priest gave a sermon on
Matthew's Gospel, Chapter 10.

*Take no gold, nor silver, nor copper in
your belts, no bag for your journey,
nor two tunics, nor sandals, nor staff;
for the labourer deserves his food…
Do not be anxious how you are to
speak or what you are to say; for
what you are to say will be given to
you in that hour; for it is not you
who speak, but the Spirit of your
Father through you.*

Francis would need no further
encouragement to live the words of
the gospels. He took to the roads as a
beggar – with no money, no bag, no
spare clothing, no sandals and no
staff. However, he did soon have a
companion: Bernard of Quintavalle,
another wealthy young man from
Assisi, and the first recruit to Francis'
order of Friars Minor. Unlike the
monks who lived in monasteries –
and so, however hard they tried to
avoid it, had worldly ties – the friars
would have only the air they
breathed and the food and water
strangers gave them.

## A NEW ORDER

This "mendicant" lifestyle could
clearly be seen as an implicit criticism of the religious establishment
at a time when its institutions had
grown enormously in power and
wealth. Already, there had been signs
of restlessness, with certain heretics

***Left** St Francis maintained good relations
with the papacy. In this 13th–14th
century painting by Giotto, he preaches
before Innocent's successor, Honorius III.*

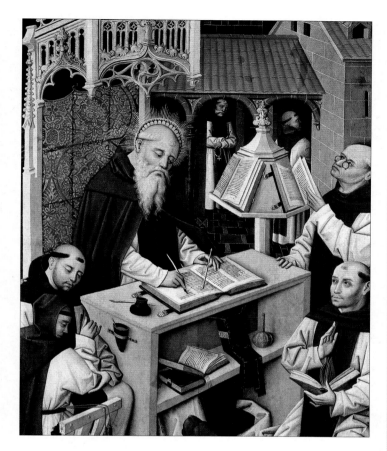

attacking the Church for its close relations with wealthy, worldly interests. The hierarchy could be forgiven for feeling defensive in the face of Francis' apparent challenge.

For his own part, however, Francis showed no interest in taking the hierarchy to task. On the contrary, he defended the institutions of the Church against all detractors and sued humbly to Pope Innocent III for his support. The Pope appears to have found Francis a perplexing character. One story claims that the Pope initially ordered the ragged, dirty vagabond before him to be sent away to tend swine; however, he then relented when Francis agreed without demur.

*Above The Dominicans, shown in this 16th-century painting by the Spanish School, were writers and teachers.*

Whatever reservations he might have had, Innocent came to the conclusion that Francis should be encouraged: that decision itself showed a certain vision on the pontiff's part. A movement that might have been profoundly destabilizing was accommodated by a Church already making conscious efforts to reform itself.

### THE DOMINICANS

St Dominic was a teacher trying to hold back the rising tide of heresy in southern France. He founded his

own order in 1214, which also took up mendicant poverty. Dominic saw that the poor were increasingly out of reach of the Church, not just in the scattered hamlets of the countryside but in the fast-growing cities. He wanted an order of young men to carry the Word to these lost sheep. Since Dominic had been placed in charge of a convent as early as 1206, these Dominican nuns actually predated the Dominican friars.

# CHURCH MUSIC

FROM THE AUSTERE GRACE OF GREGORIAN CHANT TO THE GLORIOUS
POLYPHONIES OF THE BAROQUE AND BEYOND, MUSIC HAS PLAYED ITS
PART IN THE LITURGIES OF THE CHURCH.

Both solemn and spare, the sound of plainsong (also called "plainchant") as it echoes through the aisles and cloisters is for many people the quintessential sound associated with the Catholic Church. For others, however, it will be the thunderous chorus of the Lourdes pilgrims' "Ave Maria!", or the graceful harmonies of Haydn's *The Creation* or James MacMillan's *Mass*.

## AN ORDERLY COSMOS
It seems likely that music formed part of the Christian liturgy from early on in its establishment, though in the absence of written notation from that time we have no real way of knowing for certain. Music had an almost theological significance for the people of the ancient and medieval worlds. The way in which

the different notes could resonate harmoniously was seen as analogous to the relations between the earth and the planets and stars – all set in their own rotating spheres within the overall order of God's universe. Hence the phrase, "the music of the spheres", and therefore the importance attached to music – which went far beyond the aesthetic pleasure it provided.

## SONG OF ST GREGORY
It was natural, then, that music would have its place in the monastic order, at the services offered by monks each day to mark the passage of the hours. The emphasis was on austerity: plainsong was indeed plain, involving no accompanying instruments and just a single sustained melodic line. Even so, its eerie beauty must have been an inspiration to the monks, reminding them each day of the mysterious majesty of God.

Pope Gregory the Great had encouraged the practice of singing plainsong, which, its inestimable beauties apart, helped foster the monastic virtues of co-operation and discipline. His support lent impetus to a musical genre that grew rapidly in scale and sophistication, and a rudimentary form of notation was developed during the 9th century.

Gradually, over the centuries that followed, moves were made toward simple two- and eventually more complex three- and four-part compositions – toward polyphony ("many voices"), in other words.

*Left Whether a little pipe-and-bellows affair or an elaborate one such as this from the Chapel at Versailles, the organ is the standard instrument for church music.*

mirabilia fecit ☙ aluautr si
reant cuis. 7 bractuum scum e
lonum fecit dominus saluu

*Above Much early music was performed by voice alone, as shown in this 15th-century illumination from the* Bible of Borso d'Este.

The organ added yet another voice: it is thought to have been in use since the time of Pope Vitalian in the 7th century. The organ's pure tones were the perfect complement to the human voice, and it has been the mainstay of church music ever since. As the Middle Ages gave way to the Renaissance, other instrumental sounds were introduced to church music.

## INFLUENCES ON MUSIC
Secular music was nourished by the church tradition. Though Claudio Monteverdi is famous for having composed the first operas in the 17th century, he was also a priest, and in this role brought baroque complexity to sacred music.

In his footsteps came fellow Italians, such as Antonio Vivaldi (1678–1741), a priest who wrote many of his great works for the orchestra of the Ospedale della Pietà, a church-run orphanage for girls. The kapellmeisters (or "chapel masters"), who wrote liturgical music for services at Austria's and

Germany's courts, also found time to write secular concerti, keyboard music and orchestral suites.

By this time, of course, the Reformation had swept Europe, and several of the great Baroque composers were Protestants. However, music was an ecumenical art: Catholic creativity was stimulated by the works of Bach and Handel, while the great Protestant geniuses themselves drew on the traditions of the Catholic past.

## CLASSICAL TRADITION

Religion remained an important influence into music's classical hey-day of the 18th and 19th centuries. Joseph Haydn was a committed Catholic. While he wrote many explicitly sacred works – such as his wonderful oratorio, *The Creation* (1798) – he saw the whole process of composition as an act of prayer, writing "Praise be to God" at the end of every completed piece.

His younger contemporary, Wolfgang Amadeus Mozart, may have been famously flawed as an individual, but his profound faith came through in the great *Requiem* he was working on when his own life was cut short in 1791. Franz Liszt, the great piano virtuoso and romantic composer of the 19th century, was notorious for his scandalous private life. Yet this intensely emotional man was also passionate in his attachment to Catholicism. He even took minor orders in the Church in 1865.

## SONGS OF PRAISE

What might be called the elite culture of sacred music has endured in 20th-century works by several noted composers, from France's Olivier Messiaen to Scotland's James

MacMillan. For most modern Catholics, though, Church music has taken the less sophisticated form of hymn singing. This has been more about participation than polished performance, but regardless it has been profoundly important to its participants. Communal singing can be crucial in bringing a congregation closer together, instilling in its members a sense of common purpose and common faith.

*Right With such inspiring works as the* Requiem, *Mozart created some of the most sublimely spiritual harmonies ever heard, enjoyed by Catholics and non-Catholics alike.*

*Right Many of Vivaldi's works were premiered by the girls of the orphanage he served, seen here in this 18th-century painting entitled* The Orphans' Cantata, *by Gabriele Bella.*

# HERETICS

SINCERE BELIEVERS WERE QUESTIONING THE AUTHORITY OF THE
CHURCH. THE HIERARCHY HAD TO DECIDE WHICH CRITICISMS TO
ACCEPT, WHICH TO IGNORE AND WHICH TO BRAND AS "HERESY".

An institution as far-reaching as the Church – and one with so many deeply thoughtful, idealistic individuals – was inevitably bound to have differences of opinion, even disputes, among its followers. To some extent these disputes could be contained and passionate debates took place with the Church's tacit acceptance – even its encouragement. However, some ideas were so wildly at variance with normal Catholic teaching that they could not be accommodated without the integrity of the Church being threatened. These contentious views became known as "heresies".

St Augustine had led the fight against heresy as early as the end of the 4th century, condemning the Pelagian view that humankind could earn salvation by its own efforts, without God's intervention. His view that humankind was dragged down so drastically by original sin that salvation came only and exclusively from the intervention of God

*Above Although members of a Christian faith, Waldensian followers were linked to witchcraft in this 15th-century illustration from the* Book of Occult Sciences.

was to be taken to heretical extremes in the 16th century, when it was known as Jansenism. However, the late Middle Ages turned out to be a period of particular ferment, and in hindsight we can see this as the beginnings of the Reformation.

## THE WALDENSIANS

In 1177, Peter Waldo, a prosperous merchant from Lyon, France, had undergone a spiritual crisis. Like St Francis, he had given away all his possessions and become a mendicant preacher. However, unlike the Franciscans, the "Waldensians" confronted the Church, denouncing it as representing only the richest and most powerful in society. Ultimately, they rejected the authority of its priests when Pope Lucius III banned Waldo from preaching in 1184. He and his followers set up their own Church, which survived prosecution

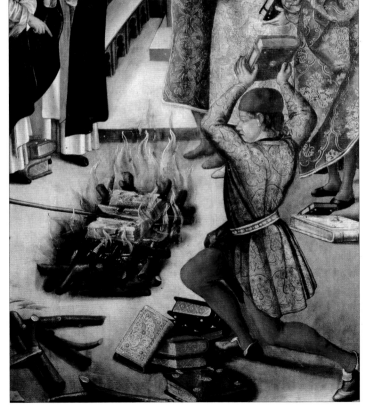

*Left Cathar books are consigned to the flames, for figurative damnation and literal destruction (*Santo Domingo y los Albigenses, *Pedro Berruguete, 15th century).*

during the following years. In 1848 the Catholic Church granted the Waldensians religious freedom.

## THE CATHARS

Southern France had by this time become the centre of another great heresy: that of Catharism. This had its roots in the Manichaeism of earlier centuries, which preached a form of dualism that combined elements from several religions. A version of the heresy had been brought West through the Balkans by Pop Bogomil and his adherents, probably dispersed along the Mediterranean trade routes. Catharism carried to extremes the Manichaean opposition between good and evil, light and darkness, the spiritual and material. For its followers, the entire earthly Creation – the material world, the body and its desires – were evil. The aim of the godly was to transcend these things.

If the Word had been "made flesh" in Christ, that could only go to show that it, too, was evil – a fact the Cathars felt was confirmed by the wealth and power of the Church. Thousands flocked to the Cathar cause, despite the arguments of the Dominicans – newly formed to

defend the faith. The violence of the official crackdown that followed (see *The Albigensian Crusade, below right*) has been condemned, but it is hard to imagine a more potent threat to the medieval order.

## THE LOLLARDS

The teachings of John Wycliffe, an English priest and scholar of the 14th century, struck a chord with many of his country's less educated people. Like Waldo, Wycliffe thought the Church had no business being rich or involving itself with the concerns of temporal government. Even in religious affairs, he argued, the Church had made too much of its own role. He wanted a scaled-down hierarchy and translations of the Bible from Latin so that people could read the Word of God themselves. He denied the doctrine of "transubstantiation". The bread and wine, he said, remained bread and wine even as they took on the nature of Christ's body and blood.

*Below An extravagant depiction of the persecution of the Lollards was illustrated in the fiercely Protestant* John Foxe's Acts and Monuments, *16th century.*

Wycliffe's followers, known as "Lollards", were seen as a threat to both secular and religious authority. Their ideas were spread into Europe by Jan Hus (or John Huss), the Czech reformer who campaigned against the sale of indulgences in the 15th century. The Lollards were a short-lived group, but their ideas were taken up by the Protestants.

---

### THE ALBIGENSIAN CRUSADE

Named after Albi, a town in the Languedoc, a region in southern France, where Catharism was officially denounced in 1178, the "Albigensian Crusade" was proclaimed by Pope Innocent III in 1208. By calling it a crusade, he equated the challenge of heresy within the Church with the threat of Islam in the Middle East and Spain. In the years that followed, the forces of the French Crown and powerful northern nobles attacked the southern peasantry and the local lords who supported them. As many as a million people may have been killed.

*Above Many atrocities were committed in the Albigensian Crusade. Here, Cathars are expelled from the city of Carcassonne (*Chronicle of France, *15th century).*

# THE INQUISITION

FEW INSTITUTIONS OF CATHOLICISM HAVE BEEN MORE FEARED THAN THE "INQUISITION", OR SO WIDELY MISUNDERSTOOD. YET THE EXCESSES OF THE "HOLY OFFICE", AS IT WAS KNOWN, CANNOT BE DENIED.

*Above Jan Hus is burnt at the stake for his heretical beliefs in this illustration from Ulrich von Reichenthal's* Council Chronicle, *15th century.*

Throughout its history, the Catholic Church has fought against heresy, but it was not until the Renaissance that it formed an official institution against such preaching. The Albigensian Crusade, set up in France in 1208 in the hope of stemming the rising tide of Catharism, could be seen as a precursor to the official Inquisitions that followed. First ordered by Pope Gregory IX in 1232, an Inquisition was a tribunal ordered by the Catholic Church to suppress and punish heresy. The first inquisitors were chosen from the Dominicans and Franciscans, who were living mendicant lifestyles and therefore not influenced by worldly gains, and who were well educated in theology.

At about the same time an anti-Waldensian Inquisition followed in Italy, but then the Inquisition waned,

*Below The Inquisition was especially active in the Netherlands and Ghent, where it was an arm of the Spanish occupation, as shown in this 16th-century engraving of the Flemish School.*

to be revived in Spain and Portugal (and their overseas colonies) from the late 15th century. More of these ecclesiastical courts for suppressing heresy were constituted in France and Italy during the Reformation. The Congregation of the Holy Office, which is often shortened to the Holy Office, was formed to oversee the Inquisitions in 1542.

Although administered by the Church, the Inquisition worked with the temporal authorities. Generally, the state took the lead. Monarchs always had an interest in enforcing conformity and were happy enough to claim divine sanction for doing so. After the Reformation, religion took on a political aspect. A Protestant was no longer just a heretic but a dangerous subversive – potentially, an agent from another state in Europe.

## SPANISH ACTS OF FAITH

It was in this febrile political context that the *Leyenda Negra* (or "Black Legend") was born. Spain, the Catholic superpower at the time, was

demonized by the propagandists of northern Europe's Protestant powers. Books and pamphlets were printed, describing in lurid detail the supposed excesses of the Spanish, from their American colonies to the torture chambers of the Inquisition. However, modern scholarship has shown that many of these accounts were mere fabrications, created by over-excited pamphleteers.

However, some of the accounts, though sensationalized, cannot be dismissed. Recent research has shown the scrupulous thoroughness with which the Holy Office sought to document its cases, avoiding prosecutions based on malicious denunciations. At the same time it

*Above Spain's Grand Inquisitor, Tomás de Torquemada, was widely feared (Spanish School, 19th century).*

## THE SPANISH INQUISITION

The Inquisition in Spain had first been established in Aragon in the 13th century, but it came into its own in the 15th century under Ferdinand and Isabella, the "Catholic Monarchs". They bore that title, not because they staunchly defended Catholicism (though they did), but because by their marriage they had brought together the realms of Navarra, Aragon and Castile to form a single Spain. (The word "Catholic" originally meant "universal", "all-embracing" – hence its use for the Church of Rome.)

Ferdinand and Isabella saw the Holy Office as a way of using ecclesiastical structures as the basis for what we would now call a police state. Since the Reconquista was only recently completed, and many of the kingdom's Jews and Muslims had been converted by force, there was considerable fear that these alien groups were secretly upholding their old beliefs and practices in private meetings. Hence the drawing up of laws of *limpieza* ("cleanliness", "purity"), which anticipated the race laws of Nazi Germany. They were

*Above Torquemada received a bull of 1487 from Pope Innocent VIII, appointing him Inquisitor General of Spain.*

imposed with terrifying thoroughness by the infamous Grand Inquisitor, Tomás de Torquemada, who was appointed to the position by the pope.

confirms the integral role of torture in the proceedings (after its explicit authorization by Pope Innocent IV in 1252). Although their frequency has been exaggerated, *autos-da-fé* ("acts of faith") assuredly took place. These rituals, in which there was a public penance for the guilty, were symbolic representations of the Last Judgement acted out before large crowds. An *auto-da-fé* ended with the accused being burnt at the stake.

### OUTRAGEOUS ACTIONS

The readiness of the Church to consign its critics to the flames is easily exaggerated: the wilder claims of Reformation propaganda have proved obdurately persistent. The armies of the Albigensian Crusade did embark on a spree of slaughter, but the extent of the Church's blessing is unclear. Outraged though

it was by Wycliffe's teachings, the Church spent so long debating them that he had died of natural causes before he was denounced as a heretic.

However, Jan Hus, the Czech preacher who campaigned against the sale of indulgences, was burnt at the stake in 1415 (an act for which Pope John Paul II apologized in 1999). Nor was he alone in suffering this fate at the hands of the Church, which, with criticism mounting, was increasingly on the defensive – and all too ready to attack.

*Right St Dominic was committed to teaching – but when all else failed, the fear of death was used to persuade the people. Here, St Dominic presides over an auto-da-fé (Pedro Berruguete, c.1495).*

# THE CHURCH IN TRANSITION

THE HISTORICAL HEADLINES MAY HAVE BEEN ABOUT THE STIFLING OF DISSENT, BUT QUIETER DEVELOPMENTS WERE TAKING PLACE BEHIND THE SCENES AS CATHOLICISM REFORMED ITSELF.

*Above Convened in 1215, the Fourth Lateran Council, shown in this 19th-century engraving, introduced far-reaching reforms in the running of the Church.*

The Church in the Middle Ages had been very much the establishment. Secure in its position, it had no real interest in changing. However, this does not mean that the spiritual status quo had gone unquestioned. The heresies of the time had only been the most extreme manifestation of a ferment of debate. This concerned not just the finer points of Christian doctrine but also the place that Catholicism occupied within society, and the developing relationship between Church and State.

## COUNCILS FOR CHANGE
These issues were explored by the Church hierarchy at such gatherings as the Third Lateran Council of 1179 and the Fourth, which followed

*Below Figures representing the Seven Liberal Arts – Arithmetic, Music, Geometry, Astronomy, Logic, Rhetoric and Grammar – are shown in a 1503 publication on humanism from Gregor Reisch,* Margarita Philosophica Nova.

in 1215. These conclaves were held in the vast council chamber of the Lateran Palace, which was the pope's official residence in Rome. Leading clerics came together to discuss the changes the Church would have to make to adapt to a changing world while at the same time staying true to its original principles.

The great emphasis of the communiqués agreed by the Third Lateran Council was on the maintenance of orthodoxy, while the Fourth is today known chiefly for its decree that Jews and Muslims should have to wear distinctive garb to set themselves apart from Christians.

Yet the small print tells a slightly different story. Most of the Council's energies had gone into the attempt to get the Church's house in order. New measures were introduced to make the clergy more accountable for its actions and to control the activities of religious foundations.

## THE RISE OF HUMANISM
At the end of the 15th century, the Italian scholar Giovanni Pico Della Mirandola advanced the views that became known as "humanism". God's greatest gift to us as humans, he argued, was the capacity to reason for ourselves. It was not just our right but our duty to use that gift. Traditional Catholic scholarship, he suggested, had seen its role as essentially a passive one of interpreting and implementing the will of God. Scholars had seen that will represented in the doctrinal judgements handed down over generations within the Church, which had come to have the force of legal precedent in Catholic thought.

Instead, Pico Della Mirandola claimed, people should be thinking for themselves and bypassing tradition to consult the ancient sources. In this view, he was reflecting the contemporary attitudes of the artists and writers of the wider Renaissance (rebirth), which was taking place in Italy at the time.

Inspired by the artwork of classical Greece and Rome, men such as Leonardo da Vinci saw the human form as the highest achievement of God's Creation. Scientists, too, were finding inspiration in the writings of the Greeks and Romans, gaining the confidence to set aside the perceived assumptions of centuries and to try out new theories and experiment with new ideas.

## COUNCIL OF TRENT
Humanism, as then understood, did not dispute the greatness of God – still less his existence – but it did raise radical questions as to how he should be served. Church leaders were unsettled – not surprisingly, since humanist thinking did tempt some scholars toward the new Protestant theologies then emerging. However, in the works of writers such as St Thomas More and Erasmus, humanism offered a reinvigoration of a Catholic tradition, which had, to some extent, become fossilized over the passing years.

That the Church was capable of flexibility was to be demonstrated at the Council of Trent. Opening in 1545, when Europe was at the height of the Reformation, its sessions continued for several years until 1563. Its main conclusions were uncompromising, with the Church rejecting the theological heresies proposed by the Protestant rebels. At the same time, it tacitly acknowledged the justice of many of the criticisms of its own institution. It was these criticisms that caused the Church to institute root-and-branch reform. Measures were introduced to combat corruption, including regulation of the issuing of indulgences to prevent their sale. Diocesan seminaries were created to provide better training for priests, and disciplinary structures were formed to handle wrongdoers.

## A CHRISTIAN JOKER

Desiderius Erasmus ("Erasmus of Rotterdam") was one of the most serious thinkers of the Renaissance, but it was with a joke that he caught the mood of an amazing time. His treatise, *Praise of Folly* (1511), was a masterly exercise in irony; among the absurdities it satirized were those of the Church. Its scholars' slavish reverence for tradition, its superstitions and its corruption: all these are ridiculed in its pages. However, this only makes the more moving the book's final reaffirmation of a Catholic faith whose truth transcends the earthly limitations of the Church.

*Above* Erasmus of Rotterdam, *painted in 1523 by Hans Holbein the Younger, was a brilliant scholar and thinker. He published many works and led the humanist movement within the Church.*

*Left* The Island of Utopia, *as imagined by the great English humanist St Thomas More, was illustrated by Ambrosius Holbein and published in 1518 in the book of the same title.*

# POWERFUL POPES

THE RENAISSANCE SAW THE PAPACY AT ITS HEIGHT AS A POLITICAL FORCE – AND ITS MORAL REPUTATION AT ITS LOWEST EBB, RESPONSIBLE FOR SOME DISREPUTABLE CHAPTERS IN THE CHURCH'S HISTORY.

Today the idea of a "Renaissance Pope" suggests magnificence and political power. However, it also implies corruption on a huge scale. This is a stereotype, of course, but one that many pontiffs of the 15th and 16th centuries appear to have lived up to. To expect otherwise would perhaps have been unrealistic. The Church was the greatest institution of the day, and its leader commanded untold wealth and incalculable influence. At the same time it was very much a human institution. The meek and innocent might be blessed in heaven, but here on earth they were pushed aside by the ambitious, the unscrupulous and the ruthless.

## A FAMILY BUSINESS

Among the Church's hierarchy, favours were exchanged, inducements were offered and friends and

*Below Building the new St Peter's took many years. Antoine Lafréry's engraving (1575) shows a papal blessing being given beneath its uncompleted dome.*

relations were taken care of. It was no surprise when the nephew of Pope Eugene IV followed him on to St Peter's throne as Pope Paul II in 1464.

Pope Sixtus IV followed in 1471. He made no fewer than six of his nephews cardinals during his papacy, on top of which he gave them benefices that brought in colossal wealth. (The Church had a vast income from a range of sources, including rents, donations, bequests and burial fees, all of which were a temptation to the corrupt.) Sixtus IV also married his nieces into Italy's leading aristocratic houses, building up a powerful network of familial connections, which he was ruthless in defending. He is believed to have been complicit in a plot carried out in 1478 in which two Medici brothers were attacked with daggers while attending Mass in the cathedral in Florence. One of them, Giuliano de' Medici, died of his wounds.

A strong sense of "family" was creeping in – of dynastic continuity and of bitter feuding – alien as this

*Above Pope Sixtus IV appoints a new prefect to preside over his library, another monument to the majesty of his reign, in Melozzo da Forli's painting (1477).*

should have been to a Church with a celibate clergy. Some popes were far from chaste. Pope Alexander VI (1492–1503) fathered nine children by an unknown number of different women. His most notorious son, Cesare Borgia, was a murderous wheeler-dealer; he became a cardinal before leaving the clergy to make an advantageous marriage.

## PAPACY AND PATRONAGE

However far they may have fallen short of the principles they were supposed to serve, the Renaissance popes undoubtedly left us in their debt as the patrons of some of the most impressive Western art. It may have been extravagance, driven too much by human vanity, but their patronage had an impact on the whole history of Western culture.

Pope Sixtus IV spent a fortune beautifying the centre of Rome, which involved widening streets and constructing new churches and other buildings. His bridge, the Ponte Sisto, still spans the River Tiber.

Pope Julius II was also a great patron of the arts. It was this pope who asked Donato Bramante to design a replacement for the old

## POPE IMPRISONED

In modern times, we have tended to think of the papacy as "above" politics, to some extent protected by their holy status. However, given the political power they wielded, the popes of the Renaissance could hardly claim to be simply men of God. Clement VII paid the price for this: though a member of the Medici family, ironically, he was innocent and unworldly by the standards of the times. His attempts to steer a safe diplomatic course between the great powers ruling Europe led to a dispute between him and Charles V, King of Spain and Emperor of Germany. In 1527, Charles' forces invaded Italy and sacked Rome. Pope Clement was held prisoner at Castel Sant' Angelo, from which he escaped.

*Above* The massive walls surrounding Rome offered the city some protection, but it lacked defensive troops, as shown in The Sack of Rome, *a 1527 painting by Johannes Lingelbach.*

St Peter's Basilica, and work on the greatest church built for Christendom began only two years into his papacy, in 1505. (That the astronomical costs were to be met by the greatest granting of indulgences yet seen was a fact that would not be lost on the Church's critics.) Julius was also responsible for commissioning Michelangelo to paint the ceiling of the Sistine Chapel.

The Medici family were already famous for their artistic patronage when the son of Lorenzo (the Magnificent) de' Medici became Pope Leo X in 1513. "God has given us the papacy," Leo X is said to have commented to a friend. "Now let us enjoy it." Fortunately for posterity, his greatest indulgence was art, including history-making works by the Italian artists Michelangelo and Raphael. He encouraged music, too, and writers such as Erasmus.

*Right* Raphael's *c.1517 portrait of his patron, Pope Leo X, captures the power and authority of the man.*

# THE POPE AND THE PAINTER

THE CEILING OF THE SISTINE CHAPEL IS UNIVERSALLY ACCLAIMED AS A MASTERPIECE. IT HAS ALSO BECOME THE ARCHETYPE FOR THE DIFFICULT RELATIONSHIP BETWEEN THE ARTIST AND HIS PATRON.

If its ceiling had never been painted by Michelangelo, art lovers would still flock to see the Sistine Chapel for its frescoes by other great artists, which include Raphael, Botticelli, Perugino and Ghirlandaio. (The chapel is in the Apostolic Palace in the Vatican City, the official residence of the pope.) Some splendid tapestries, designed by Raphael, formed part of the plunder during Charles V's sack of Rome in 1527, but they were later restored and replaced. Although named after Pope Sixtus IV, who had built the structure, the chapel really found its role under Pope Julius II, who made it a magnificent showcase for the creativity of Renaissance art.

## MICHELANGELO'S TASK

Today too many tourists look past the myriad wonders that line the walls, with eyes only for the ceiling, 20m (65ft) above. Admittedly, it is an astonishing sight: the whole sweep of human existence, from Creation to Last Judgement, in crowded scenes that seem to boil over in their energy. Yet if the artist had his own way, this masterpiece would not have existed.

*Above* The Deluge and the Drunkenness of Noah *illustrates transgression and punishment, important themes for the ceiling as a whole.*

Born outside Arezzo in Tuscany in 1475, Michelangelo had never doubted his artistic genius, but he saw himself as a sculptor first and foremost. When, in 1505, Julius II asked him to design his tomb, it seemed to Michelangelo to be the dream commission. He dedicated himself to the creation of his life's masterpiece. However, he was not to be left to his work for long. To his growing annoyance, Julius enlisted his help for various odd artistic jobs – and began to talk to him about a commission for painting frescoes on the ceiling of the Sistine Chapel.

## A CONTEMPORARY REPORT

Giorgio Vasari, gossipy chronicler of the ins and outs of the Italian Renaissance art scene, says that this idea was not Julius' own. Raphael and Bramante talked him into it

*Left Michelangelo and Julius II had a fractious – but finally fruitful – working relationship. The artist and patron are shown together in this 16th-century painting by Anastasio Fontebuoni.*

mischievously, he maintained. The former was the leading painter of the time, the latter, the star architect – and both were feeling threatened by Michelangelo's prodigious talents. The pope's preference for sculpture was well known to his contemporaries, and Michelangelo's supremacy in that arena was undisputed. By getting the artist weighed down in what appeared an impossibly ambitious task for such a comparatively inexperienced and reluctant painter, his rivals saw an opportunity to level the playing field. There was even the chance that Michelangelo would blunder the job so severely that his artistic credibility would become fatally compromised.

In truth, this version of events is unlikely, but Vasari was possibly briefed by Michelangelo himself, and his account may well reflect the workings of the artist's extravagantly suspicious mind.

## A GRUDGING LABOUR

Suffice it to say that Michelangelo tried every means to avoid taking on the project. In the end, when it became clear that he was not going to be able to do so, he decided to get it over and done with as quickly as he could. It took him four years in all, which is an astonishingly short time considering the enormous scale of the work – and the fact that Michelangelo seems to have worked largely alone, apart from an assistant who mixed his colours. Even so, the pope apparently asked him constantly about his progress. *The Agony and the Ecstasy* was the name given to the famous film about this episode in the artist's life – *The Irritability and the Impatience* might have been a more accurate title.

However, if these frescoes were not a labour of love, this hardly shows in a spectacular work that takes the continuity of Christian faith and worship as its theme. Seen in the artist's all-encompassing view, the

*Above An uncompromising Christ makes his appearance as* Judge of the World: *the climactic, culminating scene of the Sistine Chapel ceiling.*

Old Testament is the prefiguring of Christ's New Covenant; Christ and his Church the fulfilment of what the prophets promised. However, Michelangelo is undoubtedly a man of the Renaissance in the way he places humanity at the centre of God's Creation and in his depiction of the beauty of the human form as the ultimate expression of God's greatness. These values are summed up in the outstretched hands in *The Creation of Adam*, where we see the moment in which God transmits life to man.

## A RICH LEGACY

Michelangelo never did get the opportunity to finish Julius' tomb – a mausoleum was built when the pope died in 1513, but it was placed in the Church of San Pietro in Vincoli, rather than St Peter's Basilica. Little of it is Michelangelo's work – although the one piece that is, an awe-inspiring Moses, confirms that this would indeed have been a special work. It is hard, though, to feel that humanity has been the loser, as the Sistine Chapel ceiling is one of the most famous and most visited artworks in the world.

*Below The ceiling's most celebrated scene is* The Creation of Adam, *where God reaches out to Adam, giving him life.*

# NEW HORIZONS

WITH OVERSEAS EXPLORATIONS AND SCIENTIFIC DISCOVERIES BEING MADE IN SUCH QUICK SUCCESSION, RENAISSANCE EUROPE WAS AN EXCITING – BUT ALSO CONFUSING – PLACE TO BE.

As the ideological certainties of the preceeding centuries were dissolving, the Church was facing an uphill struggle to maintain its old intellectual authority. The medieval period was the "Age of Faith", when men and women never questioned their duty of subservience in God's order; but then neither did they doubt their centrality in his cosmos. Paradoxically, even as Renaissance humanism proclaimed the pre-eminence of humanity, that centrality was coming under threat.

As the voyages of the great navigators pushed back the boundaries of the world known to the Europeans, astronomers explored an

*Below Columbus' discoveries opened up a New World – and its peoples – to the Europeans, such as these Native Americans from Virginia, in this late 16th-century engraving by Theodore de Bry.*

expanding universe – which might not actually be revolving around the earth as had been thought.

THE AGE OF DISCOVERY
Europeans were aware that their continent did not encompass the entirety of the world: Africa lay just beyond the Mediterranean, after all. Spices and other luxuries were brought along the Silk Route from the East: moreover, Marco Polo had brought back tidings from China in the late 13th century. However, few Europeans had followed him. The Crusades had left the Middle East a hostile environment, and the trade that continued in this region was conducted mostly by middlemen.

The soaring costs of luxuries imported overland helped motivate the search for a sea route, which receieved a boost when Prince Henry the Navigator of Portugal

*Above Despite hurricanes and mutiny, the Portuguese navigator Vasco da Gama was the first European to reach Asia by going around Africa's Cape of Good Hope in 1497/8.*

established a naval academy c.1450. Portuguese navigators made great progress with Bartolomeu Diaz finding his way down the coast of Africa to the Cape of Good Hope in 1487, while Vasco da Gama pushed on to India a decade later.

Christopher Columbus, sailing for Spain's "Catholic Monarchs", had reached the Americas, making landfall on 12 October 1492. However, he remained convinced until he died that he had found the westerly route to East Asia. The Europeans came to realize that he had instead stumbled on a "New World" – and the Old World would never be the same.

"Who is my neighbour?" Jesus had been asked by the lawyer in Luke 10:29. That question was looking harder to answer now. Difficult as it had always been to live up to Christ's injunction to love one's neighbour as oneself, now it was a conceptual challenge, too. As Gomes Eanes de Zurara, the Portuguese chronicler, put it, how could those naked "savages", of whom navigators were now bringing home reports, really

*Above Christopher Columbus prepares to set out from the port of Palos, Spain, in August 1492, in this 19th-century fresco by Antonio Cabral y Aguado Bejarano.*

be "of the generation of Adam"? Yet, shaped as they were, how could they not be? Were these strangers to be our neighbours? The European idea of the world was being challenged.

## REVOLUTIONS

Things got worse. In 1543, Nicolaus Copernicus died. Only then was his great work *De revolutionibus orbium coelestium* (On the Revolution of the Heavenly Spheres) published. Copernicus, a priest himself and one of a family of priests and nuns, had received encouragement in his astronomical researches from fellow churchmen. However, he had been nervous about releasing his conclusions and no wonder: the Church had always followed the view of Aristotle and Ptolemy that the Sun and planets revolved around a stationary Earth. Copernicus believed the Earth and planets went around the Sun in what is called a heliocentric system.

The Church has since accepted this view, but at the time there were fears that it overturned scriptural accounts of the Creation and the cosmos – or that, if it did not, it would appear to do so. When, later in the century, another priest showed support for the Copernican theory, he was tried by the Roman Inquisition. Giordano Bruno faced a range of charges, from blasphemy to heresy: he was burnt at the stake in 1600.

*Below Copernicus revealed that the true "harmony of the spheres" was produced by planets' concentric orbit around the Sun, shown in an illustration from Andreas Cellarius' Scenographia, c.1660.*

## GALILEO'S HERESY

In the early 17th century, another Catholic astronomer, Galileo Galilei, found his own observations lending fresh support to the Copernican case. For this backing he was tried by the Church for heresy in 1633 and was forced to recant his claims. In fairness, Galileo had found discreet support among leading clergy. Several members of the Church hierarchy had acknowledged their support for both the strength of Galileo's observational evidence and the force of his argument that Old Testament cosmology should be regarded more as poetry than as science. Cardinal Caesar Baronius spoke up for Galileo's ideas, joking that "The Bible teaches the way to go to heaven, not the way the heavens go." Officially, though, the Catholic Church had condemned such views.

*Above Galileo, shown in a 17th-century painting by the Flemish Justus Sustermans, fell foul of the Roman Inquisition with his public espousal of Copernican astronomy.*

# THE REFORMATION

IN THE EARLY 16TH CENTURY, MANY BELIEVERS TOOK THEIR STAND WITH THE REFORMER MARTIN LUTHER. IN ENGLAND, KING HENRY VIII PROCLAIMED HIMSELF HEAD OF THE CHURCH OF ENGLAND.

The great indulgence sale in which Pope Julius II set out to fund the rebuilding of St Peter's Basilica in 1505 caused outrage among many people across Europe. Indulgences had been around for centuries, of course, and, so too, had abuses of the system, which was widely satirized throughout the Middle Ages. It would be hard to claim that Julius' behaviour was much worse than anything that had occurred beforehand, yet it came after centuries of supposed reform – and at a time when the Church's overall authority

*Below Martin Luther's famous protest is seen as the start of Protestantism. Ferdinand Pauwels' 19th-century painting shows the reformer nailing his "95 Theses" to the cathedral door.*

was being questioned. In this climate, cleaning up such abuses within the Church's hierarchy was not going to be enough for the dissenters.

## AUTHORITY IN QUESTION

In 1517, Martin Luther, priest and university professor, nailed his "95 Theses" to the door of the cathedral in Wittenberg, Germany, as a protest against the sale of indulgences. His arguments addressed the theology that allowed such indulgences to be awarded. The Church soon found itself under sustained attack from several sides. The scientific and intellectual tumults of the age had not left the Church unscathed. Moreover, the advent of the printing press had for the first time created what might be described as a reading

*Above The pope acts as a moneychanger in the sale of indulgences and religious dispensations, as shown in this 1521 German woodcut by Lucas Cranach.*

public – before the press, few books were available, and they could often be read only by the clerical elite, educated in Latin.

There was a growing sense that men and women might want to judge things for themselves. So Luther found a receptive ear when, questioning whether or not the Church hierarchy should even exist, he argued that every Christian believer should be his or her own priest. To further that end, he took an interest in making the Scriptures more accessible to the common people. The Church released a bull in 1520, proclaiming Luther's teachings as heretical, and only a few months later he was ex-communicated by the Church.

In 1522, Luther published his German translation of the New Testament, and William Tyndale's English Bible came out in 1525. The Church condemned both of these works: its fear was that the uneducated would be led astray without the interpretative assistance of their priests. However, to an increasing number of the educated middle class now emerging, especially in northern Europe, such thinking simply reeked of condescension.

## KING HENRY VIII BREAKS AWAY

British coins still carry the abbreviation "F.D." after the name of the monarch: it means *Fidei Defensor*, or "Defender of the Faith". Ironically, this title was awarded by Pope Leo X to England's King Henry VIII in gratitude for his pamphlet, "A Defence of the Seven Sacraments" (1521), an eloquent response to Luther's criticisms. However, the failure of Henry's queen, Catherine of Aragon, to bear him a male heir led to a conflict between the king and Rome. Henry requested the annulment of their marriage, so he could wed Anne Boleyn, but it was rejected by Pope Clement VII. The king responded in 1532 by announcing that the monarch of England would also be head of the Church of England. He also confiscated the wealth in England's Catholic churches.

*Right King Henry VIII puts Pope Clement VII in his place in an approving English satirical engraving of the 16th century.*

## A SPLIT FROM THE CHURCH

These Christians became known as "Protestants", which is from the Latin word *protestari*, or "to protest". Another meaning for *protestari* is "to affirm" or "to avow", which can also be seen as appropriate for a group whose members sought to seek guidance from the Scriptures, not from the Church's teachings. They believed that the individual person should have his or her own relationship with God. Catholicism never had the right to claim proprietorship over the "keys of heaven". What mattered was the divine Word, as revealed in the Scriptures, which it was the duty of every man and woman to read.

It could be argued that they took more moral responsibility for themselves, and there was no prospect of buying indulgences, or of pattering mechanically through a set of prayers. However, there was a tendency for a self-selecting community to feel that simply by proclaiming their belief they showed themselves to be "saved" and that there could be justification by faith instead of by works.

## CALVINISM

In Geneva, John Calvin drew a distinction between the "Elect", marked out for salvation, and the rest, "pre-destined" for damnation by God himself even before they were created. That Calvin rejected Rome and all its works was just the start of his offence, as far as the Catholic hierarchy was concerned. His doctrines affronted their sense of Christian mercy and forgiveness. The way in which Calvin and his followers accepted the consignment of so many to eternal suffering seemed not just ungodly to them but inhuman.

Catholics believed that God, though indeed all-knowing, did not actually pre-ordain the sins of the souls he created, compromising their free will. This meant that the door to salvation would always be left open.

*Below The Calvinist chapel contrasted starkly with the ornate Catholic churches of old. Such a chapel is shown in this c.1565 painting by Jean Perrissin.*

# THE COUNTER-REFORMATION

IF THE REFORMATION THREW DOWN A CHALLENGE TO CATHOLICISM, IT WAS ONE TO WHICH THE CHURCH WAS ABLE TO RESPOND. AN URGENT EXAMINATION OF CONSCIENCE RESULTED IN FAR-REACHING CHANGES.

While the leaders of the Church were debating its institutional reform at the Council of Trent, a book was causing a stir in Italy. The story of *The Miraculous Life and Doctrine of St Catherine of Genoa* seemed somehow to speak to Catholicism in its crisis. It was hard to see why this should be so. Catherine had died half a century before, and she had barely registered on the consciousness of the Church in her own lifetime. Although nobly born, she had lost any status she had once enjoyed in a loveless, violent marriage; she had never taken orders as a nun. However, she had given her life to God, tending the sick and helping the poor. She had bravely faced the agonies of her last illness.

While Catherine's biography was being read in many hundreds of European homes, a very different life

was unfolding far away in a Spanish convent. There, Teresa of Ávila was experiencing visions of Christ that seemed to take possession of her whole being, body and soul. She described these visions in an autobiography in the 1560s.

## PIETY AND PASSION

The experiences of Catherine and Teresa were their own, but they can still be seen as the products of their time. The Church had been ready for two such figures. Both were comparative outsiders and women, and were remarkable not for their services to the Church establishment but for the intensity – the drama, even – of their spiritual lives. Although Catherine's path to God had been arduous and difficult, it was one that many ordinary Catholics could imagine themselves following. Moreover, the passion shown in Teresa's faith proved to be deeply moving to the many people who had been finding themselves increasingly unmoved by a religious life that had become routine.

The Catholics who embraced these women might never have dreamt of turning to Protestantism – any more than Catherine or Teresa would have done – but they were responding to some of the same underlying discontents. Luther's call to Christians was based on rejecting a Catholicism of empty forms for

*Left St Teresa of Ávila came to represent a new kind of spirituality – impassioned and intense – as shown in the* Ecstasy of St Teresa, *sculpted by Gian Lorenzo Bernini in 1645–52.*

*Above Convened in 1545, the Council of Trent instituted wide-ranging reforms within the Church. The members of the council are depicted in this 18th-century copy of a contemporary painting.*

a deep and authentic spirituality, which was founded in the faith of the individual.

## THE JESUITS

Among St Teresa's inspirations had been the Spiritual Exercises, written in the 1520s by Ignatius Loyola. This Spanish thinker is now famous as the founder of a great religious order, the Society of Jesus (*see* The Society of Jesus, *opposite page*), but he always saw faith as being rooted in the individual. His Spiritual Exercises could be seen as a sort of self-help course in Christian devotion, a regime of daily meditations and guided prayer. However, for Loyola, faith had to exist within the framework of the Church: his Exercises had to be followed under the guidance of a spiritual director.

The interconnection between the Church and its followers was perhaps the crucial insight that fuelled the Counter-Reformation. Personal faith, for all its passion, was ultimately directionless; at the same time, a large institution could have no soul without developing a fruitful relationship with the individual. What was called for, and what Loyola's Jesuits were able to provide, was a Catholicism in which these two components went together hand in hand.

The same impulse can be seen in the life and work of St Francis of Sales who, in the early 17th century,

*Above* Pope Urban VIII takes part in celebrations marking the Jesuits' centenary, shown in this c.1640 painting by Andrea Sacchi, Filippo Gagliardi and Jan Miel.

decided to tackle the Reformation head on. As Bishop of Geneva, St Francis had his seat in the very headquarters of Calvinism, but he made it his mission to convert Protestants back to the Catholic Church.

*Above* Ignatius Loyola thought of himself as a knight in the cause of Christ. This 1556 portrait of him is by Jacopino del Conte.

# ECSTATIC ART

THE COUNTER-REFORMATION GAVE RISE TO A NEW – AND INTENSELY
EMOTIONAL – AESTHETIC. ARTISTS AND ARCHITECTS LOOKED FOR WAYS
TO DRAMATIZE THE PASSION AND FERVOUR OF RELIGIOUS FAITH.

Art had been one of the issues at the heart of the Reformation controversy. Protestants tended to regard the Church's display of wealth with suspicion. While secular art was one of the vanities that the Christian should be forsaking, "religious art" was really a contradiction in terms. What mattered was the Word of God: sacred pictures and statues were seen as "graven images" that had been prohibited by the Bible, evidence of a heathen adoration of Our Lady and the saints. The Church's collection of artistic treasures was considered one of the trappings of the "Whore of Babylon", their worldly beauties temptations to the struggling soul.

So strongly did Protestants feel about this that some extremists went on sprees of iconoclasm (literally, "breaking images"), smashing statues and stained-glass windows and whitewashing over frescoes. Many English churches still bear the scars – the disfigured statues and blank replacement glass of Ely Cathedral's Lady Chapel are just one example.

*Above Flamboyant expressiveness was key to the Counter-Reformation aesthetic, as seen in this 17th-century painting,* The Virgin Appearing to St Peter Damian, *attributed to Pietro da Cortona.*

## ON THE OFFENSIVE

The Catholic Church responded by redoubling its efforts and launched what amounted to a major artistic offensive. At the same time, religious art took on an altogether different emphasis. Where once the architect had been content to suggest the grandeur of God and the splendour of his Church, the feelings involved in religious faith were now incorporated into the designs. While the artist had previously been content to commemorate worthy piety and honest service, the new spirituality was passionate and intense. Agony, ecstasy, tragedy, triumph: all of these dramatic human sensations were harnessed by artists, designed to both arrest the attention and engage the emotions.

*Left Bernini's assistant, Giovanni Battista Gaulli, nicknamed "Baciccia", painted the Il Gesù ceiling, with much of his master's flair, in 1672–85. His work can be seen continuing past the boundaries normally created by barrel vaulting.*

The element of surprise was exploited: artists and architects of this period showed an unabashed instinct for showmanship. Rome's Church of the Gesù is a case in point. Its dazzling white façade is elegant in its symmetries, but the overall effect is simple, even chaste. This only heightens the shock (no other word would be appropriate) when the visitor pushes through the doors to be assaulted by the ravishing beauty – and riotous exuberance – that can be found within.

There are frescoes, columns, statues, pilasters and so much ornamentation in marble and gilt that the scene seems to dissolve into a single disorientating vision, with every line and plane being thrown into doubt. The previously used boundaries disappear, with artwork spilling spectacularly across the demarcations made by the barrel vaulting in the ceiling overhead. Christ and his angels appear to waft heavenward through the ceiling itself.

The overall effect is staggering. Whereas the statues and stained glass of the Gothic churches had been visual "books" for instructing the unlettered, this interior was intended to take the senses – and hence the soul – by storm.

## HIGH DRAMA
Built toward the end of the 16th century, the Church of the Gesù is the spiritual headquarters of the Society of Jesus, whose founder St Ignatius has his tomb in a side chapel. Beside the altar there is an allegorical sculpture that stands almost 3m (10ft) in height, representing *Religion Overthrowing Heresy and Hatred*. This is the work of Pierre Le Gros the Younger, a French sculptor based in Rome. With the cross of Christianity in one hand and thunderbolts of heavenly anger in the other, Lady Religion stands slightly off balance as she kicks out at Heresy, represented as an ugly old man. Sent

*Above What might have been a stagey and schematic scene becomes a powerful human drama in the c.1696 statue* Religion Overthrowing Heresy and Hatred *by Pierre Le Gros the Younger.*

sprawling, he appears to be falling over the edge of the sculpture's pedestal: the rules of gravity do not seem to apply. Hatred, a withered old woman, flinches away in fear before Religion's righteous anger. At bottom left, a little angel busily tears up books by the Protestant writers Ulrich Zwingli and Martin Luther.

## TOO SENSATIONALIST?
Le Gros' impressive creation is all but overwhelming in its impact. The technical accomplishment involved is also awe-inspiring. It is hard to believe that so obviously schematic a work could be so powerful or that such dynamism could be captured in a lump of cold stone. Yet the miraculous transformation of marble to moving drapery, warm flesh and breathing life seen in this statue was achieved even more astonishingly in Gian Lorenzo Bernini's famous *Ecstasy of St Teresa* (1645–52), another great sculpture of the period.

Inevitably, there have been some criticisms that such sculptures are shallow and sensationalist, being no more than exhibitionistic tours de force by artistic virtuosos. However, these objections miss the real point of the works. They were created by an avowedly evangelizing aesthetic that used sheer emotional force to compel an intensely personal engagement between God and the followers of the faith.

*Below Talented Renaissance sculptors could coax strong emotion out of cold stone. The 1674* Beatified Lodovica Albertoni, *by Gian Lorenzo Bernini, is a stunning example of the artist's work.*

# TEMPORAL AUTHORITY

ALTHOUGH THE CATHOLIC CHURCH WAS GROWING IN POWER AND
MAJESTY AT ITS CENTRE IN ITALY, ELSEWHERE IN EUROPE ANARCHY
AND WAR MADE IT HARDER FOR THE CHURCH TO GAIN PRIMACY.

The Church was a powerful force in Rome partly due to two donations. Although it was exposed as a forgery in the 15th century, for several centuries it was thought that the Donation of Constantine had given temporal authority over Rome and its possessions to the papacy. This misconception enabled the Catholic Church to wield an impressive political authority in Rome.

A different donation, made by the Merovingian king Pepin I, was genuine. He reigned over most of France and also over the western part of Germany and northern Italy. In 754, he had given the Church

*Below Fought in 1634, the Second Battle of Nördlingen was one of many such encounters in the Thirty Years' War. The battle is depicted in a mid-17th-century painting by Pieter Meulener.*

temporal authority over the Duchy of Rome and adjacent regions. Under the Holy Roman Empire, which was established by Pepin's son Charlemagne, these privileges had been upheld and even increased. By the time of Pope Innocent III in the 13th century, the Papal States embraced the whole of central Italy and much of the north-east.

These possessions brought the papacy not just great wealth but also considerable political power: great Renaissance popes such as Alexander VI and Julius II stood on an equal diplomatic footing with Europe's greatest monarchs. However, this was not always such a comfortable place to be, as Clement VII was to discover in 1527, when he was imprisoned during the sacking of Rome. Any idea that the Church was somehow spiritually removed, above politics

*Above Posing with a miniature Aachen Cathedral in an 1825 painting by J.P. Scheuren, Emperor Charlemagne did much to build the bond between sacred and secular power in Europe.*

and the grubby machinations of international diplomacy, could not credibly be maintained when the pope was practically a king.

## CONFLICTS OF INTEREST

Tensions between these secular and religious roles were inevitable. In the early 17th century, for instance, the papacy found itself in dispute with Venice. The city-state had remained Catholic in its allegiances; but, because its economy was based on trade, it was important it kept open its commerce with the Protestant states of central Europe. Also, as a republic, it did not see why it had to be in the control of an external authority.

In 1606, Pope Paul V placed the city under an "interdict" – this effectively excommunicated all its people, denying them the sacraments. This inflicting of a spiritual punishment for what amounted to a rejection of temporal authority was extremely unpopular, not just in Venice but elsewhere, too. While the modern opposition of Church and State had yet to be formulated explicitly, it is clear that, at some level, the pope was seen to be abusing his power.

## THE THIRTY YEARS' WAR

Such goings on in southern Europe soon became parochial when the centre of economic power shifted to the north. Since Charlemagne had founded the Holy Roman Empire, Germany and Italy had been associated, but Germany was now emerging as the greater force. However, as far as the Church was concerned, it was a country that could no longer be relied on, because many of its rulers had embraced the Lutheran cause. The Peace of Augsburg in 1555 had only delayed the showdown struggle between the Catholic and Protestant principalities of what had been the Holy Roman Empire. By the time Pope Gregory XV was enthroned in 1621, war was under way in Germany. Emboldened by the spirit of the Counter-Reformation, the Catholic princes, supported by the Church, had seen their chance to sweep away the Protestant presence in their midst. However, power politics is never so simple: individual rulers pursued their own agendas, and peripheral states were drawn into a rapidly escalating conflict.

The war continued for 30 years, turning the heart of Europe into an inferno. Civilians bore the brunt as mercenary armies embarked on sprees of rape and pillage. One-fifth or more of Germany's people were killed, some slaughtered in the carnage, others caught up in the famines and plagues precipitated by the war and the large-scale population movements it brought with it.

## A HOLLOW TRIUMPH

The Catholic powers won, having made significant territorial gains, especially in France. Humanity had, of course, been the loser. Paradoxically, so too had the Church. Under

the terms of the Treaty of Westphalia (1648), the principle of *cuius regio, eius religio*, or "whose region, his religion", was set in stone. Protestantism became embedded in several states and even Calvinism was protected.

The Catholic rulers, meanwhile, were ceasing to side automatically with Rome. They had their own strategic aims: France, for instance, had seen the war less as a religious crusade than as a way of containing the expansion of (Catholic) Spain. To thwart the Habsburgs, it had chosen to form an alliance with Protestant Sweden, ignoring the outrage of the pope. This, it seemed, was the shape of things to come: Catholic kings would support their Church when it suited them – and only then.

*Above Urban VIII was pope through the most difficult period of the Thirty Years' War. A sculpture of the pope by Gian Lorenzo Bernini sits by his tomb in St Peter's Basilica, Rome.*

*Below Signed at Münster on 24 October 1648, the Treaty of Westphalia finally brought the hostilities of the Thirty Years' War to a close.*

# POLITICAL RAMIFICATIONS

THE REFORMATION REPRESENTED A SEISMIC SHOCK FOR THE CATHOLIC CHURCH, BUT ITS REPERCUSSIONS CERTAINLY DID NOT STOP THERE. ITS POLITICAL CONSEQUENCES WERE ALSO PROFOUND.

There was no separating the religious sphere from the political world in Renaissance Europe. The stability of the social order rested on the unquestioning respect for authority that the Catholic Church had previously enshrined. With division between the European states, the Church was losing ground.

## SECULAR REACTION

Such a blow to the Church's standing compromised the security of the state as far as the Spanish establishment saw it. The Crown in Spain linked its authority explicitly with that of the Church: to be a Protestant was not just to be ungodly but also to

*Below Half a millennium's Catholic culture came to an end with the Dissolution of the Monasteries. These ruins are all that is left of Fountains Abbey in Yorkshire, England.*

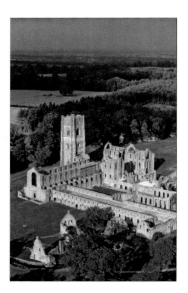

be un-Spanish. Given the extent of the country's empire in the Americas and the Pacific, the sponsorship of Spain was not to be dismissed lightly. Meanwhile, demands from French Protestants, known as Huguenots, for religious toleration were met with blunt refusal. In 1572, with an explosion of ferocity, thousands were murdered in the St Bartholomew's Day Massacre. While Henri IV had allowed the Protestants to practise their faith in peace, announcing the Edict of Nantes in 1598, that measure was rescinded by Louis XIV in 1685. The Huguenots saw their property confiscated and their churches closed down; more than 200,000 left the country to live in exile.

Northern Europe, which was the Reformation's heartland, was also a place of political division. In the Netherlands, which was a Spanish territory at the time, the people embraced Protestantism partly in a spirit of nationalist resistance.

## REACHING A COMPROMISE

Germany, Luther's homeland, was in theory a single entity under the Holy Roman Empire, but it was actually a patchwork of smaller states. Protestantism had been embraced with genuine enthusiasm in many of these areas. Several local rulers aligned themselves with the new religion to build up their own political power. A compromise was reached in 1555, when the Peace of Augsburg originally agreed the principle *cuius regio, eius religio* ("whose region, his religion"). Where a ruler was Catholic, in other words, Catholicism should hold sway; but where the king was a Lutheran, that religion would prevail in his country.

*Above Huguenots are being killed in the St Bartholomew's Day Massacre in this 19th-century painting by François Dubois.*

Instead of a recipe for tolerance it was one for systematic persecution, as rulers cleansed their countries along sectarian lines. Catholic kings were by no means innocent, but in the Protestant states of Germany and in Switzerland, home of Calvinism, priests were burnt at the stake and Catholicism was suppressed.

## DISSOLVED IN ENGLAND

The English Reformation had been opportunistic in its origins. King Henry VIII had not disagreed doctrinally with the Church; his conflict was based on his marriage status. Yet Catholicism quickly became identified as a threat to the country and its Crown, and its adherents punished its followers without mercy. Under the Act of Supremacy (1534), Henry became official head of the Church of England, and this allowed him to close Catholic foundations and confiscate their wealth. The Dissolution of the Monasteries shattered an ecclesiastical infrastructure that had been built up over centuries.

The Dissolution had opposition: 1536 saw the Pilgrimage of Grace – an uprising in Yorkshire (where there was to be a second rebellion, the Rising in the North, in 1569). Catholicism was reprieved in 1553, when Henry's daughter, Mary I, succeeded him and sought to turn the clock back. In the event, the wave of counter-repression she ordered against Protestantism succeeded only in seeing her branded with the nickname "Bloody Mary".

In 1593, Queen Elizabeth I, a non-Catholic, introduced legislation against "recusants" who refused to accept the authority of the Church of England. Those who remained Catholic included many of the country's leading families, especially in the north and the West Country. The father of William Shakespeare is believed to have been a recusant, and there has been speculation that England's greatest playwright was one as well.

King Philip II of Spain, Mary's widower, had supported his wife's mission to re-convert England. It was

*Below The Michelade was a massacre of Catholics in Nîmes, after St Michel's Fair in September 1567. Franz Hogenberg captured it in this 16th-century painting.*

*Above Protestant Elizabeth I sits in splendour before her Parliament. To her left stands Sir Francis Walsingham, a ruthless hunter of "recusants".*

with the intention of restoring Catholicism to England that, in 1588, he dispatched the Spanish Armada, hoping to invade the country. In the event, the *Armada Invencible* ("Invincible Fleet") was stopped by the English navy and dispersed by a "Protestant wind".

## UNDERCOVER CLERICS

English priests were trained in continental seminaries and then smuggled back into the country. They slipped in disguise from one private house to another around the country to give Mass. It had to be held in secret because participants never knew when they might be denounced by a suspicious neighbour or a servant with a grudge.

Although a number of these houses had hiding holes for visiting priests, many were caught and executed. Typically, they were hanged, drawn and quartered. Ordinary Catholics were killed, too, but they were often tortured first in hopes that they would give up the whereabouts of other Catholics, particularly their priests. The missionaries were feared by the authorities, not just as religious dissidents but as enemy agents. It hardly helped that the headquarters of English Catholicism were abroad, at Douai in France, and Valladolid in Spain.

*Above A number of English houses had hiding holes, so priests could quickly be concealed from the authorities. This hiding hole is in the King's Room in Moseley Old Hall, Staffordshire.*

s.Catherina
Iris.

# A WORLD RELIGION

The Catholic religion underwent a major cultural and geographical shift when a Middle Eastern sect became the European Church of Rome. As horizons widened, missionaries ventured out into the farthest reaches of Asia, the Americas and Africa, bringing the Word of God to some of the millions who had not yet heard it.

For a long time in Europe the idea of a godless universe had been – quite literally – unthinkable. In the 17th, 18th and 19th centuries, intellectuals, scientists and politicians began to place their faith in "reason". Christianity was so much superstition, said the rationalists, an instrument of oppression; the Church was a reactionary force. When two secularist ideologies – fascism and communism – plunged the world into chaos in the 20th century, the Church was caught up in the accompanying conflicts. Peace did return, at least for Western Europe and North America, where a new generation grew up in affluent societies. In the consumerist society, everything was a matter of choice – including religious belief and personal morality. Yet most of the world still lived in poverty and the Church had a duty to those people, too.

In the new millennium, Catholicism finds itself facing huge challenges, as it has throughout its history. Time and again, it has shown its capacity to recover from its setbacks and learn from its mistakes while holding firmly to its founding principles to be a guiding light of faith for a struggling world.

*Above When the Europeans became established in the Americas, Catholicism quickly spread throughout Latin America. Sister Juana Inés de la Cruz, a Mexican poet, scholar and nun, was painted in the 17th century by an unknown Mexican artist.*

*Left European explorers introduce the Cross – and Christianity – as they come into contact with previously unknown civilizations in the New World. Théodor de Bry illustrated scenes of these meetings in his 1592 Americae Tertia Pars.*

# MISSIONS TO THE EAST

THE APOSTLES WERE THE FIRST CHRISTIANS TO SPREAD THE GOSPELS.
FROM THE 15TH TO 17TH CENTURY, EUROPEANS BEGAN TO TRAVEL
FARTHER EAST, WHERE THEY SPREAD THE MESSAGE OF THE CHURCH.

"Go therefore and make disciples of all nations…" was Christ's command (Matthew 28:19). To the apostles the missionary impulse was part of Christianity. They spread Christ's message through Syria and Asia Minor, and westward to Rome, the centre of an extensive empire. There was even a tradition that St Thomas carried the gospels to India. Christian communities thrived in Iraq and Iran, too, but in the 5th century their Church no longer recognized the authority of Rome when it embraced Nestorianism, a heresy that believes

*Below China's Mongol emperor Kublai Khan greets the Polo brothers on their visit to China. In this c.1412 illustration from the* Book of the World's Marvels, *they receive a letter to deliver to the newly elected Pope Gregory X.*

Christ is divided into two: the divine and the human. It was now time for missionaries to carry the gospels to the farthest corners of Asia.

## CENTRAL ASIA

The willingness of the Mongols to adopt Nestorianism may have contributed to the rise of the legend of Prester John *(see right)*. In 1289, Pope Nicholas IV dispatched John of Montecorvino to take messages to Kublai Khan of China and other Mongol leaders. He was the first Roman Catholic missionary in China and translated the New Testament and Psalms into the Mongol language. Missionary work appealed to the enterprising spirit of the new Franciscan and Dominican orders, who sent missions to western and central Asia from the 13th century.

*Above St Francis Xavier (1506–52) did more than anyone else to carry the Christian message to the East. This 17th-century portrait is by an unknown painter.*

### PRESTER JOHN
By the 12th century, the failure of the Crusades and the growing strength of the Islamic world had left western Christendom in a state of demoralization. People were prepared to clutch at straws – even the legend that, somewhere in the East, there was a powerful empire ruled by a Christian king. Prester John had even written a letter, it was said, promising to come to Europe's rescue, attacking the Muslim enemy from the rear. So vague were the stories, and so inexact the geographical knowledge of Europe at this time, that Prester John's realms were variously reported as lying in Ethiopia and Central Asia. In 1177, Pope Alexander III went as far as writing a letter to Prester John seeking his assistance, but his messenger appears to have been lost somewhere in the vastness of Asia.

## SPREADING OUT

The missions into Asia were bold but small-scale ventures. Anything more was unrealistic, given Christendom's political and geographical situation. Europe was effectively "boxed in": by Islam on its eastern frontier, by Africa's Sahara to the south and by an apparently infinite Atlantic Ocean to the west. However, the Age of Discovery changed all that, opening a door upon a much wider world. This was a period between the early 15th century and the 17th century in which Europeans explored the oceans, seeking new trading routes. As these great voyages broadened horizons, they brought Christians into contact with nations which had never heard the Gospel Word.

The evangelizing impulse was never lost and found fresh impetus in the 16th century. The Counter-Reformation brought a new spiritual energy, with the Jesuits leading the way. St Francis Xavier founded a mission in Goa, on the coast of India, in 1542. The "Apostle of the Indies" went on to preach Christianity in Indonesia and, from 1549, Japan. The other orders were by now well-established in Malacca and Malaysia, and Augustinian friars had a mission in the Philippines from 1565.

## THE CHINESE ENDEAVOUR

The greatest challenge for the missionaries at the time was China, a vast and complex country that had an ancient history and strong religious traditions of its own. In 1552, St Francis Xavier was preparing to embark on another mission, this time to China, when he died on an island off Guangdong, on its southern coast. However, 30 years later, his fellow-Jesuits, Michele Ruggieri and Matteo Ricci, established their own mission in Beijing.

The Jesuits were under no illusions about the huge scale of the task that awaited them, and not merely

*Above* Many missionaries paid the ultimate price for their devotion to their religion. An unknown 17th-century Japanese artist illustrated Jesuits being martyred in Japan in 1622.

*Below* Jesuit missionary Matteo Ricci and scholar Li Paul Xu Guangqi became friends, shown together in this 17th-century engraving. They translated key works of Western science into Chinese.

because of the enormous population of the country. Chinese society was sophisticated and its sense of cultural identity secure. There could be no pretence that these were "savages" in need of civilization.

## A CULTURAL EXCHANGE

The Westerners sought out the Chinese scholarly elite and, addressing them as equals, opened up a dialogue on just about every aspect of life and thought. In the process, they introduced the Chinese to the whole range of Western culture, from art and literature to mathematics and science. They earned the respect and trust of China's rulers — and several Jesuits were even given posts in the imperial administration. Many Chinese intellectuals willingly converted to Christianity.

Sadly, as time went on, dissension between the Jesuits and Franciscans ended up hampering the effectiveness of both. In 1644, moreover, Manchu invaders swept away the old Qing dynasty in China and inaugurated a new order that was far less tolerant toward foreign faiths.

# MISSIONS IN THE AMERICAS

THE DISCOVERY AND EXPLORATION OF THE NEW WORLD DURING THE
16TH TO 18TH CENTURIES BROUGHT WITH IT THE DISCOVERY OF NEW
NATIONS AND CULTURES — AND ANOTHER WAVE OF MISSIONS.

*Above Fray Bartolomé de Las Casas
(1484–1566) became Catholicism's
conscience in the Americas, with his
impassioned pleas for humanity toward
the native peoples (artist unknown).*

The newly discovered peoples of
the Americas were the subject of an
important debate held in Valladolid,
at that time the capital of Spain, in
1550–1. Two Dominicans, Juan
Ginés de Sepúlveda and Bartolomé
de Las Casas, argued the burning
question of the day. Were the native
peoples of "New Spain" really men
and women, like Europeans? They
looked like humans, but they apparently went unclothed, like animals,

*Below After Columbus' first landfall in
the Caribbean, Christianity soon spread
down through South America.*

and their customs were alien to
Europeans. Should they be treated as
equals, or put under subjection?

There were good grounds for
taking the latter view, Sepúlveda said.
Had not Aristotle himself written
that some peoples were by their very
nature slaves, and needed to be
subjected for their own good? On
the contrary, Las Casas maintained.
He believed that the "Indians" were
entitled to exactly the same treatment as Europeans, but these rights
were being scandalously ignored.
Both in his Valladolid address and
in a series of polemical writings on

the subject, Las Casas catalogued
every kind of exploitation and abuse
that the native peoples were being
subjected to. From Columbus' voyages to the Caribbean islands to the
conquests of Mexico and Peru, by
Cortés and Pizarro respectively, the
native peoples, including the Taino,
Aztec, Maya and Inca, were harshly
treated by the Spaniards.

## NEW WORLD, NEW WAYS

Both sides of the debate claimed
victory, but the controversy went on
for years. The Church was divided:

*Below Spanish conquistadors massacre
the Inca after capturing their capital,
Cuzco, in 1532. The event is captured
in this 1602 engraving by Théodor
de Bry from the* Historia Americae.

NORTH AMERICA

to Lisbon

Gulf of Mexico

Bahama
Islands

from Seville

Cuba

Puerto
Rico

Jamaica    Hispaniola    Virgin Islands

Honduras    Caribbean Sea

ATLANTIC
OCEAN

Trinidad

Panama

Tenochtitlán    Cempoala

Chollolan    Tlaxcala

Veracruz

Tumbes

San Miguel    Caxamarca

SOUTH AMERICA

PACIFIC OCEAN

Cuzco

Chiquitos

N

Taruma

Guaraní

→ Columbus' first voyage (1492–93)
→ Cortés' conquest of Mexico (1519)
→ Pizarro's conquest of Peru (1531–33)
✠ Jesuit missions in South America

0 · · · · 1000 mi
0 · · · · 1500 km

in some places it had become an arm of oppression, while elsewhere it had become a fighter for the indigenous peoples and their rights. An encomienda system was established, in which Europeans took land for themselves, in effect enslaving its indigenous occupiers.

In theory expropriation came with a duty of guardianship. Some took this obligation seriously: the Society of Jesus led the way in trying to make the New World a better one. The Jesuits reigned over *reducciones* ("reductions") that covered most of what is now Paraguay, along with vast tracts in Uruguay, Brazil, Bolivia and Argentina. There they had the rights of the representatives of the colonial power. However, instead of enslaving the indigenous peoples, they settled them around their mission stations, giving them schools and establishing farms to teach skills in agriculture.

The Jesuits' approach could be accused of high-handedness, but their paternalism was preferable to the outrageous exploitation going on elsewhere. The indigenous peoples made it clear where their preferences lay, flocking to the *reducciones* in large numbers. Neighbouring colonists had no alternative but to improve conditions radically if they were to have any hope of hanging on to their subject Indians. As Bishop

*Above* Made for Aztec offerings, this casket cover found a new role in the Christian liturgy. It is now kept in the Templo Mayor Museum, Mexico City.

of Michoacán, Mexico, from 1537, Bishop Vasco de Quiroga introduced a system of his own. Along with a foundation in Christian education, he had "his" indigenous people taught craft skills, each village being given a different speciality, from weaving and metalwork to pottery. His subjects even had a degree of political autonomy.

Not surprisingly, such utopias sparked controversy and other Europeans lobbied against them. There, lobbying was so successful that in the middle of the 18th century the Jesuits were formally expelled from Spanish and Portuguese America.

## NORTHERN MISSIONS

Along North America's eastern sea coast, the main colonial power was Protestant England – with the exception of the colony of Maryland, which was founded by Catholic refugees from the same country in 1633. Farther north, in Canada, the French were in charge. Their intrepid priests played a major part in exploring the interior, venturing up the St Lawrence River to the Great Lakes.

The west coast, though nominally Spanish-ruled, saw little sign of European settlement at first. It was not until the 18th century that encroachments were made down the coast by Russian traders, which created nervousness at home.

In 1769, Father Junípero Serra set out from San Diego with the Spanish soldier and official Gaspar de Portola to build a chain of missions. They founded 21 missions in total, up and down what became known as the *Camino Real*, or "Royal Road". Junípero Serra set up nine of them personally, travelling an estimated 38,000 km (23,600 miles) in the 15 years before he died.

*Below* A figure of founder Junípero Serra stands before the Mission Church of San Diego de Alcalá, San Diego – California's first church, established in 1769.

### THE HURON CAROL

In 1643, the Jesuit priest and explorer Jean de Brébeuf wrote his "Huron Carol", referring to God as Gitchi Manitou – the great deity of the Algonquin people – and giving the Christmas story a new setting in Canada.

*Twas in the moon of wintertime when all the birds had fled*
*That mighty Gitchi Manitou sent angel choirs instead;*
*Before their light the stars grew dim, and wondering hunters heard the hymn:*
*Jesus your King is born, Jesus is born, in excelsis gloria...*

*Within a lodge of broken bark the tender babe was found;*
*A ragged robe of rabbit skin enwrapped his beauty round*
*But as the hunter braves drew nigh, the angel song rang loud and high:*
*Jesus your King is born, Jesus is born, in excelsis gloria.*

# THE GOSPEL IN AFRICA

THE STORY OF CATHOLICISM IN AFRICA IS TIED UP INEXTRICABLY WITH THAT OF COLONIALISM IN THE 16TH TO 19TH CENTURIES. TODAY'S CHURCH MUST LOOK BACK ON A RECORD THAT IS DECIDEDLY MIXED.

*Above To many Africans, such as these slaves photographed in Zanzibar in the 1880s, the Christian message could give meaning to a downtrodden life.*

Exploration of sub-Saharan Africa by Europeans came late. Prior to the 19th century, Africa was for the most part considered only as a place for buying slaves. Sea captains of different nations sailed down the hazardous coast, but generally stopped for only as long as it took to load up with their helpless human cargo. Then the ships set off again – some sailing to the plantations of British North America, but many to the New World colonies founded by Catholic Portugal, Spain and France.

Although this slave trade was a monstrous business, at the same time it was immensely profitable, and the American venture was central to the strategic aims of these great powers. So closely were the clergies of these conquering countries involved in this project that few seem to have questioned its moral implications for Christians. Although a succession of popes did condemn the trade – such as Gregory XIV in 1591, Urban VIII in 1639 and Benedict XIV in 1741 – with so much at stake they failed to make their message heard.

### AFRICAN CATHOLICISM?
Some efforts were made to preach the gospel: indeed, Portuguese priests made great strides in the Kingdom of Kongo (which included much of what is now Angola, as well as parts of the modern Republic of the Congo and Democratic Republic of the Congo). However, in a spirit of tolerance, the Church allowed the incorporation of elements of African religion, and soon Kongolese Catholicism was barely recognizable as Catholicism at all. At the start of the 18th century, for example, a woman named Kimpa Vita mobilized the masses, claiming to be the reincarnation of St Anthony of Padua. She insisted that Christ had been Kongolese, and that St Anthony was a deity alongside him.

*Left A contemporary cartoonist addressed the imperial ambitions of the wealthy businessman Cecil Rhodes: Europeans were tripping over one another in their "Scramble for Africa".*

## A SPIRITUAL SCRAMBLE

The exploration of Africa's vast interior began in real earnest in the 19th century, when it was still seen as a "dark continent" by many Catholics. Nevertheless, the Church was equipped: a wealth of missionary experience had been acquired in the Americas and Asia, and in 1622 a co-ordinating Congregation for Propagation of the Faith had been founded. (In the 20th century this was renamed the Congregation for the Evangelization of Peoples.)

The Catholic Church had competition. The most famous British traveller in Africa, David Livingstone, though today generally thought of simply as an explorer, was just one of many highly motivated Protestant missionaries. Livingstone's explorations, moreover, are difficult to disentangle from the wider British effort to colonize the African interior. Cecil Rhodes' boastful ambition to build a railway "from the Cape to Cairo" typified the colonialists' view of Africa as a blank canvas on which to capture their grand designs. Catholic and Protestant missionaries had brought with them, along with the gospels, an unmistakable message of European supremacy.

> ### ABUSIVE RULERS
> The presence of the French Archbishop Charles Lavigerie in Tunisia, a French statesman once remarked, "is worth an army to France". Lavigerie had once said, "as missionaries we also work for France". Where Catholic powers prevailed, the Church often acted as an arm of the colonial administration. Terrible atrocities were committed when the French ruled in what is now the Republic of the Congo.
>
> Still worse was the holocaust committed by Belgium's King Leopold II in the south in his so-called Congo Free State, now the Democratic Republic of the Congo. Mass rape and mutilations were carried out by troops to discourage dissent and boost productivity on the plantations and in the mines. By 1908, up to ten million citizens had been killed by the troops.

These missionaries were fighting a (sometimes unseemly) turf war, analogous to the great colonial "Scramble for Africa" itself, where Europeans competed to claim African territories as their own in the late 19th century until World War I. In some places this had tragic consequences. In Buganda, the main kingdom of what is now Uganda, the local king – a despot of hideous cruelty – kept himself in power by playing Protestant and Catholic missionaries off against one another.

The Catholic missionaries at work in Africa belonged to the Society of the Missionaries of Africa, which was better known as the "White Fathers". The society was founded in 1868 by the Archbishop of Algeria, Charles Lavigerie, who was originally sent to work in French North Africa. The distinctive white garb for which its members were named was modelled on the robes of the desert nomads. Also in the vanguard were the priests of the Society of African Missions, which was founded in 1850 by Bishop Melchior de Marion-Brésillac.

*Below French White Fathers pose amid a congregation of local converts outside their traditionally built mission in Urundi (now Burundi) in the years before World War I.*

**Above** *A French missionary bulletin of 1878 sends an uplifting message to encourage generosity from back home.*

# THE ENLIGHTENMENT ASSAULT

FROM THE SCIENTIFIC, INTELLECTUAL AND POLITICAL COMMUNITIES
CAME TRENCHANT CRITICISMS OF CATHOLICISM: SOON THE CHURCH
WAS STRUGGLING TO HOLD ITS OWN.

The Copernican revolution, in which the 16th-century astronomer claimed that the Earth revolved around the Sun – which meant that the Earth was not, as the Church believed, the centre of the universe – had been only a foretaste of the formidable challenges to come. In 1687, the English scientist Sir Isaac Newton published his *Philosophiae Naturalis Principia Mathematica* ("Mathematical Principles of Natural Philosophy"). While Newton was not an atheist, it was hard to resist a feeling that his far-reaching theories could be suggesting a universe that was governed not by God but instead by mathematics and science.

*Below Sir Isaac Newton's theories transformed perceptions of the universe – and, inevitably, of God. This 1687 frontispiece is from the* Philosophiae Naturalis Principia Mathematica.

The English poet Alexander Pope, a Catholic, had no difficulty in reconciling his fellow countryman's new science with his deeply felt religious views on the Creation:

> Nature and Nature's laws lay hid
>   in night,
> God said "Let Newton Be!" and
>   all was light.

In a perverse sort of way, it probably helped that the poet was living in a Protestant country in which anti-Catholic feeling was rife. Catholics had even been blamed for the Great Fire of London of 1666. Under the Penal Laws then prevailing, the poet was not allowed to live in London, but had been forced to take a house outside the city, at Twickenham. Pope's faith was almost certainly steeled by the humiliations he had to undergo.

*Above Brilliant in his thinking, vicious in his satire, Voltaire became the scourge of the Catholic Church. This 1811 portrait is by Jacques Augustin Pajou.*

### THE FRENCH "INFAMY"
In Catholic France, the situation was different: there the Church was closely identified with a monarchical establishment that oppressed the poor and repressed all freedoms. In such circumstances, young intellectuals were more predisposed to regard religion as superstition and to dismiss the liturgy and sacraments as mumbo-jumbo. These intellectuals, and soon the general French public, were quick to adopt anything that seemed to offer a rational explanation for the wonders of creation. *Écrasez l'Infâme* ("Crush the Infamy") became the war cry of François-Marie Arouet, who is much better known today by his pseudonym Voltaire. The infamy he was referring to was the alliance of the Church and Crown against freedom, justice and the rule of reason.

Voltaire was the most famous of the 18th-century *philosophes*, whose work extended far beyond the realm of philosophy as normally understood into just about every area of

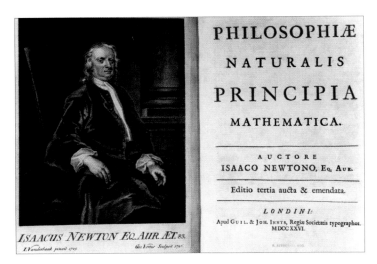

PHILOSOPHIÆ
NATURALIS
PRINCIPIA
MATHEMATICA.

AUCTORE
ISAACO NEWTONO, Eq. Aur.

Editio tertia aucta & emendata.

LONDINI:
Apud Guil. & Joh. Innys, Regiæ Societatis typographos.
MDCCXXVI.

ISAACUS NEWTON EQ. AUR. ÆT. 83.

life and politics. Other prominent *philosophes* included Jean Jacques Rousseau, who said "Man was born free, but he is everywhere in chains". These metaphorical chains were not just those of tyranny but of public institutions, even of morality: children were born innocent, he said, then corrupted by their education. He also claimed that no institution did more to blight the pure soul than the Catholic Church, which was steward of a morality that destroyed the very virtue it claimed to save.

## COMPREHENSIVE CRITIQUE

By 1750, under the leadership of Denis Diderot, a group of scholars worked on a great, multi-volume *Encyclopédie*. This was to be a "systematic dictionary of the sciences, arts and crafts", and it was to be drawn up, said Diderot, "without regard to anybody's feelings". They wanted to include every branch of human knowledge.

The Encyclopedists questioned Christianity's most fundamental tenets, arguing that theology was just another branch of philosophical investigation, and that religious doctrine should be submitted to the same sort of scientific testing as anything else.

*Above An intimidating late 18th-century French illustration shows an army sapper and a revolutionary exhorting "Liberty, Equality and Fraternity…Or Death".*

## REVOLUTION

The *Ancien Régime* was finally swept away in 1789. Although the French Revolution did bring a sort of freedom, it also brought its own infamy, too, in the Reign of Terror. The new Republic was defiantly secular in its approach. The idea of *laïcité* was

established: France was to be run by and for lay people, not the clergy. Christian values were to be replaced by those of *Liberté, Egalité* and *Fraternité* ("Liberty", "Equality" and "Fraternity").

Religion was not actually outlawed (as it would be later in some communist countries), but it was restrained and no longer enjoyed special favours from the state, and it was certainly not allowed to set the tone for ruling the country. Catholicism was given the same slightly grudging tolerance as the Protestants: gone were the days when its cardinals and bishops were active participants in the government of the state.

In the absence of any real understanding developing between the state authorities and the Church hierarchy, the concept of "Ultramontanism" soon grew among the Catholics in opposition to *laïcité*. *Ultramontane* literally means "beyond the mountains": the range in question was the Alps, on the other side of which lay Italy and Rome. French Catholics were told by their clergy that, whatever their state might try to tell them, its authority was trumped by that of their Church.

## THE IMPERIAL CATECHISM

In 1804, Napoleon Bonaparte overthrew the revolutionary state, installing himself as Emperor Napoleon I. However, any hopes that the Church might find its old authority restored were cruelly dashed. On the contrary, the ultimate ignominy came in 1806 with the "Imperial Catechism", rewritten by the emperor himself and imposed on France's Catholic educators:

*What are the duties of Christians toward those who govern them, and in particular toward Napoleon I, our emperor?*

*Christians owe the princes who govern them – and we in particular owe Napoleon I, our emperor – love, respect, obedience, fidelity, military service, and the taxes levied for the preservation and defence of the empire and of his throne…*

**Right** *Pope Pius VII and his legates suffered the indignity of being obliged to be present during Napoleon's Coronation in 1804. The pope is the subject of this 1807 painting by Jacques Louis David.*

# HOLDING BACK THE TIDE

THE 19TH AND 20TH CENTURIES SAW THE CHURCH ENGAGED IN AN
INCREASINGLY FRANTIC REARGUARD ACTION TO DEFEND ITSELF
AGAINST FREE–THINKING LIBERALISM AND REFORM.

The Church's identification with its conservative causes was to leave a lasting legacy that would be difficult for Catholicism to live down. It has always insisted that it was no enemy of science or reason – only to the "rationalism" that makes an idol out of human thought. Although Catholicism would come to terms with the discoveries of Newton and his successors, during the 19th and early 20th centuries the clergy often found itself acting as apologists for scientific backwardness, which only seemed to confirm the charge that the Church stood for superstition.

## CONSERVATIVE VIEWS

It hardly helped that the most obvious product of the "Enlightenment" had been bloody revolution in Catholic France. The ferment there

*Above* Giuseppe Garibaldi led the Italians in their 19th-century struggle for nationhood. Most could not understand why the Church opposed this movement.

was viewed with consternation in other countries, whose rulers saw their own authority under threat. Rome's unease at the rise of *laïcité* may have been understandable, but it also placed the Church firmly in the camp of the conservatives.

Under the guise of resisting revolution, the Habsburg rulers of Austria, for instance, set themselves against every kind of social change. Backed by the state chancellor and Emperors Francis I and Ferdinand I, they refused the ambitions expressed by subject populations for national sovereignty – not just in Hungary and the Balkans but also in Italy.

## THE *RISORGIMENTO*

In 19th-century Italy, a resurgence of national feeling, known as the *Risorgimento*, arose among a people who had for too long lived under Austrian domination. The movement received no encouragement from the Church, which saw any attack on authority as corrosive of its own. Conservatives in Italy shared

*Left* By the 1860s, Pope Pius IX was completely dependent on French backing. He blesses Bourbon troops outside the Royal Palace in Naples in this 19th-century painting by Achille Vespa.

this view, but as time went on and the ferment rose, theirs became an increasingly unpopular position. Because the Vatican identified itself more closely with despotic rulers in Vienna than with the overwhelming will of the Italian people, it severely damaged the Church's reputation.

Pope Pius IX still insisted that, as pope, he was temporal ruler of the Papal States, the central Italian territories traditionally under the rule of the Vatican. Increasingly, the Italians disagreed and, in 1849, Pius IX needed military intervention by France's Emperor Napoleon III to secure his position. Repeatedly, he had to rely on the support of foreign imperialists – sometimes the French, sometimes the Austrians – against the Italian freedom fighter Giuseppe Garibaldi and his patriotic Red Shirt army. Finally, in 1871, papal rule in the city of Rome came to an end. The tiny enclave of the Vatican apart, the former territories were annexed by the state. Rome was now the capital of a unified Italy.

## SET AGAINST CHANGE

The episode left a bad feeling behind. Liberals saw the Catholic Church not as a champion but as the foe of freedom; workers saw it as the enemy of change. The Church itself

had been wounded and it lashed out, responding to threats to its authority with a flurry of authoritarian pronouncements. Already, in 1864, Pius IX had issued his Syllabus of Errors, a catalogue of new liberal ideas that he felt were damaging. He summed up by rejecting any notion that the Church should take steps to accommodate "progress…liberalism, or recent civilization". (Called in 1869 to ratify the Syllabus, the First Vatican Council sprang another surprise when, in a statement of 1870, Pius IX proclaimed the dogma of papal infallibility, claiming that popes are divinely guided, so infallible.)

In Protestant-dominated countries, the Church's political position might be more subtly nuanced. For the most part, though, it was identified with conservatism. In Spain, the poor knew better than to look to the Church for support in bettering their situation. They had learned to see the black-garbed priests as scavenging, flesh-eating *corvos* ("crows"). When Civil War broke out in the country in 1936, priests and nuns were massacred in their hundreds.

*Below General Franco greets some of his clerical supporters with studied courtesy: relations were not quite so warm between Spain's working people and the Church.*

### THE WORKERS' POPE

Despite the conservative stand taken by the Church, there was one pope who held a different view. Pope Leo XIII's proclamations on behalf of the world's workers would put many a socialist to shame. He himself was anything but a democrat, putting down one dissenting adviser with an unceremonious *Ego sum Petrus* ("I am Peter") but he saw the need for radical change, if only to rescue the status quo.

In his 1891 encyclical *Rerum Novarum* ("Of New Things"), he addressed the condition of the working classes as one of the great issues of the age. Reasoning that failure to reform would lead to revolution, he called for far-reaching changes in the way modern economies were organized. Denouncing the glaring gulf between rich and poor, he spoke out in support of workers' rights and trade unions, expressing his sympathy for those who went on strike to ensure the welfare of their families.

*Above Addressing the Church – and looking to the future – Pope Leo XIII is shown recording his blessing by phonograph in this 1903 print by Achille Beltrame.*

# DARK TIMES

WITH FASCISTS MARCHING ON ROME ITSELF, NAZISM ON THE RISE IN GERMANY AND COMMUNISTS IN EASTERN EUROPE, THE FIRST HALF OF THE 20TH CENTURY WAS A TUMULTUOUS TIME FOR THE CHURCH.

*Above At the height of his power, Benito Mussolini visits the Vatican in 1932 to meet Pope Pius XI and his officials.*

In 1922, cheering crowds turned out to welcome Benito Mussolini and his "Blackshirts" – the nickname given to members of his Fascist paramilitary – as they made their triumphal entrance into Rome. However, Italy's senior churchmen were rather more muted in their welcome: they had little in common with the young thugs who were following *Il Duce* ("The Leader").

Even so, there was something in Fascism to which these churchmen found themselves able to respond: its reverence for authority, its avowed respect for established tradition. Years of liberalism, with its vaunted freedoms, had brought the country only incessant labour unrest and public immorality – and a press that held the Church and all its values in clear contempt. Worse still, there was evidence everywhere in Europe of the

*Below Cardinal Pacelli, the future Pope Pius XII, signs the infamous Concordat with Germany in 1933 on behalf of Pope Pius XI.*

advances made by the Communists, who had already established an atheistic state in the Soviet Union.

## SENT BY PROVIDENCE

The Holy See had refused to acknowledge Italy's annexation of Rome in 1871, spending the next six decades in denial – and in endless wrangling with successive governments. Under the terms of the Lateran Treaty of 1929, Mussolini agreed compensation for the loss of the old Papal States. Mussolini had discarded the Catholicism of his upbringing, and privately despised it, but he also recognized its importance to the conservative Italians he wanted on his side. He made Catholicism the state religion, made criticism of the Church a crime, outlawed divorce and made religious education mandatory in all schools. All state legislation would be reviewed to ensure that it conformed with canon law. Pope Pius XI declared that *Il Duce* was "a man sent by providence": there were some

who did not question the moral price the Church would have to pay for this arrangement.

Both Mussolini and Hitler were lapsed Catholics. Like Mussolini, Hitler saw Christianity as a weaklings' creed, but he recognized the value of good relations with the Church. Pius XI signed a Concordat – an agreement between pope and secular ruler on religious matters – with Hitler's government in 1933, eager to have another ally in resisting the Communist advance.

However, the Nazis made more uncomfortable bedfellows than the Italian Fascists, especially when the ugliness of their anti-semitism became evident to all. In 1937, the pope sent out a letter to be read in German churches. *Mit Brennender Sorge* ("With Burning Sorrow") contained a forthright condemnation of the Nazis' attacks on the Jewish population as well as their attempts to establish control over the Catholic Church within Germany.

## STANDING BY?

The ensuing Holocaust was one of the darkest episodes of modern history, and the Church is one of many institutions that emerged with its reputation tarnished. Pope Pius XII, who succeeded Pius XI in 1939, has rightly been condemned. Broadly speaking, any good he did was done by stealth; he was guarded in his public denunciations. He had a love for Germany and its culture (earlier in his career he had been Papal Nuncio – akin to a Vatican ambassador – in the country) and held Hitler's populism in deep disdain. Yet the uncomfortable fact remains that what really excited his moral ardour was the threat represented by Communism in the East. Nazism appeared to him to be the lesser of two evils.

While acknowledging Pius XII's attempts to relieve the plight of World War II's victims, including Jews, some critics charge him and the Catholic Church with a failure of moral leadership. Although there were heroic efforts made by individual priests and nuns, these critics saw the institution as being weak during the war. There was general approval within the Church when, on a visit to Jerusalem in 2000, Pope John Paul II made a heartfelt apology to the Jewish community.

## AFTER THE WAR

Fascism had been all but vanquished by the end of World War II, though authoritarian governments endured for a few decades in Spain and Portugal. The Communists gained a strong hold in Eastern Europe, putting the Church there in a weak position. After the lessons of the Nazi era, the Church became outspoken critics of Communist oppression. Yet the Church's earlier links with Fascism meant some Western liberals remained sceptical that the Church's opposition to Communism was truly rooted in principle.

*Above Pius XI and Mussolini agree upon the Lateran Treaty, as illustrated on the cover of the March 1929 edition of* Simplicissimus, *a liberal satirical magazine published in Germany.*

### CATHOLICS UNDER COMMUNISM

The Soviet Union had been among the victors of World War II in 1945. With Communism's avowedly materialist principles, there was no place in the Communist scheme for the religious institution. In Russia itself, the established Church had been Orthodox, and its more independent-minded clergy was quickly hounded out by the Soviet authorities. A collaborationist congregation was created in its place. In the Ukraine, Romania and Czechoslovakia, Catholics were forced to join this officially sanctioned pseudo-Church in the tens of thousands, though many of the faithful continued their accustomed worship underground. In Poland, too, a "silent Church" clung on precariously in a mutually uncomfortable co-existence with the Communist state.

*Above Pope John Paul II visited the "Hill of Crosses" in 1993. On several previous occasions the Soviet authorities had attempted to remove this massive memorial to the Lithuanians' faith.*

# THE MODERNIZERS

THE 20TH-CENTURY POPES BROUGHT ABOUT RELIGIOUS CHANGES, AND THEIR REFORMS TRANSFORMED BOTH THE PROFILE OF THE CHURCH AND THE EXPERIENCE OF BEING CATHOLIC.

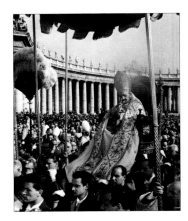

Though Pope Pius XII's pontificate is considered controversial now, in the 1950s his authority seemed impregnable. The pope who had brought the Church through World War II was naturally regarded with gratitude – his own personal role, and that of his Church, were as yet unexamined. In the Cold War climate, moreover, his uncompromising stand against Communism had won him respect well beyond the boundaries of his Church. As the first "media Pope", he became known to the world through newspaper pictures, television appearances and radio broadcasts. Within the Church,

his power was immense, even by papal standards, because he had surrounded himself with elderly and like-minded cardinals.

## A CONVENTIONAL CHOICE

Pius XII's unabashedly conservative Church was a frustrating place for the young and the radical. When he died in 1958, some saw a chance to advance reforms. However the cardinals elected Angelo Roncalli, Patriarch of Venice, to serve as Pope John XXIII. The new pontiff was already 77 years of age, and in a long career he had shown himself a meek and unquestioning servant of his

*Above Pope John XXIII blesses the crowd as he is carried in to officiate at the opening of the Second Vatican Council in 1962.*

superiors. He was not the breath of fresh air the progressives had been wanting. All the evidence indicated that this was what had recommended him as Pius' replacement: he could be relied upon not to rock the boat.

The only issue that appeared to stir up any passion in the new pope was that of Christian unity. John mourned the gradual disintegration of Jesus' Church down the centuries and longed to build bridges with Catholicism's "separated brethren". Hence, he arranged meetings with England's Archbishop of Canterbury and had talks with representatives of other churches. This, though clearly a worthy cause, was hardly an exciting one. There was no immediate prospect of real change.

## SECOND VATICAN COUNCIL

John XXIII's dream of Christian unity has remained elusive to this day. However, it was to have one very real and immediate consequence.

*Left The scene inside St Peter's Basilica at one of the climactic moments of the Vatican Council. Pope John is enthroned beneath the baldacchino in the distance.*

In 1962, the pope called together the Second Vatican Council, and from then onward the Catholic Church would never be the same.

Although some critics might see the changes as superficial, the Council re-emphasized (in some ways reinforced) the hierarchical nature of the Church. At the same time, it acknowledged the need for "top-down" directives to be supplemented by "bottom-up" reform. There was a new tone of openness, and a genuine receptiveness to criticism – lay observers, including women, were encouraged to be involved. Ordinary Catholics were to play a fuller part in the conduct of their faith, and there was to be a drive to make the Scriptures more widely available in the vernacular (people's own languages).

Measures were also taken to give lay Catholics a greater role in the Mass, and in the liturgy, too, there was to be a vernacular component. This process was completed under Pope Paul VI in 1969 when, along with a full transition to the vernacular, the practice of having the priest face the congregation when saying Mass was introduced. Previously, he had faced the altar, which was typically at the eastern end of the church, in the direction of Jerusalem (just as Muslims orientate themselves

*Above In 1976 the reactionary Archbishop Marcel Lefebvre defiantly celebrated the traditional Tridentine Mass. This celebration has been encouraged by recent popes.*

toward Mecca for daily prayers). Worshippers might feel a sense of wonder at being present for such a sacred ritual, but the new Catholicism wanted to draw parishoners in to make them feel involved.

### THE BACKLASH

The Second Vatican Council was in many ways less far-reaching than has since been assumed. Issues that were already becoming controversial, such as contraception and divorce, were mostly unaddressed. Yet Catholicism now had a completely different feel, and Pope John XXIII's critics were in no doubt that there was substance in the changes.

The French Archbishop Marcel Lefebvre led a movement within the Church to return to the old ways and the Tridentine Mass, the Latin liturgy approved by the Council of Trent in the 16th century. Ultimately, he had to lead it from outside the Church. In 1988, he was excommunicated by Pope John Paul II (himself a conservative) after the archbishop consecrated four new bishops without official sanction.

### POP RELIGION

The new-look Catholicism was taken up with great enthusiasm, its advent corresponding with that of the 1960s' pop culture. Guitars strummed, children acted out scriptural scenes and kisses of peace were freely exchanged at self-consciously informal "folk masses". This occurred nowhere more so than in Liverpool, England, home of the Beatles and, from 1967, of a thoroughly modern "Metropolitan Cathedral of Christ the King". Although shaped like a stylized crown with a spectacular stained-glass lantern, its circular ground plan was inclusive and democratic. Poet Roger McGough caught the mood with his poem of dedication: "O Lord on Thy New Liverpool Address". The poem has a reference to a priest wearing the cassock, concluding that if it is worn, "Then let's glimpse the jeans beneath".

*Above In the modern design of the Liverpool Metropolitan Cathedral, stained-glass windows in the roof complement the colourful lighting that highlights the altar.*

# THE CHURCH MILITANT

THE CHRISTIAN'S DUTY TO HELP THE POOR IS CLEAR, BUT JUST HOW
FAR THE CATHOLIC CHURCH SHOULD BE PREPARED TO GO WAS A
QUESTION RAISED BY LIBERATION THEOLOGY.

In the 20th century, many South Americans lived in deprivation and from this arose Liberation Theology. It challenged the Church to make the spirit of the Beatitudes prevail by helping to overthrow established political and economic systems.

> He has put down the mighty from
> their thrones and exalted those of
> low degree;
> He has filled the hungry with good
> things, and the rich he has sent
> empty away.

This is one of the most remarkable passages in the gospels, from Mary's "Magnificat" (Luke 1:46–55).

*Below Óscar Romero, Archbishop of San Salvador, was an advocate for the poor and victims of the country's civil war. He was killed in 1980 while celebrating Mass.*

Our Lady's words celebrate the Christ who, for all his divine greatness, would keep company with prostitutes and lepers. He is the Christ who, for all his gentleness and his injunction to "turn the other cheek", was moved to violence by the sight of the moneychangers in the Temple. Further, he is the same Christ who, while summoning all to salvation, warned the rich young man that it is easier for a camel to pass through the eye of a needle than for a rich man to enter the kingdom of heaven.

## MARX'S "GOSPEL"

Was Jesus not just a saviour but also a revolutionary? It is easy to see why many should have thought so, although it is harder to see what form a real-world Christian revolution would actually take. Especially given that, from the 18th century onward, the revolutionary orthodoxy has seen religion not as an aid to humanity but as a great part of the problem. Karl Marx, the renowned founder of Communism, notoriously saw religion as "the opium of the people" – though to put this into context, it should be noted that he was writing at a time that was lenient toward taking recreational drugs. His suggestion that religion was "the sigh of the oppressed creature", "the heart of a heartless world" showed at least a degree of sympathy for those who sought religious comfort. However, he saw that comfort as illusory.

Marx's later followers took a less nuanced view and settled into the conviction that religion was a cruel hoax designed to reconcile the people to their oppression. In the false hope of salvation hereafter, they

*Above Russia's Bolsheviks expressed their antagonism to religion in no uncertain terms, shown in this 1930 print by Achille Beltrame, from the Italian newspaper* La Domenica del Corriere.

would accept their lot on the earth: a dismal status quo was thus perpetuated. It was not difficult to find supporting evidence, not just in the sufferings of the world's poor but in the cosy relations between religious leaders and those who held great political power.

## 20TH-CENTURY RADICALS

That the Church might be letting down the poor had, of course, occurred to many in its history. Even in the 19th century, Pope Leo XIII had met the labour movement halfway with his *Rerum Novarum*, a letter that addressed the condition of the working classes. However, in the 1960s, radicalism was present around the world: this was a time of student sit-ins and anti-war demonstrations. African Americans (as well as Catholics in Protestant-dominated Northern Ireland) marched in the thousands to demand their civil rights; there were general strikes and student riots in France. The aims of the activists might have been vague, but the mood of rebellion was infectious, and many Catholics – the young in particular – felt they should be making their own contribution to the "struggle".

## SOUTH AMERICAN LIBERALS

In Latin America, many millions were living in abject poverty while a helpless Church hierarchy looked on. By contrast, the leftists were able to report real achievements. In 1959, Fidel Castro, Che Guevara and their guerrilla army overthrew a repressive regime in Cuba. As proclaimed by Gustavo Gutiérrez, a priest from Peru, Liberation Theology called for a Catholicism that, not content with promising salvation in the next life, would do whatever it took to bring about revolutionary change in this one on earth.

There is no doubting the movement's sincerity in trying to improve the living conditions of the South

*Below Pope John Paul ll listened to a speech made by Daniel Ortega, leader of the Sandinistas, when the pontiff visited Nicaragua in 1983.*

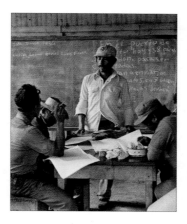

*Above Many Catholics reasoned that Christ would have approved of the Nicaraguan Literacy Campaign run by the Sandinistas, but the Church took issue with the Sandinistas' wider aims.*

American people – or, for a time, its real significance. Thousands of priests, nuns and lay Catholics were inspired by the Liberationist message, and several important

Catholic figures died for their beliefs. Archbishop Óscar Romero, who had led the popular opposition to El Salvador's oppressive military regime, was gunned down at the altar as he was saying Mass on 24 March 1980. Catholic clerics were well represented among the Sandinistas, who came to power in Nicaragua in the 1980s, including the famous poet-priest Ernesto Cardenal.

However, it was inevitable that the hierarchy of the Church would look askance at such developments, and not only through ingrained conservatism. Liberation Theology failed, as the Marxists would say, because of its contradictions. Despite certain common aims, the marriage of Communism and Christianity was always going to be problematic given the former's refusal to acknowledge any existence of a spiritual dimension. No one could see this more clearly than Pope John Paul II, who had experienced the tyranny that resulted when Communism set out to establish heaven on earth.

### CAMILO TORRES

"If Christ were alive today, he would be a guerrilla," claimed Camilo Torres. Born in 1929, and a priest since the early 1950s, he had become disillusioned with the Church's failure to relieve the sufferings of the poor. Deciding that radical action was needed – even violent action if need be – he went as far as enlisting with his country's Marxist guerrillas. The ELN (*Ejército de Liberación Nacional*, or National Liberation Army) was engaged in open war with the Colombian government. However, Torres was killed in 1966 during his first operation with the ELN, becoming the Liberation Army's most famous martyr.

# THE PEOPLE'S POPE

TODAY'S PAPACY HAS BEEN INFLUENCED LARGELY BY ONE PARTICULAR POPE, JOHN PAUL II – THE CHARISMATIC HOLY FATHER WHO BECAME A FATHER FIGURE FOR THE WORLD.

Although the final decades of the 20th century posed new challenges for the papacy, the development of modern technology had presented unprecedented opportunities as well. Pope Pius XII was recognized around the world thanks to television and press images. Pope Paul VI, the first pope of the jet age, was able to embark upon important foreign tours. However, where these previous popes had more or less uncomfortably gone through the motions as media performers, Pope John Paul II took to stardom with the utmost ease.

### AN UNEXPECTED STAR

This was in some ways surprising. John Paul II was the first non-Italian pope in half a millennium and he was an intensely serious, scholarly man whose faith had a strongly private, even mystical aspect. The youngest of three children, he was born in Poland in 1920 and named Karol Wojtyla. He had been afflicted in childhood by the loss first of his mother and then of a much-loved elder brother. He'd lost all his family members before he became a priest. In youth, Wojtyla had been a brilliant student

*Below A "rock-star" reputation was in many ways ill-suited to a deeply serious, spiritual man, but there was no denying John Paul II's popular appeal. Here he blesses the crowd at St Peter's in 1982.*

*Above At the time when Karol Wojtyla was a young seminarian in 1942, in Kraków, Poland, the city was under German occupation.*

and, more broadly, an intellectual. He was fluent in a number of languages, was widely read, and wrote both poems and plays himself. Wojtyla loved sport, too (playing as a goalkeeper for a soccer team), and had a sociable side that he was able to draw on when making his public appearances as pope.

## FREEDOM AND OBLIGATION
His early bereavements apart, the great formative experiences in Wojtyla's life were those of totalitarianism in two different forms. As a young seminarian he lived underground for months at the time of the Warsaw Uprising against the Nazis. He pursued his vocation under Communism and rose to the position of Archbishop of Kraków in a Church that had to keep silent if it was to continue to exist. Wojtyla emerged as an individualist – not an egotist, but a firm believer in the importance of the private voice of conscience. He could never accept that this should be subordinated either to the "collective will" of the Fascists or to the "dictatorship of the proletariat" of the Communists.

*Above Pope John Paul II was identified with* Solidarnosc *("Solidarity"), the free trade union that helped bring down Communism in Poland and beyond.*

It might be expected that John Paul II had little time for Latin America's Liberation Theology. However, those who dismissed him as an old-fashioned reactionary were wide of the mark. He was generally more than ready to condemn the Western powers when the occasion demanded. He was forthright in denouncing the invasion of Iraq in 2003. He was also withering in his assessment of the capitalist system, which he considered was responsible for intolerable economic inequalities and which encouraged a consumer culture that exercised a tyranny all its own.

However, this prophet of freedom had managed to disappoint Western liberals by his refusal to give ground on such issues as contraception, divorce and same-sex marriage. He could never accept that human sexuality could diverge from Church norms. Likewise he resisted calls for married clergy and women priests, reforms that might seem commonsensical to others. He argued that the Church was not just an institution to be brought up to date like any other, but one that was bound by laws lain down by Christ himself.

## WIDESPREAD POPULARITY
It was gall to his more progressive critics that John Paul II was so unrestrainedly loved, not just among Catholics but beyond the Church. This was attributable not only to his immense charisma but also to his instinctive gifts as a communicator. He visited 129 different countries, taking his papacy to ordinary people around the world. Wherever he went, he kissed airport runways, cuddled babies, showed himself to vast crowds in his "popemobile" and said Mass to millions at a time. Conservative as his attitudes may have been, his belief that ordinary Catholics should have access to his papacy was entirely in the spirit of the Second Vatican Council.

## THE SAINT MAKER
John Paul II's enthusiasm for canonizing saints has been derided (it was said that he beatified more men and women than all his predecessors put together, but incomplete records make this hard to establish). This may speak of an old-fashioned view of Christian heroism, but at the same time it also suggests John Paul II had an utterly modern understanding of media culture. Not since the early Middle Ages had there been such an interest in icons – even if the new ones were singers, models and sports stars. In giving the peoples of the world new saints, the pope was giving them exemplars from their own cultures whose courage and commitment they could aspire to and emulate.

Most of all, his supporters looked up to John Paul II himself, beyond any doubt one of the most popular popes in modern history. This was the man who, as Ireland's young people chorused in their hundreds of thousands at the open-air Mass in Dublin's Phoenix Park in 1979, appeared to have "the whole world in his hands".

*Above John Paul II rides in his popemobile during a tour of the United States in 1995. Everywhere he went he drew enormous and ecstatic crowds.*

# REACHING OUT TO OTHER FAITHS

IN THE 20TH AND 21ST CENTURIES, THE CATHOLIC CHURCH HAS BEEN EXCHANGING VIEWS WITH OTHER CHRISTIAN COMMUNITIES — AS WELL AS WITH LEADERS OF THE DIFFERENT GREAT WORLD FAITHS.

With the exception of Poland, the Christians of Eastern Europe have historically looked to the Orthodox Church rather than to Rome. The Polish people have always defined themselves against their Russian neighbours (who were often also their oppressors). Their Catholicism was a matter not just of religious faith but of patriotic pride. Yet the Poles were Slavs as well, and Pope John Paul II, who always remembered his Polish origins, was mindful of that ethnic inheritance. The desire for reconciliation with the Eastern Church ran as deep in his heart as, so many years before, it had run in that of Pope John XXIII.

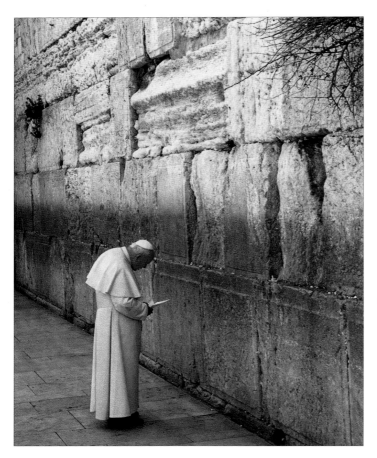

*Above An ecumenical service at Paris' Notre-Dame Cathedral is celebrated by leading Catholic prelates alongside an Orthodox metropolitan bishop (centre) and a Protestant minister (right).*

## A DIVISIVE DIPLOMAT?

In more than a quarter of a century as pope, John Paul II accomplished much for the Catholic Church, but his particular dream of reconciliation had to be deferred. It has been suggested by his critics that the pope himself had created part of the problem: his own instinctive authoritarianism rendered impossible the soft approach that would have been required. It was the same, some critics believe, with his approach to the Church of England, whose doctrine was not so far removed from that of Rome's. Although the decision of the Anglican Church to ordain women priests caused dissension between the two communities, liberal critics have claimed it was a matter in which a less stubborn pope would have found some type of accordance.

On the other hand, John Paul II's charisma propelled Christianity back on to the front page of many of the big newspapers, reminding jaded Westerners that religion could still hold relevance in a modern society. Elsewhere, adherents of the other world religions could find evidence

*Left In 2000, Pope John Paul II visited Jerusalem and the Western ("Wailing") Wall, where he begged forgiveness on behalf of the Catholic Church for centuries of anti-semitic persecution.*

in his energy and enthusiasm that the Christian West was not entirely sunk in cynicism and apathy.

Ultimately, his love of humanity – and the love that humanity felt for John Paul II – made him a more effective bridge-builder than anyone might have expected. His impetuous style certainly helped his cause. A more cautious man might never have dreamt of making his historic (and, at the time, controversial) visit to the Auschwitz concentration camp in 1979. The first-ever papal visit to Israel followed in 2000, where John Paul II's heartfelt apology for centuries of Christian persecution of Jews opened the way to a new era of discussion and co-operation.

## COMMON CAUSE

There are, of course, limits to how much progress can be made between different communities. The Catholic creed professes that it is the "one" true Church. John Paul II's successor, Pope Benedict XVI, maintains that, while other Christian Churches and non-Christian religions may offer aspects of the truth and may thereby be instruments of salvation, the

*Above In 2006, Pope Benedict XVI met the Orthodox Patriarch in Istanbul, Turkey. It was his first official visit to a Muslim country.*

whole truth is to be found only in Catholicism. Although working hard to find points of contact, he has left no doubt that he sees the world's other faiths as fundamentally misdirected, for all their undoubted honesty and zeal.

If anything unifies the world's religions, as far as Benedict XVI is concerned, it is their rejection of modern secularism and the culture it has fostered. The consumerist irreligion, he argues, says that everyone should live as he or she chooses, without reference to any higher laws. Believers of every faith have not just the right but also a duty to make a common cause against this "dictatorship of relativism".

## THE POPES AND THE IMAMS

When the Ayatollah Khomeini died in 1989, Pope John Paul II called for his achievements to be reflected upon "with great respect and deep thought". There have been more effusive eulogies, perhaps, but the pope's was still strikingly cordial in the circumstances. John Paul II had refused to lend his authority to other Christian leaders who earlier that year had expressed sympathy with the leader of Islam in Iran. The Ayatollah had issued a *fatwa* – a religious decree – calling for the killing of author Salman Rushdie for writing his novel, *The Satanic Verses*, which was said to be blasphemous. The years that followed would find John Paul II continuing his dialogue with Islam's leaders, and in 2000 he became the first pope to pray in a Muslim mosque.

Contact with the Muslim world has continued during the papacy of Benedict XVI, despite the offence caused by his quotation from an anti-Islamic text by a medieval writer in a talk at the University of Regensburg, Germany, in 2006. Relations soon recovered, and in 2008 Muslim scholars were invited to a joint seminar with Catholic thinkers held in Rome.

*Right Pope Benedict XVI clasps hands with the head of Turkey's Religious Affairs Directorate after talks about Catholic–Islamic relations and terrorism.*

# NEW CHALLENGES

THE NUMBER OF CATHOLICS DECREASED IN MANY WESTERN
SOCIETIES DURING THE LAST CENTURY. THE INFLUENCES OF CAPITALISM
AND CONSUMERISM ARE PERHAPS PARTLY TO BLAME.

In recent years, the Church has seen its support ebb away in the advanced industrialized societies. In the mostly Protestant and Anglo-Saxon countries of Europe, Catholicism was long regarded as a peasant creed that was associated with "backward" regions: southern Italy, Spain, remote parts of France – and pre-eminently with Ireland. Yet Christ had always loved the poor, and the poor had always reciprocated, offering their sons and daughters into his service.

## CHANGING SOCIETIES

When a previously poor region begins to thrive, no one mourns the passing of mass poverty – however, economic development often brings

*Below Sardinians process through their village as they have done for so many centuries, but can Catholicism offer more than history and local colour?*

problems as well as benefits. In some places, historical tendencies can be traced. For example, that most Spaniards say they no longer bother to go to Church may reflect resentments dating back to the Franco era and beyond. Italy is another country in which the Church's most visible adherents recall an authoritarian past. Although comparatively few Italians have rejected the Church outright, it is for many now no more than a part of their cultural rituals – baptisms, marriages and funerals – and is otherwise ignored.

Increased wealth has resulted in population shifts, which have created their own impact. The old over-crowded communities of the cities have been dispersed to suburbs, where more secular attitudes have prevailed. One example can be seen in St Anthony's parish in Jersey City in New Jersey, USA. In the 1950s, a

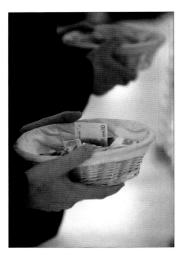

*Above Falling levels of attendance and reduced collections have sent parochial incomes tumbling, a formidable challenge for the Church in the new century.*

typical Sunday Mass was attended by around 10,000 Christians; today, less than 300 people turn out.

The problem has partly been that there is so much more to do at weekends for families with cars and money to spend – but who have precious little quality time together. Although Christ was clear in his insistence that material wealth was not spiritually enriching, Catholics are not immune to the attractions of material consumerism. Nor are they immune to the consumeristic attitude that encourages people toward the various spiritual options available these days, from yoga and meditation to New Age practices.

## A DECLINE IN CLERGY

Something is clearly wrong with the Church when Ireland is running out of priests. In 2007, 166 priests died, while only 9 new ordinations were made. The priests constitute an ageing population: in the next generation, their numbers are bound to fall further. This is because as societies prosper, life expectancy increases and families feel more secure. With this security, families tend to have fewer children. This has happened in many industrialized countries, regardless of religious culture. It has certainly occurred in Ireland, which has enjoyed great economic success in recent decades. The youths who would once have gone into the Church no longer exist in such abundance, and they have other life choices and distractions. Ireland faces the kind of administrative adjustments with which Catholics in the United States and Great Britain have become familiar, with small groups of priests and lay helpers taking charge of sprawling parish clusters.

## NEW OPPORTUNITIES

The difficulties can hardly be denied, yet given the age of the institution, talk of doom and gloom is misplaced. In 2,000 years, Catholicism has come through many more challenging times. Despite all its claims for apostolic continuity, the Church has shown the capacity to reinvent itself again and again down the centuries.

*Above Once Vancouver's Holy Rosary Cathedral dominated the skyline. Today the Christian message risks being lost amid the pressures and distractions of modern life.*

*Below A businessman finds comfort confiding with his priest in the confessional, something that many middle-class Westerners have decided is not for them.*

That it will have to do so again has become clear, with its great structures perhaps learning to accommodate a more administratively flexible, "small is beautiful" community-based system. There could be scope for lay Catholics to play a far greater role in their local communities, which has been an official goal ever since the time of the Second Vatican Council.

### THE SINS OF THE FATHERS

The Church has admitted it has not always been worthy of its members' trust. Catholics have been rocked in recent years by a series of allegations of sexual impropriety on the part of members of its clergy. From the mid-1980s onward, a series of scandals in the United States, Ireland, Australia and other countries focused attention on alleged sexual abuse of young people by diocesan priests and members of the religious orders. In some cases the Church hierarchy was accused of attempting to cover up accusations, and even of moving sexual abusers away from one scandal and into a position where he or she could offend again.

In the United States, the Church made financial settlements of $2 billion to victims of sex abuse in the past 60 years. In the largest settlement, in 2007, the Archdiocese of Los Angeles paid $660 million (£324 million) to settle 508 cases of alleged sexual abuse.

Pope Benedict XVI has departed from this shameful stance. He has gone out of his way to meet members of victims' groups and to express his shame and sorrow on behalf of the Catholic Church.

# FACING COMPETITION

IN TODAY'S SOUTH AMERICA AND AFRICA, THE CATHOLIC CHURCH IS BEING CHALLENGED BY OTHER CREEDS THAT MAY APPEAR MORE ENERGETIC, AND MORE IMMEDIATELY RELEVANT TO PEOPLE'S LIVES.

***Above*** *A worshipper is energetically welcomed to a Pentecostal congregation in Rio de Janeiro. Latin Americans have been flocking to the new chapels in their thousands.*

As recently as a generation or so ago, South America was one of the bastions of world Catholicism, a region consecrated to Christ and the Virgin Mary, utterly loyal to the pope. The idea of a Protestant Brazil or Chile was practically unthinkable. Catholicism was in the culture, in the air the people breathed.

Nevertheless, Pentecostalism has spread like wildfire throughout the region in recent decades. This new form of Christianity first appeared in the United States at the beginning of the 20th century. Rooted in a range of different Protestant churches, Pentecostalism is a faith of enthusiastic evangelism that demands that the believer be born again in the Holy Spirit – just like the disciples at the first Pentecost.

## AN ALTERNATIVE CREED

The explanations given for such a quick expansion in South America vary. Pentecostalism is strongly emotional in its emphasis, which offers the individual Christian a spiritual (or, perhaps, merely psychological) high. Catholicism has always tended to distrust this type of extravagant emotionalism. Yet the importance of the ecstatic sense of self-worth it brings to the Pentecostalist convert can hardly be exaggerated. However, in some ways, it is the logical outcome of the attentions given by dedicated missionaries, hard at work for decades among poor people who may well feel that their traditional religious leaders have often taken them for granted.

Some South Americans have pointed to the remoteness of a conservative clergy, reluctant to involve itself with the problems of the masses. Others have seen the failure of ideologically driven Liberation Theology to see the poor as real people. Either way, the Protestant missionaries have made huge strides.

By 2005, an estimated 13 per cent of Latin America's huge population had embraced Pentecostalism; that is, 75 million out of 560 million people. This overall figure conceals the fact that there are areas in which Catholicism has been in headlong retreat. In some of Rio de Janeiro's poorest districts, Protestant chapels now outnumber Catholic churches in a ratio of seven to one.

## A PLACE OF SAFETY

In some areas, politics have certainly played a part. For example, through the many long years of vicious state repression in Guatemala, courageous priests and nuns made a stand against the military, which also made them targets. The conspicuously apolitical stand of (overwhelmingly American) Pentecostalist missionaries made their church a refuge from the violence and turmoil of the time. Middle-class Guatemalans, who were instinctively uneasy at the thought of any association with the leftists, have turned to Pentecostalism in large numbers. Today about 20 per cent of the population now considers itself Protestant; that figure rises to almost one-third among the urban middle class.

## COMPETITION FROM ISLAM

In West and Central Africa, the main competition is not from Pentecostalism but from Islam. This is not surprising since Islam's history in the region is at least as long as Catholicism's. Muhammad's faith was first brought south across the Sahara by

***Left*** *Pentecostalism is not just for the poor. These bourgeois Brazilians have crossed the ocean to be baptized in the sacred waters of the River Jordan.*

desert traders; nomadic tribes there-after carried it farther to the south. A kind of frontier has long existed across this part of the continent, with – broadly speaking – Islam to the north, Christianity to the south. In reality, this border has been highly porous, with any number of communities to be found on the "wrong" side, and with close contacts, even family relations, between the two.

## MODERN RADICALS

Peaceful co-existence has until recent history been maintained, but the emergence of Islamic fundamentalism has altered the dynamics. With its agenda being as much political as religious, radical Islamic groups have engaged in direct competition for converts with Catholicism, and their evangelization has to some extent paid off.

Conflict has flared as well, most famously in the Sudan, whose Islamic Khartoum government has for years been at war with the Catholic communities of the south. Elsewhere, too, there has been trouble, most notably perhaps, in parts of Nigeria, where attempts have been made to introduce the full rigour of Sharia law.

## RESPONDING TO CHANGE

Ultimately, the only way for the Catholic Church to respond to such changes will be to change itself, while staying true to the central principals of so many centuries. Rome may remain its centre, but a Eurocentric Church will hardly be able to provide Catholicism with the worldwide guidance and support it needs. The ethnic mixture of the hierarchy has already been transformed by the addition of new African, Asian and

South American faces, and more changes may occur in the years to come. It would seem strange indeed if the first great world religion were unable to meet the challenge of globalization. Despite its past difficulties, the Catholic Church appears well placed to face the future.

*Right Théodore-Adrien Sarr celebrates Mass after being made a cardinal by Pope Benedict XVI in 2007. Senegalese Muslims also joined in acclaiming the new Cardinal.*

*Right Followers of Islam gather to pray outside the main mosque in Asmara, Eritrea. Islam is on the rise across much of North and Central Africa.*

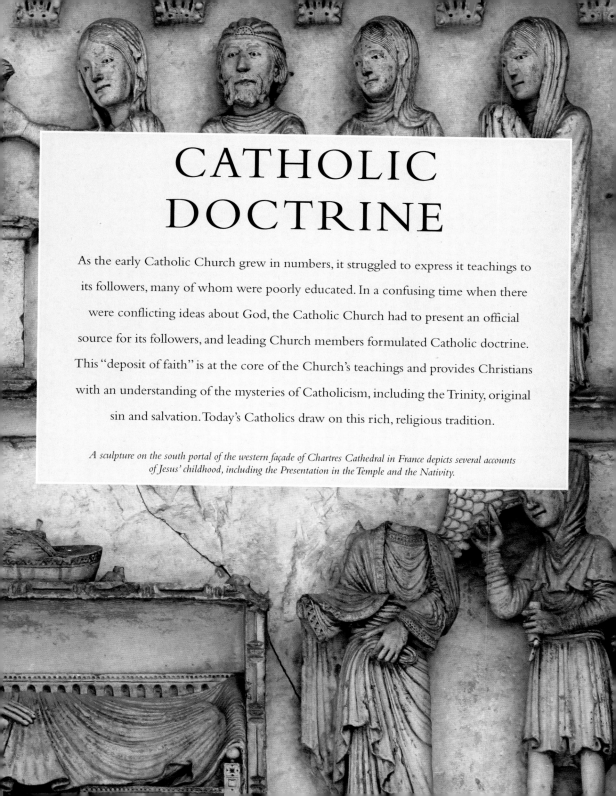

# CATHOLIC DOCTRINE

As the early Catholic Church grew in numbers, it struggled to express it teachings to its followers, many of whom were poorly educated. In a confusing time when there were conflicting ideas about God, the Catholic Church had to present an official source for its followers, and leading Church members formulated Catholic doctrine. This "deposit of faith" is at the core of the Church's teachings and provides Christians with an understanding of the mysteries of Catholicism, including the Trinity, original sin and salvation. Today's Catholics draw on this rich, religious tradition.

*A sculpture on the south portal of the western façade of Chartres Cathedral in France depicts several accounts of Jesus' childhood, including the Presentation in the Temple and the Nativity.*

# THE MYSTERY OF FAITH

As the nascent Catholic Church began to develop its doctrines in the first centuries after Christ's death, it was faced with many challenges, including persecution, the difficulty of communicating abstruse concepts, such as the Trinity, to an uneducated and superstitious populace, and the constant threat of heretical beliefs and teachings. Such challenges forced early ecclesiastics and Catholic theologians to be vigilant and proactive as they formulated and disseminated Church doctrine.

The early Church councils acted as both the universities and the senates of the Church to standardize beliefs and promulgate them as law. The early Church was blessed with a number of brilliant early thinkers such as Sts Augustine, Athanasius, Jerome and Thomas Aquinas, whose devotion to understanding Christ and his teachings, as well as to the development of the Church, was absolute. As Catholic beliefs developed into officially disseminated teachings and practice, they became part of the "deposit of faith", the vast bulwark of accepted Church tradition that had its genesis in the earliest oral apostolic teachings, the canons of the New Testament and in the decisions and decrees of the Church councils.

At the core of Church doctrine are the Trinitarian nature of God, the Incarnation of Christ as God-Man, his real presence in the Eucharist, his suffering and death, and his resurrection for our salvation. All other Catholic beliefs and teaching are nourished from the deep wellspring of these particular articles of faith.

*Above The Eastern European influence on the early Roman Church is evident in this Byzantine-style, mid-8th-century Russian illustration of the First Ecumenical Council of Nicaea, which convened in Turkey in AD 325.*

*Left The three persons of the Trinity – Christ, the Holy Spirit (in the form of a dove) and God – are the focus of this 17th-century painting by Pierre Mignard. Christ's bare chest alludes to his crucifixion, when he was stripped of his garments.*

# GOD IN THREE PERSONS

CATHOLICS BELIEVE IN THE TRINITY OF GOD, OFTEN TRADITIONALLY PORTRAYED WITH THE FATHER AS A REGAL OLDER MAN, THE SON AS A YOUNG, SORROWFUL MAN AND THE HOLY SPIRIT AS A DOVE OR FLAME.

Belief in the Trinity is an absolutely central tenet of the Roman Catholic faith, but it is also an item of doctrine that has a controversial past among Christians. It is a paradox that is difficult to understand rationally. The doctrine states that there is only one eternal, almighty God, who exists without beginning or end, and who is the creator of all that exists. However, there are three "persons" – the Father, the Son and the Holy Spirit – existing "one in being" as that God. The three are equal and eternal, each existing without beginning or end.

## THE SAME BUT DIFFERENT

As stated in the Nicene Creed, which deals specifically with the nature of Christ, the Son is said to be "eternally begotten" of the Father, but "not made", emphasizing that there was never a time when he did not exist and that he partakes of the substance of the Father even while he is another person. The Holy Spirit "proceeds" from the Father and the Son – this is an active verb that emphasizes a continuous being, a kind of eternally advancing horizon of existence. The Greek word for

*Above In this 13th-century French image, the "Creator of heaven and earth" takes the measure of his raw materials with a compass. This image may have influenced William Blake's 1794 Ancient of Days.*

proceed emphasizes "movement out of". The Greek word *perichoresis*, meaning "permeation without confusion", is also used by theologians to express how the persons of the Trinity interpenetrate each other, yet remain distinct.

### DIVINE BEINGS

The three persons of the Trinity are perceived by most Catholics as having particular, appropriate divine aspects. The Father is the Creator, the maker of all and the interlocutor with Adam and Eve. The Son's defining attribute is that he was made man. He demonstrated the infinite depth of divine love by becoming human, walking among us and acceding to an agonizing sacrifice of his simultaneously human and divine self as an

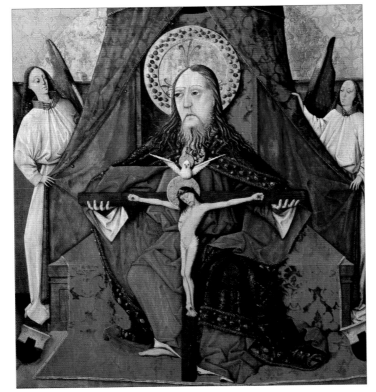

*Left The Catholic mystery of the Trinity is shown in this 15th-century European painting. They are intimately connected yet distinct, with God the Father holding his crucified Son, while the Holy Spirit as a dove rests on Christ's halo.*

offering to re-open the possibility of man's freedom from Adam and Eve's original sin.

The Holy Spirit, as implied by his name, is the only divine persona without a human form in traditional Catholic iconography. He is usually artistically represented as either a dove or a tongue of flame, the form in which, ten days after Christ's ascension to heaven, he descended to inspire the apostles as teachers of the Word of God (the day now known as Whitsunday, or more commonly in Catholic theology, Pentecost). Metaphorically, in his role as bringer of grace and an inspirer of wisdom, he is spoken of as a mighty wind or as the inspiration or breath of God. He is also known as the "Paraclete", or advocate, which refers to his role as a spiritual teacher or guide.

## A CONTROVERSIAL TIME

The doctrine of the Trinity was fiercely debated by the bishops and Church fathers in the early days of Christianity. The 4th-century controversy surrounding Arianism – a heresy that claimed the Son of God

*Above* The Holy Spirit is the only person of the Trinity who never speaks, but we can almost hear the whirr of his wings in this graceful French c. 1490 illumination by Jean Colombe.

*Above At Jesus' baptism, the heavens opened, the Holy Spirit descended and the Father spoke, "This is my beloved son…" Giovanni Guercino's 17th-century painting shows a powerful God the Father.*

was not truly God but was created by God – in particular, served as a spur to bishops to set and define the immanent divinity of the three persons of the one God as a crucial and defining Catholic doctrine.

Arianism argued that Christ was inferior to the Father in that "there was a then when he was not" – in other words, there was a time when Christ did not exist. Christ was described as the first of the Father's created beings, not "eternally begotten", but simply "begotten", thus denigrating his divine nature as a being without beginning or end.

The Council of Nicaea was convened in AD 325 by Constantine, Emperor of Rome, in large part to counteract Arianism. The Nicene Creed that was formulated at the council, then finalized at the Council of Constantinople in AD 381, is still the familiar creed recited in Roman Catholic churches today.

Even more contentious was the relationship of the Holy Spirit to the Father and the Son. The Nicene Creed of AD 325 merely stated "we believe in the Holy Spirit". In AD 381, the "filioque" ("and the son") clause was added, stating that the Holy Spirit "proceeds from the Father and the Son". It was disagreement about this "dual procession" doctrine that caused the Eastern Christian Church to split from the Roman Church in the Great Schism of 1054.

### THE TRINITY

The term "Trinity", from the Latin noun *trinitas*, meaning "three at once", does not occur in the Bible, but the gospels do contain references to the divinity of the Father, Son and Holy Spirit. For example, after Christ rose from the dead, he bid the apostles to "go forth and teach all nations, baptizing them in the name of the Father, and of the Son and of the Holy Spirit" (Matthew 28:20). The term Trinity in relation to the Godhead was first used by Tertullian, the 3rd-century son of a Roman centurion and an early convert to Christianity, who was a prolific writer and contributor to evolving Christian theology in the early centuries after Christ's death.

# CHRIST THE REDEEMER

IN CATHOLIC THEOLOGY, ORIGINAL SIN IS THE METAPHORICAL "STAIN"
ALL HUMAN BEINGS ARE BORN WITH — AND IT IS THE REASON WHY
CHRIST SACRIFICED HIMSELF TO REDEEM THE HUMAN RACE.

Original sin is inherited, like a genetic disease, from the first man – our ancestor Adam – and all humans have inherited it. The Catholic catechism says, "The whole human race is in Adam". This does not mean that original sin is a sinful action of Adam that we imitate or recreate. It is, rather, our tragic patrimony, meaning that we have been born deprived of the original grace that was God's initial endowment to our ancestral parents, Adam and Eve. The poet John Milton (although not a Catholic himself) expressed it well:

> *Of man's first disobedience,*
> *and the Fruit*
> *Of that Forbidden Tree,*
> *whose mortal taste*
> *Brought Death into the World,*
> *and all our woe…*

**Left** *Eve, having already eaten from the forbidden fruit, colludes with the serpent, who places the apple in her waiting hand as she draws Adam close. This detail is from a 16th-century German triptych.*

## FORBIDDEN FRUIT

The actual sin, described in Genesis, was eating the fruit of the Tree of Knowledge of Good and Evil, the only tree in paradise prohibited by God to Adam and Eve. Eve was tempted by Satan in the guise of a serpent, who told her she would be like a god and understand good and evil. Adam then took the fruit from Eve and ate as well.

As a result of Adam and Eve's wilfully disobedient act, Catholicism teaches that we are born fallen, with our souls deprived of sanctifying grace, not fully and freely open and receptive to God's love. The fall of the first man infused not just humanity but the entire world – the originally harmonious world made by God became discordant. Instead of every type of fruit tree, God prophesied that the earth would bring forth thorns and thistles. Instead of being blissfully unaware of their nakedness, Adam and Eve perceived it as shameful and hid. Original sin set man against himself and the earth – first intended to be our garden of delight – against man.

Catholics believe that death became part of life with original sin. As a direct response to Adam and Eve's disobedience, God pronounced, "In the sweat of thy face shalt thou eat bread till thou return to the earth out of which thou wast taken: for dust thou art, and into dust thou shalt return" (Genesis 3:19).

**Above** *Because of original sin, death gained power over us and took us from the garden of paradise. In Evelyn de Morgan's 1890* The Angel of Death, *death has wings.*

## BODY AND SOUL

Although the concept of original sin already existed, it was first defined as a doctrine in the 5th century AD by St Augustine of Hippo. Augustine had lived a dissolute life before his conversion from Manichaeism (a type of gnostic religion) to Catholicism, so he was particularly alert to man's sinful nature. The Second Council of Orange in AD 529 specified that while death of the body was the punishment for original sin, death of the soul was the sin itself.

Death of the soul is emphasized because original sin is responsible for destroying our first intimate union with God. Adam and Eve's action deprived them of the original grace that was their birthright, and this loss introduced the tendency toward corruption into the world, as though the previously perfect fabric of Creation was rent with a fatal flaw, weakening it so that it easily became tattered. Original sin is also responsible for allowing our

## CHRIST'S CRUCIAL SACRIFICE

At both the Council of Orange in AD 529 and the Council of Trent in 1546, the Church fathers defined the doctrine of justification. This emphasized that our redemption was not possible without Christ's mediation, or the merit that he obtained for us by his obedient death, to make restitution for our disobedience. Redemption is not possible by human good works and good behaviour alone. The Church fathers pronounced anathema (a kind of doctrinal condemnation) on anyone who believed humans could save themselves without Christ – specifically, Pelagius, an Irish monk whose heretical beliefs triggered the Council of Orange's pronouncements.

Pelagius believed we could save ourselves by our good works and he de-emphasized the role of God's Grace. The Catholic Church teaches that we need the grace that Christ first obtained for us by his sacrifice. Additionally, we also require the sanctifying grace that fills our soul in baptism, the educating aid of the Holy Spirit that comes to us through participation in the sacraments, and continuous obedience to God's commandments in order to avoid damnation and find eternal life with God.

*Above* Pelagius (AD 355–425) believed that original sin was not every man's inheritance, and that man could save himself without Christ's sacrifice.

inferior worldly and carnal desires, known as "concupiscence", to prevail over our reason.

### SEEKING REDEMPTION

The counterpoint to this tragic fall from grace is our ability to essentially re-enact our first parents' temptation and choice – but this time, individually, because we still retain the free will with which they were endowed by God, to choose to turn toward God, or *conversio ad deum*. The possible redemption of each individual is a direct result of the offering Christ made of himself to the Father: as man out of his own free will chose to turn away and reject God's love (*adversio ad deum*) and instead act to satisfy his own egotistical desire, Christ out of his own free will did not resist actual torture on the Cross to pay the price to redeem man. The Latin word *redemptio* is related to Hebrew and Greek words meaning "a ransom price".

*Right* Our first defence against original sin comes through the grace of baptism. In this late 16th-century painted stone, St Augustine, once a libertine, and his illegitimate son Adeodatus are baptized by St Ambrose.

# THE EUCHARIST

LIKE THE HOLY TRINITY, THE DOCTRINE OF THE EUCHARIST, WHICH
CELEBRATES JESUS' LAST SUPPER WITH HIS APOSTLES, IS ONE OF THE
MOST IMPORTANT, CENTRAL BELIEFS OF THE CATHOLIC CHURCH.

The Roman Catholic catechism calls the Eucharist "the source and summit of the Christian life". Most Catholics would probably agree that the Eucharist is a particularly special doctrine. It is one that each practising Catholic is introduced to at an early age, and it continues through the years, becoming a customary thread of the faith drawing together generations of families.

Almost any person brought up in the Catholic faith will have specific memories of their first Holy Communion, because it is a joyful day that has delightful worldly celebrations

*Above The most sacred moment of the Mass is the consecration, when the bread and wine are transubstantiated into the body and blood of Christ, as seen in this 15th/16th-century image by Giovanni di Giuliano Boccardi.*

surrounding it. It is also the first time that a child is called to participate in one of the central mysteries of the faith, the Eucharist. This is a particularly special occasion, when the child is first asked to try to extend his or her perception to encompass a numinous dimension of the infinite by participation in a very specific individual act.

THE LORD'S SUPPER
The word "Eucharist" comes from the Greek *eucharistein*, or "grateful, thankful". It is the name given to the communion that has been repeated through the centuries at every Catholic Mass. Its origin lies in the Last Supper, the story of which is engraved on the consciousness of every Catholic. The Last Supper is described in almost the same words in Matthew 26:26–28, Mark 14:22–24 and Luke 22:17–20. Celebrating the paschal meal with his apostles, and well aware that he was about to be betrayed and put to death, Christ took bread, broke it and offered it to his apostles, saying, "Take

## THE LAST SUPPER

Leonardo da Vinci's renowned mural painting, *The Last Supper* (1495–8), depicts the paschal supper at which Christ broke bread and offered wine. The painting dramatizes the moment described in the gospels when Jesus, "troubled in spirit", announces "Amen, amen, I say to you, one of you shall betray me." The disciples therefore looked upon one another, doubting of whom he spoke.

Despite the press of the apostles around the table and the apparent furor caused by Christ's words, there are two figures who remain alone with their thoughts. Judas' hand hovers slightly above a dish, illustrating Christ's words, "he that dippeth his hands with me in the dish, he shall betray me". All the other apostles lean toward Christ or toward each other, exchanging glances. Judas leans away from Christ without touching anyone else, and while the others look at Christ beseechingly, Judas simply stares. Christ's arms extend down with his palms turned upwards in a gesture that is one of submission, yet he also seems to be gathering power from the heavens toward which his hands open. Although Christ's gaze is directed away from Judas, the entire side of his face is angled toward him, almost as if he were offering a cheek to be kissed – and, of course, it is with a kiss on Jesus' cheek that Judas will betray him to his captors on the following day.

*Above Da Vinci's late 15th-century painting* The Last Supper *not ony recalls the last meal between Jesus and his apostles but is also full of symbolism, referring to the momentous event that will occur when Judas betrays Christ.*

ye, and eat. This is my body." Taking the chalice, he gave thanks, and gave it to them, saying, "Drink ye all of this. For this is my blood of the new testament, which shall be shed for many unto remission of sins." During this supper, Christ spoke the simple words, "Do this in memory of me." This quiet command is the genesis of the Eucharistic sacrifice around which a great world religion has been formed. In allusion to the Last Supper, communion is sometimes called the Lord's Supper.

Christ prefigured these actions before his death when he fed a crowd of people that had come to hear him preach and who were hungry, yet with little food. In the hands of Jesus, on that day the five loaves and two fishes available miraculously became enough to feed the multitude. When preaching in the synagogue at Capharnaum soon after performing this miracle, Jesus said, "I am the bread of Life…. He that eateth my flesh and drinketh my blood have everlasting life: and I will raise him up in the last day."

## BREAD AND WINE

Through the centuries, the central act of Mass has been the priest's consecration of wheaten bread and grape wine into Christ. The Council of Trent in 1546 defined the Eucharist as "the Body and Blood, together with the Soul and Divinity of our Lord Jesus Christ, and therefore the whole Christ, is truly, really and substantially contained in the sacrament of the Holy Eucharist."

Various theologians over the years have attempted to define the Holy Eucharist as a symbol of the body and blood of Christ (16th-century Zwinglians), or as a dynamic trans-

*Right A literal interpretation of the doctrine that the host is transubstantiated into the entirety of the body and blood of Christ can be seen in this 14th-century painting by Ugolino di Prete Ilario.*

ferral of the efficacy of Christ's body and blood to the souls of the elect at the moment of reception of the host (Calvinists), but the Church declared all such limitations on the definition of the Eucharist to be heresies.

## THE CONSECRATION

Catholic doctrine is specific regarding the holiest moment of Mass. This is known as the consecration, when the priest repeats the words of Christ at the Last Supper. "This is my body" is spoken when the priest raises the

*Left The first Holy Communion is an inspiring milestone in the lives of Catholic children. In this late 19th-century painting by Carl Frithjof Smith, a young girl proudly wears her new crucifix.*

bread and "This is my blood" is uttered with the wine, and at each and every Mass a miracle occurs and the bread and wine are changed, or "transubstantiated", into the body and blood of Christ. How the change occurs when the priest speaks the words is a mystery known only to God. What is changed is the entire substance – the being – of the bread and wine into the entirety of the substance, or being, of Christ, with only the "species", or appearance, of bread and wine remaining.

The Church holds that, in essence and in actuality (not symbolically), Christ is present in the Eucharist. In order to skirt an association with cannibalism, the Church does not usually emphasize (but it would not deny) that Christ is physically present (like the person sitting next to you in Church, for example), but that he is substantially present, which is known as the "Real Presence".

# THE CLASSIC CREEDS

THERE ARE THREE CLASSIC CREEDS OF THE CATHOLIC CHURCH: THE
APOSTLES', NICENE AND ATHANASIAN CREEDS. EACH WAS DEVELOPED
TO SHIELD THE CHURCH FROM A SPECIFIC HERESY.

Many modern Catholics can usually repeat by rote the Nicene Creed, imprinted on their memory since childhood. However, they may not realize that in the early centuries after Christ's death, when Christianity was still seeking to define and establish itself in the face of uncertainty, danger and opposition, creeds were developed and perceived as true badges of faith. They were developed to fight heresies, to establish, teach and promote right doctrine, and, in the words of the Catholic catechism, to be "the spiritual seal, our heart's meditation."

THE FIRST SYSTEM OF BELIEF
The Apostles' Creed is the oldest. It originated in the first century after Christ's death and sets forth the teachings of the Church under the leadership of St Peter, the first pope.

During the Middle Ages it was believed that the first 12 apostles had composed the Creed on Pentecost, the day that the Holy Spirit descended to inspire them; however, this is probably a legend.

About two-thirds of the Apostles' Creed sets forth in straightforward language beliefs about the identity of Jesus Christ. This is because, during the first five centuries of the Church's existence, when the Apostles' Creed was formulated, Gnosticism was an influential heresy. Followers of this faith believed that the material world was completely corrupt (beyond the "tendency to sin" of the doctrine of original sin) and, therefore, although they were willing to believe that Jesus was God, the Gnostics denied that he had ever been a true man, a flesh and blood corporeal man who had died, as well as being divine.

*Above* St Athanasius, shown in this 18th-century Greek icon, was an Egyptian theologian known as the Father of Orthodoxy. His fight against Arianism was influential in the development of the doctrine of the Trinity.

*Below* The ravaged body of Christ, showing he was flesh and mortal, stands out in a contemporary landscape, an attempt by a 16th-century French artist to help refute the Gnostic doctrine that Christ had never been truly mortal.

By denying Jesus' humanity, the followers of Gnosticism were also denying that he died for us, which was a blatant contradiction of a bedrock Catholic doctrine. The Apostles' Creed refutes this Gnostic heresy by dwelling on the corporeal history of Christ on earth, stating that he "suffered, died and was buried". This creed may have been used as a profession of faith for early Christians about to be baptized, and even today the Apostle's Creed is part of the baptismal rite.

## ONE IN BEING
The second of the classic creeds, the Nicene Creed, which is also known as the Niceno-Constantinopolitan Creed, clarified Jesus' standing. It was developed in the 4th century and endures today in both the Roman and Eastern Catholic Churches. During the 4th century, Arianism – essentially the belief that Jesus, while divine, was an inferior divinity to the Father – became such a widespread and contentious issue that it threatened the stability of the Roman Empire itself. In the Edict of Milan (AD 313), Constantine declared that Christians were free to practise their religion, so the disputes over Catholic doctrine, freed from the earlier need for secrecy, became even more acrimonious than before.

Constantine ordered a council of bishops to be convened in Nicaea (in present-day Turkey) to make a ruling on the heated issue. The Nicene Creed, which was developed at that conference, declared in its

*Above Simon Magus, shown in this 14th-century French manuscript, was a Gnostic teacher and magician known as the "first heretic". Legend says he fell to his death from the Roman Forum while trying to prove to St Peter that he could fly.*

most significant line that Jesus was "one in being with the father". The most significant Greek term used in this phrase was *homoousios*, or "consubstantial", meaning of the same substance, not *homoiousios*, which means "similar" (but not the same) substance.

In AD 381, the creed was revised to expand its definition of the Holy Spirit. The earlier AD 325 version had only noted "We believe in the Holy Spirit", somewhat short-changing the third person.

## THE STERNEST CREED
The newest of the three classic creeds, the Athanasian Creed, is a resolute profession of doctrines on the nature of the Trinity and of the Incarnation (particularly with regard to the divinity and humanity of Jesus). It also declares the absolute necessity of belief in these doctrines in order to achieve one's salvation.

The creed was written in a series of declarations that were clearly and inclusively formulated in an obvious attempt to stifle all the various heresies on the Trinity and the nature of Christ that plagued the Catholic Church, among them being Arianism, Modalism, Sabellianism, Apollinarianism and Eutychianism. To emphasize that this was a serious matter, the creed contains a series of clauses that outline two stark choices: belief, or the road to damnation. It concludes: "This is the Catholic faith, which except a man believe faithfully and firmly, he cannot be saved."

*Below The large hands of the Madonna protectively enfold the Christ child in this 15th/16th-century painting by Giovanni Bellini. He grasps his mother's thumb, even as he asserts his divinity by offering a blessing.*

### OF UNKNOWN ORIGIN
The Athanasian Creed is also known as the Symbol Quicunque for its first Latin words, "*Quicunque vult salvus esse…*" ("Whosoever wishes to be saved…"). Tradition has ascribed the Athanasian Creed to Athanasius, the 4th-century Bishop of Alexandria, but this has been proved untrue. Although many plausible theories have been put forward as to its origin, none have been conclusive. However, scholars tend to agree that it was written in France *c.* mid-5th century.

# THE CATECHISM

TO HELP THE FAITHFUL LEARN THE BELIEFS OF THE CATHOLIC CHURCH, ALL ITS GREAT THEOLOGICAL TEACHINGS HAVE BEEN SUMMARIZED IN WHAT IS POPULARLY KNOWN AS THE CATECHISM.

"Catechetics" comes from the Greek *katechesis*, meaning instruction by word of mouth. A "catechumen" is the person being instructed in religious doctrine. The New Testament portrays the 12-year-old Jesus as an exceptional catechumen:

*And it came to pass, that, after three days, they found him in the temple, sitting in the midst of the doctors, hearing them and asking them questions. And all that heard him were astonished at his wisdom and his answers. (Luke 2:46)*

## THE WORDS IN WRITING

A catechism is doctrinal instruction provided in written form. It is in a question and answer format because the Church considers it the best method for ensuring that the doctrine being taught is correct and uniform – which is important in a religion where shades of meaning are crucial and confusion can unwittingly lead to heresy.

In Catholicism's early history, written doctrinal instruction was generally sparse, a deficiency that contributed to the Church's

*Above A youthful Jesus turned the usual catechetical order inside out by teaching the rabbis. In this 15th/16th-century painting by Albrecht Dürer, Jesus amazed them with his preternatural wisdom.*

vulnerability to the Reformation. Fifteenth-century parish priests, who were often poorly educated in abstruse Church doctrines themselves, were usually unable to help their confused parishioners. Poor instruction and misunderstanding of the complexities of the doctrines, including the plenary indulgence, enabled corrupt practices, such as selling indulgences for money. Martin Luther was one of the reformers who pounced on these practices, and many left the Church to join the reformers as a result.

The first-ever Catholic catechism was published in Vienna in 1555 by Peter Canisius, a Dutch Jesuit. Canisius compiled a single volume

*Left Peter Canisius (1521–97), shown in this 17th-century Flemish painting, wrote three Latin and German catechisms and helped to found the University of Fribourg, Switzerland, still an influential school of Catholic theology.*

that contained 222 questions and 2,000 scriptural quotations. This catechism is still a favourite of theologians and historians centuries later; however, at the time it was first published, it was too sophisticated to be of much help to the ordinary priest and parishioner.

## EDUCATING THE CLERGY

The Church recognized the need for, in the words of the 16th-century Council of Trent, "...a formulary and method for teaching the rudiments of the faith, to be used by all legitimate pastors and teachers". This was to take the shape of a simpler catechism that would be helpful for ordinary priests as they cared for the souls of their flocks. The resulting Roman catechism was published in 1566 and translated into the vernacular languages used by all Catholic countries.

The Roman catechism was intended to educate the clergy, and parish priests were ordered by their bishops to memorize it and to pass on that rote knowledge to their parishioners. It was the work of a number of distinguished theologians and cardinals of the day, and the authority of the Roman catechism was considered unimpeachable.

### THE DISCIPLINE OF THE SECRET

In the early centuries of the Church, during and just after the Roman persecutions, admission to the mysterious doctrines and rites of the new religion called Christianity was treated with great reserve. Scriptural support for a gradual revelation of the mysteries was provided by Matthew 7:6: "Give not that which is holy to dogs; neither cast ye your pearls before swine, lest they trample them under their feet, and turning upon you, they tear you."

The gradual revelation of the doctrines and rituals of the Church was known as the Discipline of the Secret. In particular, early Christians considered that the teachings of the Trinity and the Eucharist should be revealed to postulants only after careful preparation, because the doctrines imparted to the poorly prepared could easily be misconstrued as tritheism (the Trinity) or cannibalism (the Eucharist). As Christianity became more established, the practice of the Discipline of the Secret began to diminish and it was for the most part finished by the 5th century AD.

## MODERN VERSIONS

New catechisms continue to be developed. The catechism familiar to Americans is the Baltimore Catechism. In 1829, American bishops asked for a catechism adapted to the needs of the diverse American Catholic audience. *A Catechism of Christian Doctrine, Prepared and Enjoined by Order of the Third Council of Baltimore*, was issued in 1855 and became the standard United States catechism. A modernized edition of the Baltimore Catechism is still available today.

Another new catechism, entitled *Compendium of the Catechism of the Catholic Church,* was started on the 20th anniversary of the Second Vatican Council, brought to completion by Pope John Paul II and published by Pope Benedict in 2005.

*Below Founded in 1253 by the Chaplain of Louis V, the Sorbonne was an institution of education, famed for its influential, but conservative, school of theology.*

*Below A nun from the Missionaries of Charity, the order founded by Mother Teresa, is engaged in the traditional catechetical method of oral instruction.*

# IN ACCORDANCE WITH THE SCRIPTURES

CATHOLICISM VIEWS THE SCRIPTURES AS THE WORD OF GOD, PASSED ON BY WRITERS INSPIRED BY THE HOLY SPIRIT. THEY ARE CONSIDERED DIVINE REVELATION IN WRITTEN FORM.

The Scriptures that form the sacred canon are the biblical books accepted by the Church as genuine. Catholicism sees the Old Testament, which existed years before the birth of Christ, as part of a divine plan, calling the Old Testament an "active and steady preparation" for the revelations of Christ in the New and credited with tilling the ground for the coming of the Messiah. According to the Catholic catechism, this is a covenant that is "strikingly fulfilled" in the New Testament. It says the Old Testament books:

> ...give expression to a lively sense of God, contain a store of sublime teachings about God, sound wisdom about human life, and a wonderful treasury of prayers, and in them the mystery of our salvation is present in a hidden way.

"Typology" is the term that describes seeing the revelations of the New Testament prefigured in the books and stories of the Old.

## THE DEPOSIT OF FAITH

Unlike Protestant Christianity, the Catholic Church does not view Scripture as the sole source of divine revelation. This was a major issue during the Reformation, with the Protestant reformers claiming that all belief required specific evidence or *sola scriptura* ("scriptural proof"). The Catholic Church, in contrast, argued that scripture should be read from the perspective of a sacred tradition, and that it should include the non-scriptural compendium of teachings and traditional beliefs – referred to by the Church as the "deposit of faith". These teachings and beliefs were revealed by Jesus

**Above** *Moses keeps a protective arm around the second tablets of law written by the hand of God in this 17th-century painting by Laurent de la Hyre. Moses had smashed the first tablets when he saw his people worshipping a golden calf.*

to the apostles and passed down through the apostles and early Church fathers to become Catholic customary belief and practice through the centuries.

At the same time, the Church does not encourage individualistic interpretations of Scripture, especially when they are not supported by valid study and scholarship. Instead, the ultimate authority for scriptural interpretation is the magisterium, or the teaching authority of the Church comprised of the pope and the bishops of the Church. The magisterium's scriptural interpretations, according to Church doctrine, are infallible because they are inspired by the Holy Spirit. That said, the Catholic Church does encourage serious biblical study, so that readers will not react to the Bible only according to their own subjective emotional responses.

**Left** *Pope Benedict XVI provided an extensive commentary on modern methods of Biblical exegesis in his 1988 Erasmus lecture, "Biblical Interpretation in Crisis".*

## THE BACKGROUND

In "The Interpretation of the Bible in the Church", a 1993 document written by Cardinal Joseph Ratzinger (who became Pope Benedict XVI in 2005), the cardinal freely asserted that the Bible would be more fully appreciated if its readers had a working knowledge of the society, history, languages and geography that influenced its writers. Of this "historical-critical" approach, Cardinal Ratzinger pointed out that the "eternal word" of God, the Bible, was brought into being during specific historical periods, and that readers of the Bible must necessarily be grounded in the cultural and social details of those eras for proper and accurate comprehension of the text.

However, an overemphasis on these methods could obscure what the Church refers to as the "spiritual sense", a dimension of the Scriptures that extends far beyond the reality of other human texts. Benedict warned that modern historical-grammatical methods of interpretation can lead to the distancing of God's original words if too much emphasis is put on the human dimension of the words.

Benedict went on to assert that while approaching biblical exegesis (or interpretation) with the proper respect for the texts, as God's Word requires, all the possible methods of interpretation – historical, philological, sociological – should also be given their due. It is essential for Catholics to keep in mind that the principal aim of their studies should be the deepening of their faith.

### DIFFERENT TESTAMENTS

The Protestant and Catholic Bibles differ in the number of canonical books contained in their respective Old Testaments. Catholic Bibles have 46 books, Protestant Bibles, 39. The reasons for the discrepancy go back to ancient political and religious history. Early Christians accepted as divinely inspired the *Septuagint* (Greek for 70, referring to the 70 translators from Hebrew into Greek) version of the Jewish Old Testament. When the *Septuagint* was translated from Hebrew into Greek, it contained seven newer Greek books that had never been in the Hebrew language, but they were still considered part of the divinely inspired canon by Jews at the time of Jesus.

In AD 100, Jews purged their canon of these non-Hebrew books, known as the Deuterocanonical (for second canon, because they were newer) books. Christians chose to keep the seven, because at the time of Christ, they had been considered inspired texts. However, in 1517 during the Reformation, Martin Luther advocated the old Hebrew canon, partly because he objected to references to Purgatory in some of the Deuterocanonical Books. Even today, many Protestant Bibles include the seven disputed books only at the back of the volume and refer to them as the Apocrypha (hidden) books. The Seven Books of the Apocrypha are Baruch, Maccabees I and II, Tobit, Judith, Ecclesiasticus (or Sirach) and Wisdom.

*Below The English translation of the New Testament by William Tyndale (1494–1536) was the first based on Hebrew and Greek texts.*

*Above Biblical exegesis – the critical explanation of the text – takes many forms. This medieval French Bible Moralisée from c.1230 features brief biblical passages interspersed with moral or allegorical lessons.*

# THE EVANGELISTS

THE "FOUR EVANGELISTS" – MARK, MATTHEW, LUKE AND JOHN – ARE
CREDITED IN THE TRADITION OF THE CATHOLIC CHURCH AS THE
AUTHORS OF THE GOSPELS IN THE NEW TESTAMENT.

"Evangelist" is from the Greek for "one who proclaims good news", so the title when referring to the gospel writers emphasizes they are spreading the word of Jesus' life to inspire others to believe in Jesus as God. The earliest Gospel, Mark, was written about 40 years after Jesus' Resurrection. In that intervening time, accounts of Jesus were passed on orally, and all the Evangelists used this oral tradition for the content of their gospels. The four gospels were composed from about AD 65 to 100.

## AUTHOR UNKNOWN

Secular biblical scholars generally agree that the actual authorship of the gospels is anonymous; the titles "according to…" (not "by") Matthew, Mark, Luke or John, were added in the late 2nd century. Secular scholars also believe that the gospels were written according to the oral traditions of, rather than written by, the particular Evangelists. Yet the Church, while acknowledging the likely accuracy of the historians' position, has essentially declared that scholarly

*Above A portrayal of the four Evangelists eschews symbology and shows the four as reverent scholars, each cradling his precious gospel (Greek school, 18th century).*

debate over the specific human authorship of the gospels is beside the point. In *Dei Verbum* (or "Word of God"), a "dogmatic constitution on divine revelation" issued by Pope Paul VI in 1965, the Church stated that as whoever "wrote" the gospels was inspired by the Holy Spirit, the real author of the gospels is God – and as such, the Church accepts them in their entirety as sacred and canonical. In other words, the authors, no matter who, were divinely inspired.

## THE ORATORS

Tradition describes the Evangelists as four distinct people: Mark was a missionary with Paul, and Peter's follower. Matthew, one of the apostles, was a tax collector from Galilee. Luke, another missionary with Paul, was a Greek doctor, and is also believed to be the first Christian

*Left Tradition says that St Luke painted some of the earliest icons of the Virgin Mary. This has become a popular subject in art, as in this 16th-century painting by Maerten van Heemskerck.*

## FOUR CREATURES BOUND TOGETHER IN SPIRIT

For centuries, the four Evangelists have been magnificently illustrated in Christian iconography and art as the "four living creatures" that flank God's throne in Revelation and Ezekiel. Described as six-winged and "full of eyes", the living creatures are fierce testaments to God's majesty and power. Traditionally, the first living creature, a lion, symbolizes Mark; the second, an ox, Luke; the third, a man, Matthew; and the fourth, an eagle, John. Each creature encompasses certain virtues: Mark's lion is royal and courageous; Luke's ox represents endurance and sacrifice; Matthew's man suggests the primacy of human intellect; and John's eagle, spirit and aspiration.

*The Book of Kells*, the superb 9th-century illuminated manuscript produced by Irish monks on the island of Iona, devotes a full page to the four living creatures. They frequently guard the portals of medieval cathedrals and glow in the light of ancient stained-glass windows. The symbols of the Evangelists are most often seen together, reflecting the beautiful words of St Irenaeus of Lyons (AD 120–202), "He who was manifested to men, has given us the gospel under four aspects, but bound together by one Spirit."

*Right The symbols of each of the four Evangelists are shown in this introductory page to the Gospel of St Matthew, from* The Book of Kells.

painter (he is often portrayed holding a brush and is said to have painted the Black Madonna of Czestochowa, now the centrepiece of a Polish shrine). John was the beloved youngest apostle of Jesus.

### THE "SYNOPTIC GOSPELS"

The first three gospels, Mark, Matthew and Luke, which are similar in content, are known as the "Synoptic Gospels", meaning they "see with the same eyes". Scholars believe the Synoptics have a common, lost source document, which is referred to as "Q" (from the German *Quelle*, or "source"). The Gospel of John, which is notably different, is known as the "maverick" gospel.

Each gospel was developed with unique characteristics. Mark is referred to as the "action" gospel,

because it contains the most miracles and has a quick narrative pace – in fact, the word "immediately" appears 39 times. Luke contains more parables, and, as befitting a doctor, has a somewhat scientific tone. Its opening words state that it is intended as an orderly account for attaining knowledge. Matthew opens with a genealogy of Jesus, with frequent references to the Old Testament, and it emphasizes that Jesus is the prophesied Messiah. His work appears to have been written for a Jewish audience.

John opens with the famous passage, "In the beginning was the Word: and the Word was with God: and the Word was God." John is the most spiritual of the four gospels and the only one to state an evangelical purpose, "that ye might believe that Jesus is the Christ, the son of God; and that believing ye might have life through his name". John is also the only Gospel not to describe Jesus offering bread and wine at the Last Supper (the acts that instituted the Eucharist). In its place is the account of Jesus washing the apostles' feet.

*Right Christ walking on water, as depicted in this 20th-century painting by Frederic Montenard, is described in the gospels of Matthew, Mark and John. The miracle is prefigured in the Old Testament when the River Jordan parts for Joshua. "Jesus" is Latin for the Hebrew name Joshua.*

# OUR LADY

MANY OF TODAY'S CATHOLICS GROW UP SURROUNDED BY IMAGES OF THE VIRGIN MARY, BUT IT WAS NOT UNTIL THE 5TH CENTURY AD THAT MARY'S UNIQUE STATUS AS GOD-BEARER WAS EVEN RECOGNIZED.

Mary's eminent position in the Catholic pantheon was slow to develop. St Paul does not mention Mary, mother of Jesus, in any of his epistles. The Bible does not mention Mary's ultimate fate after Christ's death on the Cross. The last mention of Mary is in Acts 1:14, when she was present with the apostles as they persevered in prayer after Jesus' Ascension and just before Pentecost. We do not know where, how or even if Mary actually died. The Scriptures are silent on all of these things.

## THE GOD-BEARER

Mary's status in the Church began to develop after she was declared *Theotokos* (Greek for "God-bearer") by the Council of Ephesus in AD 431. As was their wont, the early Church

*Below Mary spreads her cloak in a gesture of protection in this detail from a c.1422 painting by Jean Miralhet. The* Sub Tuum Presidium, *a hymn dating from the 3rd century, begins, "Beneath thy compassion, we take refuge, O Theotokos".*

fathers debated for a long time before endowing Mary with this title. Its ultimate conferral was yet another means for the Church fathers to promulgate the concept of Christ as God-man, indivisibly true man and true God. By officially proclaiming Mary "God-bearer", it meant that she did not give birth to just the "man" aspect of God, as believed by Nestorius, the 3rd-century Bishop of Constantinople. Calling Mary *Theotokos* was just one more way to affirm the indivisible divine–human nature of Christ.

## A PRAYER FOR MARY

It was only after the Council of Ephesus that liturgical feasts were held in Mary's honour, though the earliest known prayer to Mary, the *Sub Tuum Praesidium* ("Beneath Thy Compassion"), dates from *c.* AD 250. The prayer is a plea to Mary in her role as an intercessor for humanity with God. Pope John Paul II mentions this important mediatory role of Mary in *Redemptoris Mater*, his 1987 encyclical letter concerning Mary, noting that she intercedes "…not as an outsider, but in her position as mother". Mary, as both mortal woman and mother of the God-man, has a special attentiveness to the needs of mankind as well as a unique intimacy with her son. As a suffering mother, she has earned the right to be an adviser – even to God.

## CONCEIVED WITHOUT SIN

There are three Catholic doctrines regarding Mary. The Immaculate Conception claims that alone among human beings, Mary was conceived without the inherited stain of original sin. It states "…the most

*Above As he hung on the Cross, Christ placed Mary under the protection of the apostle John, shown in this painting by Rogier van der Weyden. Christ spoke words to each in turn, "Woman behold thy son…Behold thy mother."*

Blessed Virgin Mary, from the first moment of her conception, by a singular grace and privilege from Almighty God and in view of the merits of Jesus Christ, was kept free of every stain of original sin."

This dogma sets forth the utter singularity of Mary. No other human being received this privilege from God. Besides the logic that the woman who was to bear and raise God would be free of a fallen nature, this doctrine also endows Mary with a special role, if not of our Redeemer, as is Christ, then as the one who made redemption possible through her obedience.

## PERPETUAL VIRGINITY

Mary was a virgin at Christ's conception and remained so despite his gestation and birth and indeed for the rest of her life. Known as Perpetual Virginity, in the words of the Lateran Council (AD 649), Mary conceived "without any detriment to her virginity, which remained inviolate even after his birth". Mary's lasting virginity was accepted by most of the early Church fathers, although Tertullian disagreed with it.

The doctrine provided a prototype for the monastic movement as it gained strength in the Church, starting *c*. the 4th century with St Anthony. Mary's celibacy is also representative of the metaphor of being "wedded to Christ", or so devoted to Christ that this relationship subsumes all others. The Church is known as the Bride or Spouse of the Lamb, nuns are brides of Christ and the Church continues to insist on the celibacy of priests, so that their devotion to God remains completely unchallenged by earthly vows.

## THE ASSUMPTION

Celebrated by Catholics each year on 15 August, the Assumption is the doctrine that "…at the end of her

*Below The Eastern Catholic tradition of the Dormition (falling asleep) of Mary teaches that she died a natural death, surrounded by all of the apostles except Thomas, who was late. The scene is shown in this 14th-century Byzantine mosaic.*

earthly course, Mary was assumed into heavenly glory, body and soul". This is the 1950 definition given by Pope Pius XII, in a decree (*Munificentissimus Deus*) whose solemnity is apparent from the fact that it is the only ex-cathedra invocation by a pope since the doctrine of papal infallibility was established in 1870.

Pius XII's decree leaves vague the question of whether or not Mary actually died before she was raised by God into heaven. A variety of early non-scriptural accounts of the Assumption exist, some written by early saints, such as Gregory of Tours and John of Damascus.

Eastern Orthodox Catholics tend to favour more explicit stories concerning Mary's actual death, stating that she was surrounded by 11 of the apostles at the moment of her death. They refer to this death as Mary's Dormition, but believe along with Western Catholics that she was bodily assumed into heaven after her burial; the Dormition is also celebrated on 15 August. In any case, the Assumption is viewed by most Catholics as prefiguring the final redemption of all observant Catholics on the Last Day.

### MOTHERLY LOVE

Despite all the unusual doctrines that surround Mary, the Catholic fascination with this figure seems to be related to something intimate and simple: her motherhood. The familiar enveloping motherly relationship and the idea that Jesus had a special fondness for Mary were illustrated when he did favours for her (turning water into wine at the wedding at Cana). Some of his last words as a living man were spoken to her as he hung from the Cross, where he appointed his apostle John to care for his mother. These actions seem to simplify Jesus' humanity into something that we can understand, even while he maintains his godliness. A simple emotion in powerful people is always resonant, and through Mary we can find this in Christ.

*Above Mary rests her cheek on the head of her thriving son, whom she closely resembles. This early 16th-century* Madonna and Child *by Raphael emphasizes the natural maternal bond.*

# Marian Apparitions

APPARITIONS OF THE BLESSED VIRGIN MARY HAVE BEEN REPORTED FOR MANY CENTURIES. THE CATHOLIC CHURCH REFERS TO SUCH VISIONS AS "PRIVATE REVELATIONS".

Probabably the earliest of the Marian revelations dates back to AD 40. It occurred before Mary's Assumption into heaven, when the apostle James, who was in Spain trying to spread the gospel, had a vision of the Virgin atop a marble pillar. She instructed him to build a church on the site, and that church today is said to be the first of the thousands of churches that have been dedicated to and named for the Blessed Virgin.

## GUADALUPE

The three most influential Marian apparitions occurred at Guadalupe in Mexico, Lourdes in France and Fatima in Portugal. Guadalupe is notable because the visionary, Juan Diego, was an Aztec and a recent convert to Christianity. Mary appeared to him in 1531 at the site of a former temple to the Aztec gods,

and as a proof of her appearance she left her image mysteriously imprinted on Juan Diego's tilma, a type of cactus-fibre cloak. The image and the cloak have never decomposed and even today, more than four centuries later, the cloak (protected by bullet–proof glass) can still be seen at the basilica that was built in Guadalupe. Juan Diego's vision was influential in converting many indigenous Mexicans to Christianity, although these people were initially disinclined to do so because of their subjugation by the Spanish.

## LOURDES AND FATIMA

Probably the best-known Marian vision occurred at Lourdes in 1858. The lady who appeared to a poverty-stricken and sickly shepherd girl said very little, mainly directing her supplicant to pray the rosary and to do penance. Yet the simple, intense, committed (and lifelong) piety and certainty of Bernadette Soubirous so impressed the clergy who examined her that Bernadette remains today the exemplary believable visionary in the eyes of the Church. Lourdes is also known for Massabielle, the spring blessed by the Virgin that has been responsible for dozens of otherwise inexplicable cures.

Fatima is remarkable for both the number of the visions and the loquacity of the Virgin Mary. Appearing six times in 1917 to three young children, Mary foretold the end of World War I but warned of a

*Above Our Lady, atop a pillar carried by angels, is illustrated in a c. 1629 painting by Nicolas Poussin. She appeared to the apostle James as he prayed by the banks of the Ebro River in Zaragoza, Spain.*

worse war to come. She provided the children with a brief vision of hell and requested that Russia (this was during the Russian Revolution) be consecrated to her Immaculate Heart. Pope John Paul II, who felt that Our Lady of Fatima was

*Left The Basilica of Guadalupe in Mexico is the most visited Catholic shrine in the world; on the feast of Our Lady of Guadalupe, millions make the pilgrimage – some on their knees.*

responsible for his own survival from an assassination attempt that occurred on the feast of the Lady of Fatima, did perform such a consecration in May 1984. As a gesture toward Russia, he mentioned the nations that "particularly needed to be… consecrated" in the consecration.

## THE DEPOSIT OF FAITH

The Church teaches that even the private revelations they dub "worthy of belief" do not constitute part of the "deposit of Faith" (the approved doctrines) of the Catholic Church, and that Church members are not bound to believe even the "approved" apparitions. The Church holds that the sum total of crucial Catholic revelations was given in apostolic times and, in particular, is contained in the doctrines of Christ's birth, death and Resurrection. Cardinal Ratzinger (who is now Pope Benedict XVI) commented in 2000 that the "…mystery of Christ as enunciated in the New Testament" was the utter, complete revelation of God to humanity, and that the Church neither needs nor expects anything more. There is no need for further divine manifestations. The Church feels that revelation is complete and that "secrets" revealed by visions cannot add to it.

## MODERN REVELATIONS?

The attitude of the Catholic Church to Marian apparitions is cautious. The amount of attention paid to contemporary apparitions (such as the "disapproved" manifestations in Bayside, Queens, New York City) can quickly get out of hand due to the speed and widespread nature of modern publicity and ease of travel for pilgrims. The Church is concerned

*Left A personal supplication to St Bernadette of Lourdes (1844–79) is inscribed on this little holy card, together with an image of Bernadette (shown with a halo) after the pious woman entered the Sisters of Charity.*

Sainte Bernadette

*Ton sourire divin illumine ma vie
Et lorsqu'au dernier jour vers toi prenant l'essor
Mon âme aura quitté l'exil pour la patrie
O Vierge Immaculée viens me sourire encor*

that such charismatic phenomena will spread false doctrine and corrupt its magisterial authority. In essence, the devotees of particular Marian visions run the risk of developing into cultists.

Catholic doctrine also teaches that private revelation is not something to aspire to. St Teresa of Ávila

(though she herself had visions) reflected the sentiments of the Church when she said, "They desire to see; faith holds on without seeing." In other words, you should not need visions to believe. Christ himself said, "More blessed are they who have not seen and have believed."

Modern-day investigations of Marian apparitions are instituted by the bishop of the relevant diocese. If the messages being relayed by the apparition to the visionary are in any way contrary to the accepted doctrine of the Church, that alone is enough to have the apparition declared invalid. Investigations will also probe the mental, physical and spiritual health of the visionary and consider whether the messages being conveyed by the apparition are considered beneficial to the spiritual health of the faithful.

*Right Our Lady of Fatima asked the three shepherd children to whom she appeared to pray the rosary daily; today there are nightly candlelight processions to the shrine, where the participants pray.*

# ALL SAINTS

THE MOST FAITHFUL SERVANTS OF GOD WHILE THEY WERE ON EARTH
ARE KNOWN AS SAINTS, AND CATHOLICS BELIEVE THEY ARE REWARDED
WITH A PARTICULAR INTIMACY WITH GOD IN HEAVEN.

The word "saint" comes from the Latin *sanctus*, or "holy, consecrated". In the general sense, the Catholic Church believes that anyone who has died and been accepted into heaven has earned the status of saint. However, there are also people who have been judged worthy of canonization by the Church hierarchy here on earth because of their exemplary behaviour as Christians. These saints are considered to have an especially intense beatific vision of God.

## THE FIRST SAINTS

In the early centuries of Christianity, saints came from the ranks of the martyrs, those who in Roman times chose death rather than renounce their faith. After Christianity was legalized by the Edict of Milan in AD 313, the learned of the faith such as bishops or theologians ("doctors") were often considered for saint-hood. Anchorites, or hermits, were also likely to achieve the designation by popular reputation. A saint chosen

*Above St Matthew was stabbed in the back by a hired assassin while saying Mass in the church he built in Ethiopia. He is a saint by virtue of being an apostle and a martyr. This 14th-century illustration is from an altarpiece of St Matthew showing scenes from his life.*

by reputation would be venerated by the people, who might visit the person's tomb or celebrate the day of his or her death.

After many years, the ecclesiastical authorities became involved and eventually created an official process for declaring someone a saint. The first saint for whom official canonization documents exist is St Udalricus, who was canonized in AD 973. In the early days of canonization, it was part of the practice to exhume the presumed saint's body and place it under an altar, apparently to facilitate the practices of veneration and pilgrimage that often resulted. An alternate way to express canonization is "to be

*Left In this 15th-century painting, the bones of King Louis IX of France are disinterred (for reburial under an altar) by Pope Boniface VIII, who later canonized Louis.*

## THE LONG ROAD TO CANONIZATION

There is a set procedure to follow for a person to be made a saint. First there is The "Opening of the Cause", which occurs when the diocesan bishop agrees that there is enough evidence to initiate an investigation into the life of a deceased resident of his diocese, by popular opinion known as outstandingly holy. Usually, there is a five-year waiting period after the candidate's death, but in the case of Pope John Paul II, Pope Benedict XVI waived this waiting period. At this point the candidate can be called "a servant of God". The report that results from the investigation is sent to the Congregation for the Causes of Saints, the Vatican investigative body that vets saintly nominees. If the Vatican agrees the report profiles a saint in waiting, the candidate is called "Venerable".

A posthumous miracle, evidence of the candidate's intercessory influence with God, must be verified. After verification, the candidate is beatified. Mother Teresa was beatified in 2003. After beatification, the candidate is called "Blessed". The Congregation for the Causes of Saints must verify that a second miracle occurred after the beatification before the candidate can be called a "Saint".

*Above The widely held conviction that Pope John Paul II was an exceptionally holy man caused Pope Benedict XVI to open the cause for canonization only weeks after John Paul's death.*

raised to the full honours of the altar". Even today, saintly bodies reside under altars in some of the most surprising places – the body of St Mother Mary Frances Cabrini, for example, is under the altar of the chapel at Mother Cabrini High School in New York City.

VENERATION OR WORSHIP?
The modern Church recognizes saints as people of exemplary holiness who are worthy of veneration, which is not the same as worship. The act of worshipping a saint would violate the first commandment – "thou shalt not have strange gods before me". Catholicism is emphatically a mono-theistic religion. The Church makes a specific distinction between *latria*, or "worship", due only to God, and *dulia*, which is "honour or venera-tion", due to saints. The Blessed Mother has her own intermediate category, known as *hyperdulia* – a very high degree of veneration due only to her.

*Right St Anne's status as grandmother of the Holy Family means that she is asked to intercede on family matters. Shown here in this 17th-century French painting, she is patroness of expectant mothers, women in labour and of the sick.*

Worship and veneration can seem similar, since their practices (prayers to the worshipped or venerated, for example, or kneeling before statues, and feast days) are alike. However, the difference between worship and veneration is found in the believer's heart. When he or she worships, he or she is recognizing that the object of worship is divine. There is an element of awe rather than respect. When you venerate or honour, you are recognizing that the object of your veneration is due your respect – in the case of the Blessed Mother, the highest respect – but there is no awe and no intent to confer or recognize divinity.

Catholics who pray to saints do so not to obtain grace or favour straight from the saints themselves, but to ask the saint to intercede with God. This is because the saint is so close to God that their intercession is likely to smooth the way of the prayers of the petitioner.

# A STATE OF GRACE

An individual's state of grace (whether or not he or she will receive sanctifying grace from God) depends on his or her efforts to gain salvation by turning to God through free will. Yet, one has to only briefly consider contemporary scandals that fill the newspapers' headlines to realize that humankind's sinful nature has not changed much over the centuries since early ascetic monks and doctors of the Church, such as Thomas Aquinas, created the Christian vocabulary to talk about sin. The seven "deadly" categories still apply – pride, avarice, greed, lust, gluttony, envy and sloth – leading men and women into both public and private trouble and strife. What has changed over the centuries is the emphasis that the Church places on forgiveness rather than punishment, and most particularly on the manner in which it defines not only punishment, but reward.

Also enduring is the human metaphysical longing for answers to ultimate questions and the craving to put our faith in something that is unified, peaceful and eternal. Catholicism defines this as the Trinity, the ultimate end of our seeking. The emphasis that the modern Church places on our personal relationship with God and on our eventual either beatific union with or desolate divorce from him is evidence that the Church has shifted the promise of heaven's glory and the threat of hell's fires and mutilations from the pointedly physical to the ineffably spiritual. The Church offers the heaven of rest and union with God.

*Above The seven deadly sins all imply gross self-absorption. This attribute is evident in the oblivious expression and callous disregard of the child's pleas displayed by the overstuffed man in a scene depicting gluttony from Hieronymous Bosch's late 15th-century Tabletop of the Seven Deadly Sins and the Four Last Things.*

*Left In contrast to many paintings of the Harrowing of Hell, Giotto di Bondone portrays Christ as a tender and kind, rather than glorious and triumphant, liberator in his c. 1320–5 painting, Descent into Limbo.*

# THE SOUL REDEEMED

CATHOLICS HAVE DISAGREED ON WHAT PEOPLE NEED TO DO TO GAIN
REDEMPTION FROM ORIGINAL SIN. IN ADDITION TO CHRIST'S SACRIFICE,
INDIVIDUALS MUST ALSO CONTRIBUTE TO THEIR OWN SALVATION.

Debates between Christians on what sinful humans need to do to attain salvation involved some of the most divisive issues of the 16th century, leading to the Protestant Reformation. Shuffled around in the debates were issues of grace, faith and the relative significance of human good works, along with the role of Christ's sacrifice on the Cross. The Catholic Magisterium, or teaching authority, and Martin Luther – the Catholic priest responsible for starting the Protestant Reformation by nailing his influential 95 Theses to the door of a church in Wittenberg – agreed on one important issue: that Christ's ultimate sacrifice on the Cross was the absolutely necessary prerequisite for human redemption.

*Above* Faithful Catholics pray before The Way of the Cross, *a sculpture that emphasizes the physical reality of Christ's sacrifice. The weight of the Cross seems to drive Christ into the ground, with only the help of Simon of Cyrene keeping him from falling.*

### GOD'S GIFT

As a result of original sin, humans are viewed as helpless to effect their redemption on their own. (Pelagius, a 5th-century theologian, disagreed and thought that people could handle their redemption without God's intervention; the Catholic Church declared him a heretic.) Both Catholics and Lutherans also agreed that salvation is a gift from God. God has no obligation or need to save sinful humanity.

Fortunately, even the grievous fact of original sin was not enough to destroy God's love for humanity – his Creation – and his infinite goodness is displayed in the mystical balance of Christ's redemptive sacrifice. As the 20th-century theologian Jaroslav Pelikan has noted, Christ's obedient passion and sacrifice on the tree of the Cross undid the damage that humankind had done next to the tree of disobedience.

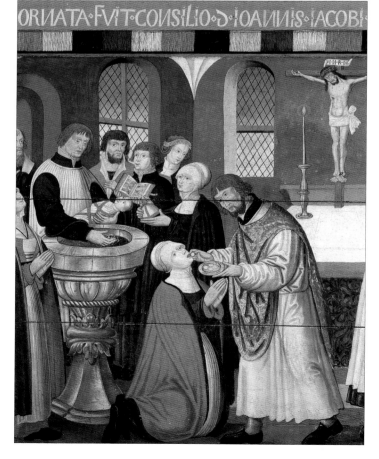

ORNATA·FVIT·CONSILIO·D·IOANNIS·IACOBI

*Left The Catholic Church recognizes seven sacraments, while the Lutheran Church practises only two – baptism and the Eucharist. In this detail from a 1561 altar front from Torslunde, Denmark, Martin Luther, who was once a Catholic monk, performs both.*

## HAVING FAITH

Luther believed that *sola fide* (or "faith alone") was the sole active principle in humankind's salvation. People would be saved by their faith in Christ's life, death and Resurrection. Christ basically earned redemption that is "imputed", or credited, to us if we have faith. Although Luther agreed that due to their faith in Christ, people develop a disposition to do good works, known as the process of sanctification, he thought that these human good works would never be enough to have any active effect on our redemption. Christ's sacrifice, and our faith in it, are all that matter. Luther is said to have declared, "Good works are useless."

## CATHOLIC BAPTISM

In contrast, Catholicism teaches that not only can we be active contributors to our own salvation, but in fact, we must be so, in order to be saved. Faith alone will not be sufficient. Catholics view salvation as a process, so unlike Protestants they do not say, "I've been saved". Their ultimate salvation will be decided on their particular Judgement Day.

Catholicism teaches that we are redeemed through the progressive and co-operative interactions of first (and most crucially) Christ's initial sacrifice, the prerequisite that has made our personal redemption possible. Next we need to participate in a baptism, which is like our first purifying bath to cleanse us of original sin and infuse us with an initial dose of sanctifying grace. This act of baptism can be seen as an introductory step toward the process necessary for spiritual salvation.

## JUSTIFICATION

Catholic theologians call what happens at baptism "initial justification". Justification is defined as making a person righteous in the eyes of God. However, to keep the spiritual introduction received at baptism

***Above*** *On the day of the final judgement, Catholic tradition declares that soul and body will be reunited. This 15th-century fresco by Giovanni Canavesio shows bodies rising from their graves on this ultimate day.*

vigorous, Catholicism teaches that we need to participate actively in the Church and its sacraments, especially attendance at Mass, reception of the Eucharist and good works. Through these sincere acts of participation in the Catholic community, we become more immune to sin – and we also turn into more vigorous spiritual beings. This level of participation is known as "progressive justification".

***Above*** *The scallop shell is the traditional Catholic symbol of baptism. John the Baptist is said to have baptized Christ with water poured from a scallop shell. Here Pope John Paul II baptizes a child in the Sistine Chapel in 2001.*

# THE NATURE OF SIN

CATHOLICISM RECOGNIZES DIFFERENT TYPES OF SIN, FROM THE
ORIGINAL SIN OF ADAM AND EVE TO THE UNFORGIVABLE SIN. IT IS OUR
CHOICE TO TURN TO GOD AND NOT SIN OR TO TURN AWAY FROM HIM.

To understand how sin is viewed in Catholic doctrine, one needs to consider the concept of *aversio ad deo*, or "turning away from God". Sin is an insult to God, an almost unimaginable rudeness when considering that, in the Catholic view, God has offered us the most superb gift, his love. Sin is perverse, in that it says "no" to the love of God; the Catholic catechism says that sin contradicts the love of God.

Sin is the refusal to accept this priceless love and to choose instead to turn down the blind alley of self-love or toward a false attraction to worldly objects or persons. It is a disordered perception (as a result of original sin) of the value of attractions of the temporal world that we

*Below Man's fallen nature leaves him vulnerable to the attractions of the temporal world, including riches, corporeal delights and secular power, shown in Jean de Gerson's 1462* Mirror of Humility.

mistakenly define as love. The more complete the degree of turning away from God, the more distance we put between ourselves and the grace we receive in his presence, and thus the more likely we are to continue to sin.

## PERSONAL SIN

When we resist or turn away from God's love for us, we cannot receive his grace, and without God's grace we lose the most effective means to avoid our tendency toward personal sin. While original sin is inherited from our ancestral parents, personal sin is our own production (though we can blame Adam and Eve for the fact that we were born imperfect). Regardless of excuse, Catholic doctrine teaches that after Adam and Eve's fall from grace, humanity retained, in weakened form, its free will. Since we still have free will, even in a fallen world we can choose to "turn toward God", or *conversio ad deo*, and not sin.

*Above A 15th-century Italian illustration shows Jesus uttering the famous words, "He that is without sin among you, let him cast the first stone at her".*

## VENIAL VERSUS MORTAL

Catholics classify sins as either venial or mortal (theologians break these sins down into smaller categories, but for most of us the mortal/venial distinction is sufficient). To continue the metaphor of turning away from God, a venial (from the Latin word *venia*, or "forgiveness, pardon") sin would be a slight acknowledgement, and a mortal (from Latin *mortalis*, or "death") sin would be turning one's back, which is the rudest of cuts that would sever all social ties (*see Before the Mortal Blow, opposite*). Biblical reference to the venial versus mortal sin distinction can be found in 1 John 5:16–17:

> He that knoweth his brother to sin a sin which is not to death, let him ask, and life shall be given to him, who sinneth not to death. There is a sin unto death: for that I say not that any man ask.

Venial sins (those little rudenesses to God) do not in and of themselves sever all ties and destroy our hope for eternal life with God. However, like any rudeness, they can damage the relationship between us and him and lead in time to the final rift unless

## BEFORE THE MORTAL BLOW

Unconfessed and therefore unforgiven mortal sins cause the death of the soul and consign the sinner to hell – eternal punishment. However, God is fair and just, so mortal sins are not easy to commit. You cannot "accidentally" commit a mortal sin. Before you turn away from God and choose the devil, three ominous conditions must be present:

**Grave Matter:** The act, to any person of normal reason, would be understood as evil.

**Full Knowledge:** The potential sinner must know that the act is evil. A person with a mental illness, such as schizophrenia, for example, may not have full knowledge that an act he is about to commit is heinous.

**Deliberate Consent:** It is up to us. The choice is ours, because God endowed us with free will. We can choose to turn toward the Dark or the Light. If you hit someone with your car accidentally and kill him or her, that is not a mortal sin; but if the accident happened because you drank alcohol at a party, knowing that you planned to drive home, then the accident is a mortal sin because you acted irresponsibly.

*Right St Augustine thought one of the most terrible results of the fall of man was* libido dominandi, *or "the lust for dominance". Cain, son of Adam, enacts a tragic result of that lust – fratricide – in* The Killing of Abel, *a detail from the 1379–83 Grabower Altarpiece by Master Bertram of Minden.*

we mend our ways. As this particular passage makes clear, mortal sin leads to the death of the soul.

### THE UNFORGIVABLE SIN

The New Testament refers to an eternal, or unforgivable, sin. In Mark 3:22–30, Christ says, "All sins will be forgiven the sons of men, and whatever blasphemies they may utter; but he who blasphemes against the Holy Spirit never has forgiveness, but is subject to eternal condemnation." Christ also refers to unforgivable sin in Matthew 12:3–32, when Pharisees, who witness Christ cast out demons, claim Christ had the power of Beelzebub (the devil).

The unforgivable sin is connected to a wilful rejection of God in the face of all the manifest good that is clearly vouchsafed to us. This sin consists of seeing good and perversely calling it evil. It blasphemes against the Holy Spirit in his role as a "convincer of sin", which is what Pope John Paul II called the Holy Spirit in the 1986 encyclical, *Dominum et Vivificantem*. John Paul pointed out that the Holy Spirit's role is to purify humankind's consciences, so that they are able to call good and evil by their proper names. When we radically reject the Holy Spirit, we are no longer able to see our good and our salvation even when they stare us in the face. This is the unforgivable sin.

*Right A 14th-century biblical illumination shows the fool who said, "There is no God" (Psalm 53). The sin of apostasy, or rejecting God, is called the unforgivable sin.*

# THE SEVEN DEADLY SINS

SINCE THE 5TH CENTURY, CATHOLIC THEOLOGIANS HAVE DISCUSSED A
LIST OF PARTICULAR SINS FOR THE FAITHFUL TO AVOID, BUT IT WAS ONLY
IN THE 12TH CENTURY THAT A CREED LISTED THE SEVEN DEADLY SINS.

Although the list of the seven deadly, or cardinal, sins has traditionally been paired with a list of virtues, it is the sins that are remembered. The seven deadly sins (and the corresponding virtues), in the order of descending gravity, are: pride (humility), avarice (generosity), envy (kindness), wrath (patience), lust (chastity), gluttony (temperance) and sloth (diligence).

The Catholic catechism refers to these sins as capital vices, noting that they are capital because they produce other sins. In fact, the seven deadly sins are actually categories of sin, and

*Below Hieronymus Bosch's 15th-century* Tabletop of the Seven Deadly Sins and the Four Last Things *shows the deadly sins balanced with four medallions of the four last things: death, judgement, heaven and hell.*

sins falling within those categories are not always mortal. For example, eating two desserts when you really needed only one – or none – would be a sin classified as gluttony, but it would not be enough to send you to eternal punishment (unless it was a symptom of a much larger problem).

## EARLY MENTIONS
The tradition of the seven deadly sins originated in the writings of John Cassian, a 5th-century monk and ascetic. In his book *Collationes*, he provided a list of eight vices that were particularly tormenting to ascetic monks, as follows: gluttony, impurity, covetousness, anger, dejection, accidia (or boredom), vainglory and pride. Pope Gregory the Great included a similar list in his book *Moralia on Job.* Cassian and Gregory

*Above The virtue of flourishing generosity is seen in opposition to the deadly vice of avarice in this 1945 illustration,* Allegory of Generosity and Avarice, *by Rémy Hetreau.*

may have been influenced in turn by *Psychomachia*, an allegorical poem by the 4th-century Roman Christian poet Aurelius Prudentius Clemens. His poem featured a battle between personified virtues and vices in the style of the *Aeneid*. Prudentius may have influenced later authors who made specific use of the deadly sins in their writing, in particular, Geoffrey Chaucer and Dante Alighieri. Of the church fathers, Thomas Aquinas in his *Summa Theologiae* (1265–73) paid attention to the seven deadly sins, for example, analysing multiple manifestations of gluttony, such as *studiose*, or "eating too daintily", and *laute*, or "eating too expensively".

## BY COUNCIL DECREE
The wide dissemination and subsequent popularity in public discourse of the seven deadly sins can be traced back to the Church's Fourth Lateran Council (1214). One of the decrees of the council was the

## SEVEN SINS OF THE 21ST CENTURY

In 2005, the Church published a "Compendium of the Social Doctrine of the Church", which reasserted the humanist position of the Catholic Church on all social issues. The widely publicized list of the seven "social sins" derived from this compendium. The social sins of the 21st century are:

1: Bioethical violations, such as birth control
2: Morally dubious experiments, such as stem cell research
3: Drug abuse
4: Polluting the environment
5: Contributing to the widening gap between rich and poor
6: Excessive wealth
7: Creating poverty

The compendium states that social sin falls into two categories: "On the one hand, the all-consuming desire for profit, and on the other, the thirst for power, with the intention of imposing one's will upon others." Bishop Gianfranco Girotti also stated that, "While sin used to mostly concern the individual, today it has mainly a social resonance, thanks to the phenomenon of globalization."

requirement that Catholics attend yearly confession. In order to make a good confession – or any confession at all – the ordinary communicant needed to be educated in the concept of sin and given a vocabulary to talk about it. Parish priests as well had to learn the language of sin. In the Lambeth Constitutions of 1281, Archbishop of Canterbury John Peckham provided the clergy with a syllabus that included the seven deadly sins (as well as the seven virtues and the seven sacraments).

## THE NUMBER SEVEN

Many Christians have asked why there are only seven deadly sins and have noted some considerable

*Above St Thomas Aquinas, one of the Church's most erudite theologians, provided an exhaustive analysis of the seven deadly sins in his* Summa Theologiae. *This portrait of Aquinas is by Alessandro Botticelli (1445–1510).*

omissions from the list, such as cruelty to others. This is because seven was considered a number of significance in the Old Testament, starting with the creation of the world in seven days, and it has reappeared in many other guises as an important ordering principle in Scripture, in particular, in the "Book of Sevens", Revelation. Seven is generally considered a number of high sacred significance.

*Above The oil industry often displays social sin. It pollutes the Earth in its desire for great wealth.*

# JUDGEMENT DAY

ACCORDING TO CATHOLICISM, EACH PERSON IS JUDGED AT DEATH
(PARTICULAR JUDGEMENT). CHRIST WILL RETURN ON JUDGEMENT DAY
TO JUDGE THE LIVING AND THE DEAD (GENERAL JUDGEMENT).

The Catholic vision of Judgement Day is a particularly specific one. Catholic tradition teaches that there are two separate and specific judgements: the particular and the general. The particular judgement, as the name implies, has more significance for the fate of each person, while the general judgement is the Judgement Day that will see the Second Coming of Christ and the end of the world as we know it.

## AT DEATH

Particular judgement happens at the exact moment of individual death, when the soul separates from the body. Catholic sacred tradition teaches that the particular judgement is instantaneous, so that the soul will simply know, immediately, what the verdict is and go on its own in the right direction. The choices are heaven, which is reserved for the perfectly pure; Purgatory, for the vast group of the imperfectly pure

(those with venial sins that are still unconfessed and unforgiven); and hell, for the definitely not pure (those with mortal sins that remain unconfessed and unforgiven).

## A PAPAL BULL

This belief in the prompt fulfilment of the sentence was a controversial one within the early Church. Some Church fathers argued that either the bliss of the beatific vision (for example, the intuitive knowledge of God) or the suffering of the tormenting fires of hell would be postponed until the general judgement. Pope Benedict XII convened a commission to decide the question, and after four months of testimony

*Below During the Second Coming of Christ, saints will be rewarded with the beatific vision of Christ, implied in this early 15th-century German painting by his larger size in relation to the others and the blissful expression of the saints.*

*Above Aided by its guardian angel, this soul is slipping away to its judgement (fresco detail from the* Last Judgement, *Voronet Monastery, Moldavia, Romania). The soul will be reunited to the body it leaves behind at the general judgement.*

from various theologians, he issued the 1336 papal bull, *Benedictus Deus*. This bull proclaimed, once and for all, that your fate was indeed determined right away.

## GENERAL JUDGEMENT

The judgement that has been traditionally depicted in Western art – full of angels, demons, writhing naked bodies and a just Christ sitting on a throne with a group of saints in attendance – is known as the general judgement. It is a popular theme of medieval and Renaissance paintings.

Church tradition teaches that at the general judgement, all bodies, both the saved and the damned, will be rejoined to their immortal souls. The wicked, unfortunately, will not be happy to meet their bodies again, as noted in Revelation 9:6, "The wicked shall seek death, and shall not find it, shall desire to die, and death shall fly from them…"

Scripture specifically assigns the general judgement as a role for Christ. In John 5:28, it states, "…for the hour cometh wherein all that are in the graves shall hear the voice of the Son of God." This is why the general judgement is also referred to as Christ's Second Coming.

It will be during the general judgement that the Godhead's ultimate purpose for mankind will finally be fulfilled.

The general judgement appears to have the same function as a public trial: although a particular judgement has already been pronounced, the general judgement is needed so that all may witness the justice of the final decrees. General judgement features an aspect of public proclamation, as described in the Athanasian Creed, "at whose coming all men must rise with their bodies and are to render an account of their deeds". The general judgement is the day of public accounting and is a final judgement.

THE FINAL JUDGEMENT
Catholicism teaches its followers that when Christ returns, it will be for the final judgement and that the resulting reign will be eternal and in heaven. Over the centuries, however, Christians have held different

*Below Weighing souls after death, shown in this 12th-century Catalan fresco, was an ancient belief of Egypt and Greece as well as early Christianity. Traditionally, the archangel Michael escorted souls to God on Judgement Day and weighed them.*

views on what will happen during the final judgement (*see* Final Judgement and the Millennium, *below*). Pre-millennialism describes this as an actual return of Christ for a thousand years, before the final judgement. However, post-millennialism prefers to describe an achieved perfection on earth due to the preaching of the gospel, as a result of which the entire earth will be Christianized. After the thousand years of earthly Christian perfection, then Jesus returns to conduct the final judgement. Pre-millennialism posits a return and reign of Christ on earth prior to

*Above A phalanx of saints are in attendance above, the mouth of hell gaping is on the right and delight or dismay (as applicable) are shown on earth in The Last Judgement by Bartholomaeus Spranger (1546–1611).*

the final judgement, whereas post-millennialism believes in a period of achieved perfection on earth prior to the final judgement.

The Catholic Church refutes pre-millennialism and also rejects the post-millennial view that there will ever be a period of perfection on earth prior to the final judgement (this view would contradict the

### FINAL JUDGEMENT AND THE MILLENNIUM
The Book of Revelation, and Chapter 20 in particular, is problematic for Catholics. This difficult chapter describes a thousand-year period when Satan will be bound with chains in a pit, after which he will be "loosed for a little while" and emerge to deceive again. This thousand-year period when Satan will be bound is known as the millennium. There are many gradations of opinion (much of it Protestant evangelical) on the millennium, but most understand it as a thousand-year "golden age" of the triumph of Christianity, a reign of Christ himself (pre-millennialism) or of the Christian religion (post-millennialism) on earth that will be distinct from the final judgement and distinct from eternity.

# VISIONS OF HEAVEN

THE WRITERS OF THE BIBLE REFERRED TO HEAVEN AS A PHYSICAL PLACE, GOD'S FIRMAMENT. HOWEVER, TODAY'S CATHOLIC CHURCH DESCRIBES HEAVEN AS A STATE OF BEING.

The Bible uses several descriptive phrases when referring to heaven, including a kingdom, a crown, the city of God, a reward and even an inheritance. This metaphorical variety on the part of biblical writers shows that the early Christians felt a certain liberty in their attempts to imagine heaven, as long as it provided a good image.

In the popular imagination, both in the past and present, heaven is often seen as being palatial, expressed in the term "pearly gates", which derives from the opulent description of heaven as the "New Jerusalem". In Revelation 21:21, its gates "are twelve pearls, one to each: and every several gate was of one pearl". In paintings and movies, heaven is

*Above* Orderly groups of saints approach the fortified portal of paradise in this 1480 detail from the Last Judgement, Voronet Monastery, Moldavia, Romania.

dreamy, awash in clouds that are often shot through with pastel rays of effulgent light. In common usage, "heavenly" is the adjective of choice for anything highly pleasurable, from pizza ("a slice of heaven") to relaxing in a hot bubble bath.

## GOD'S FIRMAMENT

Despite these images, the etymology of the word "heaven" derives from words referring to "a roof or covering", confirming the majority view that heaven is above us. Genesis 7:10 describes God making the "firmament", which serves as a vast buttress that divides the elemental regions of the earth: "And God made a firmament, and divided the waters that were under the firmament, from those that were above the firmament… And God called the firmament heaven…".

*Left* St Augustine, in one of his most influential works, Civitate Dei, described two opposing cities, the earthly and the heavenly. These are shown in this early 15th-century French illustration, La Cite de Dieu, or "City of God".

This soaring support of the world came to be associated with the abode of God, "...a building of God, a house not made with hands, eternal in heaven" (2 Corinthians 5:1). Medieval cathedrals aspired to represent in earthly architecture the inspiring span and lofty height of heaven.

## A STATE OF BEING

Catholic doctrine, however, is circumspect in describing heaven as an actual physical place. No doctrine of the Church has ever attempted to establish the latitude and longitude of heaven, and although it is the traditional concept, the modern Church is even cautious in describing heaven as the dwelling place of God. This is because by doing so, it would imply that God can be contained in a particular place.

Instead, the Church describes heaven as a state of being achieved only by those who are pure of all sin. The Catholic catechism says that when we enter into the state of being of heaven, we will have a "beatific vision" of God. Unless God makes himself open to an individual for contemplation, God cannot be seen. If this contemplation takes place, our spiritual and intellectual perceptive capacity will be unbound from its earthly limitations so that we will be able to perceive and receive God – this is a beatific vision. Such an encounter "is what the perfect happiness of heaven will consist of".

In 1336, Pope Benedict XII defined belief in the beatific vision (for those who attain heaven) as a dogma of the faith. Theologians, however, put limits on even the beatific vision. They state that while we will see God (such as in the Trinity) entirely, our vision will not have the absolute and infinite clarity with which God perceives himself. The Church also believes that there are degrees of beatitude granted to the Blessed; saints have a more extensive vision of God.

*Above New residents, borne on the backs of obliging angels, are welcomed to heaven with open arms in this 15th-century work from* Hastings Book of Hours.

## BEING REUNITED

There is also a more homely aspect to heaven. The Church teaches that in heaven we will be reunited with our beloved family and friends who have gone there before us, and the language of some of the prayers for the dead in the Church emphasizes that heaven is the true home of the righteous and that our arrival in heaven will actually be a homecoming. In the service that is given for the dead, the Prayer of Commendation states:

*May you return to [your Creator] who formed you from the dust of the earth.*
*May holy Mary, the angels, and all the saints come to meet you as you go forth from this life...*
*May you see your Redeemer face to face.*

The sense is of a family's loving, eager greeting to one of its members who has been too long away. Heaven is also a homecoming in that we return to our first home, paradise, redeemed from a long sojourn in the fallen world. St Augustine said, "Thou hast made us for Thyself (O God) and our heart is troubled till it rests in Thee."

*Below The Madonna and saints contentedly work, read and play in a walled garden in this c. 1410 German painting,* Paradise Garden. *The garden is the earthly mirror of paradise, which is from the old Persian word for "a walled garden" or "park".*

# PURGATORY

CATHOLICS BELIEVE THAT AFTER DEATH THERE ARE MANY SOULS THAT ARE NOT DESTINED FOR HELL BUT THAT ARE NOT READY TO ENTER HEAVEN WITH GOD – THEY GO TO PURGATORY TO BE CLEANSED OF SIN.

The Catholic doctrine regarding the concept of Purgatory has developed from the Catholic belief that God is both merciful and just. Because God is merciful, sinners can atone for their non-mortal sins even after death, but because he is just, this atonement is a requirement that must be met.

Purgatory (from the Latin word *purgare*, "to make clean, to purify") is where that atonement happens. The Church teaches that Purgatory is where those who die without mortal sin on their soul, but also without making full satisfaction to God for their sins, must suffer for a time to purify their souls and to make recompense to God. Purgatory is different from hell because it is temporary. Souls suffering in Purgatory know that eventually they will be with God. In traditional teaching, Purgatory is a place; however, in more contemporary teaching it is a state of being.

## A DEVELOPING CONCEPT
The early church Councils of Lyons (1274), Florence (1438–43) and Trent (1545–63) all made statements describing, with varying degrees of

*Above Few theologians were as aware of the struggle between good and evil as St Augustine. In this 15th-century French woodblock print, he focuses on his work despite the clamour of demonic distractions around him.*

specificity, the Church's developing concept of Purgatory. In *The City of God*, St Augustine expressed his belief that there would be temporal punishment after death, and Pope (later St) Gregory the Great, influenced by Augustine, was principally responsible for refining the idea of *purgatorius ignis*, or the "cleansing fire", into doctrine.

Going to Purgatory is not completely inevitable. The pure do not go to Purgatory, and Catholics also believe that those who, through no fault of their own, have suffered terribly in life (say an unjustly convicted prisoner), essentially pay recompense for their sins by experiencing Purgatory here on earth. However, those who have been less than pure will go to Purgatory.

## PURGING OUR SINS
Purgatory is necessary, in most cases, even if you have made an appropriate confession of your sins and have been forgiven. The Catholic concept of penance is that temporal punishment is required to discharge our debt

*Above Purgatorial punishments match the earthly sin. In an illustration in* Le Trésor de Sapience *by Jean de Gerson (1363–1429), the prideful are pushed into the ground and trodden on, expiating their arrogance by being forced to grovel in flames.*

of sin as a necessary condition of absolution. The Church makes the point that Purgatory is necessary not because God is vengeful but because our sins, like a stain, have worked into our essence. Only the spiritually clean can truly see God, and being spiritually cleansed is difficult work, a sense expressed by the early Church father, Gregory of Nyssa, in his reflections on Purgatory:

> …we may figure to ourselves the agonized struggle of that soul which has wrapped itself up in earthy material passions, when God is drawing it, his own one, to himself, and the foreign matter, which has somehow grown into its substance, has to be scraped from it by main force, and so occasions it that keen intolerable anguish.

## INTERCEDING SAINTS

Catholicism also teaches that the prayers of the faithful still residing on earth can help the souls in Purgatory. The Communion of Saints refers to the belief that all faithful members of the Church, whether living or dead, are united as members of a single spiritual community and can help one another; therefore, the saints in heaven can intercede with God to help us on earth, and by offering suffrages – our prayers, fasting and works of charity on earth – we can obtain divine mercy for the souls in Purgatory, perhaps even hastening the time that they will be released into heaven.

*Above Part of a larger panoramic 15th-century French painting by Enguerrand Quarton,* The Coronation of the Virgin, *this detail depicts Purgatory in an unexpected location – just beneath the walled city of Rome. It includes a few fortunate penitents who have completed their time in Purgatory and are rising from the depths, with the aid of angels.*

## HEAVEN SHOULD NOT BE FOR SALE

Indulgences, or remission of time spent in Purgatory, became a hot trading commodity during the early 16th century. The trade in indulgences reflected the extreme concern with the afterlife during this era when the Black Death (plague) had decimated Europe's population. Pope Leo X took advantage of this situation to enrich the Church coffers by selling indulgences – though selling them is a mortal sin (Leo, a member of the Medici family, was extremely corrupt). Leo was selling plenary indulgences, a particular type of indulgence that provides total remission of the temporal punishment (time in Purgatory).

Indulgences are legal in the Church, but because of this earlier history they are often misunderstood as being a kind of coupon for time off from Purgatory that the Church offers in exchange for cash. However, what many do not understand is that even forgiven sins may result in some time in Purgatory after death, before an individual is in acceptable spiritual shape for heaven. Plenary indulgences can free you from that prospect, but there are conditions attached. First, they should never be offered solely in exchange for money. Sins must be forgiven by confession; the person receiving the indulgence must go to confession and receive Communion for a week, and the person must perform charitable works prescribed by the Church.

*Above Johann Tetzel, a Dominican prior, sells indulgences in Germany in this 18th-century woodblock print.*

# VISIONS OF HELL

MODERN CHURCH DOCTRINE ON HELL IS RELATIVELY TAME IN COMPARISON TO THE LURID VISION OF ETERNAL DAMNATION THAT HAS GRIPPED THE POPULAR IMAGINATION SINCE THE MIDDLE AGES.

The Scriptures contain a number of references to a hell with a fearsome aspect, describing it as a place of fire and darkness. Among these are: "pool of fire" (Revelation 19:20), "everlasting fire (Matthew 18:8; 25:41; Jude 7), "unquenchable fire" (Matthew 3:12), "furnace of fire where they will weep and gnash their teeth" (Matthew 13:42, 50),

"exterior darkness" (Matthew 7:12; 22:13; 25:30) and "mist" or "storm of darkness" (2 Peter 2:17; Jude 13).

### ETERNAL DAMNATION

These are all arresting descriptions, particularly when coupled with the concept of being never ending, because hell, of course, is eternal. Contemporary Catholic clergy are

***Above*** *The license allowed in portraits of Satan is evident in this 15th-century rendition, which depicts him with belled horns, wings like ribbed leaves and tusks.*

unlikely to dwell for long on these descriptions. However, in medieval times and up to the Second Vatican Council (1962–5), priests and nuns often invoked the grim spectre of hell in an effort to scare their congregations into good behaviour. The Church considered meditation on the "Last Things," which are death, judgement, heaven and hell, as salutary to spiritual health.

We are indebted to the medieval period for many of our images of hell as a place of gruesome punishments and apocalyptic landscapes. The vision literature of the Middle Ages featured an entire genre of texts that recounted personal tours of hell, featuring horrible retributions that were tailor-made to suit the sin. This early vision literature influenced the great Florentine poet Dante, who in his *Inferno* described hell as a series of nine concentric circles, with limbo, the least severe, at the outer rim and Satan confined at the centre.

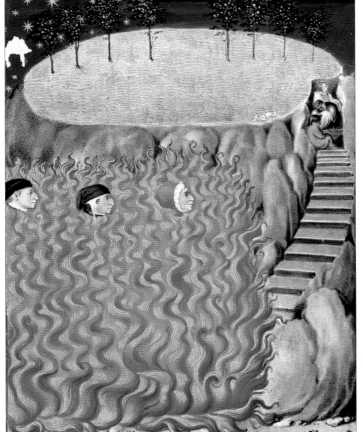

***Left*** *A 14th-century image from Dante's* Divine Comedy *shows stars in paradise, terraces in Purgatory and fire in hell.*

*Right A demon delivers a new soul to hell to join eternally tormented souls in this detail from a 15th-century painting by Enguerrand Quarton.*

## HELLFIRE

The fires of hell are supernatural: they do not require fuel and they do not consume those they burn, but blaze eternally. Traditional Catholic theology describes hellfire as *poena sensus*, meaning the "pain of sense". *Poena sensus* is considered a corporeal pain, because Scripture specifies that after the last judgement, the damned will be rejoined to their bodies. Some have noted that *poena sensus* was an appropriate pain, because mortal sin is often allied to excessive desire for physical and material pleasures.

## THE CHURCH'S VIEW

The Second Vatican Council did not mention hell, but the gentling of Church rhetoric on hell dates from then. The current Catholic

*Above The damned make their way to hell and the pure to heaven in Rogier van der Weyden's 15th-century painting of the Last Judgement.*

definition of hell, as noted by Pope John Paul II, states that the ultimate punishment for sin itself is hell, and that it is "more than a physical place". Hell represents the state of those who have chosen freely and completely to "separate themselves from God".

The Catholic catechism describes hell as a state of being where the individual chooses to reject God's love, thereby dying in mortal sin. By choosing to exclude him or herself from God, and by not repenting, he or she will be separated from God for eternity – this is hell.

To older Catholics whose lifetime spans the expositions of both the older eternal, infernal physical punishment vision of hell from before the Second Vatican Council and today's metaphysical "eternally separated from God" hell, the difference can be striking. This is a situation in which the Catholic Church has exercised its magisterial authority to interpret Scripture. Here we see the evolution of Church tradition at work.

John Paul II also went on to say that we need to understand the meanings presented by the images of hell in Scripture, which illustrate an empty and frustated life if living without accepting God. The Pope calls the scriptural words on hell

"images" and says, not that they "are" hell, but that they "show" a state of being. So, heaven is unity with God and hell is separation from God. Although John Paul II did not repudiate the old concept of hell, he did go so far as to redefine the terms of the discussion.

### THE PAIN OF LOSS

*Poena damni*, or the "pain of loss", refers to psychic pain. The Church describes *poena damni* as a real, intense pain, rooted in the loss of the beatific vision. The damned still retain the human need for God, even if they have rejected this desire, and so are tormented eternally by the unquiet described by Augustine in his *Confessions*, "…You have formed us for yourself, and our hearts are unquiet until they find rest in you." The disquiet of the damned can never be stilled, so they burn with eternal despair. It is the *poena damni* that Pope John Paul II emphasized in his definition of hell. "Damnation" comes from the Latin word *damnum,* which means "loss", emphasizing that the essence of hell is in the pain of loss.

# VISIONS OF DAMNATION

THE ARTISTIC REPUTATION OF PAINTINGS OF HELL HAS ALWAYS ECLIPSED
THOSE OF HEAVEN. BLISS SEEMS TO LEAVE ARTISTS AT A LOSS, BUT THEY
APPEAR TO HAVE A PASSION FOR PAINTING ETERNAL PUNISHMENT.

Hell was by no means an unusual
subject in religious art. Two popular
themes are of "The Harrowing of
Hell", when Christ descended into
hell after his Crucifixion, before his
Resurrection, and the Last Judgement.
Numerous artists, including Giotto di
Bondone (c.1267–1337), Fra Angelico
(c.1387–1455), Hans Memling
(c.1440–94) and Michelangelo (1475–
1564), have depicted hell. Giotto's hell
is a fiery nether region dwarfed by a
conquering Christ who was enthroned in an orderly heaven with
the righteous in attendance.

Memling's triptych *The Last
Judgement* depicts hell as a flaming
pit into which the undifferenti-
ated bodies of the damned tumble,

superintended by colossal and well-
armed demons. Jesus holds centre
stage as the archangel Michael
weighs the souls. The left panel shows
the pure being led to heaven, while
the right panel shows the damned.

Fra Angelico's hell is honey-
combed with flaming caverns where
bleeding, naked people are bound,
speared and burnt by gleeful demons
resembling diabolical monkeys, or
the unfortunate occupants are eaten
in great gulps by Satan himself,
looking like a great ape.

### THE MASTER OF HELL

Pre-eminent among all the painters
of the horrors of hell is Hieronymus
Bosch (c.1450–1516). He was an
unassuming Dutchman who never
travelled far from 's-Hertogenbosch,
his village in the duchy of Brabant
(modern-day Netherlands). In a
small house on the market square,
besides making devotional wood-
cuts, he painted hell and its countless
demons in endlessly inventive, start-
lingly modern, gruesome detail.

In contrast to many of the other
illustrations of hell, Bosch's chaotic,
brightly coloured depictions are
typically overrun with life, albeit
in monstrous forms: strange demons
that resemble insects or sea creatures,
monstrous birds, odd plants with
pod-like excrescences, enormous
ears, mussel shells, eggs, unusual ice
skaters and odd little bathyspheres
with grilles for doors. One representative Bosch monster is a fish
swallowing another fish, with lobster
legs and a spiny tail.

Bosch's demons tend to have long
whip-like tails resembling the sting-
ers on stingrays. The damned are not
simply burnt or bound, but are

*Above The descent into the mouth of
hell was a standard subject of medieval
"doom" paintings. In a detail from Hans
Memling's 15th-century version, the
damned souls tumble with arms and legs
extended in almost balletic poses.*

tortured in an indescribable variety
of obscene manners by a wealth of
phantasmagoric creatures. Hellfire
burns on the outskirts of Bosch's
canvases, in dark regions shot with
red light; unlike the typical painting
of hell, the flames are not the
principle torture of the damned.

### THE FIRST SURREALIST

Because he married an heiress, Bosch
did not depend on the Church hierarchy for commissions of his work,
unlike many other artists. Free from
the need to submit his compositions
to the censorship of the Church,
he was able to produce beautifully
painted works featuring imagery not
found in any Scripture.

Bosch's technique came to him
naturally: several of his relatives were
also painters, including his grandfather, father, brother and three
uncles. The Flemish style of slender,
restrained human bodies and of

*Above The damned are subjected to
various forms of torture applied by tiny
demons, from being suspended by the hair
to the racking of bare skin, in this detail
from Giotto di Bondone's c.1303
painting, The Last Judgement.*

meticulous attention to detail is evident in his work. However, Bosch's iconography is like no other religious painter's and is a precursor in its hallucinatory specificity to the early 20th-century work of the Surrealists, artists that were hailed as "revolutionary" more than five centuries after Bosch.

## A DEVOUT BROTHER

Surprisingly, the little-known story of Bosch's life suggests that he participated in the conventional pious observances of society: he was a sworn member of the Society of Our Lady, a devout brotherhood founded in 1318. The society was a powerful but exclusive group, and

Bosch was allowed to become a member upon marriage because his wife was already one. The studies of the brotherhood may have contributed to Bosch's obsession with hell: they were said to conduct daily readings of accounts of hell.

Despite his deeply unconventional work, during his lifetime Bosch became enormously popular among the laity, if not the Church itself. King Philip II (1527–98), the Spanish monarch known for his collection of saintly relics, was a particular admirer of Bosch. He was a keen collector of his works and kept Bosch's painting of a wheel depicting the seven deadly sins in his bedroom at the Escorial Palace.

*Left Only in the hell of Bosch would one find what resembles a penguin on ice skates, as seen in this 1503–4 detail from* Die Hölle. *The horror of Bosch's hell is its complete lack of logic and reason – all the universe is askew.*

*Above Fra Angelico's vision of hell exemplifies the "cooking and eating" motif, with a cauldron of unfortunates being boiled, Satan gorging on their flesh and lesser demons contemplating bodies massed for their delectation.*

# LIMBO

A REGION ON THE EDGE OF HELL, LIMBO WAS RESERVED FOR THOSE WHO DIED FREE FROM SERIOUS PERSONAL SIN, YET, THROUGH NO FAULT OF THEIR OWN, WERE STILL IN A STATE OF ORIGINAL SIN.

The name "limbo" derives from the Latin *limbus*, meaning "hem", "border" or "edge", reflecting its juxtaposition with hell. The concept of limbo was developed as an extension of the doctrinal importance that the Church ascribes to original sin and baptism, added to its belief that only those who are free of all vestiges of sin will be worthy of the beatific vision of God.

There are two categories of candidate that can go to limbo. These are either virtuous people who died before Jesus redeemed them from original sin, or babies who died before being baptized.

## GOD'S GIFT

Original sin is an inescapable fate for all humans, with only the Virgin Mary being conceived without it. Romans 5:18 says, "Therefore, as by the offence of one, unto all men condemnation; so also by the justice of one, unto all men justification of life." This scriptural syllogism makes clear the direction of the Church's thinking: if salvation, that gift of God, is going to apply to all people, then so must the unfortunate predecessor to salvation: the hereditary stain that marks all the unbaptized as exiles from God. In other words, the unbaptized are at risk.

*Above The halo over Mary in Pietro Lorenzetti's 14th-century painting,* The Birth of the Virgin Mary, *is a clue that she was conceived without original sin.*

## THE TWO LIMBOS

Catholic tradition originally taught that there were two limbos: *limbus patrum*, for virtuous but unbaptized adults (*patrum* refers to "fathers"), reflecting the belief that the Old Testament patriarchs – including Abraham – would go there, and *limbus infantium*, for unbaptized infants. The two limbos were required because *limbus patrum* would end with the Second Coming, whereas *limbus infantium* was permanent. The fathers could not be baptized because Jesus Christ had not yet redeemed man. The babies were not baptized because they had died before anyone had baptized them.

In fact, this is why the Church teaches that in an emergency, anyone can baptize a baby by making the sign of the cross over the infant and

*Left Abraham holds the souls of the righteous in this 12th-century French manuscript. Because he lived before Jesus was born, Abraham was not redeemed before he died and went to limbo.*

speaking the words, "I baptize thee (NAME) in the name of the Father and of the Son and of the Holy Spirit." Many doctors, nurses and midwives have performed such baptisms over newborns they feared would not survive.

## INNOCENT BUT IN LIMBO

The ultimate fate of the innocent but unbaptized was controversial, as were so many theological issues before their applicable doctrines were established. St Augustine was the most severe: this 4th-century theologian believed that the innocently unbaptized would be punished, though more mildly than the truly damned. The theologian Peter Abelard (1070–1142) believed that the innocent but unbaptized suffered no physical pain, only the pain of the loss of God, and Pope Innocent III (1160–1216) agreed.

St Thomas Aquinas held an even more soothing concept, stating that limbo was a place of "natural happiness", but with the crucial exception that its residents were deprived of the transcendent joy of true union with God (known as

supernatural happiness). However, the Council of Florence (1438–43) seemed to backtrack, stating, "the souls of those dying in actual mortal sin or in original sin alone go down at once into hell, to be punished, however, with widely different penalties". Yet the teaching of Aquinas remained the somewhat equivocal general Church position – crucially, it was never a definitive doctrine – right up until the 21st century and the pontificate of Pope Benedict XVI.

### A 21ST-CENTURY DEBATE

Centuries of debate about limbo continue. In April 2007, the International Theological Commission, an advisory panel to the Vatican (previously headed by Cardinal Ratzinger, now Pope Benedict XVI) published a report endorsing the belief that *limbus infantium* was too limiting when it came to salvation. The report affirmed the superabundance of God's Grace over sin, noting that Christ's relationship with humankind must be stronger than any links with Adam. In a contest between original sin and salvation where no personal guilt is involved, the power of Christ's mercy vanquishes the power of Adam's sinfulness. The report, however, does not repudiate the Church's doctrine of original sin or the need for baptism. Instead, it theorizes that in the case of unbaptized infants, God can give his Grace without the need of the sacrament being given in baptism.

*Above* In the Harrowing of Hell, between death and Resurrection, Christ went to limbo to free the just who died before him. It is depicted in this 15th-century fresco.

*Above* The theologian Peter Abelard, shown in this 19th-century engraving, supported the idea of limbus infantium. Pope Innocent III accepted his view.

# PRACTISING CATHOLICISM

One of the world's biggest institutions, the Catholic Church has a huge hierarchy.

As leader of the Church, the pope rules from the Vatican, the centre of the Church's

government. From there, the pope provides guidance to the bishops in their dioceses,

the priests in their parishes, the monks and nuns in their monasteries and missionaries,

and ordinary lay people in their everyday activities. People from all these walks of life

seek inspiration from the Church as they practise their faith and celebrate the holy

days that occur throughout the liturgical year.

*The Eucharist, along with baptism and confirmation, is a sacrament of initiation into the Catholic Church. These girls are taking their first Holy Communion in Charlotte, North Carolina, in the United States.*

IN·HONOREM·PRINCIPIS·APOST·PAVLVS·V·BVRGHESIVS·ROMANVS·PONT·MAX·AN·MDCX

# INSTITUTIONS OF THE CHURCH

On Easter Day, tens of thousands of Roman Catholics pack into St Peter's Square in Vatican City, Rome, to hear the pope celebrate Mass and give his Easter address. The event is broadcast live around the world: the address and the Apostolic blessing that follows it are termed *Urbi et Orbi* ("to the City [of Rome] and to the World").

As spiritual leader of the Roman Catholic Church, the pope heads a vast global organization. Pope Benedict XVI's third Easter address, delivered on 23 March 2008, was televised in 57 countries, and he followed it by giving Easter greetings in no fewer than 63 languages. According to figures released by the Church hierarchy in March 2008, more than one in six people worldwide – 17.4 per cent of the global population – is Roman Catholic. This percentage is equal to around 1.13 billion people.

For these people the pope's authority is supreme. As well as being Europe's only absolute monarch, ruler of Vatican City (the world's smallest independent state), he stands at the head of the Holy See, the Church's machinery of government, and its administrative structure, the Roman Curia. He is at the peak of the great Church hierarchy of cardinals and archbishops, bishops, priests and deacons that also includes the many thousands of priests, monks, friars, nuns and religious sisters in the Church's religious orders. He is nothing less than the Vicar of Christ, his representative on earth. Yet in all these roles, the pope is called to humility and service: among his official titles is "Servant of the Servants of God", in line with the passage in St Matthew's Gospel (20:27) where Christ declares "whoever would be first among you must be your slave".

*Above* Standing in the central loggia of St Peter's Basilica, Pope Benedict XVI gives the Urbi et Orbi *blessing that follows the Easter Sunday Mass.*

*Left A vast crowd of the Roman Catholic faithful attend open-air Mass in St Peter's Square at the Vatican on Easter Sunday.*

# THE HOLY FATHER

THE POPE HAS ULTIMATE AUTHORITY OVER ROMAN CATHOLICS AND OVER THE CHURCH. HE IS ONE OF A LONG SUCCESSION OF POPES, ELECTED TO THIS POSITION BY THE COLLEGE OF CARDINALS.

The title "pope" derives from the words in Late Latin (*papa*) and Greek (*pappas*) meaning "father", and his position is similar to that of a father in a patriarchal family. The pope is addressed as "Your Holiness" and "Holy Father". In addition, the pope has eight formal titles listed in the official directory of the Holy See (the central government of the Catholic Church): Bishop of Rome, Vicar of Jesus Christ, Successor of the Prince of the Apostles, Supreme Pontiff of the Universal Church, Primate of Italy, Archbishop and Metropolitan of the Roman Province, Sovereign of the State of Vatican City and Servant of the Servants of God.

## SUCCESSOR OF ST PETER

Bishop of Rome and Successor of the Prince of the Apostles are two titles that reflect the fact that for Roman Catholics the pope is a spiritual descendant of the apostle St Peter. Pope Benedict XVI, who has

been pope from 19 April 2005, is said to be the 265th pope in an unbroken succession of popes from St Peter.

According to biblical accounts, Christ renamed Simon, son of John, Peter, based on the Greek *petros*, or "rock", because the Church was to be built with his strength. In later tradition, Peter was recognized as the leader of the 12 disciples who established the Christian Church in Italy, becoming the first Bishop of Rome. He was also buried in Rome, in the place where the high altar in St Peter's Basilica now stands.

## CHRIST'S REPRESENTATIVE

The pope is also called the Vicar of Christ, meaning his representative – a person acting in his place.

*Below Under rules introduced in 1970 by Pope Paul VI, only cardinals aged 80 or below can vote for a new pope. In 2005, 117 cardinals were eligible to vote when Pope Benedict XVI was elected.*

*Above The name conclave comes from the Latin cum clave ("with a key"). At one time the cardinals were locked away until a new pope was elected.*

For Roman Catholics, the pope serves as Christ's officer, with supreme authority over the Church, because he occupies the place of St Peter, who was originally given the authority to serve in this way. Pope Gelasius I (served AD 492–6) was the first to assume the name "Vicar of Christ"; before his time Christians had reserved the title for the Holy Spirit and popes were referred to as "Vicar of St Peter". The other titles reinforce the pope's position as supreme ruler of both the Catholic Church and the Vatican.

Roman Catholics believe that – just as the pope is the successor of St Peter – the archbishops and bishops of the Church are the successors of the apostles. The archbishops, bishops and the pope receive from the Holy Spirit the gift of infallibility – the capacity to discern what is right, and to be free from mistakes in morals and matters of faith when they jointly proclaim a doctrine. By this remarkable gift they share a part of Christ's own infallibility. The pope as leader of the bishops possesses a unique infallibility that makes it possible for him to make a definitive decree on doctrine that concerns matters of faith or morals.

*Above* During a conclave in the Sistine Chapel at the Vatican to appoint a new pope, ballot papers are placed in these ballot boxes by the cardinals.

*Below* Pope John Paul II greets the faithful during his first public appearance at the Vatican after his election to the papacy on 16 October 1978.

## RITUALS OF ELECTION
The pope is elected by the College of Cardinals in a series of closed sessions called a papal conclave, held in the Sistine Chapel in the Vatican Palace. The cardinals vote by writing the name of their preferred candidate on ballot papers beneath the words *Eligo in Summum Pontificem* ("I Elect as Supreme Pontiff"). They carry on voting until one man has the votes of two-thirds of the cardinals plus one. However, if the process becomes prolonged, the cardinals can agree to elect by simple majority.

When one name is agreed, the cardinal in question is asked if he accepts election as Supreme Pontiff. If he replies yes, he then gives the papal name by which he will be known, and the other cardinals pay him their respects.

The pope blesses the crowd and is then ceremonially installed in a service a few days later. At one time this was a grand coronation, but since the time of Pope John Paul I (served for 33 days in 1978), this has been replaced with a simpler ceremony in which the pope is invested with the papal robe, called the pallium, during a Papal Inauguration Mass.

# THE VATICAN:
# A PLACE APART

THE ROMAN CATHOLIC CHURCH'S CENTRE OF GOVERNMENT, GENERALLY KNOWN AS "THE VATICAN", IS IN VATICAN CITY. IT HAS ITS OWN MILITARY CORPS, GOVERNMENT AND INFRASTRUCTURE.

Vatican City is a city-state set within the Italian capital Rome. The world's smallest independent state, the Vatican covers about 44 hectares (109 acres) and has a population of between 800 and 1,000 people. The city-state is mostly enclosed by high stone walls that separate it from Rome. It is the sovereign territory of the Holy See (the Church's central government), and heads the Church's machinery of spiritual and pastoral rule.

While the Holy See has a history dating to the time of St Peter, Vatican City was created only in 1929 under the Lateran Treaty signed by the Kingdom of Italy and the Holy See. Its official name is *Stato della Città del Vaticano* ("the State of Vatican City").

*Below St Peter's Basilica looks down on St Peter's Square. The basilica's majestic 45m (150ft)-high façade was built by Carlo Maderno in the 17th century.*

Vatican City is run as an elected monarchy that is ruled by the pope. One of the pope's formal titles is Sovereign of the State of Vatican City. Roman Catholic clergymen serve as the city-state's chief functionaries. The official state flag is the yellow and white papal banner.

## MOUNT VATICAN

Vatican City takes its name from the hill in north-western Rome on which it stands. This area was known as *Mons Vaticanus* ("Mount Vatican") by the Romans in the pre-Christian era. The city contains the magnificent domed church of St Peter's Basilica, which by tradition stands over the burial place of St Peter, as well as the vast Vatican Palace (also known as the Apostolic Palace). With more than 1,000 rooms, this is an impressive structure that contains the pope's apartments, the

*Above Indoors, the vast scale of St Peter's Basilica impresses upon worshippers the power and grandeur of God – Father, Son and Holy Spirit.*

Church's government offices and several chapels, as well as the Vatican Museum and the Vatican Library.

Within the complex is the Sistine Chapel, famed for its ceiling frescoes of scenes from the book of Genesis that were painted by Michelangelo in 1508–12. It also has a papal reception suite decorated with frescoes by Raphael and the artists of his studio, from 1508 onward, and the Borgia Apartment, a suite decorated with frescoes by Pinturicchio in 1492–5 for Rodrigo Borgia, Pope Alexander VI. The Vatican Museum contains a wealth of statuary, including the ancient Roman statues of *Apollo Belvedere* (350–325 BC) and of *Laocoön and His Sons* (160–20 BC).

Adjacent to the museum, the Vatican Archive houses religious and historical documents dating back over centuries, including the report on the Church trial in 1633 of mathematician and astronomer Galileo Galilei, whose promotion of the theory that Earth and other planets revolve around the Sun was condemned by the Church on the grounds that it conflicted with Scripture. The complex also holds the Vatican Library, which has one of the world's most valuable collections of manuscripts and early books.

A number of other buildings belong to Vatican City but are situated beyond the city walls. These include the pope's summer villa in Castle Gandolfo, 24km (15 miles) south of Rome, as well as the churches of St John Lateran, St Mary Major and St Paul's Outside the Walls, all in Rome. The Church of St John Lateran is Rome's Cathedral Church and the ecclesiastical seat of the Bishop of Rome – that is, of the pope.

## PROTECTING THE CITY

Vatican City has its own military corps known as the Pontifical Swiss Guard. The guardsmen, who are all Swiss and Roman Catholics, maintain a 24-hour watch over the pope and the Apostolic Palace. The Swiss Guard's role in protecting the pope dates back to the time of Pope Sixtus IV in the late 15th century. The guardsmen wear a Renaissance-style uniform that is sometimes said to have been designed by Michelangelo, but in fact was created in 1914. Technically, the Swiss Guard is a unit of the Holy See, not Vatican City.

The city has its own security and civil defence services department. It encompasses a police and security force called the Gendarme Corps of Vatican City-State, as well as its own fire brigade.

## RUNNING THE CITY

The Vatican has the infrastructure and machinery of government necessary to run an independent country: a diplomatic corps; a court system; its own bank and independent postal,

*Above As well as protecting the pope and the Apostolic Palace, the Pontifical Swiss Guard are responsible for controlling access into and out of Vatican City.*

telephone and telegraph services; its own water supply; street-cleaning and lighting; and a railway system. The railway is a stretch of track about 270m (885ft) in length, used for carrying freight. There is even a Vatican jail and a printing plant.

The Pontifical Commission for the State of Vatican City, a group of cardinals appointed by the pope, has responsibility for the state's domestic administration, while foreign relations are handled by the Secretariat of State of the Holy See.

The Vatican City newspaper *L'Osservatore Romano* (The Rome Observer) has been published since 1 July 1861. It was initially independently run, but since 1885 it has been owned by the Holy See.

*Right The elaborate Vatican Library was established by Pope Nicholas V in 1448. It holds some of the most important books from the earliest days of the Church.*

# HIERARCHY OF THE CHURCH

FROM PAPACY TO PARISH, THE CATHOLIC CHURCH'S HIERARCHY IS A VAST PYRAMID CONNECTING THE POPE AT ITS SUMMIT THROUGH PRIESTS AND DEACONS TO MEMBERS OF THE FAITHFUL AT THE BASE.

As Vicar of Christ on Earth, the pope holds supreme and universal power over the Roman Catholic Church. As Bishop of Rome and successor to St Peter, he is foremost among, and leader of, the bishops of the Church.

### THE UPPER HIERARCHY

Bishops, archbishops and cardinals are at the top of the hierarchy. The pope has ultimate authority for the appointment of bishops. With them he shares what is termed "collegiate" responsibility for leading the Church.

*Below On ordination a bishop becomes a member of the College of Bishops and takes on his share of responsibility for governing the Church.*

The bishops together form the College of Bishops. They are viewed as the successors of Christ's apostles and have a duty to teach the faithful.

Each bishop is in charge of an ecclesiastical area known as a diocese, which contains several individual parishes. His principal task is to care for the faithful in his area, like a shepherd cares for sheep. The main church of the diocese is known as a cathedral and is the ecclesiastical seat (base) of the bishop. In some metropolitan areas, an "ordinary bishop" is the principal bishop and is assisted by a team of auxiliary bishops.

The pope appoints some bishops as archbishops. They have control of an even larger area known as an

*Above Archbishop Egan leads his first service as archbishop in St Patrick's Cathedral, New York, on 19 June 2000. Archbishops are responsible for presiding over Mass in their ecclesiastical seat.*

archdiocese, which contains a number of dioceses. The pope is also responsible for appointing some senior bishops as cardinals. They form the College of Cardinals. Some care for dioceses, while others serve the pope as advisers and administrators in Rome. When a pope dies or if a pope abdicates, the cardinals meet in closed session (conclave) to elect one of their number as the next pope.

### PRIESTS AND DEACONS

Beneath the bishops are two further ranks in the ordained orders: priests and deacons. Priests have the same principal responsibility as a bishop, which is to care for the faithful in the area. Priests proclaim the gospels, lead community prayer and worship, celebrate Mass and the other sacraments for their congregation and teach the faith. Some are members of religious orders, while others are diocesan priests devoted to service in a particular diocese. Most serve in parishes but some instead serve as chaplains in hospitals, universities, prisons or the armed services.

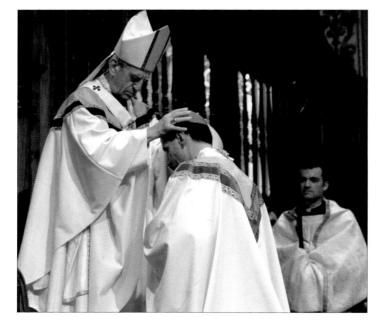

Both priests and bishops are assisted by deacons. In the early Church, deacons also held a special responsibility for charitable work, but as the role of deacon evolved, it became no more than a stage in training to become a priest. However, reforms introduced in 1967 by Pope Paul VI have re-established a group of permanent deacons in the Church. These deacons are men not called to be priests. They often have full-time jobs outside the Church, and whereas priests must be celibate, some deacons may be married.

## WITHIN THE RANKS

Ecclesiastical duties are restricted by rank. Only bishops can perform ordination – that is, make others a bishop, a priest or a deacon through the sacrament of Holy Orders, which is centred on the laying on of hands and a prayer of consecration. Only bishops or priests can say Mass or hear confession.

Deacons have a special responsibility for reading the gospel in Church and for working with the poor. Deacons can preach, perform baptism and conduct marriage services – in the latter case they technically act as witnesses, because the bride and groom administer the sacrament of Holy Matrimony to one other.

## CHURCH GOVERNMENT

The pope is the head of the Holy See, the Church's central machinery of government. The Holy See's administrative structures are collectively known as the Roman Curia. The Roman Curia is divided into several departments, the most important of which is the Secretariat of State, which performs political and diplomatic work for the Holy See.

*Right* Pope Benedict XVI presides over the Roman Curia at the Vatican. Curia (from medieval Latin) means "court" – as in "royal court".

### CANON LAW

The Roman Catholic Church has its own legal system, complete with its courts, judges, lawyers and legal code. The code derives its authority from the council of bishops as descendants of the apostles and the pope as successor of St Peter and Vicar of Christ.

The code has its original source in canons (rules) adopted by Church councils, supplemented by papal decretals or letters that state legal decisions, and input from Celtic, Saxon and other legal traditions. The material was formulated as a code and promulgated by Pope Benedict XV in 1917, then revised in the 1960s to 1980s and repromulgated by Pope John Paul II in 1983.

Parts of the code were adapted from Roman Law as codified on the order of Byzantine emperor Justinian I in AD 529–34. Church courts follow the Roman law style practised in continental Europe, with panels of judges and inquisitorial or investigative proceedings, as distinct from the adversarial proceedings with a single judge and a jury followed in law courts in the United Kingdom and the United States.

*Above A canon law tribunal hears a case. Roman Catholic canon law is the world's oldest continuously used legal system.*

The Secretariat is split into the Section for General Affairs, which holds responsibility for appointments, documents and so on, and the Section for Relations with States. The latter is responsible for interacting with governments of countries from around the world as well as with international bodies, such as the United Nations.

# THE PATH TO PRIESTHOOD

A MAN CALLED TO THE PRIESTHOOD UNDERGOES TRAINING THAT OFTEN TAKES SEVEN OR MORE YEARS AND INCLUDES STUDY IN A SEMINARY AND PASTORAL WORK IN A PARISH.

The journey to the priesthood starts by receiving a call from God to serve as a priest. The calling is known as a vocation (from the Latin *vocatus*, which is the past participle of *vocare*, or "to call"). The call to become a priest is only one of four possible vocations that are recognized by the Roman Catholic Church.

The other three are the calls to life as a brother or sister in a religious order; the call to marriage, with husband and wife sharing faithful love; and the call to single life, embracing celibacy and living either alone, with family or with other single faithful.

These four vocations are viewed as being equal but different. Each faithful Catholic will receive a call by God to one of the four forms of life. The task is to discern the calling and then test it to be sure that a person is

*Below During an ordination service, ordinands prostrate themselves to symbolize their personal unworthiness, humility and reliance on the Grace of God.*

truly being called to that particular pathway. The training to become a priest is known as his formation. The details of the training vary from place to place, but the process typically encompasses several stages.

## PASSING THE TEST

If a young man acts upon a calling to become a priest, he must be willing to embrace a life of celibacy and prayer. He must be ready to commit to proclaiming the gospel, teaching the Catholic faith and doing his utmost to build his faith community. This is a lifelong commitment, so first the young man will need to test his vocation during a period of enquiry and preparation.

He is expected to pray to God for guidance and to be open and patient in waiting for a response. He will discuss his vocation with his local priest and either through him or independently can make contact with the specialist vocations director of the diocese or of a religious order if he feels called to join one.

*Above Young men training for the priesthood pray in a seminary chapel. The word "seminary" comes from the Latin* seminarium *("bed of seeds").*

## EARLY EDUCATION

If he is convinced that he has a vocation, the next stage is to apply to a seminary, a theological college specializing in training priests. A young man who wants to become a diocesan priest applies to a seminary through his local diocese. If he wants to become a priest in a religious order, such as the Franciscans, he applies directly to the order. The application process for a seminary generally includes academic assessment, interviews and psychological tests.

If the young man is accepted into the seminary, he begins his priestly education. The amount of time this takes depends on many factors, including the level of his previous education. His studies will include philosophy, theology, history and Scripture. The training will usually encompass a pre-pastoral stage of study for a year or two, followed by a pastoral stage in which the student serves in a working parish – perhaps returning to his own parish.

## TRANSITIONAL DEACON

The next stage is to train as a deacon. For many years being a deacon was a stage in training to be a priest, but following Pope Paul VI's reforms there has been a return to the practice – common in the early Church – of maintaining a group of permanent deacons who are not destined to be priests. For this reason, students training to be priests who become deacons are now referred to as transitional deacons to distinguish them from permanent deacons.

After training the student is ordained a deacon. He will then serve for some time – at least six months, but often longer than that – as a transitional deacon before being ordained as a priest.

## CALLED AS A PRIEST

At the completion of his training a student is called to be a priest by his bishop. If the bishop makes the decision not to call a student to become a priest, his action establishes that the young man did not truly have a vocation to the priesthood.

Young men must normally be at least 25 years old to become priests. Bishops have the authority to lower this age limit by one year, but only the Holy See can authorize the ordination of anyone younger than 24 years old.

*Below A deacon assists at the Mass. Transitional deacons become familiar with the priestly functions they will perform once they have completed their ordination.*

### TAKING VOWS

At ordination priests take vows of celibacy and of obedience to their bishop. Priests in religious orders take a vow of poverty in addition to those of obedience and celibacy. Before they can actively serve, priests have to be "incardinated" by a bishop or certain other religious superiors, such as the head of a religious order. This word derives from the Latin word for "a hinge", and when a priest is incardinated it means he is attached to and subject to a religious superior.

In practice, the priest will promise obedience to the bishop during his ordination service. However, if the priest has already made a vow of obedience to the superior of a religious order, then he will also acknowledge this pre-existing vow during his ordination.

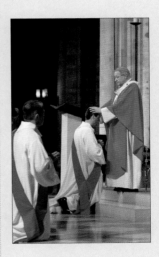

*Above After a priest takes his vows of celibacy during his ordination, the bishop will practise laying on of hands – this is a symbolic gesture that has been used since the Old Testament.*

# MARRIED TO THE CHURCH

A PRIEST IS EXPECTED TO EMBRACE A CELIBATE LIFE. BEING CELIBATE
ENABLES HIM TO AVOID WORLDLY DISTRACTIONS AND CONCENTRATE
ON DEDICATING HIS LIFE TO SERVING GOD.

Roman Catholics believe that a priest's celibate life is a reflection of heaven. Priests are said to be married to the Church. The catechism declares that priests who embrace celibacy are "called to consecrate themselves with undivided heart to God…and give themselves entirely to God and to men" and that when it is accepted "with a joyous heart", "celibacy radiantly proclaims the Reign of God". Celibacy is a gift from the priest to God and to the people, to be made in a spirit of service.

The Church stresses that requiring celibacy in priests does not devalue the sacrament of marriage.

*Below Both brothers and sisters in Christ make sacrifices in adapting their lives to harmonize with the Church's teachings.*

Being a priest or entering married life are among the four vocations recognized by Catholics – and no one vocation is said to be superior to any of the others.

## BIBLICAL JUSTIFICATION
There is a principal source often cited by the Church in support of a call for clerical celibacy, a biblical passage found in Matthew, Chapter 19. In this passage Christ gives a description of marriage as a divinely ordained union between man and woman, and declares that any man who divorces his wife on grounds other than "unchastity" and then takes another is committing adultery. The disciples then say that if this is true it is surely better not to marry. In his response Christ apparently agrees, saying "Not all men can receive this saying, but only those to whom it is given" – that is, not everyone can accept this. He then adds, in the key verse (Matthew 19:12) that is generally cited by Roman Catholics:

*For there are eunuchs who have
been so from birth, and there are
eunuchs who have been made
eunuchs by men, and there
are eunuchs who have made
themselves eunuchs for the sake
of the kingdom of heaven.
He who is able to receive this, let
him receive it.*

By the word that is translated as "eunuchs", Christ is thought to mean men who are celibate, who have freely chosen not to have sexual relations. Priests are an example of those in Christ's third category, who are celibate "for the sake of the kingdom of heaven".

*Above A priest consecrates himself to a
new life and adopts celibacy, as stated in
the catechism, "for the love of God's
kingdom and the service of men".*

Another key biblical justification for the celibacy requirement can be found in the writing of St Paul in the First Letter to Corinthians (7:32-4): "The unmarried man is anxious about the affairs of the Lord, how to please the Lord; but the married man is anxious about worldly affairs, how to please his wife, and his interests are divided." These verses clearly support the Church's position that a celibate life frees a priest to concentrate on serving God and man.

## PRESSURE ON THE CHURCH
In the late 20th and early 21st centuries, critics inside and outside the Church have questioned the requirement of celibacy in priests. In an era of sexual liberation through much of Western society, the vow of celibacy has apparently made it more difficult to attract young men to the priesthood. There has been a mounting crisis in vocations, with the Church unable to replace priests who die and a number of parishes being left without priests.

## THE CHURCH HOLDS FIRM

Nevertheless, the requirement of sexual abstinence by priests has been repeatedly reaffirmed by the Church hierarchy. The Second Vatican Council's Decree on the Ministry and Life of Priests in 1965 addressed the issue and claimed that celibacy was a charitable act of the priest, one that provided "a source of spiritual fruitfulness in the world".

In 1967, Pope Paul VI expressed in his encyclical *On Priestly Celibacy* that when a priest dedicates himself to God through celibacy, he can form a more profound relation with God, and this would benefit humankind. The priest would be better prepared to devote himself to his parishioners. In 1979, Pope John Paul II declared in a letter to priests that in order to serve their fellow humans, the priests must be free in their hearts – and that celibacy is a sign of this freedom.

*Right* Pope Paul VI called celibacy a special kind of asceticism that is more exacting than the sacrifices demanded of other Christians.

*Below* Pope Paul VI, enthroned, opens the Second Vatican Council in 1965. In its deliberations, the Council made notable pronouncements on celibacy.

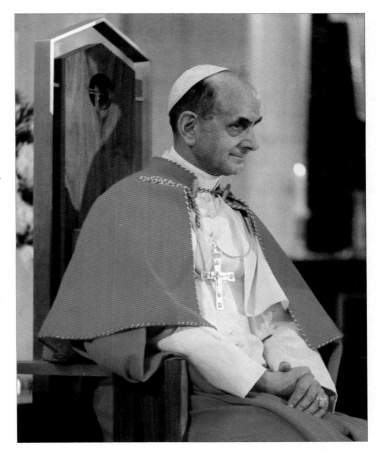

### MARRIED PRIESTS?

There are some exceptions to the strict requirement of celibacy. Certain Protestant ministers who are married and then convert to Catholicism are allowed to serve as priests while married if they are given authority by the pope. Men of mature age who are married may be ordained and serve as permanent deacons — that is, they may be deacons but may not become priests. Men who have been ordained deacons while single may not later marry.

# CALLED TO SERVE

IN THE SACRAMENT OF HOLY ORDERS, CANDIDATES ARE ORDAINED AS BISHOP, PRIEST OR DEACON. THE PROFOUND, BEAUTIFUL CEREMONIAL CONTAINS MOMENTS OF POWERFUL VISUAL THEATRE.

There are three types of ordination: as bishop, priest or deacon. On his ordination the candidate will join the relevant order – of bishops, priests or deacons. The word "ordination" means the incorporating of an individual into an order.

Only bishops have the power to perform ordinations. The essential rite of the sacrament is when the bishop lays his hands on the head of the candidate, or ordinand, and pronounces the prayer of consecration. It is traditional, but not required, for

*Above* An ordinand puts his clasped hands between those of his bishop as a sign of faithfulness to his ecclesiastical superior.

the ordination to take place during a Mass; ordinations are often held on a Sunday in the cathedral of the presiding bishop.

## THE ORDINAND'S EXAM

In the usual service of ordination, the ordinands are called forward to the altar after the reading of the gospel. The presentation follows, when the bishop asks a series of questions to establish that the candidates have passed through the necessary levels of training in their formation as priests and that they are worthy to become priests. The bishop then "elects" – that is, chooses – each candidate and offers the prayer: "We rely on the help of the Lord God and our Saviour Jesus Christ and we choose this man, our brother, for priesthood in the presbyteral order." The congregation present then signals its support by applauding.

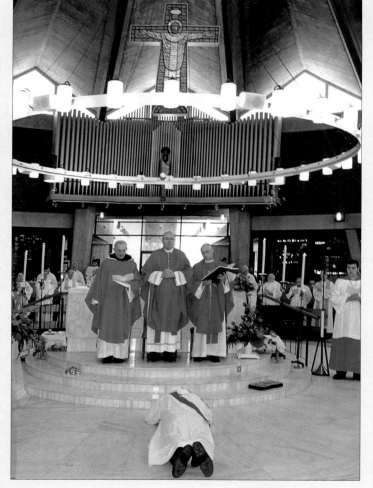

*Left* Prostrating himself while the bishop prays the Litany of the Saints, the ordinand shows his reliance on the Holy Spirit and the support of the faithful.

The candidates sit while the bishop delivers a homily (sermon) on the nature of priesthood and the role of the priest. The candidates then come forward to the altar once more for the examination, in which the bishop asks whether they are willing: to discharge the office of the priesthood; to celebrate Christ's mysteries; to exercise the ministry of the Word; and to consecrate their lives to God through Christ the High Priest. They reply each time "I am".

## VOW OF OBEDIENCE

Each ordinand goes forward and, putting his hands in those of the bishop, promises to respect and be obedient to the bishop and his successors. (In some forms of the ordination service, when the candidates are being ordained as priests in a religious order, rather than as diocesan priests, they instead make a vow of obedience to the superior of the religious order to which they belong.) The bishop prays, "May God who has begun the good work in you bring it to fulfilment."

Next the ordinands lie prostrate on the floor while the bishop and assembled faithful recite the Litany of the Saints. The ordinands lie face down to symbolize their unworthiness to be a priest (or bishop or deacon, depending on the service) and the fact that to take on and succeed in the job they depend on the grace of God, and the prayers both of the saints and martyrs and of the Christian Community on Earth.

## LAYING ON OF HANDS

The ordinands kneel. The ordaining bishop places his hands on the head of each ordinand in silence. The already ordained priests helping at the service do likewise. The laying on

*Right The laying on of hands is a principal ritual that symbolizes the granting of priestly authority and the descent of the Holy Spirit.*

of hands is an ancient ritual going back to Old Testament times, when it was used by Jews to install their priests. The gesture is symbolic of the bishop's prayer to the Holy Spirit to descend on the candidate, and also of the long tradition of sacerdotal, or priestly, authority running right back to the time of the apostles.

The bishop says the Prayer of Consecration. He prays to the Holy Spirit to descend on the priest-to-be, to give him gifts needed for the ministry to which he is called.

## THE NEW PRIEST

Priests who are newly ordained now put on the stole and chasuble, the vestments worn by priests when celebrating Mass. The bishop anoints the hands of each new priest with chrism (consecrated oil), which is symbolic of Christ himself as High Priest The newly made priests then wipe the chrism from their hands on cloths. (They usually give these to their mothers in recognition of the women's sacrifice in giving their sons to the service of the Church.)

The new priests are given patens and chalices that have been brought forward by the people. The bishop prays: "Accept from the holy people of God the gifts to be offered to Him.

*Above A newly ordained priest receives from the bishop the chalice and paten he will use to celebrate his first Mass.*

Know what you are doing, and imitate the mystery you celebrate: model your life on the mystery of the Lord's Cross."

The bishop makes the sign of peace to the newly ordained priests. They then join with the bishop in celebrating the Eucharist. At the close of the Mass service the bishop will kneel before the altar and the priests will give him their blessing. The priests can now share in Christ's own eternal priesthood: they have now been ordained to serve the Church as Christ did many centuries earlier.

# UNDER ORDERS

MEMBERS OF RELIGIOUS ORDERS UNDERTAKE TO FOLLOW A RELIGIOUS
RULE OR WAY OF LIFE UNDER THE LEADERSHIP OF A SUPERIOR. THEY
MAKE A FORMAL DEDICATION OF THEIR LIVES TO GOD.

*Above Franciscan friars confer in the
cloisters of Santa Chiara in Naples,
Italy. They share the complex with nuns
of the Poor Clares.*

Religious orders are also known as
Institutes of Consecrated Life. Their
members take solemn public vows of
chastity, poverty and obedience
under Church law. Some members of
religious orders are also ordained as
priests or deacons, but if they are not
they are considered to be members of
the laity rather than clergy.

Within a religious order, authority is centralized in a superior or
general house, which holds jurisdiction over geographically distributed
dependent houses. However, a major
exception to this general rule is the
Order of St Benedict, in which there
is no single superior house with
overall authority and each of the
individual abbeys is autonomous.

## THE RELIGIOUS ORDERS

Some members are known as monks
and nuns, or simply monastics, and
live in enclosed communities. They
devote their lives primarily to prayer
and devotions. Others are known as
friars and religious sisters, or mendicants, and live in a more open context
and engage in social, medical or
educational work. Historically, the
monastics are self-supporting, while
the mendicant orders rely on alms
for their upkeep.

There is also a distinction between
canons regular and clerks regular.
Those known as canons regular live
in either a closed community or as
secular canons in open society.
Although they are first and foremost
monks, some of them are priests.
They devote themselves primarily to
the monastic life, which is centred
on celebration of the liturgy and on
contemplation. Conversely, clerks
regular are first and foremost priests,
but they choose to live in a community following a religious rule, in
a similar manner to monks. Clerks
regular devote themselves primarily
to the ministry of the priesthood.

## TAKING OF VOWS

Members of religious orders take
what are known as solemn vows of
obedience, chastity and poverty.
Under solemn vows they renounce
the right to own property. Members
of another type of order, called religious congregations, take "simple"
vows. In practice, those who swear
simple vows retain the right to
own material possessions, but they
hand over the administration of
the possessions to the congregation.
Simple vows can be for a limited
period, whereas solemn vows are for
life. Those serving as novices, who
are in the process of becoming a

## RULE OF LIFE

The "rule of life" is a set of guidelines that govern all aspects
of behaviour by members of a religious order. Major
examples in the Roman Catholic tradition include:

• The Rule of St Francis of Assisi, which is followed by
  those in the Franciscan tradition, such as the Order of
  the Friars Minor
• The Rule of St Benedict, followed by the Benedictines
• The Rule of St Augustine, which is traditionally
  followed by the Augustinians.

*Right Benedictine monks harvest flowers in the grounds of the
11th-century Abbey of Santa Maria Assunta at Praglia, near
Padua, Italy.*

*Above Jesuits are led from Rome by the Superior General, who holds the office for life. Spanish father Adolfo Nicolas was appointed in 2008.*

monk or nun, swear simple vows for a limited period before professing solemn vows for life.

There is another kind of religious community in which members do not take any vows. This is called a Society of Apostolic Life. A bishop grants this kind of society authority to operate in his diocese. An example is the Catholic Foreign Missionary Society of America.

## SOCIETY OF JESUS

Jesuits are an important example of clerks regular. They are members of the Society of Jesus, which was established in the 1530s by Spaniard Ignatius Loyola in Paris. Today the society is governed from its headquarters in Rome, the General Curia, by the Superior General (also known as Father General), who is confirmed in his position by the pope. The Father General is assisted by an advisory council in Rome;

around the world, the order is split into geographic provinces, each one led by a Father Superior.

The Society is the largest religious order of priests in the Catholic Church. About 13,500 of its 20,000 members are priests, with around 1,800 brothers, 3,000 students and almost 1,000 novices. From its early days the society combined strong central authority with mobility. Jesuits place emphasis on obedience to the pope – they are said to take a "fourth vow" (in addition to those of poverty, obedience and chastity) of particular obedience to the pope. Because Loyola had a military background, and due to this particular reverence for the papacy's authority, the Jesuits are sometimes referred to as the "Foot soldiers of the pope".

*Right A statue of Father John Carroll sits in front of the Jesuit university of Georgetown. He founded the private university in 1789.*

## JESUIT EDUCATION

Priests and brothers engage in many kinds of evangelical work, including missions and social work in less developed countries, but they are associated with education. Their first university, the Pontifical Gregorian University, or Gregorianum, in Rome, has been providing education since its foundation in 1551.

The Jesuits staff and run many schools, colleges, seminaries, universities and theological colleges. They work in more than 112 different countries around the world, and their education work is particularly important in India and the United States. In India, the Jesuits maintain colleges and schools in Mumbai, Calcutta, Delhi and Goa. In the United States, the Jesuits run more than 50 universities, colleges and schools, including the celebrated Georgetown University, which was founded in Washington, D.C., and Fordham University, which is located in New York City.

# BROTHERS IN CHRIST

ONE BRANCH OF THE RELIGIOUS ORDERS STRESSES THE SPIRITUAL BENEFITS OF COMMUNITY LIVING. MONKS FOLLOW A RELIGIOUS RULE CENTRED ON CELEBRATING THE LITURGY OF THE HOURS TOGETHER.

St Benedict of Nursia, author of the *Rule of St Benedict*, is often celebrated as being the founder of Western monasticism. Modern Benedictines are the successors of the 6th-century monks for whom Benedict, founder of the monastery at Monte Cassino in Italy, wrote his rule of life in *c*. AD 535–40.

In a prologue and 73 chapters, the *Rule of St Benedict* directs monks to divide their time mainly between common prayer, prayerful meditative reading and manual work. The monks are expected to work six hours a day with their hands. The Rule, which St Benedict calls "a school of the Lord's service", also gives detailed guidance on acceptable sleeping arrangements, food and drink, clothing and caring for the sick, as well as hospitality for guests and recruitment. Although

*Below The brothers of Bec Abbey at Le Bec-Hellouin, a Benedictine abbey in France, are joined for Mass by the sisters of the nearby Monastère de Ste Françoise Romaine.*

modern Benedictines do not follow the rule so strictly, they do still use it to guide their lives.

### THE ORGANIZATION

From early on the Benedictines were organized to allow for local decision-making. Each monastery or "house" is autonomous, and the houses are grouped in 21 congregations. In 1893, Pope Leo XIII established the Benedictine Confederation of the Order of St Benedict, which is a confederation of the autonomous congregations, and appointed an abbot primate as its head. The abbot primate does not have direct jurisdiction in Benedictine monasteries but has a general concern for the wellbeing of Benedictines worldwide. The headquarters of the confederation is in Rome.

### A LIFE GOVERNED BY VOWS

Benedictine monks take three vows: of obedience, that they promise to live according to the Rule of St Benedict; of stability, that they will endeavour to remain in the

*Above St Benedict's great legacy was his inspired and moderate Rule for monastic life. He wears a plain cloak in this 15th-century illustration by Andrea di Bartolo.*

Benedictine order for life; and of conversion, that they will seek to follow Christ's example in all things, and will transform their life by adopting poverty and chastity.

In a typical Benedictine house, the monk's day is structured around six church services in the Liturgy of the Hours, with intervening periods of work and private prayer with meditative reading (known as *lectio*

*divina*). The typical day includes four hours in liturgical prayer, five hours in private prayer and spiritual reading, six hours of labour and eight hours of sleep. The remaining hour is set aside for eating.

A monk is required to attend the liturgical services. The first service is the "night office" of matins, which is prayed while still dark, and this is followed by the "morning office" of lauds at dawn. The monks work in the morning, and meet for midday prayer. They then work again in the afternoon, and celebrate Mass together in the late afternoon. The evening services are vespers (evening prayer) and compline (night prayer), which is said and sung before the monks retire to sleep.

The monks view their times of prayer and reading as their true work, but they are also required by the Rule of St Benedict to work. It warns that idleness can be dangerous to the life of the soul and urges brothers to keep themselves busy, sometimes at manual labour and at other times, in spiritual reading. The Rule specifically calls on the monks to work with their hands, but in modern monasteries the work done varies according to circumstance. Many Benedictine houses run schools in which monks work as teachers and administrators; there is also a good deal of practical work in and around the monastery: in the gardens, kitchens and laundry. In some houses, the monks also run a parish and keep a retreat house. They also often perform social work with local people.

## BECOMING A MONK

A young man who wants to become a monk typically starts by staying in the monastery for a period as a visitor, then progresses to being a

*Right The Rule of St Benedict encourages brothers to work with their hands each day. A monk works prayerfully in his pottery studio.*

postulant. As a postulant he commits to living in the monastery alongside the monks for three to six months.

He may leave after six months, or commit to being a novice. As a novice he is "clothed": this means he is given his monk's habit or cloak. After one or two years as a novice, the young man may be asked to renew his simple (temporary) vows for three years. After three years he may take solemn (life) vows and become

*Above Brothers share a meal. Their communal life is known as cenobitic monasticism, from the ancient Greek words* koinos *and* bios *("common" and "life").*

a monk. He can continue as a novice for six or nine years, but after that period he must take life vows or leave the monastery. At any point when the applicant is free to leave, he may also be asked to leave if the abbot thinks he is not suited to monastic life.

### DECLINING NUMBERS
Membership of the Roman Catholic Church is on the rise, but the number of those living a monastic life is in decline. Figures released in February 2008 showed that the number of members of the consecrated life fell a little under 10 per cent in 2005–6 to 945,210. There are many more nuns and sisters than brothers and friars. Of those in the consecrated life, around 750,000 are women compared to approximately 190,000 men. Today, around 8,400 men and 14,600 women live in monastic communities. They follow different rules of life.

# A CONTEMPLATIVE CHRISTIANITY

IN THE TRADITION OF CONTEMPLATIVE MONASTICISM, MONKS LIVE IN AN ENCLOSED COMMUNITY AND COMMIT TO A LIFE OF SELF–DISCIPLINE AND PRAYER ON BEHALF OF THE CHURCH AND THE WORLD.

Contemplative monks have no active ministry in terms of pastoral or missionary work or charitable enterprises, and they have little social interaction except through prayer. They generally live under strict rules governing their interaction. They spend large parts of the day alone and endeavour to live largely in silence. They usually work to produce goods by which they wholly or partially support themselves.

Members of the Carthusian Order (or the Order of St Bruno) live a life of this kind. The order was founded by St Bruno of Cologne in 1084 and takes its name from Chartreuse in France, where Bruno established his first hermitage with six companions. Carthusian monasteries are headed by a prior. They contain a community of cloister

*Below The mother house of the Carthusian Order is the remote monastery of La Grande Chartreuse, which is based in the Chartreuse Mountains of eastern France.*

monks (sometimes called fathers), who commit to greater solitude, and brothers (or lay brothers), who have a less solitary life and take on the material tasks necessary to the running of the house.

In England, Carthusian monasteries are called charterhouses. The order is open to women as well as to men. There are currently 24 charterhouses worldwide – 19 monasteries, holding 370 monks, and 5 nunneries, holding 75 nuns.

## LIFE IN A HERMITAGE

In a typical charterhouse, each of the cloister monks has his own hermitage, or living quarters, which usually has two storeys. Below is a workshop and wood for the wood-burning stove that is the hermitage's source of heat. The main room, above, is the cubiculum. The hermitage also has its own water supply and lavatory.

In the cubiculum, the monk prays, studies, sleeps and eats. He follows most of the Liturgy of the Hours, using full ceremony as if in

*Above St Bruno was a brilliant theologian and teacher. In this detail from a 17th-century painting by Nicholas Regnier, he is receiving the order.*

public, although three daily services are celebrated communally in the chapel attached to the monastery. The monk enters the cubiculum through a small antechamber, which is known as the Ave Maria. This symbolizes the fact that in prayer the monk comes to Christ by way of the Blessed Virgin Mary. He begins all his offices and other prayers with intercessions to the Virgin. In the workshop area, the monk performs work for at least two hours a day.

The hermitage adjoins a walled garden in which the cloister monk meditates and grows vegetables and flowers. Each of the hermitages gives

**TRAPPIST MONKS**
Another well-known group of contemplative monks is the Order of Cistercians of the Strict Observance. Its members are known as Trappists, from the name of La Grande Trappe (La Trappe Abbey) in Normandy, France, where the order was established in 1664. Trappists are contemplative monks who follow the Rule of St Benedict. Like the Cistercians, they divide their day between prayer and work. Trappist monasteries are known particularly for their production of celebrated ales, such as Chimay, which is made in Scourmont Abbey in Forges, Belgium, and Orval, made in the Abbaye Notre-Dame d'Orval monastery, also in Belgium. The order is open to women as well as to men. There are currently about 2,500 Trappist monks and 1,800 Trappist nuns (known as Trappistines) housed in about 170 monasteries worldwide.

on to a communal cloister through a turnstile: food and other materials can be left in this area without disturbing the cloister monk, which allows the contemplative monk to maintain absolute solitude.

Unlike the monks, the brothers of the community spend less time in prayer and more maintaining the monastery. They are responsible for managing food and other supplies, preparing meals, organizing the library and delivering books to cloister monks, carrying out repairs around the charterhouse and so on.

### SILENCE
The monks attempt to live in silence. Although they do not take a vow of silence, they try to speak only when strictly necessary. They aim by this discipline to cultivate inner serenity.

Each cloister monk leaves his hermitage three times a day for services in the main chapel. These are the night offices (matins), the morning Eucharist and vespers in the evening. Occasionally, he meets his superior for a conference. On feast days and Sundays, all the monks meet for a community meal, held in silence. Once a week the brothers participate in a four-hour walk in the countryside around the charterhouse. They are permitted to speak on the walk: they walk in pairs, and change partners every 30 minutes. Two times a year the monks join in a

*Above A documentary film* Into Great Silence *(2005) provided an insight into the lives of Carthusian monks at La Grande Chartreuse.*

community day of recreation and once annually they receive a visit from family.

### THE SOLITARY LIFE
The Carthusian motto is the Latin *Stat crux dum volvitur orbis* ("The Cross holds steady while the world turns"). It celebrates the idea that silent contemplation and solitary prayer can create a place of sacred stillness amid change. The place of stillness serves to sanctify the wider world.

The monks endeavour to interiorize the silence amid which they live. They report that by a spiritual paradox, in solitude they can experience unity with all God's Creation. Through this experience their hearts are expanded to the dimensions of the love felt by Christ himself, for all people and all creatures.

The Carthusians live by a rule known as the Statutes. It declares that the hermitage is on holy ground and is a place where the monks can talk to God, where "earth meets heaven, and the divine meets the human". Carthusians aim to live in a state of constant and pure prayer, to exist in the presence of God and to maintain their hearts as an altar from which prayer rises constantly to God.

*Above A monk at La Trappe Abbey in Normandy, France, reads in front of a 1692 portrait of Father de Rancé, who was the founder of the Trappists.*

# WORKING IN THE WORLD

ANOTHER BRANCH OF THE RELIGIOUS ORDERS, KNOWN AS THE MENDICANTS, MAKES IT A PRIORITY TO PREACH THE WORD OF GOD AND TO PERFORM GOOD WORKS IN SOCIETY.

The mendicant orders are distinct from the monastic orders. The calling of monastic orders, such as the Benedictines or the Carthusians, is to live a life of self-disciplined routine and devotion in a monastery. While many monastic orders minister to the world through schools, parishes and retreat houses attached to their monasteries, the mendicant orders follow a call to engage directly with the wider world. They traditionally rely on the charity of others for support as they administer their work.

The mendicant orders also have a different organization. Brothers are attached to a province rather than to an individual monastery. They are answerable to a provincial superior general instead of to the abbot or prior of their own religious house.

Brothers and priests in the mendicant orders are known as friars, which distinguishes them from their counterparts in the monastic orders, who are called monks. "Friar" comes from the French *frère* and the Latin *frater* (both meaning "brother").

### THE FOUR GREAT ORDERS

Of the mendicant orders, four of them in particular are referred to as the "great orders": the Franciscans, the Dominicans, the Carmelites and the Augustinians. They were recognized as the four Great Orders at the Second Council of Lyon (the Fourteenth Ecumenical Council of the Roman Catholic Church) in 1274. There are other mendicant orders, which are generally known as the lesser mendicant orders (*see Catholic Mendicant Orders, left*).

The Franciscans were founded in about 1209 by St Francis of Assisi. They are sometimes called the Friars

*Above Franciscan friars gather to follow the Via Dolorosa ("Way of Grief") in Jerusalem on Good Friday. Devotions are the ground from which good works grow.*

Minor because Francis called his followers *fratres minores* ("lesser brothers") to place stress on their humility. They are traditionally called the Grey Friars because they wear a grey habit. The Dominicans were established in around 1215 by St Dominic; they are often called the Black Friars because they wear a

*Below A Carmelite friar from Aylesford Priory in Kent, England, leads local children in learning and worship. The priory was founded in the 13th century.*

## CATHOLIC MENDICANT ORDERS

The great and lesser mendicant orders are listed below, with the year they were established:

- Franciscans, founded in 1209
- Dominicans, founded *c.*1214
- Carmelites, founded *c.*1155, mendicant order from 1245
- Augustinians, founded in 1256
- Minims, founded in 1474
- Conventual Franciscans, founded in 1517
- Capuchins, founded in 1520
- Third Order Regular of St Francis, founded in 1521
- Discalced Carmelites, founded in 1568
- Discalced Trinitarians, founded in 1593
- Order of Penance, founded in 1781

*Right* *Children orphaned by the tsunami disaster of 2004 can attend a new nursery that has been set up by the Salesians of Don Bosco in Sri Lanka.*

black *cappa*, or "cloak", over a white habit. The Carmelites were founded in about 1155, originally as a contemplative order, but they became mendicants in 1245. They are also called the White Friars because they wear a white cloak over a brown habit. In 1255, the Augustinians were founded as a mendicant order from various groups of hermits by Pope Alexander IV and follow a rule based on the writings of St Augustine. They wear black garments too.

## THE FRIARS' WORK

Many thousands of friars in the mendicant orders engage with needs across the world. Augustinian friars work as teachers, missionaries and also as parish priests; there are more than 2,700 Augustinian friars serving in about 40 countries. Franciscan friars work in virtually every country in the world. They have a special calling to work with the poor, in shelters, hospitals, schools and in programmes supporting justice and peace.

Dominican friars have a special calling to preach the gospel – indeed their official title is the Order of Preachers. They are also strongly committed to communal religious life, which they see as an essential support for their preaching work. According to their constitutions, they commit themselves to study assiduously, to celebrate the liturgy and especially the Eucharist together, to persevere and "to live with one mind the common life".

Dominican friars live in priories under an elected prior, where they sing the Mass and Holy Liturgy

*Right* *Street children from Nairobi enjoy working the land at a youth centre founded in 1994 by the Salesians of Don Bosco in Langata, Kenya.*

together and share their meals and times of recreation. They commit to spreading the gospel wherever their work takes them, whether it is in hospitals, prisons, universities or schools. They see publishing books and dissemination of the gospel on the Internet as part of their work. These friars aim to emulate their founder, of whom it was said that he was always either talking to God or about God.

## TEACHING ORDERS

Some religious orders are devoted particularly to teaching in schools and colleges. The De La Salle brothers, which was founded in 17th-century France by St Jean-Baptiste de La Salle, a canon at Rheims Cathedral, runs schools in 80 countries teaching more than 900,000 students.

The Salesians of Don Bosco, which was founded in 19th-century Italy by St John Bosco, are committed to working with young people in need. The Salesians number more than 16,000 priests and brothers who work with the young in 128 countries.

The Salesians run a large number of secondary or high schools, including: in London, Farnborough and Bolton in England; in Los Angeles and Richmond, California, and New Rochelle, New York, in the United States; at Imphal and Calcutta in India; and one in Hong Kong. They also run college-level educational establishments, which include DeSales University in Pennsylvania.

# BRIDES OF CHRIST

WOMEN ENTER RELIGIOUS ORDERS TO SERVE GOD THROUGH PRAYER, DEVOTIONS AND GOOD WORKS. WOMEN CALLED TO RELIGIOUS SERVICE ARE CALLED "BRIDES OF CHRIST".

When women commit themselves to religious life they can choose to become nuns or religious sisters. The words "nun" and "sister" are often not distinguished in common usage, but strictly speaking a nun is a woman who has taken vows, committing herself to an enclosed life of prayer and contemplative devotions within a convent, while a religious sister has chosen a much more actively engaged life of service, caring for the sick, starving, poor and otherwise needy.

## LIFE IN A CONVENT

Nuns live in a monastery or a convent. A monastery is normally thought to be a community of monks

*Below* Sisters of contemplative orders work tirelessly and devotedly through prayer to bring peace and God's love to a troubled world.

and a convent to be a community of nuns, but some communities of monks are also called convents and some communities of nuns are referred to as monasteries, especially in the Benedictine tradition. (Religious communities of nuns were once also called nunneries, but this word is now archaic.)

Nuns live an enclosed life. They are not generally permitted to leave the convent or to receive visitors, although some do carry out teaching or other ministries as permitted by the constitution or rule of their particular community. Strictly, convents should be built so that the inner courtyards and gardens cannot be seen from without and the windows do not open on to public roads.

The convents are independent of one another, with each community headed by a Mother Superior. She is usually elected for life, but

*Above* Today's nuns still follow the advice of the 16th-century nun St Teresa of Avila, who taught sisters that Christ "has no hands on earth but yours".

in some constitutions the Mother Superior is subject to re-election every three years.

If the community is an abbey, she is known as an abbess, and if it is a priory she is a prioress. The distinction made between abbey and priory depends on differences in the particular religious orders and in the community's level of independence.

## STEPS TO SISTERHOOD

If a young woman feels she has a calling to the religious life as a nun or sister, she becomes a postulant for six months to a year. During this time she usually lives in the community, following the life of the nuns and sisters closely, but takes no vows. If she and the order then determine that she has a vocation, she is generally given the habit (clothing) of the order and lives for one to two years as a novice; at this point she still takes no vows. The next stage is to take temporary vows for one year or

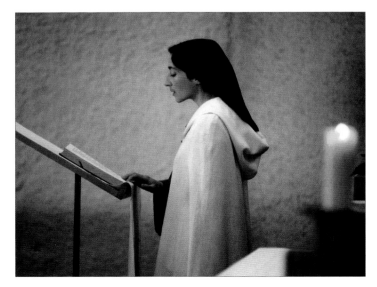

*Right Work is a form of prayer for nuns, such as for these English Benedictine sisters attentively labouring over the ironing.*

more, up to six years. The last stage is to take final vows and make perpetual profession.

The vows the nuns take will vary from one order to another. In the Benedictine tradition nuns, such as Trappistines and Cistercians, take a threefold vow of stability (to remain a member of the community), of obedience to the Mother Superior and of conversion of life (to adopt poverty and chastity). Franciscan and Dominican nuns take a vow of poverty, chastity and obedience. Some nuns take an extra vow specific to the kind of work they do or the character of their order.

## TYPES OF ORDERS

There are contemplative orders and charitable orders. Most of the strictly enclosed congregations of nuns are members of contemplative religious orders who are devoted to seeking union with God through prayer and contemplation. The Carmelite nuns, the Redemptoristines and the Poor Clares (or Order of Poor Ladies) are all examples of contemplative orders. They sometimes undertake enclosed ministries by supporting a particular type of work through prayer in the convent: for example, the Redemptoristines pray for the work of the Redemptorist friars. They often support themselves by labour in the convent — for example, by making liturgical items, such as church candles and vestments.

Women in the charitable orders are committed to performing works of charity and mercy, teaching and caring for the sick or aged. Examples include the Little Sisters of the Poor, Ursulines and the Sisters of Charity.

## THE DEVOTION OF ST THÉRÈSE

St Thérèse of Lisieux was a French Carmelite nun of the late 19th century whose spiritual autobiography, *L'histoire d'une âme* ("Story of a Soul"), published in 1898, inspired great popular devotion. She was canonized in 1925 by Pope Pius XI and in 1997 Pope John Paul II declared her a Doctor of the Universal Church. She is one of three women among the 33 Doctors of the Church.

Thérèse, who is today popularly known as "the Little Flower of Jesus", became a Carmelite novice in April 1888 at the tender age of 15, following her sisters Pauline and Marie into the order. She died of tuberculosis on 30 September 1897 when just 24 years old. Thérèse is celebrated for her "Little Way" of devotion and love, which promotes the need for trust and absolute surrender. She wrote:

*Love shows itself in deeds.... Great deeds are beyond me. The only way I can show my love is by throwing out flowers and these flowers are each a small sacrifice, each look and word, and doing of the very least thing simply for love.*

*Right St Thérèse was a teenage novice when she posed for this picture at the Carmelite house in Lisieux, c.1890.*

# LIVING FOR OTHERS

WOMEN IN THE RELIGIOUS ORDERS DEDICATE THEIR LIVES TO GOD IN CHRIST AND TO PRAYING FOR AND SERVING THOSE IN NEED BECAUSE OF POVERTY, SICKNESS OR IGNORANCE OF THE GOSPEL.

Whether nuns or religious sisters are members of a contemplative or charitable order, their religious life is intended to reach out to help other people. Enclosed orders seek to ease suffering in the world through devoted prayer, while charitable orders provide care, shelter, education and love to the needy.

### IN AN ENCLOSED ORDER

The Poor Clares, which was established in 1212 by St Clare of Assisi and St Francis of Assisi, is an enclosed contemplative order of Franciscan nuns who are committed to a life of prayer without possessions. These nuns pray the Holy Liturgy and

*Below Sisters in the Poor Clares dedicate themselves to service through prayer. Some undertake strict acts of penance, fasts and other austerities.*

celebrate Mass together. They see intercessionary prayer as an important part of their calling, and they accept prayer requests from outside the convent and pray daily for the Church and the world.

Some houses keep retreat centres in the grounds of the convent. They also work in their convent to maintain the community as well as to support themselves. To this aim, they might make candles, vestments, greeting cards or religious pictures. The nuns follow a rota for cooking, gardening, cleaning, answering calls and so on.

The nuns view the enclosed life they live as a vital spiritual discipline that expresses their love for God. They leave the enclosed community only when it is absolutely necessary – perhaps to visit the doctor or dentist or to see a parent who cannot

*Above A sister distributes medicine at an Ursuline orphanage in Guyana, South America. The Ursulines have a special calling to education and healthcare.*

travel. They are permitted to receive visits by close family members as allowed by the abbess.

### CARING FOR THE POOR

Among many orders of nuns dedicated to charitable work in the world, the Missionaries of Charity, a religious order with a special calling to serve the extremely poor, is one of the most celebrated in modern times. The order was established in 1950 by Mother Teresa of Calcutta, and today it includes 4,500 nuns working in 133 countries.

These nuns care for orphans, lepers, victims of AIDS, refugees, former prostitutes, street children, the mentally ill and those suffering in the wake of famine and natural disasters. In Calcutta, the place of their foundation, they maintain no fewer than 19 homes, including ones for the dying, for lepers and a school for street children. The nuns in this order take the conventional vows of poverty, chastity and obedience. They also take a fourth vow to offer "wholehearted and free service to the poorest of the poor".

### CARING FOR THE OLD

The Little Sisters of the Poor is a religious order with a particular calling to care for the elderly. The order

## MOTHER TERESA

Albanian Agnes Gonxha Bojaxhiu (later Mother Teresa) was a Roman Catholic nun who went to India as a missionary and took her solemn vows in 1937. She reported that she received a call from God to work with the poor in Calcutta in 1946, and in 1950 she received permission from the Vatican to establish the Diocesan Congregation of the Calcutta Diocese, which became the Missionaries of Charity. She opened her first home for the dying in Calcutta in 1952. In the 1960s, the order expanded through India and around the world. In the 1970s, she was internationally recognized for her work and received the Nobel Peace Prize in 1979. She died on 5 September 1997 and was beatified by Pope John Paul II in 2003 under the name Blessed Teresa of Calcutta.

*Right Mother Teresa declared that her mission was to care for the hungry, destitute and those without homes, for all people who feel that others do not want or love them.*

was established in 1839 in France by Jeanne Jugan, but they have a strong presence in many cities in the United States. Today the order has approximately 4,000 sisters caring for more than 22,000 elderly people in 34 countries, including India, Hong Kong, Taiwan and the United Kingdom. In the United States alone, the Little Sisters of the Poor are responsible for running 32 homes for the elderly, including houses in San Francisco, Washington, D.C., New Orleans, Indianapolis and Pittsburgh.

The Little Sisters of the Poor put into practice their founder's instuctions to always show kindness toward others, but particularly to those who are sick. Jeanne Jugan had stressed that the calling to serve the sick was a great sign of God's Grace, and she declared that because the infirm were God's creatures, when the sisters cared for the sick they were serving God himself.

The nuns rely on charitable contributions to support their work, and they generally tour the area around their home in a "begging van", in which they collect gifts not only of food but also of medical and other important supplies.

*Right The Benedictine sisters in this early 18th-century French painting by Louise Madeleine care for the sick.*

In addition to vows of obedience, chastity and poverty, the sisters take a fourth vow of hospitality. They endeavour not just to give their residents shelter, food and comfort, but also to cater for their spiritual, psychological and social needs.

### PRAYER AND DEVOTION

Sisters in charitable orders, such as the Missionaries of Charity and the Little Sisters of the Poor, anchor their active life in a routine of prayer and contemplative devotions. The Little Sisters of the Poor, for instance, will typically start the day with meditation and morning prayer, and then hold a daily Mass at the end of the morning. Residents in their homes are welcomed to this service. The sisters also take time for regular prayer throughout the day and they engage in meditative religious reading, or *lectio divina*. In addition, they meet for evening prayer at the end of the day.

# THE MISSIONS

A NUMBER OF ROMAN CATHOLIC RELIGIOUS ORDERS ARE DEDICATED
TO MISSIONARY WORK. THEY WORK ACROSS THE WORLD IN BOTH
DEVELOPED AND DEVELOPING COUNTRIES TO SPREAD THE GOSPEL.

There are many Catholic missionary orders, but the Missionaries of the Sacred Heart, an order founded in France in 1854 by French priest Jules Chevalier, is particularly notable.

## WORLDWIDE MISSION

The Sacred Heart has about 2,000 brothers and priests working around the world in more than 50 countries from Australia to Venezuela, inspired by their founder to find opportunities to serve Christ in the depths of the world's need. Chevalier was convinced that Christians could have as profound an experience of God's

*Below The brothers of some missionaries are active in helping the poverty-stricken, such as these from the Missionaries of the Poor, repairing roofs in Kingston, Jamaica.*

Grace in the world as they would in an enclosed religious community, and he declared that when brothers were helping the poor, the great power of God's love and of the Sacred Heart of Jesus would flow forth as needed. The greater the difficulties the brothers encountered in doing God's work, the greater the help God would provide.

Brothers still work in Papua New Guinea, where the order sent its first missionaries in 1882. They run the St Joseph Training Centre at Fissoa on the island of New Ireland, in which young men, many the sons of subsistence farmers from rural villages, study mathematics, English, music and religion while majoring in mechanics or carpentry. The young men also learn agricultural skills.

*Above The Sacred Heart of Jesus provides spiritual inspiration to the brothers of the Missionaries of the Sacred Heart.*

Many are given scholarships, paid from a fund set up by two of the Sacred Heart brothers.

The brothers, who are sometimes better known as MSC from the initials of their name in Latin, *Missionarii Sacratissimi Cordis*, declare that they see their work as "to be on Earth the heart of God", to meet need in whatever form they encounter it. In missions in England, Wales and Ireland, for example, they work with migrants and refugees in ecumenical interfaith initiatives and widely in education and parishes. Their motto is: "May the Sacred Heart of Jesus be everywhere loved."

On 1 September 2004, Pope John Paul II wrote to the Sacred Heart to mark its 150th anniversary, praising its founder and its work. He said that the organization's founder, Father Chevalier, established the Sacred Heart as a place for God to meet humankind, and expressed his wish that the community continue to inspire and have strength for its spiritual work. He also declared that they had a wonderful history worth remembering, but also "a great history still to be accomplished".

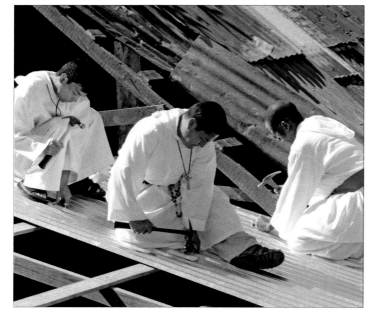

*Right A priest from the Catholic Foreign Missionary Society of America (Maryknoll) greets those attending a wedding Mass in Kibera, Nairobi, Kenya.*

## MARYKNOLL

Formerly known as the Catholic Foreign Missionary Society of America, Maryknoll sends more than 550 priests and brothers to work around the world, especially in Africa, Latin America, Korea, Japan and China. The order was founded in 1911 in the United States by Fathers James Anthony Walsh and Thomas Frederick Price.

In their mission statement, the brothers declare that, wherever they have travelled, they have been touched by the strength of human perseverance and greatly empowered by their experience of Christian faith in times of need. They work with them in declaring their faith in Jesus. The Maryknoll brothers commit themselves to standing in solidarity with the poor, to entering inter-religious dialogue, to serving as witnesses of Christ, to celebrating the Church's liturgy and to proclaiming the gospel and teaching the faith.

The society is linked to the Maryknoll Sisters of St Dominic, a group of religious sisters founded in 1912, in the United States. More than 700 Maryknoll Sisters work in 30 countries, including Albania, Panama, Nepal, Sudan and Taiwan. The sisters are associated with setting up convent schools. Widely known examples are Maryknoll Convent School in Kowloon Tong, Hong Kong, and Miriam College in Quezon City, Manila, the Philippines.

## OTHER MISSIONS

The larger religious orders, while not formed primarily to carry out missionary outreach, do a great deal of

work of this kind. Among many examples, Capuchin Franciscans maintain missions in Central America (Panama and Nicaragua) and in South Africa. In Pretoria, South Africa, for example, they run the Damietta Peacemaking Initiative to promote non-violence and peace, from Padre Pio Friary in Rietvallei.

The Jesuits spread the gospel through their outreach work in educational establishments, orphanages, hospitals and community centres as part of their overseas missions – notably in Guyana, Zimbabwe and South Africa. The Carmelites also maintain several missions, including ones in Kenya, Mozambique, Indonesia, East Timor,

Burkina Faso, Cameroon and the Democratic Republic of Congo. In Kenya, for instance, the Carmelites have established an enclosed monastery in Machakos and a house of formation in Ngong diocese.

Another notable order is the Missionaries of La Salette, which was founded in 1852 in La Salette, near Grenoble, France, where a shrine to the Blessed Virgin Mary was established. The order has around 1,000 nuns, priests and lay members working in support of healing and reconciliation in North America and Europe, as well as performing missionary work in countries such as Madagascar, the Philippines, Bolivia, Myanmar, Namibia and Angola.

*Right Franciscan sisters demonstrate God's love for the helpless by running an orphanage school in northern Egypt.*

# LAY GROUPS

THE CHURCH ENDORSES THE WORK OF SEVERAL ORGANIZATIONS THAT WERE ESTABLISHED TO HELP LAY CATHOLICS FOLLOW THE GOSPEL IN THEIR RELIGIOUS WORK AND FAMILY LIVES.

The largest lay group, Opus Dei (Latin for "God's work") is a Roman Catholic organization of predominately lay people who seek to grow closer to God and achieve sanctity through work and everyday activities, including family life. There are around 87,000 members worldwide, in 80 countries; 98 per cent are lay people and just 2 per cent priests. Approximately 30 per cent of lay members (called numeraries) are celibate and live in Opus Dei centres, while roughly 70 per cent (called supernumeraries) are married and serve God in family life.

The movement was founded in 1928 in Spain by Roman Catholic priest Josemaría Escrivá and received approval in 1950 from Pope Pius XII.

In 1982, Pope John Paul II declared the organization a personal prelature within the Church, under the name the Prelature of the Holy Cross and Opus Dei. This means that it functions like a religious order. The Church governs Opus Dei members through a prelate, who is appointed by the pope, and has a status equivalent to that of a superior general in a religious order. The members remain part of local church congregations.

As an organization, Opus Dei runs high schools, colleges, university halls of residence, business and agricultural schools, and it also does charitable work. In Spain, it founded and runs the University of Navarre at Pamplona. It also runs a university at Piura in Peru.

**Above** *Pope John XXIII stands between St Josemaría Escrivá and Msgr Álvaro del Portillo, another leading Opus Dei figure, in 1960.*

### A SECULAR ROUTINE

Josemaría Escrivá encouraged people to try to "convert their work into prayer". He described a dream in which God's children could sanctify themselves although they lived as ordinary citizens. It was through regular work and the mundane routine of everyday life that people could find God's love.

Escrivá died in 1975. Pope John Paul II beatified him in 1992 and proclaimed him a saint in 2002. John Paul II declared Escrivá the "saint of ordinary life", adding that he disseminated through society the awareness that a calling to holiness is received by all, with no distinctions of culture, racial identity, social class or age.

### SPIRITUALITY

Opus Dei members are expected to follow a set form of personal devotions every day, including Mass, and to attend a weekly confession. They should also attend an annual spiritual retreat of three weeks for numeraries and one week for supernumeraries.

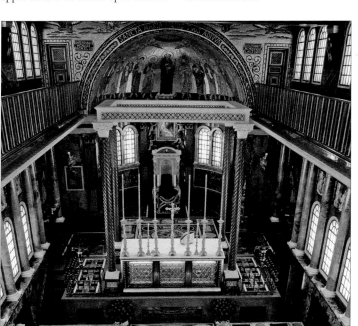

**Left** *The Church of Our Lady of Peace in Rome is the headquarters of Opus Dei. Many pray at the crypt of St Josemaría Escrivá.*

Spiritual practice for a member of Opus Dei often includes an element of sacrifice by voluntarily offering discomfort or pain to God. This can simply involve self-sacrifice in terms of self-denial and charity in dealing with others. However, some celibate numeraries are said to practise physical mortification by either wearing a spike metal chain known as a cilice on the upper thigh or by flailing themselves with a woven cotton strap known as a discipline.

## A CRITICIZED PRACTICE

Self-mortification is one of many areas in which Opus Dei has been criticized. Opponents attack the practice as being akin to masochism and even liable to undermine spiritual development by fostering

*Above A statue of St Josemaría Escrivá, founder of Opus Dei, stands in an alcove of the basilica façade within the Vatican.*

pride. However, defenders of the practice respond that it is a valued way of identifying with Christ's physical suffering, has been used by Christians for centuries and is more used today in the Roman Catholic Church than is generally known.

## A SECRETIVE SOCIETY

Opus Dei has been accused by some of being both secretive and manipulative. They claim that a number of leading politicians around the world are members of the society, although few make public statement of their membership. Some people suggest that the organization dominates members and uses overly aggressive recruitment techniques. Opus Dei, however, states that members are not coerced into joining and people are free to leave if they want to.

## OTHER LAY GROUPS

Many of the major religious orders also support lay associates: for example, the Dominican laity have their own rule, the Rule of the Lay Fraternities of St Dominic, first issued in 1285, while Franciscan lay

followers are members of the Secular Franciscan Order and follow a rule established for secular followers by St Francis himself in 1221. Secular Franciscans have a novitiate and formal profession, but they are not bound by their religious vows, and can be married and live ordinary lives in the community.

Among the other Catholic lay bodies is the Catenian Association, which is an international brotherhood of Catholic professionals and businessmen. It was established in 1908 in Manchester, England, and now has about 10,000 members in Australia, Ireland, South Africa, Malta, Zimbabwe and Zambia, as well as in the United Kingdom.

Their aims are to develop social bonds and foster brotherly love among members. The association grants bursaries to provide partial support for young Catholics who are performing community work. The Catenians also maintain a Public Affairs Committee that monitors and speaks out on any proposed legislation that would contradict Catholic teaching.

*Above The Catenian Association has sponsored projects to help the needy in Mexico and Africa, such as at this children's home in Zambia.*

---

### IN RECOGNITION FOR CHRISTIAN SERVICE

The Association of Papal Orders is an organization for people who have been awarded papal knighthoods. These awards are made at five levels to people who have provided a great service to the Catholic Church. The five levels are:
• Supreme Order of Christ
• Pontifical Order of the Golden Spur
• Pontifical Order of Pius IX
• Pontifical Order of St Gregory the Great
• Pontifical Order of Pope St Sylvester.
Notable recipients of the awards include Prince Rainier III of Monaco (Pontifical Order of the Golden Spur), former German Federal Chancellor Helmut Kohl (Pontifical Order of St Gregory the Great) and the Hollywood entertainer Bob Hope (Pontifical Order of Pope St Sylvester).

# LIVING THE SACRAMENTS

There are seven sacraments through which practising Catholics receive God's Grace. These are baptism, confirmation, the Eucharist, penance and reconciliation (popularly known as confession), "the anointing of the sick", holy orders and Holy Matrimony. According to the *Catechism of the Catholic Church*, the sacraments were "instituted by Christ and entrusted to the Church". They are stages in the spiritual life – from new birth as a Christian in baptism and confirmation, through to the anointing of the sick, often administered at the end of earthly life before the final journey into eternal life. The sacraments help individual Catholics make spiritual progress and grow in holiness.

Most people do not receive all seven sacraments: only some have a priestly vocation and receive holy orders, for example, and all who receive holy orders (except already married deacons) cannot receive Holy Matrimony. Individuals must be prepared to receive the sacraments. God's Grace may be blocked from working if someone is not disposed to receive it. For a sacrament to be effective, a person must have faith in it, although at the same time the sacraments in themselves strengthen and give expression to a person's faith.

Particular objects used by the clergy, including the special robes or vestments that a priest or bishop wears when celebrating the Eucharist or the Liturgy of the Hours, are termed "sacramentals". They are material things blessed or set apart to summon the respect believers should have for the sacraments of the Church – in the words of the *Baltimore Catechism* (a Catholic school text in the United States) "to excite good thoughts and increase devotion".

*Above The last rites performed for a dying person include celebration of the Eucharist, depicted in Hieronymus Bosch's 15th–16th-century painting* Death and Last Rites.

*Left The Eucharist is central among the sacraments. All seven sacraments are connected to Christ's paschal mystery – his redemptive sacrifice that is re-enacted in the Eucharist.*

# GOD'S HOUSE

THE FIRST CHRISTIANS WORSHIPPED IN PRIVATE HOUSES, BUT OVER TIME CHURCHES HAVE DEVELOPED INTO SUBSTANTIAL PUBLIC BUILDINGS THAT SERVE AS THE CENTRE OF ROMAN CATHOLIC LIFE.

The earliest public churches were built after Christianity was adopted as the state religion of the Roman Empire in the 4th century AD. They were based on the Roman basilica, a large roofed public building often used as a courthouse or market. Like the basilica, the early churches had a central hall, known as the nave, with a timber roof and an aisle on each side, which were separated from the nave by a line of columns.

A wooden altar was established toward one end of the nave. In the first churches, the altar was typically at the west end of the nave, in imitation of the arrangement in the Jewish Temple in Jerusalem. The bishop or

***Above** The Jewish Temple in Jerusalem, shown in this c. 1728 Jewish manuscript, was an inspiration to early Christians, who based part of their church layout on it.*

priest celebrating the Eucharist faced east – on the grounds that it was the direction of the heavenly Jerusalem and thus it was from this direction that Christ would return in glory – and so he always looked toward the congregation. For unknown reasons, in about the 6th century the arrangement was reversed, with the altar at the east end of the nave.

Beyond the altar was the apse, basically a semicircular or sometimes rectangular recess, usually vaulted, occupied by the bishop and priests during services. When celebrating the Eucharist, the bishop or priest, who continued to face east, looked toward the apse and away from the worshippers in the nave. The area around the altar, which was set aside for the clergy, became known as the presbytery or sanctuary.

***Left** The west front of Lincoln Cathedral in England incorporates elements dating from 1072. The main part of the cathedral is 13th-century, in the Gothic style.*

At the west end, a long entrance porch called the narthex ran across the full width of the nave and led into the nave. Unbaptized believers and penitents generally remained in the narthex, where they were separated from clergy and other believers.

## THE BEMA AND THE CHOIR

There were many variations of these areas. In some churches, a wooden platform called the bema was built in the centre of the nave. The clergy sat in this area and read lessons and delivered sermons from the lectern on the bema. In some large churches, the eastern end of the nave began to be fenced off with a small railing to form an area for the choir, and sometimes the choir area was attached to the bema. This arrangement survives to this day in the Basilica di Santa Maria Maggiore (AD 430–40) in Rome. More typically, the choir area became a separate architectural feature connecting the nave and sanctuary.

## CRUCIFORM PLAN

In some churches, a transept was added on a north–south axis, perpendicular to the nave, to form a church shaped like a cross. The point at which the transept cuts across the nave was known as "the crossing": the nave usually extended to the west of the crossing and the choir and sanctuary lay to the east. The arms of the crossing were called north

*Above* The altar stands at the centre of the Metropolitan Cathedral of Christ the King, Liverpool, England, surrounded on all sides by seats. The designer was aiming to help the congregation feel more linked to the liturgy.

transept and south transept: at each end of these, additional altars were added in honour of particular saints. Often a dome was built above the crossing. A good example of this design is the magnificent 11th-century Basilica of San Michele Maggiore in Pavia, Italy. In some cathedrals – for instance at Lincoln (built 1092–1311) and Salisbury (1220–58), both in England – a second, smaller transept was built to the east of the main one.

## HALL CHURCH

In Italy in the 15th and 16th centuries, the hall church design was developed to reduce the long distance between entrance and altar. At this time, during the Counter-

Reformation (the Catholic Church's response to the rise of Protestantism), Church authorities wanted to promote the importance of preaching: a pulpit was introduced halfway down the nave and large side chapels were built nearby. A fine example of this design is the Church of the Gesù in Rome, the mother church of the Society of Jesus, or Jesuits, built in around 1568 by Giacomo da Vignola and Giacomo Della Porta.

## GREEK CHURCH DESIGN

From early times, many Eastern churches were built on the plan of a Greek cross – a cross with four arms of equal length. Rather than have the crossing toward one end of a long nave, these churches had four equally sized wings meeting at a central crossing. The crossing point was generally square and domed. One good example is the 6th-century Church of Hagia Sophia in Istanbul (which eventually became a mosque and is now a museum).

This design returned to relevance in Western churches of the late 20th century, many of which put the altar toward the centre of the church to symbolize the centrality of the Mass in Catholic life. Two examples include the Metropolitan Cathedral of Christ the King in Liverpool, England (1958–70), and the Cathedral of Saint Mary of the Assumption, which was built in San Francisco, California (1967–71).

## THE ROOD SCREEN AND REREDOS

In many medieval churches, a wooden screen separated the faithful in the nave from the clergy and other celebrants in the choir and sanctuary. The screen consisted of a large carved cross (or "rood") with an image of Jesus upon it, often flanked by carvings of the Blessed Virgin Mary and St John looking on. The structure was called the rood screen or choir screen. Many churches also had decorated screens behind the altar in the east. This often profoundly beautiful structure was called an altar piece or reredos.

*Right* The intricately carved rood screen in the Gothic church of Saint-Etienne-du-Mont in Paris, France, has spiral staircases on either side.

# GREAT CHURCHES

FROM ROME TO LOS ANGELES, FROM THE 4TH TO THE 21ST CENTURY,
THE BASILICAS AND CATHEDRALS OF THE ROMAN CATHOLIC CHURCH
ARE AMONG THE WORLD'S MOST INSPIRATIONAL BUILDINGS.

Traditionally, the apostle Peter went to Rome and became the Church's first bishop. He was martyred in Rome and was buried in a Christian cemetery on *Mons Vaticanus*, where the Vatican now stands. Emperor Constantine built a basilica on the site in AD 326–33. However, by the end of the 15th century this building was in poor condition.

## ST PETER'S BASILICA

The Basilica di San Pietro diVaticano, better known as St Peter's Basilica, was built on the same site as the original basilica over more than a century, 1506–1626, and was consecrated in 1628. Among its many architects were Donato Bramante, Michelangelo and Gian Lorenzo Bernini. It stands withinVatican City – reputedly with St Peter's grave beneath its altar – and is considered the most holy church for Catholics

worldwide. Many popes, including John Paul II in 2005, have been buried in this basilica.

## MEDIEVAL CATHEDRALS

In the Middle Ages, the pope was often at odds with the Holy Roman emperor. During this time the great St Peter's Basilica in Rome was rivalled by the imperial church at Aachen (which is now part of western Germany), the most historic cathedral in northern Europe. At the heart of this church is the Palatine Chapel, which was founded by Charlemagne, King of the Franks, in 792 and consecrated to the Blessed Virgin Mary in 805 by Pope Leo III. German kings (and later emperors)

*Below Filippo Brunelleschi's breathtaking dome at Florence Cathedral contains 4 million bricks. With the lantern at its top, it is 114.5m (375ft) high.*

*Above The throne of Charlemagne on which Holy Roman emperors were crowned stands in the upper gallery of the Palatine Chapel in Aachen, Germany.*

were crowned in the Palatine Chapel for more than 600 years, between 936 and 1531.

Charlemagne himself was buried in a vault beneath the cathedral on his death in 814, and the cathedral became an attraction for pilgrims throughout the Middle Ages, when it was known as the Royal Church of St Mary at Aachen. The golden Shrine of St Mary was built in the choir in 1220–39 to contain four sacred relics: Christ's swaddling cloth, his loincloth, Mary's cloak and the beheading cloth of John the Baptist. Every seven years to the present day the relics are removed from the shrine and put on display for pilgrims.

There are other great European cathedrals of the Middle Ages and Renaissance, including the grand 13th-century Gothic cathedral of Chartres in France, celebrated for its magnificent stained-glass windows, and the Basilica di Santa Maria del Fiore, also known as Florence Cathedral, with its glorious 14th-century campanile (bell tower) partly designed by Giotto, the bronze doors of 1403–24 on the baptistery by

*Above* The Basilica of Our Lady of Peace in Yamoussoukro, Ivory Coast, was built with the finest Italian marble as well as 7,000sq m (75,350sq ft) of stained glass.

*Above* Light falling through the glass roof creates striking patterns in the Catedral Metropolitana Nossa Senhora Aparecida.

Lorenzo Ghiberti and the octagonal dome that was built in 1420–36 by Filippo Brunelleschi.

## MODERN RIVALS

The cathedral at Florence was built to rival St Peter's Basilica in size and grandeur, and this desire survived into the late 20th century. The Basilica of Our Lady of Peace in Yamoussoukro, Ivory Coast, Africa, was modelled on St Peter's, built in 1985–90 and consecrated by Pope John Paul II on 10 September 1990. It was designed to be the greatest Catholic church in the world: it covers a slightly larger area than St Peter's – 3 hectares (7.4 acres) compared to 2.3 hectares (5.7 acres). However, critics point out that the area includes a villa and rectory, which are not part of the church, and that the Ivory Coast basilica has a smaller capacity at 18,000 people, compared with 60,000 for St Peter's.

In Liverpool, England, the Metropolitan Cathedral of Christ the King was built in the 1960s to a design by Sir Frederick Gibberd. Its circular plan was drawn up in response to the call by the Second Vatican Council for increased participation by the laity in the sacred liturgy. The cathedral was consecrated on the Feast of Pentecost, 14 May 1967. Another strikingly modern, circular cathedral is the Catedral Metropolitana Nossa Senhora Aparecida in Brasilia, Brazil. It was designed by Oscar Niemeyer, built from 1958 onward and was consecrated on 31 May 1970.

### OUR LADY OF THE ANGELS

The greatest Roman Catholic church dedicated in the early 21st century is surely the outwardly austere, inwardly beautiful Cathedral of Our Lady of the Angels in downtown Los Angeles, California. It was begun in 1997 to designs by Spanish architect José Rafael Moneo, and opened in September 2002. It incorporates a plaza of 1,860sq m (20,000sq ft) and a main sanctuary 100m (333ft) in length and up to 30m (100ft) high. It has superb bronze doors, created by artist Robert Graham, which pay homage across the centuries to Ghiberti's bronze doors in the Florence baptistery.

*Right* The Cathedral of Our Lady of the Angels is 12 storeys high and is specially designed to resist earthquake damage.

# THE ALTAR OF GOD

THE ALTAR, AT WHICH THE PRIEST CELEBRATES THE EUCHARIST, IS THE FOCAL POINT OF THE SANCTUARY. IT IS REVERED BY CHRISTIANS AS THE *MENSA DOMINI* ("TABLE OF THE LORD").

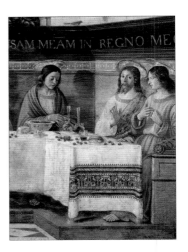

The sanctuary itself is the area set aside for the priest celebrant, deacons and other ministers. It is usually raised above the rest of the church, with its area demarcated by a low rail. Within the sanctuary, the altar is the principal furnishing. The altar represents the table at which Christ shared the Last Supper with his apostles and instituted the Eucharist.

The Church teaches that the altar also stands for Jesus himself and for the Cross on which his sacrifice was made: for these reasons, it is

*Above* The altar stands in for the table used at the Last Supper by Christ and the apostles, which is shown in Domenico Ghirlandaio's 15th-century painting.

honoured with incense. Numbers are often symbolic to Catholics, and the five crosses carved on it represent Jesus' Five Sacred Wounds.

The table or horizontal top of the altar is normally made of natural stone because it embodies Christ, described in the First Letter of Peter as "that living stone, rejected by men but in God's sight chosen and precious" (1 Peter 2:3–4). Although the support of the tabletop can be of any material, the altar should honour Christ by being simple and beautiful.

## SANCTIFIED BY RELICS

The altar stands on a raised platform called the predella. This is often made of wood. For symbolic reasons, the steps leading up to it are normally an uneven number – three, five or seven – and each about 15cm (6in) high. The steps may be of stone, wood or

*Left* Three steps mount to the main altar in St Patrick's Cathedral, New York City. The sanctuary was renovated in the 1930s to 1940s, when the elegant baldacchino (canopy) was added.

brick. If there are three steps, they are used to distinguish between ranks of ministers at the Eucharist: the celebrant will stand on the predella, the deacon on the second step and a subdeacon or another lower-ranking minister on the third step.

Beneath the altar is a box called the sepulchrum, used for containing a holy relic and other specific objects. The box has a gold, silver or lead reliquary to hold part of the bodily remains of a saint, together with three grains of incense and a parchment certifying that the altar has been consecrated. If possible, the relic is of the saint in whose name the church was built. The relics were traditionally placed within the altar, but they are now set beneath it. Catholics do not worship the relics or saints. The saints are honoured as men and women of great holiness, exemplars of the Christian life. The relics remind believers that the Eucharist celebrated on the altar is a source of God's Grace, the grace that enabled the saints to live such holy lives.

## MARKING A CELEBRATION
For a celebration three white cloths are laid on the altar. Two candles are lighted to celebrate a Low Mass, one

*Below A burning candle marks the presence of the blessed sacrament within the tabernacle (centre). Its presence further sanctifies the altar as the table of the Lord.*

spoken by a priest without incense or the presence of a deacon or subdeacon; but six candles are required for a High Mass, a solemn celebration with music.

## THE TABERNACLE
The gifts of the bread and the wine are consecrated during the Mass and distributed to the people. Some consecrated bread and wine – the blessed sacrament – is reserved in the tabernacle, a small carved metal container. The tabernacle is usually kept within the sanctuary, on the altar or at the side, but in some churches it is kept in a separate side chapel. It is sometimes kept beneath a small canopy or conopaeum.

A candle must always be kept burning above the tabernacle. This is called the altar lamp, or sanctuary light. The light reminds the faithful of the presence of Christ in the blessed sacrament and it embodies Christ, called in the Gospel of John "the true light that enlightens every man" (John 1:9). The light is an expression of the burning love of the faithful for their Lord. Although more than one light may be on the tabernacle, there are always uneven numbers lit: three, five, seven and so on.

## GOSPEL AND SERMONS
In many churches, a raised pulpit stands at the front of the sanctuary, on the left-hand side of the church as

you face the altar. The gospel and sermons or homilies are traditionally delivered from this pulpit. On the right-hand side of the sanctuary as you face the altar is usually a lectern, from which the Epistle is generally read. Although lay people can use the lectern, only members of the clergy can use the pulpit. Some churches do not have pulpit and lectern. Instead, they have a single podium, called an ambo, in the space otherwise occupied by the pulpit.

### PRIESTLY CHAIR
The sanctuary also contains a chair for the priest celebrant. Although this chair should not be grandiose, it should reflect the dignity of the priest's role in administering the sacrament of the Eucharist. In a cathedral, the bishop has a permanent chair called the cathedra and another chair is placed alongside for other priest celebrants. Additional chairs are provided for deacons and other ministers.

*Above The sanctuary of the 13th-century St Asaph Cathedral in Denbighshire, North Wales, contains the bishop's seat.*

# VESTMENTS

WHEN CELEBRATING THE LITURGY OF THE CATHOLIC CHURCH, MEMBERS OF THE CLERGY WEAR SPECIAL ROBES OR VESTMENTS THAT SYMBOLIZE ASPECTS OF A PRIEST'S SPIRITUAL ROLE.

The celebrant's vestments distinguish him from the people and remind him of his vocation and duties, and the holiness of the acts he undertakes. The wearing of priestly vestments has historical roots going right back to the early days of Christianity – and even beyond to the Old Testament age, when the Jewish priests of Aaron wore ritual garb.

To celebrate the liturgy and in processions, clerics traditionally wear a cassock, a long, close-fitting cloak with buttons down the front, so-called from the Italian *casacca* for "greatcoat". Priests generally wear a black cassock, while bishops wear a purple one and cardinals a red one (or a black one with red piping). The pope's cassock is always white.

## VESTMENTS FOR EUCHARIST
To celebrate the Eucharist, a priest also wears an alb, a cincture, a stole and a chasuble. An alb is a full-length white linen gown worn over the priest's cassock. It is a descendant of the white toga worn by the ancient Romans and takes its name from the Latin word *albus*, meaning "white". The alb's colour symbolizes purity. Around the waist the priest secures the alb with a braided linen or woollen cord called the cincture, from the Latin *cinctura*, meaning "girdle". It is usually white, like the alb. The cincture is worn to symbolize the priest's chastity.

Around his neck and across his shoulders, the priest wears a long decorated strip of material called a stole. It should be approximately 200cm (80in) long and 5–10cm (2–4in) in width. The stole generally has a cross embroidered at each end and in the middle (the part worn behind the neck); the middle cross is required because the priest must

*Below Kneeling deacons wear the alb (full-length white gown), cincture (cord belt) and stole (strip across shoulder and chest).*

*Above Many priests still wear a black cassock for day-to-day duties, but some wear a suit with shirt and clerical collar.*

kiss this when putting on the stole. Bishops wear the stole in the same manner as priests; deacons wear it over the left shoulder and diagonally across the chest.

The priest wears a decorated outer garment called the chasuble over his vestments. The chasuble is usually made of silk or velvet and often has a large cross on the back. Its name derives from the Latin *casula*, which means "little house", because the over garment provides protection or shelter for the priest. The chasuble symbolizes the yoke of Christ and the virtue of charity.

he censes the priest and the paten. The priest lifts the Host and then places it back on the paten on the altar and kneels in adoration.

The priest raises the chalice and recounts Christ's actions in taking a cup of wine, giving thanks and praise to the Father in heaven, then giving it to the disciples, stating, "Take this all of you and drink from it". The priest refers to the contents in the cup as "the blood of the new and everlasting covenant" and continues by stating that blood was shed for humankind so that its sins will be forgiven. At this point, an acolyte once again rings a bell to signal the moment of consecration, and if incense is being used, he will cense the priest and chalice.

## COMMUNION RITE

Before the congregation receives the Eucharist, all join in repeating the Lord's Prayer, then they share a sign of peace according to local custom. The priest breaks the Host and puts a piece in the chalice in what is called the rite of fraction, and prays: "May this mingling of the body and blood of our Lord Jesus Christ bring eternal life to all who receive it."

*Below In today's Mass, communicants receive the consecrated Host when the priest places it on the tongue.*

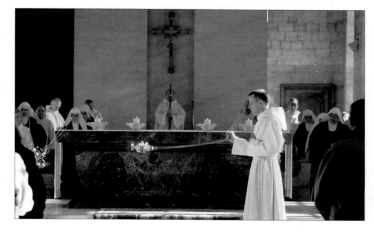

*Above Incense signifies the sanctity of the altar and of the gifts of bread and wine that become the Lord's body and blood.*

The priest says a prayer of personal devotion, then presents the Host (consecrated bread) to the congregation with the words, "This is the Lamb of God who takes away the sins of the world. Happy are those who are called to his supper." All present respond with the words, "Lord I am not worthy to receive you" and finish off with "say the word and I shall be healed".

The priest receives Communion himself and distributes it to other ministers and deacons, and then to the congregation, who usually

come forward in procession. Each communicant bows, then receives the Host on the tongue (in the past it was sometimes received in the hand); the priest declares "the body of Christ" and the communicant responds "Amen". The communicant is offered the chalice and the priest declares "the blood of Christ".

It is possible for communicants to receive only the Host, and for the priest to dip the Host into the wine and present it in that form, laying it on the communicant's tongue; this is called intinction. Usually, the congregation sings a Communion song throughout this period.

Afterward, the chalice, paten and other vessels are washed and dried and placed on the altar and the priest declaims a prayer after Communion. At this point notices are read out, then the priest gives one of a choice of blessings on the people and pronounces one of a choice of dismissals. All include the phrase "Go in peace"; the variant based on the original Latin dismissal (*Ite, missa est*), which gives the Mass its name, is "The Mass is ended. Go in peace". The congregation responds, "Thanks be to God." Then the priest kisses the altar, makes a customary reverence with other ministers and leaves. A hymn is often sung at the close of the service.

# BAPTISM

IN THE SACRAMENT OF BAPTISM, AN INDIVIDUAL IS REBORN AS A
CHRISTIAN AND GAINS A SANCTIFYING GRACE THAT ENABLES HIM OR
HER TO SHARE IN THE LIFE OF GOD – FATHER, SON AND HOLY SPIRIT.

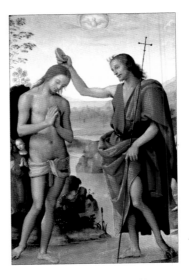

*Above When Jesus was baptized by
John the Baptist, the Holy Spirit
descended upon him. Perugino captured
the scene in this* c. 1500 painting,
Baptism of Christ in the Jordan.

Most Catholics are baptized as
infants, but those who convert to
Catholicism can be baptized as an
adult if they have not previously been
baptized in another Christian
denomination. With confirmation
and Holy Communion, baptism is
listed as one of three sacraments of
initiation that prepares an individual
for life as a Christian.

According to the *Catechism of
the Catholic Church*, baptism is the
backbone of the complete Christian
life, "the gateway to life in the spirit";
through baptism people are united
with Christ and are "incorporated
into the Church and made sharers in
Her mission". In baptism, people join
the priesthood of believers.

## A NEW BIRTH

One of the key biblical texts that
supports baptism is from Jesus'
words to Nicodemus, "Truly, truly,
I say to you, unless one is born of
water and the Spirit, he cannot enter
the kingdom of God" (John 3:5).
Baptism is a symbolic rebirth: and
only through baptism can believers
come to the other sacraments of
Christian life.

According to Catholic doctrine,
baptism frees an individual from
original sin (the mark of human sinfulness with which all are tainted, and
which derives from the disobedience
to God's commandments of the first
people, Adam and Eve, in the Garden
of Eden). For this reason, practising
Catholics believe they must baptize
their children as infants; should the
children die unbaptized, they would
remain tainted by original sin and
their salvation would be prevented.
Baptism also liberates people from
their own sins and from any punishment deriving from these.

## RITE OF BAPTISM

In normal circumstances, the rite of
baptism involves friends or relatives
of the child's parents as "godparents";
they hold a responsibility to help the
parents in raising the baptized child
as a Christian. The bishop, priest or
deacon greets both the parents and
godparents and reminds them of
the responsibilities attendant on
bringing an infant to baptism, which
include training the infant "in the
practice of the faith" and keeping
God's commandments "as Christ
taught us, by loving God and our

*Below Our Lord explains the necessity
of being "born of water and the Spirit" to
Nicodemus, depicted in this 17th-century
painting by Crijn Hendricksz Volmarijn.*

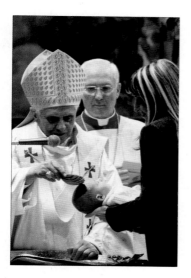

*Above An infant is baptized by Pope Benedict XVI. The catechism teaches that by being baptized "we are freed from sin and reborn as sons of God".*

neighbour". He then leads the parents (and godparents if desired) in tracing the Cross of Christ on the infant's forehead.

Readings from the Holy Gospel and a homily or sermon follow. The celebrant leads the prayer of the faithful that calls on God to "bathe this child in light" and give the child "new life of baptism" and asks that the child is welcomed into the holy

Church. The prayers also call on God to "renew the grace of our baptism in each one of us".

The celebrant invokes the Blessed Virgin and the saints, and proceeds to a prayer of exorcism and anointing before baptism in which he calls on God to free the child from original sin and "make him (or her) a temple of your glory". He then anoints the infant with oil in Christ's name.

SACRED WATERS

At the font, the celebrant recites an introductory prayer. The priest blesses the water in the font, then once again reminds the parents and godparents of their responsibility to raise the infant in the Catholic faith. He asks them to make three professions of their faith: in God the Father; in Jesus Christ; and in the Holy Spirit. As he says this he refers to the Catholic Church and the communion of saints, as well as Jesus' Resurrection and everlasting life. All present then announce their belief in these things: "This is our faith. This is the faith of the Church." They then declare that they are proud of their profession.

Then the celebrant baptizes the infant, saying the child's name and declaring, "I baptize you in the name of the Father and of the Son and of the Holy Spirit." At each naming of God, he either pours water over

*Above A Catholic convert leans over a font as she is baptized in the Cathedral of Notre-Dame de Paris — the celebrant is using a traditional scallop shell.*

the infant's forehead or immerses the child in the water of the font. The celebrant anoints the infant with chrism, or holy oil, and clothes him or her in a white garment as an "outward sign of Christian dignity". The baptism usually concludes with the celebrant reaffirming that the infant has been reborn in baptism, leading the congregation in the Lord's Prayer, then giving a blessing.

## SYMBOLIC WATER

When the main baptism takes place at the font, the celebrant's introductory prayer identifies water as a symbol of God's grace and a "wellspring of holiness". The waters of baptism are likened to those that existed before the Creation and on which God breathed, to those of Noah's flood, to the waters of the Red Sea that parted as the Israelites were led out of Egypt, to those of the Jordan in which Christ himself was baptized and to the waters mixed with blood that flowed from his side on the Cross.

*Right A font holds holy water used for baptism — this 12th-century Belgian font depicts Jesus' own baptism.*

# CONFIRMATION

PEOPLE WHO RECEIVE THE SACRAMENT OF CONFIRMATION ARE
ANOINTED WITH HOLY OIL. THE RITE CONFIRMS AND STRENGTHENS
THE GRACE THEY DERIVED FROM BAPTISM.

Confirmation is the second of the three sacraments of initiation, and is traditionally delivered after baptism and before the Eucharist. In the early Church and the Eastern Church today, these three sacraments are delivered in a single occasion in early childhood, but in the Western Church (in the Latin Rite) confirmation is delayed until late childhood, at a time when the recipient can understand the significance of the sacrament. When adults are baptized, they usually receive the three sacraments at the same time and in the traditional order.

In most cases in the Western Church, only a bishop can administer the sacrament of confirmation, but priests have been authorized to confirm adult converts and children who are at risk of death; the priest uses chrism or holy oil blessed by the

*Below* The laying on of hands is a key part of confirmation. As descendants of the apostles, bishops perform the rite.

bishop. The chrism is blessed in a special service, the Chrism Mass, on Holy Thursday during Easter Week.

## THE GIFT OF THE SPIRIT
The Church places an emphasis on the connection between confirmation and the Feast of Pentecost, when the Holy Spirit descended on Christ's apostles. Bishops, as successors to the apostles, administer confirmation. There is also a biblical precedent for the practice of bishops imparting the Holy Spirit to others through the laying on of hands. Acts 8:15–17 describes when the apostles Peter and John went to the Christians in Samaria and "prayed for them that they might receive the Holy Spirit, for it had not yet fallen upon any of them; they had only been baptized in the name of the Lord Jesus. Then they laid hands on them and they received the Holy Spirit."

In the Latin Rite used by the Western Catholic Church, the confirmation service begins with those

*Above* A bishop anoints candidates for confirmation with chrism, signifying the mark of the Holy Spirit, in this 15th-century painting by Rogier van der Weyden.

ready for confirmation, known as confirmands, renewing their baptismal vows and professing their faith. The bishop extends his hands over them and prays: "All-powerful God, Father of our Lord Jesus Christ, by water and the Holy Spirit you freed your sons and daughters from sin and gave them new life…". Then he anoints each confirmand with chrism. The bishop says, "Be sealed with the gift of the Holy Spirit." The anointing is accompanied by a laying on of hands by the bishop. The phrase "be sealed" signifies that the newly confirmed belongs to Christ in God. The seal marks the Christian as being enrolled in Christ's service and also provides a promise of divine protection. At the close of the service the bishop makes the sign of peace over the newly confirmed Christians.

In the Eastern Catholic Church, a priest generally administers the sacraments of baptism, confirmation (usually referred to as Chrismation) and Communion in a single ceremony. The priest will use chrism blessed by the bishop, anointing the recipient on the forehead, eyes, nose, ears, lips, breast, back, hands and feet, each time, declaring "The seal of the gift that is the Holy Spirit".

## ITS BENEFITS

The sacrament is called confirmation in the Western Church because it confirms, completes, strengthens and deepens the grace imparted by baptism. In confirmation, according to the catechism, baptized members of the faithful are "more perfectly bound to the Church", "enriched with a special strength of the Holy Spirit" and thereby "more strictly obliged to spread and defend the faith by word and deed".

The sacrament connects believers "more firmly to Christ" and unites the faithful in "divine filiation" (the condition of being a child of God). While baptism brings Christians into the priesthood of believers, confirmation perfects this priesthood and, according to St Thomas Aquinas, "The confirmed person receives the power to profess faith in Christ publicly and as it were officially (*quasi ex officio*)."

## FIRST COMMUNION

In the Western Church, the occasion on which a young person receives Holy Communion (when he or she participates in the Eucharist) for the first time, is often celebrated with a family party. Especially in the United States and Ireland, these celebrations can be lavish: boys dress in a suit and girls wear a special white dress with a veil and gloves. In some countries, a girl wears a dress handed down from her mother or sister; in others, she will take First Communion in school uniform plus veil and gloves. In many Latin American countries, boys dress in a uniform with military-style aigullettes (braided cords) for the ceremony.

## CONFIRMATION AFTER FIRST COMMUNION

The traditional order in which the three sacraments of initiation were received was: baptism, confirmation, Communion. However, in the early 20th century, Pope Pius X encouraged Catholics to allow children to receive the Eucharist as soon as they reached the age of reason (generally understood to be about the age of seven years). As a result, many young people received Communion before they were confirmed. However, in the late 20th and early 21st centuries, there has been a return to the traditional order.

*Above* Girls wear white dresses, sometimes with veils and gloves, for first Communion. The colour symbolizes their purity.

It is also traditional for the young person to receive a present to mark the occasion – perhaps a prayer book, icon or rosary.

*Below* The Eastern Catholic Church emphasizes the Christian initiation by delivering baptism, Chrismation (confirmation) and the Eucharist together.

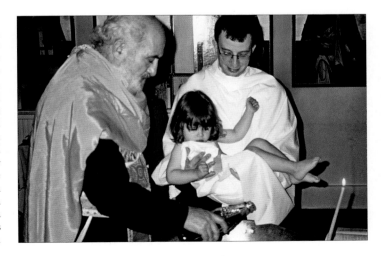

# HOLY MATRIMONY

THE SACRAMENT OF HOLY MATRIMONY GIVES A COUPLE THE DIVINE
GRACE THEY NEED TO ACHIEVE HOLINESS IN THEIR MARRIED LIFE. THE
"AUTHOR" OF THE MARRIAGE IS GOD.

***Above*** *In the Eastern Catholic Church,
the sacrament is called the "Crowning".
The crowns worn by bride and bridegroom
are a sign of the marriage covenant.*

In marriage, husband and wife receive the Holy Spirit, which helps the married couple to keep their vows. As the *Catechism of the Catholic Church* puts it, "The Holy Spirit is the seal of their covenant, the ever available source of their love and the strength to renew their fidelity."

## WITNESS TO THE UNION

In the Latin Rite of the Western Church, the wedding ceremony takes place before a priest and at least two witnesses: strictly speaking, the ministers of Christ's Grace in this sacrament are the husband and wife, and the priest is a witness. However, in the Eastern Catholic Church, the minister of the sacrament will be the presiding bishop or priest, who crowns husband and wife. There are two variants of the Latin Rite Catholic marriage ceremony: one with Mass, lasting about one hour, and one without Mass, which lasts around 20 minutes.

## RITE OF MARRIAGE

When both husband and wife are Catholics, they are encouraged by the Church to have a wedding Mass. The priest usually meets the couple at the door of the church and leads them to the altar. The next stage is to celebrate the liturgy of the Word, in the course of which the priest delivers a homily on the mystery of marriage, the responsibilities of husband and wife and the dignity of love between a married couple.

Then the priest begins the rite of marriage. He addresses the couple: "You have come together in this church so that the Lord may seal and strengthen your love in the presence of the Church's minister and this community." He will question the

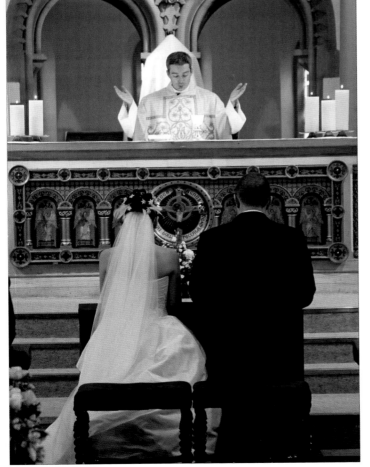

***Left*** *Catholic marriages are usually
celebrated during Holy Mass. In their
marriage, bride and bridegroom are
inspired by Jesus' self-sacrifice. They
become one body in Christ.*

couple's condition and intentions, asking them to confirm that they are joining "freely and without reservations", that they will "love and honour each other as man and wife for the rest of [their] lives" and that they will accept children from God and bring them up in the law of Christ and his Church.

Then the couple exchange vows, each promising "to be true…in good times and in bad, in sickness and in health" and declaring, "I will love and honour you all the days of my life". The words of the vows may vary. The priest blesses the couple, asking Jesus to strengthen their consent and fill them with blessings. The priest then blesses the rings and the couple exchange rings, which are worn as a sign of mutual love and fidelity.

### NUPTIAL BLESSING

The service proceeds by way of general intercessions into the liturgy of the Eucharist. After the Lord's

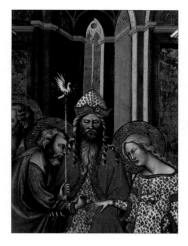

*Above Joseph and Mary exchange rings in this 14th-century detail of* Wedding of the Virgin Mary *by Bartolo di Fredi. From early on, the Catholic Church has taught that couples should love with a "supernatural…and fruitful love".*

*Below God blesses married love; its purpose is for procreation. A married couple receive a child from God in this 15th-century French miniature.*

Prayer the priest proclaims the nuptial blessing, calling on Jesus to bless bride and groom individually and as a couple joined in a holy bond and married in Christ to one another. The priest reminds all that marriage is a holy mystery that symbolizes the marriage of Christ to his Church, the one blessing of those given to Adam and Eve that was not "forfeited by original sin or washed away in the flood", and asks that the husband trust his wife and recognize that "she is his equal and heir with him to the life of grace". The priest prays, if the woman is of childbearing age, that the couple be blessed with children and have a long life, and after happy old age achieve fullness of life with the saints in heaven.

Then the couple receive Holy Communion. At the end of the service the priest blesses them once more before husband and wife kiss. All sing a hymn as the couple process out of the church. When a couple chooses a marriage service without Holy Communion it largely follows the outline above, but omits the celebration of the Eucharist.

### SPECIAL DISPENSATION

Those who come forward for marriage should normally be baptized Catholics. However, a dispensation, usually granted by the priest himself, is possible for a "mixed marriage" between a Catholic and a baptized non-Catholic (a Christian of another denomination) as long as the couple have chosen freely to marry, have the intention of remaining together for life and being faithful to one another, and are planning to have children if the bride has not passed the childbearing age. If one partner is Catholic and the other is not baptized (perhaps a non-Christian or a person of no religion), a church dispensation for disparity of cult is required from the local bishop.

# "WHAT GOD HAS JOINED…"

FOR CATHOLICS, HOLY MATRIMONY CREATES A PERMANENT AND INDISSOLUBLE BOND BETWEEN HUSBAND AND WIFE. GOD CREATED MARRIAGE AS THE FULFILMENT OF LIFE FOR MOST MEN AND WOMEN.

As part of the blessing of the married couple during the sacrament of Holy Matrimony, the priest may state, "What God has joined together, let no man put asunder", which is a direct quotation from Christ's own teaching on marriage (Mark 10:9). The *Catechism of the Catholic Church* is also unequivocal, stating that once a marriage between a baptized couple has been consummated, it "can never be dissolved".

Like the other sacraments, Holy Matrimony has both outward and inward signs: the outward sign is the marriage contract, which is the

*Below By participating in the wedding at Cana in Galilee, shown in this 14th-century painting,* The Marriage Feast at Cana, *by Duccio di Buoninsegna, Jesus confirmed the holiness of the marriage bond.*

agreement made verbally between both husband and wife when they exchange vows before the priest and witnesses; the inward sign is the grace it delivers. The Church's teaching accepts that marriage can bring many challenges; however, it also stresses that God's Grace is sufficient to help husbands and wives overcome their difficulties.

## DIVINE INSTITUTION

The Church teaches that God created man and woman for one another and that married love is in the image of God's love. Christ attended the wedding at Cana in Galilee, where he performed the first of the many signs that confirmed his status as the Son of God by turning water into wine (John 2:1–11). The Church interprets this event as confirmation

*Above A blessing is given to both man and woman in this 15th-century detail from* Engagement of the Virgin *by Michael Pacher. Both must freely give their consent to be married.*

of the goodness of marriage and a proclamation that marriage is a sign of Christ's presence.

For Catholics, marriage is both a natural and a divine institution. It is a natural institution because it has existed in the form of a lifelong union between a man and a woman in all societies and cultures through history. Yet it is also a divine institution created by God, sanctified by Christ at Cana, and sealed through the sacrament of Holy Matrimony by the action of the Holy Spirit.

## IN PREPARATION

The Church instructs that both parties to a marriage must have a clear understanding of what they are doing when they take their marriage vows. Husband and wife are required to attend preparatory meetings with the priest who will witness their marriage. These meetings are known as pre-Cana meetings – a reference to the wedding at Cana.

A course of pre-Cana meetings can be held over a single weekend or be spread over six months or so.

## ANNULMENT OF A MARRIAGE

The key condition for a marriage is that husband and wife give their consent to be married freely and are free to give their consent. In cases where the parties to a marriage can show that either of these conditions were not met, a Church tribunal can grant an annulment of the marriage. Annulment is not the same as divorce: the judgement does not dissolve the marriage, for marriage is an indissoluble bond; it determines that the marriage did not ever take place.

The two parties must understand what they are doing and must have given the matter some consideration; they must have a genuine intention to keep the vows they swear – to form a permanent and faithful union, inclusive of sexual acts intended for the purpose of procreation. Various impediments to the marriage are grounds for annulment. Examples include husband and wife being close blood relatives, one partner being already married at the time of the wedding or one partner being in a psychological state that precludes an ability to give free consent.

*Right* Henry VIII's wife Catherine of Aragon is shown in The Divorce of Henry VIII, *by Eugene Deveria. Theirs was one of several marriages Henry had annulled.*

The priest and the married couple discuss the sanctity of marriage, their faith and life in the Church, plans for children and so on; they may be asked about financial matters. Nearer to the time, husband and wife, if both are baptized Catholics, are expected to receive the sacrament of penance and reconciliation in preparation for their wedding. With these preparations, both husband and wife should enter marriage prepared to maintain their vows – married life should present no surprises.

### WHEN A MARRIAGE FAILS

The Church recognizes that in some cases a marriage can deteriorate so badly that husband and wife can no longer live together. In this situation, they should live separately and the members of the Church should help them live as best they can in a Christian fashion. The estranged husband and wife are not free to

divorce or remarry, and they should remember that the preferred solution in the eyes of the Catholic Church would be for the couple to reconcile their differences.

If a Catholic divorces and makes a second (civil) marriage, the Church views the person as committing adultery against the first marriage partner. He or she is in contravention of God's law and cannot receive the Eucharist. Nevertheless, that person should be welcomed to church if he or she wants to come: priests and the whole Church community should be attentive toward that person.

*Right* God intends man and woman to join permanently in marriage; once joined, they should not seek separation. *A 19th-century engraving,* The Ages of Life, *shows how a married couple honour their vows throughout life.*

# THE SANCTITY OF LIFE

CHURCH TEACHINGS ON MARRIAGE, SEX AND CONTRACEPTION, ABORTION AND HOMOSEXUALITY ARE UNDERPINNED BY BELIEF IN THE SANCTITY OF ALL LIVES CREATED BY GOD.

The Catholic faithful believe that sex has a divinely ordained place within a couple's marriage: its purpose and function is for the procreation of children. Married love is blessed by God and meant to be fruitful. This teaching is based on verses in Genesis, Chapter 1:

*So God created man in his own image, in the image of God he created him; male and female he created them. And God blessed them, and God said to them, "Be fruitful and multiply, and fill the earth and subdue it." (Genesis 1:26–29).*

## AT THE SERVICE OF LIFE

Parents are called not only to procreate but also to educate: having brought children into the world, they must give them instruction in moral and spiritual matters. Parents should serve their children in love. The *Catechism of the Catholic Church* states

*Below The pope holds a fatherly position to Catholics. Married couples entrust their children to the care of God and his Church.*

that one of the main functions of marriage and family is "to be at the service of life".

There are some married couples who have not had children, but this does not devalue their marriage in any way. They can still aim to live a life of service through hospitality, self-sacrifice and charity. Other people are called to chastity. This does not devalue marriage, either. The vocation to chastity and the vocation to married life both come from God, and both should be equally valued. The two ways of life reinforce one another.

## CONTRACEPTION

The Church's teachings on contraception arise from the understanding that Catholics should only have sex within marriage and that the main function of sex is for procreation. Using contraceptives, such as a condom or the contraceptive pill, is directly against Catholic teaching. This is because these methods interfere with the natural law of God's Creation and split sex from its proper procreative role.

However, Catholics are allowed to use natural methods of birth control – chiefly by having sex only when the wife is at a low-fertility part of her cycle. Natural birth control is allowed because it is in harmony with the natural law of God's Creation and uses God-given powers, such as self-control, rather than chemical interference (as with the pill) or a physical barrier (such as a condom). Catholics must be responsible and correctly motivated in using this method: for example, it would be acceptable to use the method to space out children in a

*Above In this 14th-century detail from* The Creation of Adam *by Master Bertram of Minden, God is shown instructing Adam about his duty to procreate and father children.*

### HOMOSEXUALITY

The Church recognizes that some men and women have deep-seated homosexual tendencies: the catechism calls these tendencies "intrinsically disordered" and "contrary to natural law". Sexual relations between people of the same sex are not approved because they "close the sexual act to the gift of life" and "do not proceed from a genuine affective and sexual complementarity". The Church believes that homosexual people are called to chastity: they are required to develop self-mastery and they are expected to pray for support. In these circumstances, they can rely on God's sacramental grace to help them reach Christian perfection.

*Right Catholic parents bring their children to Christ in Lucas Cranach the Elder's* Christ Blessing the Children *(c.1540). Parents are responsible for teaching their children the Catholic faith.*

family, but to do so to avoid having children in order to have more spending money would be immoral.

The Church also teaches that sex has a unifying function – it brings the husband and wife into a close spiritual, mental and physical union. By using artificial contraception, according to the teaching, the couple are violating this function and preventing themselves from giving completely to each other.

In addition, according to the Church, the use of contraception has a number of negative effects. Among these it promotes immoral behaviour, damages marriage as an institution, makes men respect women less, and gives people the idea that they can achieve total control over bodily processes of reproduction when this control rightly belongs to God.

Opponents of the Church's position argue that contraception has benefits for people both as individuals and collectively. The Church's response is that using contraception is evil and that it is never the correct approach to do evil, even if you believe good may come of it.

### RIGHT TO LIFE

The Church takes a very strong position against the use of abortion. Catholics believe that a new life begins at the moment in which a woman's egg is fertilized by a sperm. The fertilized egg is a human being independent of mother and father. According to Pope John Paul II in his 1995 encyclical *Evangelum Vitae* ("The Gospel of Life"), abortion is

*Right The catechism teaches that God's Grace helps married couples "attain holiness in their married life and in welcoming and educating their children".*

"a grave moral disorder" because it involves the intentional killing of an innocent person. Church teaching states that every individual, including a foetus, has an inalienable right to life – and this right extends from the moment of conception until the person's physical death. In canon law, a person who procures an abortion is excommunicated.

# PENANCE AND RECONCILIATION

DURING THE SACRAMENT OF PENANCE AND RECONCILIATION, WHICH IS OFTEN REFERRED TO AS CONFESSION, CATHOLICS CONFESS ANY WRONGDOINGS TO THEIR PRIEST AND RECEIVE ABSOLUTION.

*Above The penitent admits any wrongdoing, but also humbly confesses (acknowledges and honours) God's profound holiness and great mercy.*

Confession provides spiritual healing for people who have been distanced from God by their sins and restores to them the Grace of God. The sacrament has two effects or aspects: outer and inner – the outer aspect is that the penitent believer receives absolution from his priest, either by remission of sin or the punishment due to sin; the inner aspect is that through repentance and confession the believer is reconciled to God.

In addition to being known as confession, penance and reconciliation can also be called the sacrament of conversion (because, according to the *Catechism of the Catholic Church*, it

*Below After his Resurrection, Christ tells his disciples that they have the power to forgive sins, as seen in this 14th-century panel by Duccio di Buoninsegna.*

"makes sacramentally present Jesus' call to conversion") and the sacrament of forgiveness. Along with the anointing of the sick, confession is one of two sacraments of healing. Through these two sacraments, according to the catechism, the Church continues Christ's work of "healing and salvation, even among Her own members".

Christ instituted the sacrament of confession on Easter Day, when after rising from the dead following his Crucifixion he appeared to the apostles and said, "Receive the Holy Spirit. If you forgive the sins of any, they are forgiven; if you retain the sins of any, they are retained" (John 20:22–23).

There is another biblical precedent for this sacrament, found in the episode described in the Gospel of

Matthew (9:2–8) in which Jesus publicly forgave the sins of a paralytic man brought to him for healing and cured him of his paralysis.

## WHEN TO CONFESS

Catholics must receive the sacrament of confession when they are aware that they have committed a mortal sin and in any case at least once a year. They are encouraged to go to confession once a month. (Mortal sins are distinct from venial sins. Mortal sins are those that condemn a soul to hell because they cannot be forgiven without repentence; lesser venial sins, if unconfessed and so not absolved, cause separation from God but not eternal damnation.)

Catholics are also required to receive the sacrament of confession before they receive the Eucharist for the first time. In Lent, the Church urges believers to receive the sacrament of confession as part of their preparation for Easter. Catholics are generally keen to receive confession because, as one of the seven sacraments instituted by Christ, it delivers God's Grace to those who receive it and so is a vital aid in living a good Christian life.

There are four key elements to the sacrament. Firstly, penitent individuals are required to be contrite; that is, to feel sincere remorse for their sins. They must have a genuine intention not to commit the sins again. Secondly, they must confess the number and kind of their sins to a priest. Thirdly, they need to receive absolution from the priest. Lastly, they must perform satisfaction or the acts of penance that were prescribed by the priest.

## ABSOLUTION FROM SIN

A priest (or bishop) does not himself have the power to forgive sins. However, he exercises the power on behalf of Christ through the sacrament of penance if he is ordained validly and has proper jurisdiction over the penitent who makes confession. In administering the sacrament, the priest acts in *persona Christi* ("in the person of Christ").

*Below In delivering absolution, a priest acts on Christ's behalf. As well as receiving God's pardon, the penitent is reconciled with the Church.*

The priest hears the confessions of his parishioners or other members of the faithful at set times, and the normal form of confession is for the penitent individual to say, "Bless me Father for I have sinned" and then to specify the period that has elapsed since his or her last confession. The penitent has to confess all mortal sins committed in that period and is encouraged to confess venial sins, too. The prayer of confession begins, "O My God I am heartily sorry…".

The priest then delivers absolution. One form describes a merciful God, who "through the death and resurrection of his Son" has become reconciled to humankind and has sent the Holy Spirit among people "for the forgiveness of sins". It goes on to state that through the Church's ministry God may pardon the person and give him or her peace. The priest ends by absolving the person from his or her sins in the three names of the Holy Trinity.

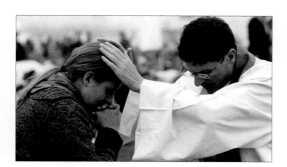

### SEAL OF THE CONFESSIONAL
The priest is bound by the absolutely inviolable seal of the confessional – he cannot reveal what he has been told in confession, even under threat of death. A priest who does so is automatically excommunicated from the Church. In criminal matters, for example, if a person admits to murder in the confessional, the priest cannot tell the police or other authorities, but he can encourage the penitent to give himself or herself up and can withhold absolution as a means of leverage.

# ANOINTING OF THE SICK AND THE LAST RITES

GOD'S GRACE IS DELIVERED TO THE SEVERELY ILL THROUGH THE ANOINTING OF THE SICK AND LAST RITES, WHICH HELP THEM COPE WITH SICKNESS OR DEATH AND RESIST THE FEELING OF DISCOURAGEMENT.

In the sacrament of the anointing of the sick, a priest anoints a seriously ill Catholic person with holy oil. Along with penance and reconciliation (or confession), the anointing of the sick is one of the Catholic Church's two sacraments of healing. Through the anointing of the sick, an ill person is united with the suffering of Christ, and even permitted to share in the redemptive work performed by Christ's Passion. The sacrament will bring spiritual and sometimes physical healing – and also forgiveness of sins.

All the sacraments draw on biblical precedent. The central text in support of the anointing of the sick is in James 5:14–15:

**Below** *The sacrament delivers grace to strengthen the ill person, bringing courage, peace of mind and, subject to God's will, physical healing.*

*Is any among you sick? Let him call for the elders of the Church, and let them pray over him, anointing him with oil in the name of the Lord; and the prayer of faith will save the sick man, and the Lord will raise him up; and if he has committed sins, he will be forgiven.*

## RECEIVING THE SACRAMENT

Only a priest or bishop can administer the sacrament of the anointing of the sick. According to canon law, he can give the sacrament to any member of the faithful who has reached the age of reason and is in danger of death either though illness or old age. If a person receives the sacrament when close to death, then recovers, he or she can receive this sacrament a second time if the illness strikes again. Equally, a person can receive the sacrament a second time

**Above** *Christ comforted and healed the sick, as illustrated by James Tissot in his 19th-century painting,* In the Villages the Sick Were Brought unto Him.

if a continuing illness worsens, and a person about to have serious surgery may also receive the sacrament.

The priest can also use his pastoral judgement to determine whether or not it is appropriate to administer the sacrament a second time or even more often when a person is chronically ill or very old and weak. He can administer the sacrament to a person at home, during Mass or while in a hospital and may give it to a group of the seriously ill if desired.

## ADMINISTERING THE SACRAMENT

The priest uses olive or vegetable oil that has been blessed by the bishop in the Chrism Mass on Holy Thursday (the Thursday of Holy Week). In the Latin Rite of the Western Church, the priest usually anoints the sick person on the forehead, marking the shape of the Cross, and says: "Through this holy anointing may the Lord in his love and mercy help you with the grace of the Holy Spirit. May the

*Above A priest visiting a seriously ill person will carry all the equipment he needs to perform anointing and to celebrate the Eucharist.*

Eucharist should always be the last sacrament of the earthly journey, the *viaticum* for 'passing over' to eternal life." The sacrament of the anointing of the sick is also called *sacramentum exeuntium* ("the sacrament of those departing"). It is the last of the holy anointings of the Christian life, and follows on from the anointings of baptism and confirmation. "This last anointing," according to the catechism, "fortifies the end of our earthly life like a solid rampart for the final struggles before entering the Father's house."

Lord who frees you from sin save you and raise you up." He may anoint other parts of the body, without using the verbal formula.

## LAST RITES
When the sick person is in immediate danger of death the anointing is considered to be one of the "last rites", which also includes penance and reconciliation and the Eucharist. The normal procedure is for the priest to hear the person's confession, then anoint him or her, before giving him or her the Eucharist. In some cases, when a person is too ill to confess, the priest can pronounce absolution – but this is believed to be effective only if the dying person inwardly feels contrition for the sins.

The Eucharist given to a seriously ill person is called *viaticum*, a Latin word meaning "provision for the voyage" and referring to the final journey of this earthly life – through death into eternal life. In the words of the *Catechism of the Catholic Church*, "As the sacrament of Christ's Passover, the

*Right In addition to anointing, those near to death confess their sins and receive the Eucharist, as in this 15th-century painting by Rogier van der Weyden.*

# DUST TO DUST

WHEN A PERSON DIES, CATHOLICS GIVE THANKS FOR THE GRACE OF GOD EVIDENCED IN HIS OR HER LIFE. CATHOLIC FUNERAL SERVICES COMPRISE A VIGIL, A MASS AND A BURIAL OR COMMITTAL.

*Above During a funeral Mass, the presiding priest censes and blesses the coffin as the Church expresses its communion with the departed.*

The three forms of funeral service have been authorized in the *Ordo exsequiarum* ("Order of Christian Funerals") of the Catholic Church's Roman Rite. Each form has its proper place: the vigil is usually held at home; the funeral or requiem Mass in the Church; and the committal in the cemetery. All three forms express what the catechism calls the "paschal character" of death. This refers to a Catholic's understanding of death in terms of Easter, in the light of Jesus' death and Resurrection.

## VIGIL, MASS, COMMITTAL

The vigil is a gathering for prayers and biblical readings, with a sermon, that is held before the day of the funeral Mass and committal, often at the home of the deceased person. One or more eulogies on the dead person's life are shared. These should not praise the individual but concentrate on the workings of God's Grace in his or her life. The vigil is often held as part of a wake.

*Below After the funeral Mass, a priest blesses the coffin before it is transported to the cemetery for the committal.*

The funeral Mass is often called a requiem Mass. Those gathered pray for the forgiveness of sins and the salvation of the soul of the departed. The service takes the name *requiem* from the Latin wording at the beginning of the first section, the Introit: *Requiem aeternam dona eis, Domine, et lux perpetua luceat eis* ("Grant them unending rest, O Lord, and may light perpetual fall on them"). Requiem Masses can also be held as a memorial for a deceased person and to mark an anniversary of a person's death.

The rite of committal consists of prayers and Bible readings as the body is buried in a cemetery, or before cremation. In the committal the faithful bid farewell to the deceased person; the Church commends him or her to the care of God.

## FULFILMENT OF A LIFE

Catholic teaching views death as the end and fulfilment of a devout person's sacramental life. His or her religious life has been structured to lead to this end: death is the fulfilment of the new birth of baptism, of the new life that was confirmed and strengthened by the anointing of the Holy Spirit at confirmation, and the participation in the heavenly feast anticipated every time he or she received the Eucharist. During the funeral, the Church, which has carried the devout person through life, like a mother would care for a growing child, now offers him or her to God the Father, in Christ.

The liturgy and ceremonial of the requiem Mass generally follows that of the standard Mass, but omits its more joyful expressions, including the gloria and the Creed and certain doxologies, or hymns of praise. A key element of the Mass in this setting is the funeral homily, which must be delivered by a bishop, priest or deacon, and which explicates the meaning of death in the context of Christ's own death and his triumphant Resurrection.

Celebrating Mass is central to the funeral because the Eucharist lies at the very heart of a Catholic's understanding of death. In the Eucharist, a member of the faithful will have communion with Christ and with the departed person. The gathered faithful will then pray for the forgiveness of the deceased person's sins, and ask that he or she enjoy the heavenly feast to which the Eucharist looks forward: in doing this, and in

*Right The funeral, followed by burial or cremation, is illuminated by belief in "the resurrection of the dead, and the life of the world to come".*

receiving the Eucharist, the faithful at the Mass will learn to exist in communion with the departed.

## ATTITUDE TO CREMATION
For many centuries the Catholic Church did not allow cremation because it held the practice to be counter to belief in the resurrection of the body. The official position was that cremation was a pagan practice. However, in 1963 the Vatican began to permit the use of cremation as long as the reason for choosing it did not go against Catholic beliefs.

The initial requirement was that all funeral services had to be carried out in the presence of the dead body, which would then be cremated afterward. This was changed in 1997 and since then the funeral liturgy can be used in the presence of cremated remains of the body. The Church does not permit the scattering of ashes after cremation; it teaches that the ashes should be entombed in a grave or mausoleum.

## DRESSED FOR A MASS
Bishops or priests that celebrate requiem Masses were traditionally expected to wear black vestments and ornaments. Black is considered to be the colour of the most profound grief, and is also worn for services on Good Friday. Today, clergy often wear white to symbolize the glory of the Resurrection.

## MUSICAL HERITAGE
Requiem Masses are often sung, and there is a very rich heritage of musical settings of requiem Masses, including works by the notable composers Wolfgang Amadeus Mozart, Hector Berlioz and Gabriel Fauré.

The revised form of the Latin Rite for the requiem Mass, which was introduced following the Second Vatican Council (1962–5) and is used generally today, does away with a number of elements of the traditional requiem that are familiar to people who know the service chiefly through these magnificent musical settings.

One example is the sequence beginning *Dies irae, dies illa, Solvet sæclum in favilla* ("Day of anger, day when the world turns to ashes..."). This is a powerful part of classical requiems by Mozart and Verdi, but was made optional and then dropped from the requiem Mass following the Second Vatican Council as part of changes designed to tone down elements suggestive of despair and fear of judgement while emphasizing hope and belief in the Resurrection. The *Dies irae* was part of the requiem Mass in the Roman Missal 1962 (prior to the Second Vatican Council) and so is still heard in churches that celebrate the Tridentine liturgy in use before the Council.

*Left A memorial Mass for Pope John Paul II was held in the Church of the Holy Sepulchre (the church in which Jesus is traditionally believed to be buried), in Jerusalem, on 6 April 2005. Latin Patriarch Michel Sabbah presided, and some 200 heads of state, heads of government and royalty gathered to attend the pope's funeral.*

# PRAYER

IN PRAYER, CATHOLICS CAN COMMUNICATE WITH THEIR CREATOR. BELIEVERS CAN BUILD AND MAINTAIN A LIVING AND PERSONAL RELATIONSHIP WITH GOD THE FATHER, SON AND HOLY SPIRIT.

Prayer can be public or private: it can be a shared communal experience or a personal and solitary formal rite, spoken aloud or a more fluid, silent interior activity. Public forms of prayer include the Mass and the Liturgy of the Hours. Among private forms are the use of the rosary and the practice of *Lectio Divina*, which is a meditative reading of the Scriptures developed as a form of devotion by medieval monastics. The Catholic Church teaches that the chief sources of and inspirations to prayer are the Word of God in the Bible, the liturgy of the Church and the virtues of faith, hope and charity.

## HOW TO PRAY

Catholic authorities stress that it is essential to pray but that the kind of prayer does not matter. Pope John Paul II, in writing about how to pray, said that it was a simple thing to do and recommended that you pray "any way you like, so long as you do pray". Prayer may be a very personal outpouring. The catechism quotes St Thérèse of Lisieux:

*For me prayer is a surge of the heart; it is a simple look turned towards heaven, it is a cry of recognition and of love, embracing both trial and joy.*

Prayer is not just self-expression. Elsewhere, the catechism states that prayer is not something to be turned into a "spontaneous outpouring of interior impulse". The Holy Spirit instructs the faithful in how to pray through "a living transmission" (Sacred Tradition) within the Church.

*Above In Jacob Cornelisz van Oostsanen's 1523 painting,* Adoration of the Trinity, *a Christian (right) prays with hands clasped together.*

Prayers of all kinds must be made in the name of Jesus, for these have access to God the Father through Christ. The Holy Spirit teaches believers to pray to God the Father through the Son, and that through the many different kinds of prayer the one Holy Spirit acts.

## BENEFITS OF PRAYER

The Church teaches that prayer leads the faithful away from sin toward salvation. In prayer, a believer turns to God and receives direction from the Holy Spirit; without this guidance the believer is trapped in sin. According to the Church, people who pray with eagerness and call on God cannot sin, therefore they are saved; those who do not pray are trapped in sin and are in the way of damnation.

Praying by repeating the name of Jesus in the Jesus Prayer has the effect of summoning Christ within the believer. Whereas in the Old Testament, the Jews were forbidden

## THE JESUS PRAYER

The catechism states, "There is no other way of Christian prayer than Christ." St Paul exhorted Christians to "pray constantly" (1 Thessalonicans 5:17), to attempt to keep one's life in God's presence and under his eye: a favoured way of doing this is through "prayer of the heart". One example used for centuries by Christians in both the Eastern and Western Churches is the Jesus Prayer, an invocation based on repetition of the Lord's name. The Jesus Prayer developed in a variety of forms, the most common of which is "Lord Jesus Christ, Son of God, have mercy on us sinners". Praying this prayer while being active in the world sanctifies every action.

*Above Catholics are encouraged to pray in Jesus' name, who spread the Word, as shown in this 17th-century Greek icon.*

to utter the name of God, in Jesus, God adopted human form and delivered his name to humanity: the name Jesus contains the divine presence. The catechism explains: "The name 'Jesus' contains all: God and man and the whole economy of creation and salvation…whoever invokes the name of Jesus is welcoming the Son of God who loved him [or her] and who gave himself up for him [or her]."

## PRIVATE PRAYER

The Church also teaches that private meditative prayer complements and sustains the public prayer of the liturgy. In his apostolic letter *Rosarium Virginis Mariae* ("Rosary of the Virgin Mary"), which was witten on 16 October 2002, Pope John Paul II described the rosary as a good introduction and an accurate echo of Church liturgy. He added that praying the words of the rosary as taught by the Church involves carrying on an inner meditation on

the glories and hidden meanings of Christ's life and this lets the believer take part in a deep study of Christian mystery that amounts to a profound and practical training for a holy life.

*Above A prayer book, shown in this 16th-century detail from* Portrait of the Artist's Sister in the Garb of a Nun *by Sofonisba Anguissola, is an indispensable aid for some Catholics devoted to private prayer.*

Pope Benedict XVI emphasized the fact that private prayer, contemplation and religious devotions do not distract from loving service in the world but in fact provide an essential underpinning and support for that service. He used the example of Mother Teresa of Calcutta and the work of her order, the Missionaries of Charity, as an example. In his first encyclical, *Deus Caritas Est*, written in December 2005, he declared that the example of Teresa of Calcutta illustrates the fact that when we devote time to God in private or public prayer, it does not distract us from serving our neighbours in love, but rather is a limitless source of loving service.

*Left In prayer, the believer reaches out to God. The Church teaches that calling on the name of Jesus summons his presence within us.*

# THE SACRED HEART

CATHOLICS USE THE SACRED HEART OF JESUS AS A FOCUS FOR THEIR INTENSE DEVOTIONS IN WHICH THEY SEEK TO MAKE REPARATIONS TO JESUS FOR THE SINS OF HUMANKIND.

The Sacred Heart of Jesus is a symbol of God's love for humanity. God's love was expressed in Christ's suffering, and the Sacred Heart is pierced by human sins. Through prayer and contemplation, Catholics can consecrate themselves to the Sacred Heart.

In Catholic art, the Sacred Heart is usually shown to be aflame and shining with light, injured by the lance

*Below The apostles showed human frailty when they failed to keep watch with Jesus. They are asleep in Barna da Siena's 14th-century painting,* Christ in the Garden of Gethsemane.

that stabbed Jesus' side on the Cross, with a crown of thorns around it and blood falling from it. This image is often superimposed on Jesus' chest, with his wounded hands pointing to the heart. The light and flames represent the power of divine love.

## DEVOTION TO THE HEART

Those who want to express their devotion to the Sacred Heart usually seek to receive Communion often. They commit to establish a "first Friday" routine – to go to confession and then receive the Eucharist on the first Friday of the month for

*Above Many Catholic homes, churches and other institutions contain Sacred Heart statues to remind the faithful of Jesus' profound love and suffering.*

nine consecutive months. They may also partake of Holy Hour devotions on Thursdays. The Holy Hour is an hour-long prayer vigil, usually conducted in the presence of the Holy Sacrament. It is intended to make amends to Jesus for the hour in the garden of Gethsemane when he prayed alone, and returning to his disciples found them asleep. He reproached Peter: "So, could you not watch with me one hour? Watch and pray that you may not enter into temptation; the spirit indeed is willing, but the flesh is weak" (Matthew 26:40–41).

Sometimes the devout partake in a ceremony at home known as the enthronement of the Sacred Heart. A priest visits the home to set up ("enthrone") an image or statue of Jesus bearing his Sacred Heart: it reminds those living in the house that they have been consecrated to the Sacred Heart.

## PAPAL TEACHINGS

In his encyclical *Annum Sacrum* (On Consecration to the Sacred Heart) of 25 May 1899, Pope Leo XIII

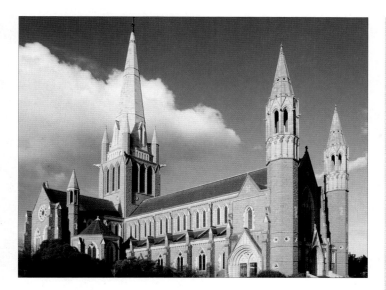

consecrated all humans to the Sacred
Heart of Jesus. He described the
Sacred Heart as a comprehensible
symbol of Christ's endless love and
declared that it was right that
Catholics should dedicate themselves to the Sacred Heart; when the
faithful do this, he added, they offer
and bind themselves to Jesus. Many
Catholic organizations, including
churches, colleges and missionary
and teaching orders, are dedicated to
the Sacred Heart.

Pope Pius XII delivered a teaching
on the mystical aspects of revering
the heart of Jesus in his encyclical
*Haurietis Aquas* (On Devotion to the
Sacred Heart) in 1956. He declared
the heart of Jesus to be a symbol of
God's threefold love in the Father,
Son and Holy Spirit; he wrote that
believers should look devoutly upon
the divine Redeemer's heart as an
image of Jesus' love and a witness of
our salvation in the events of Easter,
and as a kind of mystical pathway
along which we climb upward to be
embraced by our Saviour.

Pius XII also declared in this
letter that devotion to Jesus' Sacred
Heart was the foundation on which

*Above The Sacred Heart Cathedral at
Bendigo in Victoria, Australia, is one of
many Catholic institutions named after
the Sacred Heart.*

individual believers, their families
and whole nations could construct
the kingdom of God.

FEAST DAY
The feast of the Sacred Heart was
established in the church calendar
in 1856 by Pope Pius IX and is
celebrated 19 days after Pentecost.
Because Pentecost falls on a Sunday,
the feast of the Sacred Heart takes
place on a Friday. On this feast day,
devout Catholics will meditate on
the devotional aspects of the Sacred
Heart of Jesus.

They say the prayers laid out in
the Act of Reparation to the Sacred
Heart, which begins "Most sweet
Jesus, whose overflowing charity for
men is requited by so much forget-
fulness, negligence and contempt,
behold us prostrate before Thee,
eager to repair by a special act of
homage the cruel indifference and
injuries to which Thy loving Heart is
everywhere subject…".

*Above As a nun, St Marguerite
Marie Alacoque had an intense
mystical experience of Christ's
suffering, captured in this 1888
painting,* Beatified Marguerite
Marie Alacoque's Vision of
Jesus' Heart, *by Antonio Ciseri.*

# STATIONS OF THE CROSS

THE STATIONS OF THE CROSS IS A SET OF 14 PENITENTIAL MEDITATIONS
ON CHRIST'S PASSION, WHICH ARE OFTEN PERFORMED DURING LENT,
ESPECIALLY ON FRIDAY EVENINGS.

The 14 meditations are each linked to a specific scene that illustrates one of the series of events that included Christ's condemnation to death, passage to Calvary and his Crucifixion. They are performed before paintings or statuary that represent the scene in question. The paintings or statues are usually carefully arranged around the walls of a church or chapel; however, they can also be laid out as a series of images along a pathway, for example, near a shrine.

By praying at the Stations of the Cross, the Catholic believer can make a spiritual pilgrimage. The Church teaches that the prayers and meditations before the Stations of the Cross should be performed in a spirit of reparation – in an attempt to clear away humanity's sins.

In 1928, Pope Pius XI wrote in his encyclical *Miserentissimus Redemptor* that Catholics had a duty to offer reparation to Christ for the sins that have been committed against him. In 2000, in a letter marking the 50th anniversary of the Benedictine Sisters of Reparation of the Holy Face, Pope John Paul II called the effort to make reparation for the sins committed every day against Jesus an attempt to place oneself alongside the infinite number of crosses on which the son of God is still crucified. The meditations made at these Stations often seek to focus on the positive effects of the acts of atonement that Christ performed, as well as consider the grave sins of humankind that have been the reason for Christ's suffering.

*Above* Pope John Paul II bears a cross during the first part of the Stations of the Cross in the Colosseum in Rome on 5 April 1996.

*Above* The 5th station: Jesus is judged by Pilate. These images are from a fresco by an unknown artist of the 15th century.

*Above* The 6th station: Jesus is mocked, beaten, blindfolded and crowned with thorns by enemies.

## THE OLD SEQUENCE

The traditional sequence of the Stations of the Cross was used by Catholics for centuries. It was as follows: Jesus is condemned to death (1), is given the Cross (2), then falls for the first time under the weight of the Cross (3); Jesus encounters his mother, the Blessed Virgin Mary (4), and Simon of Cyrene is forced to carry the Cross (5); Veronica (Berenice), a pious Jerusalem woman, gives Jesus her veil to wipe his face (6); Jesus falls down for a second time (7); he addresses the daughters of Jerusalem (8); he falls for a third time (9), then he is stripped of his garments (10); Jesus is nailed to the Cross (11); Jesus dies on the Cross (12); his body is removed from the Cross and laid in the arms of his mother (13), and then laid in the tomb (14).

This sequence was altered by Pope John Paul II in 1991 because the traditional sequence included six scenes (3,4,6,7, 9 and 13) not backed by Scripture. The first five of these do not appear at all in biblical accounts, while station 13 – the scene of Jesus laid in his mother's arms, represented so famously and beautifully in the many Pietà statues of art history – is a misrepresentation, for in biblical accounts Joseph of Arimathea was working alone when he took down Jesus' body and laid it in a tomb.

## THE REVISED SEQUENCE

John Paul II devised a new (though not obligatory) sequence called the Scriptural Way of the Cross. The 14 scenes of this sequence are as follows: Jesus prays in the Garden of Gethsemane (1), then is betrayed by Judas Iscariot and arrested (2); he is condemned by the Jewish judicial body, the Sanhedrin (3); St Peter denies Jesus (4), then Jesus is judged by Pontius Pilate (5) and is whipped and given a crown of thorns (6); Jesus takes the Cross (7), then Simon of Cyrene carries it (8); Jesus speaks to the women of Jerusalem (9); he is crucified (10); he promises the "good thief" being crucified with him, "Truly, I say to you, today you will be with me in Paradise" (11), entrusts his mother to his disciple John with the words, "Woman, behold, your son!" and to the disciple, "Behold your mother!" (12); he dies on the Cross (13); his body is put in the tomb (14).

## GOOD FRIDAY

Catholics are generally encouraged to pray and meditate at the Stations of the Cross on Good Friday. John Paul II made a practice of performing public devotions at Stations of the Cross set up in the Colosseum, Rome, each Good Friday. In 1991 and thereafter, he prayed the new scriptural sequence outlined above. Initially, the Holy Father himself carried the Cross from station to station, but in later life his age made it necessary for him to watch the devotions from a stage while others carried the Cross. In 2007, Pope Benedict XVI approved the new sequence of the Stations of the Cross for use by Catholics.

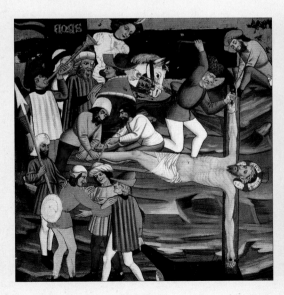

*Above* The 10th station: Jesus is bound and nailed to the Cross during his Crucifixion.

*Above* The 14th station: Jesus' body is placed in the tomb with the help of Joseph of Arimathea.

# THE ROSARY

FOR CENTURIES DEVOTED CATHOLICS HAVE USED THE ROSARY – A
ROUND OF PRAYERS THAT ARE CENTRED ON THE BLESSED VIRGIN
MARY – IN BOTH PUBLIC AND PRIVATE DEVOTIONS.

The rosary is also a physical object
that enables believers to keep track of
their prayers. It consists of a small
crucifix on a circular string with a
medal and a series of beads of various
numbers. The beads are divided into
groups of ten beads called decades,
each group preceded by an individual
bead set apart slightly from the others.
It is used to say the prayers that form
the rosary. The central prayer of the
rosary is the Hail Mary:

> *Hail Mary, full of Grace, the Lord is
> with thee; blessed art thou amongst
> women, and blessed is the fruit of thy
> womb, Jesus. Holy Mary, Mother of
> God, pray for us sinners now and
> at the hour of our death.*

The other key prayers used in the
rosary to complement the Hail Mary
are the Lord's Prayer beginning "Our
Father, who art in Heaven…" and
the Apostles' Creed beginning "I
believe in God, the Father Almighty,
creator of heaven and earth…".

## PRAYING THE ROSARY

The usual pattern of prayers is an
introduction, then five decades of
the rosary and a conclusion. During
the introduction, believers hold the
crucifix as they pray the dedication
"In the Name of the Father, and of
the Son and of the Holy Spirit:
Amen" and the Apostles' Creed.
Then they progress along the four
beads after the crucifix, saying one
Our Father and three Hail Marys.

Then they begin on the five
decades. At each bead they say one
Our Father and at each decade
one Hail Mary. At the conclusion
they hold the medal as they pray one
of many other prayers to Mary, then
return to the dedication "In the
Name of the Father, and of the Son
and of the Holy Spirit: Amen".

## THE MYSTERIES

While praying the decades of the
rosary, believers meditate inwardly
on the mysteries of the lives of
the Virgin Mary and Jesus. These

***Above*** *A Luminous Mystery: Peter,
James and John see Jesus in his true light
in Pietro Perugino's 15th–16th century*
The Transfiguration.

meditations were divided into three
groups of five: the Joyful Mysteries
(of Jesus' birth), the Sorrowful
Mysteries (of Jesus' Crucifixion) and
the Glorious Mysteries (of Jesus'
Resurrection). However, in 2002
Pope John Paul II proposed a new set
of mysteries, the Mysteries of Light,
or Luminous Mysteries, following
key events in Christ's ministry.

In each group, one mystery is
aligned to one decade of the rosary,
so when praying the entire rosary
once, believers can meditate on one
set of five mysteries. There is a pattern
for meditating on the mysteries: the
Joyful Mysteries are considered on
Monday and Saturday, the Sorrowful
Mysteries on Tuesday and Friday, the
Glorious Mysteries on Wednesday
and Sunday and the Luminous
Mysteries are optional for Thursdays.

***Left*** *Pope John Paul II declared that the
rosary prayer encompasses in its words
the depth of the Holy Gospel's message.*

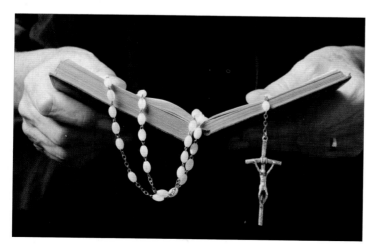

*Right A Glorious Mystery: The Virgin is carried to heaven and crowned in this c.1500 Flemish illustration,* Assumption and Coronation of the Virgin.

## ORIGINS AND REVIVAL

The Hail Mary is also known as the Ave Maria, which comes from its first words in Latin *Ave Maria, gratia plena, Dominus tecum.* The prayer combines three main parts, the first being the salutation delivered by the archangel Gabriel to the Blessed Virgin at the Annunciation. The second part, "Blessed is the fruit of thy womb, Jesus", derives the greeting of Elizabeth to Mary (Luke 1:42); and the third part, the prayer "Holy Mary, Mother of God…" was, according to the *Catechism of the Catholic Church,* developed by the Church.

By tradition, the rosary was developed by St Dominic when combating the heresies of the dualist Cathars in 13th-century France. It has been refined over many years, but it reached its modern form by the 15th century when the Dominican

*Below A Joyful Mystery: the Virgin Mary gives her consent to God's planned Incarnation at the Annunciation in Melchior Broederlam's 14th-century* Annunciation and Visitation.

preacher Alan de la Roche promoted its use. In 1520, Pope Leo X gave the rosary his official papal backing.

In 1858 in Lourdes, France, Marie-Bernarde Soubirous (St Bernadette) saw apparitions of the Blessed Virgin Mary, who urged her to say her rosary, and to tell others to pray, perform penances and say the rosary for the salvation of sinners. Lourdes is now a centre of pilgrimage for Catholics.

### THE WORDS OUR SAVIOUR GAVE US

Also known as the paternoster and the Our Father from its initial words in English and Latin, the Lord's Prayer is based on the one taught by Jesus to the apostles. According to the accounts in Matthew 6:9–15 and Luke 11:2–4, it runs:

*Our Father who art in heaven,*
*Hallowed be thy name.*
*Thy kingdom come,*
*Thy will be done,*
*On earth as it is in heaven.*
*Give us this day our daily bread.*
*And forgive us our trespasses,*
*As we forgive those who*
*    trespass against us.*
*And lead us not into temptation,*
*    but deliver us from evil.*

The Catholic version does not include the doxology or hymn of praise "For the kingdom the power and the glory are yours, now and forever" that appears in some other versions.

# THE BLESSING

THERE ARE CENTURIES OF TRADITION AND LAYERS OF SYMBOLISM
BEHIND CATHOLIC PRACTICES, SUCH AS THE BLESSING GIVEN BY THE
CLERGY, MAKING THE SIGN OF THE CROSS AND USING HOLY WATER.

When Roman Catholic priests are
ordained, their hands are anointed
with chrism, holy oil that has been
blessed by a bishop. After receiving
the sacrament of Holy Orders
through this and other related rituals,
priests are able to share in Christ's
own priesthood: their hands have the
power to bless people and objects. In
the act of blessing, the clergy can
sanctify both people and objects, and
dedicate them to God's service.

*Above Jesus gave numerous blessings, as
shown in Fernando Gallego's 15th-century
Christ Blessing, and with a gesture of his
hands worked many miracles.*

The long-held practice of sanctifying both people and objects
through the act of blessing has many
biblical precedents. God blessed his
Creation and after the Flood blessed
Noah, while priests of the Jewish
faith delivered blessings on their
people. Christ himself and the
apostles gave blessings to the sick and
needy and to their followers. The
Church teaches that blessing is the
chief sacramental, a rite or object
through and with which the sacraments are administered.

### THE POWER TO BLESS
In general, only bishops and priests
can deliver blessings, except in one
exception under which a deacon is
empowered to bless the paschal
candle on Holy Saturday. Certain
types of blessing are reserved for
more senior clergy. Only the pope

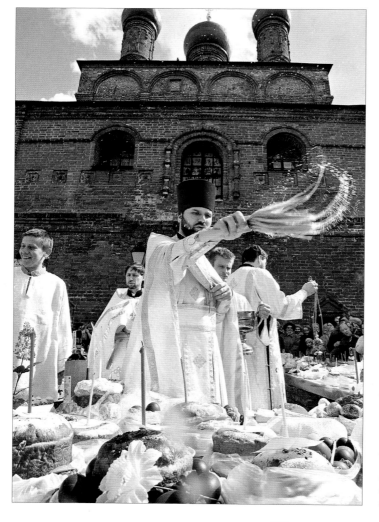

*Left In Moscow, a priest of the Eastern
Catholic Church blesses cakes and coloured
eggs with holy water as part of the Easter
celebrations. By blessing these objects, he is
removing original sin from them.*

can deliver some blessings – for example, those to which are attached an indulgence or remission of temporal punishment due to sin.

The pope's *Urbi et Orbi* blessing to the city of Rome and to the world, which is delivered every year on Easter and Christmas, has an indulgence attached for all Catholics who hear it in person, on television or on radio. Only bishops can deliver another class of blessings – for example, blessings on churches, cemeteries, chalices and vestments.

## PRIESTLY BLESSINGS

There is a wide range of blessings that can be made by priests. They include blessings for the sick or for women due to deliver a baby and for people at various stages of Church life. There are also blessings for sanctifying objects used in religious devotions, such as crosses, images of Jesus, bells,

***Above** Pope Benedict XVI delivers the papal* Urbi et Orbi *blessing. He prays that God's blessing should settle on the listening faithful and be with them always.*

medals, candles, rosaries and so forth. There are blessings for animals, food, buildings, such as schools or hospitals, and public objects, such as bridges, ships, stores, planes and so on.

The Church teaches that blessing is necessary and efficacious because people, animals and objects are all part of the Creation touched by sin after the Fall and therefore vulnerable to evil spirits. The blessings counter this effect by invoking the name of God, Father, Son and Holy Spirit and usually also by using the sign of the cross, a symbol of God's mercy and of Christ's victory over sin.

## THE SIGN OF THE CROSS

When Catholics make the sign of the cross, they are honouring the Cross of Calvary and the redemptive sacrifice of Jesus. The Cross is a symbol of both God's mercy and his victory through Christ over sin.

Individual believers make the sign of the Cross on their own bodies as an expression of devotion. The most common form is to touch forehead, breastbone or stomach, left shoulder and then right shoulder in sequence. Usually the believer prays "In the Name of the Father" when touching the forehead, "And of the Son" when touching the stomach, "And of the Holy Spirit" when touching the left and right shoulders in sequence.

## HOLY WATER

Sometimes a person will touch his fingers in holy water before making the sign of the Cross. When the faithful arrive at church for Mass, they dip their fingers in the bowl of holy water that is kept in a font near the entrance and make the sign of the Cross on head and torso.

The holy water has been blessed by a priest, and in this action the faithful bring to mind their baptismal promises as they seek to purify themselves before preparing to receive the Eucharist. Holy water is sometimes used to bless the faithful by sprinkling them with an aspergil (silver water sprinkler) during the Mass, especially during the Easter season. It is also used in blessings to sanctify places, objects and people.

---

### DIMINUTIVE CROSSES

A variant form of the ritual is to use the thumb to make a small sign of the Cross three times over forehead, lips and chest, sometimes while praying quietly "May Christ's words be in my mind, on my lips and in my heart". This is the normal usage when the gospel is proclaimed during Mass. A third kind of Cross made by the clergy is a small sign, traced with the thumb, for example, on the forehead of a baby in the sacrament of baptism or on the Holy Gospel during the liturgy of the Word in the Mass.

***Above** A priest makes the sign of the Cross on a child's forehead using his thumb. The sign assures the child of God's protection.*

# THE CATHOLIC YEAR

The Catholic liturgical year has been shaped by events in the life of Christ. Although the actual historical dates of these events are uncertain, over the centuries a chronology has evolved that reflects the principal milestones of Christ's life as described in the Scriptures. However, at the same time it considers the manner in which human progress through time has fluctuated with the seasonal cycles. Thus "Christ our Light" was born after the deep night of the winter solstice, and our redemption from despair and damnation came in spring, after the full moon of the equinox. In the Catholic calendar, these natural cycles have assumed a religious dimension as they are allied to the life of the God-man who Catholics believe died for humankind's eternal salvation.

Just as in the life of each individual, "ordinary time" is also a component of the liturgical year. During ordinary time, no specific events in Christ's life are celebrated, although holy days of obligation such as All Saints' and the Assumption of Mary do fall within ordinary time. Strictly speaking, "ordinary" here refers to ordinal, or numbered, time; it encompasses the period from the evening of Candlemas (2 February) until Shrove Tuesday, and again from the Monday after Pentecost until vespers the night before Advent. Ordinary time pays homage to the simpler days that Christ spent on earth and reminds us to consider, even now, how we go about our normal daily lives.

*Above Mary presides over ranks of saints in this fresco in the baptistery dome of Padua Cathedral, with her eminence emphasized by an enveloping golden aureole.*

*Left Youthful Christians bear a massive wooden cross in Jerusalem's Church of the Holy Sepulchre, built at the site of Christ's Crucifixion. The original 4th-century church was built by Constantine; the present structure dates from the Crusades of the 12th century.*

# HOLY DAYS

ROMAN CATHOLICS CONSECRATE EACH DAY OF THE YEAR TO REMEMBRANCE OF AN EVENT IN THE LIFE OF CHRIST OR THE BLESSED MOTHER, OR TO ONE OF THE SAINTS.

There are around 10,000 Catholic saints, and in the Catholic year, which is known as the liturgical year, each day has some sacred significance relating to a saint. Catholics nourish their spiritual consciousness by meditating on the particular virtues and mysteries that are invoked by the history of the saint on each new feast or saint's day.

## THE FIRST HOLY DAYS

The tradition of saints' days dates back to the first centuries of the Catholic Church during the Roman persecutions. The first saints were the Christian martyrs, and early Christians often honoured their sacrifice by celebrating the day of their death, also known as their "birthday into heaven". During the Middle Ages, saints' days were a common method of dating, so "St Martin's Tide", or "Martinmas", referred to a date near 11 November, the feast day of St Martin of Tours; "Bartholomew Tide" meant a date

*Below Farm labourers, such as the one in this 15th-century image from the* Historia Naturalis, *often stopped working on the many holy days in medieval times, so holy days were unpopular among landowners.*

in the waning days of summer, on about 24 August (commemorating St Bartholomew, patron of printers).

The Church classifies the daily liturgical observations as solemnities, feasts, memorials and commemorations. Solemnities, as their name implies, are the most important, but of the 13 yearly solemnities, only 6 are classified as holy days of obligation in the United States and 10 in Europe. (This group of six does not include ordinary Sundays, when Catholics are obliged to attend Mass each week, in honour of the day Christ rose from the dead.)

The Catholic Church mandates that Catholics must attend Mass on holy days of obligation, and refrain from "unnecessary servile work", often defined as physical labour. This prohibition is the genesis of today's word "holiday", which is an obvious contraction of "holy day". In feudal times serfs were freed on holy days of obligation so they could attend Mass.

## MEDIEVAL HOLY DAYS

By the Middle Ages, holy days were so numerous and engrained in the observances of society that in some quarters they came to be considered a nuisance. The prohibition against servile work was taken up by the populace with enthusiasm, and soon medieval lawmakers found themselves having to issue stern decrees to make "exemptions" from the command not to work on holy days so that crucial work, such as harvesting, did not come to a standstill. The *Catholic Encyclopedia* notes that from the 13th to the 18th century, some dioceses observed more than 100 feast days – days in which no work was done. Celebrations of the

*Above St Bartholomew is associated with books, as in this 14th-century illustration by Andre Beauneveu, because of a printers' celebration, the Wayzgoose. It is held on 24 August, the time of year printers began to work by candlelight.*

"octaves" of major Catholic holy days, such as Easter, could cause work to stop for more than a week. Complaints reached a crescendo in

### EARLY "FAIRS"

Not all Catholics abstaining from work on holy days were involved in reverent contemplation. The Latin *feria*, meaning "religious holiday", evolved to become "fair", a word that is still used to refer to a leisure activity, not to religious observance. One prelate suggested that while holy days gave Catholics a chance to "…receive the food of the Word of God, which they sorely need", they were instead using their holy days to relax or set up impromptu markets – and some of these were held within the churchyards themselves.

the 16th century, and finally in 1642 Pope Urban VIII bowed to the inevitable and issued an encyclical, *Universa per Orbem*, that reduced the number of holy days to 36 (not including Sundays).

Even priests are subject to normal human nature, and in 1858 Pope Pius IX had to issue a second encyclical – this time to order priests to offer Mass on the "suppressed" holy days. This was issued because some priests had decided to take a holiday of their own and had ceased to celebrate Mass on feasts that were no longer holy days of obligation, although to do so was still their responsibility.

## EUROPEAN HOLY DAYS

Holy days of obligation vary from country to country and year to year. In Europe, holy days are often celebrated with opulence. In Rome, for example, the Feast of Sts Peter and Paul (29 June) is a general holiday for the entire city, marking the day in AD 64 when both saints were martyred for their faith (Peter by being crucified upside down and Paul by beheading). Today, Romans observe the holy day with extravagant decoration of the 4th-century basilicas dedicated to each saint, and each year the pope presents palliums (from the Latin for "stole") to the city's bishops. The palliums are newly woven from wool shorn from lambs, and they symbolize the lamb carried over the shoulders of the good shepherd, reminding the bishops they are the shepherds of their pastoral flock, just as was Peter, Rome's first bishop.

## AMERICAN HOLY DAYS

The holy days of obligation in the USA are fewer than in Europe. This is, in part, because the tradition of their celebration is shorter than in many European countries, where Catholicism has been the majority religion for many centuries. In the early years of the United States,

Catholics were a minority, widely scattered in a vast country, and victims of prejudice. Puritans did not celebrate holy days because they had been offended by the excesses that they had observed in Europe. American bishops took such realities into account and reduced the number of holy days.

In the United States, if All Saints' Day or Ascension falls on a Saturday or Monday, the obligation to attend Mass is rescinded. The American Conference of Bishops has also suppressed certain holy days that are still active in Europe: the observances for Epiphany (6 January), Corpus Christi (the Thursday after Trinity Sunday), St Joseph (19 March) and the apostles Sts Peter and Paul (29 June) have been moved to the next following Sundays.

American holy days of obligation, with the exception of Christmas, are normally celebrated in a low-key manner simply by going to Mass. However, in certain American ethnic enclaves, old traditions of celebration on a saint's day still endure; for example, the feast of San Gennaro is usually celebrated with a street fair in Manhattan's Little Italy.

*Above* On the feast of Sts Peter and Paul in Rome, Pope Benedict XVI drapes a pallium made of new woven wool over the shoulders of an archbishop.

*Below* The September feast of San Gennaro, here celebrated in New York's Little Italy neighbourhood, home of many Italian-Americans, honours the 4th-century martyrdom of Januarius, the patron saint of Naples.

# The Festive Calendar

The feasts of the Catholic calendar have marked the days of the year for centuries. Some feasts occur on the same day each year, but others move depending on the lunar cycle.

Like the saints that they honour, Catholic feast days have been ranked and classified. Solemnity is the highest ranking of the holy days, but depending on the country it is not always a holy day of obligation. A feast day is the next highest rank of holy days, with celebrations that honour Jesus, Mary and the saints. A memorial is the lowest rank of holy days, a way of honouring saints without giving them fully fledged feast

days. Below is a key to symbols that indicate if the feast has a fixed or moveable date, and when a day of obligation is celebrated by most countries or only those in Europe.

## KEY
✧ moveable feast
⌘ fixed feast
O Holy Day of Obligation
❖ Additional European Holy Day of Obligation

*Above A calendar of saints' days from a 14th-century French Bible highlights the numerous days that were celebrated.*

## JANUARY
1 Solemnity of Mary Mother of God ⌘O
6 Solemnity of Epiphany ⌘❖
13 Feast of Baptism of Jesus ⌘
25 Feast of the Conversion of St Paul ⌘

## FEBRUARY
2 Feast of Candlemas (Presentation) ✧⌘
5 Shrove Tuesday ✧
6 Ash Wednesday ✧

## MARCH
2 Laetare Sunday ✧
16 Palm Sunday ✧
19 Spy Wednesday ✧
19 St Joseph ✧
20 Maundy Thursday ✧
21 Good Friday ✧
23 Easter ✧
25 Solemnity of the Annunciation ⌘

*Left St Paul's conversion to Christianity, captured in this 15th-century painting by Hildesheim, is celebrated on 25 January.*

*Above* *Many feast days celebrate Jesus and the Virgin Mary, depicted together in this Byzantine painting.*

## MAY

1  Ascension ✧○
11  Pentecost ✧
18  Feast of Trinity Sunday ✧
22 Solemnity of Corpus Christi
     ✧❖
30  Sacred Heart of Jesus ✧
31  Immaculate Heart of Mary ✧

*Above* *In Valencia, Spain, the feast of Corpus Christi is marked with processions of* rocas, *carts decorated with holy statues.*

## JUNE

29  Solemnity of Sts Peter and
     Paul ❖

## AUGUST

15  Solemnity of Assumption
     of Mary ⌘○

## SEPTEMBER

18  Birth of the Virgin Mary ⌘
29  Mass of archangels Michael,
     Raphael and Gabriel ⌘

## NOVEMBER

1  All Saints' Day ⌘○
2  All Souls' Day ⌘
23  Feast of Christ the
     King ⌘
30  First Sunday of Advent ✧

## DECEMBER

7   Second Sunday of Advent ✧
8   Feast of the Immaculate
     Conception ⌘○
14  Gaudete Sunday (Third
     Sunday of Advent) ✧
21  Fourth Sunday of
     Advent ✧
25  Christmas Day ⌘○
28  Solemnity of the Holy
     Family ✧

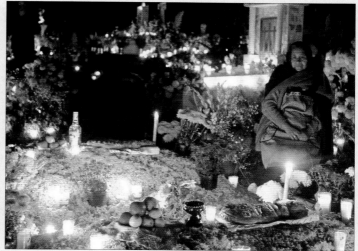

*Above* *The holy days of All Saints and All Souls are celebrated in Mexico with graveside offerings, including* pan de muertos – *bread made for the dead.*

*Above* *Michael, Raphael and Gabriel, the only archangels in the Scriptures, share a feast day in September. They are shown in this 15th-century image by Domenico di Michelino with Tobias, an encounter described in the* Book of Tobit.

*Left* *Christmas in midwinter, lights against the darkness – despite the debate and uncertainty about the true date of Christ's birth, it is celebrated around the world on 25 December.*

# A CHILD IS BORN

CHRISTMAS, A SEASON THAT CATHOLICS DEVOTE TO THE CELEBRATION OF JESUS' BIRTH, ENCOMPASSES TWO PERIODS IN THE CATHOLIC CHURCH: ADVENT AND CHRISTMASTIDE.

Advent is a season of preparation that is about four weeks long, although it is sometimes a little shorter, depending on the day of the week the 25th falls on. It will always include four Sundays. Christmastide is the period from Christmas Day to the feast of the Epiphany on 6 January – the traditional 12 days of Christmas.

## CELEBRATING ADVENT

Like the secular Christmas, the Catholic Christmas (from Old English *Cristes Maesse*, or "Mass of Christ") involves weeks of preparation. However, unlike the frenzied weeks of shopping promoted by the worldly media, the four weeks of Advent (from the Latin *Adventus*, or

*Above* The Magi, probably Persian kings, visited Christ when he was nearly a year old – not in the stable, as some traditions suggest. Gerard David captured the visit in his Adoration of the Kings, c. 1515.

"coming") involve steady spiritual preparation, marked by a certain amount of sober sacrifice and longing in the beginning, but as Christmas Day approaches, a mounting sense of joy. On the third Sunday of Advent, known as Gaudete (or "Rejoice") Sunday, the heightened anticipation is symbolized by a change in the colour of the priest's vestments from purple to rose.

Celebration of Advent originated in the 5th century, when Bishop Perpetuus of Tours decreed a fast, known as "St Martin's Lent", from St Martin's Day (11 November) to Christmas. In the 6th century, Pope Gregory the Great shortened Advent to four weeks, its modern duration, and strict fasting gave way to a less rigorous abstinence from meat and dairy. The liturgy of Advent emphasizes that preparation for Christ's first coming at his birth prefigures the preparations that Christians should make for his Second Coming.

## THE NATIVITY

One of the most widely known and beloved stories is that of Christ's Nativity. The tradition of the divine birth in a primitive stable in the

## DOMESTIC RITUALS

The domestic rituals of Advent evolved as expressions of the longing and expectation that characterize the season. The colourful family ceremonies are particularly attractive to children, helping them to focus on the spiritual rather than the commercial meaning of the season. The Advent wreath is a circular wreath of evergreens with four evenly spaced candles, three violet and one rose, to represent the four weeks of Advent. The violet symbolizes penitence, and the rose, lit on the third Sunday known as Gaudete Sunday, represents joy at the imminent approach of the Nativity. Families gather at a weekly Sunday dinner to light the candles, a new candle as each week passes, and dine by their light in the December evening. Some modern wreaths also include a white candle, symbolic of Jesus, that is lit on Christmas Eve. The familial ritual reminds Catholics of the intimate scene of the Holy Family within the snug stable.

Nativity scenes are usually small enough to fit on a table or mantelpiece. Some are simple and homemade, others are heirloom sets crafted by old world-artisans. The stable, the barn animals and the manger are arranged before Christmas, and Mary and Joseph are allowed to set up housekeeping, but the infant Jesus and the Magi must await the day appointed for their arrival in Scripture. Meanwhile, each day children add a few wisps of straw to the manger. By Christmas Eve, the manger will be comfortable for the infant figure, who arrives on time and with ceremony – gently placed in the manger at midnight on Christmas Eve. On Epiphany, the royal visitors from the East arrive, and the three kings are added to the stable scene.

*Right* The weekly ritual of lighting the Advent wreath in church or at home helps children understand the spiritual significance of the Advent season.

*Right* Although born in a humble setting, the Christ child seems to transfix the gaze of all in this 15th-century illustration by Rosello Franchi and Filippo Torelli.

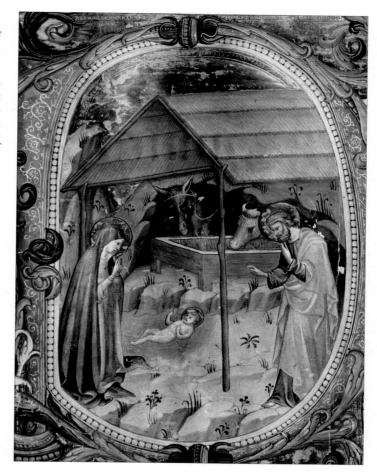

depth of winter concentrates the sense of mystery and delight that Catholics experience during this season. However, despite the hold that the Nativity story has on the popular imagination, the date of Jesus' birth is still unknown, and the only gospel to describe the Nativity is Luke, Chapter 2, in just a few words that have echoed down the centuries:

*And she brought forth her first born son and wrapped him in swaddling clothes and laid him in a manger: because there was no room for them in the inn.*

Around this quiet description, combined with the telling in Matthew, Chapter 2 of the wise men from the East who saw the star of the King of the Jews and travelled to seek and adore him, has arisen the vast tradition of the Christian Nativity in story and especially in art.

## A DATE IN QUESTION

In the early centuries of the Church, Christmas was not celebrated; some early theologians, such as Origen (AD 185–254), viewed celebrating the birthday of Christ with disfavour, calling it a pagan custom. The actual date of Christ's birth was also much disputed. Scriptural evidence for the date of the Nativity is inconclusive, and many scholars have argued that shepherds would not have kept their flocks in the fields at night in winter. The choice of 25 December was a compromise. Because the Church identified Christ with the coming of the light of redemption, it seemed most natural to celebrate the birth of "Christ Our Light" at a time when light was reborn after the solstice on 21 December. The date also takes advantage of a deep-rooted human

urge to celebrate at this time; the Roman holiday of *Sol Invictus*, or the birth of the Unconquered Sun, and the birthday of Mithras, the Persian God of Light, were both celebrated in December. By the 4th century, Christ's birth was celebrated in Rome on 25 December; early celebrations of Christmas were often combined with the older celebrations of Epiphany on 6 January.

*Right* The birth of Christ Our Light, after the winter solstice, reached its fruition at the Transfiguration, when Christ shone before his apostles. Fra Angelico painted the scene in The Transfiguration, *1436–45.*

# CARNIVAL!

THE MOST JUBILANT OF ALL OF THE CATHOLIC FESTIVALS, CARNIVAL IS INEXTRICABLY LINKED TO LENT, THE MOST AUSTERE. CARNIVAL HAS BEEN CELEBRATED BY CATHOLICS FOR SEVERAL CENTURIES.

As the predecessor to Lent in Catholic countries, carnival is a riotous indulgence of role reversal and licentious behaviour that has occurred for centuries. The word "carnival" probably derives from the medieval Latin phrase *carnem levare*, meaning "to remove meat". The linking of carnival and Lent in the calendar expresses an apparently innate human desire for cycles of feast and famine.

Some historians suggest that the Catholic Church was aware that carnival, which originated in southern European countries, was simply the ancient Roman pagan festival of Saturnalia under another name, yet tolerated the festival in order to smooth the transition from old pagan observances to those of the new religion. However, it is also true that the Catholic Church, especially when compared to the more sober Christian sects, such as Puritans or Quakers, has always had an appreciation of festival and pageantry.

## EARLY CELEBRATIONS

Contemporary carnivals are often associated with Rio de Janeiro – which mixes the European tradition with native American and African cultures: Venice, New Orleans and the Caribbean – and they almost always include vast costume parades with elaborate floats. However, carnival celebrations in Catholic countries have a long history – the Venetian carnival is mentioned in documents from 1092. In ancient times, carnival is said to have begun just after Epiphany (6 January) and lasted until Shrove Tuesday (*see* Shrove Tuesday, *below*), but in Rome the carnival was permitted to last for eight days, from the Monday of the week before Lent until Shrove Tuesday.

*Above Like carnival, the Roman festival of Saturnalia was officially approved and served as an antidote to a more solemn time – Saturnalia was held in midwinter; and carnival before Lent.*

## THE POPE AND CARNIVAL

Right up through the 19th century, Rome held a famous carnival that was supported, sometimes implicitly and sometimes explicitly, by the popes. No Roman carnival could begin without a papal edict, and depending on the reigning pope, that edict might be withheld.

Some popes, such as the 15th-century Pope Paul II, were involved in planning for carnival. Paul II ordered the Jewish people of Rome to pay a yearly tax of 1,130 gold

---

## SHROVE TUESDAY

The British version of carnival, which is held on the day before the first day of Lent, is Shrove Tuesday. It takes its name from the verb "to shrive", meaning to absolve of sin and give penance. Medieval custom was to confess and receive penance just before Lent in order to approach the austere week in a state of penitent purity.

A more whimsical name for Shrove Tuesday is Pancake Day because fasting was practised during Lent, and pancakes were a convenient way to use up any remaining eggs, milk and butter. This particular Tuesday has many aliases and is also known as Mardi Gras, which is French for another common name, Fat Tuesday. New Orleans is renowned for its Mardi Gras, its carnival celebrations that culminate on Fat Tuesday.

*Right A 19th-century vignette by Basile de Loose shows the making of pancakes, enjoyed by young and old.*

*Above* The pre-Lenten celebration of carnival reaches its apotheosis in Rio de Janeiro's sambodrome, a custom-built parade ground for carnival extravaganzas.

florins (the 30 added to recall Judas and the 30 pieces of silver), and the money was spent on carnival. Paul II also paid, straight from the papal treasury, for races for the elderly, children, asses and bulls. Conversely, Pope Sixtus V (elected in 1585) directed that gibbets and whipping posts be erected on the piazzas as a warning not to let carnival licentiousness to verge to the criminal.

In the 16th century, the Church attempted to steal carnival's thunder by holding a 40-hour prayer service on Monday and Shrove Tuesday – however, the 40 hours of prayer did not have a lasting negative effect on carnival's popularity.

## RACES AND CANDLES

The high points of the Roman carnival, popular from the 17th century onward, were the race of Berber horses and the Race of the Candles, both held in the Via del Corso. The riderless horses were released, wearing balls full of sharp pins hanging from their sides to goad them on down the crowded Corso. In 1882, 15 people were killed when the horses charged into the crowd, and that put an end to this tradition.

The Festa dei Moccoletti (candles) was held on the last night of carnival, when the people dressed in costume, and carrying candles and lanterns, swarmed through the streets trying to put out others' candles while keeping their own lit. The custom also ended in the 19th century, but children in Rome still celebrate it by going to school in costume.

*Above* The Race of the Candles involved three wooden pillars – representing Sts George, Ubaldo and Anthony – raced to the basilica. They seem ready to topple in this 19th-century Italian illustration.

# ASH WEDNESDAY AND LENT

LENT IS AN AUSTERE PERIOD OF SPIRITUAL PREPARATION LEADING UP
TO EASTER. IT STARTS ON ASH WEDNESDAY, AND DEVOUT CATHOLICS
FAST DURING THIS 40-DAY PERIOD.

Lent is a period of penitence and self-denial. It developed as an adaptation of an ascetic period of study and prayer followed by early postulants converting to Christianity. They undertook this period before being baptized on Easter eve. Pre-baptism instruction in these early centuries also included exorcism; descriptions of such initiation preparations are found in the 3rd-century *Apostolic Tradition*, a written collection of early Christian practices attributed to St Hippolytus. The word "Lent" derives from Middle English *Lenten*, or "spring", and is related to the German root for "long", because the days in spring get longer.

*Below A 16th-century Flemish artist has portrayed carnival as a corpulent figure among revellers. He is armed with a spitted fowl, ready to do battle with the opposing force of Lent, who thrusts a baker's paddle bearing fish toward him.*

## THE PERIOD OF LENT

Lent lasts for a total of 40 days, in imitation of the number of days Christ was in the wilderness, fasting and withstanding the temptations of Satan (Matthew 4:1–2, Mark 1:12–13, Luke 4:1–2). Until the 600s, Lent always began on Quadragesima Sunday, 40 days before Easter, but Pope Gregory the Great moved the start to Ash Wednesday to achieve 40 days without counting Sundays, which are feast days, when fasting is relaxed. During Lent, fasting was general: law courts were closed (in AD 380, the Roman emperor Gratian decreed that all legal proceedings be suspended for 40 days); theatres were shuttered; and hunting and military manoeuvres were all forbidden.

## THE START OF LENT

On Ash Wednesday, priests smear the foreheads of penitents with ash (made by burning the palms used in

*Above Jesus' 40-day fast in the desert, when he was tempted by the devil, is captured in this 19th-century painting by Ivan Nikolaevich Kramskoy. It is the model for the 40-day period of Lent.*

the previous year's Palm Sunday celebration) in the shape of a cross, saying "Remember that you are dust, and to dust you shall return" (Genesis 3:19), a reminder to those who have revelled in the excesses of Mardi Gras. Expressing penitence by using ashes is a custom inherited from ancient Jewish observance. In the Old Testament, Job expresses penitence to God with the words, "Therefore I despise myself and repent in dust and ashes" (Job 42:6).

*Right Lent's sobriety is represented by this stark composition of ash and palm, invoking the two celebrations of Ash Wednesday and Palm Sunday.*

In the early days of Christianity, ashes were used for those who had declared serious sins and asked to be shriven; the penance imposed began on Ash Wednesday and exiled the penitents from society for the 40 days of Lent; this custom is the genesis of the word "quarantine". The ashes were not smeared in a cross but sprinkled on the heads of the sinners. Over time, a public display of humility and penitence by the mark of the ashen cross became widespread.

## FASTING DURING LENT

Lent has always been associated with fasting; there is a scriptural basis for this, as in Matthew 9:15, Christ, when questioned why his disciples, unlike the Pharisees, did not fast, commented, "Days will come, when the bridegroom shall be taken away from them, and then they shall fast." It was after Jesus' departure that Christians began fasting. By the 12th century, St Bernard of Clairvaux noted that Lenten fasting was general: "kings, and princes, clergy and laity…" all fasted. When King Wenceslaus of Bohemia needed to eat meat during Lent due to ill health, he first sought dispensation from the pope. The "Black Fast" referred to one meal, taken in the evening, consisting of bread, herbs and water. Rules for fasting have become more lenient over time, but devout Catholics will still fast on Lenten Fridays.

## MODERN FASTING

For today's Catholics, 40 days of Lenten fasting in imitation of Christ's trial and temptation in the wilderness can be a particularly instructive experience, as we are so accustomed to relative plenty. A strict fast today is defined as only one meal, with two smaller meals that taken together would not equal a full meal. Animal foods, except fish, are avoided. As Christ lay in the tomb for 40 hours, the devout undertake a total fast for 40 hours just prior to Easter.

Catholics often undertake fasting as a family affair (although children under 14, according to canon law, are not required to fast), with the entire family choosing to give up meat, dessert, television or video games, then donating the money saved by this abstinence to charity, following the ancient Lenten tradition of almsgiving. Catholics are also encouraged to allow a sort of spiritual plenty to fill the space no longer occupied by temporal delights – Lent is a time of prayer and meditation. For this little time, Catholics follow the rigorous practice of monks, hoping to achieve some of the same religious insight.

Participating in fasting and other forms of abstinence are understood to be physical self-control that mirrors spiritual discipline. The Catholic catechism describes fasting as an "interior penance" and "spiritual preparation" that prepares Catholics for the arrival of Christ in the Eucharist, at his Resurrection and at the Second Coming.

*Below On Ash Wednesday, the first of Lent's 40 days, Catholics wear a cross of ash on the forehead, a symbol of penitence since Old Testament times.*

# HOLY WEEK

THE WEEK LEADING UP TO EASTER IS A PERIOD IN WHICH CATHOLICS
REMEMBER AND MOURN THE SUFFERING OF JESUS, WHEN HE WAS
SACRIFICED ON THE CROSS TO REDEEM HUMANKIND.

The week before Easter begins with Palm Sunday and extends to the vigil of Easter at sunset on Holy Saturday; it is known as Holy Week. During Holy Week devout Catholics follow along with Christ in a respectful attempt to take on the burden of the agony that he accepted as the price for their redemption.

Before the agony in the garden, anticipating the trial about to come, Christ said to Peter and the sons of Zebedee, "I am sorrowful even unto death....Stay you here and watch with me" (Matthew 26:38). The apostles, though, fell asleep, leaving Christ alone; he reproached them with, "Could you not watch one hour with me?" (Matthew 26:40). The liturgy and customs of Holy Week draw Catholics along with Christ's Passion, so that they "watch" with Christ and try to make reparation for that original abandonment.

## IN MOURNING

The stark and mournful tone of Holy Week is marked in many churches by obscuring all statues and crucifixes in purple veiling. The custom derives from the European tradition of hiding the altar crucifix behind a

*Above Judas was paid 30 pieces of silver to betray Christ. He is shown with the apostles' money bag in this 16th-century fresco by Eglise St Sébastien Plampinet.*

hanging that would be dropped to the ground during Palm Sunday, and reading from Matthew 27:51: "And behold the veil of the temple was rent in two from the top even to the bottom." This was one of the cataclysms that followed Christ's death. The liturgical atmosphere is of a community in mourning: the altar is not decorated with flowers, and the Te Deum and gloria are not sung.

## FROM PALM SUNDAY

In Scripture, Holy Week begins with the entry of Jesus into Jerusalem, his way strewn with palms and lauded with the Hosannas of the multitude, an event described by all four Evangelists. However, the triumph was short-lived; by Friday, Jesus would hang from the Cross. Today the entry into Jerusalem is commemorated as Palm Sunday. Palms are distributed at Mass, and some palms are saved to burn to make ashes for the next year's Ash Wednesday, symbolically linking

*Left After the Last Supper, Christ washed the apostles' feet. The ritual of washing feet, shown in Giovanni Agostino da Lodi's painting, 1500, symbolizes repentance.*

triumph (palms) and penitence and death (ash). Wednesday of Holy Week is also known as "Spy Wednesday", referring to Judas and his agreement to betray Christ for 30 pieces of silver.

## THE HEART OF THE WEEK

Easter Triduum (*triduum* is Latin for "three days") refers to the three days at the heart of Holy Week: Maundy Thursday, Good Friday and Holy Saturday. In Anglo-Saxon times, the Triduum was called "The Still Days", referring to the sorrow Catholics feel at this time, as well as to the time Christ lay in the tomb.

Maundy Thursday has tremendous significance for the Catholic Church, because it is on this day, at the paschal meal of the Last Supper, that Christ instituted the Eucharist. "Maundy" from the Latin *Mandatum*, or "commandment", refers to Christ's injunction to the apostles at the Last Supper, "A new commandment I give unto you, That ye love one another; as I have loved you" (John 13:34).

In John's Gospel, there is also a description of Christ humbly washing the apostles' feet on this day, and some churches commemorate Holy Thursday by a ritual in which the diocesan bishop washes the feet of 12 parishioners. In monasteries, the tradition was for the abbot to wash the feet of an ordinary monk.

After Thursday evening Mass, known as the Mass of the Lord's Supper, the altar is stripped of all cloths and candles, and the Eucharist in its chalice is removed from the tabernacle on the central altar and set in an unobtrusive side altar, known as the "altar of repose". The central altar remains bare and desolate of the sacred presence for all of Good Friday, the day marking Christ's Crucifixion and his death. Many churches remain open so that their parishioners can stay and pray quietly, "watching" with Christ in his time of need.

*Above A cross is borne through the streets in Corsica, France, on Good Friday.*

No masses are celebrated on Good Friday – the only day of the liturgical year on which it is forbidden to celebrate the Mass. Good Friday observances often include the Way of the Cross. Parishioners and clergy assemble in the late afternoon (Scripture notes that Christ died at the ninth hour, or 3 p.m.) at some public meeting place outdoors and carry a large cross in procession through the streets, stopping at designated points along the route to recite the Stations of the Cross. This public ritual is another example of the effort Catholics make during Holy Week to share and make reparation for the agony that Christ experienced for their sake.

### THE TENEBRAE SERVICE

Although the events commemorated by Holy Week occurred around 2,000 years ago, the Tenebrae is designed to help Catholics bridge the emotional distance and experience Christ's Passion as though they were there. "Tenebrae" means "shadows or darkness", and the service makes its participants feel as though a dark cloud has just passed over the sun.

The elements of the Tenebrae date from the 5th century. The original Tenebrae services were held in monasteries in the earliest morning hours. Today the service is held on either Maundy Thursday or Good Friday, usually at dusk. The church is in semi-darkness, the only light source a triangular candelabra known as the hearse, from the Middle English *herse*, or "harrow" (the two were similar in shape). As the service of sorrowful psalms, chants and lamentations is read, the candles are extinguished one by one until only a single lit candle remains. Then the celebrants, making no sound, leave the altar, marooning the congregation in the dark, silent church. Suddenly, a rough, clattering noise, known as the *strepitus* (Latin for "wild din" or "crash") is heard. It represents the convulsion of the earth at Christ's death. The congregation file from the church in silence, their way lit only by a few candles as they depart.

*Right Since the 13th century, the hearse has held candles during the Tenebrae service. "Hearse" later came to refer to a candle frame over a coffin, and from that to the vehicle that carries a coffin.*

# THE RESURRECTION AND EASTER

AFTER THE SOMBRE HOLY WEEK, CATHOLICS AROUND THE WORLD CELEBRATE EASTER, A JOYOUS OCCASION COMMEMORATING THE RESURRECTION OF CHRIST OUR LIGHT.

To Catholics, Easter is the greatest Catholic celebration and completes the meaning of all that came before and all that followed and is to come in Christian history. Without Easter, Catholic doctrine has no point, but all of Christianity is enlivened by the Resurrection of Christ on Easter.

The name "Easter" in Germanic languages is derived from old English and Germanic root words referring to the East and dawn. *Eastre* or *Ostara* was also the Anglo-Saxon Teutonic goddess of spring and fertility. In France, Easter is known as *Pâques*, and all Romance language names for Easter are from *Pascha*, for "Passover".

## HE IS RISEN

The Easter story can be simply told: two days after Christ was placed in the tomb of Joseph of Arimathea and a big stone rolled across the entrance,

Mary Magdalene, Mary, the mother of James and Salome, and "the other women" (the gospels differ on who was with Mary Magdalene) visited the tomb to anoint the body with spices, only to find the stone rolled away and the sepulchre empty. An angel sitting on the stone informed them that Jesus had risen (*see Easter: The Quem Quaeritis, opposite*).

## A DATE IN DISPUTE

Easter was first known as "Pasch", and the earliest references to it date from the 2nd century. Easter is a moveable feast, meaning that its date varies each year according to the lunar calendar (all of the other major Christian holidays follow the solar calendar). During the first centuries of Christianity, the correct date was disputed, but the First Council of Nicaea in AD 325 finally decreed that

*Above* The unleavened bread of Passover has become in Catholicism the unleavened bread transubstantiated into the Eucharist. The bread is being made in this 15th-century detail from the Schocken Bible.

Easter was to be celebrated the first Sunday after the 14th day of the moon (approximately the full moon) following the date of the spring equinox (assumed to be 21 March). Therefore, Easter can come as early as 22 March or as late as 25 April. The dates of other holy days, such as Pentecost, depend on the Easter date. Easter's date is linked to the Jewish celebration of Passover, because the Last Supper, three days before Christ's Resurrection, was a Passover Seder.

## CHRIST OUR LIGHT

After the darkness of the events of Holy Week, Catholics express their jubilation at the Resurrection in the traditional Easter vigil service. Near midnight on Easter eve, Catholics gather in a dimly lit church, symbolizing the darkness of Christ's tomb, and wait. Outside the church, a new fire is kindled and blessed. At midnight, priests light the paschal candle, marked with the Cross and the alpha and omega, symbols of Christ, from the new fire and process

*Left* Andrea Mantegna's dramatic 15th-century painting of Christ's Resurrection is scripturally inaccurate — according to the Bible no man or woman witnessed Christ coming forth from the tomb.

## EASTER: THE QUEM QUAERITIS

Four lines of dialogue beginning in Latin *Quem Quaeritis*, or "Whom do you seek?" were the genesis of the theatrical tradition of miracle and mystery plays that began in the 10th century. The Quem Quaeritis is a trope, or elaboration, of the part of the Easter liturgy that describes Mary Magdalene and "the other women" finding Jesus' tomb empty, with an angel sitting on the great stone.

> *Whom do ye seek in the sepulchre, O followers of Christ?*
> *Jesus of Nazareth, the Crucified, O heavenly ones.*
> *He is not here; he is risen, just as he foretold.*
> *Go, announce that he is risen from the sepulchre.*

The original adapted dialogue has come down to us in manuscripts from the monks at the 10th-century Abbey of St Gall and in actual stage directions written *c.*AD 965 by Bishop Ethelwold for Benedictine monks at Winchester. The original four-line vignette was performed, in Latin, by priests in the church sanctuary. Such dramatic renditions by the clergy of parts of the Easter liturgy were so popular that the subject matter was expanded to dramatize episodes from the New Testament and the lives of the saints. Responsibility for productions was removed from the clergy and taken over by the guilds of medieval towns, who performed the plays in English, with non-reverent elements.

*Above Mystery plays, adaptations of biblical scenes, were produced in public squares on moveable stages known as pageant wagons, as depicted in this 16th-century English illustration.*

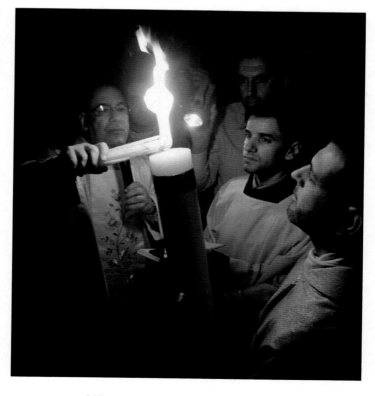

into the dark Church, symbolizing the Resurrection of Christ our Light. Easter is also traditionally associated with the baptism of new converts to Christianity, and Easter vigil services often incorporate baptisms of new Catholics on this auspicious day. The custom of wearing new clothes at Easter derives from the fresh white robes worn by the newly baptized.

The association of light with Christ's Resurrection is also the symbolic basis of the sunrise services, a variation of the Easter vigil. Often held on a hilltop, the faithful wait to see the new light of dawn pierce the dim sky; after dawn, a mass is celebrated outdoors. Joyful Catholics may be greeted by their priest with the ancient traditional Easter greeting, "Christ is risen indeed!" The one greeted then replies with "And hath appeared unto Simon!"

*Right An Easter vigil opens with the kindling of a new paschal candle, a large white candle symbolizing the return of the light of Christ, which is relit throughout the year to mark sacred rites.*

# CHRONOLOGY OF POPES

SINCE ST PETER, THE FIRST POPE, THERE HAS BEEN AN ALMOST CONTINUOUS SUCCESSION OF POPES. THE FOLLOWING IS A CHRONOLOGICAL LISTING OF ALL THE POPES WHO HAVE HEADED THE ROMAN CATHOLIC CHURCH.

*Above St Peter, the first pope, was traditionally supposed to have been crucified upside down, as in this fresco by Leonhard von Brixen, 1470.*

*c.*32–66 Peter
*c.*66–78 Linus
*c.*79–91 Anacletus
*c.*91–101 Clement I
*c.*101–109 Evaristus
*c.*109–16 Alexander I
*c.*116–25 Sixtus I
*c.*125–36 Telesphorus
*c.*138–42 Hyginus
*c.*142–55 Pius I
*c.*155–66 Anicetus
*c.*166–74 Soter
*c.*174–89 Eleutherus
*c.*189–98 Victor I
*c.*198–217 Zephyrinus
217–22 Callistus I
222–30 Urban I
230–5 Pontian
235–6 Anterus
236–50 Fabian
251–3 Cornelius
253–4 Lucius I
254–7 Stephen I
257–8 Sixtus II

260–8 Dionysius
269–74 Felix I
275–83 Eutychian
283–96 Caius
296–304 Marcellinus
*c.*306–8 Marcellus I
*c.*310 Eusebius
311–14 Miltiades
314–35 Silvester I
336 Mark
337–52 Julius I
352–66 Liberius
366–84 Damasus I
384–99 Siricius
399–401 Anastasius I
401–17 Innocent I
417–18 Zosimus
418–22 Boniface I
422–32 Celestine I
432–40 Sixtus III
440–61 Leo I
461–8 Hilarius
468–83 Simplicius
483–92 Felix III
492–6 Gelasius I
496–8 Anastasius II
498–514 Symmachus
514–23 Hormisdas
523–26 John I
526–30 Felix IV
530–2 Boniface II
533–5 John II
535–6 Agapetus I
536–7 Silverius
537–55 Vigilius
556–61 Pelagius I
561–74 John III
575–9 Benedict I
579–90 Pelagius II
590–604 Gregory I
604–6 Sabinian
607 Boniface III
608–15 Boniface IV
615–18 Adeodatus I
619–25 Boniface V
625–38 Honorius I

638–40 Severinus
640–2 John IV
642–9 Theodore I
649–53 Martin I
654–7 Eugene I
657–72 Vitalian
672–6 Adeodatus II
676–8 Donus
678–81 Agatho
682–3 Leo II
684–5 Benedict II
685–6 John V
686–7 Conon
687–701 Sergius I
701–5 John VI
705–7 John VII
708 Sisinnius
708–15 Constantine
715–31 Gregory II
731–41 Gregory III
741–52 Zachary
752 Stephen II
752–7 Stephen III
757–67 Paul I
768–72 Stephen IV
772–95 Hadrian I
795–816 Leo III
816–17 Stephen V
817–24 Paschal I
824–7 Eugene II
827 Valentine
827–44 Gregory IV
844–7 Sergius II
847–55 Leo IV
855–8 Benedict III
858–67 Nicholas I
867–72 Hadrian II

872–82 John VIII
882–4 Marinus I
884–5 Hadrian III
885–91 Stephen VI
891–6 Formosus
896 Boniface VI
896–7 Stephen VII
897 Romanus
897 Theodore II
898–900 John IX
900–3 Benedict IV
903 Leo V
904–11 Sergius III
911–13 Anastasius III
913–14 Lando

*Above St Francis of Assisi presents the regulations of his new order to Pope Innocent IV in this 18th-century painting by Niccolo Ricciolini. Innocent IV was a strong pope, affirming papal authority.*

***Right** Pope Clement V was responsible for moving the papacy to a new seat in Avignon, France, in 1305. This statue tops his tomb in Bordeaux's St André Cathedral.*

**Above** *Pope Clement VII suffered being taken prisoner in 1527. Giuliano Bugiardini's portrait, c. 1532, shows him six years later, in more dignified times.*

914–28 John X
928 Leo VI
928–31 Stephen VIII
931–5 John XI
936–9 Leo VII
939–42 Stephen IX
942–6 Marinus II
946–55 Agapetus II
955–63 John XII
963–5 Leo VIII
964 Benedict V (deposed)
965–72 John XIII
973–4 Benedict VI
974–83 Benedict VII
983–4 John XIV
985–96 John XV
996–9 Gregory V
999–1003 Sylvester II
1003 John XVII
1003–9 John XVIII
1009–12 Sergius IV
1012–24 Benedict VIII
1024–32 John XIX
1032–44; 1045; 1047–8
  Benedict IX
1045 Sylvester III
1045–6 Gregory VI
1046–7 Clement II
1048 Damasus II
1049–54 Leo IX
1055–7 Victor II
1057–8 Stephen X

1058–61 Nicholas II
1061–73 Alexander II
1073–85 Gregory VII
1086–7 Victor III
1088–99 Urban II
1099–1118 Paschal II
1118–19 Gelasius II
1119–24 Callistus II
1124–30 Honorius II
1130–43 Innocent II
1143–4 Celestine II
1144–5 Lucius II
1145–53 Eugene III
1153–4 Anastasius IV
1154–9 Hadrian IV
1159–81 Alexander III
1181–5 Lucius III
1185–7 Urban III
1187 Gregory VIII
1187–91 Clement III
1191–8 Celestine III
1198–1216 Innocent III
1216–27 Honorius III
1227–41 Gregory IX
1241 Celestine IV
1243–54 Innocent IV
1254–61 Alexander IV
1261–4 Urban IV
1265–8 Clement IV
1271–6 Gregory X
1276 Innocent V
1276 Hadrian V
1276–7 John XXI
1277–80 Nicholas III
1281–5 Martin IV
1285–7 Honorius IV
1288–92 Nicholas IV
1294 Celestine V
1294–1303 Boniface VIII
1303–4 Benedict XI
1305–14 Clement V
1316–34 John XXII
1334–42 Benedict XII
1342–52 Clement VI
1352–62 Innocent VI
1362–70 Urban V
1370–8 Gregory XI
1378–89 Urban VI
1389–1404 Boniface IX
1404–6 Innocent VII
1406–15 Gregory XII
1417–31 Martin V
1431–47 Eugene IV

**Right** *Pope Urban VIII was a temporal leader as well as a spiritual ruler, with his own coinage. This gold coin was produced in Avignon, France.*

1447–55 Nicholas V
1455–8 Callistus III
1458–64 Pius II
1464–71 Paul II
1471–84 Sixtus IV
1484–92 Innocent VIII
1492–1503 Alexander VI
1503 Pius III
1503–13 Julius II
1513–21 Leo X
1522–3 Hadrian VI
1523–34 Clement VII
1534–49 Paul III
1550–5 Julius III
1555 Marcellus II
1555–9 Paul IV
1559–65 Pius IV
1566–72 Pius V
1572–85 Gregory XIII
1585–90 Sixtus V
1590 Urban VII
1590–1 Gregory XIV
1591 Innocent IX
1592–1605 Clement VIII
1605 Leo XI
1605–21 Paul V
1621–3 Gregory XV
1623–44 Urban VIII

1644–55 Innocent X
1655–67 Alexander VII
1667–9 Clement IX
1670–6 Clement X
1676–89 Innocent XI
1689–91 Alexander VIII
1691–1700 Innocent XII
1700–21 Clement XI
1721–4 Innocent XIII
1724–30 Benedict XIII
1730–40 Clement XII
1740–58 Benedict XIV
1758–69 Clement XIII
1769–74 Clement XIV
1775–99 Pius VI
1800–23 Pius VII
1823–9 Leo XII
1829–30 Pius VIII
1831–46 Gregory XVI
1846–78 Pius IX
1878–1903 Leo XIII
1903–14 Pius X
1914–22 Benedict XV
1922–39 Pius XI
1939–58 Pius XII
1958–63 John XXIII
1963–78 Paul VI
1978 John Paul I
1978–2005 John Paul II
2005– Benedict XVI

**Left** *Pope Benedict XVI, who was elected pope after one of the shortest conclaves in Catholic history, must face the challenge of giving leadership to the world's Catholics in an age of increasing secularism.*

# RELIGIOUS ORDERS

THERE ARE A GREAT MANY DIFFERENT ORDERS WITHIN THE CATHOLIC CHURCH. BELOW IS A LIST OF THE MAJOR RELIGIOUS ORDERS AND THEIR FOUNDERS, ARRANGED CHRONOLOGICALLY.

## BENEDICTINES
The first great order of monks, founded by St Benedict of Nursia in 529.

## CARTHUSIANS
Enclosed order, including both monks and nuns, established by St Bruno of Cologne, 1084.

## CISTERCIANS
Reformist monastic order, founded by Robert of Molesme in 1098 and greatly expanded by St Bernard of Clairvaux.

## CARMELITES
The Brothers (and Sisters) of Our Lady of Mount Carmel, founded in the 12th century on Mount Carmel, Israel.

## TRINITARIANS
Order of the Holy Trinity, an order of priests, monks and nuns that was founded by St John de Matha in France in 1198.

## FRANCISCANS
Friars (Mendicant Brothers), founded by St Francis of Assisi in 1209.

## POOR CLARES
The Order of Poor Ladies, founded in Assisi, Italy, by St Clare with the help of St Francis in 1212.

## DOMINICANS
Friars, predominantly a teaching order; established by St Dominic in southern France in c.1215.

## AUGUSTINIANS
A group of monastic orders, incorporated as a "Grand Union" in 1256.

## CAPUCHINS
The Order of Friars Minor Capuchin, following a back-to-first-principles re-foundation of the Franciscans, started by Matteo di Bascio in 1520.

## THEATINES
The Congregation of Clerks Regular of the Divine Providence, known as the Theatines from their foundation in Chieti (Theate), Italy, founded in 1524 by St Cajetan.

*Above* St Benedict of Nursia can be seen teaching his Rule to his monks in this 13th-century French illustration.

## JESUITS
The Society of Jesus, founded by St Ignatius Loyola in 1534.

## URSULINES
Order of nuns, devoted mainly to the teaching of girls, established in Italy by Ste Angela de Merici in 1535.

## SISTERS OF LORETO
Order of nuns founded by Mary Ward, an Englishwoman in French exile, in 1609.

*Above* St Bruno, founder of the Carthusian order, prays in the wilderness at Chartreuse, France, in this 17th-century painting by Nicolas Mignard.

*Right* A 14th-century sculpture shows St Bernard of Clairvaux, a leading Cistercian, carrying the chapel of Clairvaux, the abbey that he founded.

*Above St Ignatius Loyola presented the rule book for his newly established Society of Jesus to Pope Paul III (1534–49), shown in this anonymous painting.*

## CONGREGATION OF THE MISSION

Also known as the Lazarists or Vincentians, this order of priests was established by St Vincent de Paul in 1624.

## DAUGHTERS OF CHARITY

Often referred to as Sisters of Charity, a congregation of nuns formed by St Vincent de Paul in 1633.

## TRAPPISTS

An order of monks and nuns, a Cistercian offshoot named for France's La Trappe Abbey, where their famous rule of silence was first introduced in 1664.

## LOVERS OF THE HOLY CROSS

Order of nuns, founded in 1670 in Vietnam and centred in the Far East.

## REDEMPTORISTS

The Congregation of the Most Holy Redeemer, who are missionaries to the poor; the order was founded in Italy by St Alphonsus of Ligouri in 1732.

## CONGREGATION OF CHRISTIAN BROTHERS

Commonly known as Christian Brothers, a congregation of lay brothers within the Roman Catholic Church, dedicated to educating poor boys worldwide; it was established by Edmund Ignatius Rice in Waterford, Ireland in 1808.

*Above Trappist monks perform their religious office at the Abbey Notre-Dame d'Aiguebelle, France. Prayer is an important part of their routine.*

*Above An Indian nun from the Missionaries of Charity ministers to Calcutta's poor. Founder Mother Teresa won international renown for the charity's work with the destitute.*

## SOCIETY OF MARY

The Marist Fathers (the Marist Brothers are an offshoot), an order of teachers and workers dedicated to the poor, founded by William Joseph Chaminade in France, 1817.

## LITTLE SISTERS OF THE POOR

Order of nuns dedicated to the care of the poor – especially the elderly – founded in France by Jeanne Jugan in 1839.

## SOCIETY OF AFRICAN MISSIONS

Founded by Melchior de Marion Brésillac in 1850.

## WHITE FATHERS

More formally, the Society of the Missionaries of Africa, founded in Algeria by the French cardinal Charles Lavigerie in 1868.

## MISSIONARIES OF CHARITY

An order of nuns established in 1950 by Mother Teresa of Calcutta to help the poor.

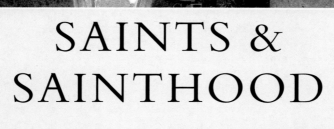

# SAINTS &
# SAINTHOOD

For hundreds of years, starting with the first martyrs of the early Church, saints were

chosen by public acclaim. Gradually the bishops, and finally the Vatican, took over

authority for approving saints, using a process known as Canonization. Being given the

title of saint tells us that the individual lived a holy life, is in heaven, and is to be

honoured by the Church. Canonization does not make a person a saint; it simply

recognizes what God has already done.

*The Last Supper (Leonardo da Vinci, c. 1495–98) is a mural painting that represents a scene from the final
days of Jesus with his apostles – 12 men chosen to be ambassadors of his teachings around the world.
Eleven of the apostles later died cruel deaths for their faith, and many churches are dedicated to them.*

# SAINTHOOD

The company of saints is filled with souls from all walks of life. These former human beings have been granted the highest accolade that their fellow Christians can give in honour of their holiness and worldly achievements.

In this section, Sainthood, there is a clear explanation of the qualities a person must show before they are officially recognized as a saint. Many have devoted their lives to spreading the word of God, others have sacrificed their own well-being for the welfare of their fellow men, women and children. Believers choose candidates for sainthood from a spontaneous understanding of their superior qualities as humans, but the Church is more circumspect in granting this status.

Official and non-official attitudes within the Church are given a full history, and the religious beliefs surrounding saints are clearly described. Also covered is the alteration of custom and religious practice brought by the religious wars of the Reformation, a change that affected the regard in which saints are now held. Ritual expressions of faith, such as pilgrimages and the veneration of shrines and relics, are analysed in both historic and modern expressions. Feast days and the festivals that have developed around these occasions are discussed. The reasoning behind certain saints being selected as patrons of nations, professions and causes is explained. This is not a history of the Church, but a revelation of the role saints play in art and the prayers of the faithful.

*Above* Twelfth Night Altarpiece *on wood. St Ursula and companions (left), the Adoration of the Kings (middle) and St Gereon with companions (right) (Stefan Lochner, c.1440).*

*Left Detail of* Procession in St Mark's Square *(Gentile Bellini, c.1500).*

# WHAT IS A SAINT?

A SAINT IS A DEAD INDIVIDUAL WHOSE EXCEPTIONAL HOLINESS
CHRISTIANS BELIEVE HAS EARNED HIM OR HER A PLACE IN HEAVEN.
THERE, SAINTS ACT AS CELESTIAL AGENTS. THE FAITHFUL MAY PRAY
TO THEM AND BESEECH THEM TO CONVEY THEIR PRAYERS TO GOD.

*Above Detail from the* Communion
of the Apostles, *a 15th-century
fresco at Platanistasa in Cyprus.*

Saints are not gods, they are not
worshipped. But they are
believed to exist so close to God
in heaven that they fulfil a key
role as intermediaries for the
Roman Catholic and Eastern
Orthodox Churches.

Lacking the temerity to
approach God directly, worshippers call upon these holy souls for
assistance. In 1545, the defining
Council of Trent stated that the
saints, who "reign" with Christ,
offer people's prayers to God to
obtain his benefits.

A Christian mystic once
described the feelings of all
believers when he said, "We
worship Christ, as the Son of
God; as to the saints, we love them
as the disciples and imitators of
the Lord."

## CULT FOLLOWING

From the earliest days of the
Church, the cultus of veneration
developed to include figures
besides Jesus who were deemed to
be holy. Their lives, which showed
great piety and humility, served
as inspiration to the inchoate
community of believers.

On the day of their death,
these holy individuals were
believed to have been reborn into
God's presence. Possessing this
elevated status, the saints quickly
developed cult followings. Their
death was commemorated with a
feast day at which time typically

*Right From the early Renaissance,*
Madonna Enthroned with Saints
*(Domenico Ghirlandaio, 1484).*

the faithful would gather at the
saint's tomb. The bodily remains,
or relics, were believed to possess
power. Not only were saints in a
privileged position to get prayers
answered, they could also work
fabulous miracles.

## MARTYRS

The judgement of an individual's
imitation of Christ in this early
period of Christianity was
concerned as much with the
manner of their death as with the
conduct of their life. A martyr —
he who dies for the Christian
faith — became an automatic
choice for the company of saints.
As the Church grew, especially

once the pope became the sole
authority in conferring such status
in the 2nd millennium, other
factors became as important, if not
more so, in determining a saint.

## HEROIC VIRTUE

Those who did not die a martyr
had to be shown by their cultus to
have led a life of "heroic virtue",
as it is defined by the Vatican. In
Christian terms, this means they

must have abandoned worldly interests. Whatever their station in life, whether prince or pauper, their devotion to faith in Jesus had to be manifest in their humility, charity and prayer.

As bureaucracy and suspicion played ever greater roles in the assessment process, so fewer saints were created. The late John Paul II did much to rationalize and clarify the procedure of canonization (literally, adding a name to the canon of saints).

### SINNERS REDEEMED

Not all saints led virtuous lives from beginning to end. Some were formerly tyrants, thieves or prostitutes before they turned to Christ. Even St Paul once cheered the stoning of the martyr St Stephen. St Pelagia was a harlot.

But these lives inspire believers, who feel hope when they learn that anyone might be redeemed through devotion. Perhaps St Paul summed up the quality of sainthood best when he said, "I live, yet not I, but Christ liveth in me."

*Right A panel showing Christ and the apostles at Pentecost (Georgian School, 12th century).*

### SAINTS IN OTHER FAITHS

Veneration of holy people, as messengers of the Almighty, has a place outside the Christian faith, too. Judaism refers to a category of holy figures known as Tzadikkim. In Islam, certain holy men, known as *Sufis*, are remembered with festivals. Thousands of Muslims in Pakistan, for example, commemorate the life and death of a 12th-century Sufi, Lal Shahbaz Qalandar, with sacred songs and dances performed by dervishes (followers of Sufism).

In Hinduism, *Sadhus*, or holy men, are considered to have reached saintly status while still alive. Likewise in Buddhism, *Arhats* are monks who are considered to have reached a state of nirvana.

Although there are some similarities in concept between the faiths, each has its own meaning. None are identical with that of Christian sainthood, which constitutes a unique doctrine of heavenly community.

*Right Dancing dervishes from a Persian miniature (c.1650).*

# SAINTS IN THE EARLY CHURCH

THE FIRST CHRISTIANS WERE FORBIDDEN TO PRACTISE THEIR FAITH
AND WERE CRUELLY PERSECUTED BY THE ROMANS. MANY EVEN
DIED FOR THEIR BELIEFS. THESE MARTYRS WERE HONOURED AS
SAINTS BY THEIR FELLOW BELIEVERS IN THE EARLY CHURCH.

There has never been any argument over the saintly status of the Holy Family, or the apostles and friends of Jesus on earth, but other saints have had slower recognition, or their status has been disputed. The earliest figures chosen for sainthood were usually those who died as martyrs.

Christianity was born in Palestine, a land that was then part of the Roman Empire. The Roman authorities who had condemned Jesus to death forbade any practice of his faith. Periodic state persecutions of Christians were merciless.

Whole communities who refused to abandon their faith were massacred, and some individuals suffered hideous torture. Some, dressed in rags with no weapon, were pitted against well-armed Roman gladiators, or fierce beasts. Thousands were murdered. While the names of many survive, we know few details beyond the date, and perhaps the place, of their death.

Records of these martyrs, the first Christians, can be read in the grave inscriptions found in the catacombs of Rome where the dead were laid to rest.

## EARLIEST MARTYRS

The first martyr (protomartyr) known to us was murdered about five years after the death of Christ. St Stephen was carried to the outskirts of Jerusalem and stoned to death. As he fell to his knees, he cried out, "Lord, lay not this sin to their charge." Thus, in his dying, he showed his belief in

*Above St Agnes, fellow virgins and singing angels in an altarpiece from the Upper Rhine (c. 1460).*

Jesus' message of love and forgiveness towards the wrongdoer. Many of the early martyrs showed a similar courage in their deaths. St Catherine of Alexandria endured the cruel spikes of a wheel. St Lucy refused to forsake her faith, even under torture, and was savagely beheaded.

It must be accepted that many legends grew up around the martyrs. For instance, although Lucy's tormentors had gouged out her eyes, it was said that she could fit them back into their sockets. Likewise, it was said that divine intervention broke Catherine's wheel, rescuing her from pain. Sebastian survived being tied to a column and shot through by a shower of arrows. And when Januarius was thrown to the lions, the beasts refused to attack him, instead laying quiescent at his feet. There are accounts of saints being thrown into vats of boiling oil and

*Below The martyrdom of St Erasmus as illustrated in the* Golden Legend, *a 13th-century hagiography of saints written by Jacobus de Voragine.*

emerging unscathed. Others who suffered a beheading were said to have merely replaced their heads.

## BLESSED VIRGINS

Many of the earliest female saints were chosen not only for their status as martyrs, but also for their purity in imitation of the Blessed Virgin. The importance of virginity has always been a strong (but not essential) consideration in the sainthood of women. As late as the 15th century, when St Joan of Arc claimed this status, she was given humiliating physical inspections to test the truth of her words.

During the Roman persecutions, St Agnes, at the age of 14, consecrated her virginity to Christ. She refused marriage, and both her faith and innocence were put to the sword. St Irene, a young girl, was forced by the Romans to go naked into a brothel, but she radiated such purity that no man dared go near

her. She was martyred in AD 305. In the same century the most extravagant legend of proud virgins involves the British St Ursula and her 11,000 virgin companions. Forced to flee their homelands to avoid "violation" through marriage, they finally reached Germany. There they were martyred for their beliefs, yet they died joyously.

## TRUTH IN LEGEND

Sceptics tend to dismiss these tales. But Christians honour them because they symbolize the superhuman courage and piety of the persecuted, and confirm that all suffering is eased by faith in Christ. As the novelist Sir Arthur Conan Doyle once said, "a legend however exaggerated upon fact is its own fact, witnessing belief." Although in many cases these stories are embellishments of a terrible reality, they still hold a certain truth for believers.

## CATACOMBS OF ROME

Beneath the city of Rome lies a great labyrinth of caves and tunnels. Probably first used by pagans as burial grounds, the early Christians tunnelled into this underground world to lay their dead. Some of the catacombs had been dug out to form large halls with connecting chapels. Recesses were hollowed out to hold three or four bodies apiece. They were sealed with slabs of marble or tiles bearing inscriptions and motifs. The labyrinth was also used as a place of refuge to escape Roman persecutors. By the late 4th century AD, the catacombs were no longer burial vaults but pilgrimage sites, which are still visited today.

*Above* The interior of a catacomb in Rome dating from the 3rd century AD.

*Left* One of the 40 martyrs of Sebaste being killed in AD 320, during the Roman persecution of Christians under the rule of Emperor Licinius (Byzantine, 12th century).

# DOCTORS OF THE CHURCH

LEADERS EMERGED FROM THE EARLY CHRISTIAN COMMUNITIES TO HELP DEVELOP THE STRUCTURE OF THE CHURCH. LEARNED WRITERS AND THINKERS AMONG THEM WHO MADE SIGNIFICANT CONTRIBUTIONS WERE CALLED "DOCTORS OF THE CHURCH".

A landmark change in the fortunes of the Church occurred early in the 4th century AD when Emperor Constantine I converted to Christianity. His edict permitting the worship of all faiths meant saints were no longer chosen primarily for their martyrdom. More important was the purity of a life dedicated to Christ. Some did so by renouncing the world, others played key roles in developing the Church for the benefit of the flock.

Scholarly writers and thinkers worked on formulating doctrine for the Church. Some helped develop new forms of prayer and

*Above* St Augustine of Hippo *(Piero della Francesca, 15th century).*

ritual. The greatest among these learned Christians were the early "Doctors of the Church", a term meaning great teachers. Unlike other saints who are championed by the people, the Church authorities alone decide who is worthy to receive this title.

## GREAT TEACHERS

To be recognized as a Doctor, the saint must formulate a special doctrine. Alternatively, he or she may make a profound interpretation of the faith, as well as having a "remarkable holiness" of life.

St Jerome (c.AD 341–420), who started his life as a monk, translated the Bible from Greek into Latin. St Ambrose interpreted the significance of the sacraments, and

*Left* Detail of St Ambrose from the *fresco* Doctors of the Church *(Giotto di Bondone, 13th century).*

defended the authority vested in the office of the pope. St Gregory the Great (c.AD 540–604) was a successful missionary, notably directing the conversion of the English. St Augustine of Hippo's interpretation of Christ's message profoundly influenced Christian moral principles.

## MODERN DECLARATIONS

Recognition as a Doctor of the Church could be a long process, sometimes taking centuries to complete. Sts Ambrose, Jerome, Augustine of Hippo and Gregory the Great all lived before the 8th century, but they were not declared Doctors until Pope Benedict XIV came to office in 1740.

The tradition of creating doctorships still continues today. St Theresa of Lisieux (1873–97) was declared a Doctor by John Paul II in 1997 for her simple but inspirational devotion. She is now one of the most popular of saints.

*Above* St Gregory in the Golden Legend *(Jacobus de Voragine, c. 1370).*

## DESERT FATHERS

Christ said, "If any man will follow me, let him deny himself, take up his cross and follow me" (Mark 8:34). In the first centuries of Christianity, there were believers who took these words as a direction to forsake all earthly pleasure. They followed the example of John the Baptist in hoping that hardship would wash away their sinful selves, and isolated themselves from society by living in deserts and other uninhabited places.

They led harsh lives, with little food. Legends say they were fed by ravens or wolves, and that water gushed from stony wastelands. The genuine humility and devotion shown by these ascetics attracted others, and soon groups of hermits chose to inhabit huts and caves close to each other.

From these loose communities, particularly those in Egypt, emerged teachers known as the "Desert Fathers". First among them was St Pachomius who lived alone on the banks of the Nile until other ascetics gathered around him. Some were so fanatical in their contempt for their own bodies they risked starvation and madness. To impose some constraints, Pachomius set up a community of 100 followers who committed to abide by his "Rules". To vows of chastity, poverty and obedience, he added orders of prayer and routine.

By his death, c.AD 346, Pachomius had founded ten monasteries, among the first such Christian institutions. Another popular Egyptian hermit of the 4th century, St Antony, also organized a monastic community. Over the centuries many other founders have established similar orders.

*Above* This 12th-century wall painting from Macedonia depicts St Antony, sometimes referred to as "the eremite" for his desert life.

# EASTERN SAINTS

THE CHURCHES OF RUSSIA, EASTERN EUROPE AND THE MIDDLE EAST DEVELOPED THEIR OWN THEOLOGY, VARYING FROM THAT OF ROMAN CATHOLICISM. EASTERN SAINTS FORM A DISTINCT COMPANY AND EVOKE A PARTICULAR KIND OF VENERATION.

*Above Mosaic detail in the apse of the Basilica Eufrasiana in Porec, Croatia (4th century). The work draws the eye to focus on the Blessed Virgin and the Christ child.*

The Eastern Church treats its saints in a slightly different way from that of Rome. Saints are not approached primarily as a means of conveying prayers to God, but rather to bring the believer closer to the reality of God. The reason for this difference lies in the Eastern Church's separate development in history from the West.

A formal schism between Western and Eastern Christians in 1054 led to the formation of a branch of Christendom known as the Eastern Orthodox Church. The two branches of Christianity had different beliefs about the dual nature of Christ, as both man and God.

The Roman Catholic and Orthodox Churches both believe that Christ is the Son of God who nevertheless assumed human form. The Orthodox interprets this to mean humans can attain the spiritual

*Left An icon of St Gregory Palamas (Russian School, 19th century).*

qualities of God; the Roman Church believes humans can only strive for these qualities.

The Orthodox Church has not altered its dogma or ritual since the 8th century. So tradition is paramount, and the saints form a key part of their worship.

### EARLY HOLY FIGURES
Pre-eminent among the Eastern saints is the Blessed Virgin. But everyone who is in heaven is a saint for the Orthodox, including pre-Christian Jews such as Moses. Popular early saints, such as John, Nicholas of Myra, George and Christopher, are common to both branches, but post-medieval saints are not.

The Orthodox categorize their saints according to type: prophets (those who foretold the coming of

*Left Detail from a manuscript showing St Sergius of Radonezh overseeing the building of a church (Andrei Rublev, 15th century).*

Jesus), the apostles, martyrs, Church Doctors (or Fathers), monastics (Desert Fathers) and the just (those who imitate Christ).

St John Chrysostom is highly honoured as a preacher and teacher. In AD 398, he was elected as archbishop of Constantinople (now Istanbul) and is recognized as a Doctor of the Church.

Another Doctor is St Basil the Great (c.AD 330–79) who laid down rules of organization for monastic life. His friend, St Gregory of Nazianzus, also ranks high among Orthodox saints.

## BYZANTINE MYSTICS

St Gregory's spiritual theology was developed by Simeon the New Theologian (d.1022) to reach a high point in Byzantine mysticism. Another Gregory, of

*Below The transfiguration of Christ in an Armenian manuscript (1362).*

Sinai (d.1346), devised new methods of meditation that influenced Orthodox practice. Other saints include Sergius of Radonezh (c.1315–92), monastic founder beloved of the Russians.

Mount Athos in Greece has a tradition of saintliness. Here the monk St Gregory Palamas (d.1359) founded an ascetical order, Hesychasm. Controversially it claimed visions of God's "uncreated light", an idea later accepted.

# CANONIZATION

AS THE CHURCH GREW, ITS COMMUNITIES REVERED MORE AND MORE DEVOUT FIGURES AS SAINTS. THE NEED TO CONTROL THE CREATION OF SAINTHOOD RESULTED IN THE ESTABLISHMENT OF A SYSTEM OF UNIVERSAL RECOGNITION IN A CANON OF HOLY SOULS.

Although some living people are described as saints, to be a real saint, the person must be dead. Up until the 4th century AD, when Christianity was adopted as the official religion of the Roman Empire, the devout were made saints only if they had died for their faith, for example were martyrs.

In the early, unstructured Church, groups began to identify individuals who, in their life and particularly in their death, imitated Christ. Such a group, known even today as a "cult" or "cultus", acknowledged the saintly qualities of the individual at their death.

The cultus prepared a joyous burial at which the death was celebrated with the eucharist. The

*Below Pope John Paul II canonized 120 Chinese martyrs in a ceremony held in St Peter's Square, Rome, on 1 October 2000.*

earthly remains, or relics, of the saint were carefully wrapped in an effort to preserve them. Every anniversary of the death called for a reunion of followers, and this day came to be known as the saint's "feast day".

## GROWTH OF CULTUSES

The proclamation of these devout members of local communities as saints was based on no established criteria in the early period. Vague ideas of holiness based on manner of life and death were frequently supported by claims of miracles and visions.

By the 4th century AD, local priests or bishops were being drawn into debate on the worthiness of these decisions. In some cases, for instance, there was suspicion that a person had committed suicide in the hope of being granted the glory of a martyr-

*Above Pope Pius II canonizes St Catherine of Siena (Pinturicchio, 16th century).*

saint. This was a particular problem among the desert hermits of North Africa. So priests began to assess the claims of the cultuses.

Bishops saw formal procedures of investigation as the best way to tackle the growth of false cultuses. Priests kept records of saints and the reasons for their sanctification.

## PAPAL SAINTS ONLY

At last, in the 12th century, the right to confer, or "canonize", sainthood was reserved for the Holy See, the office of the pope.

The official implementation of this development was attributed to Pope Alexander III (1159–81), though recent scholarship prefers Innocent III (1199–1216). From the 13th century, papal commissions were ordered to investigate claims to sainthood. The cultuses continued to select an individual but the commission required evidence that the candidate had lived a life worthy of Christ. Any claims to miracles were to be thoroughly investigated by the Church. These rules are followed to this day, although in 1983 Pope John Paul II streamlined the regulations, making them more precise.

MAKING A SAINT

Step One: The cultus makes its choice of saint, but the local bishop does not automatically accept it. For five years after the candidate's death, he conducts research into his or her virtues, or the circumstances of martyrdom. This allows time for a calm assessment of the candidate's life and death.

Then, the bishop's approval is submitted to the Congregation for the Causes of Saints, a panel made up of theologians and cardinals of the Church. If the panel

### DECANONIZATION

The Holy See knows the early saints have poor records, if any, to support their status. But it generally accepts the situation.

However, the Holy See did decanonize St Barbara in 1969 and Simon of Trent in 1965 because they were purely legendary characters. St Brigid of Ireland was accused of being a pagan figure, and so she too was decanonized.

Official announcements are often ignored. Cultuses can remain attached to saints, despite formal abolishment. In recognition of this loyalty, the Church has allowed certain cultuses to venerate "their" saint, but has withdrawn universal recognition.

Some decanonized saints in history include: Barbara, Brigid of Ireland, Christopher, George, Philomena, Simon of Trent, Valentine and William of Norwich.

approves, the name is submitted to the pope who then declares the candidate "Venerable".

Step Two: Martyrs will be canonized by the pope, but the Venerable must now be supported by a written claim from the recipient of a purported miracle performed by the holy candidate.

This miracle must occur after the death of the candidate. The believer must avow that they prayed to the Venerable who then interceded with God in answer to that prayer. This is seen as proof that the dead one's spirit is close to God. The pope approves the beatification of the candidate, who

*Above* Detail from a fresco showing the canonization of St Francis by Pope Gregory IX (Giotto di Bondone, c.1295).

can now be venerated by his or her cultus as "Blessed". Mother Teresa of Calcutta is an example.

Step Three: The third and last step towards sainthood needs evidence of one more miracle. When the pope has this, he agrees to canonize the beatified who is then named a saint. This status identifies the person as one who lived and died in imitation of Christ, and is officially in heaven. He or she can be honoured by all.

# MYSTERIES AND MIRACLES

LEGENDS OF MIRACLES AND EXTRAORDINARY BRAVERY ARE WELL-
KNOWN ATTRIBUTES OF THE SAINTS, BUT SOME WERE WITNESSED
MANIFESTING MYSTERIOUS POWERS AND PHYSICAL CHANGES THAT
DEFY SCIENTIFIC EXPLANATION.

Saints were so named because they led lives in imitation of Christ. It followed therefore that, like Jesus, they might be capable of performing miracles. The early saints were credited with having all sorts of supernatural powers. Evil spirits, disease, mortal ene-mies and wild animals were all claimed to be overcome. The per-ceived holiness of saints and their closeness to God led the faithful to believe that their prayers might be answered, and in miraculous fashion, too. Once a devout Christian had been declared a

*Above* St Denys is said to have carried his severed head to his burial place, as shown in this stained glass window in St Aignan Church, Chartres, France.

saint, their lives often became embellished with events of the miraculous, such as inexplicable cures or angelic assistance.

## VOICES AND VISIONS
St Joan of Arc claimed she had heard the voices of three saints instructing her to save France. The mystic and writer St Hildegard of Bingen described heavenly visions she experienced during her life. Crowds of people in Milan heard a unearthly child's voice calling out repeatedly, "Ambrose for bishop." The divine message persuaded them to elect Ambrose, despite him being unbaptized.

Another account of a divine apparition involved St Isidore the farmer, a humble, browbeaten peasant. He was so tired and in

*Left* St Januarius visited in prison by Proculus and Sosius (*Francesco Solimena*, c.1700).

such pain from beatings he could not work, but two angels appeared and ploughed the fields for him.

St Clement was said to have experienced a vision of Jesus while suffering extreme thirst digging a quarry under Roman coercion. The vision which came in answer to the saint's prayers was accompanied by a spring of water gushing suddenly from the rocks.

## HEALING

The more obvious imitation of Christ involves miraculous cures reminiscent of his ministry, such as healing disease. St Odile, for example, was said to have been born blind, but was given sight after her baptism. During her life, she restored the sight of others.

Saints' relics were believed to have the power to effect miraculous cures. Pilgrims travelled great distances to be in the presence of a saint's tomb, so that they might receive the healing power believed to reside within the corpse.

The relics of St Martin, for instance, were said to ooze curative oil and the faithful would flock to his tomb for a mere dab. Likewise, in the 7th century, oil was said to weep from the tomb of St John the Baptist and bore the odour of the honey upon which he had survived.

## RESCUE

Miraculous cures save the body from physical peril. Closely associated in terms of salvation are the rescues of individuals or whole communities from evil, frequently in the shape of a human enemy.

A painting of Our Lady of Czestochowa, commonly referred to as the Black Madonna, became the focus of Polish nationalism in the 14th century. When the Hussites overran the monastery of Jasna Gora (Mount of Light) in 1430, the painting was said to resist all attempts to destroy it. Every subsequent siege failed and Our Lady of Czestochowa was officially named Queen of Poland.

In times of war, saints are invoked for their protection, especially in great peril. And when victory comes against all odds, guardian angels and patron saints often receive the credit.

The blood of St Januarius has been revered in Naples ever since 1631 when Mt Vesuvius erupted. Subsequent prayers to the saint are believed to have prevented any repetition of such a disaster. Every year the vial containing the blood is displayed. If it liquefies the year will be free from disaster.

## THE STIGMATA

The appearance of wounds on the hands, feet and in the ribs, in imitation of those made by the nails that pinned Christ to the Cross, are a phenomenon known as the stigmata. St Francis of Assisi was the first Christian to manifest the marks, in 1224, which remained on his body for two years until his death. Since then, the Catholic Church has recognized 62 men and women as stigmatics. Listed below are the best-known sufferers, some saints, others Blessed.

St Angela of Foligno
Blessed Baptista Varani
Blessed Carlo of Sezze
St Catherine of Genoa
Blessed Catherine of
   Racconigi
St Catherine de' Ricci
St Catherine of Siena
St Clare of Montefalco
St Colette
St Francis of Assisi
St Frances of Rome
St Gertrude
St John of God
St Lidwina
Blessed Lucy of Narnia
St Lutgardis

St Margaret of Cortona
Blessed Margaret Mary
   Alacoque
Blessed Marie de l'Incarnation
Blessed Mary Anne of Jesus
St Mary Frances of the Five
   Wounds
St Mary Magdalene de' Pazzi
Blessed Osanna of Mantua
Padre Pio (*St Pius of Pietrelcina*)
St Rita of Cascia
St Veronica Giuliani

*Right St Francis of Assisi receiving the stigmata on the mountain of La Verna in Italy (School of Bonaventura Berlinghieri, 13th century).*

# HOLY RELICS

WHETHER SKELETON OR MERE SCRAP OF CLOTHING, RELICS WERE BELIEVED TO REPRESENT A SAINT'S PRESENCE ON EARTH. FOR THE DEVOUT, THEIR POWER WAS SUCH THAT EVEN SIGHT OF THESE ARTEFACTS WAS SAID TO EFFECT MIRACULOUS CURES.

From the earliest period of Christianity, the bodily remains of saints were venerated. A custom developed in which the saint's relics were no longer buried or laid in catacombs, but placed beneath church altars.

Churches sheltering relics were perceived by St Augustine of Hippo to be "as tombs of mortal men, whose spirits live with God". To this day, in the Roman Catholic Church, altars upon which mass is celebrated must contain the relics of a saint, according to canon law.

Gradually, the term "relic" embraced lengths of bone, scraps of burial wrappings, jewellery. Indeed, it could mean any little thing that had once belonged to the saint. The Church accepted this development because in the 1st century AD in Ephesus, Turkey,

tradition held that God had performed miracles through the handkerchiefs and aprons of St Paul. The sick believed they had been cured simply through their proximity to Paul's clothing.

The faithful believed that their prayers for forgiveness were more likely to be heard when uttered before relics or tombs. Other believers claimed the very sight of the relic summoned forth the saint who, through God, might perform miraculous cures of any ailment, from warts to infertility.

## COLLECTORS' ITEMS
Holy sites were not limited to the saints' burial places but included any site where a relic was housed. Their bodily relics became valuable, some fetching large sums, and were often plundered

***Above** A reliquary of the hand of St Thomas Becket kept at Burgos Cathedral, Spain.*

## THE HOLY HOUSE
The story attached to the "Holy House" of Loreto in Italy indicates the crazed, but profound, attachment medieval Christians had for their greatest saints.

According to the extravagant legend, an angel lifted the house in Nazareth where Joseph and the Virgin Mary had once lived, and carried it away. The house landed in random places before finally coming to rest in Loreto. The event was precisely recorded as ending on 7 September 1295. So many pilgrims flocked to see this wondrous relic, coined the "Holy House", that the authorities constructed an imposing church on the site. It continues to attract visitors.

***Right** The Basilica (Holy House) of Loreto, Italy, is one of the most revered sites in the Christian world. It was built in 1469 to house what is believed to be the miraculously transported home of the Virgin Mary.*

by clergy and believers who strove to build up collections. In the process relics were moved – "translated" – from one place to another. There could be a finger at one church, a shinbone elsewhere, while a third might claim to have a saint's sandal or cloak.

The faithful might ideally have wished to visit tombs, but a relic would serve just as well. It held the power of the saint. Even the churches of Jerusalem, whose significance rested on their association with the sites of Jesus' passion, boasted ownership of the relics of the True Cross upon which the Saviour had suffered crucifixion.

Every Christian pilgrim longed to visit the shrine of a saint, and many collected relics. The more precious items were kept in beautiful caskets, known as reliquaries, shaped like small tombs.

These containers were wrought in precious metals and adorned with jewels and enamelled images. Many are treasured to this day in Roman Catholic and Eastern Orthodox churches, although most are housed in museums across Europe and the USA.

## STRANGE AND BIZARRE

Some of the more interesting relics include a small carving of St Foy (also known as St Faith), from the 9th century. The figure is covered in gold plate and, over the centuries, believers bedecked the surface with precious emeralds, pearls and amethysts. This martyr was just 12 years old when she died. In the back of the carving there is a cavity containing her tiny wrapped skull.

Pope Urban V had the head of St Cassian encased in an elaborate casket. But Charlemagne (Charles the Great AD 747–814), emperor of the Holy Roman Empire, did better than that. He built a cathedral to house his huge collection of relics.

Among them, he claimed, were the cloth that once wrapped the decapitated head of John the Baptist, the tunic of the Virgin Mary, and swaddling cloths of the Infant Jesus. His collection of relics was displayed every seven years for a week in July. Vast crowds visited the church in Aachen, formerly Aix-la-Chapelle. The custom is still followed, revealing 200 relics every seventh year.

*Right A reliquary of St Foy (also known as St Faith) made of gold and jewels, held in the church in Conques, France (9th century).*

*Above left This reliquary depicts the martyrdom of the Roman St Candidus. It is made of nutwood and covered in gold and silver (c.1165).*

*Above Reliquary of St Stephen with enamel work from Limoges (12th century).*

# MEDIEVAL PILGRIMAGE

A JOURNEY TO VISIT THE SACRED RELICS OF A SAINT WAS AN IMPORTANT ACT OF DEVOTION IN THE MIDDLE AGES. THE HEALING POWER BELIEVED TO RESIDE IN THEM, AND THE SPIRITUAL ENERGY ASSOCIATED WITH THEIR SHRINES, DREW HORDES OF PILGRIMS.

Early Christians believed it an important act of piety to pray at the places where the Saviour and his company of saints had lived and died. A pilgrimage involved hardship. It was a form of penance, a humble mission to offer prayers of contrition, and call on the saints to intercede with God. From as early as the 2nd century AD, records tell of Christians travelling great distances on foot to the Holy Land in order to visit Bethlehem and Jerusalem.

They would have had a hard job, for these sites in Palestine were lost after AD 132, when the Roman emperor Hadrian demolished Jerusalem and rebuilt the city with temples dedicated to Roman gods. Only in AD 326, when Emperor Constantine I ordered Christian bishops to find the sites of Christ's passion, were shrines and churches built there.

One such site, the Holy Sepulchre, built by Constantine himself, stands to this day, albeit with some modification. The emperor's mother, St Helen, also a convert, founded churches in the Holy Land which drew yet more pilgrims.

## HEART OF THE EMPIRE

Outside the Holy Land, the most significant destination was Rome. Here the tombs and relics of the Holy Martyrs, including Sts Peter and Paul, were located. In AD 326,

*Above* The chapel at Aachen Minster was built AD 788–805 for Emperor Charlemagne to house his huge collection of relics.

St Helen brought to the city a marble staircase taken from the judgement hall of Pontius Pilate in Jerusalem. Purported to be the very steps upon which Christ had trodden as he went to his trial, these Holy Stairs were installed in the church of St John Lateran, and are said to be stained with Christ's blood. To this day, pilgrims climb the 28 stairs on their knees.

## ROADS THROUGH EUROPE

In England, thousands trekked to Canterbury to see the relics of St Thomas Becket, or made their way to Norfolk to pray before the holy shrine of Our Lady of Walsingham. Pilgrims took the Via Francigena, a popular route from Canterbury to Rome.

On the way was Paris, with Christ's crown of thorns, and Chartres, which held the holy tunic of the Virgin Mary. Pilgrims

*Left* An illustration from John Lydgate's The Troy Book and The Siege of Thebes, *shows pilgrims leaving Canterbury for London (1412–22).*

flocked to Tours, where the relics of St Martin were kept. And Cologne, in Germany, possessed the relics of the Magi, the three wise men who visited the stable to pay homage to the baby Jesus.

Once in Italy, pilgrims could glimpse the Holy Shroud of Jesus in Turin. And travelling on southwards, they would throng the streets of Assisi where St Francis was buried. From all over Europe, devout Christians journeyed to Santiago de Compostela in Spain, where the relics of St James the Great lay in his tomb.

## IMPACT OF REFORM

Pilgrimage had become so popular, even hysterical in its folksy enthusiam, that the whole activity invited disdain in some quarters. The bishop of Salisbury was moved to describe the veneration of relics as "abominable idolatry".

In 1517, the German priest Martin Luther introduced a radical idea. He argued Christians

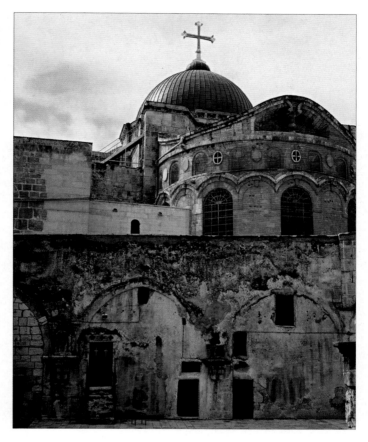

### NEW MARTYR SAINTS

A major consequence of the Reformation (1517–1648) was that new martyrs joined the company of saints. Hundreds of Welsh and English Roman Catholics were burnt, crushed between milling stones or beheaded by Protestants during the religious strife.

Some deaths were political in intent, and since then 200 have been named as martyrs. In 1970, Pope Paul VI found 40 to be worthy of canonization. They are known as the Forty Martyrs of England and Wales. Of these, 13 were priests, 20 monks and friars, and the remaining 7 consisted of lay men and women.

could approach God for forgiveness, without the intercession of the saints. So began the great division in the Church, the Reformation, which separated Christians into Roman Catholics and Protestants.

As Christendom became a battlefield, shrines were destroyed and relics burnt. In England, the shrine of St Thomas Becket was melted down to enrich the king's coffers, and the beautiful shrine in Walsingham violated.

Even Luther, the angry reformer, was distressed at such destruction wrought by the mobs. After these calamitous events, relics no longer gripped the reli-

*Above The Church of the Holy Sepulchre in Jerusalem, c.AD 335, commemorates the tomb of Christ and is a special place of pilgrimage.*

gious mind. Pilgrimages, too, lost their worldly appeal and were not the major social events they were in the pre-Reformation period.

Instead, pilgrimages reverted to being the pious causes of penance they had once been. Modern believers still honour relics, even venerate them, especially on feast days. Some recently canonized saints, such as the Aztec peasant Juan Diego, command huge followings of pilgrims who come to witness their relics.

# Important Feast Days

FEAST DAYS, TRADITIONALLY SET TO MARK THE DAY OF THE SAINT'S DEATH, ARE A CELEBRATION OF BIRTH INTO HEAVEN. CHURCHES CONDUCT SPECIAL MASSES, AS WELL AS PUBLIC EVENTS OUTDOORS. PROCESSIONS, MUSIC AND DANCE INVOLVE THE WHOLE COMMUNITY.

Roman Catholics and members of the Orthodox Churches venerate the saints' feast days in their liturgy. Important saints are celebrated on these days with special processions, particularly when the church houses their relics and images.

*Above* Thomas Aquinas being received into the Dominican order *(German School, 16th century). His feast day is 28 January.*

### JANUARY
Gregory of Nazianzus, Basil the Great 2
Genevieve 3
Elizabeth Seton 4
Sava 14
Antony of Egypt 17
Sebastian 20
John the Almsgiver 23
Thomas Aquinas 28

### FEBRUARY
Brigid of Ireland 1
Agatha 5

*Below Russian priests celebrating the feast day of St Cyril and St Methodius, known as "apostles to the Slavs", in 2007.*

Jerome Emiliani 8
Valentine, Cyril and Methodius 14
Martyrs of China 17

### MARCH
David of Wales, Gregory of Nyssa 1
Katharine Drexel 3
Patrick, Joseph of Arimathea 17
Joseph (husband of Mary) 19
Cuthbert 20

### APRIL
Isidore of Seville 4
John-Baptist de La Salle 7
Teresa of Los Andes 12
Bernadette of Lourdes 16
Anselm 21
George 23
Mark 25
Catherine of Siena 29

### MAY
John 6
Pachomius (West) 9
Helen with Constantine (East) 21
Rita of Cascia 22

Madeleine Sophie Barat, Bede 25
Philip Neri, Augustine of Canterbury 26
Bernard of Montjoux 28
Joan of Arc 30

### JUNE
Justin 1
Martyrs of Uganda 3
Boniface 5
Martha (East) 6
Columba of Iona 9
Antony of Padua 13
Thomas More 22
John the Baptist 24
Peter and Paul 29

### JULY
Thomas 3
Athanasius the Aconite 5
Benedict 11
Mary Magdalene 22
Bridget of Sweden 23
Christopher, James the Great 25

Anne (West) 26
Martha (West) 29
Ignatius of Loyola 31

## AUGUST
Jean–Baptiste Vianney 4
Fourteen Holy Helpers,
  Dominic 8
Edith Stein 9
Clare of Assisi 11
Maximilian Kolbe 14
Mary, the Blessed Virgin
  (Assumption) 15
Stephen of Hungary 16
Rose of Lima 23
Augustine of Hippo 28

## SEPTEMBER
Gregory the Great 3
John Chrysostom (West) 13
Hildegard of Bingen 17
Matthew 21
Padre Pio 23
Sergius of Radonezh, Firmin 25
Wenceslas 28
Archangel Michael 29

*Below The running of the bulls in
Pamplona takes place on 7 July, the
day the relics of St Fermin, a popular
local saint, came to the town.*

*Above St Athanasius the Aconite, a
Greek Father of the Church (print,
16th century). His feast day is 5 July.*

## OCTOBER
Theresa of Lisieux 1
Francis of Assisi 4
Denys of Paris, Martyrs of
  the Spanish Civil War 9
Edward the Confessor 13
Teresa of Ávila 15
Luke 18
Crispin and Crispinian 25
Simon, Jude 28

## NOVEMBER
All Saints 1
All Souls 2
Malachy 3
Vincent Liem 7
Leo the Great (West) 10
Martin of Tours (West) 11
John Chrysostom (East) 13
Albert the Great 15
Elizabeth of Hungary 17
Cecilia 22
Alexander Nevski 23
Andrew 30

## DECEMBER
Francis Xavier 3
Nicholas of Myra 6
Ambrose (West) 7
Eulalia of Mérida 10
Lucy 13
John of the Cross 14
Thomas 21
Stephen (West) 26
John 27
Holy Innocents (West) 28, (East) 9
Thomas Becket 29

*Below The Feast of St Lucy (Carl
Larsson, 20th century). On 13 December,
the oldest girl in a Scandinavian family
wears a crown of candles.*

# HEROES AND MARTYRS

REVERENCE FOR RELICS AND DEEP ATTACHMENT TO THE SAINTS DID
NOT SIT WELL WITH ALL BELIEVERS. PROTESTANTS REGARDED THESE
PASSIONS AS IDOLATRY, AN AFFRONT TO THE TRUE FAITH, AND THREW
OUT THE SAINTS. YET THE IDEA OF HONOURING HEROES REMAINS.

*Above A portrait of Martin Luther,
the priest who started the Protestant
movement (Lucas Cranach, the Elder,
1529). He is greatly honoured for his
brave and radical reforms.*

For more than a thousand years, Christendom guarded and reigned over Europe, Russia and Eastern Europe. The pope, his bishops, archbishops and clergy played a major role in economic and political life. The vast majority of the people recognized the authority of the Church. Even kings and queens, believed to be anointed by God to rule, formed an integral part of the system.

But by the 14th century, the Church was not the fervent, disciplined institution it once had been. Popes lived in splendour and

*Below Protestant Martin Luther is
shown here in triumph over Catholic
Pope Leo X (woodcut, 1568).*

priests were corruptible. The Reformation started as a call to return to the "purity" of early Christianity, and was not intended to create a major rift. However, great differences of opinion arose, and during the 15th and 16th centuries Christendom became a realm of war and disorder.

## CRY FOR REFORM

Reformers insisted the individual was important to God and no person needed the intercession of saints or priests to reach him. They insisted that veneration of the saints was contrary to the teachings of the Bible. As a result, the Protestants, as reformers came to be known, refuted the need for

saints as intermediaries, and dismissed the rule that priests be ordained by the pope. In acts of rebellion against the Roman Church, Protestants in countries across northern Europe forbade all worship relating to saints: relics, shrines and pilgrimages were all considered unnecessary and banned. Even images of the Blessed Virgin were prohibited.

## EVENTS IN ENGLAND
However, the Church of England was born out of political need rather than religious fervour. Henry VIII (1491–1547) chafed under papal rule and rejected the authority of Rome.

A period of killings and torture of Roman Catholics under Henry was followed by a similar persecution of Protestants by Mary Tudor (1516–58). By the death of Elizabeth I in 1603, most English subjects had learnt to accept that their monarch, and not the pope, was the head of their Church. However, English Protestants did not reject all the practices of the Roman Church. Indeed, in the Preface to their new Book of Common Prayer, the English Church emphasized the continuation of "the main essentials".

Priests continued to be ordained (though not by the pope), and the saints were not abandoned. The English simply decided not to create any more. Their Church proclaimed that images, relics and the "invocation of the saints is a fond thing vainly invented…but rather repugnant to the Word of God".

## CATHOLIC CUSTOMS
Despite this general antipathy towards sainthood, the English Church does acknowledge feast days for the Blessed Virgin and the apostles in the Book of Common Prayer. Obscure regional customs also hint at an English attachment to the old saints.

For instance, in Derbyshire, to avoid the charge of idolatry, it was rumoured that people would create temporary icons of the saints. It is thought that in former remote places, such as Buxton,

Eyam and Tideswell, the villagers dressed the village wells with intricate images of flowers that represented an apostle, a saint or the Blessed Virgin. These decorations appeared on the feast days.

The habit of honouring the most devout Christians in the community was hard to abandon, too. Consequently, in rejecting the title of saint, the Church of England chose instead to define

such people as "Heroes and Martyrs". On 9 July 1998, Queen Elizabeth II, Supreme Head of the Church of England, accompanied by the highest priestly officer of her Church, the Archbishop of Canterbury, unveiled ten statues of 20th-century martyrs. The list was cross-denominational, and in fact none of the men and women so honoured were members of the Church of England.

### 20TH-CENTURY MARTYRS
Instead of saints, the Church of England recognized heroes and martyrs. Statues of ten heroes and martyrs were erected on the façade of Westminster Abbey in London.

**Grand Duchess Elizabeth of Russia:** Murdered in 1918 during the Russian Revolution.
**Manche Masemola:** Killed in 1928 by her parents in South Africa for converting to Christianity.
**Maximilian Kolbe:** Polish priest murdered in 1941 in a Nazi concentration camp.
**Lucian Tapiedi:** Peasant from Papua New Guinea murdered in 1942 by Japanese troops.
**Dietrich Bonhoeffer:** German pastor murdered in 1945 by the Nazis.
**Janani Luwum:** Teacher murdered in 1977 by Idi Amin in Uganda.
**Esther John:** Indian missionary martyred in 1960.
**Dr Martin Luther King Jr:** Civil rights campaigner assassinated in 1968 in the USA.
**Wang Zhiming:** Chinese pastor killed in 1973 by the government.
**Archbishop Oscar Romero:** Murdered in 1980 in San Salvador.

*Above The martyrs' statues at Westminster Abbey: Martin Luther King Jr, Oscar Romero, Dietrich Bonhoeffer, Esther John and Lucian Tapiedi.*

# NEW WORLDS

EXPLORATIONS BEYOND EUROPE HELPED SPREAD THE CHRISTIAN FAITH TO THE AMERICAS, AFRICA, INDIA AND THE FAR EAST. MISSIONARIES AND THEIR CONVERTS FACED HARDSHIP, EVEN MARTYRDOM, AND INEVITABLY THE COMPANY OF SAINTS EXPANDED.

The apostles set a pattern of evangelism, making it a duty for Christians to spread the Gospel. Whether Roman Catholic, Eastern Orthodox or Protestant, churches have always treated this duty as a serious commitment.

The faith of these missionaries was tested during the widespread explorations of the Europeans in the 17th and 18th centuries. Adventurers and merchants first traded with, then colonized, far-flung lands, and Christian evangelists followed in their wake.

### MISSIONARY MARTYRS
Modern secular opinion asserts that these missions forced their faith on people for mere political purpose or to exploit natural resources. This may be true of

*Below A Catholic nun in Africa teaches children how to use knitting needles during the 1920s.*

ambitious leaders, but thousands of lowly religious gave their lives to the service of the indigenous people of these lands. Frequently, the missionaries protected their flock from both colonial masters and local warlords.

In remote, uncharted parts of the world, nuns and monks from Ireland, France, Portugal and Spain suffered the same hardship as their flock. They also filled non-religious roles as nurses and educators. Many paid the ultimate price of martyrdom and were canonized for their faith.

St Francis Xavier was among the first to be venerated for his life as an evangelist beyond the bounds of old Christendom. He travelled through the Far East, spreading the gospel, and was martyred. As other Europeans followed his example through the Americas, Asia and Africa, so the company of saints expanded.

### NATIVE CONVERTS
The legends of the saints were told to inspire converts and it mattered not that the Blessed Virgin was depicted with Chinese or Mexican features. With the infant in her arms, she became a universal symbol. Regardless of ethnic features, St Francis was recognized with his stigmata, and St Roch with the dog at his feet.

One of the earliest New World converts to inspire a cultus was Blessed Kateri Tekakwitha, a Native American who died in 1680 and was beatified in 1980. Similarly, a cultus developed after

*Above A Chinese representation of* The Nativity *(Lu-Hang-Hien, 19th century).*

the death of the Spanish Dominican St Joachim Royo, who died in China in 1748.

In Japan, Paul Miki and his companions, converts of St Francis Xavier, suffered relentless persecution before finally being tortured and crucified in 1597. Survivors venerated the blood-stained clothes of these 26 victims who were all canonized.

In Uganda, Charles Lwanga and his 21 companions, all under the age of 25, were burned alive for their faith in the 1880s. As they faced their horrific deaths, "their exemplary courage and cheerfulness were comparable with those of the early Christians". They were canonized in 1964.

The first native saint of the USA, Elizabeth Seton, died in 1821, and was canonized only in 1971 for her charity towards deprived children.

St Josephine Bakhita was taken into slavery in Africa, but found refuge in a convent in Italy. Her

*Right Missionaries and their catechumens experience floodwater in Hindustan, north India, in 1910.*

work as a nurse, together with her humility, attracted a cultus after she died in 1947. She was canonized in 2000.

## MASS CANONIZATION

Pope John Paul II recognized the neglected martyrs of the New and Developing Worlds. Tireless in visiting Catholic communities and in reinforcing the Universal Church, the late pope created more than 480 new saints. Through this pope's concern for his global flock, victims of mass persecution have been sanctified. He canonized 117 martyrs of Vietnam, all of whom gave their lives between 1745 and 1862. The Martyrs of Mexico, 25 Christians killed between 1915 and 1937, were also made saints in 2000.

Furthermore, he initiated the process of sanctification of the estimated 6,832 priests and religious put to death during the Spanish Civil War (1936–39). By creating native sainthoods, the pope hoped to encourage the Church in those parts.

*Above A painting of the Madonna on animal hide, made by Pueblo Indians in a traditional style (1675).*

*Left An armed ship carrying missionaries under the monogram of Jesus off the coast of New Granada, modern-day Colombia (artist unknown, 18th century).*

# MODERN PILGRIMS

THE MODERN ERA HAS SEEN A REVIVAL IN PILGRIMAGE AS A CHRISTIAN DUTY. NOT SINCE THE 16TH-CENTURY REFORMATION OF THE CHURCH HAVE SO MANY PILGRIMS UNDERTAKEN THE LONG JOURNEYS TO SHRINES FOR CURES, PENANCE AND PRAYER.

*Above Pope John Paul II celebrated mass with a million believers in front of a statue of the Virgin in Fátima, Portugal, on 12 May 1991.*

The pious duty of pilgrimage, although never abandoned by Roman Catholics, regained some of its former popularity during the Victorian era. The Ottoman Islamic hold on Palestine had weakened, and in 1855 a cross was borne through Jerusalem for the first time since the Crusades.

Pilgrims began visiting again the holy sites of Jerusalem, Bethlehem and Nazareth. By 1900, the traveller Gertrude Bell described a hostelry "packed with pilgrims tight as herrings sleeping in rows on the floor".

## VISIONS OF MARY

Various extraordinary events have contributed to this latter-day increase in the popularity of saints. In 1876, more than 100,000 pilgrims attended the dedication of the church at Lourdes, in south-west France, where St Bernadette received a vision of the Virgin Mary. Three years later, at Knock in Ireland, 15 people saw a vision standing on the village chapel roof of the Virgin accompanied by St Joseph, St John and a lamb. A shrine there now attracts more than a million pilgrims every year.

In 1917, the Blessed Virgin was said to have visited three children at Fátima in Portugal and entrusted them with three secrets. Now five million pilgrims a year visit their shrine. Believers claim that the Virgin told the children about forthcoming mass death in a second world war and an

*Below Catholic pilgrims during the Holy Week praying at the first Station of the Cross on the Via Dolorosa in Jerusalem (Erich Matson, c.1900).*

attempted assassination of a pope – both of which prophecies have come true.

## ECHOES OF THE PAST

Modern pilgrims, in imitation of the difficult conditions of their medieval counterparts, and also to show penitence, may choose to walk the "pilgrim's way" to particular shrines.

A popular route is the trek to Santiego de Compostela on the Atlantic coast of Spain. During their journey, they may pass other places of pilgrimage, such as the shrine to the Virgin Mary in Vézelay and at Conques, and can see the relics of the martyr, St Foy.

The main aim of the pilgrimage is to visit the tomb and relics of St James the Great at Santiago de Compostela. The Church gives a certificate to those pilgrims who have walked the last 100km/ 60 miles or cycled the last 200km/ 120 miles of the route. These awards echo the medieval habit of rewarding successful pilgrims with distinctive clothes and badges.

## RECENT DEVELOPMENTS

Ever since 1717, the most devout have walked about 110km/70 miles from Warsaw to the Jasna Gora monastery in Poland to see the miraculous icon of Our Lady of Czestochowa, reputedly painted by St Luke. But since the ending of Communist rule in the late 20th century, many more throng the route. An estimated million pilgrims a year now go to the site.

The biggest crowds are found at Zihuatanejo in Guadalupe, Mexico, where St Juan Diego had a vision of the Virgin. Ten million pilgrims pay homage to Our Lady of Guadalupe at this shrine every year. And seven million people travel to the tomb of the humble stigmatic, St Padre Pio, at San Giovanni Rotondo in south Italy.

## PERSONAL JOURNEYS

Other holy sites and shrines draw those seeking a significance particular to themselves. The pilgrim might be named after the saint, or be seeking one who is patron of a disease or other affliction.

Many visit Assisi, Italy, for St Francis, although an earthquake has left this site damaged. Pilgrims travel to the abbeys at Montserrat in France, or Trier in Germany, to seek intercession from the saints and wonder at the glorious holy

### BEING A PILGRIM

Modern Roman Catholic and Orthodox pilgrims are serious in their intent when they undertake journeys to the places associated with the saints. This is often the site where their relics are enshrined. Pilgrims seek penance and offer prayers of gratitude, or request their intercession.

Walking the route to a shrine, the faithful will take time to pray or undergo some physical hardship in penance. They venerate those shrines they pass as they head toward their final destination. If that is Rome, they will climb, on hands and knees, the hard marble steps of the Holy Stairs of St Peter's Cathedral.

Popular pilgrimages are those to Assisi, the shrine of St Francis, or to places that honour St James the Great in South America, or visits to sacred sites of the Holy Land. But in the 21st century, the sites and festivals that attract most visitors are those associated with the Virgin Mary, the one figure from the company of saints who seems to have sustained an imaginative hold on believers – and non-believers.

*Above Pilgrims kneel with crosses at the pass of Roncesvalles, Spain, on their way from south-west France to Santiago de Compostela.*

buildings. Today, pilgrimages to the Holy Land have become almost as dangerous as they were during the Crusades.

Many aspects of modern pilgrimage resemble the medieval experience, as Chaucer described in his poetic work *The Canterbury Tales*. Hostelries proliferate along the routes, especially near the shrines, just as they did in the Middle Ages. Translators and guides find work, while merchants are busy selling souvenirs, often facsimiles of medieval relics.

*Right Souvenir of the pilgrimage to Lourdes, made for the International Exhibition in Paris in 1867.*

# THE BLESSED

THE CHURCH DOES NOT GRANT SAINTHOOD LIGHTLY. HOLY SOULS MAY REMAIN FOR DECADES, EVEN CENTURIES, IN THE RANKS OF THE BLESSED OR THE VENERABLE, WHILE THE CLAIMS MADE ON THEIR BEHALF ARE CAREFULLY SCRUTINIZED BY THE VATICAN.

Mother Teresa of Calcutta lived a life that even the secular acknowledge was saintly. In the minds of many believers she is a saint. Yet she has not been canonized. Until a second miracle is officially attributed to her, she remains among the Blessed. Likewise, in the Rotunda of the Capitol Building in Washington, D.C., USA, stands a statue of the Blessed Father Joseph Damien de Veuster. This man was, and still is, deeply venerated by lepers and their families. For 16 years he nursed the lepers of Moloka'i in Hawaii. His gentle devotion and Christian faith were recognized as

*Above A photo of Blessed Father Joseph Damien de Veuster in 1873.*

being worthy of a saint. He died in 1889 and was eventually beatified in 1995 by Pope John Paul II, but Catholics in Hawaii already regard Father Damien as a fully fledged saint.

## UNKNOWN BUT HOLY

These are but two individuals who led lives of public service. Many others do not have national or global recognition. Cultuses have sometimes asked for obscure, private individuals to be named as saints. One such is Pierre Toussaint who was born a slave in Haiti in 1776 and taken by his master, John Berard, to live with him in New York. There Berard taught Pierre to read and write.

When Berard died, Pierre continued to care for the family of his late master by working as a barber. When Mrs Berard married again, Pierre set up his own home and with his wife cared for the homeless and destitute.

They purchased the freedom of many slaves, opened a school, and set up a religious order for black

*Left The procession of the Beatified in The Last Judgement (Giotto di Bondone, 1303).*

women. After his death in 1853, Toussaint became the only layman to be buried in the grand precincts of St Patrick's Cathedral in New York. He was recognized as Venerable by the Church in 1996, but in the local community people know him fondly as the "Barber Saint".

WILD MYSTIC

An Indian girl, Kateri Tekakwitha, endured a short wretched life, spent poor and lonely. Her father was a Mohawk chief and her parents died of smallpox. She survived but was scarred and left partially blind. Yet she claimed always to be filled with the joy of her faith.

Kateri, a mystic, revelled in the great prairie wilderness that was her home. She came to be known as the "Lily of the Mohawks", though some called her the "Mystic of the Wilds".

When she died in 1680, the local Jesuit missionaries were astounded to find her corpse transformed into the gracious form of a beautiful young woman. Their witness to her devotion and spiritual power formed the ground for her being granted beatification in 1980.

*Right A statue of Blessed Kateri Tekakwitha, a Native American mystic who died in 1680.*

*Left A watercolour portrait of Pierre Toussaint, fondly known as the "Barber Saint" (c.1825).*

PATRONS OF CAUSES

In some cases, the Blessed have been allowed to become patrons of causes. Maria Teresa Ledóchowska, who was born into a 19th-century noble Polish family, nevertheless devoted herself to mission work, especially to the abolition of slavery. The countess founded a community, first called the Sodality, now known as the Institute of St Peter Claver. Having taken vows as a nun, Maria worked tirelessly against slavery. She was beatified in 1976 by Pope Paul VI who declared her the patron of Polish missions.

Many saints are honoured for giving to the poor, but Blessed Bernardino of Feltre (d.1494) helped those too proud to accept welfare. He took over the Church's faltering little pawnshops, the *montes pietatis*, started in 1462 by Barnabas of Terni. Under Bernardino's care, the pawnshops were properly run and became very successful. They charged very low rates of interest and profits were used for charity. For centuries the shops could be found all over western Europe. His cultus was approved in 1728.

## MOTHER TERESA OF CALCUTTA

Even as a small child in Skopje, Macedonia, Teresa showed a religious turn of mind and, at 17, announced she wanted to become a missionary. She was sent to India and took her vows as a nun in 1937.

Teresa worked as a teacher until 1946, when she claimed she heard the voice of Jesus calling for her help. Further voices told her to found the Missionaries of Charity. For the rest of her life she devoted her energies to the care of the ill and dying poor of Calcutta.

So inspirational was her example that her followers opened other centres of Missionaries of Charity, first in Venezuela and Tanzania, then in other countries. Women took vows as nuns, and laymen were encouraged to help. Later the Missionaries of Charity Brothers was founded for priests. Mother Teresa died in 1997 and her tomb in Calcutta is a site of pilgrimage. She was beatified in 2002.

*Below Mother Teresa in Calcutta, India, in 1976.*

# PATRON SAINTS

EACH BELIEVER NURSES A PARTICULAR AFFECTION FOR ONE OR MORE SAINTS, AND TURNS TO THESE HOLY SOULS FOR HELP AND PROTECTION. EVERY ASPECT OF LIFE IS UNDER SAINTLY GUARDIANSHIP, WHETHER IT IS BABYHOOD, COURTSHIP, DOG BITES OR LOST POSSESSIONS.

Early Christians, believing the saints to be alive in heaven, found it logical to see them as patrons for mortals on earth.

Saints were thought to look after certain sectors of society, as well as support themes or activities with resonance in their personal story.

*Above St Jerome Emiliani, the patron saint of lost children, with a young orphan boy (Giovanni Domenico Tiepolo, 1780).*

**Abandoned children** – Ivo of Brittany, Jerome Emiliani

**Asylums for the mentally ill** – Dympna

**Alpine travellers** – Bernard of Montjoux

**Babies** – Holy Innocents, Maximus, Nicholas of Tolentino, Philip Zell

**Beggars** – Giles

**Birds** – Gall

**Blind people** – Thomas the Confessor, Cosmas and Damian, Archangel Raphael

**Blood donors** – Mary, the Blessed Virgin, Our Lady of the Thorns

**Booksellers** – John of God

**Boys** – Dominic Savio

**Breastfeeding** – Basilissa, Giles

**Brides** – Dorothy

**Cemeteries** – Michael, Anne

**Childbirth** – Margaret of Antioch, Raymund Nonnatus, Leonard of Noblac, Erasmus

**Children, longing for** – Rita of Cascia

**Children, lost** – Jerome Emiliani

**Criminals** – Dismas

**Degree candidates** – Joseph of Copertino

**Dentists** – Apollonia

**Difficult situations** – Eustace

**Dog bites** – Ubaldo

*Left Ferdinand III ruled as a king in Spain in the 13th century (illuminated manuscript, c.1250). He is the patron of prisoners and the poor.*

# DIRECTORY OF SAINTS

The first Christian saints were recognized soon after Christ's death over two thousand years ago and new names have been added ever since. This Directory lists a selection of major saints chronologically in order of their deaths. A strong historical sense emerges from studying these biographies, while changing cultural systems form a background to their stories.

Many saints are surrounded by myths of super-human strength and startling powers of endurance. These legends can be viewed as entertaining tales, yet they linger in the mind because these impossible acts are underwritten by a sincere faith. But, generally, the lives show the humanity of the saints. Some were short-tempered, some had brilliant minds, while others were confused and bewildered. We see kings becoming humble, scullery maids honoured for their integrity, and pious illiterates making an impact on the world.

The difficulties and problems encountered in their lives mirror the political and social worlds they inhabited. The persecution of Christians during the Roman Empire is familiar to most readers, but perhaps less well known is the persecution of later times that proved equally horrific.

The company of saints is varied and complex, filled with eccentric personalities, but all are alike in their pious attachment to God.

*Above* A bejewelled casket containing the relics of Thomas Becket (c.1190).

*Left* St Francis Expels the Devils from Arezzo (Giotto di Bondone, c.1297–1299).

# ARCHANGEL RAPHAEL

THIS ARCHANGEL IS THE HERO OF A LEGEND IN WHICH HE HELPS A POOR, BLIND MAN. HIS NAME MEANS "GOD HEALS", AND HE IS TRADITIONALLY SEEN AS BOTH A HEALER AND PROTECTOR.

**KEY FACTS**
*Divine messenger of God*
DATES: *Not human but a manifestation of God*
PATRON OF: *Travellers, young people leaving home, sad people, health inspectors, the sick, the blind and against eye disease*
FEAST DAY: *29 September*
EMBLEM: *Holding a bottle, carrying a fish or a staff, accompanied by a boy*

The Gospel of John tells us that in Jerusalem there was once a pool called Bethesda where, at a certain time every year, "an angel" stirred its waters. The first people to enter the pool after this visit would be cured of their illness or disability. By tradition, Raphael is credited as this very angel.

In the Apocryphal Book of Tobit, there are many stories about Raphael. Disguised as a man, he takes a journey with a boy, Tobias, and his dog. They travel to recover a debt owed to

*Above* Tobias and the Angel (*Andrea del Verrocchio, c.1470–80*).

the boy's blind grandfather, and have many adventures. On their return home, Raphael restores the old man's sight by asking him to eat a particular fish. Most paintings of this archangel show him with a fish, the boy and the dog, and he is a patron of travellers.

# ARCHANGEL MICHAEL

THE ARCHANGEL MICHAEL SAVED HEAVEN BY VANQUISHING THE DEVIL WHO WAS INTRUDING WHILE DISGUISED AS A DRAGON.

**KEY FACTS**
*Divine messenger of God*
DATES: *Not human but a manifestation of God*
PATRON OF: *Ambulance drivers, bakers, mariners, paramedics, soldiers and battles*
FEAST DAY: *29 September*
EMBLEM: *Frequently dressed in armour carrying a gatekeeper's staff, sword, scales, banner, dragon*

The Old Testament describes Michael as the protector of Israel, "always interceding for the human race". He was the angel who spoke to Moses on Mount Sinai. The New Testament says he "has authority over the people" and "gave them the law".

Archangel Michael fought the Devil when war broke out in heaven. Michael defeated the beast and the angels siding with it, so he was given the right to judge souls seeking entry into heaven.

Many medieval images show Michael weighing human souls

*Above* The Archangel Michael Defeating Satan (*Guido Reni, c.1600–42*).

brought before him for judgement. He is very often pictured fighting the dragon. Michael is the patron of battles and soldiers, as well as those believed to be "possessed by the devil".

Archangel Michael appeared in visions at Monte Gargano in Apulia, Italy, in the 5th century AD. Many churches worldwide, especially those built on hilltops, are dedicated to him, such as Mont-St-Michel in France.

# ARCHANGEL GABRIEL

THE ARCHANGEL GABRIEL DELIVERS SOME OF GOD'S MOST IMPORTANT MESSAGES TO MAN. HE INFORMED BOTH ELIZABETH AND MARY THAT THEY WOULD SOON GIVE BIRTH.

**KEY FACTS**
*Divine messenger of God*
DATES: *Not human but a manifestation of God*
PATRON OF: *Communications, postal workers, journalists, broadcasters*
FEAST DAY: *29 September*
EMBLEM: *Trumpet, often carries a lily, shield or spear*

In the Old Testament, Gabriel was present at the burial of Moses and at an Israelite victory over the Assyrians. He visited the prophet Daniel to warn him of the coming of the Messiah, saviour of the Israelites. He also helped Daniel interpret a dream that rescued the Israelites.

In the New Testament, the archangel Gabriel was charged with telling Zachary that his wife Elizabeth would bear a son who would play an important role in the Messiah's life. This son was John the Baptist.

## THE ANNUNCIATION

The most important message Gabriel delivered was to the Virgin Mary. He appeared before her to announce she had been chosen, above all women, to give birth to Jesus, the Son of God. His greeting to Mary, reported in the Gospel of Luke, has become the start of the "Hail Mary".

The Annunciation, Gabriel's visitation to the Virgin Mary, has been the subject of hundreds of paintings. The archangel always has wings and often wears a courtier's clothes, or a white tunic covered by a cloak.

Some traditions hold that, accompanied by "a multitude of heavenly hosts", Gabriel appeared above the hills of Bethlehem where shepherds were tending their flock. He announced the birth of Jesus to them.

In an ancient chapel on the Appian Way in Rome there is an early image of Gabriel. Some medieval depictions show him carrying the staff of a doorkeeper to show that he is a guardian of the Church.

His feast day used to be 24 March, date of the Annunciation. In 1969, the pope decided he should share a feast day with archangels Michael and Raphael.

*Below The archangel Gabriel appears before Mary for the Annunciation (Sandro Botticelli, c.1489–90).*

"HAIL MARY, FULL OF GRACE.
THE LORD IS WITH THEE.
BLESSED ART THOU AMONGST WOMEN,
AND BLESSED IS THE FRUIT OF THY WOMB, JESUS.
HOLY MARY, MOTHER OF GOD,
PRAY FOR US SINNERS, NOW AND AT THE HOUR
OF OUR DEATH."

GABRIEL'S GREETING TO MARY MAKES UP THE FIRST TWO
LINES OF THE "HAIL MARY" PRAYER

# THE HOLY FAMILY

JOSEPH, MARY AND THE INFANT JESUS MAKE UP THE HOLY FAMILY.
THE GOSPEL OF MATTHEW SAYS THAT THE MESSIAH WILL BE
DESCENDED FROM THE HOUSE OF DAVID. THE SPIRITUAL RELATIVES
OF THE HOLY FAMILY ARE THE HOLY TRINITY.

Joseph and Mary were humble and loving parents of the infant Jesus. They brought up their son in the Jewish faith and Jesus was taught to be a carpenter by his earthly father, Joseph.

### OF ROYAL DESCENT?
In the first 16 verses of his gospel, Matthew demonstrates a direct line of descent from King David of the Israelites to Joseph and Jesus. Such an ancestry was essential if the Jewish prophecy that the Messiah would come from the House of David was to be fulfilled. The same royal connections are ascribed to Mary, although nothing is known of her origins. Details of the lives of her mother, Anne, and of her father, Joachim, come only from apocryphal sources.

### THE BIRTH OF JESUS
When the Roman authorities held a census of the population, Joseph was obliged to travel to

*Above* The Holy Family
*(Luca Signorelli, 1486–90).
Christ is shown as a diligent child.*

*Below A fresco depicting* The Flight into Egypt, *from the Lower Church at Assisi in Italy (Giotto di Bondone, 14th century).*

Bethlehem, the city of David, to record his name. The journey was slow because of his young wife's pregnancy. Mary was very close to giving birth, but as Joseph hurried round Bethlehem at nightfall all he heard was the cry, "No room at the inn". Many other people had crowded into the town to fulfil the Romans' demands.

At last, a kindly innkeeper led him to the stables and told the tired girl that she could rest there. It was here in the stable, alongside cows and donkeys, that Mary gave birth to Jesus and laid him in a manger for lack of a cradle.

Shepherds arrived because angels had told them to visit the new Messiah. A bright star hung over the stable and guided the shepherds who brought the baby the gift of a lamb. The Holy Family received more guests with the arrival some time later of the three Magi, or wise men. They had read signs and warnings that told them where to find the new "King of the Jews". They brought him costly gifts of gold, frankincense and myrrh.

*Below Stained glass showing the holy family in the carpenter's shop, Steeple Aston, England (19th century).*

*Above A Nativity scene from the Bellieu Orthodox Church in Samokov, Bulgaria (16th century).*

After Jesus was born, Joseph received a warning that Herod was planning to kill the baby, so the Holy Family fled to Egypt. Herod carried out his threat, killing all male infants in Bethlehem under two years, but the Holy Infant was not among them.

## NO ORDINARY CHILD
Because the archangel Gabriel had appeared to both Mary, at the Annunciation, and to Joseph to explain the importance of their son, they knew that Jesus was a special child. In spite of this they were still horrified to find, a day

into their return journey from the annual trip to Jerusalem for Passover, that the 12-year-old Jesus could not be found among the family group.

Joseph and Mary returned immediately to the city and after searching for three days found him in the temple in the midst of doctors and rabbis, listening to the teachings and asking questions. Jesus calmly asked his mother why she had been so worried when she knew that he would be "about my Father's business".

## THE CRUCIFIXION
We know from St John's Gospel that the Blessed Virgin was accompanied by her sister, Mary of Cleophas during her vigil at the foot of the cross. As Jesus hung from the cross, he asked the apostle John to care for his mother. This implies that she had no other sons or a husband to care for her after Jesus' death. By tradition Mary became surrogate mother to John, and travelled with him on missionary work abroad.

*Below Twelve-year-old Jesus debating with the rabbis in the temple (Adolph Friedrich Erdmann von Menzel, 1851).*

# MARY, THE VIRGIN

MARY IS THE UNIVERSAL SYMBOL OF PURITY AND MOTHERHOOD. MANY CHRISTIANS BELIEVE SHE WAS FREE OF SIN FROM THE MOMENT SHE WAS CONCEIVED, A DOCTRINE KNOWN AS THE IMMACULATE CONCEPTION.

## KEY FACTS

*Mother of the Son of God*
DATES: *1st century BC*
BIRTH PLACE: *Unknown*
PATRON OF: *Motherhood, virginity*
FEAST DAY: *15 August*
EMBLEM: *Blue robes, crown, lily*

The image of Mary, the Blessed Virgin, is instantly recognizable, whether as a mother with her child in her arms or with her dead son laid across her lap. A mother nurtures her child, and her suffering for the sake of that child is intense. Mary, in the role of the Holy Mother, represents feelings understood by everyone. No saint can match the mother of the Son of God.

### EARLY LIFE

Little is known about Mary's early life. There are no dates for her birth or her death, and mention of her parents Anne and Joachim is only found in the apocryphal 2nd-century AD Gospel of James.

We do know, from the Bible, that the Blessed Virgin was a young Jewish girl, and that like her future husband Joseph, she was said to be descended from the family of the great Israelite king, David.

### MOTHER OF CHRIST

It was the angel Gabriel who told Mary that she was to be the mother of Christ, an event known as the Annunciation. The angel said that the child would be

*Left Mary and the baby Jesus are depicted as playful and loving in this stained glass from Eaton Bishop, England (14th century).*

*Left A sculpture of Mary cradling the body of her dead son (I. Günther, 18th century). Artistic images of this moment are known as "the Pietà".*

the Son of God, not of a man. Mary accepted this extraordinary fate with great faith and courage.

The Roman population census obliged Mary and Joseph to travel to the home of their ancestor, David. Mary gave birth to Jesus in a stable in Bethlehem, surrounded by animals. Shepherds and later three wise men, the Magi, came to worship the young Messiah.

After the Nativity, Mary is mentioned only a few times in the gospels. Mary and Joseph took Jesus for his presentation at the Temple of Jerusalem, as was the custom. With Joseph and Jesus she fled to Egypt to save their child from slaughter by Herod's men. At the marriage feast at Canaan, Mary asked Jesus to intervene when the wine ran out. And when Jesus hung dying on the cross, Mary kept vigil close by.

The Blessed Virgin was also with the apostles at Pentecost, the time after Christ's Ascension when the Holy Spirit is believed to have descended upon them. There is no mention of Mary living with Jesus and his apostles or teaching during this time.

### LEVELS OF VENERATION

Mary, the Mother of God, is universally admired by Catholic believers. The Catholic Church accords different levels of honour. The highest level is adoration, or latria, and is reserved for God and the Trinity (God the Father, God the Son and God the Holy Ghost). Veneration of the Blessed Virgin is granted the Church's second highest honour and is known as hyperdulia, as theorized by Thomas Aquinas. Veneration of the company of all other saints is known as dulia.

*Above A detail from* Wedding at Canaan, *the occasion when Jesus performed his first miracle by turning water into wine at the request of Mary (Paolo Veronese, 1563).*

## A MOTHER'S PLACE
Although nothing is known of Mary's death, members of the Roman Catholic and Eastern Orthodox Churches hold that she was lifted body and soul into heaven. This event is celebrated as the Assumption. Her role as the mother of Jesus placed her very close to God in heaven.

Many believers think that if a person asks Mary to intercede on their behalf, her great influence is bound to bring God's forgiveness and redemption of their sins.

## MARY IN ART
In earlier times Mary's image could be seen widely throughout Christendom. During the early medieval era, depictions of the Virgin Mary and the infant Jesus

*Right Mary with the twelve apostles and two archangels in a Russian icon showing* The Ascension *(c.1450).*

were generally richly decorated with gold. They were portrayed as formal, grand and majestic.

Images from the late medieval and early Renaissance periods show a tender young woman with a baby. She is often clothed in a heavenly blue gown and the child is naked. Images of the Virgin Mary in the developing world more recently often show her dressed in the most admired style of the local people.

In today's Catholic and Orthodox worlds, Mary is still remembered when many other saints are neglected. Holy icons and festivals held in Mary's honour continue to attract millions of believers across the globe.

# JOSEPH

THRUST INTO THE UNIQUE ROLE OF EARTHLY FATHER TO THE SON OF GOD, JOSEPH PROVED A KINDLY HUSBAND AND CARING PARENT. HE PROTECTED HIS YOUNG FAMILY BY FLEEING FROM KING HEROD.

**KEY FACTS**
*Husband of the Virgin Mary*
DATES: *1st century BC*
BIRTH PLACE: *Palestine*
PATRON OF: *Canada, Peru and Mexico, families, fathers, manual workers (especially carpenters), the homeless, exiles, travellers*
FEAST DAY: *19 March and 1 May*
EMBLEM: *Bible, branch, carpenter's tools, ladder, lamb, lily*

Joseph, husband of the Virgin Mary, was a godly man. He is most often portrayed as both honourable and compassionate.

He makes few appearances in the New Testament. The Gospels of both Mark and Luke describe his royal descent from the House of David, although a carpenter by trade. According to the Jewish prophets, the Messiah would come from this House.

Joseph's age is unknown. As the betrothed of a young woman, it may be fair to assume he was also relatively young at the time of his engagement. An indication of his noble character is given by the nature of his reaction when he learned Mary was pregnant. Not wishing to shame her, he decided to end the betrothal quietly. His distress was dispelled when an angel appeared and explained the intervention of the Holy Spirit.

## THE FLIGHT INTO EGYPT
After the Nativity and the visit of the Magi, an angel interpreted one of Joseph's dreams, warning him of Herod's order to murder all the small boys in Bethlehem. This led Joseph to flee his home to save his wife and the baby Jesus. Numerous paintings depict Joseph as very protective of his family.

Later in Egypt, an angel let Joseph know when it was safe to return to Palestine, and he settled in Nazareth. He followed Jewish custom when he took his wife to the purification ceremony that all women underwent after giving birth. The scribes do not record Joseph's death but it is assumed he died sometime before the crucifixion of Jesus, as Joseph is not mentioned as present on this day.

## OTHER INTERPRETATIONS
Joseph's actions show him worthy of his role as protector of the Son of God. Despite this, some apocryphal writings represent him as an old man and parent of other children. The travelling players of medieval theatre liked to present him as a clownish old fool.

Veneration for Joseph grew, however, and in 1870 he was declared patron of the Roman Catholic Church. A special day, 1 May, was dedicated to him as patron of manual workers.

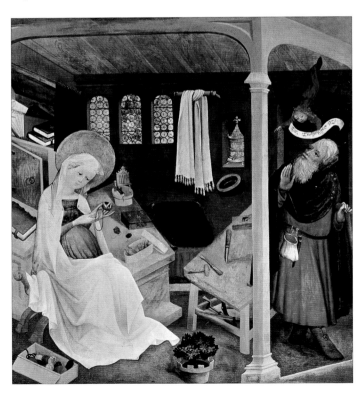

*Left A small angel reassures Joseph in* The Doubt of St Joseph *(French School, c.1410–20).*

# ANNE

THE MOTHER OF THE BLESSED VIRGIN IS NOT MENTIONED IN THE
CANONICAL GOSPELS, BUT APOCRYPHAL SOURCES PRAISE HER AND
SHE HAS A LOYAL FOLLOWING NONETHELESS.

**KEY FACTS**
*Mother of the Virgin Mary*
DATES: *1st century* BC
BIRTH PLACE: *Unknown*
PATRON OF: *Childless women,
horsemen and miners*
FEAST DAY: *26 July (West)*
EMBLEM: *Basket, door*

There is no firm evidence to determine the parentage or place of origin of the mother of the Virgin Mary. Yet believers longed to have information about the earthly grandmother of Jesus. There is an apocryphal text, the Gospel of James, that mentions her as a saint. Gregory of Nyssa, the brother of St Basil the Great and a saint in his own right, also refers to her with reverence.

In the Gospel of James, Anne is described as childless, and she "mourned in two mournings, and lamented in two lamentations". Her desperate prayers were answered when an angel visited her house to tell her she would bear a child.

Anne responded with the words, "As the Lord my God liveth, if I beget either male or female I will bring it as a gift to the Lord my God; and it shall minister to Him in holy things all the days of its life." So the Virgin Mary was consecrated to God even before her birth.

In the *Golden Legend*, stories of the saints from the 13th century, Anne's husband Joachim dies shortly after the birth of Mary. Anne remarries twice. She has a daughter by each of these new husbands, and both these girls are given the name of Mary. The girls grow up to produce many cousins for Jesus and two boy cousins become apostles. Despite the fictitious nature of both these sources, Anne became sufficiently important in the Church for her relics to appear at the church of Santa Maria Antiqua in Rome.

*Above A young Mary is shown
reading to her mother in this
manuscript drawing (15th century).*

*Below The story of Mary's birth
is here imagined within a
contemporary Venetian domestic setting
(Vittore Carpaccio, 1504–8).*

## LATER INFLUENCE

The figure of Anne remained in the public mind and artists favoured her as a subject. Paintings and stained glass illustrations show Anne as a tender mother to her little girl. Other images depict Anne teaching Mary how to weave and read.

An unexpected cultus grew in Constantinople (Istanbul) during the 6th century AD when Emperor Justinian I dedicated a shrine to St Anne. She was venerated in Europe from the 13th century. When England's King Richard II (1367–1400) married Anne of Bohemia in 1382, the English bishops petitioned the pope to grant a feast day for St Anne. Later, the official status of such an unsubstantiated figure aroused great anger in Martin Luther.

# JOACHIM

JOACHIM IS HONOURED AS THE HUSBAND OF ANNE AND THE FATHER OF MARY. HIS POPULARITY GREW IN THE WEST IN THE MIDDLE AGES AS THE CULTUS OF THE BLESSED VIRGIN FLOURISHED.

**KEY FACTS**
*Father of the Virgin Mary*
DATES: *1st century BC*
BIRTH PLACE: *Unknown*
PATRON OF: *Fathers, grandfathers*
FEAST DAY: *26 July (West)*
EMBLEM: *Elderly man holding doves, lamb*

This man became a saint by virtue of being the husband of St Anne and the father of the Blessed Virgin. In Hebrew, his name means "the Lord will judge". The sources of information for him are entirely fictitious, as they are for his wife.

In the *Golden Legend*, Joachim is given a picturesque history. This book tells how he was expelled from the Jewish temple because, after 20 years of marriage, he and his wife remained childless.

Desolate and believing God had cursed him, Joachim went to seek refuge with a band of shepherds. He decided to fast for 40 days. An angel visited and comforted him with the news that his wife would bear a child. Excited, Joachim hurried home.

*Above* Charlemagne, and the Meeting of Saints Joachim and Anne at the Golden Gate *(the Master of Moulins, c.1500).*

*Below right* Presentation of the Virgin at the Temple *(Philippe de Champaigne, 1639–40). Mary would have been taken to a synagogue, but this image depicts a Christian setting.*

*Below left A fresco scene showing Joachim among the shepherds (Giotto di Bondone, c.1303–10).*

But Anne, his worried wife, was wandering through Jerusalem looking for her husband. An angel appeared and advised her to go to the Golden Gate. There, Anne found her husband. After this happy reunion, she conceived the child who would become the Mother of God.

## LATER RECOGNITION

The cultus of St Joachim began in the East and was more popular there than in the west. For several centuries the Eastern Orthodox Church has celebrated his feast day on 9 September. The Roman Catholic Church was less eager to grant him sainthood, but the large cultus could not be ignored. Pope Gregory XV (1554–1623) allowed him status as a saint, and Joachim shares a feast day with his wife.

# ELIZABETH

ELIZABETH WAS ELDERLY AND GENERALLY ASSUMED TO BE BARREN WHEN SHE BECAME PREGNANT WITH THE BOY WHO WOULD BECOME JOHN THE BAPTIST. THE ARCHANGEL GABRIEL DELIVERED THE NEWS.

**KEY FACTS**
*Wife of Zachary,
mother of John the Baptist*
DATES: *1st century BC*
BIRTH PLACE: *Probably Palestine*
PATRON OF: *Pregnancy*
FEAST DAY: *5 November*
EMBLEM: *Elderly woman*

It is assumed that Elizabeth was close to menopause when Gabriel announced that she was carrying a child. She was known to be childless, and the news must have brought her great joy.

Elizabeth, a descendant of the patriarch Aaron, is said to have been related to the Blessed Virgin. Their friendship was cemented by their fates as well as by blood.

Numerous paintings show these women together. Elizabeth was the first person to recognize Mary as the mother of the future Lord.

*Left A detail of St Elizabeth from the church of Santa Maria di Porto Fuori, Italy (Ercole de' Roberti, c.1480–81).*

# ZACHARY

INITIALLY DOUBTFUL, ZACHARY WAS JOYFUL AT THE PROMISE OF A CHILD AND NAMED HIM JOHN.

**KEY FACTS**
*Father of John the Baptist*
DATES: *1st century BC*
BIRTH PLACE: *Probably Palestine*
FEAST DAY: *5 November*

The father of John the Baptist was a Jewish priest. He and his wife Elizabeth had long been married, but had no children.

Zachary was visited by the archangel Gabriel in the temple in Jerusalem, who announced that Elizabeth was to give birth to a child who would "make ready a people prepared for the Lord". Zachary doubted the words of the angel and was struck dumb.

At the baby's circumcision Elizabeth insisted that he was to be called John, going against the Jewish tradition that a child should be given a family name. Zachary supported her by writing on a tablet, "His name is John". Immediately, he regained his voice and began praising God. His words, known as the Benedictus, form part of the Church liturgy.

"AND THOU, O CHILD, SHALL BE CALLED THE PROPHET OF THE MOST HIGH; FOR THOU SHALT GO BEFORE THE LORD TO PREPARE HIS WAYS, TO GIVE HIS PEOPLE KNOWLEDGE OF SALVATION THROUGH FORGIVENESS OF THEIR SINS . . ."

THE BENEDICTUS
(CANTICLE OF ZACHARY)

*Left In this Flemish early Renaissance painting, Zachary is displayed in the fine clothes of a medieval baron to indicate his high status as the father of John the Baptist (Jan Provost, 1510).*

# JOHN THE BAPTIST

JOHN THE BAPTIST DEVOTED HIS LIFE TO WARNING PEOPLE TO "REPENT, FOR THE KINGDOM OF GOD IS AT HAND". HE DECLARED THAT THE MESSIAH WOULD SOON APPEAR AMONG THEM.

**KEY FACTS**
*Baptized Jesus*
DATES: *d.c.AD 30*
BIRTH PLACE: *Nazareth*
PATRON OF: *Pilgrims to the Holy Land, Knights Hospitallers, hoteliers, birdwatchers*
FEAST DAY: *24 June, 29 August*
EMBLEM: *Lamb, cross, a scroll*

The writings of Sts Jerome and Augustine of Hippo suggested that John the Baptist was sanctified in the womb and never committed a sin. He certainly chose a "heroic" life of hardship and poverty, dressing only in animal skins and living on food he could scavenge.

John devoted his life to telling people to prepare for the coming of the Messiah and his Kingdom.

He must have had a charismatic personality with great energy and determination, for he attracted a large following.

### BY THE JORDAN

His youth was spent as a hermit, surviving on a diet of locusts and wild honey, a lifestyle that closely resembled that of some of the prophets of the Old Testament.

Crowds came to hear him preach, and John began to baptize them by dipping them in the River Jordan. When Jesus came through the crowd, a dove hovered over his head.

John took this bird to be a sign of the Holy Spirit, so he knew Jesus was the Messiah. He then baptized Jesus, saying he was "the Lamb of God who takest away the sins of the world". In paintings, John is often shown pointing at a lamb and holding a cross.

John the Baptist was later put in prison for denouncing an incestuous marriage between the governor of Galilee, Herod Antipas, and his niece, Herodias. His stepdaughter, Salome, pleased Herod so much with her dancing that he offered her anything she wanted. At her mother's prompting, the girl requested the head of John the Baptist. It was delivered to her on a platter.

### TEACHINGS

The teachings of John the Baptist prepared the way for the work of Jesus. John preached about the presence of a "messianic kingdom" and the need for all to repent their sins. His lessons were

*Left* St John the Baptist in the Wilderness *(Hieronymus Bosch, c.1504–5). John the Baptist is shown in a landscape of strange plants with a lamb, one of his emblems.*

rooted in the Jewish belief that one day the Almighty would send a messiah to lead the people to righteousness. Many Jews who heard John speak were therefore sympathetic to the arrival of Jesus and accepted him as their long-awaited leader.

A large number of disciples followed John and imitated his severe ascetic mode of life. He taught them methods of prayer and meditation. Many ordinary, humble families were moved by his message, too.

Historians believe that John the Baptist's wanderings took him to the Dead Sea. Lessons similar to his message are recorded in the Dead Sea Scrolls – papyrus writings dating from the early Christian era. In Samaria, there is evidence of a community, the Mandaeans, or Sabaeans, who defined themselves as "Christians according to John". It seems these people preserved ideas and traditions that confused John the Baptist with Jesus.

*Below* Salome with the Head of Saint John the Baptist *(Bernardino Luini, c. 1525–30). Salome is shown as a young woman with a sly and cunning expression.*

Medieval Christians prayed to John the Baptist, believing that through him, Christ would enter their souls. He is reputedly buried in Sebaste, Samaria. Alone among the saints, his feast day is held on his birthday. However, the date of his death is also celebrated in the West on 29 August.

An important saint, some of his relics are claimed to be held in St Sylvester's Church in Rome, and in Amiens, France. Many churches in Britain and Europe have been dedicated to him.

*Left* Saint John the Baptist *(Titian, c. 1540). John may be dressed in skins and rags, but he is here presented as a powerful man and leader. The lamb lies at his feet.*

## THE MEANING OF BAPTISM

Baptism is a religious purification ceremony in which a person is either immersed in water, or has water poured over their head. Baptism is part of the Christian tradition, but can be seen to have a precursor in the Jewish tradition of undergoing a *mikvah*, or cleansing ritual, for instance on conversion to Judaism.

Baptism has been subject to many interpretations by different Christian churches, and as a result has varied meanings. It can be seen as a path to salvation and a process by which a person is cleansed of their sins. In this way, baptism may help a convert to Christianity put their past behind them and start afresh.

Similarly, baptism may be seen as a symbolic death and rebirth, an interpretation put forward in the Bible by Paul who says that we share in the death, burial and rebirth of Jesus Christ through baptism. Baptism can also function as a symbol of conversion, through which a believer declares their faith and their membership of a particular church.

*Right* Mosaic in the dome of the Arian Baptistry in Ravenna, Italy (5th century AD). The Holy Spirit, visible as a dove, hovers above the head of Christ during his baptism by John.

# DISMAS

JESUS COMFORTED DISMAS, THE "GOOD THIEF", AS TOGETHER THEY
SUFFERED DEATH BY CRUCIFIXION. DISMAS FELT THAT UNLIKE JESUS
HE DESERVED HIS PUNISHMENT AS HE HAD COMMITTED A CRIME.

**KEY FACTS**
*Crucified next to Christ*
DATES: *d.c.AD 30*
BIRTH PLACE: *Probably Galilee*
PATRON OF: *Thieves, condemned
criminals, undertakers*
FEAST DAY: *25 March*
EMBLEM: *Tall cross, naked on cross*

Dismas, a common thief, was nailed to a cross next to Jesus on the day of the Crucifixion and spoke with him. The Eastern Orthodox Church has put in their litany the words that Dismas uttered to Jesus, "Lord," he said, "remember me when you come into your kingdom". Jesus gave the reassuring answer, "Today thou shalt be with me in Paradise".

Luke records the story in his gospel. Dismas reprimands the other thief, Gestas, who asks Jesus, as the Messiah, to prove it and save all three of them from death. According to a medieval story, some time previously, Dismas, in awe of the infant Jesus, had even ordered his fellow bandits to leave the Holy Family unmolested as they made their escape to Egypt.

In the Middle Ages, Dismas came to be seen as the patron saint of prisoners and thieves.

*Right* The Crucifixion
*(Francesco Botticini, c.1471).*

# VERONICA

AN ORDINARY WOMAN WITH A KIND HEART TRIED TO SOOTHE
CHRIST AS HE CARRIED HIS CROSS ON THE WAY TO HIS CRUCIFIXION
AT CALVARY. THE VEIL SHE USED BECAME AN IMPORTANT RELIC.

**KEY FACTS**
*Wiped the brow of Christ*
DATES: *1st century AD*
BIRTH PLACE: *Probably Galilee*
FEAST DAY: *12 July*
EMBLEM: *Veil with Christ's
image upon it*

There is a strong possibility that Veronica is a legendary figure. Even her name is likely to be a combination of *vera*, meaning "true" in Latin, and *icon*, meaning "image" in ancient Greek. However, she figures in the Stations of the Cross, the 14 events that mark the journey of Christ carrying his cross to the Hill of Calvary.

Veronica was a woman in the mob who followed Jesus on his last earthly trip. The crowds pushed and shoved to catch a glimpse of this man, the so-called "King of the Jews", and many yelled insults in bloodthirsty tones. But scattered among the crowds were frightened, anxious

and distressed Christians. Veronica was one of these. Pitying Jesus as he sweated and struggled under his burden, she took off her veil and wiped his brow.

An imprint of his face was left on the veil and it was taken to St Peter's Basilica in Rome in the 8th century. The veil became a popular relic in the 14th and 15th centuries. Claims that Jesus had once cured Veronica of a blood illness remain unproven.

*Left St Veronica's veil is clearly
imprinted with the image of Jesus
Christ (the Master of Saint Veronica,
Germany, c.1420).*

# JOSEPH OF ARIMATHEA

A SECRET BUT WEALTHY CONVERT TO CHRISTIANITY RESCUED THE
BODY OF CHRIST AFTER THE CRUCIFIXION. HE LAID IT TO REST IN
THE TOMB HE HAD PREPARED FOR HIMSELF.

**KEY FACTS**
*Cared for the dead body
of Jesus*
DATES: *1st century AD*
BIRTH PLACE: *Jerusalem*
PATRON OF: *Grave diggers,
burial, cemetery keepers and
caretakers*
FEAST DAY: *17 March*

Joseph was a wealthy Israelite who had secretly converted to Christianity. He did not take part in the Jewish condemnation of Jesus, nor did he speak against it.

Following the arrest of Jesus, the situation in Jerusalem was tense. Jewish leaders were calling for the punishment of this person who claimed to be the Messiah. But Pontius Pilate, the Roman governor, was reluctant to sentence Jesus to death.

To mark the Jewish festival of Passover, Pilate offered to pardon one prisoner, giving the Jews a

*Below Joseph of Arimathea preaches
to the inhabitants of Britain (William
Blake, 18th century).*

choice between Jesus and the common thief, Barabbas. Pilate was shocked by their choice and washed his hands to indicate his innocence. "Let his blood be upon us," the irate crowd replied. No doubt many Christians, like Joseph of Arimathea, did not dare face the mob.

## THE TOMB OF CHRIST
Overwhelmed by shame at his cowardice after the Crucifixion, Joseph went to Pontius Pilate and asked for the body of Jesus. It was the custom to throw the bodies of criminals as carrion for animals to devour. But Joseph bought the mutilated body before this happened, and took it to a garden he

owned, close to Calvary where Jesus had died. Here, Joseph had carved out a rocky sepulchre intended as his own burial place. He wrapped the body in clean linen, pushing a huge rock against the opening to close the tomb.

## LEGENDARY TRAVELS
It is said that the apostle Philip sent Joseph on a mission to England where he founded a church at Glastonbury and grew a tree that is said to flower on Christmas Day. Joseph is included in the Arthurian legends.

# MARY MAGDALENE

LOVED FOR HER DEVOTION TO JESUS, MARY MAGDALENE IS THE
GRAND EXAMPLE OF THE REFORMED SINNER. HER LIFE SHOWS THAT
ANYONE MAY BE TRANSFORMED IF THEY TRULY REPENT.

Mary Magdalene was one of the many women who accompanied Jesus and the apostles on their travels, caring for them and supporting them. She was close to Jesus and played a major role in the events surrounding his death and resurrection.

## CONTROVERSIAL FIGURE
Over the centuries Mary Magdalene has aroused much controversy among theologians.

In Western Christianity, she is often identified both as the sister of Martha of Bethany and as the sinner who dried Christ's feet with her hair. But in Eastern Christianity, Mary Magdalene, Martha of Bethany and the sinner are three different women.

Despite these problems, the existence of Mary Magdalene is not questioned. She is known for her sincere conversion, generous heart and contemplative mind.

**KEY FACTS**
*First witness to the risen Christ*
DATES: *1st century* AD
BIRTH PLACE: *Possibly Magdala,
Palestine*
PATRON OF: *Repentant sinners,
hairdressers, perfume-makers,
contemplatives*
FEAST DAY: *22 July*
EMBLEM: *Jar of ointment,
loosened hair*

*Above Detail of Mary kissing Jesus' feet from* Life of Saint Mary Magdalene *(attr. to Giotto di Bondone, Palmerino di Guido and others, 14th century).*

## REPENTANT SINNER
The story of the sinner is perhaps the most significant of the earlier accounts thought to relate to Mary Magdalene.

While Jesus was dining at the home of a Pharisee called Simon, a woman crept in and knelt before him. Simon was angered by this interruption from a woman who was a known sinner.

The woman began to kiss Jesus' feet and weep, begging to be forgiven for her transgressions. She dried his feet with her long hair and rubbed them with

*Left* Mary Magdalene Reading *(attr. to Ambrosius Benson, 1540).*

*Above* Christ on the Cross with Saints *(Luca Signorelli and Pietro Perugino, 1482).*

expensive perfumed ointment. Jesus told the distraught woman that all her sins were forgiven.

## MESSENGER OF CHRIST

To modern Christians, both Orthodox and Catholic, Mary Magdalene is important because she was a devoted and committed follower of Christ who witnessed some of the most significant moments of his life. She accom-panied Jesus on his last journey to Jerusalem and was present at the Crucifixion, keeping vigil.

Three days after his death, Mary went to his burial cave, intending to anoint his body. When she arrived she found the rock that closed the cave opening had been rolled away and the body was gone. Mary ran to question a gardener nearby. But when he spoke she realized that he was the risen Christ. Jesus gave her the glory of telling the disciples that he had been resurrected.

## PREACHER AND HERMIT

Eastern legend claims that, after the Resurrection, Mary Mag-dalene travelled to Ephesus with the Blessed Virgin and the apostle

> "SAINT MARY MAGDALENE, TEACH US TO FORGIVE OURSELVES, AND THEN TO FORGIVE OTHERS."
>
> PRAYER TO ST MARY MAGDALENE

*Above* Mary Magdalene carried by angels *(Simon Vouet, 17th century).*

John, where she later died and was buried. According to a Western legend, however, Mary, along with her sister Martha and brother Lazarus, travelled by boat to France. They landed in Provence and proceeded to Marseilles, where they preached the Gospel. Mary is said to have retired to a nearby cave to live as a hermit. When she died, angels carried her to the oratory of St Maximus near Aix-en-Provence.

## MARTHA

Martha was either the sister of Mary of Bethany or, as in the Western Christian tradition, the sister of Mary Magdalene. Jesus was said to enjoy visiting Martha's house and loved her and her siblings. It was Martha's brother, Lazarus, whom Jesus raised from the dead.

A popular story reveals Martha's busy nature. On one of Jesus' visits to their home, she bustled about preparing food, while Mary sat in rapt attention at the feet of Christ. When Martha expressed irritation at her sister's idleness, Jesus rebuked her. He told her that Mary had made the better choice; the contemplative life is preferable to an active one that allows no time for thought or prayer.

*Above* The Raising of Lazarus *(the Coetivy Master, c.1460). Martha was chief among the mourners to witness the miracle.*

# THE APOSTLES

THE 12 MEN CHOSEN BY JESUS TO AID HIM IN HIS WORK WENT OUT
TO PREACH THE GOSPEL WITH AUTHORITY AFTER HIS DEATH.
IT WAS EACH APOSTLE'S DUTY TO LIVE IN IMITATION OF CHRIST.

and rocks, as a secret sign. *Icthys*, the Greek word for "fish", is an acrostic, or word puzzle, consisting of the initial letters for five other words that described Christ to his believers: *Iesous Christos Theou Yios Soter* (Jesus Christ, Son of God, Saviour).

## ROLE OF THE APOSTLES

Jesus defined the purpose of the work of his chosen few. They were to teach his message, to baptize, to rule by guiding the faithful, and to sanctify the grace of God through prayer. These roles were to be passed on to successors when an apostle died or became frail.

Roman Catholics believe that Jesus appointed these "men of the apostolate" to administer his Church. He put the organization into their hands with Peter, the first pope, as his chief. Peter was to rule the whole Church, make judgements and name his successor. This division of duties has remained the basis of the administrative structure of the Church ever since. All popes are believed to be Peter's successors.

Jesus had at least 120, possibly thousands, of disciples. They were ordinary men and women who followed him wherever he went, learning from his teachings. He selected 12 special men to be his apostles (derived from the Greek word for "ambassador") from among these people. They became his closest companions and were witness to some of the most significant moments of Christ's life and resurrection.

## FOLLOWERS OF JESUS

The earliest followers of Christ were two pairs of brothers – Peter and Andrew, and James and John – fishermen who worked along the coast of the Sea of Galilee. Tax collectors were generally despised at the time, and yet that was the profession of Matthew, the next apostle to be called.

*Above A very early fresco of Jesus Christ and his apostles, found in a church in Cappadocia, Turkey.*

It is thought that 11 of these 12 men were Galileans. Judas Iscariot, their treasurer and the man who betrayed Jesus, was the only non-Galilean. After the Crucifixion, Peter oversaw the replacement of Judas by Matthias.

## FISHERS OF MEN

When Jesus called Peter and Andrew he said that if they followed him he would make them "fishers of men". Many Christians consider these words to be a metaphor for the apostles' role: to bring people to Jesus as a fisherman catches fish.

In the years of persecution, cautious Christians used the image of a fish, scratched on walls

*Above Christ calming a storm and saving fishermen in stained glass from Exeter Cathedral, England.*

## JUDAS ISCARIOT

This apostle is infamous for betraying Christ to the Jewish authorities. But it was his method of identifying his leader, Jesus, that is perceived as particularly repugnant. Judas knew that Jesus and the apostles had spent the night praying in the garden of Gethsemane. At dawn, he and the temple guards approached the group, and Judas told the guards, "The one I kiss is the man you want". For the sum of 30 pieces of silver, he kissed Jesus, who was then led to his death.

It was said that Judas, crazed with remorse, threw the "blood money" into the temple and then hanged himself. The kind of tree to which he tied his noose is still known as a Judas tree, and the field where Judas died is called "Áceldama" – the field of blood. His name is given to traitors, while any act of betrayal is often termed "the kiss of Judas".

*Right* The traitor's kiss is hewn from stone on this church wall in France.

Protestants were, and are, more ambivalent about the role of the individual apostles. Some credit them with divine authority. Other sects say they are simply the first evangelists or preachers. They are seen as early missionaries who were given significant qualities to fulfil their role as heralds of the gospel message.

### SPREADING THE WORD

Soon after he had chosen the 12, Jesus gave his apostles the power to cast out evil spirits and cure disease. He sent them out in pairs to preach and use their gifts in the towns of Galilee, instructing them to "take nothing for their journey, except a mere staff".

After the Resurrection, the apostles dedicated themselves to spreading the teachings of Jesus around the known world. Peter was the first of them to perform a miracle and was also one of the first apostles to set out into the world as a missionary.

All the apostles undertook arduous journeys to fulfil their appointed roles. They set high standards of obedience, poverty and chastity, avoiding all worldly pleasures that might distract them from their mission.

### DYING FOR THEIR FAITH

Such was the conviction of these men that they were prepared to die cruel deaths for their faith. A total of 11 apostles were martyred. The work of these brave men proved productive. After 300 years of continued apostleship the Emperor Constantine I made Christianity the religion of the Roman Empire, and from then on the "new" religion spread rapidly.

*Below* All the apostles were present with Jesus at the Last Supper (Justus van Gent, 1473–74).

# JAMES THE GREAT

ABANDONING HIS FISHING NETS IN ORDER TO BECOME A "FISHER OF MEN", JAMES WAS ONE OF THE EARLIEST DISCIPLES TO FOLLOW JESUS, AND THE FIRST APOSTLE MARTYR.

There were two apostles named James. One became known as James the Less and the other, James the Great – so-called because he was the elder of the two. James the Great was one of the leading apostles.

James and his brother John were fishermen who abandoned their nets to follow Jesus. Both brothers were known to be quick-tempered, hence their nickname "sons of thunder".

James also had qualities of reliability, leadership and loyalty. He witnessed the major events of Christ's life. He was one of those present at the Transfiguration, and was in the garden of Gethsemane to comfort his master during his most despairing moments.

The details of James' life after the Crucifixion are uncertain. He may have gone to Judea and Samaria to spread the Christian

*Above The shell and pilgrim's staff identify St James the Great (Hans Klocker, c.17th century).*

*Below Apostles Philip and James are often portrayed as men of learning (School of Fra Bartolommeo, c.1400).*

**KEY FACTS**
*Apostle*
DATES: *d.AD 44*
BIRTH PLACE: *Galilee*
PATRON OF: *Spain, Guatemala, Nicaragua; and, with Philip, of Uruguay*
FEAST DAY: *25 July*
EMBLEM: *Shell, sword, pilgrim's staff, pilgrim's hat*

message. But it is known that he was beheaded by Herod Agrippa in Jerusalem.

His body, it is said, was carried to the shore where a boat suddenly materialized. His disciples placed the body in this miraculous vessel and it floated to the coast of Spain. There, Christians found the relics and buried them in a forest where the city of Santiago de Compostela now stands.

The shrine containing his relics in Compostela was of great importance during the Crusades, because soldiers believed St James could grant military prowess. Santiago de Compostela remains a major site of modern pilgrimage.

## GROWTH OF HIS CULTUS

According to Spanish tradition James appeared to fight the Moors when they invaded Spain in AD 844. He rode through the sky on a white horse, holding a shield bearing a red cross and a sword. With his help, the Spanish vanquished their enemy.

In the 16th century, sailors allegedly saw St James resting on a cloud. It hovered protectively over the galleons carrying early Spanish explorers across the Atlantic to the Americas. He inspired them to convert the American people they encountered. The feast day of St James the Great is celebrated in major national festivals in South America to this day.

# JAMES THE LESS

THIS APOSTLE IS IDENTIFIED AS "THE SON OF ALPHAEUS" BUT HE
SLIPS QUIETLY, ALMOST ANONYMOUSLY, THROUGH THE CHRISTIAN
STORY. SOME SOURCES IDENTIFY HIM AS CHRIST'S BROTHER.

**KEY FACTS**
*Apostle*
DATES: *d. AD 62*
BIRTH PLACE: *Galilee*
PATRON OF: *The dying*
FEAST DAY: *3 May*
EMBLEM: *Fuller's club*

There is little mention of James the Less during Jesus' ministry. But after the Crucifixion and Resurrection, this James communicated closely with Jesus before his Ascension into heaven.

James became an important figure in the new Christian community in Jerusalem where St Paul relied on his leadership. During the Council of Jerusalem (c.AD 50), James supported Paul in the call to accept Gentiles as Christians without demanding these converts be circumcized. This decision caused much controversy at the council. As men brought up in the Jewish tradition, the apostles tended to regard circumcision as an important symbol of faith.

James was stoned or possibly clubbed to death. Another version says James was thrown from a temple top, but as he lay dying, he forgave his tormentors. Even Jewish leaders of the time believed the city faced calamity after the death of this fine man. James is often linked with the apostle Philip, and many churches are dedicated to "Philip and James".

*Right* The Communion of the Apostle James the Less *(Niccoló Bambini, 1720).*

# PHILIP

THIS PRACTICAL-MINDED APOSTLE HELPED IN THE FEEDING OF THE
5,000, AND THE SEARCHING QUESTIONS HE ASKED JESUS CLARIFIED
IMPORTANT POINTS OF FAITH.

**KEY FACTS**
*Apostle*
DATES: *1st century AD*
BIRTH PLACE: *Bethsaida*
PATRON OF: *Uruguay*
FEAST DAY: *3 May (West)*
EMBLEM: *Loaf of bread, large cross, a dragon*

Philip heard John the Baptist preach and then sought out Jesus. Philip seems to have been an energetic and practical man. He arranged appointments, and introduced Nathanael, later St Bartholomew, to Christ.

When Jesus wanted to feed a crowd of 5,000 people who had gathered to hear his message, Philip commented, "Two hundred pennyworth of bread is not sufficient for them". But when a small boy offered five loaves and two fishes, Philip helped distribute the food, believing this would feed everyone as Jesus said.

*Above* The Apostle Philip *(Georges de La Tour, 1620).*

At the Last Supper, Philip asked, "Lord, show us the Father". The answer came from Jesus, "I am in the Father and the Father is in me."

Philip preached in Phrygia and is thought to have killed an evil dragon brought by the Scythians. He possibly died a martyr in Hierapolis (in Syria), but his relics are held in Rome. He is closely associated with James the Less. The two apostles share a feast day.

# BARTHOLOMEW

BEST-KNOWN FOR THE CRUEL MANNER OF HIS DEATH FROM BEING FLAYED ALIVE, THIS SINCERE AND LOYAL APOSTLE IS THOUGHT TO HAVE PREACHED AS FAR AFIELD AS INDIA.

**KEY FACTS**
*Apostle*
DATES: *1st century AD*
BIRTH PLACE: *Probably Galilee*
PATRON OF: *Tanners*
FEAST DAY: *24 August*
EMBLEM: *Butcher's knife*

When Jesus first met Bartholomew, also known as Nathanael, he observed a man "in whom there is no guile". Bartholomew never doubted the truth of Jesus' teachings and was one of the early apostles. He was present at the Pentecost and then travelled to spread the message.

Bartholomew is said to have preached in Armenia and India, where he may have left behind a copy of the Gospel of St Matthew. Tradition says he defeated demons in India that encouraged idol worship. He converted the local king Polemius and his family. This action enraged the king's brother,

Astrages, who captured him and ordered Bartholomew to be flayed alive and then beheaded.

Michelangelo shows Bartholomew holding his own flayed skin in *The Last Judgement* in the Sistine Chapel, Vatican City. His relics were enshrined on an island in the River Tiber in Rome.

*Left A curved butcher's knife forms part of this statue of Bartholomew in San Gennaro in Italy, referring to his cruel death.*

# JUDE

TRADITIONALLY BELIEVED TO BE THE AUTHOR OF THE EPISTLE OF JUDE, THIS APOSTLE IS NOW BEST KNOWN AS THE PATRON SAINT OF LOST CAUSES. HE IS OFTEN TURNED TO BY THOSE IN DESPAIR.

**KEY FACTS**
*Apostle*
DATES: *1st century AD*
BIRTH PLACE: *Palestine*
PATRON OF: *Hopeless causes*
FEAST DAY: *28 October (West)*
EMBLEM: *Club, holding a boat*

The apostle Jude is not mentioned with any great frequency in the gospels, but he has a large modern cultus. For uncertain reasons, this apostle gained a reputation for offering sympathy and hope to those in despair. Worshippers turn to him when they are in dire trouble.

His name is often followed by the words "not Iscariot", so that he is not confused with Judas. He is also known as Thaddaeus.

It is claimed he wrote the *Epistle of Jude*. This tells of a mission to Persia with another

apostle, Simon, who apparently was his cousin. Jude was martyred by being clubbed to death, although there is little evidence to verify how he died.

Sometimes Jude is pictured holding a ship while his cousin clutches a fish. These signs indicate that the men were both former fishermen.

*Left A detail of* The Apostle Thaddeus *from Siena Cathedral (Duccio di Buoninsegna, 1308).*

# THOMAS

CHIEFLY REMEMBERED AS "DOUBTING THOMAS", THIS APOSTLE NEEDED PROOF BEFORE ACCEPTING ANY TRUTH. HE WAS THE FIRST TO ACKNOWLEDGE CHRIST'S DIVINITY AFTER THE RESURRECTION.

**KEY FACTS**
*Apostle*
DATES: *1st century AD*
BIRTH PLACE: *Probably Palestine*
PATRON OF: *Architects, carpenters, surveyors, builders, sculptors*
FEAST DAY: *3 July (West)*
EMBLEM: *Incredulity, holding T-square as a builder*

Thomas questioned things but, once he was given a satisfying answer, remained firm in his belief. He asked Jesus, "Where are you going? How can we know the way?" Jesus answered, "I am the way, the truth, and the life." Fiercely loyal, Thomas was ready to die with Jesus.

The apostle is most famously known as "Doubting Thomas" because he could not believe the Resurrection of Christ. When he met the Lord after his death, Thomas asked to touch the wounds left by a soldier's lance as he hung on the cross. Christ allowed him to do so and, now convinced of the reality, Thomas became ardent in his belief. Indeed, he was the first to publicly acknowledge the divinity of Christ by calling him "My Lord and my God".

A legend says that because Thomas did not witness the Blessed Virgin's Assumption to heaven, she appeared in person to reassure him. As a token of proof, she gave him her belt.

His life after the Pentecost is mysterious. There are claims that he travelled to India where he

*Below A patient Christ offers proof of his resurrection in the painting* Doubting Thomas *(Gian Francesco Barbieri, 1621).*

preached and built a cathedral for a prince. Such stories are perhaps confirmed by a community of Christians in Kerala, south India, who identify themselves as the "St Thomas Christians".

In 1522, Portuguese travellers claimed to have seen his grave in Mylapore near Madras. The *Acts of Thomas*, a document from the 3rd or 4th century, says he was killed by a lance. His relics ended up in Persia (Iran), but Ortona, in Italy, also laid claim to them.

# PETER

CHRIST DESCRIBED PETER AS THE "ROCK OF THE CHURCH". AS THE
LEADER OF THE APOSTLES, HE IS THE EARTHLY FATHER OF THE FAITH,
AND IS SAID TO HOLD THE KEYS TO THE KINGDOM OF HEAVEN.

## KEY FACTS

*Leader of the apostles; called the
rock of the Church by Jesus*
DATES: *d.c.AD 64*
BIRTH PLACE: *Bethsaida,
Sea of Galilee*
PATRON OF: *Fishermen, papacy*
FEAST DAY: *29 June*
EMBLEM: *Keys, ship, fish, cockerel*

Peter was warm and impetuous by nature, yet also rather cautious. He needed reassurance that Jesus was indeed the Messiah.

To his eternal shame, he was so overwhelmed by fear during the trial of Jesus that three times he denied his friendship with him. But Peter's passion and general boldness made him leader of the apostles. His name, Cephas in Aramaic, means "rock" and Jesus chose him as the "rock" upon which the Church was built.

Known as Simon Peter, he fished with his brother Andrew on the Sea of Galilee. Jesus came to them one day when they had failed to catch any fish. He told them to lower their nets and to their surprise they hauled up an enormous catch. "Come with

*Above A mural showing Peter's denial of Christ and the cock crowing (from the Church of the Holy Cross at Platanistasa, Cyprus, 15th century).*

*Below Peter enthroned and six scenes from the lives of Jesus and St Peter (the Master of St Peter, 1280).*

me," Jesus said, "and I will make you fishers of men." After this, Peter began his ministry with Jesus, and he is mentioned frequently throughout the gospels. He was very close to Christ and became the leader of the 12 apostles. He was with Jesus during the Agony in the Garden, the night

Christ spent in tormented prayer before his arrest and death. And when the soldiers came that dawn to make the arrest, Peter was so enraged that he sliced off the ear of Judas Iscariot, the man who had betrayed Jesus to the authorities to his eternal shame.

Peter was one of three apostles to witness the Transfiguration when Jesus was surrounded by light with the prophets, Moses and Elijah, on either side. A voice said, "This is my beloved Son… Listen to Him." And after Pentecost, when the Holy Spirit gave the apostles the gift of tongues, Peter was the first to speak to the crowds.

## FIRST CHURCH LEADER

Peter took administrative control of the apostles after Christ's death and chose Matthias to replace Judas Iscariot. He sent Paul and Barnabas to the Mediterranean as disciples and evangelists.

Peter cured a beggar who had suffered all his life from a lame leg, thus becoming the first apostle to perform a miracle. More significantly, he was ready to sit at a meal with a non-Jew, or Gentile. Peter converted a Roman centurion, Cornelius, who was the first Gentile to become a Christian believer.

The admittance of Gentiles caused controversy among the other apostles who had preached only to other Jews. They regarded the diet of non-Jews as unclean. But Peter had the support of Paul, who, like him, was determined to spread Christianity to everyone. Peter's frequent public preaching led to his arrest by Herod, who imprisoned him under heavy guard. But the apostle escaped, helped – it was said – by an angel who broke his chains and opened the prison doors.

This convinced Peter that he had truly been chosen to lead. He wrote letters and preached unceasingly, while organizing from Jerusalem the appointment and missions of evangelists.

Some authorities credit Peter with introducing the concept of "episcopal succession". In finding a replacement for Judas Iscariot, he began a system of choosing leaders from men who were familiar with the first apostles. This gave rise to the tradition that bishops and priests had a special closeness to Christ, and ensured that the status of priests remained separate from their flock.

When Peter visited Rome, he was arrested for his Christian activities and tried by the

*Below Peter is dressed in papal splendour as he observes the Crucifixion (Ottaviano di Martino Nelli, 1424).*

## CORNELIUS

Cornelius (not to be confused with the Gentile Roman centurion) was an heir to Peter who became "bishop" of Rome in 251. He followed Peter in teaching that the Church must be conciliatory in its embrace. He favoured a lenient approach towards Christians who had lapsed. Another priest, Novatian, thought those who committed adultery, murder or even made a second marriage, should be expelled from the Church. Cornelius asserted that the Church had the power to forgive and welcome the repentant back to the community. The inscription "Cornelius martyr" inscribed on his tomb can be seen in the crypt of Lucina, in Rome.

*Right This reliquary of St Cornelius, dating from 1350–60, is made of gold and silver.*

> "YOU ARE PETER
> AND UPON THIS ROCK
> I WILL BUILD
> MY CHURCH."
>
> JESUS SPEAKING TO PETER

Emperor Nero, who condemned him to death by crucifixion. Legend has it that Peter asked to be hung upside down on the cross because he was not worthy of dying in the same way as Christ.

Some claim that he died on the same day as Paul, and they share a feast day. For two centuries after

Peter's death, letters which were supposedly written by him were distributed in order to revive his lessons and maintain his influence.

He was buried in a tomb beneath the Vatican. Believers consider him the keeper of the gates to heaven, the saint who can let them enter the kingdom, or deny them entry when they die. Peter's enduring popularity is shown by the dedication of 1,129 churches to him in England alone.

*Below Peter was the first apostle to perform a miracle. In this painting St John and St Peter heal a lame man (Masolino da Panicale, 1425).*

# SIMON

SIMON LIVED TO A GREAT OLD AGE AFTER A SUCCESSFUL LIFE AS A WELL-TRAVELLED MISSIONARY.

Simon is featured in a number of legends and has long been venerated, especially in the East. He is also known as the Zealot or the Canaanite, possibly because he had belonged to a strict Jewish sect. He appears in the New Testament as one of the apostles, but is not much mentioned after the Pentecost, when the Holy Spirit granted Christ's followers the gift of tongues.

One story says he travelled with Jude and that they took their mission as far as Persia (Iran).

*Above* The Apostle Simon *in a chiaroscuro drawing (Mair von Landshut, 1496).*

**KEY FACTS**
*Apostle*
DATES: *1st century AD*
BIRTH PLACE: *Probably Galilee*
FEAST DAY: *28 October (West)*
EMBLEM: *Boat, sometimes the weapon of his murder, a falchion — a short sword bent like a sickle*

Here, pagan priests slaughtered both men. Some sources say Simon was sawn in two, others that he was stabbed to death.

A further interpretation has Simon dying in battle when he was bishop of Jerusalem, while others claim that the apostle trekked across North Africa until he reached the age of 120 years and was finally martyred.

# BARNABAS

CHRIST DID NOT CHOOSE BARNABAS AS AN APOSTLE. HOWEVER, HIS MISSIONARY WORK OUTSIDE PALESTINE, FIRST WITH PAUL, THEN ALONE, BROUGHT HIM THE TITLE OF HONORARY APOSTLE.

**KEY FACTS**
*Apostle*
DATES: *1st century AD*
BIRTH PLACE: *Unknown*
FEAST DAY: *11 June*
EMBLEM: *Sometimes associated with a type of thistle that flowers on his feast day (in England)*

Barnabas was a Cypriot Jew who took the newly converted Paul to meet the other apostles in Jerusalem. Though not one of the 12 apostles, Barnabas was one of the earliest evangelists.

Peter described Barnabas as "a good man, full of the Holy Ghost and of faith", and sent him to Antioch. From there Barnabas sailed with Paul to Cyprus, where Barnabas showed the people what "wonders God had wrought".

He is believed to be the founder of the Church in Cyprus. He may have been martyred at Salamis in AD 61. *The Epistle of Barnabas* carries his name, but its authorship is uncertain.

*Below* Paul and Barnabas (attr. to Rombout van Troyen, 17th century).

# ANDREW

PETER'S BROTHER ANDREW WAS THE FIRST OF THE DISCIPLES JESUS CALLED. THE CRUEL MANNER OF HIS REPUTED MARTYRDOM ON A SALTIRE CROSS IS COMMEMORATED ON THE SCOTTISH FLAG.

**KEY FACTS**
*Apostle*
DATES: *d.c.AD 60*
BIRTH PLACE: *Bethsaida, Galilee*
PATRON OF: *Scotland, Greece and Russia, fishermen*
FEAST DAY: *30 November*
EMBLEM: *Small saltire cross*

Andrew heard John the Baptist preach and longed to meet Jesus. He and his brother Peter (then called Simon), worked as fishermen on the Sea of Galilee.

Initially, the brothers only joined Jesus at his preaching from time to time. But finally they abandoned their families and their work to follow him. The Greek Orthodox Church calls Andrew "Protoclete", meaning "first-called". They venerate him highly, as do the Roman Catholic and Russian Orthodox Churches.

Jesus granted the Miraculous Draught of Fishes to Andrew and Peter. This occurred when, after a day of poor fishing, the presence of Jesus produced a great haul for the two men. Andrew also played a part in the feeding of the 5,000 with loaves and fishes. Being an intense believer, he encouraged Gentiles to meet the Messiah, too.

## MISSION AND DEATH
After the Crucifixion, it seems much of Andrew's mission work was in Greece, but he also went to Constantinople (Istanbul), a key place in the history of the early Church. Medieval worshippers claim he founded the Church there. Some believe he preached as far as Kiev in Ukraine before moving on to Scotland, but there is no evidence for this.

Legend gives Andrew a brave martyrdom at Patras. With dignity, he disrobed himself and knelt before the cross as his persecutors prepared him for crucifixion. He was bound to the wooden beams

*Above* Martyrdom of the Apostle Andreas *from Westphalia (artist unknown, c.1500).*

of the saltire (X-shaped) cross. Even in his agony, Andrew is said to have carried on preaching. The crowd begged the consul to show mercy and take the dying man down. This he did after two days.

In 1204, Crusaders siezed Constantinople and took St Andrew's supposed relics to Amalfi, Italy. However, some say that St Regulus journeyed "to the ends of the earth" carrying his relics. Then an angel led him to Scotland, to the place now named after him, St Andrews.

*Below* St Andrew and St Peter Responding to the Call of Jesus, *Byzantine mosaic (6th century).*

# PAUL

INITIALLY A PERSECUTOR OF CHRISTIANS, AFTER HIS DRAMATIC CONVERSION PAUL BECAME THE CHURCH'S FIRST MISSIONARY. HIS LETTERS DEVELOPED AND EXPOUNDED CHRISTIAN THEOLOGY.

**KEY FACTS**
*Great missionary and theologian*
DATES: *d.AD 64–65*
BIRTH PLACE: *Tarsus in Cilicia*
PATRON OF: *Malta, Greece, Catholic missions and lay teachers*
FEAST DAY: *29 June*
EMBLEM: *Sword and book; generally portrayed as elderly and balding with a long beard*

On meeting Paul, a Roman centurion was struck by the apostle's air of nobility and courage. Others described him as having the spirit of a strong man who was generous and eager to create a cheerful atmosphere.

Paul was born in Tarsus to a strict Jewish family and was named Saul. His upbringing was steeped in strict Jewish Law. Although he applauded the killing of the Christian martyr, St Stephen, Saul was confused. How could this man find the strength to defy the Law, simply through the love of Jesus Christ? Even so, Saul decided that no one should break the laws that bind society.

### CONVERSION
Saul tried to find Christians and deliver them to possible death. On one such errand Saul was travelling along the road to Damascus

*Above This portrait of St Paul captures the expression of a noble man (Etienne Parrocel, c.1740s).*

*Below Paul travelling on the road to Damascus with his troops in search of Christians to persecute in* The Conversion of St Paul *(Pieter Bruegel the elder, 1567).*

when suddenly he was blinded by a great light and overcome by the presence of Jesus. He understood from this vision that his mission was to spread the Christian faith to Gentile, non-Jewish people.

His sight was miraculously restored three days later, and shortly afterwards he was baptized. He then spent several years in Arabia living as a hermit.

He returned to Damascus and began to preach about Jesus, and took the name of Paul as a mark of his change. His preaching, however, aroused the fury of local Jews. Paul was forced to escape with the help of fellow disciples who lowered him in a basket over the city wall.

He travelled to Jerusalem to meet Peter who chose him and Barnabas as travelling evangelists.

### APOSTLE TO THE GENTILES
Paul's first journey took him to Cyprus and Syria before he returned to take part in what came to be called the Council of Jerusalem in about AD 50. Here, he found Peter and others in dispute over the rules of conversion.

The apostles, all born as Jews, had tended to preach only to other Jews about Jesus the Messiah. Peter wanted Gentiles, or non-Jews, to be brought into the fold. Paul, who agreed Christ brought redemption to all of humanity, managed to find a compromise. The Church, he argued, should be as catholic (universal) as the Roman Empire.

The disciples agreed that Gentiles must adopt certain Jewish rules, especially those regarding food. But they decided that the Gentiles must never be denied access to the Lord's message. Paul's diplomacy possibly saved Christianity from remaining a mere sect of Judaism, and opened the way for a whole new religious belief system.

Paul spent years travelling around the Middle East and the Mediterranean coast, preaching the gospel. He was shipwrecked, mocked, arrested, but never deterred. While travelling, he wrote numerous letters which are included in the Epistles of the New Testament. These letters were read at gatherings so people might be inspired by his words to convert to the new faith.

His teaching was intimate and personal, related to his own experience of the vision of Jesus. His writings say that Jewish Talmudic Law teaches knowledge of sin, provoking people to dwell on evil thoughts. But the message

"FOR I AM PERSUADED THAT NEITHER DEATH, NOR LIFE NOR ANGELS, NOR PRINCIPALITIES, NOR POWERS, NOR THINGS PRESENT, NOR THINGS TO COME, NOR HEIGHT, NOR DEPTH, NOR ANY OTHER CREATURE, SHALL BE ABLE TO SEPARATE US FROM THE LOVE OF GOD, WHICH IS JESUS CHRIST OUR LORD."

ROMANS 8

**Above** St Paul's, Christopher Wren's magnificent cathedral in London, is dedicated to the man regarded as the greatest apostle of the Church.

of Jesus, said Paul, is one of love, "written on the heart". Jesus works inwards and outwards on people's thoughts, and Christians are "inspired to God-likeness".

## ARREST AND DEATH

While visiting Jerusalem, Paul's preaching enraged the Jews who handed him over to the authorities. As a Roman citizen, he was able to claim trial in that city, though shipwrecked in Malta on the way. He was placed under house arrest and after some years, he was put on trial. Sources vary, and it was possibly on a later visit to Rome after further travels that he was found guilty of "anti-imperial activities" and beheaded.

It was claimed that his head bounced three times, and at each bounce a spring gushed from the earth. The place of his beheading is called Tre Fontane, in Rome. Tradition claims he died on 29 June in AD 64 or 65, the same

day as Peter's martyrdom (also in Rome), and thus they share their feast day.

Paul is the first great missionary and theologian of Christianity. He is regarded as second only to Jesus in inspiring Christian faith.

### SAINT TITUS

St Paul's importance is confirmed by the enormous church dedicated to him in London. Yet little is heard of his close disciple, Titus, the Gentile who attended the decisive Council of Jerusalem where the apostles agreed that Gentiles should be accepted into the faith.

Titus travelled with Paul as secretary and companion on a mission and was entrusted with setting up a community in Crete. Paul warned him to be firm in converting the surly Cretans. Titus was to spend most of his life there, although he lived for a while in Dalmatia. He is recognized as the first bishop of Crete and was buried there in Gortyna. His head was taken as a relic to Venice in AD 823.

**Above** Titus helped Paul to escape the city walls of Damascus in a basket.

# MATTHEW

THE PRESUMED AUTHOR OF THE
FIRST GOSPEL WAS A FORMER
TAX COLLECTOR.

There are few stories about Matthew, also known as Levi. Little is known too about his life as an evangelist. He is presumed to be the author of the first gospel, written in an easy style for public reading.

Matthew was a tax collector, one of the hated class of Jews who collected money on behalf of the Roman authorities. His fellow Jews not only regarded this close contact with Gentiles as unclean, but also distrusted tax-men and believed they were corrupt. When Jesus approached Matthew, and

*Above* Saint Matthew *from* The Book of Kells, *an illuminated manuscript,* c.AD 800.

was even prepared to eat with him, he immediately rose from his counting table and followed him.

**KEY FACTS**
*Author of the first gospel*
DATES: *1st century*
BIRTH PLACE: *Capernaum*
DEATH PLACE: *Possibly Ethiopia*
PATRON OF: *Bankers, accountants, tax collectors, bookkeepers*
FEAST DAY: *21 September*
EMBLEM: *Angel or man with wings, money bag, spear or sword*

After Christ's Ascension to heaven, Matthew became a missionary like the other apostles but his journeys are not recorded.

An apocryphal story says that Matthew was martyred in Ethiopia defending an abbess. His reputed relics were transported to Salerno in Italy via Brittany. Others say he died in Persia.

---

# JOHN

THE DISCIPLE WHOM JESUS LOVED AND ENTRUSTED HIS MOTHER TO
AFTER HIS DEATH IS THOUGHT TO BE THE AUTHOR OF THE FOURTH
GOSPEL, THREE EPISTLES AND THE BOOK OF REVELATION.

John and James the Great were two fiery-tempered brothers, sons of Zebedee. Both were called from mending their fishing nets to follow Jesus.

John's ardour could turn him to brave and reckless endeavours. However, Jesus' faith in John was apparent at the Crucifixion. When he was facing death, Jesus put his mother, Mary, the Blessed Virgin, into John's care rather than choose anyone else.

The belief that he was a favourite disciple is confirmed by the facts of John's life. He was with Jesus at the Miracle of the Loaves and Fishes. With Peter and James, he witnessed the Transfiguration, and he was by the side of Jesus during the Agony in the Garden of Gethsemane.

John was placed at the right hand of Christ at the Last Supper, and he was the only disciple not to desert Jesus during the horrors

*Left This woodcarving depicts John's anguish and horror during Christ's crucifixion at Calvary (Ferdinand Maximilian Brokof, 18th century).*

**KEY FACTS**
*Author of the Fourth Gospel and the Book of Revelation*
DATES: *1st century AD*
BIRTH PLACE: *Galilee*
PATRON OF: *Booksellers, writers, artists, knights, theologians, typesetters*
FEAST DAY: *27 December (West)*
EMBLEM: *Eagle, chalice, sometimes a book*

of the Crucifixion. He kept vigil at the foot of the Cross, and then showed no hesitation in accepting Jesus had risen from the dead.

After the Ascension, John worked with St Peter organizing the early Christian Church. After some years, he was exiled to Patmos, a Greek island. One of the greatest Christian evangelists, it is thought he died at a great age in Ephesus, Turkey.

# MARK

THE AUTHOR OF THE SECOND GOSPEL INTERPRETED AND RECORDED PETER'S TEACHING.

Mark was young when he first met Jesus. His mother's house was a favourite meeting place for the apostles and Jesus often visited.

Although Mark was not an apostle, he seems to have been charming and affectionate, though not brave or confident. It was rumoured that he ran away from the Roman soldiers who arrested Jesus. And he abandoned a difficult mission with St Peter to Cyprus. But when older, he gave St Paul much support during his arrest in Rome. St Peter even referred to him fondly as his son.

Mark travelled widely as an evangelist, visiting Jerusalem, Rome and Egypt. He may have travelled to Alexandria and become the first bishop of that city. Mark's gospel incorporates many of Peter's teachings and memoirs, so it is likely it was written in Rome where the two men spent long periods together.

Despite Mark's important role in the Christian story as the writer of the Second Gospel, his place and manner of death are uncertain. He is thought to have died sometime after Jerusalem was destroyed in AD 70. A legend claims he was tied round the neck and dragged through the streets of Alexandria. His bodily relics were carried by the Venetians to Venice where they were placed in the basilica named after him, St Mark's Basilica.

*Right St Mark's famous emblem, the winged lion, sits at his feet (the Ulm Master, 1442).*

The relics survived a fire in the church in AD 976, and were installed in the new building. A series of mosaics in the church tell the story of St Mark and the translation of his relics.

**KEY FACTS**
*Writer of the Second Gospel*
DATES: *d.c.AD 74*
BIRTH PLACE: *Jerusalem*
PATRON OF: *Notaries, translators, opticians, glass workers, Venice*
FEAST DAY: *25 April*
EMBLEM: *Winged lion*

*Left A statue of St Mark by the early Renaissance sculptor Donatello (1411–15). St Mark's image appears widely in Italy.*

His emblem is a winged lion. This refers to the inspiration Mark derived from John the Baptist, who lived in the wilderness with animals. Mark became the patron saint of Venice. His lion emblem can be found on the façades of many buildings across the Greek Ionian islands, where medieval Venice held dominion.

# LUKE

THE PHYSICIAN AND WRITER OF THE THIRD GOSPEL WAS A MOST SYMPATHETIC MAN WHO, UNUSUALLY FOR THE TIME, INCLUDED IN HIS WORK THE WOMEN WHO WERE IMPORTANT IN THE LIFE OF JESUS.

**KEY FACTS**
*Writer of the Third Gospel*
DATES: *1st century AD*
BIRTH PLACE: *Antioch, Syria*
PATRON OF: *Surgeons, doctors, painters and glass artists*
FEAST DAY: *18 October*
EMBLEM: *Winged ox*

St Luke was a Greek doctor. His writings contain observations of women and human suffering, and reveal him to be gentle and sensitive. St Paul probably converted Luke, a Gentile of Antioch, and persuaded him to travel with him on evangelical voyages around the Mediterranean.

More than any other New Testament writer, Luke shows us the women in Jesus' life. Thanks to him, we know more about Mary Magdalene and about the widow whose son Jesus restored to life.

Luke tells the story of Mary and the Annunciation, and also mentions Elizabeth, mother of John the Baptist. He is deeply respectful of the Virgin Mary and apparently knew her. The words

*Above* This enamel plaque showing St Luke was made in the workshop of the Kremlin (17th century).

*Below* St Luke Drawing the Virgin (Rogier van der Weyden, 15th century). Luke was a talented painter as well as writer.

he puts into her mouth when he describes the Annunciation are known as "Mary's Prayer", and have become part of the liturgy.

## A HUMANE APPROACH

Luke emphasizes gentle aspects of the faith. He repeats the most moving parables that Jesus told to show examples of goodness and kindness. However, his gospel does open with the story of the bull sacrificed by Zachary to celebrate the birth of his son, John the Baptist. This accounts for Luke's emblem, a winged ox.

He also wrote *The Acts of the Apostles*, a mixture of history and prophecy describing the spread of Christianity. He explains how the faith broke with Judaism, and extended beyond Jerusalem to Rome in the West.

Luke also has a reputation as a painter. There are many portraits of the Virgin attributed to St Luke in the Christian world, though unfortunately none are authenticated. The church of St Augustine in Rome has several such portraits. It is said Luke lived to a great age and never married.

"MY SOUL DOTH MAGNIFY THE LORD, AND MY SPIRIT HATH REJOICED IN GOD MY SAVIOUR"

LUKE 1:46

# STEPHEN

THE FIRST CHRISTIAN MARTYR
WAS CRUELLY STONED TO DEATH
IN JERUSALEM FOR HIS BELIEFS.

The first ever Christian martyr was a learned Jew and one of the first deacons. After his conversion, Stephen took control of almsgiving to elderly widows in his community. When he began to preach he often criticized some aspects of Jewish Mosaic law.

After Stephen had made some particularly hostile allegations, his Jewish listeners became outraged. He accused them of resisting the true Spirit and being responsible for the death of Christ.

## KEY FACTS
*First martyr*
DATES: *d.c.AD 35*
BIRTH PLACE: *Jerusalem*
PATRON OF: *Bricklayers, stonemasons, builders, deacons*
FEAST DAY: *26 December (West)*
EMBLEM: *Stones, the palm of martyrdom, a book*

The mob stoned him to death with the consent of a man called Saul, a Roman Jew. Saul later converted and became Paul, the great Christian leader.

*Left The stoning of St Stephen as depicted in a stained glass window (St Edmundsbury Cathedral, Suffolk, England, 19th century).*

# EUSTACE

THE HERO OF THIS LEGEND CHASES A STAG THAT BEARS THE CROSS
OF CHRIST WITHIN ITS ANTLERS. THIS EXPERIENCE LEADS TO HIS
CONVERSION AND HIS UNTIMELY DEATH.

Fabulous stories surround the figure of St Eustace. Named Placidas at birth, he became a high-ranking Roman soldier and was a keen huntsman.

One day he stalked a stag deep in the forest. As he lifted his bow, the stag turned. A gleaming crucifix grew between its antlers. Then the stag said, "I am Jesus, whom you honour without knowing".

Placidas, his wife and children converted to Christianity and he was baptized as Eustace. They suffered many misfortunes and Eustace's faith was tested to the limits. His wife was seduced (or raped) and his children sold into slavery. Later, their luck changed for the better when Eustace was

## KEY FACTS
*Miracle appearance of the crucifix*
DATES: *Unknown*
BIRTH PLACE: *Unknown*
PATRON OF: *Hunters and those in difficult situations*
FEAST DAY: *2 November (West; officially de-canonized)*
EMBLEM: *Stag bearing a crucifix*

reunited with his family in Rome. He was honoured for a military victory, but unfortunately this good luck did not last, and when he refused to make a pagan sacrifice, he and his family were thrown to the lions in the arena. The beasts refused to attack, so the entire family was burnt inside a brazen bull – a form of execution devised by the ancient Greeks, akin to being boiled alive.

*Left The Vision of Saint Eustace (Albrecht Dürer, 16th century).*

# POLYCARP

A TRUE SHEPHERD TO HIS FLOCK, THE BISHOP OF SMYRNA WAS ONE OF THE APOSTOLIC FATHERS OF THE CHURCH. HE GUIDED IT THROUGH DANGERS OF HERESY AND INTERNAL DISPUTES IN ROME.

**KEY FACTS**
*Apostolic Father of the Church*
DATES: c.AD 69–155
BIRTH PLACE: *Possibly Syria*
FEAST DAY: *23 February*

Polycarp knew the apostles, particularly St John. He was the living link between those who had known Christ in the flesh and the next generation of believers. This made him an Apostolic Father, and with this authority he played a significant role in the early Church.

During a wave of paganism in Asia in the 2nd century AD, Polycarp kept an strong hold on the essentials of Christ's teaching. He fought heretical or radical interpretations and practices, and his firm stand strengthened the spread of the Church in the East.

A heretical sect leader who wished to have a debate with Polycarp was rebuffed with the phrase, "I recognize you as the first-born of Satan". In his own writing, Polycarp explained, "For every one who shall not confess that Jesus Christ has come in the flesh is the antichrist".

St Irenaeus of Lyons was a child when he first heard Polycarp preach and recount his memories of the apostles. Irenaeus has left letters mentioning Polycarp, who was the bishop of Smyrna for almost 50 years. These letters give

*Left* Saint Sebastian and Saint Polycarp Destroying the Idols *(Pedro Garcia de Benabarre, 15th century). Broken idols litter the floor.*

glimpses of his life and his high standing in the Church. Ignatius of Antioch, awaiting martyrdom in Rome, trusted Polycarp to receive and forward secret letters on his behalf.

In old age, Polycarp was called to Rome to discuss the timing of feast days, especially that of Easter. He met Anicetus, bishop of Rome. They agreed to disagree, and Polycarp returned to Smyrna, believing his community could now peacefully use the calendar that it preferred.

## MARTYRDOM

He was over 80 when a mob bayed for his blood. Excited by pagan festivities that included lions attacking Christians, they shouted, "This is the father of the Christians". The Roman consul refused to throw Polycarp into the arena, but conceded to a death by burning. At the stake, Polycarp said, "May I be received among the martyrs in your presence today as a rich and pleasing sacrifice." A soldier stabbed him in order to spare him the pain of burning. Christians gathered relics from the ashes, and wrote an account of the trial and death of this martyr-saint, giving evidence of an early cultus.

*Left* St Polycarp spread the Christian faith in the sometimes rugged terrain of Palestine (left) and Syria.

# JUSTIN

THIS CHRISTIAN PHILOSOPHER
EXPLAINED THE MESSAGE OF
CHRIST IN HIS WRITINGS.

Justin was well educated and
sought answers to life's problems through philosophy. But the
teachings of Pythagorus, Plato
and the Stoics brought him no
closer to the Almighty.

## CONVERSION

A chance encounter with a
stranger directed him to look for
meaning in the message of
Christ. When Justin converted to
the faith he was about 30 years
old. The Christians he met were
reluctant to discuss their rituals
with an outsider. Justin said, "It is
our duty to make known our
doctrine, lest we incur the guilt
and the punishment of those who
have sinned through ignorance."

Justin wrote the *Apologies* and
*Dialogues*, important fragments of
which have survived. In these
writings, he sets out the moral
values of the faith and presents a
philosophical proof of its truth.

He is recognized as the first
Christian apologist. Dressed as a
philosopher, he preached and
taught throughout Palestine, Syria
and other regions.

## TRIAL AND DEATH

In Rome, he had a public debate
with another philosopher, named
Crescens. Justin presented the
more convincing argument, and
his adversary is believed to have
later instigated his arrest. A record
of his trial survives. The martyr
confessed his faith unhesitatingly,
and gave courage to six other
Christians who were also on trial.
Justin was decapitated, in accordance with Roman law.

### KEY FACTS
*Apologist (vindicator) of the faith*
DATES: *c.AD 100–65*
BIRTH PLACE: *Flavia Neapolis
(now Nablus, Palestine)*
PATRON OF: *Philosophers*
FEAST DAY: *1 June*
EMBLEM: *Philosopher's clothes*

*Left* A stained-glass window depicting
St Justin preaching to fishermen in
stormy weather.

*Below* A Sailor Offering a
Model Boat to St Justin *(Domenico
Robusti Tintoretto, son of Jacopo,
c. 17th century).*

# IRENAEUS OF LYONS

THE BISHOP OF LYONS WAS AN INFLUENTIAL THEOLOGIAN WHO HELPED THE CHURCH TO CLARIFY THE ARTICLES OF CHRISTIAN FAITH, IN PARTICULAR THE UNITY OF THE FATHER AND THE SON.

**KEY FACTS**
*Venerated as a martyr*
DATES: *c.AD 130–200*
BIRTH PLACE: *Possibly Smyrna*
FEAST DAY: *28 June (West)*
EMBLEM: *Bishop's clothes*

As a theologian St Irenaeus was not only able to defend and explain Christianity theoretically, he could also preach it to laymen.

Irenaeus worked as a priest in Lyons. He was sent to Rome on a peacemaking mission by his bishop Pothinus in AD 177. He took a message to the pope to show leniency towards the North African Church whose practices differed from those of Rome. He also brokered a compromise between the East and Pope Victor III who wanted Rome to decree the dates for Easter.

On his return, Irenaeus became Bishop of Lyons as his predecessor had been killed. Under his care the faith spread through this rich merchant city. He was the first to make a systematic organization of Catholic beliefs. His writings distinguished faith from the then popular heresy, Gnosticism, and he enhanced the unity of the faithful.

He wrote the "rule of faith" that encompasses all "the riches of Christian truth", still delivered at baptisms. He died at Lyons, but unfortunately his shrine was destroyed in the Reformation.

*Above St Irenaeus resurrects and baptizes a girl in this Belgian tapestry.*

# COSMAS AND DAMIAN

THE TWIN DOCTORS WHO NEVER CHARGED FOR THE MEDICAL CARE THEY GAVE HAVE LONG BEEN VENERATED FOR THEIR HEALING SKILLS AND THEIR KINDNESS. AS SUCH, THEY ARE PATRONS OF DOCTORS.

**KEY FACTS**
*Doctors, miracle cures*
DATES: *Unknown*
BIRTH PLACE: *Syria*
PATRON OF: *Doctors, dentists, barbers, chemists, hairdressers*
FEAST DAY: *26 September (West)*
EMBLEM: *Ampoules and medicine jars*

A widespread cultus followed Sts Cosmas and Damian in the 5th century AD. They practised as doctors in Cyrrhus, Syria, where a famous basilica was erected.

With wonderful powers of healing, aided by the Holy Spirit, they were known as the "holy moneyless ones" because their medical care was free. They also looked after sick animals.

Although Cosmas and Damian were persecuted by the Romans, it was said that rocks thrown at the twins simply flew backwards. Neither did the torture rack function. A further account says that after their eventual deaths by

beheading, the twins returned to earth to save Justinianus, deacon of their church. He lost a leg and they replaced the pale limb with another one from a black-skinned Ethiopian man. Differing versions of this story have been depicted by artists over the years.

Sick believers took to sleeping in the twins' church, hoping this "incubation" would cure them – a practice known also to occur in other religions.

*Right* Healing of the Deacon Justinianus by the Saints Cosmas and Damian (*Fra Angelico, 1440*). *The new black leg is clearly visible.*

# PERPETUA

A YOUNG MOTHER RECORDED
HER EXPERIENCES AND VISIONS
WHILE AWAITING MARTYRDOM.

**Above** *The shrine of St Perpetua is transferred to the Church of Bouvignes after the Siege of Dinant in 1466 (Flemish School, 15th century).*

**KEY FACTS**
*Martyr*
DATES: *d.AD 203*
BIRTH PLACE: *Carthage*
FEAST DAY: *7 March*

The daughter of a wealthy pagan in Carthage, Perpetua was arrested during a Roman persecution of newly converted Christians. Perpetua was first placed under house arrest, then imprisoned, even though she was the mother of a young baby.

She was 22 years old when she wrote about her extraordinary experiences. The work, finished anonymously, is an authentic record of Christian martyrdom.

She mentions her worries about her father and baby and describes vivid dreams of ladders to heaven and her dead brother, but the most inspiring vision was one of herself, changed into a man, fighting the devil.

Perpetua was allowed to send her baby home before her death. Some say she entered the arena at Carthage singing joyfully. She was wounded by a mad heifer, then despatched by the sword.

# FELICITAS

ST PERPETUA'S HANDMAIDEN RISKED HER OWN LIFE AND THAT OF
HER UNBORN CHILD WHEN SHE ACCEPTED THE CHRISTIAN FAITH.
SHE WAS MARTYRED AT THE SAME TIME AS HER MISTRESS.

**KEY FACTS**
*Martyr*
DATES: *d.AD 203*
BIRTH PLACE: *Carthage*
FEAST DAY: *7 March*

This young woman was a slave of St Perpetua in the Roman colony of Carthage. When her mistress was arrested, Felicitas (or Felicity) went with her to prison.

Felicitas was heavily pregnant at the time of their detention. Her husband, Revocatus, and two other slaves, Saturninus and Secundulus, were also caught up in the persecution. While under house arrest, they were all baptized before their transfer to prison.

Incarcerated in a filthy cell, Felicitas went into a difficult labour and brutal warders jeered at her pain. She knew her fate and that of her husband was death in the arena, so was grateful to give birth beforehand. A free Christian adopted the baby girl.

**Above** *The ancient Punic city walls of Carthage in present-day Tunisia. For the saints' martyrdom in the city's arena, leopards and bears were prepared to attack the men, and a mad heifer directed toward the two women.*

# DENYS OF PARIS

CREDITED WITH THE FOUNDING OF THE CHRISTIAN CHURCH IN PARIS, THIS VIRTUOUS MAN WENT ON TO BECOME A BISHOP AND WAS LATER MARTYRED FOR HIS FAITH.

## KEY FACTS

*Early mission to France*
DATES: *d.c.AD 250*
BIRTH PLACE: *Italy*
PATRON OF: *Paris and France, headaches*
FEAST DAY: *9 October*
EMBLEM: *Head held in his hands*

Said to be a fearless preacher, the Italian-born St Denys (or Dionysius) of Paris was sent on a dangerous mission to revive the persecuted Church of Gaul (France) in AD 250. Together with the deacon Eleutherius and the priest Rusticus, he established a Christian community on an island in the River Seine, close to Roman Paris.

St Denys' mission led to countless conversions, arousing the anger of the local pagan priests

**Below** *The interior of the 12th-century monastery dedicated to St Denys, built on the site of his death in Paris. It is a fitting tribute to the patron saint of the city and France.*

**Above** *This baroque statue of St Denys is one in a group of the Fourteen Holy Helpers. Denys is shown carrying his severed head, still preaching, in accordance with the story.*

who pushed for the missionaries to be stopped. The saint and his companions were eventually imprisoned and tortured before being beheaded on Montmartre (Martyrs' Hill) where the church of the Sacré Coeur now stands.

According to legend, a great miracle then occurred: St Denys picked up his head and walked two miles, preaching as he went. He eventually lay down and was buried with his fellow martyrs by a pious woman named Catulla.

Another version of events states that after they had been murdered the bodies of the martyrs were thrown into the Seine and retrieved and buried by converts. In both accounts, a shrine was built over the burial place, to be covered years later (c.AD 630) by a great abbey and church. This building, the Basilica of St-Denis later became the burial place of the kings of France.

## A NATIONAL FIGURE

St Denys had become a figure of national devotion by the 9th century. This was partly due to a great medieval mix up. The Emperor Louis I of France had been given the writings of a certain Dionysius (or Pseudo Dionysius) in which the author claimed to know the apostles. To the people of the time this would have identified the author as Dionysius the Areopagite, who was converted to Christianity by St Paul.

When Louis commissioned Hilduin, Abbot of St-Denis, to write a biography of St Denys in 835, he asked the abbot to use the works of Pseudo Dionysius as his source. In Hilduin's book, Dionysius the Areopagite and St Denys became the same man. This fiction persisted for 700 years, until it was discovered that Pseudo Dionysius was in fact a 5th-century theologian and philosopher, and St Denys was a significant figure in his own right.

# VALENTINE

TWO DIFFERENT VALENTINES WERE MARTYRS DURING THE ROMAN PERIOD, AND IT WAS ONLY DURING THE 14TH CENTURY THAT THE SAINT'S NAME BECAME ASSOCIATED WITH LOVERS.

**KEY FACTS**
*Representative of hidden love and courtship*
DATES: *3rd century AD*
BIRTH PLACE: *Unknown*
PATRON OF: *Lovers, betrothed couples, greetings*
FEAST DAY: *14 February*
EMBLEM: *Heart, birds, roses*

There seem to be two saints with this name. One was a 2nd-century bishop of Terni, Italy, the other a 3rd-century priest in Rome; both were martyred. Some hagiographers claim they were one and the same person.

The 3rd-century Valentinus was reportedly imprisoned for helping Christians, then tried to convert the Emperor Claudius II, cured his jailer's daughter of blindness, and was beheaded outside Rome's Flaminian Gate.

No one is sure why Valentine is associated with lovers. It may follow Lupercalia, an old pagan festival, celebrated in mid-February. On the eve of the Lupercalia, all the young women's names would be put into a container, and each young man would draw out a name. He would then be paired with the woman he had chosen for the remainder of the festival.

Another theory associates the courtship with a line by the English medieval poet Chaucer, who observed that birds choose their mates on 14 February.

*Right St Valentine (painted glass, Hungarian School, 19th century).*

# VICTOR OF MARSEILLES

THIS CONVERT, A SOLDIER, WAS SEVERELY PUNISHED FOR HIS FAITH AND HAD A STRONG CULTUS IN THE MEDIEVAL ERA. HIS TOMB BECAME A POPULAR PILGRIM SHRINE.

**KEY FACTS**
*Venerated as a martyr*
DATES: *3rd century AD*
BIRTH PLACE: *Marseilles, France*
PATRON OF: *Millers, lightning, torture victims, cabinet-makers*
FEAST DAY: *21 July*
EMBLEM: *Windmill, millstone*

Archaeological evidence points to the burial of a total of three martyrs beneath the church of St Victor in Marseilles. Tunnels and caves show early habitation, probably of monks.

Victor may have been a Moor in the Roman army who was converted. His fellow soldiers, fearing for his life, begged him to return to traditional Roman beliefs, but he refused. Legend says he was betrayed by other militia.

He was thrown into prison but his profound faith converted the two military wardens charged with guarding him. These two

*Below Victor of Marseilles is shown as a brave soldier of the faith destroying false idols (Hermen Rode, 1481).*

men were executed, and legend describes the cruel treatment meted out to Victor. He was put on the rack, and burned. His foot was hacked off and then he was crushed and ground between two large millstones.

Many miracles were claimed in his name and he developed a wide cultus in the medieval era. His tomb became one of the most visited pilgrim centres in what was then Gaul, and St-Victor Church can still be visited today.

# CECILIA

ANGELS AND HEAVENLY MUSIC
HELPED CECILIA TO CONVERT
HER HUSBAND AND OTHERS.

When she was a young woman, Cecilia's family refused to accept that she had taken a vow of virginity and forced her to marry a pagan. During the wedding, Cecilia sang silently to the Lord, "My heart remain unsullied, so that I may not be confounded". The bride vowed that her marriage would never be consummated.

Cecilia kept strong in her faith and told her husband, Valerian, that an angel was guarding her. She said God would be angry if Valerian touched her, but if he desisted, God would love him. Furthermore, if her husband were baptized, he would see this angel.

Valerian converted and angels appeared and placed flowers on the heads of the young couple. Cecilia's brother Tiburtius chose to become a Christian after this incident. In fact, the two men became so ardent in their faith that the Romans beheaded them, as Christianity was proscribed. Cecilia buried the two martyrs at her home. She, too, attracted anger

*Above A terracotta statue of Cecilia in the cathedral in Le Mans, France (Charles Hoyay, 17th century).*

from the state, but officials sent to arrest her were so overwhelmed by her faith that they converted.

Cecilia converted 400 people who were later baptized by Pope Urban in her home, which was later dedicated as a church.

The authorities did not abandon their persecution of Cecilia. They tried locking her in her own bathroom and burning the furnaces high. She lived through this ordeal, and then survived for three days after a soldier hacked at her neck with a sword.

There is little firm evidence for Cecilia's story. Her patronage of music comes from the heavenly sound she heard in her head while the organs played at her wedding.

## KEY FACTS
*Virgin martyr*
DATES: *3rd century AD*
BIRTH PLACE: *Rome*
PATRON OF: *Musicians, singers, composers*
FEAST DAY: *22 November*
EMBLEM: *Organ or lute*

### ANASTASIA
Virgin martyrs such as Ursula and Cecilia have attracted legends of heroism and miracles. Other martyrs give their names to churches, or else linger in the religious folk memory.

One such figure is St Anastasia. Nothing is known about her. It is possible she was martyred at a place now known as Srem Mitrovica, Serbia. Her name is in the Roman Canon. A prayer is said to her at Mass, and a few antique Byzantine churches carry her name. She was a "matron", not a "maiden", so she is not counted as one of the virgin martyrs.

*Below A stained-glass window depicting the martyrdom of St Anastasia (20th-century copy from a 13th-century original).*

*Left St Cecilia's tomb. Her body was found lying in this position in 1599, and the statue copies it exactly.*

# GEORGE

THE POTENCY OF HIS STORY ENSURES THAT ST GEORGE HOLDS A PLACE IN THE COMPANY OF SAINTS, BUT THE CHURCH SUSPECTS THAT THIS CHIVALROUS KNIGHT MAY BE MERELY A LEGEND.

In the 6th century, St George was described as good in so many ways that all his "deeds are known only to God". Sadly, most things about this saint remain known only by his maker, because evidence of his life is so sparse.

It seems certain, however, that George was a real martyr, a knight who came from Cappadocia in Turkey and died in Lydda (site of modern-day Lod) in Palestine.

### GEORGE AND THE DRAGON

In what is undoubtedly his most famous legend, George was riding through Libya when he heard cries of mourning. Townspeople told him that they were being tyrannized by a dragon that they had to feed with two lambs a day. Now they had no lambs left and the dragon was demanding a human meal. They had drawn lots from the maidens and the king's daughter had been chosen. Dressed in a beautiful bridal gown, the princess had gone forth to meet her doom. St George dashed into action and crippled the monster by thrusting his lance into it. Tying her girdle round the dragon's neck, the princess led it limping to the town. The terrified citizens prepared to run, but George told them that if they would be baptized, the dragon would be slain. They all agreed. It was alleged that approximately 15,000 people were baptized. Four ox carts moved the beast's body to a distant meadow.

*Right* St George and the Dragon (Paolo Uccello, c.1439–40).

*Above St George as depicted in a fresco in the Church of our Lady of the Pasture, Asinou, Cyprus (late 12th century).*

### CULTUSES AND CRUSADES

There are signs that St George's cultus was widespread early in Christian history. He was venerated across Europe and known in England before the Norman Conquest of AD 1066. His image can be found all over the Middle East, the Balkans and Greece.

During the Crusader battle of Antioch in AD 1098, Frankish (German) knights were blessed with a vision of George and another knight, St Demetrius. Possibly on his return from the Third Crusade a century later, Richard I promoted the veneration of St George in England.

### PATRONAGE

St George is now the patron saint of England, as well as of boy scouts and soldiers, and many churches bear his name. In 1914, together with St John Chrysostom and St Roch, St George was declared a patron of Constantinople (Istanbul).

Because so little is actually known of St George, the Church downgraded him in 1960, and today his feast day is reduced to prayers during mass. But his name and his story of chivalry are loved across the world. His flag, a red cross on white background, was well known by the 14th century and is the national flag of England.

## KEY FACTS
*Knight martyr*
DATES: *d.c.AD 303*
BIRTH PLACE: *Cappadocia, Turkey*
PATRON OF: *England, Istanbul, boy scouts, soldiers, and many other groups*
FEAST DAY: *23 April*
EMBLEM: *Red cross on white background, dragon*

# VITUS

A CHILD WHO DEFIED HIS PARENTS TO BECOME A CHRISTIAN, VITUS CURED SUFFERERS OF MENTAL ILLNESS AND EPILEPSY. FOLLOWERS DANCED ON HIS FEAST DAY TO ENSURE A YEAR OF GOOD HEALTH.

**KEY FACTS**
*Miracle worker*
DATES: *d.c. AD 303*
BIRTH PLACE: *Sicily*
PATRON OF: *St Vitus' dance, actors, comedians, against lightning and storms, against epilepsy, protection against dangerous animals, Sicily*
FEAST DAY: *15 June*
EMBLEM: *Dog or cockerel*

It is said that Vitus was a young boy when he elected to be baptized without his parents' knowledge. His angry parents beat him and threw him into a dungeon when he refused to give up his faith.

*Above The façade of the neo-Gothic Cathedral of St Vitus in Prague.*

Angels, dancing in a dazzling light, came to comfort him. His furious father visited him and tried to persuade Vitus to abandon the faith. But the angry man was blinded by the light and flitting movements of the dancing angels. He restored his father's sight, but this did not bring Vitus any peace.

As various other miracles were attributed to him, he found that officials became suspicious of him. Fearing for his safety, he fled from his birthplace in Sicily. He landed with two companions at Lucania in Italy where they stayed a while, preaching to the people. Finally they reached Rome, where Vitus cured Emperor Diocletian's son by expelling evil spirits that possessed the child.

But after this healing, Vitus was expected to make a thanksgiving sacrifice to the Roman gods who, it was presumed, had given him the power. Vitus refused, and so was branded a dangerous sorcerer.

Vitus and his companions were subjected to various unsuccessful tortures and were reputedly lifted to safety by an angel during a great storm. The site of their death or martyrdom remains unclear. Both St-Denis in Paris and Corvey in Saxony claim to hold his relics.

# DYMPNA

A PRINCESS WHO FLED FROM HER OBSESSED FATHER BECAME PATRONESS OF THE INSANE.

*Above This intricate decorated altar is found in the St Dympna Church in Gheel, Belgium (c. 1490–1500). It is called the Passion Altar, and it depicts the last days of Christ on earth.*

**KEY FACTS**
*Virgin, miracle worker*
DATES: *c. 7th century*
BIRTH PLACE: *Possibly Celtic Britain*
PATRON OF: *The mentally ill, against epilepsy and possession by the devil, sleepwalkers*
FEAST DAY: *30 May*

Legend explains that Dympna was a princess, the daughter of a Celtic or heathen king. She grew up to be beautiful, but she also bore an uncanny resemblance to her dead mother.

Her father developed a perverted passion for his daughter, and so she fled with her confessor or teacher, St Gerebernus. The two fugitives made their way to Gheel, near Antwerp, in Belgium. They lived as hermits but the king traced them and demanded her return. When the king's request was refused, he ordered his guards to murder Gerebernus and he beheaded his own daughter. Years later, the bones of the victims were discovered. After visiting these relics, numerous epileptics and lunatics claimed to be cured.

# CHRISTOPHER

THE PATRON SAINT OF TRAVELLERS DERIVES HIS NAME FROM A GREEK WORD MEANING "ONE WHO CARRIES CHRIST". CHRISTOPHER IS LOVED FOR THIS HONOURABLE TASK.

**KEY FACTS**

*Carried the child Jesus across a river*
DATES: *Unknown*
BIRTH PLACE: *Unknown*
PATRON OF: *Wayfarers, travellers and motorists*
FEAST DAY: *25 July*
EMBLEM: *Pole to aid walking through the river, carrying a child on his shoulder*

One of the best-known saints, Christopher is now deemed legendary and no longer included in the Roman Calendar. However, this "de-canonization" has not stopped the popular veneration of St Christopher, whose image adorns cars and key rings. Travellers everywhere continue to pray for his intercession.

According to some stories, Christopher was a tall, muscular man. He is described in the *Golden Legend* as having a "fearful face and appearance".

*Below This image from a German illuminated manuscript gives a realistic view of the agony St Christopher endured as he carried the small, but extraordinarily heavy infant Jesus across the river (15th century).*

## BECOMING A CHRISTIAN

Christopher found "a right great king" to serve, but soon observed he made the sign of the cross whenever hearing the word "devil". Christopher felt that needing such help was hardly fitting for a great monarch. So instead, he sought this powerful devil and worked for him.

With the devil leading him, Christopher travelled through the desert. The discovery that a cross, thrust into the sands, frightened the devil prompted Christopher to seek an explanation. A holy hermit told him about the power of this cross, and then converted him to Christianity.

Because of his size, Christopher dreaded fasting. Nor could he accept long hours of prayer and short periods of sleep. The hermit asked if Christopher could carry travellers across the river. In this way, the *Golden Legend* explains, he found a way to serve the Lord.

## CARRYING CHRIST

A child once asked Christopher to carry him, so he hoisted the little boy on to his shoulders and stepped into the water. The child grew heavier, but Christopher persevered. On reaching the other bank, he felt "all the world upon me; I might bear no greater burden". The boy replied, "Thou hast not only borne all the world upon thee, but thou hast borne Him that made all the world, upon thy soldiers. I am Jesus Christ."

Christopher went to Lycia (southern Turkey) to preach but was arrested. He survived burning by iron rods, and when they shot him, the arrows stopped in mid-air. Finally they beheaded him.

The truth about Christopher is sparse. He was martyred in the Middle East, honoured in the 3rd century AD, and a church was dedicated to him in the 4th century AD. Early Christians prayed to his image to ensure safe travel, which has led to the practice today.

*Below St Christopher is gaunt but noble in this sensitive wood carving (Gothic-style winged altar in the Kefermarkt, Austria, c.1490).*

# CHILD SAINTS

THOUSANDS OF CHILDREN HAVE DIED ALONE OR WITH THEIR CHRISTIAN FAMILIES IN DEFENCE OF THEIR FAITH. YET FEW NAMES SURVIVE FROM THIS GROUP OF YOUNG MARTYR SAINTS.

**M**any children were named as saints not only for the purity and innocence of their youth, but for the horrible deaths they suffered as martyrs.

It is safe to assume that thousands of unnamed children, together with their families, were slaughtered by the Roman authorities. Some attracted a cultus and their names live on. These children mostly come from the early years of the faith when its members were subject to horrific, intermittent persecution.

## EARLY MARTYRS
Legend describes St Foy (or Faith) as a defiant child who is said to have lived in Agen, Gaul (France) in the late 3rd century. Legend states that she was roasted alive and beheaded for her belief. Her bravery was venerated and thousands made the journey to visit her relics in Conques, France. Crusader soldiers, especially, pleaded for her protection.

The story of St Irene tells that this brave Macedonian girl was about 13 when she was arrested with her sisters

*Left A sculpture of St Philomena made out of gilded wood (1890).*

*Above The Abbey church of St Foy in Conques, France, which holds her gorgeous relics.*

in *c.*AD 303. While her sisters were killed, Irene was spared because she was so young. She was sent naked into the soldiers' brothel where no man dared approach her. She was eventually burnt alive in AD 304.

Although the 4th-century St Pelagia of Antioch is named in the church litany, all we know about her is that, when she was 15, soldiers invaded her home. To escape from them and avoid dishonour, the young virgin sacrificed her life by jumping off the roof of her house.

St Philomena's history is also obscure, but even now pilgrims visit her shrine in Naples. Her relics were unearthed in 1802 near an inscription bearing her name in the Roman catacombs. Her relics were subsequently moved to Naples, and miracles began to occur.

Because of controversy surrounding the relics of St Philomena, in 1961 the Holy See removed her from the liturgical calendar of saints and wanted to dismantle her shrine; yet she continues to attract pilgrims.

Son of Coenwulf, King of Mercia (AD 796–821), Prince Kenelm was next in line for the throne. But according to legend his sister, Quendreda, was jealous of the seven-year-old Christian prince and ordered the boy's tutor to murder him so she would inherit the throne. It was said that a dove carried a document to Rome telling of his death, and his relics were translated to Winchcombe in Gloucestershire. His wicked sister's eyes fell out and she was blind for the rest of her life.

## CHILD MARTYRS
*Names with age at death; those in bold refer to martyrs described on these two pages:*

Agape (Charity), 9
**Agnes**, 13
Christodoulos, 14
**Dominic Savio**, 15
Elpis (Hope), 10
Eulalia Mérida, 12
**Foy** (or **Faith**), unknown
Gabriel Gowdel, 7
**Irene**, 13
Justus of Beauvais, 9
**Kenelm**, 7
Kizito, 13
**Maria Goretti**, 12
Niño de Atocha, unknown
Pancras of Rome, 14
Paul Lang Fu, 9
**Pelagia of Antioch**, 15
**Philomena**, unknown
Pistis (Faith), 12
Rais, 12

## 19TH AND 20TH CENTURIES

There are only a few known child saints from the 19th and 20th centuries. They are symbols of the bravery of the thousands of unnamed children who suffered for their faith during this time.

One such child is Dominic Savio. He was only 12 when he entered a Turin monastery. A cheerful, peaceful child, he was famous for the hours he spent in prayer. Dominic suffered from tuberculosis and, during a fever, experienced a vision. Before his death in 1857 he cried out, "I am seeing the most wonderful things!" He was 15.

During the Boxer Rebellion in 1900, thousands of Christians were murdered for playing a part in the foreign domination of China. One of the youngest was Paul Lang Fu, just nine years old. He ran to his mother's side as soldiers tied her to a tree, but they hacked off his arm and burnt him to death.

Maria Goretti (1890–1902) was a martyr for chastity and the Christian life. She was only 12 years old when she was murdered by a man who tried to rape her. Before she died, she forgave him his sin. He was imprisoned and after eight years he became a Christian; he was present at her canonization in 1950.

## AGNES

Agnes is probably the best-known child saint. Some stories claim she was 13 when she died in Rome around AD 305. She was buried on the Via Nomentana, and a church was built over her grave soon after her death.

This young Christian girl refused to marry the son of a Roman prefect because she had dedicated herself to Christ. When the son complained, the father tried to force the marriage. Agnes remained steadfast in her refusal. According to legend she was then dragged naked through the streets to a brothel, but her hair grew and hid her body. One man who tried to rape her was blinded, but Agnes prayed for him and his sight returned. The Romans finally put her to death by piercing her throat with a sword after flames would not burn her.

Agnes is often painted with a lamb to symbolize her purity and every year, on her feast day, two lambs are blessed inside her church in Rome. Their wool is woven by the nuns of St Agnes' convent into bands which the pope confers on bishops as a sign of authority. The superstitious believe virgins who go without supper on the eve of the feast of St Agnes will dream of the man who will become their true love.

*Left St Agnes holding the palm of martyrdom (Lucas van Leyden, 1510).*

# EULALIA OF MÉRIDA

THIS YOUNG SPANISH GIRL DARED TO CONFRONT A ROMAN JUDGE, BOLDLY REPROVING HIM FOR HIS PERSECUTION OF CHRISTIANS. SHE WAS ACCOMPANIED AT HER DEATH BY A WHITE DOVE.

## KEY FACTS
*Virgin martyr*
DATES: *d.c.AD 304*
BIRTH PLACE: *Mérida, Spain*
FEAST DAY: *10 December*
EMBLEM: *Oven*

Eulalia is widely venerated in Spain for being a courageous virgin, a martyr – and a child.

Early in the 4th century AD, under the Roman Emperor Maximian, the persecution of Christians was widely enforced. In Mérida, local believers were rounded up and arrested. The judge Dacian was presiding over their trials when a young girl confronted him. Her wealthy family were apparently austere and frugal, and it must be assumed they were among the persecuted. She was only 12 years old, but Eulalia was courageous and loyal to her faith and family. She informed the judge that he was wrong to condemn and oppress the Christians.

She said that his prisoners were following the way of the one true God, so the Romans should not

**Above** *The interior of the Cathedral of Santa Eulalia, Barcelona (13th–15th century). The saint commemorated by this building may be merely legendary.*

punish them. He tried to divert the child with bribes, but Eulalia became angry and stamped on the sacrificial pagan cake he offered her. Then she delivered a deadly insult. Eulalia spat at the judge.

Dacian gave orders that she be tortured by being torn with iron hooks. Finally, she was bound and burnt to death in an oven. Spectators said that, just as she was thrust into the flames, a white dove fluttered from her mouth and soared into the air. Then a short and unexpected snow fell,

**Left** Sts Eulalia and Clare *(Pedro Serra, 14th century).*

soothing her burns and covering her body. Christians dug her body from the icy mound and buried her remains with the oven in which she had died. The burial site is in Mérida.

## THE CULT OF EULALIA

Thousands of medieval pilgrims visited the young saint's shrine, and many sites claimed to house her relics during the 6th and 7th centuries. Numerous churches and monasteries were dedicated in her name.

Artists favoured her gruesome death as a subject. The cathedral of Palma and the Catalonian art gallery in Barcelona have paintings of Eulalia. The Venerable Bede refers to this child-martyr in one of his hymns, saying "scorched by fierce flames, Eulalia endures." The Spanish poet, Prudentius, describes the flight of the white dove from Eulalia's mouth.

## FALSE CLAIMS

From time to time, it seems the longing to proclaim sainthood for a friend or relative overwhelms a community. There are examples of "duplicate saints" being given the name and even the legend of a known saint.

For instance, another girl named Eulalia, from Barcelona, has also been claimed as a saint. She has been accorded similar legends and status by false cultuses. Scholars have decided that the young girl from Mérida is the person who probably did exist, whereas the other girl never did.

# JUSTUS OF BEAUVAIS

DURING ONE OF THE MOST SEVERE PERSECUTIONS OF THE CHURCH BY THE ROMAN AUTHORITIES, SOLDIERS CAME TO TAKE AWAY A CHRISTIAN FAMILY, BUT WERE GREETED BY A DEFIANT SMALL BOY.

**KEY FACTS**
*Child martyr*
DATES: *3rd or 4th century AD*
BIRTH PLACE: *Beauvais*
FEAST DAY: *18 October*

The persecution of Christians by edict of the Roman Emperor Diocletian in AD 303 was one of the worst in the history of the early Church.

It was possibly during this violent period that soldiers came to the family home of the young Justus demanding the arrest of his Christian father and brother. The boy, just nine years old, showed no fear, although he must have known that the soldiers were dangerous and brutal men. He refused to reveal where his family were hiding. Ignoring his youth and bravery, his persecutors lifted their swords and swiftly sliced off the boy's head.

According to legend, Justus' head continued to speak after his decapitation. The words remained defiant. Justus had a large cultus in France, Belgium and Switzerland.

*Above The grave of a martyr from the 2nd or 3rd centuries AD; the fish was a secret symbol among Christians.*

# PANCRAS OF ROME

THIS SAINT'S HISTORY IS OBSCURE YET HIS NAME LIVES ON BOTH WITHIN THE CHURCH AND IN THE SECULAR WORLD, NOTABLY AS A PARISH AND RAILWAY TERMINUS IN LONDON, ENGLAND.

**KEY FACTS**
*Child martyr*
DATES: *Early 4th century AD*
BIRTH PLACE: *Phrygia*
FEAST DAY: *12 May*

There is no hard evidence about St Pancras. A martyr of that name was buried in the Aurelian Way in Rome. Legend has it that St Pancras was only 14 when he was killed.

In about AD 500, Pope St Symmachus built a church in Rome over the tomb of St Pancras. Miracles in his name were claimed at the site. The great St Augustine of Canterbury built a church in his honour in that city. This building, too, carried an atmosphere of great spirituality.

After their conquest of England in 1066, centuries later, the Normans dedicated a church in London to the boy saint. His name was given to a parish and a railway station in London. These facts make it easier to believe that the boy did exist, and that once upon a time his bravery and the circumstances of his death were well known.

*Below An etching of St Pancras Church at Euston in London, designed by H.W. Inwood (Thomas Kearnan, 19th century).*

# DOROTHY

FEARLESS IN THE FACE OF TORTURE AND DEFIANT IN DEATH, DOROTHY RETURNED TO WORK A MIRACLE, DELIVERING A GIFT FROM PARADISE TO A MAN WHO HAD TAUNTED HER FOR HER FAITH.

**KEY FACTS**
*Virgin martyr*
DATES: *d.c.AD 304*
BIRTH PLACE: *Caesarea, Cappadocia*
PATRON OF: *Florists, gardeners, brewers and bridal couples*
FEAST DAY: *6 February*
EMBLEM: *Basket of flowers, especially roses, and of fruit*

Despite coming from a noble Roman family in Caesarea in Cappadocia, Turkey, Dorothy would not pay homage to her family's pagan gods. Punished for her Christian faith and refusal to marry, she experienced frightful torture. But the weapons used against her felt as mere feathers.

At the place of execution, Dorothy showed no fear and instead announced to the crowd around her that she was glad to leave this cold world for one that knew neither ice nor snow. A young man called Theophilus, taunted her for both her virginity

and her faith. He then challenged her to send him roses and fruit when she reached her paradise.

In the winter after Dorothy's martyrdom, an angel delivered a basket filled with roses and fruit to Theophilus. He converted but the young man, too, was executed.

*Left Theophilus taunts Dorothy in* The Flower Miracle of Saint Dorothy *(Hans Baldung, 1516).*

# VINCENT OF SARAGOSSA

SPAIN'S FIRST MARTYR SAINT WAS REVERED FOR HIS COURAGE AND STAMINA IN THE FACE OF REPEATED TORTURE. SYMBOLIC OF THIS RESISTANCE IS HIS SUPPOSED POWER AGAINST WINTER FROST.

**KEY FACTS**
*Spain's first martyr*
DATES: *d.AD 304*
BIRTH PLACE: *Saragossa, Spain*
PATRON OF: *Wine-growers, wine- and vinegar-makers, and of Portugal*
FEAST DAY: *22 January*
EMBLEM: *Dressed as a deacon holding a palm tree or on a gridiron*

There is little evidence about this early martyr saint, yet St Vincent of Saragossa was venerated across the Roman Empire. Every Christian community associated his name with Christ.

He is the protomartyr of Spain and his fate was horrible. Taken prisoner, Vincent was thrown into jail. He was kept on a starvation diet so that his body, and resolve, might weaken. Still he refused to recognize the pagan gods.

The authorities put him in the stocks, stretched him on the rack and roasted him on a gridiron. After that he was returned to his

miserable prison and left to starve. Vincent endured all this brutal violence with defiance and took a long time dying.

Vincent is credited with the power to fight winter frost, hence his patronage of wine.

*Left A depiction of the* Martyrdom of St Vincent *(French manuscript illumination, 15th century).*

# LUCY

YET ANOTHER VICTIM OF THE DIOCLETIAN PERSECUTION, LUCY
WAS BELIEVED TO HAVE BEEN RESCUED BY THE HOLY SPIRIT. SHE IS
REMEMBERED FOR THE MIRACULOUS RECOVERY OF HER EYES.

**KEY FACTS**
*Virgin martyr*
DATES: *d. AD 304*
BIRTH PLACE: *Syracuse, Sicily*
PATRON: *Against eye afflictions
and throat infections*
FEAST DAY: *13 December*
EMBLEM: *Disembodied eyes,
usually on a platter*

Lucy lost her father when she
was a child but was, by all
accounts, a resolute, devout young
Sicilian. She had a loving mother,
yet Lucy kept secret her Christian
faith and her vow of virginity.

Her mother, Eutychia, was a
wealthy noblewoman from
Syracuse. She followed tradition
by betrothing her adolescent
daughter to a local youth. This
expectation made Lucy confess
her faith and she invited her
mother to accompany her on a
pilgrimage to the tomb of St
Agatha. The two women prayed at
this shrine and Eutychia was
cured of haemorrhages from
which she suffered. Grateful and
convinced of Lucy's faith, she
released the girl from the
betrothal. But the young man was
furious at the rejection of his
marriage offer, and reported Lucy
to the authorities who promptly
arrested her.

## MARTYRDOM

The persecution by the Emperor
Diocletian was famous for its zeal
in attacking Christianity, with
many of its followers perishing.

The emperor sentenced Lucy
to be taken to a brothel. However,
it was said that the girl became
immovable. Neither a gang of
strong men nor a team of oxen
could shift her. She had been
filled by the Holy Spirit, making
her miraculously heavy.

Her wardens could not lift her
to take her to the stake for
burning. So instead, it is claimed,
they tore out her eyes and threw
them on a platter. Lucy calmly

*Above St Lucy displays her eyes on
a platter (A. Colza, 1513).*

took hold of them and put them
back in their sockets. Her sight
was magically restored. Frustrated

by the failure of their cruel methods in persuading the saint to
abandon her faith or her virginity,
the soldiers beheaded the girl.

In many paintings, Lucy holds
the platter bearing her eyes.
Otherwise her eyes are dangling
from a sprig of leaves or on her
clothes. She has long been connected with light, partly because
of the story of her eyes, and also
because her name is linked to the
Latin word for "light", *lux*.

Lucy is remembered in
Sweden on the shortest day of the
year with festivals at which young
girls carry candles in her memory.
She is likewise venerated in her
birthplace, Sicily.

*Below Detail of St Lucy resisting a
team of oxen in front of the Judge
Paschasius (Bartolo di Fredi, c. 1380).*

# PATRON SAINTS OF PROFESSIONS

IN THE WORLD OF WORK, SOME SAINTS ARE PATRONS BY CUSTOM, OTHERS BY PAPAL CONCESSION. SOME HELPED PARTICULAR PROFESSIONS; OTHERS ARE CHOSEN FOR THE LIVES THEY LED.

**Accountants** – Matthew
**Actors** – Genesius of Arles, Vitus
**Actresses** – Pelagia the Penitent
**Advertisers** – Bernardino of Siena
**Air crew** – Joseph of Copertino, Theresa of Lisieux
**Anaesthetists** – René Goupil
**Apothecaries** – Nicholas of Myra, Cosmas and Damian
**Archaeologists** – Jerome, Helen
**Architects** – Thomas, Barbara
**Art dealers** – John
**Artists** – Luke, Catherine de'Vigri of Bologna
**Astronauts** – Joseph of Copertino
**Astronomers** – Dominic
**Athletes** – Sebastian
**Authors** – John, Paul, Lucy, Francis of Sales
**Bakers** – Elizabeth of Hungary, Zita, Nicholas of Myra, Agatha
**Bankers** – Bernardino of Feltre, Matthew
**Bar staff** – Amand
**Basket-makers** – Antony of Egypt
**Beekeepers** – Ambrose, Bernard of Clairvaux, Valentine, Modomnoc
**Bishops** – Charles Borromeo
**Blacksmiths** – Dunstan, Eloi
**Bookkeepers** – Matthew
**Brewers** – Amand, Wenceslas, Augustine of Hippo, Boniface
**Bricklayers** – Stephen of Hungary
**Broadcasters** – Archangel Gabriel
**Builders** – Barbara, Blaise, Louis IX, Vincent Ferrer
**Bus drivers** – Christopher
**Butchers** – Adrian of Nicomedia, Luke
**Cab drivers** – Christopher, Eloi, Fiacre, Frances of Rome
**Cabinet-makers** – Anne, Joseph, Victor of Marseilles
**Carpenters** – Joseph, Thomas
**Civil servants** – Thomas More

*Above* St Bernardino of Siena *(Giovanni di Paolo, 1450). He is patron of advertisers.*

**Clergy** – Gabriel Possenti
**Clowns** – Genesius of Arles, Julian the Hospitaller
**Cobblers** – Crispin and Crispinian, Bartholomew
**Cooks, chefs** – Laurence, Macarius the Younger, Martha, Paschal Baylon
**Craftsmen** – Eloi, Catherine of Alexandria

**Customs officers** – Matthew
**Dancers** – Vitus, Genesius of Arles, Philemon
**Dentists** – Apollonia
**Dietitians** – Martha
**Diplomats** – Archangel Gabriel
**Doctors** – Blaise, Cosmas and Damian, Pantaleon
**Domestic workers** – Adelelmus, Martha, Zita
**Ecologists** – Francis of Assisi
**Editors** – John Bosco, Francis of Sales
**Engineers** – Ferdinand III
**Farm-workers** – Benedict, Isidore the Farmer, Eloi, Phocas of Sinope, George
**Firefighters** – Agatha, Laurence, Catherine of Siena
**Fishermen** – Andrew, Peter, Simon, Zeno, Magnus
**Florists** – Dorothy, Rose of Lima
**Funeral directors** – Joseph of Arimathea, Dismas, Sebastian

*Above* St Fiacre *(illumination, 15th century). Cab drivers in Paris plied their trade from the hotel St Fiacre and the saint has become their patron.*

*Above St Ivo of Brittany is patron of judges because he mediated in church disputes (Gaudenzio Ferrari, 1520).*

**Goldsmiths** – Dunstan, Eloi
**Grocers** – Archangel Michael, Leonard of Noblac
**Gunners** – Barbara
**Hairdressers** – Louis IX, Martin de Porres, Mary Magdalene
**Hoteliers** – Amand, Julian the Hospitaller, Martha
**Housewives** – Martha, Zita, Anne
**Huntsmen** – Eustace, Hubert
**Jewellers** – Eloi, Agatha, Dunstan
**Journalists** – Francis of Sales, Paul, Maximilian Kolbe
**Judges** – Ivo of Brittany
**Labourers** – Eloi, Isidore the Farmer, Guy of Anderlecht, Lucy
**Lawyers** – Ivo of Brittany, Thomas More, Robert Bellarmine
**Leather-workers** – Crispin and Crispinian, Bartholomew
**Librarians** – Jerome, Catherine of Alexandria, Laurence of Rome
**Locksmiths** – Dunstan, Eloi, Peter, Leonard of Noblac
**Magistrates** – Ferdinand III
**Mechanics** – Catherine of Alexandria
**Merchants** – Nicholas, Homobonus
**Midwives** – Dorothy of Myra,

*Right Limestone statue of St Maurice, the patron of soldiers and armies (Magdeburg Cathedral, c.1240).*

Brigid of Ireland, Peter of Verona, Raymund Nonnatus
**Miners** – Barbara
**Musicians** – Cecilia, Gregory the Great
**Naval officers** – Francis of Paola
**Nurses** – Agatha, Camillus of Lellis, John of God, Catherine of Siena
**Obstetricians** – Raymund Nonnatus
**Painters** – Catherine de'Vigri of Bologna, Benedict Biscop
**Paramedics** – Archangel Michael
**Paratroopers** – Archangel Michael
**Pawnbrokers** – Nicholas of Myra
**Perfumers** – Nicholas of Myra, Mary Magdalene
**Philosophers** – Albert the Great, Justin, Catherine of Alexandria, Thomas Aquinas
**Photographers** – Veronica
**Poets** – Columba of Iona, John of the Cross, Brigid of Ireland, Cecilia
**Police officers** – Archangel Michael, Sebastian
**Politicians** – Thomas More
**Priests** – Jean-Baptiste Vianney
**Printers** – Augustine of Hippo, John of God

*Above St Vincent of Saragossa is surrounded by vines and grapes to indicate his patronage of wine-makers.*

**Publishers** – John of God
**Sailors** – Nicholas of Myra, Francis of Paola, Phocas of Sinope
**Scholars** – Jerome, Brigid of Ireland, Catherine of Alexandria
**Scientists** – Albert the Great, Dominic
**Secretaries** – Genesius of Arles, Catherine of Alexandria
**Silversmiths** – Andronicus, Dunstan
**Social workers** – John Francis Regis, Louise de Marillac
**Soldiers** – Martin of Tours, George, Maurice, Fay, James the Great
**Surgeons** – Cosmas and Damian, Luke, Roch
**Surveyors** – Thomas
**Tailors** – Boniface, Homobonus
**Tax collectors** – Matthew
**Teachers** – John-Baptist de la Salle, Catherine of Alexandria, Francis of Sales, Gregory the Great, Ursula
**Veterinarians** – Eloi, Blaise, James the Great
**Waiters** – Martha, Notburga, Zita
**Weavers** – Maurice
**Wine-makers** – Amand, Vincent of Saragossa, Martin of Tours

# PANTALEON

ONCE AMBITIOUS AND WORLDLY, PANTALEON ABANDONED A SUCCESSFUL CAREER IN MEDICINE TO LIVE "IN IMITATION OF CHRIST" AND WAS EVENTUALLY MARTYRED FOR HIS FAITH.

**KEY FACTS**
*Martyr saint*
DATES: *d.c.AD 305*
BIRTH PLACE: *Nicomedia
(now Izmit, Turkey)*
PATRON OF: *Doctors, midwives,
a Holy Helper*
FEAST DAY: *27 July*
EMBLEM: *Olive branch*

The Eastern Orthodox Church honours this saint as the "Great Martyr and Wonder Worker". (In the Greek language, Pantaleon means "all compassionate".) However, although his cult was well established in the East and West from an early date, there are no surviving authentic particulars of Pantaleon's life, which has become the subject of legends.

It is thought that he was the son of a pagan father, but was brought up as a Christian by his mother. He studied medicine and later practised as a doctor in Nicomedia (now Izmit) in Turkey, eventually gaining the important position of physician to the Emperor Galerius Maximianus.

However, being young and carefree, as well as ambitious and successful, Pantaleon abandoned his faith to enjoy the worldly pleasures of the royal palace. Fortunately, one of his friends from his former Christian life, Hermolaos, persistently reminded him of the truth of the Christian faith. When Emperor Diocletian came to power and started his fierce campaign of terror against Christians, Pantaleon realized where his feelings and loyalties lay. He distributed his wealth among the poor, treated the sick without receiving payment, and changed his life to one of discipline and austerity in imitation of Christ.

## CAPTURE AND TORTURE
Other doctors, who had long envied Pantaleon for his success at court, took the opportunity to denounce him to the authorities.

***Above** The church of St Pantaleon (AD 966–80) in Köln, Germany.*

He was arrested with Hermolaos and two other friends. The other three men were all executed, but the emperor, reluctant to lose a good doctor, begged Pantaleon to deny his faith. He refused, and his statement of faith was reinforced when he miraculously cured a cripple during his trial.

According to the stories, six types of torture were devised for Pantaleon. He was thrown into deep water to drown, then burning lead was poured over him. They tried to burn him, and they set wild beasts upon him. Then they turned him on a wheel and thrust a sword through his throat. But no matter what mode of torture was employed, Pantaleon was miraculously protected from harm, suffering no wounds and feeling no pain. When at last his tormentors beheaded him, it is said that milk flowed from his veins and the olive tree to which he had been tied burst into fruit.

In Ravello, southern Italy, a reputed relic of St Pantaleon's blood allegedly liquefies every year on his feast day.

***Above** A fresco of St Pantaleon from Macedonia (12th century). Scarcely remembered now in the West, St Pantaleon is still venerated in the East, and many legends and miracles are associated with this martyr.*

# LUCIAN OF ANTIOCH

THE MAN WHO ESTABLISHED THE IMPORTANT SCHOOL OF THEOLOGY IN ANTIOCH MADE AN AUTHORITATIVE TRANSLATION OF THE OLD TESTAMENT INTO GREEK BEFORE HIS MARTYRDOM.

**KEY FACTS**
*Martyr saint*
DATES: *d. AD 312*
BIRTH PLACE: *Samosata, Syria*
FEAST DAY: *7 January (West)*
EMBLEM: *Bishop's vestments, dolphins*

Orphaned at the age of 12, Lucian had Christian parents, who it is thought may have been martyred. He became the student of a famous teacher, Macarius of Edessa. After baptism, Lucian adopted a strictly ascetic life.

## TEACHER AND SCHOLAR

His routine of disciplined habits allowed Lucian to write and study. He became a teacher, and is believed to be the man who established the school of theology in Antioch, which at that time was a significant Christian centre. One of his students was Arius, whose followers were sometimes known as Lucianists and who became the founder of Arianism.

Lucian is also known to have made an important translation of the Old Testament from Hebrew into Greek. His version, which corrected misleading translations in common use at the time, stressed the importance of maintaining the literal sense of the texts. His complete edition of the Bible, known as *Lucian Recension*, was used by St Jerome during his work on the *Vulgate*, and St John Chrysostom also regarded it as an authoritative text. Surviving manuscripts confirm this respect, and one such text, the Arundelian, is in the British Museum.

## ORTHODOXY OR HERESY?

Lucian lived at a time of conflict within the Church in Antioch. Three successive bishops were hostile to his teachings, and for some years he was excluded from major meetings of Christian leaders. However, it seems that he otherwise enjoyed wide popular support. The people respected him for his great learning as well as admiring his noble character. He was later restored to office.

## PRISON AND MARTYRDOM

During an outbreak of Christian persecution, Lucian was arrested and taken to Nicomedia, where he faced the Roman official Maximin Daza. He was thrown into prison, but, despite brutal treatment, his reputation for dignity and courage grew during the nine years he spent there. When dragged before the authorities for interrogation, he would always reply simply "I am a Christian".

At last, because he would not renounce his faith, his diet was reduced to sacrificial cake that had been dedicated to pagan idols. This he refused to eat. Some say he starved to death, but others relate that he was tortured and then beheaded. One legend even claimed he was flung into the sea and drowned, but that dolphins carried his body to shore where it was collected by his followers.

Lucian's relics were taken to Drepanum, where on the first anniversary of the saint's death, St John Chrysostom preached a tribute to this much-admired scholar and martyr.

*Left The remains of the Roman Emperor Diocletian's palace at Nicomedia (now Izmit) in Turkey. Lucian suffered during Diocletian's persecution of Christians.*

# HELEN

THE MOTHER OF EMPEROR CONSTANTINE WAS AN ELDERLY WOMAN WHEN SHE CONVERTED. AN ANGEL IS SAID TO HAVE HELPED HER IDENTIFY THE TRUE CROSS WHILE SHE WAS VISITING THE HOLY LAND.

**KEY FACTS**
*Mother of Constantine,
finder of the True Cross*
DATES: *c.AD 250–330*
BIRTH PLACE: *Drepanum (later
Helenopolis, in modern-day
north-west Turkey)*
PATRON OF: *Archaeologists*
FEAST DAY: *18 August (West)*
EMBLEM: *Crown, cross*

Helen came from humble origins, but she made a grand marriage and gave birth to a great son. According to tradition, she was born in Drepanum (later renamed Helenopolis after her, by her son Constantine) and her father was an innkeeper. Her husband, Constantius Chlorus, a Roman general, divorced her when he became Emperor of Rome in AD 292, but their son greatly honoured her.

FINDING THE TRUE CROSS
When in her sixties, Helen made a pilgrimage to Jerusalem. She had converted to Christianity by this time. Her son, who was by then emperor, had organized diggings to uncover the holy sites of Jesus and the apostles.

It is told that Helen was at the hill of Calvary, where foundations were being dug for the church of the Holy Sepulchre, when three

*Left* St Helen *(Altobello Meloni, 15th century).*

crosses were excavated. A woman with a terminal illness was touched by each of the crosses, and the True Cross cured her, thus revealing its sacred nature.

Relics of the Cross were taken to Rome, where they were housed in the Basilica of Santa Croce, built for the purpose. The Holy Stairs – allegedly the marble steps excavated from the hall of Pontius Pilate where Christ's trial was held – were also moved to Rome.

Helen was renowned for her generosity and work among prisoners and the poor, and she founded churches in both Palestine and Rome.

## CONSTANTINE THE GREAT

Some biographies of Constantine claim his mother, Helen, was his father's paramour, not a wife. Though his father was emperor, Constantine still had to fight hard to win leadership of the Roman Empire. His cause was doubtless helped by his diplomatic skills.
Although he promoted Christianity after his conversion, he was reluctant to cause strife in a predominantly pagan Rome. As emperor, he founded Constantinople (now Istanbul) on the site of the old city of Byzantium, which in time became the centre of the Christian world.

*Right* Emperor Constantine and St Helen with the True Cross *(fresco, c.8th century).*

*Above* St Helena and the Miracle of the True Cross *(attr. to Simon Marmion, 15th century).*

# PACHOMIUS

A COMPETENT ADMINISTRATOR, THIS FORMER ROMAN SOLDIER
WAS HIGHLY INFLUENTIAL IN ESTABLISHING ORDERLY COMMUNAL
LIFE FOR HERMITS IN THE REGION OF UPPER EGYPT.

**KEY FACTS**

*Founder of the first monasteries*
DATES: *c.AD 290–346*
BIRTH PLACE: *Esna,*
*Upper Egypt*
FEAST DAY: *9 May (West)*
EMBLEM: *Appearance of a hermit*

Life in the Roman army prepared Pachomius well for the path he chose to follow. Born to heathen parents in Egypt, he was conscripted into the Roman army, where he fought under Constantine the Great. He became a Christian after his return home, and immediately went to live in the wilderness, there putting himself under the guidance of an old hermit named Palemon.

Pachomius lived near the River Nile and became part of a small community of other ascetics committed to the austere life of a recluse. An angel is said to have visited Pachomius after a few years and told him to establish a monastery in the desert. It seems this Desert Father preferred the life of the community to that of the solitary. He was concerned, too, that some of his fellow hermits were extreme in their behaviour and that they were running the risk of madness from starvation and hardship.

## FOUNDING MONASTERIES

His life in the army had taught Pachomius about the organization of a dedicated community, and he also had a flair for administration. After his first monastery was founded in AD 320, he established nine others for men and two nunneries for women, and wrote rules for living in these communities.

*Above* This Byzantine mosaic *includes Pachomius' name in Latin in the design (12th century).*

The monks and nuns took vows of chastity, poverty and obedience, and regulations regarding diet and prayer were strict but humane. Fanaticism was outlawed and meditation and prayer were supervised. Members learnt by heart passages from the Psalms

and other books of the Bible. Pachomius acted as an army general might do in running the monasteries. Monks were commanded to move from one house to another, superiors were put in charge of each house, and accounts were presented every year.

The order he founded was known as the Tabennisiots, after a place near his first monastery. Pachomius' manuscripts have not survived, but his Rule was translated into Latin by St Jerome, and this influenced Sts Basil the Great and Benedict, both of whom founded great monastic orders based on St Pachomius' methods.

St Athanasius the Aconite, patriarch of Alexandria, was a friend of Pachomius and visited the monk in his monastery at Dendera, near the Nile, where Pachomius lived out his life. The Eastern Orthodox Church holds this remarkable man in high veneration.

*Right* St Pachomius (16th century).
*The saint, remembered for building the first monasteries, is shown in this fresco to be casting his saintly light on the construction of a grand tower.*

# RELIGIOUS ORDERS

MONASTERIES AND CONVENTS SUSTAIN COMMUNITIES DEVOTED TO A
STRICT RELIGIOUS LIFE. THESE RELIGIOUS ORDERS HAVE A ROLE IN
ROMAN CATHOLIC AND EASTERN ORTHODOX CHURCHES.

Although Christianity does not regard ownership of property or marriage as sinful, the Church recognizes that some people have a special calling to dedicate their lives to prayer and to God.

Those called to this religious life fall into two categories. The first are the eremites, who choose to pursue a life of solitary meditation, following the precepts formulated by St Antony of Egypt and other Desert Fathers. The second group, the coenobites, share a communal life of prayer that is influenced by the ideas of St Pachomius. Founders of the various orders laid down rules for monastic life, which continue to apply in Roman Catholic and Eastern Orthodox Churches.

The lives of all monks and nuns are guided by the primary disciplines of prayer, spiritual development, inner contemplation and physical labour.

## EARLY MODELS
The earliest monasteries were self-supporting and independent of papal authority. Many monks were not even ordained as priests.

Some early founders, such as Martin of Tours and Cassian, maintained harsh regimes. But St Benedict, who established a monastery at Monte Cassino, Italy, rejected this military-like austerity. His rules were those of a well-ordered household with routine and sympathetic discipline. He encouraged labour to sustain the community and literacy to provide an understanding of the scriptures. By the 10th century, his rule was accepted throughout Western Christendom.

The Rule of St Augustine of Canterbury was also influential. He stipulated that monks should be ordained clerics, living within an order but going into the world to work as priests.

*Above* St Zeno *(Francesco Bonaza, 17th century). St Zeno founded the earliest nunneries and encouraged women to take vows.*

*Above left* St Hugo of Grenoble in the Refectory of the Carthusians *(Francisco Zurbarán, 1633). St Hugo helped establish their house in Grenoble, France.*

Over time, monastic orders lost their independent status and were required to obtain papal blessing and authorization.

## LATE MEDIEVAL TIMES
During the Crusades, monastic rules of prayer and preaching were extended to include military and medical duties. The Knights Hospitaller of St John, which was founded in 1113, and the Knights Templar, established in 1119, both consisted of fighting men or soldier-nurses.

*Above* The monastery of Monte Cassino, originally established by St Benedict, had to be rebuilt after severe bombing by the Allies in WWII.

Other religious orders were established in the 13th century, which returned to the asceticism of the early Desert Fathers. They included the Franciscans, founded by St Francis of Assisi, the Dominicans of St Dominic, the Carmelites, and the Augustinian Hermits. These were all mendicant orders, relying on charity for survival. Although the monks were attached to a community, they functioned as individuals.

Nuns generally lived in their enclosed communities, isolated from the outside world. They followed the Rule of St Francis through St Clare, or that of the Dominicans or Benedictines.

## COME THE REFORMATION

During and after the Reformation, orders developed to strengthen the faith. Priests concentrated on teaching, nursing, leading retreats or missions. Most famous were the Jesuits, a missionary order founded by Ignatius of Loyola in 1534.

The Reformation reinforced eremitical orders. The Capuchins evolved from the Franciscans in 1525, the Trappists from the Cistercians in 1664, and the Maurists from the Benedictines in 1621. The Discalced Carmelites developed from the rule of St Clare in 1593.

*Below* A 15th-century drawing of monks wearing the distinctive habits of their orders. The Carmelites wore white, the Franciscans brown or grey, the Benedictines black, and the Dominicans black and white.

## KNIGHTS HOSPITALLER OF ST JOHN

For centuries, a nursing order ran a hospital in Jerusalem. Then, in the 1120s, Raymond du Puy turned the order into a military community known as the Knights Hospitaller of St John. Nursing was not abandoned, but during the Crusades, the monks became much-feared soldiers. Expelled from Jerusalem by the Turks in 1291, they went to Rhodes.

Later, in the 16th century, the order was forced to move to Malta, where it remained until 1798. In 1834, after demonstrating that they had left their military past behind them, the order was allowed to settle in Rome.

*Above* Order of St John of Jerusalem, a woodcut dating from the 14th century.

# ANTONY OF EGYPT

THIS SAINT IS OFTEN REGARDED AS THE FATHER OF MONASTICISM, AND WAS KNOWN FOR HIS HEALINGS, BUT IT IS HIS LIFE OF SOLITUDE, PRAYER AND GENTLENESS THAT HAS HAD THE MOST LASTING IMPACT.

**KEY FACTS**
*Desert Father, ascetic*
DATES: *AD 251–356*
BIRTH PLACE: *Coma, Egypt*
PATRON OF: *Skin diseases, domestic animals and pets, basket-makers*
FEAST DAY: *17 January*
EMBLEM: *Pig, bell*

The popular view of saintliness is embodied by St Antony of Egypt. He was not tempted by worldly goods or comfort, he did no harm to others, he was not too proud to undertake humble work, and he spent his life in prayer.

## SOLITUDE AND PRAYER

Born into a respectable Christian family in Coma in Upper Egypt, Antony was given a narrow education. When his parents died, he was 20 and heir to a considerable estate. But he recalled the words of Christ, "Go, sell what thou hast,

*Left St Antony in a stained glass from Suffolk, England (17th century). He was once a swineherd and St Antony's cross can be seen on his cloak.*

and give it to the poor, and thou shalt have treasure in Heaven." He gave away his land and wealth, keeping only enough for the care of his younger sister, and lived among local ascetics. Then for 20 years, from AD 286 to AD 306, he took to the desert, where he lived a life of complete solitude and extreme austerity, seeking the love of God in prayer and meditation.

When he was 54, Antony was asked to leave his hermitage and organize some nearby ascetics into a monastic order. Back on his mountain, the hermit cultivated a garden and wove baskets. A follower, Marcarius, guarded him from curious onlookers.

Toward the end of his life, Antony visited Alexandria to comfort persecuted Christians and refute Arianism. He was, by now, famous for his wisdom and miracles; crowds rushed to see him and many were converted.

Sufferers from ergotism (also known as "St Antony's Fire") visited his shrine at La Motte in France, where the Order of Hospitallers of Saint Antony was founded c.1100, to seek a cure.

*Left The central panel of* The Temptation of St Anthony *(Hieronymus Bosch, c.1505).*

# BASIL THE GREAT

VENERATED FOR HIS ROBUST DEFENCE OF THE FAITH, THIS DOCTOR
OF THE CHURCH WAS ALSO AN IMPORTANT FIGURE IN ESTABLISHING
MONASTIC RULES DEDICATED TO CHARITABLE WORK AND POVERTY.

**KEY FACTS**
*Doctor of the Eastern Church*
DATES: *c.AD 330–79*
BIRTH PLACE: *Cappadocia,
Turkey*
PATRON OF: *Russia, monks of
the Eastern Churches*
FEAST DAY: *2 January (with St
Gregory of Nazianzus)*
EMBLEM: *Bishop's vestments,
often pictured with other early
Doctors of the Church*

Basil's extensive writings reveal
a humorous, tender person,
yet he proved unyielding in his
fight for orthodoxy.

He was born in Cappadocia,
one of ten children in an extraordinary family: his grandmother,
both parents, and three siblings
were all destined for sainthood.

On returning from studies in
Constantinople and Athens, where
he had become good friends with
Gregory of Nazianzus, he
travelled widely, to Palestine,
Egypt, Syria and Mesopotamia,
studying the religious life, before
taking up life as a hermit in
Cappadocia. His brother joined
him there in a life of contemplation and preaching.

Basil established the first
monastery in Asia Minor, instigat-
ing a brotherhood of hard labour,
charitable work and communal
routine, a system that he believed
better served God and his faithful
than did solitary asceticism. His
rule, unchanged, is followed by
monks today in the Eastern
Orthodox Church, and forms the
basis of orders dedicated to him.

*Above An icon from Moscow shows
St Basil wearing the* omophor
*vestment of an Eastern Orthodox bishop
and holding a copy of the Gospels.*

## BATTLING ARIANISM

During Basil's lifetime, a schism
threatened the Church, caused by
the popular teachings of Arius,
which denied the divinity of Jesus.

The harsh activities of the
Arian Emperor Valens against
traditionalism brought Basil back
to Caesarea to protect his community from attack. Valens was
too afraid of Basil's reputation to
act against him, and withdrew
from Caesarea, but he continued

to promote Arianism elsewhere.
Basil preached daily to huge
crowds and produced numerous
texts on belief that remain in use
in the Eastern Orthodox Church.

During a period of drought, he
built hospitals and soup kitchens
where his monks served the poor.
But anxious that the faith might
be waning in the east, he increased
his preaching, emphasizing the
Church's beliefs. His lessons were
conveyed everywhere both by
texts and through word of mouth.

In AD 378, Valens died and was
succeeded by his nephew, Gratian,
who discouraged Arianism. As
Basil himself lay dying the follow-

ing year, he was confident that,
with the emperor on his side,
orthodoxy would prevail.

Christians, pagans and Jews all
mourned the "father and protector" of Caesarea, while the Church
honoured St Basil for keeping the
faith alive. He is one of the great
Doctors of the Church.

*Below An 18th-century altarpiece
in St Peter's Basilica in Rome shows
St Basil defiantly celebrating mass in
the presence of the Emperor Valens.*

# BARBARA

THE LEGEND OF ST BARBARA IS A ROMANTIC ONE ABOUT A BRAVE AND BEAUTIFUL GIRL WHO REFUSES ALL SUITORS FOR CHRIST. HER CULTUS WAS POPULAR IN FRANCE DURING THE MIDDLE AGES.

**KEY FACTS**
*Virgin martyr*
DATES: *Unknown*
BIRTH PLACE: *Unknown*
PATRON OF: *Gunners, artillery,
dying people, miners*
FEAST DAY: *Formerly
4 December, but removed from
Roman calendar in 1969*
EMBLEM: *Tower*

It is highly unlikely that this saint ever existed: although she allegedly lived in the 3rd century, nothing was written about her until the 7th. She was officially de-canonized in 1969.

According to the *Golden Legend*, Barbara was the daughter of a pagan, who locked her in a tower so that no man could see her. But her beauty was so renowned that men still came to court her. When Barbara became a Christian, her father was so furious that he tried to kill her, but she miraculously escaped.

*Above St Barbara (Flemish manuscript illumination, 1475).*

Eventually she was handed over to a judge, who condemned her to death and ordered her father to carry out the deed. This he did, but he was immediately struck by lightning and died.

This is the reason that Barbara is regarded as a patron of those in danger of sudden death, originally from lightning, later from cannon-balls, gunfire or mines.

# CYRIL OF JERUSALEM

THE LESSONS OF ST CYRIL FOR THOSE SEEKING BAPTISM ARE SO PROFOUND, AND HIS FIGHT FOR THE TRUE FAITH SO EARNEST, THAT HE IS HONOURED AS A DOCTOR OF THE CHURCH.

**KEY FACTS**
*Doctor of the Church*
DATES: *c.AD 315–86*
BIRTH PLACE: *Jerusalem*
FEAST DAY: *18 March*
EMBLEM: *Bishop's gown*

St Cyril was a clear thinker and an excellent teacher. But it was his misfortune to live during a time of schism among the Eastern Christian communities, when the ideas of the unorthodox Arians were gaining ground against the traditionalist concept of the Holy Trinity – the threefold godhead of Father, Son and Holy Spirit.

Cyril was born and educated in Jerusalem. After becoming a priest, his first assignment, from St Maximus, was to train converts preparing for baptism. His lessons of faith were – and indeed still are – much admired, and they brought him prestige and high office.

When he first became Bishop of Jerusalem in AD 349, strange lights were said to fill the sky over the city. But during the 35 years Cyril served as a bishop, he spent

*Left The Church of the Holy Sepulchre in Jerusalem where St Cyril was bishop during the 4th century AD. This scene has scarcely changed since.*

much of his life in hot dispute with the dominant Arians. He was first exiled in AD 357, and although he was recalled two years later, he was banished twice more and spent a total of 16 years in exile.

However, in AD 381, Cyril took part in the First Council of Constantinople, which gave official endorsement to the concept of the Trinity. St Cyril was made a Doctor of the Church in 1882.

# GREGORY OF NAZIANZUS

THE INSPIRED PREACHING AND WRITING OF ST GREGORY HELPED
TO UNIFY THE EASTERN ORTHODX CHURCHES IN TIMES OF STRIFE.
AS A RESULT HE WAS MADE A DOCTOR OF THE CHURCH.

**KEY FACTS**
*Doctor of the Eastern
Orthodox Church*
DATES: *AD 329–89*
BIRTH PLACE: *Arianzus, south-
west Cappadocia, Turkey*
FEAST DAY: *2 January*
EMBLEM: *Bishop's gown*

This shy, diffident poet-priest
was the son of wealthy
parents, Gregory, Bishop of
Nazianzus and his wife Nonna,
who were able to give him the
best education. He attended the
renowned theological school at
Caesarea and continued his studies first at Alexandria and then at
the University of Athens, where
he rekindled his youthful friendship with St Basil the Great.

### RELUCTANT PRIEST
Together, the two friends formed a
common resolve to live a contemplative life, and when Basil set up a
retreat in Pontus (now Turkey),
Gregory joined him. Together they
wrote the Monastic Rules.

After two years of the contemplative life, Gregory returned to
Nazianzus. His father, now elderly, was not happy with his son's
decision to live as a monk, and
resolved to have him home. In
AD 361, the bishop forced his son
to be ordained as a priest.

Neither did his friend leave him
in peace. Basil, who had by then
become Archbishop of Caesarea,
had Gregory consecrated as
Bishop of Sasima, most probably
to maintain his own influence in
what was a disputed area. The
place, however, was a hostile border settlement and Gregory spent
little time there. The whole affair
brought about a quarrel between
the pair, from which their friendship never fully recovered.

After the death of his parents,
Gregory, who had always desired
the contemplative life, escaped
briefly to a monastery in Seleucia.

*Above These images depict the visions
of the Old Testament prophet
Ezekiel, and are part of* The
Homilies of St Gregory, *an
illuminated manuscript held in
Paris (9th century).*

### AGAINST HERESY
Five years later, in 379, Gregory
was recalled to serve the Christian
community of Constantinople in
their battle for orthodoxy. Church
officials were determined to use
Gregory's oratorical talents in their
dispute with Arianism.

The heresy had been so
successful in Constantinople that
there was no longer an Orthodox
Church active there, and Gregory
was obliged to use his house to
hold meetings. Here, he preached
five discourses on the Holy
Trinity. These teachings helped
ensure that orthodoxy was confirmed at the First Council of

Constantinople in AD 381. For a
brief, unhappy period he was
Bishop of Constantinople, but differences of opinion with the
Eastern bishops led him to resign.

### PEACE AT LAST
Gregory spent his last years in
priestly duties in Nazianzus and in
retreat. Many of his letters survive,
as does an autobiography and some
religious poetry.

After his death aged 60, St
Gregory's relics were translated to
Constantinople and later to
Rome. He is one of the great
Eastern Doctors of the Church
alongside Sts John Chrysostom
and Basil the Great.

*Above St Gregory of Nazianzus,
overseen by an angel while working
at his desk, in a mosaic in the second
dome of the Basilica San Marco,
Venice (c.1350).*

# AMBROSE

THIS POPULAR BISHOP OF MILAN BECAME A KEY COMBATANT IN THE STRUGGLE AGAINST THE ARIAN HERESY. HE ALSO WROTE IMPORTANT TEXTS ON CHRISTIAN ETHICS AND INTERPRETATION OF THE BIBLE.

A vigorous intellect, energy and charm helped Ambrose in the murky political world he encountered as Bishop of Milan.

He was the son of a noble Roman family, and legend tells that, when he was child, a swarm of bees settled on him, which was deemed to symbolize his future eloquence (hence his patronage).

He studied law, Greek, rhetoric and poetry before becoming consular prefect of Liguria and Aemilia, with headquarters in Milan. He was a gifted administrator and diplomatic leader – and the citizens trusted him.

### KEY FACTS
*One of the four great Latin Doctors of the Western Church*
DATES: *AD 339–97*
BIRTH PLACE: *Trier, Germany*
PATRON OF: *Bees, beekeepers and those who work with wax*
FEAST DAY: *7 December (West)*
EMBLEM: *Whip, to symbolize his fight against heresy*

*Left* Enthroned Ambrose *(Alvise Vivarini, 1503).*

Then Ambrose took to studying Christianity. In AD 374, when the bishop of Milan died, he attended the council meeting to elect a successor. Ambrose was not a follower of Arianism, a sect that was strong in the Milan area, and gave a speech favouring orthodox beliefs. To his great surprise – he was not even baptized – he was elected bishop and was in office within a week.

TACKLING THE HERETICS
The new bishop took charge of a weak Church. The empire, too, was stricken by battles for supremacy between East and West.

The greatest demonstration of his moral strength was shown after the Massacre of Thessalonica in AD 390. The governor there had been assassinated and, in retribution, Theodosius, Emperor of the eastern Roman Empire, ordered thousands of citizens to be killed. Ambrose was horrified. He faced Theodosius and reminded him that God was more important than the state, and that even the emperor must submit to holy law. Contrite, Theodosius made a public penance for his savage act.

*Left* The Emperor Theodosius and Saint Ambrose *(Peter Paul Rubens, 17th century).*

# AGATHA

ALTHOUGH LITTLE IS ACTUALLY KNOWN ABOUT THIS SAINT, HER ALLEGED BRAVERY IN THE FACE OF HORRIFIC TORTURE AND DEATH ENSURED HER A WIDESPREAD FOLLOWING IN MEDIEVAL TIMES.

Although there is some evidence that a virgin martyr named Agatha died in Catania in the first years of the 4th century, little is known about this saint. However, her memory persists and she is patron of Catania.

Her legend recounts that her parents were Christians from the nobility who openly refused to offer sacrifices to pagan gods. The local consul Quintinian, who tried unsuccessfully to seduce Agatha, raised a campaign against all Christians, and the young girl was arrested. As she approached the consul, she prayed, "Jesus Christ, Lord of all, Thou seest my heart… I am thy sheep: make me worthy to overcome the devil."

Her persecutors were aware that virginity was important to their Christian victims, so Agatha was sent to a brothel. It is said that her faith and piety shone from her, and no man dared approach her.

## MUTILATION AND DEATH

Instead, she was taken away to be tortured. Agatha was not afraid of martyrdom because it meant she would soon join Christ. Quintinian devised a mutilation suited to horrify a beautiful young girl. His henchman pierced and severed Agatha's breasts.

St Peter is said to have visited Agatha and restored her breasts. However, she was then forced to walk across hot coals and shards of glass. But as she took her first step, Mount Etna erupted and an earthquake shook the earth. The watching crowd screamed for her release, convinced her God was

*Above* This marble altarpiece portrays the coronation of St Agatha in heaven (15th century).

punishing them all. Quintinian stopped the torture, but quietly starved her to death instead.

St Agatha is often the subject of paintings illustrating her mutilation. The resemblance in shape of bells to breasts is the reason for her patronage of bell founders.

*Below* Saint Agatha (*Francesco Guarino, 17th century*).

# MARTIN OF TOURS

THE SON OF A MILITARY MAN, MARTIN JOINED THE ARMY BUT CHOSE INSTEAD TO BE A "SOLDIER OF CHRIST". HE FOLLOWED HIS FAITH WITH ENERGY AND CONVICTION.

## KEY FACTS
*Monk bishop*
DATES: *c.AD 316–97*
BIRTH PLACE: *Pannonia*
*(present-day western Hungary)*
PATRON OF: *Soldiers, infantry*
*and cavalry, horses and their riders,*
*geese, wine-makers*
FEAST DAY: *11 November (West)*
EMBLEM: *Armour, sword, cloak*

This saint is traditionally commemorated as having led a life of bravery as a "soldier of God". In fact, his first career was in the army – following his pagan father's footsteps – but he came to believe that war was incompatible with his commitment to Christ. When accused of cowardice, he offered to stand unarmed between the opposing sides, but was instead discharged from the army.

Martin became known for his charity as well as moral courage. One famous legend recounts that as a soldier riding to Amiens in bitterly cold weather, he saw a poor man dressed in rags. Filled with compassion for the man's plight, he cut his heavy army cloak in two and wrapped the man in one half. That night, as he slept, Jesus appeared to him wearing that half of the cloak.

*Below* Saint Martin Sharing His Cloak with a Poor Man *(Domenico Ghirlandaio and workshop, 15th century).*

*Above* The Mass of St Martin of Tours *(Eustache Le Sueur, 1654).*

## MONK AND BISHOP
For ten years, Martin lived at Ligugé, a plot of land given to him by Hilary, the Bishop of Poitiers. Originally living a solitary life, Martin was soon joined by others, and founded a monastery there – the first one in Gaul. Then, in AD 372, at the acclamation of clergy and people, he was elected as Bishop of Tours.

After his ordination, he continued to live as a monk, moving to a solitary place, Marmoutier, where he later founded one of several other monasteries.

Martin travelled around his parish on foot and by donkey, preaching over a wide area with a desire to see the conversion of rural areas. He destroyed heathen temples and sacred trees and performed many miracles, notably healing lepers. It is said that he even raised a dead man to life.

He became involved in many doctrinal disputes. In AD 384, when some bishops appealed to the Roman authorities to execute local heretics, Martin begged (in vain) for their lives, claiming banishment was sufficient. Such a forgiving nature ensured his popularity into old age. A mausoleum marks his grave at Tours.

## HILARY OF POITIERS
In AD 356, the Arian Roman Emperor Constantius II banished this bishop, whom he had branded a "mischief-maker". Throughout his life, Hilary was fierce in his fight against the Arian heresy.

Though born (*c.*AD 315) and brought up in a pagan family, Hilary converted to Christianity in AD 350, following a long process of study. He became a bishop around three years later, and went on to produce many influential writings, particularly discourses on the Holy Trinity. He was praised by Jerome and Augustine of Hippo, and was influential in the spiritual development of Martin of Tours.

# PELAGIA THE PENITENT

THIS BEAUTIFUL AND TALENTED ACTRESS ABANDONED HER FORMER
LIFE AND WEALTH TO BECOME A CHRISTIAN. SHE LIVED THE REST OF
HER LIFE AS A RECLUSIVE HERMIT DISGUISED AS A MAN.

## KEY FACTS
*Penitent*
DATES: *5th century*
BIRTH PLACE: *Antioch*
PATRON OF: *Actresses*
FEAST DAY: *8 October*
EMBLEM: *Hermit*

In the 5th century, St John Chrysostom wrote about a glamorous harlot of Antioch who repented and became a nun. The story of Pelagia the Penitent seems to follow this tale but it comes with embellishments.

Pelagia was a beautiful and immensely wealthy woman as well as an actress, which was considered a disgraceful profession.

She liked to sway through the promenades of Antioch, dressed in marvellous clothes to flaunt her attributes. A retinue of admirers followed in her wake. One day as she passed a solemn group of bishops attending a service given by bishop Nonnus of Edessa, a leading Christian, the men turned their backs on her. But Nonnus himself stopped preaching and admired the lovely woman. He was troubled that she was clearly so successful at her chosen yet despised profession, while he felt he had failed as bishop to his Christian flock.

## PELAGIA'S CONVERSION
Nonnus prayed all through the night, then the next morning went to attend to his duties at the cathedral. Pelagia, who had heard his preaching, followed him and begged to be baptized. She was given instruction by a deaconess and accepted into the Christian community. After her baptism, she gave away all her possessions and disappeared from Antioch. She

crept off and, dressed as a man, she took up the life of a hermit on the Mount of Olives in Jerusalem.

Pelagia was forgotten by all her old companions although some Christians visited her. A deacon, known as James, was said to have sought an interview with the "beardless recluse", and afterwards wrote down her story. Only at her death did people realize that this hermit was not only a woman, but one with an infamous reputation in the city of Antioch.

The legend has been seen as a fine example of penitence. Others say it was written by a male hermit who longed for a female counterpart in his harsh life.

Pelagia's story has remained a popular one, and has been told in a number of versions over the centuries – from the fourth all the way to the thirteenth. Her name appears in many ports and villages around the Mediterranean Sea.

*Right Sts Pelagia and Euphemia in a mosaic from San Apollinare Nuovo, Ravenna, Italy (AD 561).*

# NICHOLAS OF MYRA

LEGENDS ABOUT THE PATRON OF RUSSIA CREDIT ST NICHOLAS WITH BEING A MIRACLE WORKER BLESSED WITH THE VIRTUES OF KINDNESS AND GENEROSITY – ESPECIALLY TOWARD CHILDREN.

**KEY FACTS**
*Identified with Santa Claus*
DATES: *4th century* AD
BIRTH PLACE: *Possibly Patara,
Lycia (modern-day Turkey)*
PATRON OF: *Children, brides,
unmarried girls, Russia, travellers,
sailors, maritime navigators*
FEAST DAY: *6 December*
EMBLEM: *Three balls or bags of
gold, purse, anchor, ship*

This saint is famous for his role as Father Christmas. The fact that he is patron of children may explain this status. Alternatively, the reason might lie in the legend that St Nicholas once found three dead children hidden in a brine tub and brought them miraculously back to life. There is also the story of his rescue of three young girls doomed to prostitution through poverty. As a gift, St Nicholas threw three bags of gold into their window, thus providing the girls with marriage dowries.

There is evidence that a bishop of Myra, named Nicholas, did live in the 4th century AD, but little else is known about him. Some claimed St Nicholas attended the Church's first General Council in Nicaea in AD 325. Or he may have been martyred before Constantine legalized Christianity in AD 313.

***Above*** *This fresco shows St Nicholas saving three condemned knights from death (Giotto School, c.1300–5).*

***Below*** *Saint Nicholas Protecting the Sailors (Vitale da Bologna, 14th century). He is patron saint of sailors.*

## A PEOPLE'S SAINT

Despite his lost life story, St Nicholas has been, since early Christian history, a popular saint. His image can be found all over Russia and the Christian Middle East. Churches everywhere are dedicated in his name.

His many legends depict a strong, chivalrous man. He rescued three sailors from drowning, and saved three condemned men from execution. Sailors faced with a storm called upon his name, and it is said St Nicholas appeared at the shore and calmed the waves.

His physical strength was revealed as a newborn, when he sprang to his feet and stood firm. And as a small boy, he showed deep devotion, listening attentively to the sermons of the local bishop, his uncle.

Italians stole his relics in 1095 and gave them to the church in Bari, where they remain to this day. Europeans carried his name to the New World. Linguists have observed that Dutch settlers in the USA called him "Sinte Klaas". Following European tradition, they would have given presents on his feast day, thus starting the Santa Claus tradition.

# BLAISE

KNOWN FOR HIS KINDNESS AND FOR HIS MEDICAL SKILLS, BLAISE WAS SOUGHT BY BELIEVERS TO INTERCEDE NOT ONLY FOR THEIR OWN HEALING BUT ALSO FOR THEIR PETS AND FARM ANIMALS.

**KEY FACTS**
*Martyr saint*
DATES: *4th century AD*
BIRTH PLACE: *Sebaste, Armenia*
PATRON OF: *Doctors, farmers, wool trade, laryngologists, builders, veterinarians, a Holy Helper*
FEAST DAY: *3 February*
EMBLEM: *Wool-comb, two crossed candles*

Although no historical details of his life exist, the stories of Blaise's healings have made him popular and his feast day is still celebrated in some churches.

It is said that Blaise was born into a wealthy, Christian home in the 4th century AD. Blaise became Bishop of Sebaste in Armenia while he was still young, but he lived during the reign of Emperor Licinius, a time of severe persecution of Christians.

Warned by his brethren that his life was in danger, Blaise fled to the hills, where he remained isolated from his community, and where, allegedly, wild animals would turn to Blaise when they were ill or hurt and he would heal them.

## STORIES OF HEALINGS

Among many stories is one of a countrywoman who came to the saint's cave with her small son who was choking to death on a fishbone. Blaise touched the child's throat, the bone was dislodged, and the boy survived.

Eventually, Blaise was arrested. It is told that as he was marched off to jail, he passed a wolf loping off with a pig in its mouth, while nearby a poor woman wept at the loss of her animal. Blaise ordered the wolf to drop its prey and was instantly obeyed. The grateful woman later brought the prisoner food, and a candle to light his cell. Indeed, different traditions have varied tales of St Blaise, but all tell of farmers calling on him for help with their sickly animals. Water with the blessing of St Blaise is given to sick cattle.

## PATRONAGE

The saint is also associated with mending sore throats, and some churches celebrate the Blessing of the Throat on his feast day. The priest ties ribbons to two candles, then touches the candle ends to the throat of the sufferer, saying, "May the Lord deliver you from the evil of the throat, and from all other evil."

Perhaps Blaise's torturers knew of his bond with animals because, before beheading him, along with numerous other tortures, they combed his flesh with an iron wool-comb. In time the wool comb came to be his emblem, and he became patron of the wool trade. For a long time, his feast day was celebrated with a procession in Bradford, once the centre of the English wool business.

St Blaise's cult is not known before the 8th century, but he became one of the most popular

*Above Saint Blaise (Giovanni Battista Tiepolo, 1740). His bishop's vestments give no hint of his hardships as a hermit.*

saints of the Middle Ages, most probably due to his association with miraculous cures. He was called upon to help diseased people and animals, and his name lives on in the village of St Blazey in Cornwall, England.

St Blaise also enjoys an international cultus. He is the patron saint of Dubrovnik, and in Spain he is venerated under the name of San Blas; in Italy he is known as San Biagio. He is one of the Fourteen Holy Helpers.

*Below A statue of St Blaise in Dubrovnik, Croatia (15th century).*

# JEROME

THE GREATEST BIBLICAL SCHOLAR OF HIS TIME WAS VENERATED FOR
HIS AUTHORITATIVE TRANSLATION OF THE BIBLE FROM THE
ORIGINAL HEBREW AND GREEK VERSIONS INTO LATIN.

**KEY FACTS**
One of the four great Latin
Doctors of the Western Church
DATES: c.AD 341–420
BIRTH PLACE: Strido, Dalmatia
(Balkans)
PATRON OF: Scholars, students,
archaeologists, librarians, translators
FEAST DAY: 30 September
EMBLEM: Bishop's hat, book,
stone and lion

Numerous paintings of Jerome have created an abiding image of a lean old man, bent over his books in a remote cave. At his feet a large friendly lion keeps benevolent guard. But the reality was quite different.

Jerome seems to have been a man at war with himself. He longed to concentrate on his studies but also sought academic debate. A quick temper and impatient manner made this saint unpleasantly aggressive and

*Left* St Jerome *(Theodoricus of Prague, 14th century). Often his symbol in art is a book.*

intolerant of his colleagues' ideas. Critics bemoaned his lack of Christian meekness and surfeit of sarcasm and unkindness.

### EARLY LIFE
Jerome received a classical education and went on to study further in Rome. During this time he nursed an ambition to experience the world and in order to fulfil this ambition, the young man travelled widely and actively sought out teachers and further intellectual stimulation.

At this early stage in his life Jerome was not devout, being too interested in the literature and philosophy of the Greeks. After a headstrong dispute in Rome with colleagues, he felt impelled to leave the city and travelled again, this time with two friends touring eastern Europe.

However, a chance occurrence changed his life. All three men fell dangerously ill with a severe fever. The subsequent death of both his companions had a profound impact on Jerome, who

*Left* Saint Jerome in a Landscape *(Giovanni Battista Cima da Conegliano, c.1500–1510).*

turned to the Christian faith. But his commitment to Christianity caused him great anguish.

He greatly enjoyed the company of women, and found too much pleasure in reading pagan Greek texts. Believing these joys would carry him away from God, he decided to abstain from them. To this end, Jerome went to live as a hermit in the desert where he could think and pray without distraction.

## GREAT SCHOLAR

Somewhat against his will, he was ordained and sent back to Rome in AD 382. Pope Damasus I saw that this man would never do as a parish priest but believed his scholarship could serve well.

Jerome produced important texts about traditional dogma and monasticism, and expounded the virtue of celibacy. He wrote in praise of the Virgin Mary, asserting the view that she remained a virgin throughout her life.

Posterity honours him for translating the Bible from Greek and Hebrew into Latin. His version is known as the Vulgate or Authorized Bible. Jerome was the first scholar to make the distinction between the "true" texts and the dubious, or

"SHOW ME, O LORD, YOUR MERCY AND DELIGHT MY HEART WITH IT. LET ME FIND YOU FOR WHOM I SO LONGINGLY SEEK... I AM THE SHEEP WHO WANDERED INTO THE WILDERNESS — SEEK AFTER ME AND BRING ME HOME TO YOUR FOLD. AMEN"

PRAYER OF ST JEROME

*Above* Annunciation to Mary with the Saints Jerome and John the Baptist *(Francesco Raibolini, c.1448–1517).*

"apocryphal", texts. His work has proved invaluable to theologians ever since.

As was his wont, however, Jerome became embroiled in theological dispute, this time with the heretical Arians, about whom he wrote a scathing attack. And in the process it is possible he made one too many enemies.

## SCANDAL AND FLIGHT

Jerome's promotion of a study group for girls and widows in Rome proved to be too risky. Soon rumour was rife that Jerome shared more than his religious teachings with the ladies. Despite protests of his innocence, he did not have the support of friends and was forced to flee.

Jerome travelled to Cyprus and Antioch where two Roman women, the widow Paula and her daughter, joined him. Together they went to Egypt, then returned to Bethlehem in the Holy Land.

Paula established three nunneries in Bethlehem, and she built a monastery for men which Jerome headed. Living in a cave nearby, he

continued to analyse scripture. Even from this remote spot, his sharp tongue aroused fury among fellow theologians. He went into hiding again, before returning to Bethlehem in AD 418.

By then Jerome was old and sickly. It is said he died with his head resting on the manger where baby Jesus was born. Jerome was buried under the Church of the Nativity in Bethlehem.

## JEROME AND THE LION

A lion had crept into the monastery in Bethlehem and its presence was frightening the monks. But the animal was limping, and Jerome, realizing its distress, and impatient no doubt with the squeals of his colleagues, strode over and removed a thorn from the lion's paw. For the rest of his days, the lion padded along next to him. Perhaps a dumb beast suited the saint's social temperament better than could a human. After Jerome's death, the lion protected the monastery's domestic animals.

*Above* Saint Jerome Reading *(Rembrandt Harmensz van Rijn, 1634).*

# JOHN CHRYSOSTOM

BOTH LOVED AND HATED FOR UPHOLDING CHRISTIAN PRINCIPLES, ST JOHN CHRYSOSTOM WAS A GREAT PREACHER, WHO ALSO PRODUCED PROFOUND INSIGHTS INTO SCRIPTURE.

**KEY FACTS**
*Doctor, Eastern Orthodox Church*
DATES: *AD 47–407*
BIRTH PLACE: *Antioch, Syria (site of modern-day Antakya, Turkey)*
PATRON OF: *Preaching, sacred oratory, Constantinople*
FEAST DAY: *13 September (West)*
EMBLEM: *Bishop's gown*

A man of high intellect, John Chrysostom knew how to touch the hearts of his listeners. A committed ascetic, he aroused fury among those churchmen who preferred ease and luxury to the simplicity of a devout life.

John grew up in the major Christian centre of Antioch (in Syria). After his father died, his mother brought him up as a Christian. He studied law, but opted instead for a religious life. After his baptism, *c.*AD 370, he retired to the desert.

For health reasons, he returned to Antioch where he was ordained a priest in AD 386. His eloquent preaching won him many followers in the city.

*Left Detail of* St John Chrysostom *from the Apse Mosaic, San Paolo fuori le Mura, Rome (Edward Burne-Jones, 19th century).*

## A RENOWNED TEACHER

St John Chrysostom is remembered for his preaching – his name means "golden mouth" in Greek. He emphasized literal interpretation and practical application of scripture and wrote treatises on the Psalms, St Matthew's Gospel and St Paul's Epistles. He is admired in the West, where he is one of the four Great Doctors of the Eastern Orthodox Church.

## REFORM AND OPPOSITION

In AD 398, he was appointed Archbishop of Constantinople, and began to instigate moral reform. He dedicated church money to hospitals, forbade the clergy from keeping servants, and put idle monks to work.

It was not long before he faced opposition. Empress Eudoxia took his attacks on the morals at court as a personal affront, and Theophilus, Bishop of Alexandria, demanded that John be exiled from Constantinople.

He was briefly recalled, but then banished again a year later, and eventually died of exhaustion after he was forced to travel long distances on foot in bad weather.

*Right* St John Chrysostom exiled by the Empress Eudoxia *(Benjamin Constant, 19th century).*

# AUGUSTINE OF HIPPO

THIS INFLUENTIAL THINKER FROM NORTH AFRICA WAS THE ARCHITECT OF EARLY CHURCH DOCTRINE. HIS WRITINGS, *CITY OF GOD* AND *CONFESSIONS*, BECAME FAMOUS CHRISTIAN TEXTS.

**KEY FACTS**
*One of the four great Latin Doctors of the Western Church, Bishop of Hippo*
DATES: *AD 354–430*
BIRTH PLACE: *Tagaste (now in Algeria)*
PATRON OF: *Printers and theologians, brewers, against eye diseases*
FEAST DAY: *28 August*
EMBLEM: *Bishop's staff and mitre, dove, pen, shell, child*

As a young man of Roman Carthage, Augustine had considerable intellect and charm. His vivacity brought him, by the age of 20, a concubine and small son, Adeodatus. But he matured into a disciplined theologian and bishop, kindly towards his flock.

His pagan father ensured Augustine was well educated. His mother, St Monica, was a Christian but her son rejected her beliefs. Driven by ambition, he moved with his family from North Africa to Rome, and then to Milan. He was a restless man, searching for a vocation. His widowed mother insisted he send the

"O GOD OUR FATHER, WHO DOST EXHORT US TO PRAY, AND WHO DOES GRANT WHAT WE ASK, HEAR ME, WHO AM TREMBLING IN THE DARKNESS, AND STRETCH FORTH THY HAND TO ME, HOLD FORTH THY LIGHT BEFORE ME, RECALL ME FROM MY WANDER-INGS, AND MAY I BE RESTORED TO MYSELF AND TO THEE. AMEN."

PRAYER OF ST AUGUSTINE

*Below St Augustine (the Master of Grossgmain, c.1498).*

*Above A view of St Augustine's Cathedral at Hippo Regius, a Roman town in Algeria.*

concubine, his companion of 15 years, back to Africa. Shortly after this separation, Augustine claimed to hear a heavenly child's voice bearing a divine message.

## CONVERSION

His subsequent conversion to Christianity, however, was marred by the emotional conflict between, on the one hand, his love of comfort and women, and on the other, the austerity demanded by his faith. These feelings are recorded in his autobiography, *Confessions*.

He and his son were baptized in AD 387 and, with a group of friends, retired to his estates in Africa. The group took vows of chastity, poverty and obedience, and undertook charitable work in the community. The rules that Augustine made for monastic life formed the basis of future orders.

In AD 396, Augustine became Bishop of Hippo and never left North Africa again. From this corner of the empire, he set down his beliefs about spiritual redemption, which had a lasting impact on Church teachings.

Augustine lived in a period when the Roman Empire was crumbling under the burden of invading barbarians. Civic order was breaking down. However, Christianity was spreading, albeit haphazardly, across Europe.

Augustine believed the Church to be superior to the state, because its secular duties were based on spiritual qualities. He introduced the doctrine of man's salvation through the grace of God, and his ideas laid the foundations of a Christian political culture.

# CATHERINE OF ALEXANDRIA

THIS COURAGEOUS AND INTELLIGENT WOMAN OUT-ARGUED LEARNED PHILOSOPHERS IN DEFENCE OF CHRISTIANITY. SHE WAS TORTURED ON TWO SPIKED WHEELS AND THEN BEHEADED.

**KEY FACTS**
*Virgin martyr*
DATES: *4th century AD*
BIRTH PLACE: *Unknown*
PATRON OF: *Philosophers, young female students, librarians, nannies and wheelwrights*
FEAST DAY: *25 November*
EMBLEM: *Jagged wheel and the sword that beheaded her*

The legend of St Catherine of Alexandria is a gorgeous and romantic tale of heroism and faith.

Catherine was the beautiful young daughter of King Costus of Cyprus. She was also clever and courageous. A Christian, she confronted Emperor Maxentius about his persecution of her community.

He was amused and intrigued, and challenged her to a debate with 50 philosophers. On learning that her arguments had converted these learned men, he ordered all 50 to be burnt on a pyre, and had Catherine beaten. Unfortunately for the emperor's wife, she and 200 soldiers were converted too, and also executed.

Isolated in prison, Catherine had doves come to feed her. Then she was "despoiled naked and beaten with scorpions". But no punishments affected her body or her convictions. Maxentius then tried to tempt her with wealth and status, and asked the beautiful Christian to become his wife.

### CATHERINE'S DEATH

When Catherine refused he devised a cruel death. She was to be turned between two wheels spiked with blades. But the blades broke and the splinters killed and injured the onlookers. An angel rescued Catherine. No torture could make the girl forsake her faith or her virginity. Even her beheading confounded the emperor. Instead of blood, milk flowed from her virginal veins.

Angels, or perhaps monks, are said to have lifted her body and carried it to Mount Sinai. There it remains, in a monastery built in AD 527 by Emperor Justinian.

Catherine had an early cultus in the East, possibly originating near Mount Sinai, and it seems the Crusaders brought her story to the West. Her story is featured in the *Golden Legend*.

Catherine was removed from the Church's Calendar of Saints in 1969, but people continued to venerate her as the bride of Christ (for refusing to marry) and patron of advocates and the dying. A limited recognition of her cultus and sainthood was allowed in 2001.

*Left* St Catherine poses, calm and fearless, against her torture wheel (detail from a painting by the studio of Lucas Cranach, 1510).

*Above* A medieval woman depicted as St Catherine (Dante Gabriel Rossetti, 1857).

# URSULA

THIS BEAUTIFUL DAUGHTER OF A CHRISTIAN KING OF ENGLAND IS
SAID TO HAVE TURNED DOWN AN OFFER OF MARRIAGE FROM ATTILA
THE HUN ON ACCOUNT OF HER FAITHFUL VOW OF VIRGINITY.

**KEY FACTS**
*Virgin martyr*
DATES: *4th or 5th century* AD
BIRTH PLACE: *Unknown*
PATRON OF: *Girls, students, the
Ursuline Order*
FEAST DAY: *21 October*
EMBLEM: *Crown and huddle of
women under her opened cloak*

It is uncertain in which century
St Ursula lived, or even that she
lived at all. A mound of bones in a
burial ground was uncovered in
Germany in the 8th century, and
in the 10th century an inscription
bearing the name Ursula, a
12-year-old girl, was found at the
same site. From this "evidence", a
medieval legend grew.

Ursula was a British princess
during the 4th or 5th century. As
a dedicated follower of Christ, she
vowed to remain a virgin. She is
said to have refused a marriage
arranged by the court. In other
versions she was betrothed to a
pagan and did not refuse him but,
instead, set out to convert him.

## PILGRIMAGE TO ROME

She requested that, before the
wedding, she make a pilgrimage.
Either she ran away, or was
allowed to board a ship with
11,000 young women, also
avowed to Christ and virginity.

This crowd reached Rome
where they venerated the saints
and their relics. Ursula apparently
had a meeting with the pope, one
Cyriacus (unknown in papal
records). Ursula and her hand-
maidens then turned back and
sailed the Rhine to Germany.

They stopped in Cologne but
invading Huns had taken the city.
These barbarians slaughtered the
11,000 Christian women, but not
Ursula. The princess was spared
because her beauty had been
noticed by Attila, warrior leader
of the Huns. He desired her, even
offering marriage. But her refusal,
on account of her vows angered

*Above* St Ursula Bidding Farewell
to her Parents *(the Master of the
Legend of St Ursula, before 1482).*

*Below* St Ursula and her companions
are martyred *(16th century).*

the Hun, whereupon he ordered
his archers to shoot her through
with arrows.

In Cologne, the romance of
Ursula and her maidens was supported by old rumours of an early
martyrdom of many young
women in the city. The city's
basilica was rebuilt to honour
them. The story led to a brisk cir-
culation of relics and forged
inscriptions. Then, in the 11th
century, Elizabeth of Schönau
claimed visions of Ursula, and
made revelations in her name.

The Roman Catholic Church
removed Ursula and her
Companions from the Calendar
of Saints in 1969.

# LEO THE GREAT

KNOWN TO HAVE BEEN AN ASTUTE DIPLOMAT, LEO I IS VENERATED PARTICULARLY FOR STRENGTHENING THE ROLE OF THE POPE, AND FOR HIS ARTICULATE WRITINGS ON THE INCARNATION OF JESUS.

**KEY FACTS**
*Doctor of the Church*
DATES: *d.AD 461*
BIRTH PLACE: *Rome*
FEAST DAY: *10 November (West)*
EMBLEM: *Papal clothing*

This pope embodied the belief that the Church brings a beneficial authority to affairs of state. He was diplomatic and his decisions were supported by a strong faith and conviction in the spiritual discipline of the Church.

Born in Rome, Leo took office as pope in AD 440 when the Church was in upheaval. Not helped by the destruction of the Roman Empire, he soon went to parley with Attila, leader of the invading Huns, who had reached the River Mincio, close to Rome. Leo persuaded Attila to withdraw beyond the Danube. When the Vandals invaded Rome in AD 455, Leo's diplomacy once again prevailed, preventing widespread massacre of the city's citizens. Leo's strong leadership

was important in Church affairs. The faith's foothold in Europe was shaky, and heresies were rife, especially Monophysitism (a sect declaring "one nature" of Christ).

This doctrine held that Jesus was completely absorbed by his divinity, thus had no humanity. In contrast, Leo maintained that God had made his Son a man in order to preach the truth and to suffer in a sacrificial offering to redeem the sins of mankind.

## CHAMPION OF RIGHT

Leo wrote his tome to rebut the Monophysites and presented it at the Council of Chalcedon in AD 451. His views were upheld, confirming the orthodox belief that Jesus is both man and God. Also at the Council, the balance of

power in the Eastern Church was maintained because Leo refused to grant Constantinople primacy over Antioch and Alexandria.

His energy and mission work ensured the growth of the faith in Spain, France and North Africa. Leo implemented papal authority in these countries as well as in Italy. He was convinced that for the Church to survive, believers needed to respect the spiritual guidance embodied in the papacy.

To support his conviction, Leo spoke of St Peter's role as leader. He reminded his followers that this succession had been passed in an unbroken line to every pope since St Peter. Leo's teachings, particularly those expressed in a sermon one Christmas, brought many Christians a deeper understanding of the Incarnation of the Word.

Of Leo's numerous and articulate writings, 96 sermons and 143 letters survive. It was the long-lasting influence of these texts on the Christian Church that inspired Pope Benedict XIV to pronounce St Leo as a Doctor of the Church in 1754.

*Left St Peter and St Paul can be seen floating above the scene here in* The Meeting of Attila the Hun and Pope Leo I *(Raphael, 1509–11).*

# SIMEON STYLITES

FOR 37 YEARS ST SIMEON LIVED ON TOP OF A PILLAR, FROM WHERE HE PREACHED SERMONS THAT DREW CROWDS FROM FAR AND WIDE.

This saint's story is as fantastic as any legend. Simeon was a shepherd's son who hated comfort and longed for solitude. His self-mortifications included tying plaited palm leaves round his body, causing a flesh infection that nearly killed him. He chained himself to a rock on a mountain, and spent the 40 days of Lent with neither food nor water. Priests usually had to rescue him.

His fame spread when he built a pillar, 3m/9ft high, and lived on it for four years. But feeling this altitude did not give him enough solitude, he moved to ever higher pillars until eventually he climbed atop a pillar 20m/60ft

*Right A Byzantine mosaic of St Simeon Stylites living on top of his pillar in the Basilica San Marco, Venice.*

high and 2m/6ft wide. There he stayed for 20 years until his death. Food and water were hauled up by rope. But still he had no solitude. Throngs of spectators came to gawp and ask questions. Unfazed, Simeon gave informal sermons about kindness, fairness, and not cheating on God.

*Above A monument in a sanctuary to Simeon Stylites, on the site in Syria where he lived as a pillar hermit.*

# GENEVIEVE

BARBARIAN INVASIONS OF HER HOMELAND INSPIRED GENEVIEVE TO PERFORM HEROIC ACTS OF DEFENCE IN ORDER TO PROTECT THE CITIZENS OF PARIS. IN TIME, THEY ADOPTED HER AS THEIR PATRON.

As a child, Genevieve confided to Bishop Germanus that she lived only for God. In Paris, her young life was spent in prayer and caring for the poor.

When the city was threatened by a Hun invasion, Genevieve begged the frightened citizens not to flee but to pray. To everyone's relief, the Huns turned away at Orléans and Paris was saved.

Later, Genevieve ran sorties up the River Seine to fetch food for Parisians when under siege by the Franks. She also persuaded

*Above St Genevieve praying to save Paris (French School, 17th century).*

barbarian kings to show leniency to French prisoners-of-war. In 1129, her relics were paraded through Paris during a plague of the deadly disease, ergotism. The sick were said to be miraculously cured. The event is commemorated annually in Paris, but without her relics, which were burnt in the French Revolution.

# CELTIC SAINTS

THE CELTIC CHURCH WAS THE PRODUCT OF UNCONVENTIONAL IRISH MONKS WHO, INDEPENDENTLY OF THE ROMAN CHURCH, CREATED A GOLDEN AGE OF SPIRITUALITY, ART AND LEARNING.

Christianity arrived as early as the 2nd century AD in Wales, England and Ireland, which became the Celtic branch of the Church, albeit in scattered communities. Then in the 5th century AD, the Irish missions of two saints, Patrick and Brendan the Navigator, took the faith across the North Sea to Scotland.

These Irishmen are also thought to have introduced the austere monasticism of the Desert Fathers to the British mainland. Ascetic ideals, conceived in Egypt and Syria, might have made their way to Ireland via the distribution of religious texts, or through trade and pilgrimage in Europe.

Two other saints, Finnian of Clonard (d.AD 549) and Columba of Iona (d.AD 597), played key roles in establishing monastic life in Ireland and on the British mainland respectively. By the middle of the 6th century there were

*Above St Cuthbert turns water into wine, from Bede's Life of St Cuthbert (English School, 12th century).*

*Below A Celtic cross outside the Iona Monastery, Scotland.*

"WHAT WRETCHES WE ARE, GIVEN UP TO SLEEP AND SLOTH SO THAT WE NEVER SEE THE GLORY OF THOSE WHO WATCH WITH CHRIST UNCEASINGLY! AFTER SO SHORT A VIGIL WHAT MARVELS I HAVE SEEN. THE GATE OF HEAVEN OPENED AND A BAND OF ANGELS LET IN..."

FROM BEDE'S
*LIFE OF ST CUTHBERT*

monasteries at Glastonbury and Tintagel in Cornwall. St Columba founded a community at Iona, Scotland, in AD 565. And St Aidan established the abbey of Lindisfarne, on the coast of Northumbria, in the 7th century.

## BEACONS IN THE DARK

These times were the Dark Ages. The old Roman Empire was in disarray. Rome herself was under constant attack from the Huns, and she neglected the distant Celtic churches.

The British Isles were wild, backward and uncivilized, except in the monasteries, where Latin and learning were kept alive. Irish monks were to become famous for the quality of their scholarship and all Celtic monasteries became beacons of study and literature.

When St Augustine of Canterbury's mission arrived in AD 597, the Celtic Church, though not heretical, was regarded with some suspicion. It had a peculiar administrative structure, with no dioceses, and bishops performing mainly ritual duties. Monasteries were built on land owned by the abbot, not the

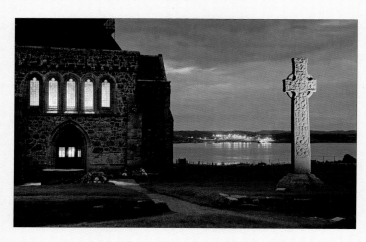

Church, and monks were not bound by rules of a founder. They lived in monasteries, which allowed, within the usual vows of austerity and obedience, independence and individual expression.

Perhaps this freedom from a more rigorous communal routine accounts for the extraordinary flowering of art and craft among the Celtic monks. Beautiful ornamental ironwork and stone work developed to a high degree of sophistication.

Some monks wrote poetry and biographies of religious figures. Others transcribed scriptural texts into lovingly made manuscripts, adorned with intricate decoration and illustration. The writing of history and biography formed an important part of the monks' literary output. The best-known examples of this genre come from a writer who was the epitome of a Celtic monk, the Venerable Bede. Bede died in AD 735 and spent his entire life within cloisters, devoting himself to scholarship and prayer. Bede is most famous for his

*Above The Venerable Bede, St Wilfrid and St Cuthbert in St Augustine's Chapel, Ramsgate, England.*

*Ecclesiastical History of the English People.* Examples of biography include Bede's *Life of Cuthbert* and Eddius Stephanus' *Life of Wilfrid*.

Christianity gradually came to replace the old pagan practices. Saxon kings of the 7th and 8th centuries AD led mass conversions,

strengthening the Church in England, especially Northumbria in the north-east.

## PRESSURE FROM ROME

As the mission of St Augustine gained ground, the Celtic Church came under pressure to conform to Roman authority. The Irish tradition, with its archaic rituals and odd calculations of the Church calendar, particularly Easter, was finally rejected at the Synod of Whitby in AD 664.

The influential monk St Wilfrid (*c.*AD 633–709) approved this turn toward Rome. And by early in the 8th century, even Iona and Lindisfarne, centres of Celtic culture in the north, had rejected the old Irish practices.

From the 9th to 11th centuries, invading Vikings destroyed many monasteries, dispersing the monks. Thus the "Golden Age" of the Celtic church was ended, and little of its identity remained.

*Left Illumination depicting three monks sitting at desks, diligently copying manuscripts (13th century).*

## CELTIC ARTISTRY

The monks of Northumbria and Ireland produced illuminated manuscripts, the quality of which has rarely been surpassed. Until the 14th century, the material used for manuscripts in Europe and the Celtic fringe was vellum or parchment. Some of the finest early medieval artwork is found in these books. Celtic monks exhibited extraordinary skill in the art of interlacing patterns of animal and geometric designs. The text, written in a script known as *literae saxonicae*, consisted of letters inked in decorative shape and subtle hue. Little illustrations appear in the margins around the text, providing a detailed record of contemporary rural and courtly life. The finest examples are the Lindisfarne Gospels, produced in honour of St Cuthbert, and the Irish *Book of Kells*.

*Right Ornamental page from* The Book of Kells *(8th century).*

# PATRICK

THE FEAST DAY OF ST PATRICK IS CELEBRATED WITH MUCH FANFARE, NOT ONLY IN HIS NATIVE IRELAND, BUT ALSO IN THE USA AND AUSTRALIA WHERE COLONISTS AND SETTLERS SPREAD HIS CULT.

**KEY FACTS**
*Missionary and bishop*
DATES: *5th century AD*
BIRTH PLACE: *Between the Rivers Clyde and Severn*
PATRON OF: *Ireland*
FEAST DAY: *17 March*
EMBLEM: *Snake, bishop's vestments, shamrock, harp*

It is said that St Patrick alone converted Ireland, and banished all snakes from the island. His own life story is also extraordinary.

Patrick grew up somewhere between the Rivers Clyde and Severn. Irish pirates kidnapped and enslaved him. He escaped after six years of servitude.

After a long period of aimless wandering he found his way home. Patrick studied the Latin Bible in preparation for joining the priesthood, but was criticized for his lack of scholarly education. He was ordained and, inspired by a dream, returned to Ireland as a missionary. He was appointed Bishop of Ireland in about AD 435.

Patrick divided the country into dioceses, and encouraged the setting up of monastic orders. He devoted himself to the delicate task of spreading the Christian faith across a land in which sun worship prevailed at the time. Every year the pilgrims of Croagh Patrick commemorate his retreat for 40 days on Cruachan Aigli.

*Right* St Patrick and a king (vellum, Irish School, 13th century).

---

# BRIGID OF IRELAND

LONG VENERATED IN IRELAND, ST BRIGID WAS SO LOVED BY THE NUNS AT HER MONASTERY THAT THEY KEPT A FIRE BURNING AT HER SHRINE IN KILDARE FOR CENTURIES AFTER HER DEATH.

**KEY FACTS**
*Founder*
DATES: *d.c.AD 525*
BIRTH PLACE: *Near Kildare, Ireland*
PATRON OF: *Milkmen, poets, cows and yard animals, blacksmiths, healers*
FEAST DAY: *1 February*
EMBLEM: *Cow lying beside her, cross made of rushes, candle*

Irish Catholics have a special affection for Brigid, placing her second only to St Patrick. Although the Church has de-canonized her, Brigid's cultus continues. Her legends reflect a generous, kindly personality, but historical facts are hard to find.

She was born, it is believed, near Kildare, and St Patrick baptized her. A very young Brigid took vows as a nun. In the convent she was a milkmaid, hence the legends of Brigid giving butter to the poor, or of cows giving her milk three times a day to cope with the thirst of visiting bishops. Brigid founded the

monastery of Kildare and helped spread Christianity through Ireland and beyond her shores. Churches dedicated in her name span Europe, showing her wide veneration. A brass reliquary of her shoe, set with jewels, is kept at a museum in Dublin.

*Left* Stained-glass windows depicting St Patrick and St Brigid (Paul Vincent Woodroffe, 1919).

# BRENDAN THE NAVIGATOR

A LEGEND CLAIMS THAT ST BRENDAN CROSSED THE ATLANTIC OCEAN IN A CORACLE. CERTAINLY, HE WAS VENERATED BY CELTIC PEOPLES FOR HIS MISSIONARY OUTREACH TO UNKNOWN LANDS.

**KEY FACTS**
*Founder*
DATES: *c.AD 486–575*
BIRTH PLACE: *Possibly Tralee, Ireland*
FEAST DAY: *16 May*
EMBLEM: *Sitting in a small boat*

Best known as the hero of an adventure legend of the 10th century, St Brendan became widely known as "the Navigator". Translated from the Anglo-Norman into several European languages, the story of his life was one of the first books to be published after Caxton's invention of the printing press in 1476.

## EARLY LIFE

Brendan was fostered by Ita, a much-loved Irish nun and saint who founded a small convent where she lived in solitude. Her nuns were encouraged to care for the sick and Ita herself educated needy boys, instilling into them her own faith.

As a youth, Brendan studied with St Erc, the bishop of Kerry. Brendan became a monk and later was appointed as abbot of Clonfert monastery. Some reports also claim he became abbot of Llancarvan in Wales.

He founded four monasteries in Ireland, one in Scotland, and evangelized in Wales and Brittany. In imitation of the apostles, Brendan was an indefatigable missionary. His life of extensive travel, criss-crossing the Irish Sea and the English Channel to France, became the source of legends about St Brendan.

## TO PARADISE

In the legend of St Brendan, he and his band of monks take to the sea in search of the Island of Promise. They sail in a traditional vessel, a coracle, made of leather stretched over a wicker frame. During the journey, unwittingly, they make camp on the back of a whale and light a fire there.

One Christmas Eve, they come upon Judas Iscariot. Every year on this night, Christ's betrayer is allowed to sit on a rock in the middle of the ocean to cool off before returning to fiery hell.

Within these stories of adventure there are hints that Brendan reached the shores of distant America. Researchers say that a close study of the text allows for an interpretation that confirms that he conducted an expedition across the Atlantic Ocean. Brendan's popularity is shown by the survival of 116 Medieval Latin manuscripts of his story.

*Below* Painting on vellum depicting St Brendan and his companions meeting a siren on their travels from the Navigatio Sancti Brendani Abbatis *(German School, c.1476).*

# BENEDICT

St Benedict created a monastic life of simplicity, work and prayer for the religious. His rules rejected the grim hardship imposed by founders of more austere orders.

**KEY FACTS**
*Founder*
DATES: c.*AD 480–550*
BIRTH PLACE: *Norcia, Italy*
PATRON OF: *Europe*
FEAST DAY: *11 July*
EMBLEM: *Black gown of his order, Rule book, broken cup containing poison*

The best way to appreciate the character of St Benedict is by studying his Rule. These guides to daily living reveal a man who understood the perils of power. He knew that extreme forms of discipline were unkind and could even drive men and women mad.

The system Benedict set up was inspired by his own experiences as a young man. Born into a good family in Umbria in the 5th century AD, he was sent as a student to Rome. However, he disliked the riotous living of the city and wandered off through the

*Left* Saint Benedict with His Monks at the Refectory *(Il Sodoma, c. 1505).*

forested valley between Lazio and Abruzzo. Finding the ruins of Nero's palace beside a lake at Subiaco, he settled in a cave there and spent most of his time in prayer and meditation.

Only one person knew of his whereabouts, a monk named Romanus, who secretly delivered him food. Gradually, knowledge of the hermit became common and his fame spread.

## MONASTIC BEGINNINGS

Benedict was persuaded to join a nearby monastery, where he was disturbed by the lax, even dissolute, ways of the monks, and set about reforming them. The monks enjoyed their easy life, and determined to poison the abbot.

Legend tells that when the deadly draught was served to Benedict he made the sign of the cross over the cup. It immediately shattered, and a raven carried the shards away.

He returned to the life of a hermit, but he was not left alone, and soon disciples gathered about him. Benedict founded 12 small monasteries, in each placing

*Left* St Benedict, *shown wearing the black garb of his monastic order (Pietro Perugino, c.1495–98).*

12 monks, over whom he served as abbot. The houses all gained a reputation for orderly, learned living, without austerity.

## RULE OF THE ORDER

Benedict perceived that prayer, routine and purposeful activity were the paths to serenity and to God. Authority was to be controlled. If a monk were to commit a major transgression, the abbot must, before fixing on a punishment, seek the advice of everyone in the monastery, even the youngest.

Though the abbot's decision was final, he must be minded that his decisions would be judged by God. Benedict recommended a simple but ample diet, though no flesh should be served, and the first meal should be around noon.

Benedict allowed for sensible hours of sleep. Property was communal, and the monks had to work, either producing food, maintaining the monastery, or spending time reading and writing the scriptures. But more important than any other duty was regular communal prayer. This he called "divine work".

## MONTE CASSINO

Soon Benedict's order became established and noble families sent their sons to his monasteries. These boys were destined to be monks and their training began

## SCHOLASTICA

Scholastica, the sister of St Benedict, followed her brother to Monte Cassino. She founded a nunnery about five miles from her brother's monastery. They met once a year, and on one visit Scholastica begged him to stay, for she longed to converse with him. But he refused, so she prayed for rain. It is said that a thunderstorm started and so he stayed the night. Alas, she died three days later, and Benedict then wrote about his conversation with Scholastica during which they discussed their faith.

*Above* John the Evangelist, Scholastica and Benedict *(the Master of Liesborn, c.1470-80).*

early. It is said that Benedict saved two of these youths from drowning by walking across water to rescue them.

They became his favourite disciples, Maurus and Placid, and were also venerated as saints. When a powerful, jealous priest

complained about the abbot, Benedict left Subiaco, taking with him a few disciples, including Maurus and Placid. He climbed a mountain above the village of Cassino. On a plateau he built Monte Cassino, the monastery that would become the centre of religious life in western Europe and which still operates today.

It was the kindly, humane interpretation of the monastic life that made Benedict so popular. He found a way of allowing the religious to live with an austerity suited to their calling, without risking their health or wellbeing.

*Left Benedictine monks walking through the monastery of Monte Cassino, Italy.*

# DAVID OF WALES

AN AUSTERE PRIEST RENOWNED FOR THE HARSHNESS OF THE MONASTIC REGIME HE ESTABLISHED IN WALES, HE NEVERTHELESS BECAME ONE OF THE BEST-LOVED SAINTS IN HIS COUNTRY.

**KEY FACTS**
*Founder*
DATES: *c.AD* 540–601
BIRTH PLACE: *Possibly Ceredigion, Wales*
PATRON OF: *Wales, poets*
FEAST DAY: *1 March*
EMBLEM: *Dove, later associated with a leek or daffodil*

St David is known as Dewi Sant in Wales, and his name is also sometimes translated as Dafydd. He is also given the title Dewi Dyfyrwr, or David Aquaticus, meaning "David, the Water Drinker". This is attributed to the teetotal regime of his monks who drank neither wine nor beer.

Tradition says David had a grand lineage. His father was thought to be of a princely family named Sant, and his mother, St Non, was also well connected. Possibly born in AD 540, David chose the life of a religious and

went to study under the Welsh St Paulinus on a remote, unidentified island. He is said to have found the old hermit blind from weeping for the sins of the world, and restored his sight.

There is another report that David made a pilgrimage to the Holy Land where he was consecrated as an archbishop by the patriarch of Jerusalem.

## AUSTERE ORDERS

When David attended the Synod of Victory at Caerleon he was uncompromising in his stand against the Pelagian movement. This heresy claimed it was possible to find salvation without the help of divine grace. A decisive victory for the established Church outlawed the British movement. David then focused on founding monastic orders.

He settled with his disciples in Mynyw, a remote corner of Wales, and set up the first of many monasteries. David's rule was renowned for its severity. His monks had to live by hard labour and were not even allowed oxen to help them plough the fields.

Their diet was bread, salt and vegetables, and only water could be drunk. Speech was permitted only when absolutely necessary. The monks prayed without break from Friday evening till dawn on

*Left Detail from a manuscript depicting St David (15th century).*

*Right Detail from a manuscript depicting St David playing the harp (French School, 11th century).*

Sundays. The monks were described as "more abstemious than Christian".

David was also a powerful preacher. Once, as he was denouncing Pelagianism to a crowd, the earth swelled into a small hill so that more people could see him. He was made head of the Church in Wales by popular acclaim, and died at Mynyw. Leeks and daffodils are worn to mark his feast day.

There are more than 50 place names and dedications to David in South Wales, with further dedications in Devon, Cornwall and Brittany. David's cult was approved by Callistus in 1120, and two pilgrimages to St David's (Mynyw) in Pembrokeshire were said to equal one pilgrimage to Rome, while three were said to equal a pilgrimage to Jerusalem.

# LEANDER

IN HIS CAPACITY AS BISHOP OF SEVILLE, THE SON OF THE DUKE OF
CARTHAGENA BECAME A PROMINENT DEFENDER OF ORTHODOXY IN
THE ARIAN DEBATE, AND DREW UP A RULE FOR SPANISH NUNS.

**KEY FACTS**
*Bishop*
DATES: *c.AD 550–600*
BIRTH PLACE: *Carthagena*
FEAST DAY: *27 February*
EMBLEM: *Bishop's vestments*

As a member of the Spanish aristocracy, Leander was well disposed to influence those around him. He was a man who carefully selected projects, then applied his energy to completing them successfully.

In about AD 584, he became Bishop of Seville and turned his attention to the unwelcome dominance of the unorthodox Arians in Spain. He used his position to ensure that, at the Council of Toledo, the orthodox concept of the Holy Trinity was officially confirmed. He then concentrated on converting the Arian Visigoths, a strong presence in the Seville region. Patiently, he set about convincing these people of the truth of the Church.

His third concern was for the lives of nuns, for whom he drew up a Rule that proved highly influential. Leander introduced the practice of singing the Nicene Creed at Mass. His younger brother was St Isidore of Seville.

*Below The region around Seville today, where Leander was a bishop in the 6th century AD.*

# JOHN THE ALMSGIVER

WHEN ST JOHN BECAME PATRIARCH OF ALEXANDRIA, HE APPLIED
IDEALS OF CHARITY AND JUSTICE TO THE ADMINISTRATION OF THE
CITY EARNING HIM THE EPITHET OF ALMSGIVER.

**KEY FACTS**
*Bishop, Patriarch of
Alexandria*
DATES: *c.AD 560–620*
BIRTH PLACE: *Amathus, Cyprus*
PATRON OF: *Formerly patron of
the Knights of Malta but replaced
by John the Baptist*
FEAST DAY: *23 January*
EMBLEM: *Bishop's vestments*

Though it is known John was born in Cyprus, it is uncertain where he lived as an adult with his wife and children. At some point he moved to Egypt where, in about AD 610, he became the Bishop and Patriarch of the archdiocese of Alexandria.

John observed that the heretical Monophysites had been busy in the city. They were persuading Christians to accept their view that Jesus had no humanity and was wholly divine.

Instead of confronting the sect, John thought to weaken them through his own example of humble but generous Christian living. His work included establishing a system of welfare reform, and the

*Above Detail from a manuscript depicting St John the Almsgiver (French School, c.550–616).*

building of maternity hospitals and homes for the aged and frail. Citizens with legal or financial problems were invited to seek John's advice at twice-weekly meetings. And he organized relief for refugees after the Persians sacked Jerusalem in AD 614.

These efforts at ameliorating hardships and difficulties much endeared him to the people of Alexandria. Many were persuaded to follow his orthodox beliefs. John died soon after retiring to Cyprus in AD 619.

# GREGORY THE GREAT

FACED WITH MILITARY THREATS FROM GERMANIC TRIBES AND UNEASY RELATIONS WITH CONSTANTINOPLE, ST GREGORY DID MUCH TO STRENGTHEN CHRISTENDOM AT A DIFFICULT TIME.

**KEY FACTS**
*One of the four great Latin Doctors of the Church*
DATES: *c.AD 540–604*
BIRTH PLACE: *Rome*
PATRON OF: *Music, protection against plague*
FEAST DAY: *3 September*
EMBLEM: *Three-tiered papal crown, dove of the Holy Spirit*

Although Pope Gregory I dreamed of a life of solitude and prayer, he was the obedient son of a wealthy family and so took up a worldly career. Self-assured and clever, he studied law and then, just 30 years of age, was appointed governor of Rome.

A year later, his father died and Gregory found himself one of the richest men in Rome. At last he revealed his true longings by giving up his position and all his wealth. His house became a monastery and he a simple monk.

The Church was reluctant to miss out on such talented leadership. First it made Gregory deacon of Rome, then an ambassador to the Byzantine court in Constantinople. He spoke no Greek and seemed to use this deficiency as a reason for living a monastic life among the monks of the city.

After a few years, in AD 586, he was recalled to Rome. Although he returned as deacon of the city, again he sought the monastic life. But when Pope Pelagius II died four years later, the people of Rome elected Gregory to succeed him. Rome was in a terrible condition when Gregory became pope. Over the previous century, the state had been conquered, sacked and pillaged many times. The city was dilapidated, without leadership or administration.

## AS POPE

When Gregory took office, a plague was raging through the city. One of his first duties was to seek penitence from the citizens in order to end the disease. And so he led a great processional litany through the ruined streets.

Soon after taking office, he wrote to all his clerics, reminding them to treat their flocks with compassion and generosity. He recommended that church money be given to those in dire straits. The granaries of Rome were filled to feed the needy in times of

*Right An altarpiece depicting Gregory the Great (Pedro Torres, 16th–17th century).*

*Below Canterbury Cathedral where Gregory based his English mission (Wenzel Hollar, c.1650).*

"AFTER HAVING CONFIRMED ALL HIS ACTIONS TO HIS DOCTRINES, THE GREAT CONSUL OF GOD WENT TO ENJOY ETERNAL TRIUMPHS."

EPITAPH ON ST GREGORY'S TOMB

*Right A detail of Saints Augustine and Gregory in* The Fathers of the Church *(Michael Pacher, 1480).*

food shortage. Jews were allowed to practise their faith and keep their property without fear of being persecuted.

## AFFAIRS OF STATE
A greater worry to Gregory was the barbarian foe. From the very outset of his papacy, Gregory had to find energy to deal with the Lombards, a well-organized Germanic group intent on settling in the Roman Empire.

Their presence threatened Christianity. Gregory induced them to remain beyond the border, and arranged an uneasy truce between their leaders and the Byzantine emperor in Constantinople. However, his relationship with the Byzantines was also tense. He resented the grand titles of office assumed by

### ANGELS IN SLAVERY
When wandering the streets of Rome one day, Gregory noticed three boys with golden hair and fair skin. They were Anglo-Saxons to be sold in the slave market. On inquiry, he was informed that the youths were "Angels".

Gregory observed, "They are well named, for they have angelic faces and it becomes such to be companions with the angels in heaven. And who is the king of their province?"

"Aella," came the reply.

"Then," announced Pope Gregory, "Alleluia must be sung in Aella's land."

He felt such pity for these little golden creatures that he determined to spread the gospel to their country.

the Patriarch of Constantinople, who he feared wanted to wrest power from the West. Gregory insisted Rome was the centre of the Church and was successful in strengthening papal authority.

### MISSION TO ENGLAND
Denied a life of solitude, Gregory found other ways to serve God directly. After once saving some English boys from slavery, Gregory set his mind on converting England. To this end, he dispatched St Augustine and 40 missionaries to Canterbury. Their success among the Anglo-Saxons gave Gregory deep satisfaction.

His writings about the liturgy were of special value, and his text is still used in the Roman Missal. Gregory died in Rome and was buried in St Peter's Cathedral.

*Below Saint Gregory the Great is visited by a dove representing the Holy Spirit as he sits writing letters (Carlo Saraceni, c.1620). The dove of the Holy Spirit is one of his emblems.*

# ISIDORE OF SEVILLE

KNOWN AS THE "SCHOOLMASTER OF THE MIDDLE AGES", ISIDORE
OF SEVILLE WAS FAMOUS FOR WRITING A HUGE ENCYCLOPEDIA,
WHICH BECAME A STANDARD REFERENCE WORK FOR CENTURIES.

**KEY FACTS**
*Bishop, historian*
DATES: *c.AD 560–636*
BIRTH PLACE: *Carthagena*
FEAST DAY: *4 April*
EMBLEM: *Bishop's vestments,
books*

The veneration of St Isidore of
Seville rests on his scientific
and historical research. For the
intellectual discipline involved in
academic work, he had to thank
his brother Leander, who
educated him.

Although not a monk, Isidore
learnt the monastic habits of deep
thinking and discipline of work.
When he succeeded his brother as
Bishop of Seville in about AD 600,
he continued Leander's mission to
lead the Visigoths away from the
unorthodox views of Arianism.
He made the Church run more
efficiently and emphasized duty
of service and charity. Above all,
believing in the importance of
education, Isidore recommended
that every diocese should have a
Church school.

## EDUCATIONIST

His writings were to become
major texts in the education of
generations of theologians,
students and researchers. Isidore
wrote 86 biographies of biblical
figures, and a handbook on morals
and theology. He also produced
various liturgical analyses.

But his most important work
was a massive encyclopedia, called
the *Etymologies* (or *Origines*). This
opus covered the arts, medicine,
law, theology, history, zoology,
anthropology, cosmology, agriculture, science and other subjects.
Almost 1,000 medieval manucripts

*Above Isidore of Seville gives a book
to his sister in this Latin manuscript.*

of the *Etymologies* are still in existence. Isidore intentionally did
not apply any original thinking
when he compiled this text. He
wished to present all the knowledge then available to the
European world and drew on
numerous sources.

His other important writings
include *On the Wonders of Nature*
and *Chronica Majora,* a history
from creation to AD 610, though
with emphasis on Spanish history.
His scholarship was admired
across Christendom and medieval
intellectuals thought him equal to
St Gregory the Great.

*Right Scenes from the Life of St
Isidore, from Le Miroir Historial by
Vincent de Beauvais (French School,
15th century).*

# CUTHBERT

A PURPORTED PROPHET AND HEALER, THE POPULAR ANGLO-SAXON
ST CUTHBERT PERSUADED HIS CELTIC FLOCK OF THE
CORRECTNESS OF FOLLOWING ROMAN CHURCH CUSTOMS.

**KEY FACTS**
*Bishop, missionary*
DATES: c.*AD 634–87*
BIRTH PLACE: *Possibly Jarrow*
PATRON OF: *Formerly of
Lindisfarne*
FEAST DAY: *20 March*

After becoming a monk in Melrose in AD 651, Cuthbert spent ten years striving to be a model ascetic. He followed the practice of the time of standing for hours waist-deep in freezing sea water, and walked miles to visit the sick, whom he was said to heal miraculously.

His appointment as abbot put him in a position of influence. His winning manner and frequent local missions laid the ground-work for replacing the ideas of the Celtic Church with those of the Roman Church. The Synod of Whitby endorsed his view.

After a spell at Lindisfarne Abbey, he retired to Inner Farne as a hermit, only to be recalled to become Bishop of Lindisfarne. The gentle monk had a special affinity with the birdlife of the Farne Islands. After he died, his body reputedly stayed incorrupt.

*Left King Siegfried visits St Cuthbert and asks him to accept the bishopric of Lindisfarne, from the Latin manuscript of* Life and Miracles of St Cuthbert *by the Venerable Bede (English School, 12th century).*

# THE VENERABLE BEDE

NO HARDY MISSIONARY OR INSPIRED LEADER, THIS HOMELY MONK
SPENT HIS ENTIRE LIFE IN CLOISTERS. YET HE BECAME THE MOST
RESPECTED HISTORIAN IN MEDIEVAL WESTERN CHRISTENDOM.

**KEY FACTS**
*Writer, historian*
DATES: *AD 673–735*
BIRTH PLACE: *Sunderland,
England*
FEAST DAY: *25 May*
EMBLEM: *Monk with pen at
a manuscript*

At the age of seven, Bede was given to a monastery in Jarrow, Northumbria, and stayed there for the rest of his life. From an early age, he loved singing, studying, reading and writing.

He produced numerous texts on many different subjects and the fame of his learning spread far beyond his native county. The best known of his works, *Ecclesiastical History of the English People*, was written in AD 731, and is still in print.

The book was compiled at a time when Christianity was still relatively new to the Anglo-Saxons

*Above Bede is shown here dictating a translation of St John's Gospel into Anglo-Saxon (James Doyle Penrose, 1906).*

of Britain, and the faith is present-ed as a unifying force for the nation. Unusually for his time, Bede took the trouble to differentiate between fact and hearsay in writing history.

An important biography was his *Life and Miracles of St Cuthbert*. His last work was a translation into Old English of the *Gospel of St John*. It is said he dictated the closing sentences of this work from his deathbed.

# RUPERT

KNOWN AS THE "APOSTLE OF THE BAVARIANS", ST RUPERT IS CREDITED WITH ESTABLISHING CHRISTIANITY IN LANDS BORDERING THE RIVER DANUBE AND WITH FOUNDING SALZBURG.

**KEY FACTS**
*Missionary, bishop*
DATES: *d.c.AD 710*
BIRTH PLACE: *Unknown*
PATRON OF: *Bavaria, Austria, Salzburg*
FEAST DAY: *27 March*
EMBLEM: *Barrel of salt*

Little is known about Rupert's early life, including his birthplace. He may have been a Frank or an Irishman. However, having committed himself to becoming a missionary, Rupert attained high office in the Church, being elected Bishop of Worms in southern Germany.

At the invitation of the Duke of Bavaria, Theodo II, the saint went to Regensburg in Bavaria. There he founded a church near the Wallersee and dedicated it to St Peter. Rupert moved on to Salzburg and gathered disciples around him. For these followers, he founded a monastery at a site

*Left St Rupert in a detail from the Altar of St Hildegard of Bingen, Chapel of St Roch (1896).*

now known as the Mönchberg, and a convent, the Nonnberg. His sister, Ermentrude, was appointed as abbess to the nuns. He built a house to accommodate clerks and dedicated another church to St Peter. It is possible that Rupert wished to emulate the great apostle in his life of fearless travel, spreading the faith.

## MISSION TO THE DANUBE

Having been appointed Bishop of Salzburg, Rupert made that city his headquarters while he travelled extensively through the lands along the River Danube. This region was still a wild part of Europe. The Frankish empire had not yet extended this far east, so Rupert was blazing a trail into hostile barbarian territory.

He must have been a charismatic preacher, for his success as a missionary was immense. He is credited, too, with opening the salt-mining industry at a place which, before his efforts, held only the crumbling ruins of an old Roman town, Juvavum. He renamed the place Salzburg. Because of this activity, paintings often depict St Rupert with a barrel of salt beside him.

*Left A statue of St Rupert located outside the Ruprechtskirche, the oldest church in Vienna.*

# BONIFACE

ONE OF THE GREAT MISSIONARY SAINTS, ST BONIFACE PLAYED A MAJOR ROLE IN ESTABLISHING CHRISTIANITY IN GERMANY WHERE HE IS SAID TO HAVE CONVERTED FOLLOWERS OF NORSE GODS.

**KEY FACTS**

*Missionary martyr, archbishop*
DATES: c.AD 680–754
BIRTH PLACE: *Possibly Crediton, Devon, England*
PATRON OF: *Germany, brewers, tailors*
FEAST DAY: *5 June*
EMBLEM: *Axe*

Boniface was born in England but he spent many years in Europe where he became known as the "Apostle to the Germans". For the first 40 years of his life he was a monk, mainly at Nursling, near Southampton. Learned and devoted to biblical studies, Boniface was nevertheless no timid scholar.

The Church recognized his qualities of boldness and effective preaching, and sent him on a hazardous mission to lands still in heathen hands. It is said that in AD 718, armed with an axe, Boniface marched into a shrine dedicated to Thor, the Norse god of thunder.

With one mighty swing of the axe, Boniface is said to have felled the oak that was a key cultic object. The amazed onlookers were so impressed with the power of this man's God that tradition says the Germanic tribes converted to his faith en masse.

## TIRELESS MISSIONARY

It is much more likely that these conversions happened over a period of time. But Boniface quickly established a reputation among the people of Bavaria, Württemberg, Westphalia and Hesse as "a man who moved with power", in the words of contemporary reports. Pope Gregory II was equally impressed and gave him the bishopric of Mainz.

*Above St Boniface is here shown in proselytizing mode with his axe (Alfred Rethel, 1832).*

Boniface summoned more male and female missionaries from his native country.

In about AD 732, the pope made him archbishop. Boniface increasingly handed over the outward missionary work to his English evangelists, while he concentrated on organizing the new Church in West Germany.

Once satisfied that Christianity had taken firm root in Germany, Boniface turned to France. Many sees were vacant or poorly managed. With the help of the Frankish King Pepin, Boniface reformed those dioceses.

He then turned northwards to Frisia, where pagan communities still existed. He was over 70 when he undertook this mission. Travelling with a small band of disciples, he stopped at a place called Dokkum. Here, Boniface and his fellow missionaries were slaughtered by the very people he had hoped to convert.

St Boniface's surviving Latin correspondence reveals a man of courage and determination, who deserves as high a profile in his native England as he enjoys in Germany. The faithful continue to make pilgrimages to his shrine at Fulda, where his remains lie.

*Right Detail from a manuscript showing Germans being baptized and the martyrdom of St Boniface at Dokkum (AD 975).*

# CYRIL AND METHODIUS

THESE BROTHERS ARE VENERATED AS APOSTLES OF THE SOUTHERN
SLAVS AND FATHERS OF SLAVIC LITERATURE. ST CYRIL GAVE HIS
NAME TO THE MODERN SCRIPT CYRILLIC, DEVISED FROM HIS WORK.

**KEY FACTS**
*Translators of Christian texts and
apostles to the Slavs*
DATES: *Cyril AD 826–69,
Methodius c.AD 815–85*
BIRTH PLACE: *Thessalonica,
Macedonia*
PATRON OF: *Europe*
FEAST DAY: *14 February (West)*
EMBLEM: *Books, Cyrillic script*

In 1980, Pope John Paul II decided the brothers, Cyril and Methodius, should share the patronage of Europe with St Benedict. Together, these three saints symbolize the religious and political unity of Eastern and Western Europe.

Cyril and Methodius were scholarly men from Thessalonika, Macedonia. Cyril studied in Constantinople where he earned the nickname, "the philosopher".

## MISSION TO MORAVIA

His older brother, Methodius, went on a mission to the Khazars of Russia. He then returned to Greece as abbot of a monastery.

At the request of Prince Rostislav of Moravia, both men were sent on a mission to the Slavic province of Moravia (now part of the Czech Republic). The two missionaries were unique in being Greek monks sent off with

*Above This icon from Bulgaria
shows Sts Cyril and Methodius in
their role as the inventors of the
Cyrillic alphabet.*

*Below A fresco depicting Cyril and
Methodius meeting Pope Adrian II
(Lionello de Nobili, 1886).*

the blessing of the pope in Rome. Until 1054, the Eastern and Western Churches remained in communion with each other.

The brothers not only preached in Slavonic but began translating the Bible and liturgy into the vernacular. Using Greek letters as a model, they invented an alphabet for Slavonic, later named Cyrillic, after Cyril, the younger brother.

But their mission, while finding converts, aroused much political and theological opposition. Their early supporters, Rostislav and Pope Adrian II, had died, and their replacements condemned the use of Slavonic, asserting that no vernacular language was suitable for use in the Church.

## METHODIUS ALONE

After Cyril died in Rome in AD 869, Methodius continued the mission alone. But he was persecuted by Bavarian princes and forces within the Church, and imprisoned by German bishops.

After he had spent two years in a damp cell, Pope John VIII had him released and he continued his work in Moravia. He endeavoured to finish translating the Bible into Slavonic but opposition went on, and he died of exhaustion. Cyril and Methodius are admired for their ecumenism – the desire to unite worshippers, East and West.

# WENCESLAS

VENERATION OF ST WENCESLAS FOLLOWED HIS RULE AS A GOOD CHRISTIAN DUKE OF BOHEMIA. HE WAS CRUELLY MURDERED FOR HIS FAITH.

*Left St Wenceslas is depicted here in armour, bearing a banner of an eagle, oil on panel (Czech School, 16th century).*

Despite the conversion of much of Bohemia (now part of the Czech Republic), pagan culture persisted and often took a political hue. When Wenceslas' father, the Duke of Bohemia, died, opposition factions mobilized. His grandmother, St Ludmilla, who had educated the boy as a Christian, was murdered and his mother was banished.

However, the people of Bohemia defeated these factions and chose Wenceslas to be their leader. He allied himself with the Christian Henry I (known as Henry the Fowler) of the Holy Roman Empire. Some nobles, including his pagan brother Boleslav, resented the power the clergy of the new court now had.

Boleslav feared his brother's marriage would produce an heir, further strengthening Christian rule and jeopardizing his own chances of power. Following celebrations at the Feast of Sts Cosmas and Damian, Wenceslas died. Boleslav was implicated in the murder but he later repented and had his brother's relics translated to St Vitus's Church, Prague.

The popular hymn "Good King Wenceslas" reflects his reputation for strength and generosity.

# ODO OF CLUNY

SO ADMIRED WAS ST ODO FOR HIS LEADERSHIP THAT EVEN THE SECULAR AUTHORITIES TURNED TO HIM FOR GUIDANCE.

Reports say Odo had a good sense of fun and was a sympathetic person. Yet he was also a leader who instilled strict monastic observances across France and Italy.

Brought up by the Duke of Aquitaine, he founded the monastery of Cluny. When Odo was made abbot, he introduced the Rule of St Benedict, with its emphasis on vows of chastity,

*Above A view of the 12th-century Benedictine monastery at Cluny in Burgundy, France.*

communal poverty and long periods of silent meditation. Cluny rose to become the most important monastery in Europe and Odo was instrumental in it.

He attained papal protection from secular interference for this monastery and others in Western Europe. By the time he retired from the world, Odo's stature was such that Italian politicians often referred to him for help as an impartial mediator in disputes.

# ULRIC

BELOVED FOR HIS GENEROSITY AND CARE OF THE POOR, ST ULRIC SERVED AS BISHOP TO THE DIOCESE OF AUGSBURG, BAVARIA, FOR 50 YEARS BEFORE DYING ON A CROSS OF ASHES.

**KEY FACTS**
*Bishop*
DATES: *c.AD 890–973*
BIRTH PLACE: *Near Zurich,*
*Switzerland*
FEAST DAY: *4 July*
EMBLEM: *Bishop's vestments*

His father placed Ulric in the care of his uncle, Bishop of Augsburg, as a child, and Ulric lived at the monastery of St Gall. He never forgot the care shown to him there.

Ulric developed a deep piety and strong sense of duty toward the poor and afflicted in the community. But his office as Bishop of Augsburg was beset with strife from constant Magyar raids on Bavaria. Ulric devoted himself to easing the hardships suffered.

He founded a number of religious houses, and built a small church where he hoped to live as a monk. However, the trappings of high office kept him from fulfilling this wish. He once caused consternation by trying to hand his bishopric to a nephew, thus infringing canonical law. As a symbol of Christian sacrificial love, Ulric died on a cross of ashes marked out on the floor. His canonization is the first known case of a pope becoming a saint.

# EDWARD THE MARTYR

COMING TO THE THRONE AT A YOUNG AGE, EDWARD WAS THRUST INTO A POLITICAL HORNET'S NEST IN ENGLAND. HIS MARTYRDOM A FEW YEARS LATER WAS RECEIVED WITH HORROR BY THE NATION.

**KEY FACTS**
*Martyr*
DATES: *c.AD 962–79*
BIRTH PLACE: *Possibly Corfe*
*Castle, Dorset, England*
FEAST DAY: *18 March*
EMBLEM: *Dagger*

Aged just 13, Edward became king of England. At such a tender age he inherited a country troubled by disputes within the Church and faced a rival claim to the throne from his stepbrother Ethelred. His bid for the throne was supported by a rebellious party led by his stepmother, Aelfthryth. Together they plotted to overthrow the young king.

Riding home one day after hunting, Edward was greeted by Aelfthryth, who offered him a chalice of wine. As he leant to take the drink, a courtier stabbed him with a dagger. Edward slumped from his horse, but a foot caught in the stirrup and he was dragged over the ground, leaving behind a trail of blood.

Though this was not technically a martyr's death, kings were regarded as representatives of God. His murder was described as "the worst deed in English history". A pillar of light was said to hover over his abandoned body, and folk claimed their ailments were cured when they visited his grave. By common consent he was deemed a martyr, while his stepmother retired to a convent.

*Left Edward the Martyr shown about to be murdered at Corfe Castle.*

# WOLFGANG OF REGENSBURG

DURING HIS LIFETIME, THE HOLY ROMAN EMPIRE EVOLVED AS A CONFEDERATION OF DUCHIES IN GERMANY. ST WOLFGANG WAS ENTRUSTED WITH EDUCATING ITS FUTURE EMPEROR HENRY II.

**KEY FACTS**
*Bishop*
DATES: c.AD 924–94
BIRTH PLACE: *Duchy of Swabia, Germany*
FEAST DAY: *31 October*
EMBLEM: *Bishop's vestments*

Though content to lead a life as an abstemious monk devoted to prayer, Wolfgang was recognized for his wisdom and qualities as a teacher. He was handed the responsibility of educating the young prince and future emperor Henry II.

Wolfgang was put in charge of the Benedictine monastery school at Einsiedeln in Switzerland before progressing to become bishop of Regensburg in AD 972. He set about reforming the lax ways of the monks and nuns in his diocese. This meant reinforcing the vows of poverty and prayer, for which Wolgang set an admirable example.

Despite Wolfgang's talents as an evangelist, his mission into Hungary was largely unsuccessful. Wolfgang's cult remains strong and his relics at Regensburg continue to attract pilgrims.

*Left A woodcut depicting St Wolfgang (P.M. Vogel, 1860).*

# OLAF

A SOLDIER KING WHO ROVED AS A PIRATE BEFORE COMMITTING TO THE FAITH, ST OLAF OF NORWAY IS CREDITED WITH INTRODUCING CHRISTIANITY TO HIS COUNTRY AT A TIME OF POLITICAL TURMOIL.

**KEY FACTS**
*King*
DATES: *AD 995–1030*
BIRTH PLACE: *Norway*
PATRON OF: *Norway*
FEAST DAY: *29 July*
EMBLEM: *Battle-axe, loaves of bread*

The son of a Norwegian lord, Olaf began his adult life as a Viking pirate raiding the shores of the Baltic and France. But one trip to Normandy ended with Olaf's conversion to Christianity.

His new faith inspired him to fight for the English who were suffering invasions from the Danes. On returning to Norway, he seized power and determined to make his country Christian.

Just though his rule was, its severity spawned dissent. Olaf's erstwhile enemy, King Cnut of Denmark and England, took advantage of the situation and sponsored a rebellion in Norway.

Their combined forces succeeded in exiling Olaf in 1029. On trying the following year to regain his throne with the aid of Swedish allies, Olaf was killed in battle. After his death, Norwegians longed for his Christian rule and claimed many miracle cures from a spring issuing at his grave.

*Left The church of St Olaf in Wasdale in Cumbria is one of the smallest churches in England. Its beams are said to have come from a Viking longship.*

# STEPHEN OF HUNGARY

ALSO KNOWN AS STEPHEN THE GREAT, THIS NATIONAL HERO IS
CONSIDERED THE ARCHITECT OF AN INDEPENDENT CHRISTIAN
HUNGARY AND FOUNDER OF A CHURCH WELFARE SYSTEM.

**KEY FACTS**
*King*
DATES: *c.AD 975–1038*
BIRTH PLACE: *Esztergom,
Hungary*
PATRON OF: *Hungary*
FEAST DAY: *16 August*
EMBLEM: *Crown*

Filled with reforming zeal,
King Stephen was inspired by
his faith and sympathy for the
oppressed. As king, he reduced
the power of the nobles and
established a semi-feudal, but
secure, social system.

If the hallmark of his rule was
charity, it was also fundamentalist.
Adultery and blasphemy were
crimes not to be tolerated, and
marriage between Christians and
pagans was forbidden. On the
other hand, he helped the poor
through his church-building
programme. By ensuring there
was a church in virtually every
diocese, tithes demanded from
landlords could feed and clothe
the underprivileged.

Stephen encouraged missions
and finished building the great
monastery of St Martin, begun by
his father. His last years were spent
in dispute over his successor,
because his only son had died.

*Right The crown of St Stephen, now
held at the Magyar Nemzeti Galeria
in Budapest (11th century).*

# EDWARD THE CONFESSOR

ADMIRED FOR HIS DEVOTION TO GOD AND CARE FOR HIS POORER
SUBJECTS, EDWARD WAS THE LAST NATIVE KING TO RULE ENGLAND
BEFORE THE NORMAN CONQUEST.

**KEY FACTS**
*King*
DATES: *1003–66*
BIRTH PLACE: *Islip, England*
PATRON OF: *Once of England*
FEAST DAY: *13 October*
EMBLEM: *Ring*

The term "Confessor" refers
to the fact that Edward lived
his life as a devout follower of
Christ. It was said that the king
and his wife, Edith, were so holy
that they did not consummate
their marriage.

Edward became King of
England in 1042 during a time
of great political turbulence.
His father-in-law, Earl Godwine,
plotted against him while the
Danish king threatened to invade
England. Edward was generous to
the poor. His subjects believed he
could "touch for the king's evil",
meaning that simply through
touch, the king was able to cure
scrofula, a kind of tuberculosis.

Another story
surrounded a ring
which the king sup-
posedly gave to a
beggar. Years later,
English pilgrims in the
Holy Land met an old
man who claimed to be
John the Apostle and he
gave the travellers the
king's ring.

Edward started building
Westminster Abbey, how-
ever he died before it was
consecrated. He was can-
onized in 1161, and since
then many sick people have
visited his shrine in
Westminster Abbey to

pray for a cure. The
worn steps to the
shrine are evidence
to the number of pil-
grims. The shrine was
dismantled during the
Reformation that
began under Henry VIII
and Edward's body was
removed. His relics lie
behind the high altar in
to this day.

*Left A sculpture of Edward
the Confessor in the church of
San Marco, Florence (Pietro
Francavilla, 1589).*

# STANISLAUS OF CRACOW

THE PATRON OF POLAND WAS A BRAVE REFORMER WHO WOULD NOT ALLOW SPECIAL DISPENSATION TO AN UNREPENTANT KING. ST STANISLAUS WAS MARTYRED FOR HIS UNCOMPROMISING STAND.

**KEY FACTS**
*Martyr saint, bishop*
DATES: *1010–79*
BIRTH PLACE: *Szczepanow, Poland*
PATRON OF: *Poland, soldiers in battle*
FEAST DAY: *11 April*
EMBLEM: *Bishop's vestments, sword*

Born into a noble Polish family, Stanislaus was well educated, possibly studying in Paris. He was consecrated a bishop in 1072, having made a reputation as a stern reformer of lapses in Christian behaviour.

In the 11th century, Boleslav II was King of Poland and said to be violent and headstrong. Once he abducted a nobleman's wife and imprisoned her in his palace.

Refusing to repent of this demeaning act, the king incurred the wrath of Stanislaus who publicly excommunicated him

*Below* The Death of St Stanislaus *(Hungarian, 15th century).*

from the Church. King Boleslav II chased his bishop from the church at Cracow and cornered him in the chapel of St Michael.

The knights who hunted down Stanislaus refused to raise their swords against him, so Boleslav committed the murder himself. The king was later deposed and Stanislaus was acknowleged as a martyr saint.

# CANUTE

KING CANUTE OF DENMARK WAS DETERMINED TO TURN HIS NATION TO CHRISTIANITY, BUT HE PAID WITH HIS LIFE FOR IMPOSING RELIGIOUS LAWS AND TAXES THAT RILED THE NOBLES.

**KEY FACTS**
*Martyr king*
DATES: *d.1086*
BIRTH PLACE: *Denmark*
PATRON OF: *Denmark*
FEAST DAY: *10 July*
EMBLEM: *Crown, dagger, lance, barefoot king with hair in a fillet*

Two passions drove this King of Denmark. He wished to impose the Christian faith on his subjects and he was determined to gain the English throne.

Twice he tried to invade England. Its countrymen, who resented the rule of French invaders brought by William the Conqueror in 1066, sided with the Danish pretender. His first attack on England was a minor raid on York, but for his second campaign, in 1085, he prepared huge numbers of men.

Not all his subjects supported the invasion. Much had been spent on church buildings, and

*Left Stained glass depicting King Canute from the west window of Canterbury Cathedral.*

new laws empowered priests at the expense of secular nobles. Annoyed by high taxes and heavy-handed religious laws, they sided with Canute's rebellious brother, Olaf. Under siege in the church of St Alban at Odensee, Canute took the sacrament. As he knelt before the altar, he and 18 followers were stabbed to death.

# PATRON SAINTS OF NATIONS

NATIONS EVERYWHERE HAVE CHOSEN PATRON SAINTS AS SPECIAL
GUARDIANS OVER THEIR COUNTRY. IN TIMES OF NATIONAL PERIL,
COUNTRYMEN ASK THEIR SAINT TO PRAY TO GOD FOR THEM.

**Albania** – Mary
**Algeria** – Cyprian
**Andorra** – Our Lady of Meritxell
**Argentina** – Francis Solano
**Armenia** – Bartholomew
**Australia** – Francis Xavier
**Austria** – Leopold III, Rupert
**Belgium** – Joseph
**Bolivia** – Francis Solano
**Borneo** – Francis Xavier
**Bosnia** – James the Great
**Brazil** – Peter of Alcantara,
  Antony of Padua
**Bulgaria** – Cyril and Methodius
**Canada** – Anne, George, Joseph
**Chile** – Francis Solano
**China** – Francis Xavier
**Colombia** – Luis Bertran,
  Peter Claver
**Corsica** – Devota
**Costa Rica** – Mary
**Crete** – Titus
**Croatia** – Joseph
**Cuba** – Mary

**Cyprus** – Barnabas
**Czech Republic** – Wenceslas
**Denmark** – Anskar, Canute
**Dominican Republic** – Dominic
**Ecuador** – Mary
**Egypt** – Mark
**El Salvador** – Mary
**England** – George
**Ethiopia** – Frumentius
**Finland** – Henry of Finland
**France** – Denys of Paris, Joan of
  Arc, Theresa of Lisieux
**Georgia** – George
**Germany** – Boniface
**Gibraltar** – Bernard of Clairvaux
**Gozo** – George
**Greece** – Nicholas of Myra, Paul
**Guatemala** – James the Great
**Haiti** – Mary
**Honduras** – Mary
**Hungary** – Stephen of Hungary
**Iceland** – Thorlac of Skalholt
**India** – Rose of Lima, Thomas
**Indonesia** – Mary
**Iran** – Maruthas
**Ireland** – Brigid, Patrick
**Italy** – Catherine of Siena, Francis
  of Assisi

*Above* Saint Rose of Lima *(Carlo
Dolci, 17th century).*

**Jamaica** – Mary
**Japan** – Francis Xavier, Peter
**Jordan** – John the Baptist
**Korea** – Joseph
**Kosovo** – Methodius
**Lithuania** – Casimir of Poland
**Luxembourg** – Willibrord
**Macedonia** – Clement of Okhrida
**Madagascar** – Vincent de Paul
**Malta** – George, Paul
**Mexico** – Our Lady of Guadalupe,
  Joseph
**Monaco** – Devota
**Montenegro** – George
**Moravia** – Wenceslas
**Netherlands** – Willibrord
**New Zealand** – Francis Xavier
**Nicaragua** – James the Great
**Nigeria** – Patrick
**Norway** – Olaf, Magnus
**Oceania** – Peter Chanel
**Pakistan** – Francis Xavier, Thomas
**Palestine** – George
**Panama** – Mary
**Papua New Guinea** – Archangel
  Michael
**Paraguay** – Francis Solano
**Peru** – Francis Solano, Rose of Lima

*Below* Detail from a 13th-century
mosaic showing scenes from the life
of St Mark.

**Far Left** St Francis Xavier Blessing the Sick *(Rubens, 17th century).*

**Left** Nicetas *(Giovanni Antonio Guardi, 18th century).*

## MARY, THE BLESSED VIRGIN

Many nations around the world have adopted Mary, mother of Jesus, as their patron, often in addition to other saints. In this feature she is listed only beside those states where she is sole patron.

Mary, the Blessed Virgin, is believed to appear in symbolic and visionary form at times of national crisis. The Philippine navy, for example, was convinced Mary hovered over their ships and helped them to repulse the enemy.

Another example comes from Albania. Catholics believe a canvas painting of the Virgin, lodged on a cliff, prevented bombs in World War II falling on their land.

**Philippines** – Rose of Lima
**Poland** – Stanislaus of Cracow, Casimir of Poland
**Portugal** – Antony of Padua, Francis Borgia
**Puerto Rico** – Mary
**Romania** – Cyril and Methodius, Nicetas
**Russia** – Nicholas of Myra, Andrew, Vladimir
**Sardinia** – Maurice
**Scotland** – Andrew, Margaret of Scotland
**Serbia** – Sava of Serbia
**Sicily** – Andrew Avellino
**Slovakia** – John of Nepomuk
**Slovenia** – Virgilius
**South Africa** – Mary
**Spain** – James the Great
**Sri Lanka** – Thomas
**Sudan** – Josephine Bakhita
**Sweden** – Bridget of Sweden, Eric of Sweden
**Switzerland** – Gall, Nicholas of Flue
**Syria** – Barbara
**Tanzania** – Mary
**Tunisia** – Mary
**Turkey** – John the Evangelist, John Chrysostom
**Uganda** – Mary
**Ukraine** – Josaphat
**USA** – Mary

**Below** *Stained-glass window depicting St Andrew from the church of St Neot in Cornwall (16th century).*

**Uruguay** – James the Less
**Venezuela** – Mary
**Vietnam** – Joseph
**Wales** – David
**West Indies** – Rose of Lima
**Zaire** – Mary

**Above** Enthroned Madonna with Child, Angels and Saints *(Lorenzetti, c.1340).*

# MARGARET OF SCOTLAND

AN ANGLO-SAXON ROYAL WHO MARRIED A SCOTTISH KING DID MUCH TO REVIVE THE FLAGGING CHURCH IN HIS COUNTRY.

**KEY FACTS**
*Queen*
DATES: *1046–93*
BIRTH PLACE: *Hungary*
PATRON OF: *Scotland*
FEAST DAY: *16 November*
EMBLEM: *Crown*

*Left A portrait of Margaret published in the* Memoirs of the Court of Queen Elizabeth *(c. 1825).*

This cultivated granddaughter of the English king Edmund Ironside was one of the last members of Anglo-Saxon royalty before the Norman Conquest. Indeed, at the invasion she fled northwards and took refuge at the court of Malcolm III of Scotland.

The king was beguiled by her charm and intelligence, and they married in 1069. Her Christian devotion inspired her to revive the Church in Scotland, which had declined since the Celtic heyday of St Columba of Iona and St Aidan. She reformed the abbey at Iona and encouraged pilgrimages and the building of monasteries.

Margaret built Dunfermline church to be a burial place for the Scottish royal family. Her adoring husband, who was at first rough and illiterate, grew to be proud of her generosity toward his subjects, and became as devout a Christian as she was.

Two of her sons became kings of Scotland. She died shortly after hearing of the death of her husband and son in battle.

# BENNO OF MUNICH

TORN BETWEEN LOYALTIES, ST BENNO HAD TO SEARCH HIS CONSCIENCE TO MAKE THE RIGHT DECISIONS. HE WAS IMPRISONED AND CASTIGATED, BUT IN ALL HE STROVE ONLY TO SERVE HIS FLOCK.

**KEY FACTS**
*Bishop*
DATES: *d. 1107*
BIRTH PLACE: *Saxony*
PATRON OF: *Munich*
FEAST DAY: *16 June*
EMBLEM: *Fish and key*

Born to a noble Saxon family at a time of political strife, Benno was frequently caught up in the agitation. Having been appointed Bishop of Meissen by the German Emperor Henry IV, Benno found himself torn between allegiances. He opted to support his fellow Saxons in their uprising against the emperor.

Henry IV promptly had Benno imprisoned, but then released him on oath of fidelity. However, he reneged on this promise, siding again with the emperor's enemies.

When, as a punishment, his bishopric was removed, Benno vowed allegiance to the anti-pope Guibert in the hope that he might

recover his position as bishop and return to his flock. When this move failed, Benno revived his loyalty to Pope Urban II.

A legend says that when the emperor was excommunicated, Benno decided the best way to stop him entering his cathedral was to throw the key into the river. Benno later found his key miraculously stored inside a fish. The saint's relics were later moved to Munich for safekeeping.

*Left The Martyrdom of St Benno (Carlo Saraceni, 1618). Benno was venerated throughout Saxony.*

# ANSELM

DESPITE FALLING OUT WITH TWO KINGS OF ENGLAND, THE ITALIAN
MONK WHO BECAME ARCHBISHOP OF CANTERBURY WAS WIDELY
ADMIRED FOR HIS LEARNING AND "PROOF" OF GOD'S EXISTENCE.

**KEY FACTS**
*Doctor of the Church*
DATES: *1033–1109*
BIRTH PLACE: *Aosta, Italy*
FEAST DAY: *21 April*
EMBLEM: *A ship, symbolizing
spiritual independence*

As a boy, Anselm longed to be a monk. After his mother died when he was 20, Anselm left home to wander as a lone ascetic. He passed through Burgundy and found himself in Normandy, where he was inspired by the teaching of the abbot Lanfranc.

He stayed at Lanfranc's monastery of Bec and in time became its abbot. It was a wealthy establishment. Once Anselm was obliged to visit England to oversee property owned by Bec, and it was on this trip that the Italian monk first met the king.

## IN AND OUT OF FAVOUR

He so impressed King William II (Rufus) that, in 1093, he made Anselm archbishop of Canterbury. Though preferring to stay in Bec, Anselm nevertheless accepted the office.

The Italian's reluctance was soon justified when William declared his hand and demanded that he, the king, should appoint all English bishops and abbots henceforth. Anselm claimed that such power resides solely within the Church, and went to Rome to discuss the problem.

In his absence, the king took his opportunity and seized the church revenues. Anselm condemned the action as theft and abandoned Canterbury to live as an exile in Europe.

In 1100, the new English king, Henry I, summoned Anselm back. Again monk and monarch disagreed over appointments, and again Anselm went into exile. By 1107, they finally reached a

*Above A 15th-century window in
Tournai Cathedral, Belgium, shows
Anselm travelling to consult the pope.*

compromise and Anselm returned to office to live out his last years in relative peace.

Exile had provided him with a chance to put down his ideas in writing. Unlike his predecessors, Anselm defended his faith by reason, rather than using scripture as his authority.

Anselm is famous for his "ontological argument" for the existence of God, in which he asserts that the mere idea that there is a God necessarily proves his existence.

Anselm's cult grew slowly, but was helped by a well-written and sympathetic biography of his life

written by his friend and disciple, Eadmer of Canterbury. In 1734, in recognition of his position as the most influential Christian writer in the period between Augustine of Hippo and Thomas Aquinas, Anselm was named a Doctor of the Church. He is admired to this day for his steadfastness and piety, and is remembered as an intellectual and philosophical man.

*Below Scenes from the* Life of
St Anselm of Canterbury, *from*
Le Miroir Historial *by Vincent
de Beauvais (French School,
15th century).*

# STEPHEN HARDING

ESTABLISHING THE MONASTIC SYSTEM OF THE CISTERCIANS WAS ST HARDING'S GREAT ACHIEVEMENT. HIS IDEAS SPREAD ACROSS WESTERN EUROPE AND REFORMED NEARLY 700 MONASTERIES.

**KEY FACTS**
*Founder of Cistercian monastic order*
DATES: *d. 1134*
BIRTH PLACE: *England*
FEAST DAY: *28 March*
EMBLEM: *Cistercian habit*

Having settled in France, Stephen Harding, who was English by birth, made a huge impact on the religious history of Europe by helping to found the great monastery of Citeaux. Under his 25-year leadership, this first of the Cistercian monasteries became a model for the austere religious life.

In a bid to return to a strict observance of the Benedictine Rule, Stephen demanded wholesale changes to the dissolute lifestyle of contemporary monks. Luxuries were banned. The monks could no longer enjoy the monastic income derived from their mills, serfs and tithes. They now had to farm the fields themselves and live on their produce alone. Many new monasteries were built in remote places to avoid contact with town folk.

Stephen expected each abbot to visit the monasteries under his care and report to Citeaux. Thus he maintained his high standards.

*Right A woodcut of the Cistercian monastery at Citeaux, France, founded in 1098.*

# NORBERT

NORBERT GAVE UP A WEALTHY LIFE TO BECOME A MONASTIC REFORMER. HE SET UP THE SO-CALLED "WHITE CANONS", WHICH SPREAD QUICKLY OVER WESTERN EUROPE, ESPECIALLY HUNGARY.

**KEY FACTS**
*Founder of order, archbishop*
DATES: *c. 1080–1134*
BIRTH PLACE: *Xanten, Prussia*
FEAST DAY: *6 June*
EMBLEM: *Bishop's vestments*

Like St Francis of Assisi, Norbert was born into a wealthy family and then abandoned his worldly privileges. Norbert almost died in a thunderstorm in 1115. This experience inspired him to give away his possessions and beg the pope for forgiveness for his past life. To atone for his sins, he became a wandering preacher in northern France and the Low Countries.

Norbert's sternness of faith and eschewing of worldly things did not endear him to all the clergy. To put his beliefs into practice, he founded a community in Prémontré in the Rhineland,

where he instituted an austere regime following the rules of St Augustine of Hippo. Norbert was a friend of St Bernard of Clairvaux and shared his reforming zeal.

Although there were clergy who resented his ideas, Norbert was generally popular. In 1126, he was appointed Archbishop of Magdeburg. His monastic order, known as the Premonstratensians, or "White Canons", after their vestments, gained ground quickly.

*Left A portrait of St Norbert from an illuminated manuscript (11th–12th century).*

# BERNARD OF CLAIRVAUX

UNDER THE LEADERSHIP OF ST BERNARD, THE CISTERCIAN ORDER GREATLY INFLUENCED THE SPIRITUAL DIRECTION CHRISTIANITY WOULD TAKE DURING MEDIEVAL TIMES.

**KEY FACTS**
*Doctor of the Church*
DATES: *c. 1090–1153*
BIRTH PLACE: *Fontaines, near Dijon, France*
PATRON OF: *Gibraltar*
FEAST DAY: *20 August*
EMBLEM: *Beehive, beekeepers, candle-makers, Eucharistic host*

St Bernard was one of the most charismatic figures of the medieval Church. His powerful preaching, energy and dedication to leading a model Christian life made him an influential force in the Church, though not one that always met with approval.

Fervent in his commitment to reforming monastic life, Bernard followed the example set by Stephen Harding, and joined his monastery at Citeaux. His clarity of vision for the developing Cistercian Order naturally led to Bernard's appointment in 1115 as abbot of the poverty-stricken Clairvaux, the third Cistercian monastery.

Critical of the gentler, parallel order at Cluny, known as the "Black Benedictines", Bernard was determined to establish an austere discipline without compromise, surviving on minimal rations and hard labour.

Starting with just 30 fellow devotees, his way blossomed despite its rigours. It is said that his charm and facility to heal the sick attracted thousands of pilgrims. By his death, the number of monks at Clairvaux alone had risen to 700, while some 400 Cistercian monasteries were established across Europe.

## POLITICS AND CRUSADE

Bernard's enthusiasm, coupled with his eloquence, inevitably drew him into church politics. At this time, the authority of the Roman Church was jeopardized by disputes over who should be pope. The princes of Europe tended to back one candidate or another. Bernard's successful promotion of Eugenius III to the papacy in 1145 did much to raise his public profile. Soon he was being asked to combat the rising Albigensian heresy in southern France, which he condemned with characteristic fervour.

Perhaps Bernard's greatest challenge was promoting the Second Crusade (1145–49) to recover the Holy Land from Muslim control. His stirring speeches inspired thousands of the good, the bad, even criminals, to "take the Cross". To protect Christians travelling to Palestine, Bernard took control of the Cistercian Order of Knights Templar and devised a chivalric code of conduct. Following the failure of the crusade, Bernard's esteem suffered a great deal, allowing his enemies to make capital out of the disaster.

Bernard's eloquent articulation of his faith is nowhere more evident than in his surviving letters and sermons, and in his treatise on the Love of God.

*Below* St Bernard of Clairvaux *(Ferrer Bassa, 14th century).*

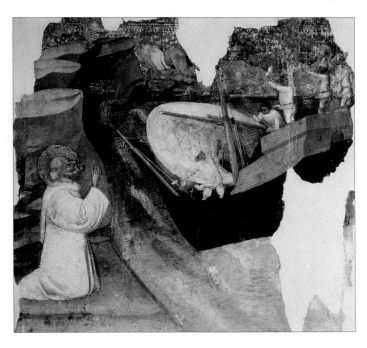

# HENRY OF FINLAND

AN ENGLISH BISHOP OF UPPSALA, SWEDEN, HENRY JOINED A CRUSADE TO FINLAND IN ORDER TO CONVERT ITS WAR-LIKE PEOPLE, AND REMAINED THERE AS A MISSIONARY.

KEY FACTS
*Martyr bishop*
DATES: *d. 1156*
BIRTH PLACE: *England*
PATRON OF: *Finland, sea fishermen*
FEAST DAY: *20 January*
EMBLEM: *Bishop's vestments*

Henry was a soldier for Christ. In 1154, he joined King Eric IX of Sweden's war against the Finns. The king saw his military expedition as a crusade and offered the Finns peace if they became Christian. They refused and were defeated in battle.

Henry stayed in Finland and he baptized many of the people. He built a church at Nousis, which became the centre of his missionary work. Eventually, he was killed by a Finnish convert when he refused to grant him forgiveness for killing a Swedish soldier. His cultus spread and he became Finland's patron saint.

*Left St Henry of Finland from the Sforza Hours, one of the most beautiful Renaissance manuscripts extant (Giampietrino Birago, c. 1490).*

# ERIC OF SWEDEN

ERIC HOPED TO INTRODUCE CHRISTIAN RULE TO HIS COUNTRYMEN BUT WAS MURDERED IN DENMARK WHEN HE TRIED TO USE HIS MILITARY MIGHT TO SPREAD HIS CHRISTIAN MESSAGE.

KEY FACTS
*Martyr king*
DATES: *d. 1160*
BIRTH PLACE: *Sweden*
PATRON OF: *Sweden*
FEAST DAY: *18 May*
EMBLEM: *Crown*

Through his marriage to Christine, of the Swedish royal family, Eric was able to claim the throne in 1156. Committed to his faith, he instituted a Christian legal system and channelled funds into the Church.

However, disgruntled Swedes opposed to his reforms sought allies abroad to back a rebellion. In 1154, one such ally arose in Denmark. Determined to spread Christianity across Scandinavia, Eric waged war against any neighbouring peoples who would not accept Christianity as their faith. He began by invading Finland. When he continued into Denmark, he was outnumbered by a united force of Danes and rebel Swedes. As Eric left Mass on Ascension Day, he was cut down by Danish soldiers. Lying humiliated at their feet, he was subjected to terrible torture and beheaded.

A cultus quickly developed around Eric. Ironically, Nordic mythology possibly played its part in raising his profile to that of national hero, residing in the heavenly abode of Valhalla.

Eric's body and kingly regalia were laid in a new cathedral built in Uppsala, and he was adopted as patron of Sweden. Until the Reformation, farmers would hold annual processions begging Eric's intercession for good harvests.

*Left The coronation of Eric of Sweden (Italian School, 19th century).*

# THOMAS BECKET

THE TRAGIC MURDER IN CANTERBURY CATHEDRAL OF THIS
DEVOUT PRIEST CREATED SUCH A SENSATION THAT PILGRIMS CAME
FROM ALL OVER MEDIEVAL CHRISTENDOM TO VISIT HIS SHRINE.

**KEY FACTS**
*Martyr, archbishop*
DATES: *1118–70*
BIRTH PLACE: *London*
PATRON OF: *Clergy*
FEAST DAY: *29 December*
EMBLEM: *Tonsured (crown of
head shaved), holding
archbishop's cross, mitre*

The clever son of a wealthy family, Thomas was a man of the world in his early career as archdeacon of Canterbury. He was just the sort of pleasure-loving priest that appealed to the young King of England, Henry II.

The king soon appointed him Chancellor of England. In this capacity, Thomas entertained lavishly and travelled abroad on diplomatic missions on behalf of his friend, the king.

*Above Detail from a medieval manuscript showing the murder of Thomas Becket (English School).*

## ARCHBISHOP

Henry ensured Thomas was made Archbishop of Canterbury in 1162 but, to his intense annoyance, Thomas repented of his former ways. Instead, he became a dutiful, austere religious, wearing a hairshirt and holding long prayer vigils.

No longer the carefree friend, Thomas began to upbraid the king on matters of taxation, reminding him of the Church's rights and privileges. Henry was further enraged when Thomas insisted God and Rome were the supreme authorities, not the King of England. Henry wished to try the clergy in the courts of England, but Thomas claimed this was unacceptable, that they had the right to appeal to Rome.

## EXILE AND MURDER

The differences between the two men descended into bitter squabbles, including disputes over money. Thomas went into exile, seeking refuge in a Cistercian monastery in France. After six years, he believed reconciliation had been reached, and returned to Canterbury in hope.

To his great dismay, he discovered his land had been appropriated and his followers alienated. But Thomas continued to assert his allegiance to God over the state. Henry, demanding and quick-tempered, was exasperated. In an outburst, his uttered wish to be rid of "this turbulent priest" was taken at face value by four nearby barons.

His henchmen sped off to the cathedral in Canterbury and, after a brief altercation with Thomas, set upon him with their swords. The king did public penance for this savage murder, but the veneration of Thomas as a martyr spread fast. Hundreds of miracles were claimed in his name and his shrine became one of the most popular in all Christendom.

*Below Henry II of England arguing with Thomas Becket (English School, 14th century).*

# HILDEGARD OF BINGEN

A MEDIEVAL RENAISSANCE WOMAN, HILDEGARD WAS A VISIONARY NUN, POET, PAINTER, MUSICIAN AND WRITER OF BOOKS NOT ONLY ON MYSTICAL THEOLOGY BUT ALSO ON BOTANY AND NATURAL CURES.

**KEY FACTS**
*Abbess, theologian*
DATES: *1098–1179*
BIRTH PLACE: *Bokelheim, Germany*
FEAST DAY: *17 September*
EMBLEM: *Books*

**B**orn the tenth child of a noble German family, the "Sibyl of the Rhineland", as she was dubbed, became aware of receiving visions as early as three years of age. At eight, she was entrusted to the care of a reclusive nun, Juetta, who lived beside a Benedictine abbey at Diessenberg in Germany.

Hildegard took vows at the age of 15, and entered a small convent established by Juetta. Under her guidance, the young nun grew in stature to eventually succeed Juetta as abbess at the age of 38.

## MYSTICAL VISIONS
The depth and quality of Hildegard's mystical experiences prompted her contemporary, St Bernard of Clairvaux, to urge her to record them on paper. This she did in abundance.

The best known of her mystical works is *Scivias* (short for *Sciens vias Domini*, "Know the ways of the Lord"). In the book

HILDEGARDIS a Virgin Prophetess, Abbess of St Ruperts Nunnerye, She died at Bingen AᴰDoⁱ 1180 Aged 82 yeares. W.Marshall sculpsit.

*Above An engraving of Hildegard (William Marshall, 1648).*

she describes visions as coming to her through "the eyes of her soul". Fully awake, she saw luminous images of figures and scripture bathed in divine light.

This light, she wrote, ignited a flame in her chest, "not like a burning, but like a warming flame, as the sun warms everything its rays touch." The experiences deepened her understanding of scripture, and she felt impelled to write widely on whatever inspired her.

Morality plays, hymns and prayers flowed from her pen. Her illustrations to *Scivias* have been likened to those of the English visionary William Blake.

## DIVERSE INTERESTS
Besides religious subjects, Hildegard compiled a survey of natural history, and a medical handbook of ailments and their treatment by natural remedy. Her breadth of knowledge prompted her to correspond with the theologian, Guibert of Gembloux, who sought her views on dogma. She gave written advice to King Henry II of England, the German Emperor Frederick Barbarossa, and even the pope himself.

Despite all this creative output, Hildegard did not neglect her duties. When it became necessary, she moved her convent to a larger building near Bingen. She founded a new house at Eibingen, and made reforms elsewhere.

Keen to pass on her spiritual insights, she preached in Germany and beyond, before dying of old age. In the modern feminist movement, she is lauded for her independence and creative energy.

*Left The Vision of St Hildegard (attributed to Battista Dossi, c.1474–1548).*

# LAURENCE O'TOOLE

THE INVASION OF IRELAND BY ENGLISH ADVENTURERS IN 1170 TURNED LAURENCE'S DUTIES FROM TENDING TO HIS FAMINE-STRICKEN FLOCK TO PROTECTOR OF THE IRISH CHURCH.

**KEY FACTS**
*Archbishop*
DATES: *1128–80*
BIRTH PLACE: *Co.Kildare, Ireland*
FEAST DAY: *14 November*
EMBLEM: *Bishop's vestments*

As abbot of Glendalough monastery, one of the five suffragan dioceses to Dublin, O'Toole was mainly involved in preventing his rural congregations from starving. But eight years after his election in 1162 as Archbishop of Dublin, O'Toole had to contend with invading Anglo-Normans led by Strongbow, Earl of Pembroke.

Two years later, the archbishop went to Rome where he was made papal legate. He also secured the pope's protection of

all Church property in Ireland. This upset the English king who had told the Irish archbishop to remind the pope that he, Henry II of the Angevin Empire, now controlled Ireland. In a tricky meeting with the king, it is a measure of O'Toole's talents that he won the king's agreement not to threaten Irish Church property.

*Left Christ Church Cathedral, Dublin (built 1172–1240).*

# DOMINIC

THE FOUNDER OF THE "BLACK FRIARS" ORDER UNDERSTOOD THAT LEADING AN EXEMPLARY LIFE OF VIRTUE WAS THE BEST WAY TO BRING CONVERTS TO THE FAITH.

**KEY FACTS**
*Founder of an order*
DATES: *c.1170–1221*
BIRTH PLACE: *Caleruega, Spain*
FEAST DAY: *8 August*
EMBLEM: *Lily, black-and-white dog*

Of noble birth in Castile, Dominic de Guzmán led an uneventful life until he joined his bishop on a mission to the heretical Cathars of southern France. The movement was growing into a menacing force.

Though avowedly Christian, the Cathars did not regard Jesus as Saviour, but merely a teacher. Other groups joined the effort but failed. A warrior knight, Simon de Montfort, mounted a crusade against them in 1208, and caused much grief and bitterness.

But Dominic took no part in such confrontation. His bishop having left him to his own devices, Dominic discovered his

*Above St Dominic (Cosmé Tura, c.1430–95).*

gift for preaching. Direct and personal, his style appealed to the listener's heart, rather than the contemporary Franciscan friars' emphasis on creation's beauty.

Basing himself in Toulouse, Dominic founded an order in which he trained priests as itinerant preachers. His eagerness to guard the teachings of Christ meant his priests were nicknamed *domini canes*, "dogs of God".

His order multiplied rapidly. Even now, Dominican men and women play an important role in teaching and preaching the faith.

393

# HOLY BEASTS

CHRISTIANITY HONOURS ANIMALS AS PART OF GOD'S CREATION.
THE SAINTS TURNED TO THEM FOR HELP AND COMPANIONSHIP, AND
STORIES TELL OF SAINTS PERFORMING MIRACLE CURES ON ANIMALS.

From the very beginning of the Christian story, beasts have played their role. Mary, the Blessed Virgin was said to have given birth in a stable, witnessed by cows and donkeys. She was visited by shepherds who brought a lamb as a gift for the infant Jesus.

Legend states that Christ trusted animals. He even used one to deliver his message. When St Eustace went hunting, his prey, a stag, turned to display a crucifix between his horns, thus converting the hunter to Christianity. The cross marking the back of the don-key is also seen as Christ's legacy to this humble beast who bore him on his final entry into Jerusalem.

*Above St Bernard dogs were used by members of the St Bernard fathers to rescue Alpine travellers from the snow.*

*Above A wooden carving showing St Roch with an angel and a dog (Antwerp School, early 16th century).*

As with Christ, so the saints' lives are linked to animals. Some saints had them as companions, others were reputed to have performed miracle cures on the sick and maimed. In turn, stories tell of animals rescuing saints from hardship and mortal danger.

## DIVINE SYMBOLS

Certain creatures came to symbolize human qualities. Dogs stood for loyalty and can be spotted in numerous paintings of saints. A lion represents courage and a dove symbolizes the Holy Spirit of peace.

St Bernard of Clairvaux is shown with a little dog at his feet. His mother, pregnant with her son, dreamt of a dog, which is regarded as the guardian of God's house, and security against evil. But the highest status in the Christian world is held by the lamb. The holiest of saints have a lamb as their attribute in emulation of Christ's figuration as

*Left Detail from* Annunciation to the Shepherds *(attributed to Simone Martini and others, 14th century).*

"PRAISE BE TO THEE, MY LORD, WITH ALL THY CREATURES."

ST FRANCIS OF ASSISI

the Lamb of God. This symbolism is based on the Paschal Lamb, sacrificed at the Jewish Passover. John the Baptist and St Agnes are both depicted with the creature.

## RESCUE AND CARE

A wolf is said to have looked after St Antony of Egypt when he lost his way in the wilderness. And St Roch was indebted to a dog. As the saint lay in a forest, dying of the plague, a little dog appeared carrying bread in his mouth and saved St Roch from starvation.

St Bernard mountain dogs, employed to track people lost in the Swiss Alps, were named after St Bernard of Aosta. In the 11th century, this saint founded a monastery in the Alps to provide shelter for crusaders trekking to the Holy Land.

As well as coming to their rescue, animals have worked closely with saints. St Antony was once a

*Below* The stag appears in The Vision of Saint Eustace *(Antonio Pisano Pisanello, 15th century).*

swineherd and St Brigid a dairymaid. The Welsh St Beuno worked with, and cared for, his cattle and sheep. At his death, these animals were taken to visit his tomb, and thereafter were said to produce strong offspring.

## TENDING TO ANIMALS

St Francis of Assisi is famous for his empathy with wild creatures. His sermon to the birds and taming of the wolf of Gubbio illustrate the saint's appreciation of creatures, which he sees as objects of God's love. St Cuthbert also had a special affinity with birds, particularly eider ducks on the Farne Islands of northern England. It was said that birds inhabiting these barren rock stacks fell under the protection of the saint who was a sort of prototype conservationist.

Famously, St Jerome drew a thorn from the paw of a lion who became his life companion. St Blaise was said to have the power to heal animals. Farmers brought him their ailing cattle, and beasts

came of their own accord. St Antony of Padua, often aloof with people, had sympathy with the animal world. He preached to fishes who were said to swarm toward him to hear his wisdom. It is said that a badly treated mule once refused its owner's fodder in indignation, but knelt at the eucharist St Antony offered it.

*Below* St Francis of Assisi Preaching to the Birds *(Giotto di Bondone, c.1295–1300).*

### PATRON SAINTS OF ANIMALS

**Animals** – Francis of Assisi, Antony of Padua
**Bees** – Ambrose, Bernard of Clairvaux
**Birds** – Francis of Assisi
**Cats** – Gertrude of Nivelles
**Deer** – Francis of Assisi
**Domestic animals** – Antony of Egypt
**Diseased animals** – Blaise
**Dogs** – Hubert
**Dogs, mad** – Sithney
**Fish** – Francis of Assisi
**Horned animals** – Cornelius
**Horses** – Martin of Tours, Giles, Hippolytus
**Rams** – Giles
**Wolves** – Francis of Assisi

# FRANCIS OF ASSISI

THROUGHOUT THE WORLD TODAY, FRANCISCAN MONKS AND NUNS
CONTINUE THE CHARITY WORK BEGUN BY THEIR FOUNDER, WHOSE
PURE LOVE OF CREATION INSPIRED A NEW ATTITUDE TO THE WORLD.

**KEY FACTS**
*First saint to receive the
stigmata, in 1224*
DATES: *1181–1226*
BIRTH PLACE: *Assisi, Italy*
PATRON OF: *Animals and birds,
ecologists, merchants*
FEAST DAY: *4 October*

Few saints are held in such high esteem for their spirit of devotion as is St Francis. The humble friar wished for nothing other than to imitate Christ. For him the world was an expression of God, and this conviction gave him a special affinity with nature.

## REJECTING WEALTH

Francis was born into a rich Italian family and as a youth enjoyed his privileged status. But in the course of a war between Assisi and Perugia, he was imprisoned and began to question his spiritual life. After the war he

*Left* Scenes from the life of St Francis of Assisi *(Bonaventura Berlinghieri, 1235). This panel is the earliest known depiction of this saint.*

started to give away money to the poor and once, so overcome with compassion, he kissed the diseased hand of a leper.

His father was so angry at this bizarre behaviour that he demanded his son renounce his inheritance. In fact, Francis was glad to do so, for he had heard a voice telling him to live without property, and to preach the word of God. Francis left his family to take up a life of poverty.

## NEW ORDER

Francis lived near the ruined chapel of St Mary of the Angels, known as the Portiuncula, near Assisi. He took shelter in a bare hut, and cared for the local lepers.

His preaching and devotion attracted followers, impressed by the simplicity and humility of Francis's faith. In 1210, Pope Innocent III authorized Francis and 11 companions to be "roving preachers of God".

Franciscans travelled in pairs preaching his philosophy of poverty and living by begging. The order soon spread across Europe as far as England.

*Left The Lower Church of San Francesco in Assisi, Italy, built in the 13th century.*

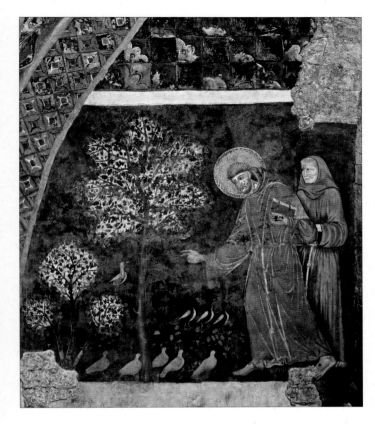

*Above* St Francis Prays to the Birds, *fresco from the church of San Francesco in Assisi (c. 1260).*

Mountains where he fasted for 40 days with his followers. While there he had a vision of an angel who enveloped him with light.

Francis then famously received the stigmata. His hands, feet and side are said to have manifested the same wounds that Christ received at the Crucifixion. The marks stayed with him for the rest of his life. In 1226, blind yet filled with joyous faith, Francis died at Portiuncula.

Despite poor health, Francis made several journeys to convert Muslims living around the Mediterranean Sea. Once, when he was taken prisoner during a battle in Egypt between Crusaders and Muslims, the local sultan was so touched by his devotion and disdain of wealth that he was released. In 1219, he reached the Holy Land, but the following year the Franciscans recalled him to Europe.

## SPIRITUAL RETREAT

The order had grown hugely in his absence and Francis handed control to the able administrator, Elias of Cortona. It was he who now maintained the Franciscan Rule, which insisted on possessing no money or property, teaching the word of Christ, and caring for the sick and needy. In 1224, Francis retreated to the Apennine

> "LORD GRANT ME THE SERENITY TO ACCEPT THE THINGS I CANNOT CHANGE, THE COURAGE TO CHANGE THE THINGS I CAN, AND THE WISDOM TO KNOW THE DIFFERENCE."
>
> ST FRANCIS OF ASSISI

> "MOST HIGH, ALL-POWERFUL, ALL GOOD, LORD!
> ALL PRAISE IS YOURS, ALL GLORY, ALL HONOUR
> AND ALL BLESSING.
>
> TO YOU ALONE, MOST HIGH, DO THEY BELONG.
> NO MORTAL LIPS ARE WORTHY
> TO PRONOUNCE YOUR NAME.
>
> ALL PRAISE BE YOURS, MY LORD, THROUGH ALL THAT YOU HAVE MADE,
> AND FIRST MY LORD BROTHER SUN,
> WHO BRINGS THE DAY; AND LIGHT YOU GIVE TO US THROUGH HIM.
>
> HOW BEAUTIFUL IS HE, HOW RADIANT IN ALL HIS SPLENDOUR!
> OF YOU, MOST HIGH, HE BEARS THE LIKENESS."
>
> THE FIRST FOUR VERSES OF THE CANTICLE OF BROTHER SUN

# ANTONY OF PADUA

THIS CHARISMATIC SAINT FROM LISBON, BELIEVED TO BE A GREAT MIRACLE WORKER, WAS MOSTLY REVERED FOR HIS PREACHING TO THE UNCONVERTED, TO HERETICS, AND TO THE MOORS OF AFRICA.

**KEY FACTS**
*Doctor of the Church*
DATES: *c.1193–1231*
BIRTH PLACE: *Lisbon, Portugal*
PATRON OF: *Portugal, lost articles, the poor, and animals*
FEAST DAY: *13 June*
EMBLEM: *Loaves of bread*

Stout and overweight, St Antony looked an unlikely person to radiate holiness. Yet it was said that when people heard his eloquent words, they were filled with the wonder of his faith.

Having joined an Augustinian monastery at the age of 15, Antony was impressed more by some visiting Franciscan friars. The simple modesty of the way taught by his contemporary St Francis of Assisi persuaded him to join their order in 1221. On a dangerous mission to Muslims in North Africa, he was lucky to suffer only fever, not martyrdom.

On returning to Italy, Antony made his way to Assisi. While staying at a nearby hermitage, he attended an ordination of Franciscan monks. Speakers who were expected to give addresses failed to appear, and Antony was prompted to step up in their place. His speech was so impressive that he was asked to become a wandering preacher.

His renown as such spread beyond his province of Romagna. Soon he was preaching against the Cathars in France, and was known as the "hammer of the heretics."

## MIRACLE WORKER

Many miracles were attributed to this popular figure. The most famous example causes the faithful to ask for his intercession now to find things lost or stolen.

Tradition says that a novice at his monastery stole Antony's psalter. When the saint prayed for its return, the thief was duly moved to do so, and rejoined the order, too. At Rimini, a mule was said to have refused its diet of oats for three days, then accepted the eucharist when Antony offered it.

It was also claimed that fish once swarmed a river to hear him preach; a tale symbolic of his powers as a preacher.

*Left* The Vision of St Anthony of Padua *(Giovanni Battista Pittoni, 18th century).*

*Right St Antony is shown here holding the infant Christ (c.16th century).*

# ELIZABETH OF HUNGARY

THE NOBLE WIFE OF A GERMAN PRINCE WAS HAPPILY MARRIED BEFORE HIS TRAGIC DEATH PROPELLED HER INTO A LIFE OF SUCH SELFLESS CHARITY AND MORTIFICATION THAT SHE DIED YOUNG.

KEY FACTS
*Princess*
DATES: *1207–31*
BIRTH PLACE: *Pressburg, Hungary*
PATRON OF: *Catholic charities, bakers*
FEAST DAY: *17 November*
EMBLEM: *Alms of a pitcher, a basket of bread, fruit, and fish, an apron of flowers*

The tragic story of Elizabeth is set in the royal society of medieval central Europe. At the birth of Elizabeth, a wandering poet-musician predicted she would marry the German prince Louis of Thuringia. Aged four, she was duly betrothed to Louis, and her father, Andrew II of Hungary, sent her to live with his family.

Expectations were fulfilled when the couple married when she was 14 and he 21 years old. Furthermore, the marriage was a happy one, with each partner allowing the other to be free to do as he or she wished.

Elizabeth was committed to helping the poor in her adoptive province. The couple's castle home was sited at the top of a cliff. Elizabeth built a hospital at the foot of this rock, and daily took down food and clothing.

She worked tirelessly as a nurse there, tending the sick and orphaned children, as well as the poor of the diocese. At her own expense, it is said, she fed over 900 people a day.

## CHANGING FORTUNES

When she was pregnant with their third child, her husband joined the Sixth Crusade (1228–29). They parted, vowing they would never marry anyone else, should anything happen to either of them. Within months of departing, Louis died of the plague. His death proved to be a turning point in her life. His brother-in-law Henry, for some unknown reason, expelled Elizabeth and her children from the castle. The family was forced into a life of hardship, without home or protection.

At last, elderly relatives came to their rescue. An uncle, the Bishop of Bamberg, let her live in his castle and provision was made for the children.

In a state of continuing grief, she assumed the life of a Franciscan tertiary (lay member). In time the urge to return to her former place of work prompted a move back to Marburg where she lived in a small hut attached to the hospital she had built. Here she resumed nursing.

Although Master Conrad of Marburg offered her protection, he was alarmed by the harsh regime Elizabeth imposed upon herself. Extreme acts of self-mortification and utter devotion to others took a toll on her health. The restrictions Conrad placed on her, and the beatings given if she disobeyed, only served to strengthen and harden Elizabeth's will.

Despite an offer of sanctuary from a Magyar noble, she could not bear to leave the place she believed the poor needed her. She died weak from lack of nutrition and austerity, aged just 23. In 1235, she was declared a saint.

*Right* St Elizabeth of Hungary *holding a basket of flowers (Ambrogio Lorenzetti, 14th century).*

# CLARE OF ASSISI

LIKE HER NEIGHBOUR, ST FRANCIS, ST CLARE ABANDONED A LIFE OF INHERITED EASE TO SERVE GOD. FOLLOWING THE FRANCISCAN WAY, SHE FOUNDED THE ORDER NOW KNOWN AS THE POOR CLARES.

**KEY FACTS**
*Founder of Poor Clares*
DATES: *1194–1253*
BIRTH PLACE: *Assisi*
PATRON OF: *Embroiderers, television*
FEAST DAY: *11 August*
EMBLEM: *Lilies for purity, holding a monstrance, and scimitar for triumph over Saracens*

Having declined two offers of marriage, Clare decided that her greatest desire in life was not to be found in the aristocratic world into which she was born, but in devotion to God. She knew that Francis in the same village of Assisi had made the same decision a few years earlier, and now she determined to emulate him.

Clare was 18 when she made her way to the chapel of the Portiuncula, where Francis based himself, two miles from Assisi. As a test of her commitment, he told Clare to don sackcloth and go and beg in the streets of her home town. Francis then asked her to dress as a bride, and in his chapel he solemnly shaved her head and received her vows.

*Above St Clare (attributed to Simone Martini and others, 14th century).*

## POOR CLARE

Francis set up a house for her nearby at San Damiano. He drew up a Rule following the example he had set himself, of poverty, chastity and obedience, and in 1216 she was made abbess.

Clare added another rule, forbidding ownership of any property, personal or communal. The order, which her widowed mother and sister also joined, was known as the Second Order of St Francis, and later the Poor Clares.

The nuns survived by begging, but the Church disapproved of this undignified public display. At the time, nuns lived in enclosed communities,

*Right The Miracles of St Clare of Assisi, fresco (Lorenzo Lotto, 1523–24).*

financed by church rents. She also struggled to have her rules of austerity approved, but eventually won her way in 1253.

However, these measures of self-denial seriously affected her health. During bouts of illness, she would lie in bed embroidering religious vestments. It was said that once, when too ill to attend Christmas Mass, Clare saw the Nativity crib projected on her cell wall and heard singing as if she were in church. As a result, she has become the patron of television.

She never wavered in her belief in God's protection. When the Saracens attacked Assisi, she was said to have held up a monstrance (vessel for the Eucharist) on the city walls in defiance, and the infidel army withdrew.

For 40 years, Clare lived with poverty and prayer, guiding her nuns, who later adopted an even harsher regime than her own. The order spread through Europe, but the English convents did not survive the Reformation.

# HYACINTH OF CRACOW

THE EXPANSION OF THE DOMINICAN ORDER OF FRIARS ACROSS NORTHERN AND EASTERN EUROPE WAS SPEARHEADED BY ST HYACINTH. HE ALSO FOUNDED THE CHURCH IN POLAND.

### KEY FACTS
*Evangelist*
DATES: *1185–1257*
BIRTH PLACE: *Kammien (Grosstein), Poland*
FEAST DAY: *15 August*
EMBLEM: *Dominican friar's habit*

A determined missionary, he was one of the key first-generation evangelizers of the Dominican Order. He helped to establish Christianity in his native Poland, and some claim he also took the faith to Russia, Lithuania and Sweden, though the historical accuracy of this is uncertain.

Legends abound of him working miracles and travelling great distances to spread the gospel. The crucial moment in his life came during a visit to Rome accompanied by his uncle, the Bishop of Cracow. Hyacinth was already a priest, but on meeting St Dominic, he was overwhelmed by the founder's strength of faith and compassion. Thus inspired, the young priest felt a profound conversion and was received into the order of preachers.

In 1221, he went to Cracow, where he set up five Dominican monasteries as centres of learning. However, his missions to the East were severley hampered by invasions from Tartar hordes that began in 1238.

*Left* Vision of St Hyacinth *(Domenikos Theotocopoulos, El Greco, late 16th or early 17th century).*

# ALBERT THE GREAT

THIS GERMAN DOMINICAN HELPED LAY THE FOUNDATIONS OF MODERN SCIENCE.

### KEY FACTS
*Doctor of the Church*
DATES: *1200–80*
BIRTH PLACE: *Swabia*
PATRON OF: *Students of the natural sciences*
FEAST DAY: *15 November*
EMBLEM: *Dominican friar, scientific instruments*

An inspiring teacher, Albert was the only scholar of his time to be called "Great". After joining the Dominicans in Padua, he taught in Germany, where Thomas Aquinas was his student.

After spells in Paris and Cologne, Albert was made Bishop of Ratisbon in 1260. But Albert longed to pursue his writings on geology, astronomy, chemistry, and geography, so asked to be released from office after just two years. His scientific observations filled 38 volumes. His theological texts also contain insight. Like Aquinas later, Albert asserted there was no conflict between faith and reason. The two are joined in harmony, he said, but some truth can only be grasped through faith. Albert was made a Doctor of the Church in 1931.

*Left* Portrait of St Albertus Magnus *(Joos van Gent, c.1475).*

# FOURTEEN HOLY HELPERS

IN THE 14TH CENTURY, THE BLACK DEATH STRUCK TERROR IN THE POPULATIONS OF EUROPE. AS A SOURCE OF RELIEF TO ROMAN CATHOLIC VICTIMS, THE POPE SET UP A SPECIAL GROUP OF SAINTS.

A magnificent chapel was built in the 18th century to house the statues of the Fourteen Holy Helpers. Within its Baroque interior, massed in a circle around the altar, stand 14 figures, each representing a saint. The Vierzehnheiligen Sanctuary was built in Germany in veneration of these saints, who were first grouped together during the Black Death of the 14th century.

## IMMORTAL PERIL
This disease was terrifying in its symptoms and caused rapid death. People were dying before they received the last rites.

"REMEMBER THE DANGERS THAT SURROUND US IN THIS VALE OF TEARS, AND INTERCEDE FOR US IN ALL OUR NEEDS AND ADVERSITIES. AMEN"

A PRAYER OF INVOCATION TO THE FOURTEEN HOLY HELPERS

This both saddened and frightened the faithful, who believed that without receiving this sacrament, they would forego the essential final step on the journey to heaven. To compensate in some measure for the lack of a priest available to serve the last rites, sufferers could call upon any one of these specified saints to intercede on their behalf for the absolution of their sins.

Some of the Helpers are martyrs, others are associated with certain diseases. Some, such as St Christopher, are even legendary. A collective feast day was assigned for all Holy Helpers on 8 August.

## MEANING THROUGH ART
As well as the statues in the sanctuary in Germany, there are many other representations of the Fourteen Holy Helpers, particularly from the 14th and 15th centuries.

Images of the figures were usually placed near church altars, often with Mary, the Blessed Virgin, cradling the Baby Jesus, or with St Christopher carrying the Christ Child on his shoulders.

*Left* St Roch Praying to the Virgin for an End to the Plague *(Jacques-Louis David, 1780).*

*Above* View of the Town Hall of Marseilles During the Plague of 1720 *(Michel Serre, 18th century).*

Paintings and sculptures often represent these saints as distorted, or holding awkward positions to indicate the symptoms they are believed to cure. Clothes or an animal companion might give a symbolic meaning or denote their traditional significance.

Indeed, some paintings are so grotesque in their depictions of diseases and suffering that the artists seem intent on bringing home the full horror of the Black Death to the viewer.

## CULTUS IN EUROPE

For centuries, these images attracted large crowds. The cultus was strong in Germany, Hungary

### THE PROTECTORS

- **Acacius** and **Denys of Paris** are called upon for headaches.
- **Barbara** intercedes for fevers and sudden death.
- **George** and **Pantaleon** protect domestic animals.
- **Blaise** guards against sore throats.
- **Catherine of Alexandria** and **Christopher** are patrons of sudden death.
- **Cyricus** helps to ward off temptation.
- **Margaret of Antioch** aids women in childbirth.
- **Vitus** prevents epilepsy.
- **Erasmus** is associated with intestinal troubles.
- **Eustace** helps out in difficult situations.
- **Giles** is invoked by lepers, the physically handicapped, and nursing mothers.

and Scandinavia. But it never commanded much of a following in Italy, France or England.

The numbers of pilgrims decreased after the Reformation. Now this group of saints is relatively obscure to most Roman Catholic worshippers.

*Above* Martyrdom of St Erasmus *(Nicolas Poussin, 1629).*

The list of saints is generally stable, but substitutions were made in some regions or cities where the veneration of particular saints was strong. The Holy Helpers were invoked to guard against specific illnesses – and these included diseases suffered by animals as well as humans.

## THE BLACK DEATH

The origin of this plague remains a mystery. It was a virulent epidemic that swept across Europe in 1348. It caused rapid putrefaction of the sufferer's body, which turned black before death occurred. In Europe, 25 million died, including one-third of the English population. The numbers of victims in Asia and North Africa are unknown.

There were other outbreaks of plague in Europe but none so devastating as the Black Death. Its cause has been attributed variously to unknown substances, germs introduced by sailors, or a predominance of rats. The lack of hygiene found in medieval cities was a major factor.

*Above* Black Death at Tournai *(Gilles Le Muisit, 1349).*

# ALEXANDER NEVSKI

A WARRIOR COUNT WAS CANONIZED BY THE EASTERN ORTHODOX CHURCH FOR HIS VALIANT DEFENCE OF RUSSIA, AND FOR ASSURING PEACE FOR HIS COMPATRIOTS DURING THE MONGOL OCCUPATION.

**KEY FACTS**
*National hero of Russia*
DATES: *1220–63*
BIRTH PLACE: *Novgorod, Russia*
PATRON OF: *Russia*
FEAST DAY: *23 November*
EMBLEM: *Knight's armour*

As the Grand Duke of Vladimir, Alexander Nevski spent much of his early life in wars against neighbouring nations of Europe. His title "Nevski" was earned by his decisive victory over the Swedes at the River Neva in 1240.

Born a prince and patriot of Russia, military pride rode next to devotion to God. Integrity of faith was an essential component of all Nevski's military expeditions. The belief that God was not on the side of force but on the side of truth and justice was one of the guiding maxims of his faith.

Major campaigns included repelling the Swedes from Novgorod and Pskov. Lithuanians were other foes, as were the Knights of the Teutonic Order, a

*Below The silver gilt tomb of Alexander Nevski, held in The State Hermitage Museum, St Petersburg (1747–52).*

*Left* Alexander Nevski *(Afanasiy Yefremovich Kulikov), 20th century.*

noble Germanic troop formed during the Crusader wars. In a triumphant battle on the banks of the frozen Lake Peipous in 1242, Nevski repelled the enemy. In so doing he put an end to all future claims of conquest by the Knights.

TARTAR OVERLORDS
Perhaps equally as important for Russia as these military conquests was the time Nevski had to spend placating the occupying Tartars. Between 1237 and 1240, these fearsome successors of Genghis Khan invaded the principalities of eastern and central Russia.

The control these menacing hordes exerted over his country posed quite a different problem, requiring careful handling. From 1240, Russia was held in servitude, paying high tribute and penalties. Through clever diplomacy, Alexander Nevski achieved some key concessions, which boosted national morale. He persuaded the Mongols to drop compulsory military service, and negotiated reductions in the tribute demanded by these overlords.

His reputation as a national hero has grown since his death. In recognition of his national status, the Russian Orthodox Church raised a division during World War II named after this patriotic saint. Many street names in Russia are also named in his honour.

# BONAVENTURE

RECOGNIZED AS THE "SECOND FOUNDER" OF THE FRANCISCANS,
ST BONAVENTURE INTRODUCED REFORMS THAT EDUCATED THE
FRIARS AND MODERATED AUSTERE TENDENCIES WITHIN THE ORDER.

The "Seraphic Doctor", as Bonaventure was known for his intellectual and mystical qualities, established a high reputation in the Church for his reforming theology. Choosing not to follow in his father's footsteps as a medical doctor, Bonaventure opted instead to become a Franciscan in 1243. It was an interesting choice for a clever man, since the Franciscan order discouraged intellectual pursuits. But he was happy to lead a life of frugal simplicity.

## REFORMS
In 1257, Bonaventure became general of the Franciscan Order in Paris, where he had studied. Because the founder, St Francis of Assisi, was detached from formal learning, there were no books to be found in the monasteries.

Yet Bonaventure could see that if the friars were to be effective as teachers they needed to be educated. They would need books and libraries to house them.

Another problem was that St Francis' Rules forbade the ownership of property. So Bonaventure had to persuade his followers to accept a different model. Being a patient man with moderate views, he was prepared to travel to the many Franciscan monasteries and Poor Clare convents to convince the religious that these changes made sense.

For the reforms he thus achieved, as well as the curbs he placed on the more austere practices of some members, he is regarded as the "second founder" of the Franciscans. Disliking high office, he once refused to become Archbishop of York, but later was compelled to be cardinal-bishop of Albano. In this role, he brokered a reconciliation with the Greek church at Constantinople.

The peace turned out to be a temporary one, though Bonaventure never knew this, since he died shortly afterwards.

**KEY FACTS**
*General of the Franciscan Friars,
known as the Seraphic Doctor*
DATES: *c.1218–74*
BIRTH PLACE: *Bagnoreggio, Italy*
PATRON OF: *Theologians, farmers,
porters, weavers*
FEAST DAY: *15 July*
EMBLEM: *Franciscan gown,
bishop's mitre. His cloak is
bordered with images of seraphim,
the highest order of angels*

*Below* Saint Bonaventure
Taking the Franciscan Habit
(*Francisco Herrera the Elder,
17th century*).

# THOMAS AQUINAS

THE "ANGELIC DOCTOR" WAS AN INTELLECTUAL GIANT OF THE
MEDIEVAL CHURCH WHO EXPANDED CHRISTIAN THINKING TO
ESTABLISH A COMPREHENSIVE DOCTRINE OF THE CATHOLIC FAITH.

This well-built man was dubbed the "dumb ox" for his gentle courtesy and because he was thought to be a little slow of mind. But as his energy and output was to demonstrate, Thomas Aquinas outstripped all his contemporaries in intellectual capacity.

One writer said that the amount of study required to produce all Aquinas' books would take several normal lifetimes. However, his aristocratic family did not share the young man's enthusiasm to join the Dominicans, a mendicant order that lived by begging.

## HOUSE ARREST
His family, who regarded the mendicants' activities as shameful, had educated Thomas at the reputable Benedictine monastery at Monte Cassino, whose abbot was related to the Aquino family. When the determined prodigy nevertheless joined the Black

Friars at the age of 21, his brothers kidnapped him and imprisoned him at the family home.

But Thomas would not relent. His family even sent a beautiful girl to tempt him from his chosen path. Paintings depict him brandishing a burning stick to ward away the temptress.

## FAITH AND REASON
Eventually released, Thomas went to Cologne, Germany, to study under St Albert the Great. This teacher provided the groundwork for much of Aquinas' theology. Thenceforth, he was to spend his

"WE SHOULD SHOW
HONOUR TO THE SAINTS
OF GOD, AS BEING
MEMBERS OF CHRIST,
THE CHILDREN AND
FRIENDS OF GOD, AND
OUR INTERCESSORS.
THEREFORE, IN MEMORY
OF THEM WE OUGHT TO
HONOUR ANY RELICS OF
THEIRS IN A FITTING
MANNER."

ST THOMAS AQUINAS

*Left* Temptation of St Thomas
Aquinas *(Diego Rodríguez de Silva
y Velásquez, 17th century).*

life moving back and forth between France and Italy as a teacher and academic.

In tandem with St Albert the Great, Thomas Aquinas believed in the harmony of faith and reason. Hitherto, theological points of debate had taken the Bible as their authority. Now Aquinas was asserting that reasoned argument was authority in itself because God gave mankind the power of reason.

## ARISTOTLE AND ISLAM

Aquinas held that everything comes from God. He said that at the end of their lives humans return to God as to their home.

A perfect life was one that combined contemplation with action, since it is only through prayer that we can know the will of God. At the time that Aquinas

*Below* St Thomas Aquinas *(Abraham Jansz Diepenbeeck, c.1640–50).*

lived, Islamic scholars were bringing ideas of the ancient Greek philosophers, such as Aristotle, back to Europe. In debate with Muslims, Aquinas produced an entire book responding to their writings.

His intellect aimed not only at the higher reaches of the Church. Some of the most beautiful hymns written for Mass have been ascribed to him and he produced prayers and expositions of the Creed for the ordinary believer. He was also a preacher, giving sermons on the Ten Commandments and key tenets of the Christian faith.

## SPIRITUAL END

In about 1266, Aquinas began his *Summa Theologica*, a study of all the Christian mysteries, which ran to five volumes. He never finished the work because in 1272 he had a profound mystical experience while attending Mass.

The effect of receiving a vision of God, as he reported, was so overwhelming that he felt his intellect no longer adequate. Indeed, he is famously reputed to have said that all he had written to date was "like straw" compared to this spiritual experience.

Not long after this event, he prepared to attend the Council at Lyons but was taken ill on the journey. He died at the abbey of Fossanuova aged 43.

*Left* St Thomas Aquinas wearing Dominican garb and praying at the altar, from Libro de Horas de Alfonso el Magnifico, *the vellum prayer book of Alfonso V of Aragon (Spanish School, c.1442).*

### SUMMA THEOLOGICA

Having produced a text, *Summa contra Gentes*, that presented the faith to non-believers, Thomas Aquinas set about writing his *magnum opus* to instruct beginners in Roman Catholic theology. Running to five volumes, *Summa Theologica* covers a great variety of subjects.

The first volume explains all that emanates from God. The second volume explains the psychology of human activity and its organization. The third asserts that humans return to God as to their natural home. The fourth volume discusses the Holy Spirit, and a life of meditation and action. And the fifth, unfinished, summarizes faith.

*Above* Title page from Summa Theologica *on vellum (French School, 14th century).*

# AGNES OF BOHEMIA

PRINCESS AGNES USED HER WEALTH TO FINANCE HER LIFE AS A HUMBLE NUN WORKING WITH LEPERS. SHE WAS CANONIZED BY POPE JOHN PAUL II IN 1989.

**KEY FACTS**
*Princess, abbess*
DATES: *d. 1282*
BIRTH PLACE: *Bohemia*
FEAST DAY: *6 March*
EMBLEM: *Poor Clare habit*

The daughter of the King of Bohemia (now part of the Czech Republic) was once betrothed to Emperor Frederick II of the Holy Roman Empire. However, this marriage was not one she wished to fulfil, so she wrote to the pope asking to be released from the engagement.

Frederick retreated with grace, and accepted that his fiancée preferred to "wed the king of heaven". Agnes' family were also supportive. On becoming king, her brother funded various projects of hers, including new monasteries, a hospital and the first Poor Clare convent north of the Alps, located in Prague.

Agnes became its abbess, having taken her vows in 1236. St Clare herself sent five nuns to help establish the convent. The severe rules of poverty demanded by the order were faithfully followed by Agnes for 40 years until her death.

*Left* St Agnes in Prison *(José de Ribera, 1641).*

# NICHOLAS OF TOLENTINO

THIS AUGUSTINIAN FRIAR SPENT MANY YEARS AS A PREACHER AND GAINED A REPUTATION AS A MIRACLE HEALER. AT TOLENTINO HE BROUGHT HARMONY TO A TOWN TORN BY STRIFE.

**KEY FACTS**
*Augustinian friar, miracle worker*
DATES: *1245–1305*
BIRTH PLACE: *Sant'Angelo, Italy*
PATRON OF: *The dying and souls in purgatory, babies and mothers, fires, sick animals*
FEAST DAY: *6 March*
EMBLEM: *Augustinian habit, basket of bread rolls, star on his chest*

On hearing an Augustinian friar preaching that the best form of love comes from beyond the world, Nicholas became so inspired that he decided to join the order.

For some years, he lived successfully as a wandering preacher in the Italian district of Ancona, on the Adriatic coast. He gradually aquired a reputation for healing people, including, in about 1270, restoring the sight to a blind woman in Cingoli.

Shortly afterwards, he heard heavenly voices calling him to Tolentino, a town devastated by

*Above* Nicholas at the Battle of San Romano *(Paolo Uccello, c. 1450–60).*

family feuds and religious schism. For the rest of his life, Nicholas devoted his energies to mending broken relations in the little town.

He fostered harmony at domestic level, caring for children and the dying and criminals. Not surprisingly, Nicholas became much loved for his kindness and sincerity of faith – it is said the entire city turned up to listen to his preaching. After a long illness, he died and was deeply mourned.

# ELIZABETH OF PORTUGAL

A SPANISH PRINCESS, MARRIED TO A PORTUGUESE KING, BECAME A SYMBOL OF RECONCILIATION BOTH AT THE DOMESTIC LEVEL AND AT THE HIGHEST LEVEL OF INTERNATIONAL DIPLOMACY.

**KEY FACTS**
*Queen of Portugal*
DATES: *1271–1336*
BIRTH PLACE: *Aragon, Spain*
PATRON OF: *Difficult marriages*
FEAST DAY: *4 July*
EMBLEM: *Crown*

The daughter of Peter III of Aragon was married at the age of 12 to King Denis of Portugal. Though her husband became cruel and abusive to Elizabeth, she followed the Christian teaching of turning the other cheek. In time, her husband converted to the faith.

Elizabeth founded hospitals and orphanages, and cared for abused prostitutes. After the death of her husband, she made a pilgrimage to

St James the Great's shrine at Compostela and became a Franciscan tertiary (lay member).

Although Elizabeth wished to live in modest obscurity, she was called upon to soothe the poor relations between Portugal and Castile. She died at Estremoz but was buried in the Poor Clares convent at Coimbra.

*Left* St Elizabeth of Portugal *(Francisco Zurbarán, 1640).*

# ROCH

THIS MYSTERIOUS SAINT, WHO WORKED HEROICALLY DURING A PLAGUE IN ITALY, WAS SAID TO HAVE MIRACULOUSLY SURVIVED THE DISEASE HIMSELF, BUT THEN PERISHED IN PRISON FALSELY ACCUSED.

**KEY FACTS**
*One of the Fourteen Holy Helpers*
DATES: *c.1350–80*
BIRTH PLACE: *Montpelier, France*
PATRON OF: *Istanbul, contagious diseases, physicians, surgeons, prisoners, cattle*
FEAST DAY: *17 August*
EMBLEM: *Plague sore on his thigh, dog at his feet, angel, bread*

Also known as Rocco or Roc, Roch is remembered chiefly for nursing plague victims in medieval Italy. It was in a time of great desperation that this young man came to do good public service. Born to a wealthy merchant family in Montpelier, France, Roch chose early in life to be a hermit and pilgrim.

It is believed he lived in Rome but was staying in Piacenza when a plague broke out. By all accounts, he exhausted himself nursing humans, and even animals, before falling victim to the disease himself. Not wishing to become a focus of concern, Roch crawled to a wood to face

*Above* St Roch is shown healing victims of the plague (Jacopo Robusti Tintoretto, 1549).

death. But legend has it that a dog brought him bread to eat and an angel cured him of the disease.

On recovering, he returned home whereupon his uncle did not recognize him, or refused to do so. Roch was then imprisoned, accused of being a fraud or spy.

He died behind bars in Lombardy. Miracle cures were later claimed at his grave, and believers started calling upon him for help at times of epidemic.

# CATHERINE OF SIENA

CATHERINE'S AGGRESSIVE SPIRITUAL BELIEFS DIVIDED PUBLIC OPINION ABOUT HER TRUE UNDERSTANDING OF THE FAITH. SOME THOUGHT HER HYSTERICAL, OTHERS AN EXEMPLARY VISIONARY.

**KEY FACTS**
*Dominican tertiary*
DATES: *1347–80*
BIRTH PLACE: *Siena*
PATRON OF: *Italy, Italian nurses*
FEAST DAY: *29 April*
EMBLEM: *Dominican tertiary habit, stigmata, holding a cross, crown of thorns, lily*

Like Hildegard of Bingen, this remarkable woman was a mystic who experienced visions and wrote meaningful religious texts. Both also became involved in worldly affairs.

Catherine was the youngest in a family of 25 children. Her twin sister died at birth. And aged six, she is said to have had her first vision of Jesus.

She used to say a Hail Mary on each step of the staircase while ascending or descending. Frightened and angered by her behaviour, her family insisted on her working incessantly, never allowing her to be alone. However, her patience

*Below* Saint Catherine of Siena Exchanging Her Heart with Christ *(Giovanni di Paolo, 15th century). Her heart is held in her fist.*

*Left* Saint Catherine of Siena *(Giovanni Battista Tiepolo, 1746).*

and obedience convinced her father of her holiness and he permitted her to become a Dominican tertiary.

## ZEAL AND STIGMATA

She lived a solitary life of prayer until 1366, when she was said to have received a vision of Mary, the Blessed Virgin, who led her to Christ. Catherine was convinced she had received a wedding ring given by Christ, though no one else could see the jewellery.

After this experience, Catherine went out into the world and began to preach. A band of followers gathered round her, referring to her as "mama".

She was energetic as a preacher and not all the citizens of her hometown, Siena, admired her style. Some thought her hysterical. But she won respect from the pope after admonishing people to go on a crusade to the Holy Land. In 1375, while visiting Pisa, Catherine suffered pangs of pain, and claimed she was marked by the stigmata (wounds identified with those of the Crucifixion). Again, none could see the scars, but on her death they became clearly visible.

## THE AVIGNON POPES

In all her contact with the public, Catherine had developed a talent for mediation, which brought her into Church politics. For some 75 years, the popes had lived in exile at Avignon. Now Catherine became involved in persuading Pope Gregory XI to return to the papal seat in Rome. Gregory responded to her quasi-mystical call and sailed for the city in 1376.

After Gregory's death, French factions in Avignon selected a rival pope in opposition to his successor, Urban VI. Catherine tried to settle the dispute but aroused such anger in her opponents they threatened her life. In 1380, she dreamt she was being crushed by a ship that symbolized the Church. Shortly afterwards, she was paralysed for days by a stroke before she died.

# BRIDGET OF SWEDEN

ROYAL ADVISOR, NURSE OF THE BLACK DEATH, AND MORAL
CRUSADER, BRIDGET STOPPED AT NOTHING IN PURSUIT OF RIGHT.
SHE PROPHESIED DAMNATION, AND EVEN CRITICIZED THE POPE.

**KEY FACTS**
*Founder of Order*
DATES: *1303–73*
BIRTH PLACE: *Uppland*
PATRON OF: *Sweden, pilgrims*
FEAST DAY: *23 July*
EMBLEM: *Monogram of Christ
(HIS), candle, book, pen, dressed
as a widow or pilgrim*

The daughter of the governor
of Uppland served in the
Swedish court as lady-in-waiting,
moral adviser to the feckless royal
family. In 1344, Bridget (or
Birgitta) went with her nobleman
husband on the long pilgrimage
to Compostela in Spain, but he
died on their return journey.

Now widowed, though with
eight children from her marriage,
Bridget for a time directed her
energy into founding a monastic
order, called the Most Holy
Saviour, or Bridgettines.

Despite the Black Death then
sweeping across Europe, Bridget
travelled to Rome and nursed the

sick there. After reputedly
receiving a vision of St Francis,
she went on to Assisi and spent
two years visiting Italian shrines.

It was said Bridget had the
power of prophecy about political
events. She is believed to have
used this facility to condemn to
damnation weak or corrupt heads
of state. The fearless nun even
dared once to criticize the pope.

*Left St Bridget in a Portuguese
vellum from the 17th century.*

# JOHN OF NEPOMUK

A DEVOUT ADVISER TO THE ARCHBISHOP OF PRAGUE UPHELD HIS
CLERICAL DUTIES TO THE POINT OF MARTYRDOM RATHER THAN
COMPROMISE THE CHURCH IN THE FACE OF A POWERFUL TYRANT.

**KEY FACTS**
*Martyr*
DATES: *c.1345–93*
BIRTH PLACE: *Nepomuk,
Bohemia*
PATRON OF: *Slovakia, of
confessors, bridges and protection
against slander*
FEAST DAY: *5 January*
EMBLEM: *Seven stars*

As vicar general, John of
Nepomuk (or Nepomucen)
became the close aide of the
Archbishop of Prague on matters
of church-state relations. When, in
1378, Wenceslaus IV became King
of Bohemia, these relations took a
turn for the worse.

A legend says that being a man
given to violent rages, Wenceslaus
became insanely jealous of his wife
and harassed John to reveal her
confessional secrets. The king so
mistrusted priests that he planned
to set up a monastery manned by
his own priests. To this end, when

the abbot of the rich Benedictine
monastery at Kladruby died,
Wenceslaus wanted to appoint his
successor in order to gain control
of the revenues from the land.

However, in anticipation, the
priests appointed a new abbot the
moment the old incumbent died.
Learning this, Wenceslaus believed
John to be the instigator.

He first beat the priests, then
tied John up, his ankles bound to
his head, and hurled him into the
River Moldau at Prague. Seven
stars were said to glow over the
site of his drowning. John was

greatly mourned
when his body
was found the
next day.

*Right A statue
of St John of
Nepomuk with a
halo of stars, on
the Charles Bridge
in Prague.*

# WARRIOR SAINTS

WHETHER SOLDIERS OF WAR OR FOR PEACE, MANY MEN AND
WOMEN SINCE THE BIRTH OF CHRISTIANITY HAVE BEEN CANONIZED
FOR DEFENDING THEIR FAITH AND GOING INTO BATTLE.

Throughout history, soldiers have often claimed that the saints have aided and protected them in battle. Many warriors have converted to Christianity and died for their faith, or fought bloody wars to protect their right to worship their God. There are others whose inspiration came from Christ himself and who took to the path of peace.

## HEAVENLY INSPIRATION
The archangel Michael, "captain of the heavenly host" and protector of Christian soldiers, has often appeared above battlefields or kept company with troops in combat. Joan of Arc identified him as helping spur her into battle.

In their long battle against Moorish invasion, the Spanish frequently called upon the apostle St James the Great, patron saint of Spain. After the miraculous victory at the Battle of Clavijo (AD 844), the soldiers claimed that James had appeared in their midst in full armour, sword in one hand and banner in the other, riding a white charger.

## SOLDIER SAINTS
Since the days of the Roman Empire, there have been military men who have rejected their earthly masters and pledged to serve only Christ.

Known in the Eastern Orthodox Church as the "Great Martyr", St Demetrius was much admired as a warrior saint. He was a soldier in the Roman army in the early 4th century, who converted to Christianity and was subsequently put to death.

*Above St Maurice, fresco detail (artist unknown, 15th century).*

A great soldier saint and inspiration to warriors and crusaders, St George is always depicted as a knight in armour. Although most of what we know is legendary, he is venerated throughout the Christian world. St George is thought to have been martyred at Lydda in Palestine around AD 303.

St Theodore, known as "the recruit", was a young Roman soldier. After his conversion to Christianity he refused to join his comrades in the worship of pagan gods. Tradition says that he also set fire to a pagan temple. He was martyred in the 4th century at Pontus (part of modern Turkey).

During birthday celebrations for the Roman emperors Diocletian and Maximian, a centurion named Marcellus threw off his soldier's belt crying, "I am a soldier of Christ, the eternal king, and from now I cease to serve you." Other Roman soldiers who

*Left Camillus of Lellis rescues hospital patients during the flooding of the Tiber in 1598 (Pierre Subleyras, 1745).*

converted expressed the same anti-military sentiments, such as St Julius who chose to die by the sword rather than serve a master on earth.

There are also great leaders who are much venerated because they were soldiers in service of Christ. St Stephen of Hungary, a skilled military strategist, set out to conquer the pagans in his country and force them to convert to the Christian faith. St Vladimir of Kiev is revered throughout Orthodox Russia as the man who brought Christianity to his country, although initially he used the army to impose the new faith.

## PEACEFUL PATH

Some soldier converts came to realize that the Christian life was not compatible with violence.

Martin of Tours, a young officer in the Roman army, asked for a discharge after his conversion. He announced, "I am Christ's soldier; I am not allowed to fight."

*Left Alexander Nevski (artist unknown, 1855).*

Much later, in the 16th century, St Camillus of Lellis was a mercenary or "soldier of fortune" who began nursing the sick and injured after his conversion. He is credited with organizing the first field ambulance unit, going into the battlefield to care for the wounded. St John of God was another mercenary whose conversion made him seek peace. He also turned to nursing and founded the Brothers Hospitallers.

During the Spanish Civil War of 1936–39, thousands of Christians fought for a country that was guided by the faith against their fellow citizens who wanted a secular regime. Hundreds of the Catholics who died were beatified by Pope John Paul II and are known as the Martyrs of the Spanish Civil War.

*Below St Demetrius (Serbian icon, 18th century).*

## THE CRUSADES

In the Middle Ages, European Christian countries mounted military campaigns to oust the Muslims from Jerusalem and give support to Christians isolated in the East.

There were eight Crusades in all, lasting from 1095 to 1272 and ending with the Muslims still in control. Vast sums of money and huge numbers of men were involved. The journey to the Holy Land involved travelling great distances and was often disrupted by battles on land and sea. The Crusaders often fought while weak with hunger and ravaged by disease.

The Crusaders believed they had God on their side and often experienced heavenly visions. They adopted St George and St Demetrius as patron saints after they appeared above the demoralized soldiers and led them to victory against the Saracens at the Siege of Antioch (1097–98).

King Louis IX of France led two disastrous crusades in 1248 and 1270. Although he was not victorious, he was venerated for his zeal in fighting for the Holy Land.

*Left The archangel Michael (Greek, c.14th century).*

*Above Manuscript illumination showing soldiers departing for the Crusades (c.1240–84).*

# JOAN OF ARC

As the girl warrior, Joan of Arc, perished in the fire prepared by Englishmen, one soldier was heard to cry out, "We are lost. We have burned a saint."

**KEY FACTS**
*Visionary, military leader*
Dates: *c.1412–31*
Birth Place: *Domrémy, France*
Patron of: *France, French soldiers*
Feast Day: *30 May*
Emblem: *Armour, battle banner*

Joan of Arc is one of the most remarkable women in history. Her life has inspired books, films, poems and paintings, yet she remains mysterious. She was courageous and indifferent to pain, a good horsewoman and deft with her sword. Yet she began as a simple illiterate peasant, at home with domestic work.

How did she convince a royal court that she could be a military leader? Where did she learn to lead an army on horseback and wield a weapon? Brought up in the Champagne area of France during the Hundred Years War between England and France, Joan was used to living in a war-torn environment.

Her village was sympathetic to the royal house of Orléans. But across the river to the south, the peasants sided with the dukes of

*Below* Joan of Arc Kissing the Sword of Deliverance *(Dante Gabriel Rossetti, 1863).*

Burgundy and the English. When she was 13, Joan said she heard God speak to her. As a result, she vowed to remain a virgin, devoted to the will of Christ.

## DIVINE VOICES

At 16, Joan claimed frequent visits by the archangel Michael and two saints, Catherine of Alexandria and Margaret of Antioch. She said the saints were dressed as queens and they instructed her to save France and crown the dauphin, Charles, as King of France.

Ignoring pleas from her father to remain, Joan prepared to travel to the court of Charles. To help her cause, she dressed as a man.

Entering the royal quarters, Joan unerringly approached the dauphin. He was a frivolous youth who hid among his courtiers to trick the girl. But she was said to have had a divine recognition of

"It is better to be alone with God: His friendship will not fail me, nor His counsel, nor His love. In His strength I will dare, and dare, and dare, until I die."

WORDS GIVEN TO JOAN IN *ST JOAN* BY G.B. SHAW

him. Confounded, the young royal listened to her announcement that God had sent her to help him and his kingdom. After close questioning from religious and military leaders, Joan won permission to raise arms.

INTO BATTLE

Stealing a sword from behind a church altar, Joan prepared for battle bearing a banner painted with the words "Jesus Maria". The people of nearby Vaucouleurs gave her a horse and a man's suit of white armour.

On 7 May 1429, Joan led her soldiers into war and banished the English from Orléans. She went on to win victories in Patay and Tours as well. But her greatest moment of triumph came when she stood beside the dauphin as he was crowned King Charles VII of France, at Rheims in July of that year. However, the indolent Charles neglected Joan, who took

*Below* The Burning of Joan of Arc on 30 May 1431 *(lithograph of the French School, 19th century).*

*Above* The Entrance of Joan of Arc into Orléans on 8 May 1429 *(Jean-Jacques Scherrer, 1887).*

it upon herself to continue the fight. But in Compiègne she was captured by the Burgundians who then sold her to the English.

WITCHCRAFT

Joan suffered nine months of brutal confinement charged with witchcraft and heresy. Her decision to dress as a man was deemed to be proof of her heresy. Barely 19 years old, the transcript of her trial in Rouen, then in English hands, makes sad reading. The court found her guilty of heresy.

As she approached the scene of her dreadful punishment in Rouen's market square, she asked for a crucifix. This she kissed and was heard to cry "Jesus" as the flames licked round her. Before her body was consumed, her corpse was displayed naked to the crowd to prove she was indeed a woman who had "wickedly" paraded as a man.

To prevent any veneration of the relics, her ashes were thrown into the River Seine. Her family petitioned to clear her name. In 1456, the pope overturned the

guilty verdict. For centuries she was popularly held to be a saint but the Church waited until 1920 before granting canonization.

Joan was not a martyr, but a virgin who lived her faith. She is the first Christian patriot, her love of country entwined with her religion. Even the English went so far as to erect a statue of St Joan in Winchester Cathedral.

VOICE OF A LEGEND

There is a tradition that Margaret of Antioch, who may never even have existed, spoke to Joan. Legend claims Margaret was a Christian exiled from home by a pagan father. She lived as a poor shepherdess until the governor of Antioch tried to seduce her. When she refused him, he tortured her. A dragon is said to have swallowed her, but she burst from it and survived. She promised divine protection, safeguards against devils, and fertility to the childless.

*Above* St Margaret *(Raffaello Sanzio Raphael, 16th century).*

# RITA OF CASCIA

AFTER CARING FOR HER WAYWARD FAMILY, ST RITA BECAME A NUN AND SUFFERED THE PAINS OF MORTIFICATION. HER RENOWN AS A HEALER MADE HER ONE OF THE FOURTEEN HOLY HELPERS.

**KEY FACTS**
*Widow, mystic*
DATES: *1377–1447*
BIRTH PLACE: *Roccaporena, Italy*
PATRON OF: *Those in desperate situations, parenthood, help for the infertile*
FEAST DAY: *22 May*
EMBLEM: *Crown of thorns, stigmata on forehead*

Born in a village in Umbria, Rita was brought up a pious girl. Indeed, she longed to devote herself to God. But she owed greater allegiance to her parents' wishes than to her own and so she submitted to a marriage that they arranged.

Unhappily, Rita found herself bound to a violent, unfaithful husband. Furthermore, their sons followed his example. Despite the difficulties she had to endure, she patiently cared for her family.

Rita prayed unceasingly that Jesus might be revealed to them. And in time the husband seemed to repent and convert to the faith, only to come home one day mortally wounded in a vendetta.

Her sons swore vengeance for his death, so Rita prayed for their death before they committed any dreadful deeds. They then fell ill. Inspired by their mother's gentle nursing, the two sons repented of their evil ways and were forgiven before they too died.

### THORN OF GOD

Now widowed, Rita applied to join an Augustinian convent in Cascia. She was refused on the ground of not being a virgin. But persistent entreaties on her part eventually succeeded and, at the age of 52, Rita was admitted to the convent.

She proved a devout sister who never flinched from the austere rules. Rita made it her special duty to nurse the sick and counsel sinners outside the nunnery. Her kindliness was said to inspire many converts.

At the age of 60, Rita attended a sermon centred on the crown of thorns. As she listened to the words describing Jesus as "king of the Jews", being forced to wear a mock crown, Rita suffered a dreadful stab of pain. She later found a wound, such as that which a thorn might cause, on the middle of her forehead.

The wound did not disappear but suppurated. It became so offensive that, for the last 16 years of her life, Rita lived largely as a recluse. On a pilgrimage to Rome in 1450, her wound disappeared, only to return when she was back

*Below Detail from* Three Depictions of St Rita of Cascia *(colour lithograph of the French School, 20th century).*

*Above Detail from* Three Depictions of St Rita of Cascia *(colour lithograph of the French School, 20th century).*

in her convent. Rita contracted tuberculosis, and thus a life of devotion, prayer and obedience was ended in 1447.

Miracles were attributed to Rita after her death. Her body, housed in a grand tomb, has remained incorrupt to the present day. A school, a hospital and an orphanage have been built around the tomb, which forms part of the Cascia convent buildings.

# FRA ANGELICO

THE PRIOR AT A MONASTERY IN TUSCANY BECAME KNOWN AS THE "ANGELIC BROTHER" FOR HIS BEAUTIFUL SPIRITUAL PAINTINGS. FRA ANGELICO REGARDED HIS ARTISTIC WORK AS ACTS OF PRAYER.

**KEY FACTS**
*Artist monk*
DATES: *1387–1455*
BIRTH PLACE: *Vicchio, Italy*
PATRON OF: *Artists*
FEAST DAY: *18 February*
EMBLEM: *Paintbrush*

Guido di Pietro, as he was christened, was born in the mountains beyond Florence, Italy. He joined the Dominican Order in Fiesole as a young man and soon became known as Fra Angelico, or "angelic brother".

An artist who thought of painting as an act of prayer, Fra Angelico produced works entirely religious in subject. Indeed, the spirituality of his work prompted the Victorian art critic, John Ruskin, to declare that the talented monk was an inspired saint rather than an artist.

## MEDICI PATRONS

Initially, the monastery trained Fra Angelico in manuscript painting under guidance from an older monk, Lorenzo Monaco. When the monks were moved to San Marco convent in Florence, the powerful and wealthy Medici family paid for enlargements of the building.

With his teacher, Fra Angelico painted the new walls with a series of murals depicting sacred scenes. He coupled the elements of medieval work with the new scientific knowledge of his own Renaissance era.

Thus his style appealed to the contemporary tastes but did not alienate traditional viewers. It is the beauty of his work, with its mystical quality, that still inspires.

In 1445, he was called to Rome to produce wall paintings at the Vatican, in St Peter's

*Above* Fresco detail from The Deeds of the Antichrist *(Luca Signorelli, c.1499–1502). In the foreground, Fra Angelico (right) is depicted standing next to Signorelli (left).*

Cathedral and the pope's private rooms. And four years later he went to Orvieto in Spain to decorate the vault of the chapel, though he was called to monastic office before finishing the work.

## PRIOR AT FIESOLE

From 1449 to 1452, he was prior of the monastery at Fiesole. He then returned to Rome, where he died after three years.

His works, which serve a contemplative purpose, are regarded as "visual prayers". They brought him recognition from a public who would gaze at them in admiration. Many are preserved in religious buildings. Almost 600 years later, at the beatification of Fra Angelico, Pope John Paul II exclaimed, "Why do we need miracles? These are his miracles."

*Right* The Annunciation *(Fra Angelico, c.1440–45).*

# CASIMIR OF POLAND

ST CASIMIR IS CLAIMED AS PATRON BY POLAND, RUSSIA AND LITHUANIA, REFLECTING THE COMPLICATED GEO-POLITICS OF MEDIEVAL EASTERN EUROPE.

KEY FACTS
*Prince of Poland*
DATES: *1458–84*
BIRTH PLACE: *Cracow, Poland*
PATRON OF: *Poland, Russia, Lithuania, the youth of Lithuania*
FEAST DAY: *4 March*
EMBLEM: *Crown*

Numerous reports from the medieval period describe well-born children possessed of a deep spirituality. But Casimir is an extraordinary example. From infancy, it was said, he had a natural tendency to be ascetic.

His father was King Casimir IV of Poland, yet his small son would admit no luxury, choosing to sleep on a bare floor and spend hours at prayer. He frequently recited a long Latin hymn in praise of Mary, the Blessed Virgin. Under plain clothes, he wore a hair-shirt to mortify the flesh. He visited the poor regularly, using his royal position to gain concessions on their behalf.

When Casimir was 15, the king appointed this unworldly son to lead the Polish army in a bid to take the throne of Hungary. As both the boy's officers and the pope were opposed to this war, Casimir decided to turn back home during the campaign. His angry father imprisoned him in Dobzki Castle for months.

Yet nothing would induce Casimir to take up arms, nor would he abandon his vow of celibacy. He continued to follow his stern, simple ways, ultimately to his death. He died in what is now Lithuania, aged 26.

*Left St Casimir of Poland (Carlo Dolci, 17th century).*

# NICHOLAS OF FLUE

POPE PIUS XII DECLARED ST NICHOLAS OF FLUE TO BE THE FATHER OF SWITZERLAND, A TRIBUTE TO HIS ROLE IN UNITING THE VARIOUS FACTIONS THAT HAD PLUNGED THE REGION INTO CIVIL WAR.

KEY FACTS
*Hermit*
DATES: *1417–87*
BIRTH PLACE: *Sachseln, Switzerland*
PATRON OF: *Switzerland*
FEAST DAY: *21 March
(25 September in Switzerland)*
EMBLEM: *Hut, hermit's clothes*

The life of St Nicholas falls into two halves. At first, he lived as a soldier, magistrate and judge in Switzerland. His family belonged to the Friends of God, a Christian brotherhood that stressed the personal union of their souls with God.

On turning 50, the second part of his life began. Nicholas decided to become a hermit. With his wife's blessing, he set off for France, but on the way observed what he described as a fiery sign calling him back to Switzerland. So he settled on a high pasture, living under the shelter of a tree.

The faithful sought him out, and built him a hut and a chapel. At this time, Switzerland was in the grip of civil war, and delegates from both sides visited Nicholas. His words are said to have resolved the political differences and a national unity was achieved by the Edict of Stans (1481).

*Left Nicholas of Flue praying in the wilderness, with a skull by his side as a memento mori (woodcut, artist unknown, 1860).*

# THOMAS MORE

AT HIS EXECUTION, THE LORD CHANCELLOR THOMAS MORE TOLD THE CROWD THAT HE WAS "THE KING'S GOOD SERVANT – BUT GOD'S FIRST". TO THE END, MORE WOULD NOT COMPROMISE HIS FAITH.

### KEY FACTS
*Martyr saint*
DATES: *1478–1535*
BIRTH PLACE: *London, England*
PATRON OF: *Politicians*
FEAST DAY: *22 June*
EMBLEM: *Lawyer's hat*

A scholar of great integrity, Thomas More was granted high office by his friend, King Henry VIII of England. He read law at Oxford University and, at the age of 23, became a Member of Parliament.

Thomas had a witty, light-hearted personality, and the king delighted in his company. When appointed Lord Chancellor, he wrote his most famous work, *Utopia*, a fantasy about an ideal community living in harmony, with equality of opportunity.

His first wife, by whom he had four children, died young but he made a happy second marriage. His family was a source of love and comfort, and Thomas drew great strength from his faith.

Much of his work was written in support of the Catholic Church and against Martin Luther's ideas of reformation. He corresponded with theologians across Europe, including Erasmus.

## RUPTURE WITH THE KING

Thomas was deeply distressed by Henry VIII's decision to break with Rome and set himself up as supreme head of the Church in England. The king's reasons were not theological.

He simply wished Rome to nullify his marriage to Catherine of Aragon, but the pope refused. Henry followed fashionable ideas of reformation and revolt against Rome, and declared religious independence.

But Thomas More was a pious man and could not support his wayward king. He resigned as

***Above** An engraving of Thomas More after a painting by Holbein (Francesco Bartolozzi, 1792).*

Lord Chancellor in 1532. Two years later, More was called to take an oath denying papal authority over English Christians. He refused and was dispatched to the Tower of London. His lands were confiscated and his family forced into poverty.

During his imprisonment there, he wrote often to his beloved daughter, Margaret Roper. He also produced his *Dialogue of Comfort*, a moving text on the meaning of faith.

The following year he was taken to Westminster Hall where he faced charges of treason because he refused to accept the king's authority over the pope's. Thomas More was sentenced to death and was beheaded in public on Tower Hill, London.

## JOHN FISHER

A distinguished scholar-priest, John Fisher was Chancellor of Cambridge University and Bishop of Rochester. He was involved in reforming the Church, but preferred dialogue to confrontation as a means of bringing change.

Fisher was a good friend of Thomas More and, like him, was asked to accept the Act of Succession, which gave Henry VIII authority over English Catholics. John refused and was taken to the Tower. While there, the pope made him a cardinal. The infuriated king condemned John to death.

The saint was so ill, he had to be carried to the executioner's block. He died in 1535, a month before Thomas More.

***Above** Portrait of Martyr and Prelate John Fisher (artist and date unknown).*

# THE SAINTS IN ART

PAINTINGS OF THE SAINTS INSPIRED BELIEVERS TO FEEL THAT, IN CONTEMPLATING HOLY IMAGES, THEY WOULD DRAW CLOSER TO GOD. PERSONAL ATTRIBUTES WERE ADDED TO IDENTIFY THE SAINTS.

Gregory the Great observed that paintings do for the illiterate what texts do for readers. There can be little doubt that the medieval faithful, most of whom could not read, were uplifted by illustrations of the saints' lives.

Despite the passing of centuries, believers who gazed upon these images were not dismayed by various artistic developments. Changes to the style of clothing worn by the saints or altered settings tended to cause no discomfort among the faithful. Neither did the portrayal of particular saints with different faces in successive paintings.

**Above** The Martyrdom of St Catherine of Alexandria *(Lucas Cranach the Elder, 1506).*

## SYMBOLS OF IDENTITY

From early in the history of Christian art, a convention arose to identify saints through symbols. These emblems served to clarify the narrative being told, and to identify the characters.

Mary, the Blessed Virgin, and infant Jesus are instantly recognizable. Likewise, Mary holding her dead son, a scene known as the Pietà, is universally understood, as is the image of the crucifix, representing the crucified Christ.

But other characters needed their individual code of identity in order to be recognized, since no one knew what the saints looked like. To modern eyes, medieval and Renaissance Christian paintings can look quaint, even bizarre.

Doves emanate rays of light, lions lie meekly on cathedral floors, and a stag might display a crucifix within its antlers. Angels have blue duck-feathered wings, and men stand, pierced by arrows or even holding their own heads. For some 1,700 years, these unlikely elements possessed a beautiful logic, easily understood by all Christians, from the bogs of Ireland to the deserts of Syria.

**Above** St Lucy with her eyes on a plate (Umbrian School, c.1550).

## LIONS TO ALABASTER

The medieval faithful knew the scholarly man with the lion was St Jerome. Likewise, the man with an arrow was Sebastian, who by tradition was shot in this manner.

The shepherdess, St Margaret of Antioch, carried a staff and was shown with a dragon because she escaped from such a beast. St James the Great had a seashell and pilgrim's staff near him. The shell

**Below** St Jerome in the Desert (Pietro Perugino, c.1499–1502).

"THE WORK SHINES NOBLY,
BUT THE WORK WHICH SHINES NOBLY SHOULD CLEAR
   MINDS,
SO THAT THEY MAY TRAVEL THROUGH THE TRUE LIGHTS
   TO THE TRUE LIGHT
WHERE CHRIST IS THE TRUE DOOR."

ABBOT SUGER (c.1081–1151)

indicated his body was found in a drifting boat, the staff that he was a journeying evangelist.

All Christendom recognized Mary Magdalene because a jar of ointment and loosened hair marked her apart. With oil of alabaster she anointed Christ's feet before drying them with her hair.

## ART AS IDOLATRY
The Church regarded artistic representations as an expression of the holiness of the saints. In the

*Below A fresco showing the popular subject of St Luke painting the Madonna (Andrea Delitio, 1477).*

Orthodox Church, they were used to concentrate the mind during meditation. But these artistic works aroused anxiety during the Reformation.

Protestant leaders forbade the erection of any kind of image in religious buildings. Images were regarded as idolatrous on the ground that the Old Testament forbids worship before idols.

Paintings, shrines and statues of saints were cleared away and frescoes were concealed behind a covering of wall paint. These zealous reformers even showed hostility toward music. The Roman Catholic Church uses

music for worship. The Eastern Orthodox Church retains a sung liturgy so revered it has remained unaltered to this day.

The reformer John Calvin declared that music had no place in a church. The less stern Martin Luther, on the other hand, composed his own church hymns.

### SAINTLY ARTISTS
There are saints who were artists, the first being the Apostle Luke, reported to have made studies of Mary, the Blessed Virgin. Perhaps the greatest painter is Fra Angelico whose spiritual paintings are famous, but the drawings and music of Hildegard of Bingen also carry a mystical quality.

Musicians and poets can be found in the company of saints. It is assumed Gregory the Great was a musician – one reason for this assumption is that the Gregorian Chants bear his name.

There are contemporary reports that describe Nicetas of Remesiana as a poet and composer who wrote the beautiful Latin hymn, *Te Deum*. He used music as a form of preaching.

*Above Manuscript illumination from Cantigas de Santa Maria (Alphonse Le Sage, 13th century).*

# ANGELA MERICI

THE ITALIAN FOUNDER OF THE FIRST ORDER OF WOMEN DEVOTED
SPECIALLY TO EDUCATING CHILDREN HAS BECOME A PATRON OF
MANY CAUSES RELATED TO THE UNDERPRIVILEGED IN SOCIETY.

**KEY FACTS**
*Founder of Ursuline nuns*
DATES: *1474–1540*
BIRTH PLACE: *Lake Garda,
Italy*
PATRON OF: *Disabled people*
FEAST DAY: *27 January*
EMBLEM: *Book*

As an orphan from an early age, Angela Merici suffered great deprivation and neglect. Vulnerable, malnourished and unloved, orphaned children were a pitiable class in Italian society at this time.

Forced to be independent as a child, Angela developed a special sympathy for the plight of orphans. While she could not help their loss of parentage, she could work to improve their lot.

To this end, she first joined the Franciscan tertiaries and then founded a special Christian community. Its members were women who were not cloistered but free to move among those who most needed education – children. The sisters, who went wherever it was convenient to deliver lessons, taught local children in the villages. Aged 42, Angela went to educate the children at Brescia.

The lay nun made pilgrimages to Rome and the Holy Land, where she was strangely struck blind. She recovered her sight on returning home.

Once again, Angela gathered a group of women in Brescia who dedicated their lives to educating children. The women made no vows of chastity or obedience, and shared no communal life. But from this nucleus grew the Company of St Ursula (known as the Ursuline nuns), named after the legendary virgin martyr.

*Right* St Angela Merici
*(Moretto da Brescia, date unknown).*

# CAJETAN

DEVOTING MOST OF HIS LIFE TO WORKING AMONG THE POOR IN THE
SLUMS OF NAPLES OPENED ST CAJETAN'S EYES TO THE REALITY OF
RENAISSANCE SQUALOR FOR LARGE SECTIONS OF THE COMMUNITY.

**KEY FACTS**
*Founder of the Theatines*
DATES: *1480–1547*
BIRTH PLACE: *Vicenza, Italy*
PATRON OF: *Job seekers*
FEAST DAY: *7 August*
EMBLEM: *Theatine habit*

Though not ordained until he was 36, Cajetan had seen enough in his working life to realize that the Church was in dire need of reform. Being an active charity worker made him acutely aware of the suffering and loss of faith in the community.

In partnership with Pietro Caraffa, a mistrusted fanatic who in fact became Pope Paul IV, Cajetan founded the Theatines (named after the diocese of Theate). This fundamentalist group of priests were trained to follow the first teachings of Christ, avoiding all sophisticated theology.

Their purpose was to preach the basics of the Christian faith in the hope of bringing back the disaffected into the Church. Cajetan also devised a system of alleviating poverty. He set up pawnshops owned by the Church to allow the poor access to loans. These non-profit organizations operated for centuries. He lived briefly in Rome but left during an invasion by troops of the Holy Roman Emperor.

Cajetan spent most of his life in Naples, then a corrupt diocese. He died there, having tried to improve its moral culture.

# JOHN OF GOD

A PORTUGUESE MADMAN RESCUED FROM AN ASYLUM TURNED
ROUND HIS LIFE BY DEDICATING IT TO THE RELIEF OF SOCIETY'S
OUTCASTS. A HOSPITAL SERVICE WAS FOUNDED IN HIS NAME.

KEY FACTS

Founder of the Brothers of
St John of God
DATES: 1495–1550
BIRTH PLACE: Monte Mor il
Nuovo, Portugal
PATRON OF: Nurses and nursing
associations, bookbinders
FEAST DAY: 8 March
EMBLEM: Poor clothing, cross

John of God, a Portuguese, spent his youth as a soldier for Spain, roaming the battlefields of Europe, before working first as a shepherd in Andalusia, and later as a merchant, peddling religious images and pamphlets in Granada.

Attending a sermon given by John of Avila, the merchant went mad with remorse for his sins. He began to scream and tear at his hair. He was confined to a lunatic asylum until John of Avila visited him, asking him to serve God. John of God began to sell wood, feeding the poor with his profits.

He built a house where he sheltered vagabonds, prostitutes, and nursed the ill.

He never founded an order, but his hospital service became the Order of the Brothers of St John of God. He tried to hide his ill health but when a noblewoman insisted on nursing him, he wept, believing he was unworthy of comfort while others suffered. When John died, all Granada followed his funeral procession.

*Right* St John of God (the School of Pedro Nolasco y Lara, 18th century).

# THOMAS OF VILLANOVA

FROM SIMPLE FRIAR TO ARCHBISHOP OF VALENCIA, ST THOMAS
ENDEAVOURED TO MEET THE NEEDS OF ALL WHO CAME HIS WAY,
REGARDLESS OF THEIR WEALTH OR STATUS IN SOCIETY.

KEY FACTS

Archbishop
DATES: 1488–1555
BIRTH PLACE: Near Villanova,
Castile
FEAST DAY: 22 September
EMBLEM: Franciscan habit,
archbishop's crook

A dreamy man by nature, fond of meditation, Thomas of Villanova was destined to join a religious order. When admitted to the Spanish Franciscan friary at Salamanca, he developed a deep faith and became a significant preacher for 25 years.

Somewhat against his will, Thomas was then appointed Archbishop of Valencia. What he found, on taking office, was a Church in need of inspiration.

A lazy, dissolute clergy required discipline, but Thomas knew that high-handed methods achieved nothing. Instead, he adopted patience and diplomacy. His gen-

*Above* The Charity of Saint Thomas of Villanova (Bartolomé Murillo, c. 1670).

tle faith served many quarters of the community. Among his congregation were disturbed *Moriscos*, Moors who had been forcibly converted to Christianity. His spirituality and reputed gift for healing brought much solace to these people.

Preferring the solitary life, Thomas asked to be allowed to step down as archbishop. But his leadership was so vital the Church ignored his requests. Worn out by duties, Thomas died in Valencia and was canonized in 1658.

# IGNATIUS OF LOYOLA

AS FOUNDER OF THE POWERFUL MISSIONARY ORDER, THE SOCIETY OF JESUS (ALSO KNOWN AS THE JESUITS), ST IGNATIUS SPEARHEADED THE COUNTER-REFORMATION IN EUROPE.

**KEY FACTS**

*Founder of the Society of Jesus, or "Jesuits"*
DATES: *c.1491–1556*
BIRTH PLACE: *Azpeitia, Spain*
PATRON OF: *Spiritual exercise and retreats*
FEAST DAY: *31 July*
EMBLEM: *Black cassock, heart pierced by thorns, the monogram of Christ (HIS), and a crown of glory*

The youngest of 11 children of a noble Basque family, Ignatius was born in the Castle of Loyola at Azpeitia. He followed the course taken by many young men of the period and trained as a soldier in the Spanish army.

But for a severe wound to his leg while fighting the French at Pamplona, Ignatius would probably have joined the ranks of the conquistadors on their expeditions to the Americas.

Instead, he was forced to take a long convalescence, during which he is said to have had a conversion

*Left Colour engraving of Ignatius of Loyola (c.1500).*

experience. Having no strong convictions of faith up to then, he reported suddenly having a vision of Mary, the Blessed Virgin, with Jesus beside her.

The experience inspired Ignatius to go to the Benedictine abbey at Montserrat. There he duly laid his sword and dagger upon the altar, and sought a cave nearby to take up life as a hermit.

## TRAINING THE SPIRIT

Ignatius imposed a harsh lifestyle on himself, going without food for long periods, scourging his body daily, and immersing himself in prayer.

As word spread, people started visiting him to seek his advice and join him in prayer. But his life of deprivation took its toll and his health suffered. He came to realize that he should not shut himself away from people, but serve them in their spiritual needs.

At the age of 32, Ignatius walked to Jerusalem, despite a permanent limp caused by his war injury. He hoped to convert Muslims but the Franciscan

*Left Detail of Heaven and angels from* The Glorification of Saint Ignatius *(Andrea Pozzo, c.1691–94).*

brothers discouraged him and, fearing for his safety, sent him home. Back in Barcelona, he took up studying and began to preach and to help the needy. However, since he was no priest, this did not endear him to the Church.

## SOLDIERS OF CHRIST

In Paris to do further studies, the ambitious young man formed a brotherhood with six friends. Among them was St Francis Xavier who would become the great missionary to the East.

Having now been ordained, Ignatius instructed the group using his own spiritual manual, *Spiritual Exercises*. This work consisted of a four-week course designed to induct new "soldiers of Christ", as Ignatius refered to the members of his brotherhood. They gave themselves to chastity and poverty, and determined to teach those without education.

Calling themselves the Society of Jesus, they also pledged to conduct missions in Europe to reclaim souls lost to the Protestant reformers. The pope gave the society his blessing in 1540, and Ignatius was chosen as its general.

## RETRIEVING CATHOLICS

Ignatius spent the rest of his life in Rome. He founded a house for converted Jews and hostels for prostitutes. But it was his work in organizing foreign missions that

earned his reputation. His writing and teaching played a pivotal role in drawing believers back to the Roman Catholic Church after the Reformation.

His conviction in the power of prayer and sympathy towards those struggling with Christian principles endeared him to believers. His influence over Church doctrine and teaching has been immense.

Yet Ignatius was criticized in some quarters for being too militaristic and authoritarian. Likewise, the Jesuits, as they were popularly known, have been attacked for their power and political meddling.

Under Ignatius' leadership, the society grew rapidly. By his death, after 16 years of development, the number of Jesuits had increased to more than 1,000 members.

*Right Detail of* The Vision of St Ignatius of Loyola *(Peter Paul Rubens, 17th century).*

*Left* St Francis Borgia Helping a Dying Impenitent *(Francisco José de Goya y Lucientes, 1795).*

### THE SOCIETY OF JESUS

This order made the usual commitments to chastity, poverty and obedience, but added a fourth vow: absolute loyalty to papal authority. It proved an effective mission in post-Reformation Europe.

Chief among their European missions was that led by St Francis Borgia (1510–72), described as the order's "second founder". St Aloysius Gonzago (1568–91) nursed plague victims and wrote important texts. And St Stanislaus Kostka (1550–68) gained fame as a Jesuit mystic.

In the 16th century, missions were set up in Brazil, China, India, Japan and Malaysia. Two martyrs, St Francis Xavier (1506–51) and St Modeste Andlauer (1847–1900), served these missions. The society has since spread worldwide.

"DEAREST JESUS, TEACH US TO BE GENEROUS;
TO SERVE THEE AS THOU DESERVEST;
TO GIVE, AND NOT TO COUNT THE COST;
TO FIGHT, AND NOT TO HEED THE WOUNDS;
TO TOIL, AND NOT TO SEEK FOR REST;
TO LABOUR, AND TO SEEK FOR NO REWARD,
SAVE THAT OF KNOWING THAT WE DO THY
  HOLY WILL."

PRAYER OF ST IGNATIUS OF LOYOLA

# FRANCIS XAVIER

THE JESUIT WHO DEVOTED HIS LIFE TO SPREADING THE GOSPEL TO DISTANT LANDS PLANTED THE FAITH AS FAR EAST AS JAPAN. HE EXTENDED THE CHURCH FURTHER THAN ANY OTHER MISSIONARY.

### KEY FACTS
*Missionary to the East*
DATES: *1506–51*
BIRTH PLACE: *Xavier Castle, Navarre*
PATRON OF: *India, Pakistan, Outer Mongolia, missions, Spanish tourism, and the pelota players of Argentina*
FEAST DAY: *3 December*
EMBLEM: *Jesuit cassock, holding a crucifix, baptism bowl, heart and pilgrim's hat*

A poor linguist and sufferer from seasickness, St Francis Xavier was nevertheless eager to carry the message of Christ to far-off lands. He was born in the Basque region and studied in Paris, where he met Ignatius of Loyola. With him and five others, they formed the Society of Jesus, popularly known as the Jesuits.

After the men were ordained as priests in 1534, Ignatius sent Francis to join Father Simon Rodriguez in Lisbon. Seven years later the young missionary set sail for Goa, western India.

After a journey lasting over a year, he landed to find a decadent Portuguese community of clerks and merchants who had abandoned their Christian ideals and virtues. Francis lived simply among the people and hoped to encourage them as converts by setting lessons to their music.

Through his example as a Christian, he tried to counteract the greed of the cruel colonists.

For seven years he travelled through southern India, Ceylon (now Sri Lanka) and Malaysia, sleeping on the floor and living off rice and water.

Always having a bowl to hold water for baptism, Francis converted many, especially among the Parava tribe, who still follow the faith to this day.

## TO THE FAR EAST
In 1549, Francis ventured to Japan where he translated the key tenets of Christianity. By currying the favour of the ruling Mikado, he was given the use of an empty

*Left St Francis Xavier (artist unknown c.1545).*

Buddhist temple to practise his faith. He established a Christian community, but it was subject to persecution in future years.

In 1552, Francis briefly returned to Goa but felt compelled to reach out to new horizons. The conviction that the unbaptized were condemned to an eternity in hell drove Francis to preach in China, then a country closed to all foreigners.

Horribly seasick during the journey, he asked to be left on a small island, Chang-Chuen-Shan, near Hong Kong. Unable to make the crossing to the mainland, he took a gamble and went with a Chinese man who promised to sneak him into China.

Alas, he was abandoned. Being exposed to bad weather and weak from malnutrition, Francis died before arriving. His coffin was packed with lime, to preserve the corpse, and taken to Goa. His body proved incorruptible and is enshrined in a church there.

*Left St Francis Xavier and his entourage in a detail from a folding screen (Japanese School, 16th century).*

# PIUS V

A STERN REFORMER WHO TOLERATED NO LAXITY AMONG HIS OWN KIND WAS JUST AS RUTHLESS IN STAMPING OUT THE MUSLIM PRESENCE IN EASTERN EUROPE.

KEY FACTS
*Pope*
DATES: *1504–72*
BIRTH PLACE: *Bosco, Italy*
FEAST DAY: *30 April*
EMBLEM: *Papal vestments*

St Pius V entered the Church when he was a youth of 15, and became a diligent priest. He held office as bishop, cardinal and inquisitor-general before being appointed pope in 1566.

At this time the Church was in a fragile state. Congregations had turned to the new churches of the Reformation. Morale was low among the clergy. The previous pope was infamous for his nepotism. The pope before him was the unpopular Paul IV, the fanatical priest Caraffa, who suppressed Protestantism by violent means.

## PAPAL POLICY

Pius V started his reign as he meant to continue it. The Church was to be an example of discipline, modest living and charity. The usual lavish party to celebrate papal ordination was cancelled. Instead, the money went to fund hospitals and the poor.

He insisted bishops live in their own diocese, not luxuriate in Rome. Priests were commanded to teach the faith to the young within their parishes. The Roman Catechism, the statement of belief, was completed after years of preparation, and translated into different languages. The Missal was reformed as well.

Although Pius's methods were stern, congregations approved of his reforms. During his papacy, he led the Inquisition, determined to stamp out Islam inside Europe. At

a political level, he allowed papal ships to join those of Spain and Venice in an alliance that defeated the Turks at the Battle of Lepanto in 1571. This victory proved decisive in breaking Muslim power in the eastern Mediterranean region.

In England, however, Pius V disappointed Catholics by not insisting they fall under the authority of the Roman Church. Indeed, his excommunication of

Queen Elizabeth I only led to further persecutions of Catholics in that country, including the destruction of their legal rights.

But in Europe, many Catholics admired his leadership. They saw him as a hero against the Turks and Protestantism, and as a pope who strengthened the Roman Catholic Church and encouraged his flock.

*Right* Pope Pius V *(Scipione Pulzone, 1570).*

# TERESA OF ÁVILA

THIS DEVOUT NUN COURTED CONTROVERSY DURING HER LIFETIME BY CHALLENGING THE ESTABLISHED CARMELITE ORDER AND BY CLAIMING NUMEROUS VISIONS AND COMMUNICATIONS WITH CHRIST.

**KEY FACTS**
*Mystic, virgin*
DATES: *1515–82*
BIRTH PLACE: *Avila, Spain*
PATRON OF: *Spain, Spanish Catholic writers, Carmelites*
FEAST DAY: *15 October*
EMBLEM: *Pen and book, an angel, burning lance or arrow*

Teresa de Capeda y Ahumada was born at Ávila to a wealthy Castilian family. She was a bright, independent girl whose piety was evident from an early age. After her mother's death, her father sent her to an Augustinian convent, where she discovered her calling to the Church. Aged 20, and against her father's wishes, she entered a Carmelite convent. Within a short time, however, Teresa was taken gravely ill and left the convent to be cared for by her family. Although she never regained full health, she returned to the Carmelites where she enjoyed the sociable, relaxed environment of the Order.

Following the death of her father in 1543, Teresa became committed to a more private,

*Below* Theresa of Ávila's Vision of a Dove (Peter Paul Rubens, c.1614).

***Above*** Detail of the Ecstasy of Saint Theresa, *held in the Church of Santa Maria della Vittoria in Rome (Gianlorenzo Bernini, c.1645–52).*

contemplative life. One particular incident changed her life: she collapsed in front of an image of Christ, later waking and realizing she must renounce all worldly emotion and live only for Him.

## VISIONARY
From the moment of her conversion, Teresa had visions and went into deep spiritual trances when she prayed. She felt misunderstood

by her fellow nuns who were dismissive of her mystic experiences. For the rest of her life she continued to have rapturous visions. In particular, she suffered a pain in her side, inflicted, she claimed, by an angel who thrust a burning lance into her heart. Her powers of contemplation developed into a deep devotion and she referred to herself as "Teresa of Jesus".

## REFORMER
After meeting Peter of Alcantara, Teresa was moved to follow his example of strict penance and mental prayer. She requested permission from the pope to open a small house. The order would be named St Joseph after her patron saint. When the secret plans were revealed, the Carmelite nuns and influential people of Ávila asked the pope to stop them. Teresa appealed to Spain's King Philip II, who resented Rome's authority. This caused angry confrontation between Church and state and Teresa was imprisoned for two

"ST THERESA, GRANT THAT MY EVERY THOUGHT, DESIRE AND AFFECTION MAY BE CONTINUALLY DIRECTED TO DOING THE WILL OF GOD, WHETHER I AM IN JOY OR IN PAIN, FOR HE IS WORTHY TO BE LOVED AND OBEYED FOREVER. OBTAIN FOR ME THIS GRACE, THOU WHO ART SO POWERFUL WITH GOD; MAY I BE ALL ON FIRE, LIKE THEE, WITH THE HOLY LOVE OF GOD."

PRAYER OF INTERCESSION TO ST THERESA OF ÁVILA

years before she was permitted to open a Carmelite sub-group. Her nuns, known as Discalced, or Barefoots, wore coarse brown habits and rope sandals to show their lives of poverty.

During the next few years, Teresa travelled across Spain establishing convents. Her nuns were separated from the world, lived on alms, were forbidden to eat meat, and were instructed by Teresa in meditation.

She founded 16 convents and 14 monasteries, because men, too, wanted to take the vows of the Discalced. These male orders were organized with the help of another mystic, John of the Cross.

*Below* The Communion of St Theresa of Ávila *(Claudio Coello, 17th century).*

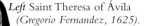

*Left* Saint Theresa of Ávila *(Gregorio Fernandez, 1625).*

Teresa's writings are testament to her great personal devotion and her thoughts on a life of prayer and contemplation. Chief among her works are *The Interior Castle* and *The Way of Perfection.* The books, which describe the journey of the "soul toward a perfect unity with God", continue to be published in numerous languages.

Teresa of Ávila died at the convent of Alba de Tormes. The odour of violets and sweet oil emanated from her tomb. It was opened and a hand was cut off illicitly, and this was found to work miracles. Her remains were reburied in 1585 in a tomb built by the Duke of Alba. Teresa was canonized by Pope Gregory XV in 1622, and declared a Doctor of the Church in 1970, the first woman to win this recognition. Her order continues to prove the need for retreat and prayer in the modern world.

## ST PETER OF ALCANTARA

St Teresa of Ávila was inspired by the life and teachings of another great mystic, Peter of Alcantara. Born Peter Garavito, he was ordained a Franciscan, but longed for a more rigorous discipline. In 1538, he became head of the strict order in Estremadura, Spain, but met with opposition when he tried to reform them further. He went on to found a small, reformed Alcantrine Franciscan order at a friary in Pedrosa. Peter encouraged Teresa to follow his rules of avoiding meat and wine, and walking barefoot. His treatise on prayer and meditation has been translated into many languages. He was canonized in 1669.

*Above* St Peter of Alcantara visited by a dove *(engraving by A. Masson after a painting by Francisco de Zurbarán, c. 1560).*

# LUIS BERTRAN

LUIS BERTRAN WAS A GIFTED PREACHER WHO CONVERTED THOUSANDS OF SOUTH AMERICAN INDIANS AND CARIBBEAN ISLANDERS TO CHRISTIANITY.

**KEY FACTS**
*Missionary in the New World*
DATES: *1526–81*
BIRTH PLACE: *Valencia, Spain*
PATRON OF: *Colombia*
FEAST DAY: *9 October*
EMBLEM: *Dominican habit*

A Dominican priest with a serious nature, Luis Bertran was a great preacher and apostle, known for his austerity. For many years, he trained Dominican novices and was admired for his teaching, profound wisdom and counselling skills. Teresa of Ávila is said to have turned to him for advice when she was reforming the Carmelite Order.

Athough he spent most of his life in his native Valencia, Luis' most significant work was carried out during his six years as a missionary to Latin America. In 1562, he was sent to a Dominican priory in Cartagena, Colombia, where he began to preach through an interpreter.

There are stories that his mission was successful because he inspired his listeners through an exhilarating combination of prophecy, miracles and talking in tongues. Certainly, his conversion rate was high – he baptized thousands of people during his travels around South America and the Caribbean Islands.

Recalled to Valencia in 1568, Louis began to train preachers for the missions. He emphasized the importance of prayer, simple Christian living and the need to reinforce words with actions.

Luis Bertran was one of the very first missionaries to speak out against the greed, cruelty and violence of many of the Spanish conquistadors. He was taken ill in Valencia Cathedral and died 18 months later.

# JOHN OF THE CROSS

JOHN OF THE CROSS IS ONE OF SPAIN'S GREATEST MYSTICAL THEOLOGIANS, LOVED FOR THE BEAUTY OF HIS POETRY AND PITIED FOR THE SUFFERING THAT HE WAS MADE TO ENDURE.

**KEY FACTS**
*Poet and mystic*
DATES: *1542–91*
BIRTH PLACE: *Near Avila, Spain*
PATRON OF: *Mystics, poets*
FEAST DAY: *14 December*
EMBLEM: *Carmelite habit, book*

Born to a poor but noble Spanish family, John of the Cross attended a Jesuit college and became a Carmelite friar in 1563.

Teresa of Ávila inspired John with her reform of the Carmelite Order, the Decalced (Barefoot) Carmelites. With Teresa's help, he set up a Decalced Carmelite friary in a hovel in Duruelo.

The Carmelite Order rejected their reforms, and in 1575 John of the Cross was imprisoned. Subjected to extremely harsh treatment, John found expression for his suffering in poetry dedicated to his search for, and love of, God. After nine months he escaped and continued his spiritual work,

founding a college at Baeza and working at monasteries in Granada and Segovia.

At the end of his life, John was once again harshly treated, this time by the Decalced Carmelites who now found his views too moderate. He died in 1591 after having written some of the most moving poetry in Christian literature, such as *The Dark Night of the Soul*, *The Spiritual Canticle* and *The Living Flame of Love*.

*Left* St John of the Cross *(Joaquín Vaquero Turcios, 20th century)*.

# PETER CANISIUS

CATHOLICS AND PROTESTANTS ALIKE ADMIRED ST PETER CANISIUS FOR HIS MODERATION DURING A PERIOD OF STRIFE AMONG CHRISTIANS IN THE 16TH CENTURY.

**KEY FACTS**
*Jesuit Doctor of the Church*
DATES: *1521–97*
BIRTH PLACE: *Nijmegen,
Holland*
PATRON OF: *Germany, Catholic
press, catechism writers*
FEAST DAY: *21 December*
EMBLEM: *Jesuit habit*

Peter Canisius rejected a legal career and marriage in Holland to join the Society of Jesus, or Jesuits. In 1552, he was sent to revive the Roman Catholic Church in Vienna, where he found deserted monasteries and many lapsed believers.

He applied all his energy to teaching the faith and strengthening the Catholic Church. He skilfully avoided confrontation with the Protestants by emphasizing a common belief in Christ's teachings. He also won the respect of the Viennese by nursing the sick during the plague.

Canisius quickly recognized the importance of the printing presses flourishing at this time. His numerous writings persuaded thousands to return to the Church, and his Catechism (1555), was translated into 15 languages. He helped found the University of Fribourg in Switzerland, where he died in 1597.

*Left* Peter Canisius the Preacher *(attr. to Pierre Wuilleret, c.1635).*

---

# PHILIP NERI

PHILIP NERI, THE APOSTLE OF ROME, WAS A MAN OF GREAT INTUITION AND HUMOUR WHOSE PATIENCE AND GOOD ADVICE WON HIM MANY SUPPORTERS AMONG THE PEOPLE OF ROME.

**KEY FACTS**
*Founder of the Congregation of
the Oratory in Rome*
DATES: *1515–95*
BIRTH PLACE: *Florence, Italy*
FEAST DAY: *26 May*
EMBLEM: *Bell, book*

Kindly and charismatic, Philip Neri founded a brotherhood devoted to welfare. In 1533, he abandoned business to live in poverty in Rome. His charisma drew loyal followers to him. In 1548, he set up a fraternity to care for the sick and the many pilgrims to the city.

After he was ordained in 1551, he formed the Congregation of the Oratory in San Girolamo. His followers took no vows and did not abandon their property or dedicate their lives to a monastic community. Pope Gregory XIII approved the order in 1575.

The Holy See called for Philip's advice in 1593 when it was reluctant to recognize Henry IV of France, a former Protestant. Philip told them to forgive the king for his lapse.

Philip died in 1595 and was so well loved that he was instantly recognized as a saint. The Oratory Order is found all over the Catholic world.

*Left The interior of the 19th-century Brompton Oratory in London, dedicated to Philip Neri.*

# Royal Saints

Many monarchs are venerated for their brave defence of Christianity. some gave their lives for that cause; others ruled with especial wisdom and benevolence.

It may be difficult to reconcile the virtuous qualities of sainthood with the characteristics of the rich and mighty, but many saints were, in fact, also powerful monarchs. In their privileged positions, these holy men and women ruled with great fortitude, promoting Christianity through example and sacrifice.

*Right Edward the Confessor in stained glass from Canterbury, England (15th century).*

## WARRIOR SAINTS
Many kings have been involved in warfare, protecting their borders and Christianity on behalf of their countrymen. Some, including Vladimir and Alexander Nevski, were soldiers. These early rulers of Russia used arms to quell invaders but proved righteous monarchs.

Henry II, another militant man, went to war to establish the borders of Germany and became emperor in 1014. After this, he turned to his religion and prayer, built monasteries, and promoted welfare for the poor. He was said to be so pious that his marriage was never consummated. Henry II was canonized in 1146, while his wife Cunegund was canonized in 1200.

Other saintly warrior kings include Stephen of Hungary, who limited the power of the nobles, reduced tribal tensions and installed a judicial system. Stephen made Hungary a Christian country, and was a heroic leader.

## SPREADING THE FAITH
As Christianity began to take root in Europe, monarchs played a vital role in imparting the faith to their subjects. English kings, such as Ethelbert of Kent and Oswald, were pioneers of the faith and venerated for encouraging the

*Left St Cunegund, empress and wife of Henry II, holding the model of a church (the Master of Messkirch, c.1530–38).*

first Christian missions. Edward the Confessor was known for his visions and miraculous cures of the ill. He devoted much of his time to the establishment of the Church and the monasteries in England and was loved for his kind and fair rule.

Norway's patron saint, King Olaf, established the Christian faith among his people and, after

"Dear son, if you come to reign, do that which befits a king, that is, be so just as to deviate in nothing from justice, whatever may befall you."

ST LOUIS, KING OF FRANCE

*Above A statue of Stephen of Hungary near the Freedom Bridge in Budapest, Hungary.*

his death in battle, was credited with miracles and a healing spring that began to flow from his grave.

## MARTYRED MONARCHS

Several Christian monarchs have been martyred for their faith. One was the English boy king, Edward the Martyr, who was killed in AD 979 in a power struggle for the throne. Another, Edmund of Abingdon, was cruelly murdered by Viking invaders when he refused to deny his faith.

Two Scandinavian kings, Canute of Denmark and Eric of Sweden, also gave their lives for their Christian beliefs. Canute's murder at an altar was followed by many miracles and wonders. Sweden became a Christian country under Eric, but he was tortured and beheaded by attacking soldiers. These Scandinavian kings had large cultuses until the Reformation, when the Protestant movement began to overwhelm the Roman Catholic Church in northern Europe.

## QUEENLY SAINTS

By the 11th century, the Scots had a pious queen. Margaret of Scotland was recognized for both her devotion to her family and her deep faith, as witnessed by her charitable work for the poor and for prisoners.

Elizabeth of Portugal was married to King Denis of Portugal. He was a violent man, but she converted him to the faith. She brought comfort and aid to orphans and "fallen women", and founded hospitals. Pilgrims and the very poor turned to her for hospitality and care.

Her distant relative, after whom she was named, Elizabeth of Hungary, likewise established hospitals, as well as founding the first orphanage in central Europe. The final part of her life was austere, poverty-stricken and devoted to prayer and charity. Her relics at the church of St Elizabeth at Marburg drew hordes of pilgrims until, in 1539, the Lutheran Philip of Hesse removed them and hid them in an unknown site.

*Right A portrait of St Vladimir (anonymous Russian artist, 1905).*

Although many later monarchs continued to support the Catholic Church and to exercise their rule with Christian values, few European kings or queens were canonized after the Reformation.

## KING LOUIS IX OF FRANCE

Louis IX took up arms for his faith, but he dedicated much of his life to spiritual causes. His subjects knew him as a man who was severe in his habits, devoting long hours to prayer. He built monasteries and a hospital for the poor. He was also admired for his efforts to show justice, even though his courtiers sometimes thwarted his good intentions. His courage in fighting for Christendom aroused great respect and he led two crusades, meeting his death at Tunis in 1270. During this last expedition, Louis tried to reconcile the Greeks to the Church of Rome.

*Above King Louis IX of France (St Louis) embarking on his first Crusade in 1248 (manuscript illumination, c.1325).*

# TURIBIUS OF LIMA

TURIBIUS WAS A TIRELESS APOSTLE, BLESSED WITH INTELLIGENCE AND A STRONG MORAL SENSE. HE SPOKE NUMEROUS LOCAL DIALECTS, WHICH ENDEARED HIM TO THE PEOPLE OF PERU.

**KEY FACTS**
*Archbishop and missionary*
DATES: *1538–1606*
BIRTH PLACE: *Mayorga, Spain*
PATRON OF: *Bishops of Latin America*
FEAST DAY: *23 March*
EMBLEM: *Archbishop's vestments*

Turibius Alfonso de Mogrobejo was born in Spain and studied law at the University of Salamanca. His reputation as a scholar and professor led to his appointment as chief judge of the Inquisition Court, and to his becoming Archbishop of Lima. He protested his inadequacy for the latter post – an unusual appointment as he was a layman – but took orders and was made archbishop before travelling to Peru in 1581.

As he visited the members of his vast new diocese, he found immorality and tyranny to be rife amongst the Spanish colonists. He saw that their Peruvian converts were not given the benefit of good Christian teaching and set about reforming the communities by building churches and hospitals. In 1591, he established the first seminary in the Americas.

Turibius was sensitive and considerate to his congregation, and his kindness encouraged trust. His implacable stand against tyranny was so effective that many converted to the faith. He died in Santa, Peru, having achieved considerable success in his mission.

*Above* The monastery of St Turibius of Lima in Potes, Spain.

# FRANCIS SOLANO

THIS DEDICATED MISSIONARY SHOWED PROFOUND COMPASSION FOR HUMAN SUFFERING AND BECAME KNOWN AS "THE APOSTLE OF AMERICA", WINNING NUMEROUS CONVERTS TO CHRISTIANITY.

**KEY FACTS**
*Missionary*
DATES: *1549–1610*
BIRTH PLACE: *Montilla, near Córdoba, Spain*
PATRON OF: *Peru, Bolivia, Paraguay, Uruguay, Chile and Argentina*
FEAST DAY: *14 July*
EMBLEM: *Franciscan habit*

Local legend has it that Francis Solano addressed his congregation in one language but was understood by everyone, irrespective of their tongue. In fact, the Franciscan priest was a gifted linguist and this talent helped him make many converts.

Ordained as a priest in Seville in 1576, Francis spent several years in the Franciscan convent before travelling to the Americas in 1589. His ship was destined for Peru but was wrecked on the way and abandoned by the Spanish crew. Francis rescued 80 African slaves, who were on board, encouraging them to cling to a section of the ship. Inspired by his prayers, they landed in Lima after two months at sea.

*Left* Seville Cathedral, Spain, where Francis Solano was ordained in 1576. It is the largest Roman Catholic cathedral in the world.

Francis spent the next 20 years evangelizing in Argentina, Chile, Colombia and Peru. He charmed his congregation by playing his lute in veneration of Mary, the Blessed Virgin, and they often joined him in song. Later, as Guardian of Lima, Francis aroused anger because of his attacks on corrupt colonists. Nevertheless, his death was the cause of widespread grief. His relics are kept in Buenos Aires and Rome.

# ROSE OF LIMA

IN 1671, ROSE OF LIMA WAS CANONIZED BY POPE CLEMENT X, THUS BECOMING THE FIRST OFFICIALLY RECOGNIZED SAINT OF THE NEW WORLD. SHE IS THE PATRON OF SOUTH AMERICA.

As a young woman, Rose was so mortified by her own beauty that she rubbed her face and hands with pepper and lye to ruin her complexion. This pious child was born to modest parents and christened Isabel, though she was always known as Rose. She chose to model herself on St Catherine of Siena by living a life of purity and self-denial. Though her parents were anxious for her to marry, Rose vowed to remain a virgin and became a tertiary of the Dominican Order. However, she remained a conscientious daughter, working to help her parents by growing flowers and making exquisite lace to sell at the local market.

## EXTREME PENANCE

To bring herself closer to God, Rose built a hut in her parents' garden and lived there in virtual seclusion. In imitation of Christ, who was forced to wear a crown of thorns, she wore on her head a circlet of silver studded inside with small spikes. She prayed for long hours, often in spiritual despair because she felt she was not worthy of God's love.

Throughout this time, she faced constant ridicule from her community and fierce opposition from her parents. Her self-inflicted penances were so extreme that she attracted the attention of the Church, which held an inquiry into her behaviour. Her friend, the archbishop St Turibius of Lima, defended her, and the Church eventually conceded that her visions and mystic exaltations were holy and true.

## CARE FOR THE SICK

In spite of her own suffering, Rose spent much time among the sick and needy of Lima. However, after many years of physical deprivation, her health declined and she was taken to live with the government official Don Gonzales de Massa and his wife, who nursed her through a long and painful illness. They later testified as to the words she used in prayer, "Lord, increase my sufferings, and with them increase thy love in my heart".

By the time Rose died in 1617 – still only a young woman at the age of 31 – her holiness was widely recognized. The people of Lima went into mourning. Dominicans, city dignitaries and officials took it in turn to carry her coffin to the grave. Her example still holds much power.

*Below A ceiling painting in Rome showing Mary crowning St Rose of Lima (Lazzaro Baldi, 17th century).*

*Left A statue of Rose of Lima outside the Mission San Francisco de Asís, California (20th century).*

# ROBERT BELLARMINE

AMONG HIS MANY ACHIEVEMENTS, THE BRILLIANT THEOLOGIAN ROBERT BELLARMINE WAS RESPONSIBLE FOR CORRECTING THE VULGATE BIBLE AND WRITING A CATECHISM, BOTH IN USE TODAY.

**KEY FACTS**
*Archbishop and theologian*
DATES: *1542–1621*
BIRTH PLACE: *Montepulciano,*
*Tuscany, Italy*
PATRON OF: *Catechists and*
*catechumens*
FEAST DAY: *17 September*
EMBLEM: *Archbishop's vestments*

This great Italian archbishop chose a life of service to God over a secular career. Despite his father's wishes that he become a politician, Robert Bellarmine entered a novitiate in Rome and went on to teach in Jesuit colleges in Rome and Florence.

## GIFTED THEOLOGIAN
After his ordination in 1570, Robert became the first Jesuit professor of the University of Louvain. It was here that his writings and lectures began to stir strong feelings and debate. The Church brought him to Milan as professor of controversial theology at the Roman College. The lectures he gave there formed the basis of one of his greatest works, *Disputations on the Controversies of the Christian Faith*, which is described as "the most complete defence of Catholic teaching yet published". It was read eagerly by all Christians, although his enemies

*Above St Robert Bellarmine, in a painting from the church of Sant-Ignazio in Rome.*

*Below The trial of Galileo by Pope Urban VIII during the Inquisition in 1633 (Italian School, 17th century).*

denounced it as being so clever it must have been the joint effort of several Jesuit scholars. The work was banned in England.

## CONTROVERSY
Robert continued to attract controversy when his stand on the power of the Church was opposed by the French and by James I of England because he insisted the pope had complete authority above that of any monarch. His *De potestate papae* on this subject was burnt by the Paris parlement. Then, contrary to other Church leaders at the time, Robert was gentle with Galileo, asking him only to produce better evidence about the sun's movements.

Appointed Archbishop of Capua in 1602, Robert dedicated his time to preaching and to attending to his parish. His last appointment, in 1605, was as Prefect of the Vatican Library.

## SIMPLE LIFE, NOBLE DEATH
All his life, Robert Bellarmine lived on the bread and garlic diet of a peasant, denied himself fires in winter and gave his possessions to the poor. In old age, he continued to write, and his *Art of Dying* was translated into many languages. He died in Rome, but he had asked beforehand that the day of his death be marked each anniversary as a time to honour the Stigmata of St Francis of Assissi. The Church granted this request.

# FRANCIS OF SALES

THE FIRST SOLEMN BEATIFICATION TO TAKE PLACE IN ST PETER'S IN
ROME WAS THAT OF ST FRANCIS OF SALES, A SAINT WHO WAS
ADORED FOR HIS GENTLE LEADERSHIP.

**KEY FACTS**
*Founder, Doctor of the Church*
DATES: *1567–1622*
BIRTH PLACE: *Château de Sales,
Savoy, France*
PATRON OF: *Journalists, editors
and writers*
FEAST DAY: *24 January*
EMBLEM: *Archbishop's vestments*

Francis of Sales was physically
frail from birth, but had a
determined spirit and an unwa-
vering faith. From an early age, he
longed to join the Church. But
his father refused his permission,
instead sending Francis to study at
the University of Paris. He later
became a Doctor of Law at Padua
in Italy. When a relative found
Francis a position as provost to the
Jesuit chapter in Geneva, his
father finally relented and Francis
was ordained.

*Left* St Francis de Sales in the
Desert *(Marco Antonio Franceschini,
c.1700–10).*

## MISSIONARY PRIEST

Francis volunteered as a missionary to Chablais, where he distributed notices explaining his work
and Christ's message to attract his
reluctant congregation. Trekking
through isolated hamlets, he met
many dangers, including an attack
by a wolf and another by an angry
mob. Yet, slowly, lapsed Catholics
began to seek his guidance.

His success was acknowledged,
and in 1602, the Church appointed him Bishop of Geneva. Francis
lived in Annecy, where he was a
popular preacher and began to
compile his handwritten texts
into books. His most famous
work is the *Introduction to the
Devout Life*. In addition to his
writing, Francis was instrumental
in the founding of the Order of
the Visitation with his friend, St
Jane Frances de Chantal in 1610.

In 1622, Francis accepted an
invitation to join the Duke of
Savoy at Avignon, hoping to gain

privileges for his community.
In every village he passed, people
wanted him to stop and minister
to them. It was bitterly cold, but
Francis continued to preach
throughout Advent and Christmas,
before becoming ill and dying at a
Visitandine convent in Lyons.

*Right* St Francis of Sales *(Noel
Halle, 18th century).*

# ROQUE GONZALEZ

ALTHOUGH ROQUE GONZALEZ SPENT TWO DECADES PROTECTING
THE FREEDOM OF INDIGENOUS PEOPLE IN SOUTH AMERICA, HE WAS
MARTYRED FOR HIS FAITH, ALONG WITH TWO FELLOW MISSIONARIES.

**KEY FACTS**
*Martyr of Paraguay*
DATES: *1576–1628*
BIRTH PLACE: *Asunción,
Paraguay*
PATRON OF: *Posadas, Argentina,
and Encarnación, Paraguay*
FEAST DAY: *17 November*

Roque Gonzalez was born into a noble Spanish family in Asunción, Paraguay, and raised a strict Catholic. He was ordained in 1599 and ten years later joined the Jesuits to pursue his dream of becoming a missionary.

### THE REDUCTIONS

Gonzalez was instrumental in founding the Reductions, an organization that created settlements for local tribes in which they could learn about Christianity. The Jesuits were passionately opposed to slavery and sought to teach, nurse and bring solace to the converts.

Without complaint, Roque endured bad weather, insects, illness and hunger, but his biggest problems came from the European "guardians". The Spanish authorities demanded that these officials be present on every mission, but they were disdainful, even brutal, toward the indigenous people. This did not reflect on Roque, whose courtesy and simplicity won the admiration of numerous converts. He taught them valuable skills such as building and farming, and established churches and schools. After three years in the

*Left A statue standing in the ruins of a Jesuit mission near Encarnación in Paraguay.*

Reduction of St Ignatius of Loyola, Roque travelled east of the Parana and Uruguay Rivers, establishing six more communities.

In 1628, he was joined by Alonso Rodriguez and Juan de Castillo, also brothers of the Jesuit Reductions. They opened another Reduction near the Ijuhi River. Juan de Castillo was selected to stay there, while Roque and Alonso trekked to an even wilder area – Caaró, now part of southern Brazil.

### OPPOSITION AND MURDER

Now, however, the missionaries met with hostility from the local medicine man, who incited some local tribesmen to attack the priest. Giving him no opportunity to defend himself, they brutally murdered him with their tomahawks. They killed Alonso, too, then dragged their bodies into the church the men had built and set it alight. A few days later, Juan de Castillo was beaten and murdered at the Ijuhi River mission.

Although these sad events were reported, the records were lost until the 19th century, when they were discovered in archives kept in Argentina. All three men were canonized as the Martyrs of Paraguay in 1988.

*Left A map of Brazil by a Dutch cartographer in the early 17th century.*

# LORENZO RUIZ

THE FIRST FILIPINO SAINT WAS AFRAID OF MARTYRDOM, BUT HIS FAITH SUSTAINED HIM SO THAT, FACING DEATH, HE PROCLAIMED, "I AM A CATHOLIC AND HAPPY TO DIE FOR GOD".

**KEY FACTS**
*Martyr of Japan*
DATES: *1600–37*
BIRTH PLACE: *Binondo, Manila, Philippines*
PATRON OF: *Filipino youth*
FEAST DAY: *28 September*

Married with three children, Lorenzo was a member of the lay brotherhood, the Holy Rosary. In 1636 he was falsely accused of murder and, fearing an unfair trial and imprisonment, he sought refuge with the Dominicans. He sailed to Japan with Father Antonio Gonzalez and others.

On their arrival in Okinawa, the Emperor Tokugawa Yemitsu ordered the ship's Christians to be arrested. Faced by a tribunal in Nagasaki, a frightened Lorenzo asked if a denunciation of Christianity would bring release.

His translator consulted the judges, but Lorenzo found his courage and cried out, "I am a Christian." His brave confession brought terrible retribution. He was burnt, hung upside down and beheaded, and his body was thrown into the sea. Lorenzo was one of 17 people martyred by the Emperor. They were canonized as Martyrs of Japan in 1987.

*Left* The Franciscan Martyrs in Japan *(Don Juan Carreño de Miranda, 17th century).*

---

# MARTIN DE PORRES

THE LIFE OF MARTIN DE PORRES WAS ONE OF HUMBLE DEVOTION. HE IS VENERATED FOR HIS CONSTANT, UNASSUMING SERVICE TO THE POOR AND HIS MIRACULOUS CURES OF THE SICK.

**KEY FACTS**
*Charity worker*
DATES: *1579–1639*
BIRTH PLACE: *Lima, Peru*
PATRON OF: *Social justice, public education, public health service, people of mixed race, Italian barbers and hairdressers*
FEAST DAY: *3 November*

Martin de Porres was one of two illegitimate children born to a Spanish knight and a freed black woman. His mother apprenticed the 12-year-old Martin to a barber-surgeon, from whom he learned to care for the sick. Three years later, he was admitted to the Dominican Convent of the Holy Rosary, first as a lay brother and later as a coadjutor brother.

Here, Martin helped to establish a hospital and an orphanage. He also welcomed African slaves, who were comforted on their arrival in Lima. Animals loved

*Above St Martin de Porres (artist and date unknown).*

him, and it was said he could feed a dog, cat and mouse from the same bowl. One of his many duties at the convent was to handle the alms for the poor, and his careful budgeting allowed him to feed and clothe hundreds of needy people in the city.

Martin was acquainted with St Rose of Lima, and when he died, as at her funeral, noblemen and Church officials were honoured to carry his coffin to its grave.

# PETER CLAVER

THIS SPANISH MISSIONARY WAS BLESSED "BY GOD WITH THOSE GIFTS THAT PARTICULARLY PERTAIN TO APOSTLES, OF MIRACLES, OF PROPHECY AND OF READING HEARTS".

**KEY FACTS**
*Missionary*
DATES: *1580–1654*
BIRTH PLACE: *Verdu, Catalonia, Spain*
PATRON OF: *Colombia; missions to slaves and African Americans*
FEAST DAY: *9 September*

In the late 16th century, the port of Cartagena in Colombia was the centre of a thriving slave trade. Thousands of captive Africans arrived at the port every month. Here, Peter Claver baptized about 300,000 enslaved people and ministered also to traders, sailors, prisoners and others in need.

Born in Catalonia in Spain and educated at the University of Barcelona, Peter Claver's spiritual journey began at the Jesuit college in Majorca. Here, he met Alphonsus Rodriguez, who foretold that they both had a future in South America.

Peter left for Cartagena in 1610, and was ordained there by the Jesuits five years later. Inspired by working alongside Father Alfonso de Sandoval, who had been ministering to the slaves for 40 years, Claver declared himself "the slave of Negroes forever".

*Below Sts Peter Claver and Aloysius Gonzaga (St Xavier Church, Amsterdam, Holland).*

*Left A stained glass showing St Peter Claver (La Chapelle de La Colombière, Chalon sur Saône, France, 1930).*

## MISSIONARY TO THE SLAVES

Peter would meet the slave ships as they came into the harbour. Conscious of the need for immediate emotional and physical care, he comforted the slaves with his gentle manner and gave them gifts of medicines, food, brandy and lemons. He carried pictures to convey Christ's life and his promise of redemption explaining to his helpers, "we must speak to them with our hands before we try to speak to them with our lips". He later visited the plantations and mines where these slaves were put to work. Refusing the hospitality of the owners, who were not all happy to see him, he stayed in the slaves' quarters.

In 1650, Peter succumbed to a plague, which left him weak and incapacitated. He was confined to his cell. He was neglected by everyone until Dona Isabel de Urbina, who had funded his charities, came to his rescue, and with her sister nursed him. Four years later, Peter took mass before falling into a coma. The people of Cartagena, realizing they were losing an extraordinary priest, were anxious to kiss his hands. Even plantation owners sensed his greatness, and after his death his cell was stripped of relics. He was canonized, along with his friend Alphonsus Rodriguez, in 1888.

# JOSEPH OF COPERTINO

CREDITED WITH POWERS OF LEVITATION, AS WELL AS WITH MANY OTHER MIRACLES, THIS SIMPLE, THOUGH MISUNDERSTOOD, PRIEST GAINED THE NICKNAME "THE FLYING FRIAR".

**KEY FACTS**
*Mystic, miracle worker*
DATES: *1603–63*
BIRTH PLACE: *Copertino, near Brindisi, Italy*
PATRON OF: *Aviation, astronauts, students and students' examinations*
FEAST DAY: *18 September*
EMBLEM: *Flying in Franciscan habit*

The story of Joseph of Copertino is a sad one. His father's death left his mother penniless and she considered the slow-witted Joseph a tiresome burden. He was widely ridiculed and known for his violent temper. He seemed incapable of learning a trade and was rejected by local monasteries until Franciscans at Grottella accepted him as a servant. The young boy became serious in his devotions and performed menial tasks without complaint.

Despite his academic struggles, Joseph was ordained in 1628 and legends began to surround him. The mere sight of religious imagery or the mention of holy names sent Joseph into a state of ecstasy during which his body would rise in the air.

*Above* Pope Urban VIII *(Gianlorenzo Bernini, c.1625–30), before whom Joseph experienced a religious ecstasy.*

*Below* St Joseph of Copertino levitates *in front of an image of the Virgin. The saint was known for such ecstasies.*

## INQUISITION AND EXILE

In Joseph's 17 years at Grottella, witnesses recorded 70 incidents of levitation. One extraordinary occurrence reportedly took place during the construction of a cross of Calvary. The centre strut was 11m/36ft high and very heavy. Ten men couldn't lift it, but during the night, Joseph flew through the air, raised the strut and fixed it to the earth.

This behaviour so worried his superiors that he was prohibited from celebrating mass, eating with his brethren or attending processions. As his trances continued, and the public interest in him increased, Joseph was taken for questioning by the Inquisitors in Naples. Finding no fault with him, they sent him to Rome, where, at an audience with Pope Urban VIII, Joseph fell into an ecstasy and the pope decided to send him to Assisi.

With crowds of people seeking out the "Flying Friar", Joseph was exiled to a monastery at Pietrarossa, and was forbidden to speak or write to anyone. When pilgrims continued to clamour for a glimpse of his miracles, he was sent to an even more remote monastery at Fossombrone, and then to Assisi, where he was kept in strict isolation. Although consoled by his visions, Joseph died in solitude. In 1767, he was canonized for his humility and patience.

# VINCENT DE PAUL

A CLEVER AND DIPLOMATIC FRENCH PRIEST, ADEPT AT PERSUADING THE WEALTHY TO BE GENEROUS TO THE POOR. TODAY, HIS SOCIETIES CONTINUE HIS TRADITION OF CHARITY AND SOCIAL WELFARE.

**KEY FACTS**

*Founder of charitable orders, hospitals and orphanages*
DATES: *1581–1660*
BIRTH PLACE: *Landes, France*
PATRON OF: *Charity workers, hospitals, prisoners, Madagascar*
FEAST DAY: *27 September*
EMBLEM: *White cloak, begging bowl*

Vincent de Paul was born in Gascony to a peasant family, but he escaped the harsh life of a farmer by studying under the Franciscans at Dax and later attending Toulouse University. He was ordained at 19 and undertook a journey to Rome, at which point he seemed to vanish for two years. Historians suspect that he obscured, or even invented, the truth about this time.

In fact, Vincent himself perpetuated the most famous account of these two years through letters he wrote to his patron, a Gascon judge called Monsieur de Comet. He claimed that, on his way from

*Above* St Vincent de Paul *(attributed to Daniel Dumonstier, 17th century).*

*Below* St Vincent de Paul and the Sisters of Charity *(Jean Andre, c.1729).*

Toulouse to Narbonne, his ship was overwhelmed by Barbary pirates. He was sold into slavery at Tunis and endured two years there before, appealing to the Christian faith of one of his captors, he managed to escape to Marseilles.

Following this uncertain period, Vincent appeared in Rome, where he was given instructions by Pope Paul V to travel to the French court of Henry IV. Vincent remained in Paris as chaplain to the queen, which gave him access to the rich and powerful members of court. He was charming and kind and able to persuade many wealthy patrons to devote funds to his worthy causes.

## CHARITY WORKER

Vincent's sensitivities to the suffering of others came to dominate his thinking. He met, and was profoundly influenced by, Francis of Sales, and expanded his work to found hospitals and orphanages. He also worked to improve the lives of galley slaves and gave missions to prisoners in Bordeaux.

Then, in 1625, he founded an order of priests to preach in remote villages, where they cared for convicts and the poor. From 1633, the men lived in small communal groups and became known as the Vincentians, or Lazarists. The order was so successful in its mission that the Archbishop of Paris

*Above An old people's home run by the Sisters of Charity at St Vincent de Paul's hospital in Peking (1900).*

asked Vincent to train priests for parish work. For 27 years, Vincent gave weekly conferences, and his priests taught at seminaries around France. They also travelled as missionaries to Madagascar, Poland, Ireland, Scotland and countries in Africa.

Also in 1633, Vincent asked his friend, Louise de Marillac, to help him form an order of women to nurse the sick. At this time, nuns lived in enclosed houses, cut off from public lives. This new order, the Sisters of Charity, took a vow of obedience for one year only,

*Above The Church of St Vincent de Paul in Paris (Rouargue Frères, 19th century).*

"IT IS OUR DUTY TO PREFER THE SERVICE OF THE POOR TO EVERY-THING ELSE, AND TO OFFER SUCH SERVICE AS QUICKLY AS POSSIBLE... OFFER THE DEED TO GOD AS YOUR PRAYER."

ST VINCENT DE PAUL

this being the time the Church allowed noviciates to enjoy social contact. They renewed their vows yearly, but Vincent's rule allowed them to take their good works into the wider world.

### INFLUENCE

Vincent de Paul had a profound effect on Church reform and was extremely popular and influential in his lifetime. He inspired countless men and women to care for the dispossessed, and the rich to fund the work. His Sisters of Charity and Vincentians continue to work all around the world, helping the homeless, the debt-ridden, orphans and prisoners. In 1833, Frederick Ozanam, a Frenchman, instituted a lay brotherhood in the name of Saint Vincent de Paul. The modern worldwide membership of SVP, as this charity is called, includes men and women, Catholics and

### LOUISE DE MARILLAC

When Louise de Marillac was widowed in 1625, she devoted herself to the charity work of Vincent de Paul. He depended on her good sense, and she helped found the Sisters of Charity, "whose convent is the sickroom; their chapel their parish church; their cloister, the city streets". She was an inspiring teacher and, under her guidance, women were committed to 40 houses of the Charity, working with the sick and giving shelter to distressed women. She was canonized in 1934. Her feast day is 15 March.

*Above Louise de Marillac distributing alms to the poor (Diogène Maillart, 1920).*

Protestants. Vincent always insisted that Protestants be treated with courtesy and understanding.

Vincent's teaching of care and service, his gentle faith, and resolute belief in the sustaining love of God brought him many friends and admirers. He died peacefully and was buried at the church of Saint-Lazare. He was beatified in 1729 and Pope Clement XII canonized him in 1737.

# SAINTLY POPES

THE FIRST POPES ARE VENERATED AS MARTYRS OF THE FAITH, BUT
MANY OTHERS ARE REVERED FOR THE WISDOM, STRENGTH AND
SPIRITUAL LEADERSHIP THEY DEMONSTRATED IN OFFICE.

The role of the papacy has often been fraught with spiritual and political strife. When Christianity was just beginning to be established, during persecution by the Roman Empire, a number of early popes were martyred for their faith. Later, popes struggled to unite the Church, which was being damaged by warring factions and corruption. Many of these holy men have been canonized in recognition of their faithfulness and spiritual leadership.

"WHEN THE WORK OF
GOD IS FINISHED, LET
ALL GO OUT WITH THE
DEEPEST SILENCE, AND
LET REVERENCE BE
SHOWN TO GOD."

FROM THE RULE OF
ST BENEDICT

### THE MARTYRS
One of the first popes, Clement I, who died around AD 100, was a contemporary of Sts Peter and Paul. He was credited with miraculous powers, and some of his writings are extant, revealing him as a thoughtful theologian. His Epistle to the Corinthians is significant because it marks the first time a bishop of Rome intervened in the business of another Church. Clement I was martyred by having an anchor tied to his neck and being pushed into the sea. Allegedly, angels built him a tomb on the seabed, and this could be seen when the sea was at low tide.

Pope Callistus was born a slave and rebelled against Roman law by promoting marriage between freeborn Christians and slaves. Kind and forgiving, he was thrown

*Above A fresco of Leo the Great (Italian School, 8th century AD).*

down a well and drowned in AD 222. Pope Cornelius was likewise resented for his policy of forgiveness to those who truly repented their sins. His attitude caused a split among churchmen, and the Romans beheaded him.

Sixtus II, who became pope in AD 257, was killed by the sword one year after he took office.

### LEADERS OF THE FAITH
One of the most influential early popes was Leo the Great. During his reign, he freed Rome from the barbarians and healed a Church fractured by war and the spread of pagan beliefs. Both the people and the clergy needed clarification on Christian dogma. In a letter to the Council of Chalcedon, Leo explained that Jesus Christ is one person, in whom the divine and the human are united, but not mixed. This became a fundamental teaching of the Church.

*Left Coronation of Pope Celestine V in August 1294 (French School, 16th century).*

The Church continued to strengthen under the rule of Pope Gregory the Great, an austere, devout man, who succeeded in establishing the primacy of Rome against claims from the Eastern Orthodox Church. He developed the Church liturgy and mounted a successful mission to England.

Gregory II, too, was an energetic apostle. He instigated reforms in the clergy, built churches and sustained the Church's authority against secular power. The monastery at Monte Cassino was revived under his care, and he built another in Rome, St Paul's-outside-the-Walls.

## DIVISION AND REFORM

The problems between the Eastern and Western branches of the Church became urgent during the office of Pope Leo IX (1002–54). Under his rule, the Church increased its independence from secular authority, and he sent legates to confer with Michael Cerularius, Patriarch of Constantinople. Leo died before the schism between the East and West had widened into total separation. Leo was a holy man, and many miracles were attributed to him after his death.

Pope Gregory VII continued his predecessors' reformation of the Church and alienated many powerful people in the process. He was determined to stop the practice of laymen appointing officers of the Church, because these laymen were often the rich

and powerful, who used the clergy to extend their secular ambitions. The German Emperor Henry IV was infuriated by this reform and tried to depose Gregory, though he later famously repented by standing at the palace gates for three days in the snow.

Peter Celestine (or Celestine V) founded the Celestine Order, but was an unwilling and unworldly pope. He abdicated his office but was still canonized for his devout nature in 1313.

In the 16th century, while the Church was still reeling from the Reformation, Pope Pius V provided vigorous leadership. A key figure in the Counter-Reformation, he helped rid the Church of heresy and corruption, controlled excessive spending by the bishops, and reformed the liturgy, making the words and rituals accessible to ordinary worshippers.

Indeed, throughout the centuries, the popes who have attained sainthood are often men who have brought remarkable devotion and wise leadership to the papal office.

*Left St Peter's Basilica and Square, Rome, as depicted in the 18th century.*

*Left Gregory the Great dictating a manuscript (illuminated manuscript, 9th century).*

## POPE PIUS X

Pope Pius X wanted "to renew all things in Christ". He opened the Church and her liturgy to ordinary people, encouraged daily attendance at Mass and welcomed children to partake of the Holy Eucharist. Church music was modernized, and on Sundays, Pius X would deliver a short sermon in a Vatican courtyard, which anyone was welcome to attend. He faced problems with the French state, and was forced to sacrifice Church property in exchange for freedom from secular control. He also restated the Christian doctrine against what he saw as heretical interpretations, in what he termed the "Modernist" crisis. After his death in 1914, a cultus came quickly into being.

*Above Pope Pius X (c. 1905).*

# MARGUERITE BOURGEOYS

THIS PIONEERING EDUCATOR, WHO ESTABLISHED THE FIRST RELIGIOUS ORDER IN CANADA AND THE FIRST SCHOOL IN MONTREAL, BECAME KNOWN AS THE "MOTHER OF THE COLONY".

**KEY FACTS**
*Educator, founder of a religious order*
DATES: *1620–1700*
BIRTH PLACE: *Troyes, France*
PATRON OF: *Poverty*
FEAST DAY: *12 January*

Born into the large family of a rich merchant, Marguerite Bourgeoys enjoyed a privileged upbringing. After her mother's death in 1639, she cared for her younger siblings but soon felt the calling of a religious vocation.

She joined a lay order of women called the Congregation of Troyes, an organization devoted to teaching the poor children of the area.

### CALLED TO CANADA
In 1652, Marguerite's future took a dramatic turn when she met Monsieur de Maisonneuve, a governor in New France (now Canada). He was recruiting teachers for an outpost called Ville-Marie, and because she was not a cloistered nun, Marguerite was able to accept the challenge.

She arrived at the fort in 1653, finding herself both teacher and nurse for the tiny community. As there was no permanent place of

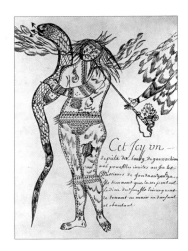

*Above An engraving of a tattooed Iroquois Indian holding a snake and smoking a peace pipe (c.1701).*

*Below Marguerite Bourgeoys with Canadian Indian converts (artist and date unknown).*

worship, she organized the building of the stone chapel of Notre-Dame-de-Bon-Secour in 1655. A year later, seeing an urgent need for education in this new land, she established the first Montreal school, teaching domestic, spiritual and academic subjects. The school thrived and she travelled back to France three times in the following years to enlist teachers.

### FOUNDING EDUCATOR
Marguerite and her fellow teachers were very courageous women, spreading their schools across the wilderness of Quebec. They were resolved to educate the children of the Iroquois tribes as well as those of the French colonists, but they faced hardships of illness, hunger, fires, and violent attacks from the very people they hoped to help. In 1676, determined to persevere with her cause, Marguerite founded the Sisters of Notre Dame.

Sadly, by 1698, she had become exhausted by hardship, and chose to resign as the superior. In keeping with the selflessness of her life, she nursed a young nun who was dying. She prayed, "God, why do you not take me instead, I who am useless and good for nought!" The young nun lived and, a few days later, Marguerite died. Thousands mourned the loss of her wise, steady guidance.

Today, giving testimony to her faith and ambition, there are 200 convents and missions around the world following Marguerite's ideals of Christian education.

# LOUIS GRIGNION DE MONTFORT

THIS UNCONVENTIONAL PRIEST ENRAGED CHURCH AUTHORITIES BUT HIS MISSIONS TO THE POOR AND INSPIRATIONAL SERMONS ENSURED HIM RECOGNITION AS A FAITHFUL APOSTLE.

**KEY FACTS**
*Missionary apostolic and founder*
DATES: *1673–1716*
BIRTH PLACE: *Montfort, Brittany*
FEAST DAY: *28 April*

As a student in Paris, Louis de Montfort experienced such squalid poverty that his future course as a missionary to the poor was decided. After his ordination in Paris in 1700, he was sent to work in Poitiers. There he founded the Daughters of Wisdom, an order of nuns that nursed in hospitals, and took his own mission to the poorest quarters.

## EVANGELIST TO THE POOR

He was very popular with the public, but his flamboyant speeches caused concern among his superiors. To enhance his lessons, Louis would make an effigy of the devil dressed as a rich woman, then burn irreligious books before it. Or he would act out the role of a dying sinner caught between the angels and the devil. His writing, too, was dramatic. The *True Devotion to the Blessed Virgin* gained a wide readership, except among theologians.

Banned from Poitiers for his evangelistic style, Louis was given the office of "missionary apostolic" by the pope. This allowed him to roam Brittany and Poitiers, which well suited his personality. The singing of the hymns that he wrote reinforced his intense and emotional preaching, and he encouraged the use of the rosary in prayer.

*Above Louis Grignion de Montfort in a church dedicated to him in Saint-Laurent-sur-Sèvres.*

*Right Pope Pius XII canonized Louis Grignion de Montfort in 1947.*

Wherever he went, churches were restored and charity to the poor was revived. Lapsed believers returned to faith after attending his sermons, while in La Rochelle, a number of Calvinists returned to the Roman Catholic Church.

In 1712, Louis founded an association of missionary priests called the Company of Mary. These men, and the women of his Daughters of Wisdom, were trained to follow his emotional approach to faith. The orders have since become highly successful international apostolic and educational missions.

Louis Grignion de Montfort died in Saint-Laurent-sur-Sèvres and was canonized in 1947.

# JOHN-BAPTIST DE LA SALLE

THIS SAINT MADE A PROFOUND DIFFERENCE TO THE EDUCATIONAL SYSTEM IN 17TH-CENTURY FRANCE, AND HIS INFLUENCE IS EVIDENT TODAY IN THE CONTINUING SUCCESS OF HIS SCHOOLS.

**KEY FACTS**

*Educator, founder of the Brothers of the Christian Schools*
DATES: *1651–1719*
BIRTH PLACE: *Rheims, France*
PATRON OF: *Schoolteachers*
FEAST DAY: *7 April*

John-Baptist de La Salle, a French nobleman, became one of the most distinguished educators in Europe. He studied in Rheims and at Saint-Sulpice, in Paris, where he was ordained in 1678.

In 1679, he met Adrian Nyel, a layman hoping to start a school for poor boys. While he encouraged him, John-Baptist did not foresee the great role he himself would play in this endeavour. He later wrote, "God, who guides all things with wisdom and serenity …willed to commit me entirely to the development of the schools."

## CHRISTIAN SCHOOLS

John-Baptist used his family home to house the schoolmasters. Patient and confident in his methods, he slowly gathered men dedicated to the profession. He sold his home, resigned as canon of Rheims, and with his 12 followers, drew up a Rule.

Teachers were to make a vow of obedience, renewable ever year, and they agreed on a name – the Brothers of the Christian Schools. Rural congregations appealed to him to train youths who would then teach in the villages, so John-Baptist opened the first training school for teachers in Rheims in 1686, followed by others in Paris and Saint-Denis. He also opened free schools for poor boys in Paris.

He drew up statutes to govern his growing institution: no Brother of the Christian Schools should be ordained a priest, and no priest should be a teacher; classes were

*Above The interior of Saint-Sulpice in Paris, where John-Baptist de La Salle studied and was ordained.*

*Below An engraving of John-Baptist de La Salle preaching (H. Jannin and P. Sarrazin, 1845).*

to be given in the vernacular, not Latin; pupils were to be silent and taught as a class, not as individuals. By 1700, there were schools across France. Today, there are more than 20,000 members, and Christian Brothers schools can be found across the French- and English-speaking worlds.

Although John-Baptist faced controversy within his brotherhood over rules and teaching methods, his contribution to the training of teachers and educational methods was significant, especially for working-class boys, who previously had been destined for manual labour. His methods of caring for delinquent boys made important advances in the rehabilitation of disturbed youth.

He died in Rheims after a short illness and was canonized in 1900. His relics lie in Rome.

# JOHN JOSEPH OF THE CROSS

HIS SOLICITUDE FOR THE UNHAPPY, AND HIS GENTLE MANNERS AS A
LEADER, BROUGHT THIS FRANCISCAN PRIEST WIDESPREAD TRUST
AND ADMIRATION AMONG THE PEOPLE OF NAPLES.

**KEY FACTS**
*Franciscan minister-provincial*
DATES: *1654–1734*
BIRTH PLACE: *Ischia, near Naples*
PATRON OF: *Naples*
FEAST DAY: *5 March*

John Joseph longed to follow the teachings of Franciscan Peter of Alcantara, and to keep rules of simplicity and contemplation. He joined the order when he was 16, but the quality of his character brought him rapid promotion. He was only 21 years old when he was placed in charge of a monastery in Piedimonte di Alife, and despite his longing for seclusion, he was ordained in 1677.

Still devoted to a contemplative life, John Joseph built hermitages where his congregation could take retreats for prayer and penance. He was sensitive in his handling of penitents, guiding them through confession and meditation. However, although he was diligent in following his duties, he begged the Church to release him from his position of authority. After a short period in Naples studying as a novicemaster, John Joseph returned to Piedimonte, becoming a menial in 1681. His leadership qualities were such that, in 1684, his fellow friars re-elected him as guardian.

## MINISTER-PROVINCIAL

In the latter part of the 17th century, the Spaniards had control of Naples, and with the pope's agreement, they insisted Spanish priests fill all high office in the Neapolitan Church. But when the Spaniards withdrew, John Joseph appealed to the pope to recognize Naples as an Italian province. He also requisitioned two large houses that the Spanish had

*Above A view of the island of Ischia, the birthplace of John Joseph of the Cross (English School, 18th century).*

claimed for themselves. In recognition of his contribution, the pope made John Joseph minister-provincial of the new province.

John Joseph applied himself to improving the discipline and organization of the monasteries, badly needed after the Spanish era. When satisfied he had done his duty, he obtained exemption from further office. He continued to help sinners and penitents, and offer spiritual counselling. The people of Naples adored him, and would gather round him when he went out in the streets. The more hysterical would try to tear patches from his ragged habit, seeking something of the holy old priest for their own comfort.

After he died, in Naples, a cultus arose, and he was canonized in 1839.

*Left This contemporary image of a Franciscan monk shows the austere simplicity of the garments that John Joseph of the Cross would have worn.*

# JEANNE DELANOUE

JEANNE DELANOUE GAVE UP A BUSY COMMERCIAL LIFE FOR ONE OF
PERSONAL SQUALOR, DEVOTING HER LIFE INSTEAD TO CARING FOR
THE POOR, PARTICULARLY OUTCAST WOMEN AND REFUGEES.

**KEY FACTS**
*Founder*
DATES: *1666–1736*
BIRTH PLACE: *Saumur, France*
FEAST DAY: *17 August*

In her earlier life, Jeanne Delanoue ran the family business, selling drapery and religious items. At the age of 26, she encountered Françoise Suchet, a religious enthusiast who claimed to have experienced visions. Inspired by this eccentric woman, Jeanne turned her home and shop into a guesthouse, transforming the cellars and caves below it into shelters for the homeless.

By 1704, Jeanne had founded an order that came to be called the Sisters of Providence. The order brought solace to homeless women, unmarried mothers, and prostitutes, and during the famine

*Right The Castle in Saumur, the city where Jeanne Delanoue was born and founded her religious order.*

of 1709 they housed 100 starving people. Each day, having slept in a filthy old shroud, Jeanne would rise at 3 a.m., pray, then tend to the needy women.

Her nickname, "the pig of Jesus", suggests a lack of care for her appearance, but Jeanne was greatly respected for her protection of outcasts, and for her care of refugees during the frequent periods of war and famine. She founded 12 communities before her death in Saumur.

# FRANCIS SERRANO

A COURAGEOUS AND FAITHFUL MISSIONARY, FRANCIS SERRANO
WAS COMPLIMENTED BY A FELLOW PRIEST FOR WORKING "AS
ENERGETICALLY AS A LION FOR THE BENEFIT OF SOULS".

**KEY FACTS**
*Martyr*
DATES: *1691–1748*
BIRTH PLACE: *Granada, Spain*
FEAST DAY: *17 February*

Francis Serrano was a Dominican priest who left Spain for the Philippines in 1725. Assigned to the post of Fujian, he showed great virtue as a missionary in a treacherous land.

Serrano was a hardy man, who had an abundance of energy, and was adventurous in spirit. His writings reveal him as a humorous, high-spirited character. He would journey unafraid through the night, crossing rivers and forests, determined to tend to his persecuted flock. He even disguised himself as a local peasant

so that he could pass unnoticed into villages to administer the Sacraments in secret.

In 1746, he was imprisoned in Fuzhou and, during 19 months of incarceration, endured violent

*Left A map of Indonesia and the Philippines (Charles Marie Rigobert Bonne, 18th century).*

beatings that badly damaged his hearing. He and other missionaries were branded on their faces, and Francis wrote, "Our hearts exulted. We were branded as slaves of Jesus Christ…these heads are no longer ours, but the Lord's. He can take them whenever He wishes." Francis, who was finally suffocated to death in his prison cell, is included among the Martyrs of China canonized in 2000.

# LEONARD OF PORT MAURICE

LEONARD WISHED FIRST, THAT HE "MIGHT LIVE FOR GOD AND LAST, THAT HE MIGHT LIVE IN GOD". TRAVELLING AROUND ITALY, HE USED THE STATIONS OF THE CROSS TO PREACH THE CHRISTIAN MESSAGE.

## KEY FACTS
*Franciscan missionary*
DATES: *1676–1751*
BIRTH PLACE: *Port Maurice, Italy*
PATRON OF: *Missions in Catholic lands*
FEAST DAY: *26 November*
EMBLEM: *Franciscan habit*

Baptized as Paul Jerome Casanova in Port Maurice, Leonard joined the Franciscan Order, basing his life on the teachings of Christ as he understood them from a close reading of the New Testament, and on the Rules of St Francis of Assisi.

In 1709, Leonard instituted reforms at the friary of San Francesco del Monte in Florence, bringing its practices back into line with the strict austerity demanded by St Francis. He attracted many followers, whom he trained and sent out to preach across Tuscany. He also established a hermitage nearby, with the purpose of enabling the friars to make biannual retreats of silence and fasting. In 1730, he was sent to Rome, where he was appointed Guardian of St Bonaventura. During his time here, he made a point of ministering to soldiers, sailors, convicts and galley slaves.

### STATIONS OF THE CROSS
In 1736, Leonard asked to be released from office, and travelled around Italy, often preaching outdoors. As a tool to spread his message, and as a symbol of his devotion, he used the Stations of the Cross, teaching his listeners how to pray before each of the

*Left Leonard of Port Maurice used the Stations of the Cross to teach his listeners about the Christian faith. The Fifth Station recounts how Simon of Cyrene helped Christ carry the cross (Giovanni Domenico Tiepolo, 1749).*

14 incidents that marked Christ's journey to the cross. It is said that he installed about 500 Stations of the Cross throughout Italy.

In 1744, Pope Benedict XIV sent Leonard to Corsica, where he encountered a hostile political atmosphere, and turbulent congregations who brought weapons to church services. The mountainous land was hard for a priest, who had to walk everywhere. Leonard's health suffered, and eventually, a ship had to be sent to bring him home.

Leonard returned to his Italian flock with renewed vigour and, in 1750, set up the Stations of the Cross in the Roman Coliseum, where he preached to a huge, excited crowd.

Soon afterward, he took a mission to the south, but the weather turned against him. Refusing an offer of shelter from some friars at Spoleto, Leonard insisted on continuing to Rome. Here he took to his bed and, exhausted by the journey, he received the last rites and a message from the pope before he died.

*Left The Gulf of Porto in Corsica. Leonard was sent to the island by Pope Benedict XIV in 1744.*

# THE MARTYRS OF CHINA

THESE MARTYRS REPRESENT THOUSANDS OF CHRISTIANS WHO
WERE TORTURED AND KILLED FOR THEIR CHRISTIAN FAITH IN
CHINA OVER A PERIOD OF MORE THAN 400 YEARS.

*Above St Jean-Gabriel Perboyre,
martyred in China in 1840 (François
Constant Petit, 19th century).*

The history of Christianity in China is a turbulent one that has involved much persecution. The first contact Chinese people had with Christianity was from the Nestorian heresy, which spread East, reaching China by the early 6th century AD.

Later, relative stability, brought by the Mongol expansion in Asia during the 13th and 14th centuries, opened up routes between the East and West and led to direct contact being established between China and Europe. Among those taking advantage of this new connection to the East were missionaries, who were eager to spread the Christian message.

## EARLY CHINESE MISSIONS

The first Roman Catholic mission to China was led by Bishop John of Montecorvino (1246–1328), who established friendly relations with the Yuan dynasty.

Unfortunately, later missionaries were not so well received. The Yuan dynasty fell in 1368, and later regimes showed violent hostility to foreigners and foreign religions. Many missionaries to China never returned. Some were defeated by the harsh conditions of travel. One such was Francis Xavier, who died in 1551 soon after being refused entry to the country. Others were deliberately targeted by the ruling powers in China. This was the destiny of Francisco Fernandez de Capillas, a Dominican, who led a mission to Fujian and was beheaded during the early Ching dynasty in 1648.

*Left A figure of
St Paul inside St
Paul's Church in
Macau, China.*

*Above Father Adam Schall von Bell
(1591–1666) was a German Jesuit
missionary to China (German
School, 17th century).*

## THE CHING DYNASTY

The Ching dynasty was particularly anti-Christian, and officials of the regime hounded Christians in China for 400 years. Among the victims were Spanish Dominican missionary Pedro Sanz, who was murdered in 1747, and Francis Regis Clet of St Vincent de Paul, who died in 1820.

Despite the killings of foreign missionaries and thousands of Chinese converts, the faith took root. Early in the 20th century, the Rev. Fang Ho collected the relics of these early Chinese martyrs and translated them to Taipei in Taiwan where they rest in the Chinese Blessed Martyrs Church in Peng Chiao.

Archives from the 19th century record details of some of the martyrs of that period. These names

> "ALMIGHTY GOD, WE GIVE YOU THANKS FOR CHOOSING MANY CHINESE FAITHFUL TO WITNESS FOR CHRIST BY GIVING UP THEIR LIVES... WE ALSO PRAY THAT WE MAY FOLLOW THE EXAMPLE OF THESE CHINESE BY REMAINING STRONG IN FAITH, HOPE AND LOVE..."
>
> EXCERPT FROM PRAYER TO THE CHINESE MARTYRS

are included among the 120 Martyrs of China. The latter were chosen to represent the thousands of anonymous victims of religious persecution. First among them is Peter Wu Guosheng, who died in 1814. Another is Agnes Cao Guiying, an account of whose torture and martyrdom in 1856 can be found in Chinese court records. She was kept in a cage so small she could not move her limbs to sit, and died in captivity.

Other known martyrs come from records dated during 1900, at the time of the Boxer Rebellion, when the Chinese rose up against everything perceived as foreign. European and Chinese Christians, nuns and priests, women and children were brutally murdered for their faith. Among them were Mary Guo-Li, who died alongside her four grandchildren and two daughters-in-law. All were beheaded on 7 July 1900. Lang-Yang and her seven-year-old son, Paolo, were stabbed and burnt a few days later. More than 30 men and women were dragged from their cathedral in Taiyuan, Shanxi Province. They were given time to take Mass and pray before they were beheaded in a mass execution on 9 July 1900. They, too, are named among the Martyrs of China.

*Above Funeral of St Jean-Louis Bonnard at the seminary of Nam-Dinh (artist unknown, 19th century).*

## COMMUNISM

The Ching dynasty was toppled in 1907, and after years of war, the Communists took power. Their persecution of Christians was as fierce as that of the previous regime. Churches were burnt, unknown thousands of Christians martyred, and it seemed that the faith had finally been eradicated. Even the ownership of a Bible could lead to imprisonment or execution. However, the faithful did not abandon their beliefs. Instead, they met in secret, risking harsh punishment.

Pope John Paul II proclaimed the 120 Blessed Martyrs of China as saints in 2000. Among them are 33 foreign missionaries and 87 Chinese, including bishops, priests, nuns, friars and 76 lay people. In 2007, the Chinese government gave the Roman Catholic Church permission to build a church, the first in more than 70 years. Christianity is now officially recognized in China and public worship is permitted in churches and cathedrals. No longer persecuted, 22 million Chinese people – Protestants and Catholics – have publicly proclaimed their faith.

## HYACINTH CASTANEDA

Hyacinth Castaneda was born in Setaro, Spain, but longed to spread the message of Christianity outside Europe. He travelled across the Atlantic, suffering from infection and seasickness, before walking across Mexico to reach the Pacific coast. From there, he travelled to the Philippines, where he was ordained, then took a boat to China. From his base in Fulcien, he started preaching and converted many people. The Chinese authorities arrested him, imprisoning him in what is now Vietnam. He was held for three years, along with fellow prisoner Vincent Liem. During this time he was branded and tortured, and he was beheaded in 1773. He is listed among the Martyrs of Vietnam.

*Below Missionaries to China were martyred in various ways: some were beheaded, others garrotted and some were burnt alive (Indo-Chinese School, 19th century).*

# GERARD MAJELLA

GERARD MAJELLA, A HUMBLE, SIMPLE LAY BROTHER FROM A MODEST BACKGROUND, HAS BEEN DESCRIBED AS THE "MOST FAMOUS WONDER-WORKER OF THE 18TH CENTURY".

**KEY FACTS**
*Miracle worker*
DATES: *1725–55*
BIRTH PLACE: *Muro Lucano,*
*near Naples*
PATRON OF: *Mothers*
FEAST DAY: *16 October*

Gerard Majella's widowed mother said of him that "he was born for heaven", and he demonstrated his religious calling from an early age, spending much of his childhood in prayer.

He initially turned down an apprenticeship as a tailor – his father's profession – to work as a servant in the house of the Bishop of Lacedogna. But the bishop was bad-tempered and unpredictable, and Gerard was neither sly nor subtle enough to withstand such a regime. So he returned home to take up his apprenticeship and worked to support his mother and three sisters.

## A SIMPLE LAY BROTHER
In 1752, Gerard fulfilled his long-held dream to join a religious order when he was accepted as a lay brother into the Congregation of the Most Holy Redeemer, or the Redemptorists. St Alphonsus

*Above Gerard Majella saving fishermen near Naples (M. Barberis, 19th century).*

*Below The Market at Naples (Domenico Gargiulo, 17th century). Gerard Majella never travelled beyond the boundaries of the city.*

Liguori, the founder of this community, had a particular empathy with peasant and illiterate congregations and Gerard found a role as a gardener, tailor and porter. His fellow priests were puzzled by his frail appearance and shy manners, and decided that he must be "either a fool or a great saint".

## MIRACLES AND CHARITY
Claims were soon circulating that Gerard could heal the sick, appear in two places at one time, read minds and tell the future. Perhaps most extraordinary of all, one story tells of his ability to levitate and fly half a mile through the air.

Despite Gerard's lowly position in the Redemptorists, he always found alms and food for the poor, and time and patience for the sick. Because of his purity and sensitivity, he was appointed as the spiritual director of numerous communities of nuns.

He remained unworldly and, when accused of lewd behaviour by a young woman, refused to defend or incriminate himself, believing silence to be the righteous response to dishonesty and injustice. The girl later admitted that the charges were false.

Gerard was only 29 years old when he died of tuberculosis. Although he had never travelled outside the kingdom of Naples, a cultus grew after his death. He is patron saint of unborn children and expectant mothers in particular, and was canonized by Pope Pius X in 1904.

# MARGARET D'YOUVILLE

MARGARET D'YOUVILLE IS KNOWN AS THE MOTHER OF UNIVERSAL CHARITY. THE FOUNDER OF THE SISTERS OF CHARITY OF MONTREAL, SHE "LOVED GREATLY JESUS CHRIST AND THE POOR".

**KEY FACTS**
*Founder*
DATES: *1701–71*
BIRTH PLACE: *Varennes, Canada*
FEAST DAY: *23 December*

From a very early age, Margaret was faced with responsibility and the rigours of poverty. Born in Varennes, Canada, she was the eldest of six children. Her father died when she was seven years old and, after a brief education from the Ursuline nuns, she helped her mother to bring up her siblings.

From this difficult start in life, she made what appeared to be a good marriage to a fur trader, François Youville. The Governor-General and other grand officials attended the wedding.

Margaret's marriage brought her great unhappiness, during which her faith sustained her. Youville was not only a drunkard and a gambler, but also illicitly traded alcohol with local Indians. The effect of this was so devastating on their community that they begged the governor for protection. Margaret bore four children, of whom only two survived. When her husband died in 1730, she found he had spent her mother's legacy and left her in debt.

## DEVOTION TO THE POOR

Margaret opened a shop to support her children and, despite her own hardships, found time to visit others in unfortunate circumstances. She tended to the sick and to criminals and, when her eldest son left home to enter the seminary (both sons became priests), she moved a destitute blind woman into his room. Her female

*Right* Montreal on the St Lawrence River in 1760. *Margaret founded her order in the city in 1737.*

friends shared her sense of duty and faith and worked as seamstresses to raise money for the poor. But Margaret still struggled to find resources to pay for her good works. She was once forced to beg for funds to pay for the funeral of an executed criminal.

*Left* The Storming of Quebec (*English School, 18th century*). *The "Grey Nuns" tended the wounded on both sides of the fighting.*

## THE GREY NUNS

In 1737, along with three young companions, Margaret formed a lay order for the service of the poor – the Sisters of Charity of Montreal, known as the "Grey Nuns". They cared for women and prisoners, nursed the sick during a smallpox epidemic, and with an all-embracing policy that made no distinction of race or status, they tended to the wounded of both sides during the war between Quebec and England that ended in 1759. The Grey Nuns' convent was burnt down twice, but the entire community funded the rebuilding.

Margaret died in Montreal, and was canonized in 1990, the first native-born Canadian saint.

# VINCENT LIEM

THIS SAINT TOOK THE NAME VINCENT LIEM OF PEACE, YET HE
CONFRONTED TERRIBLE, OFFICIALLY-SANCTIONED VIOLENCE, AND
EVENTUALLY MARTYRDOM, FOR HIS CHRISTIAN FAITH.

**KEY FACTS**
*Protomartyr*
DATES: *1732–73*
BIRTH PLACE: *Tra Lu, Vietnam*
FEAST DAY: *7 November*

In the 16th century, Christian missions from Europe entered the kingdoms of Tonkin, Annam and Cochin, now Vietnam. When Vincent Liem was born in Tra Lu in 1732, his parents were part of a well-established, but furtive Christian community that risked state persecution.

A pious child, Vincent joined the Dominican seminary when he was 12 years old. He was an intelligent and diligent pupil, and in 1753 was sent to the St John Lateran Dominican College in Manila in the Philippines, where he prepared for ordination. In 1759, he returned to his homeland and taught noviciates at the seminary of Trung Linh.

### SUFFERING PERSECUTION
The persecution of Christians was remorseless during this period, perhaps as severe as anything the early Christians suffered under the Roman Empire. Documentation of the Vietnamese martyrs is rare, but it is estimated that between the 16th and 18th centuries, more

*Above A map showing the Kingdom of Tonkin in South Asia (Charles Marie Rigobert Bonne, 1780).*

than 100,000 Christians were killed. Torture was common: limbs were cut off, flesh burnt from the living body, and some Christians who escaped death were branded on the face with the words *ta dao*, meaning "false religion".

Faced with religious oppression similar to that endured by the first apostles, Vincent followed their example, undergoing difficult journeys to spread the faith. As Sts Peter and Paul had done, he worked among non-believers, seeking converts despite the fearful dangers he risked.

Vincent was caught and imprisoned in Trung Linh, where he met fellow prisoner Hyacinth Castaneda, a Spanish priest. He was executed in 1773, the first Vietnamese-born martyr. Vincent Liem was canonized in 1988, and is one of the named Martyrs of Vietnam, representing the thousands of anonymous Christians who have been murdered in this part of the world.

*Left A coloured engraving showing the forms of torture endured by Catholic missionaries in Tonkin, China (French School, 19th century).*

# PAUL OF THE CROSS

THE SON OF A NOBLEMAN, PAUL OF THE CROSS REFUSED A RICH INHERITANCE AND A WEALTHY WIFE BECAUSE OF HIS INNER DESIRE TO FOLLOW HIS SPIRITUAL VOCATION.

**KEY FACTS**
*Founder*
DATES: *1694–1775*
BIRTH PLACE: *Ovada, Italy*
FEAST DAY: *19 October*

Paul Francis Danei refused a considerable inheritance and a promising marriage. Instead, he joined the Venetian army as a volunteer in 1714. This experience affected him profoundly and, within a year, he became a recluse.

In 1720, he emerged with a powerful vocation, determined to share with believers his profound awareness of the Passion of Christ, the suffering Jesus endured as he hung on the cross.

He was ordained as a priest and, with the help of his brother, founded the Passionist Congregation in 1727, with the aim of combining monastic virtue with active missionary work.

Paul wanted his followers to live monastic lives, even as they went forth to spread his message and minister to the sick, but papal authority was granted only after the severe rules of the order were modified. The order expanded throughout Paul's lifetime, and in 1771, an enclosed convent of Passionist nuns was approved.

**Right** *The monastery of the noviciate of the Passionist friars in Italy.*

# BENEDICT JOSEPH LABRE

PILGRIM AND MENDICANT, BENEDICT JOSEPH LABRE WAS THE EMBODIMENT OF THOSE RARE, HOLY MEN AND WOMEN WHO ARE DESCRIBED AS "FOOLS FOR CHRIST'S SAKE".

**KEY FACTS**
*Mendicant*
DATES: *1748–83*
BIRTH PLACE: *Boulogne, France*
PATRON OF: *Tramps, the homeless*
FEAST DAY: *16 April*

All faiths produce exceptional followers, who dedicate their lives to spirituality at the expense of a conventional role in society. Benedict Joseph Labre, the eldest of 15 children of a prosperous shopkeeper, was such a man.

Both the Cistercians and the Carthusians claimed that Benedict was too young and delicate to join them but possibly they sensed his eccentricity. Rejected by these monks, Benedict decided to become a pilgrim, walking from his birthplace of Boulogne to Rome, then visiting, again on foot, the holy sites of Italy, Switzerland and France.

**Above** *Nuns standing in front of the St Labre mission in Ashland, Montana (19th century).*

He slept in fields and on street corners, and accepted food when offered, but gave away any money he received. In 1774, Benedict settled in Rome, spending his days praying in the churches, his nights curled up in doorways. Eventually, due to poor health, he moved into a shelter for poor men, where he gave his food to other inmates. He collapsed in church while praying, and was carried to the shop of a friendly butcher, where he died.

The Romans recognized him as a holy man, a cultus developed, and he was canonized in 1881.

# ALPHONSUS LIGUORI

ALPHONSUS LIGUORI RECOMMENDED SIMPLICITY IN THE PULPIT AND CHARITY IN THE CONFESSIONAL. A BEGUILING PREACHER, HE WAS LOVED BY HIS CONGREGATION.

**KEY FACTS**
*Founder*
DATES: *1696–1787*
BIRTH PLACE: *Naples, Italy*
PATRON OF: *Those who hear confessions, teachers of moral theology*
FEAST DAY: *1 August*

Alphonsus' father was ambitious for his son, propelling him into a legal career in Naples. Alphonsus became a successful barrister, but after eight years a voice prompted him to "Leave the world and give yourself to me". He studied theology privately, and after he was ordained in 1726, proved to be a priest with moderate views, sympathetic to sinners.

As a preacher, he developed a clear, intelligible style, anxious that "even the poorest old woman in the congregation" should understand him. He organized Christian clubs for the unemployed of Naples and, while dining at one, advised a member not to be overzealous in his fasting, but to eat the cutlets God had provided. These comments caused rumours of extravagant goings-on at the "Cutlet Clubs" that abounded in the city. Some members were arrested, but the clubs were allowed to continue and later evolved into the Association of the Chapels.

*Above Alphonsus Liguori (artist unknown, 19th century).*

## THE REDEMPTORISTS
In 1732, aided by his friends Thomas Falcoia and Maria Celeste, Alphonsus founded the Congregation of the Most Holy Redeemer, or the Redemptorists. Unfortunately, the order was stricken by internal dissension.

This, combined with the anti-clericalism of the Italian government and the opposition of the Jansenists, left the Redemptorists in a precarious position. Despite these difficulties, however, the order survived, and Alphonsus received popular acclamation for his religious texts, *Moral Theology* and *The Glories of Mary*.

In 1762, he became Bishop of Sant' Agata dei Goti near Naples, but the congregation was corrupt and lax. Alphonsus was unbending in his reforms. During a famine, he insisted that the wealthy share food with the starving. The subsequent court actions brought against him added to his burdens.

During Alphonsus' career, he faced many professional and personal difficulties, but he never lost the support of ordinary believers. He retired from high office, in 1775, crippled with rheumatism and with his sight and hearing impaired. The Redemptorists still faced fierce opposition and, in 1780, Alphonsus was expelled from his own order when he was tricked into signing a document authorizing reforms favourable to the anti-clerical government.

Alphonsus died believing his congregation had failed, but in 1793, the order was recognized by the Neapolitan state, and it now operates all over the world.

*Left Sant' Agatha dei Goti in Campania, Italy, where Alphonsus Liguori became bishop in 1762.*

# ELIZABETH SETON

ELIZABETH SETON, EXEMPLARY WIFE, MOTHER, WIDOW AND CONSECRATED NUN, WAS THE FIRST AMERICAN TO BE CANONIZED BY THE ROMAN CATHOLIC CHURCH.

**KEY FACTS**
*Founder, first American-born saint*
DATES: *1774–1821*
BIRTH PLACE: *New York, USA*
FEAST DAY: *4 January*

Elizabeth Seton was born into a wealthy American family, respected in New York society. Her grandfather had been the Episcopalian Rector of Staten Island, and her father was the first public physician of the city.

When she was 19, Elizabeth married a wealthy trader, William Seton. Theirs was a happy marriage, but at the age of 28 she was left widowed, with five small children, after her husband died while they were on a trip to Italy.

## CATHOLIC CONVERSION

Although she had been brought up as an Episcopalian, Elizabeth found spiritual comfort in the Roman Catholic Church. Moved by the charity of the nuns she encountered in Tuscany, she underwent a conversion on her return to New York, and was baptized a Roman Catholic.

Her conversion left her an outcast from her family and her anti-Catholic community. Her religious ardour was regarded as unseemly in her sophisticated circle, and she faced some difficult years of financial trouble during which she repeatedly tried and failed to start a Catholic school in her home city.

## THE SISTERS OF CHARITY

In 1808, at the invitation of Reverend William Dubourg, she went to Baltimore to care for poor children. Here, she found her true vocation. She established

*Above An engraving showing Elizabeth Seton dressed in the costume of the Sisters of Charity (Maurindel, date unknown).*

a small religious community devoted to the relief of the poor, especially children, and to teaching in parish schools. From this grew her congregation, the American Sisters of Charity, based on the rules of St Vincent de Paul.

She took her vows as a nun, and her commitment to Christ was unswerving. Others perceived her dynamic conviction, and were inspired by her to join her cause. The Sisters of Charity is now an influential congregation, active not only in the United States, but also in Latin America, Italy and the developing world. Elizabeth died at Emmitsburg and was canonized in 1975 after prayers for her intercession brought about cures for leukemia and meningitis.

*Right The shrine of Elizabeth Seton in Emmitsburg, Maryland.*

# ANTÔNIO DE SANT'ANNA GALVÃO

MORE THAN A MILLION PEOPLE ATTENDED THE CANONIZATION OF ST ANTÔNIO, A MAN OF PEACE AND CHARITY, AND THE FIRST BRAZILIAN TO BE MADE A SAINT.

**KEY FACTS**
*Founder, miracle worker*
DATES: *1739–1822*
BIRTH PLACE: *Guaratingueto,
near São Paulo, Brazil*
FEAST DAY: *11 May*

Antônio de Sant'Anna Galvão was born into a wealthy and deeply religious family, who sent him to a Jesuit seminary at the age of 13. However, because of a strong anti-Jesuit movement in Brazil at the time, his father advised him to join the Alcantrine Franciscans.

Antônio enrolled as a noviciate at St Bonaventure near Rio de Janeiro and was ordained in 1762. In 1768, he became preacher and confessor to the laity at the St Francis Friary in São Paulo. He was also confessor to the women of the Recollects of St Teresa, where he met Sister Helena Maria of the Holy Spirit.

In 1774, inspired by this nun and her religious visions, he founded Our Lady of the Conception of Divine Providence. At this home for girls, young women could receive instruction without being required to take vows. When Sister Helena died, Antônio took sole responsibility for the

*Above An altar painting of Antônio de Sant'Anna Galvão in Brazil.*

*Below Pope Benedict XVI canonized Antônio de Sant'Anna Galvão in front of nearly a million people in São Paulo in May 2007.*

Recollects, who were subsequently incorporated into the Order of Immaculate Conception.

Over the following years, Antônio achieved high office. In 1808, he became visitator in general and president of the Franciscan Chapter of São Paulo. When, at one stage, the Church posted him outside the city, the bishop and churchgoers begged for his return.

In his old age, he returned to the St Francis Friary, but it was the sisters from the Recollects da Luz who attended him at his death.

## MIRACLE PILLS

Antônio is most famous for his "pills" – scraps of paper inscribed with prayers to Mary, the Blessed Virgin, that the faithful would swallow in hope of a miraculous cure. To this day, the pills are manufactured by the nuns of St Clare, a convent founded by Antônio in Sorocaba near São Paulo.

In 1998, the Archbishop of São Paulo tried to bring an end to what he regarded as a superstition, and ordered the nuns to stop their work. However, at the canonization of St Antônio, Pope Benedict XVI recognized the miraculous power of the saint, acknowledging two healing miracles ascribed to the pills, including a recent case of a four-year-old girl whose hepatitis had been declared incurable by the medical profession. Since the saint's canonization in 2007, the nuns have distributed as many as 10,000 pills in one day.

# MAGDALENA OF CANOSSA

MAGDALENA OF CANOSSA HAD "A MOTHER'S HEART AND AN APOSTLE'S ZEAL". HER LIFE WAS DEDICATED TO TEACHING AND EXTENDING SPIRITUAL AWARENESS.

**KEY FACTS**
*Virgin, founder of the
Daughters of Charity*
DATES: *1774–1835*
BIRTH PLACE: *Verona, Italy*
FEAST DAY: *8 May*

Although Magdalena made a vow to dedicate her life to God at the age of 17, she was compelled to take up a secular life. The third of six siblings left fatherless as children, she found herself in charge of running the family's large estate.

Despite her worldly worries, however, she could not forget her calling, and sought out friends to join her in following Christ with chastity and obedience. In 1808, in spite of family opposition, she moved to the poorest part of town to start her religious life, and built up such a following that, in 1819, she founded the Daughters of Charity. The order was dedicated to establishing charity schools, training teachers for rural areas and supporting women patients in hospital. Later, she founded the Sons of Charity for male followers.

Magdalena died in Verona surrounded by her followers. There are now 4,000 Daughters of Charity all over the world, and the Sons are active in Italy, the Philippines and Latin America.

***Above*** *St Mary's College in Hong Kong, founded by the Canossian Daughters of Charity in 1900.*

# JOSEPH COTTOLENGO

JOSEPH COTTOLENGO WILL ALWAYS BE REMEMBERED AND LOVED AS AN UNSTINTING CHAMPION OF THOSE IN NEED, WHETHER THEY BE ORPHANS, DISABLED, MENTALLY ILL OR FRAIL.

**KEY FACTS**
*Founder*
DATES: *1786–1842*
BIRTH PLACE: *Piedmont*
FEAST DAY: *30 April*

Joseph Cottolengo was ordained in 1811 and quickly demonstrated his empathy for the unfortunate. His good works began modestly, with the founding of a hospital of five beds, the "Little House", in a Turin slum.

The hospital expanded quickly, and Joseph and his followers formed the Societies of the Little House of Divine Providence. When the authorities closed the Little House during a cholera epidemic, the brothers nursed the sick in their homes. The Little House then moved to Valdocco, a suburb of Turin, where it was soon

***Above*** *The city of Turin, where Joseph Cottolengo did many great works.*

surrounded by an assortment of care homes for the deaf and dumb, orphans, elderly people, epileptics and the mentally handicapped.

Joseph also started communities of prayer to bring solace to those in mortal and moral danger. Joseph seemed carefree about finances, believing that the Lord would provide, and so it was with surprise that his successor accepted his perfectly kept account books when he retired.

Although he was only 56 years old, Joseph died of typhoid in his brother's home at Chieri only a week after his retirement.

# INCORRUPTIBLES

ALL SAINTS ARE REVERED FOR THE WONDROUS ACTS, AND OFTEN MIRACLES, THEY PERFORM WHEN THEY ARE LIVING, BUT SOME SHOW EXTRAORDINARY PHYSICAL QUALITIES EVEN AFTER THEIR DEATH.

The words "incorrupt" and "incorruptible" are used by the Catholic Church to describe bodies that do not decompose after death. The body is considered incorrupt only if no preservation techniques, such as embalming, have been used, and it is not uncommon for the body's lack of decomposition to be accompanied by a sweet smell. The discovery of an incorrupt corpse is generally made by chance, and when the body of a holy person is found intact, it is traditionally taken as a sign of sainthood.

Alongside other miraculous phenomena associated with saints, including stigmata and the healing of the sick, the survival of a saint's corpse seems to defy any scientific explanation, and many Catholic Christians believe the holiness and piety of an incorruptible saint to be the cause of divine preservation.

*Above A portrait of Rita of Cascia in the church of Santa Maria del Giglio, Venice (19th century).*

### EARLY INCORRUPTIBLES
A very early example of an incorruptible is the 3rd-century saint, Cecilia. When her tomb was opened in 1599, a thousand years after she was buried, her corpse showed no signs of corruption. Sadly, on exposure to the air, it quickly turned to dust.

*Left A portrait of Bernadette of Lourdes (19th century).*

There was frequent correspondence between Rome and the English clergy after the death of Edward the Confessor in 1066. A cultus grew around this king, and the campaign to have him canonized was strengthened when his body was found to be incorrupt in 1102. Monks from Westminster made enquiries and in 1161, Pope Innocent III finally agreed with their findings and advised that the saint's relics be translated to Westminster Abbey. In 1163, a procession carried the incorrupt body to its final resting place.

## THE BLOOD OF ST JANUARIUS
St Januarius, who was martyred in AD 305, is the patron saint of Naples, and his presence is believed to protect the port from harm. Twice every year – on 19 September and on the Saturday before the first Sunday in May – a solemn procession, led by representatives of the Church, progresses through the city displaying a vial of St Januarius's blood, which liquefies and bubbles in just the same way as fresh blood. Believers fear a calamity would hit Naples if the blood failed to liquefy. Other saints whose blood was said to show this quality include Pantaleon, Stephen and John the Baptist.

*Right Cardinal Crescenzio Sepe, Archbishop of Naples, looks at the glass vial holding the blood of St Januarius during the Feast of San Gennaro in 2006.*

*Above* The incorrupt body of Catherine Labouré, kept at 140 rue du Bac in Paris, France.

*Above* The incorrupt body of Jean-Baptiste Vianney is kept in the Basilica at Ars, France.

St Rita of Cascia (1377–1447) is another incorruptible, whose face, hands and feet survive along with much of her skeleton. Her remains are on display in the Basilica of St Rita in Cascia, Italy.

### THE LAST 200 YEARS

The body of John-Baptiste Vianney also remained intact after his death in 1859. He won the admiration of his congregation for his faith and goodness. They were amazed, too, by his meagre diet of boiled potatoes, and his habit of sleeping for a mere two or three hours a night. His extraordinary qualities in life were extended in death when his body did not decompose.

Madeleine Sophie Barat was an energetic woman who travelled widely and devoted herself to the Christian education of children. The miraculous preservation of her body, which is kept in Jette in Belgium, reflects the strength and vitality that she always demonstrated in life.

Another holy woman whose body has proved incorrupt is Catherine Labouré. This modest

*Right* The incorrupt body of St Rita of Cascia is carried around Rome during a celebration on her feast day.

> WE SHOULD SHOW HONOUR TO THE SAINTS OF GOD, AS BEING MEMBERS OF CHRIST, THE CHILDREN AND FRIENDS OF GOD, AND OUR INTERCESSORS. THEREFORE, IN MEMORY OF THEM WE OUGHT TO HONOUR ANY RELICS OF THEIRS IN A FITTING MANNER.
>
> ST THOMAS AQUINAS

nun, who is venerated as a mystic, was canonized in 1947. She died in 1876 and her body rests in the the convent where she lived for nearly half a century, in the chapel at 140 rue du Bac, Paris.

An equally humble woman whose body survives without corruption is Bernadette of Lourdes, who saw visions of the Virgin and lived piously as a nun. After her death in 1879, her corpse was removed three times from its resting place to undergo scientific examination. It now resides in a glass case in the convent at Nevers where visitors can marvel at its preserved state. Doctor Comte who examined St Bernadette's corpse in 1925 wrote, "...the body does not seem to have putrefied, nor has any decomposition of the body set in, although this would be expected and normal after such a long period in a vault hollowed out of the earth".

# JEAN-BAPTISTE VIANNEY

JEAN-BAPTISTE FAILED HIS CLERICAL EXAMS, BUT WAS ACCEPTED INTO THE PRIESTHOOD BECAUSE THE CHURCH NEEDED MEN OF SIMPLE GOODNESS AND DEVOTION AS WELL AS MEN OF LEARNING.

**KEY FACTS**
*Founder*
DATES: *1786–1859*
BIRTH PLACE: *Dardilly, near Lyons, France*
PATRON OF: *Patriarchal clergy*
FEAST DAY: *4 August*

Jean-Baptiste was a shepherd boy, who, dismayed by the treatment of priests during the Revolution, applied to join the clergy. He was conscripted into the Napoleonic army but, soon after, deserted and resumed his studies for the priesthood. This was a precarious career because anti-clerical forces in control of France remained hostile even after a ban on all monastic orders was lifted in 1810.

## VILLAGE PRIEST

Two years after his ordination in 1815, Jean-Baptiste was sent as parish priest to a remote village, Ars-en-Dombes. He had a genuine hatred of immorality, and a recital of sins would often reduce him to tears. This made him intolerant of simple pleasures, such as

*Above A contemporary drawing showing Jean-Baptiste Vianney being harassed by a demon.*

*Below A lithograph portrait of Jean-Baptiste Vianney (1866).*

dancing, and minor transgressions, such as lewd language. But villagers forgave Jean-Baptiste's severity because he revealed supernatural talents, producing miraculous supplies of food to feed to orphans, and prophesying the future. He could also read hearts and had knowledge of things happening beyond his sight. He suffered violent assaults from the Devil, who beat him and even burnt his bed.

Jean-Baptiste was so sympathetic to remorseful sinners that confessors queued for his pastoral care, and a special booking office was set up at Arles railway station to handle the 300 visitors travelling every day to visit the wonder worker. He started work at 11 o'clock each morning and spent long hours in the confessional. He wanted to develop his spiritual meditations and tried three times to become a monk, but returned each time to Ars.

Years of listening to the sins of penitents eventually moderated his views on frivolity and pleasure, and he turned his full attention to teaching his flock about the enduring love of God and the significance of Church liturgy.

Jean-Baptiste was a modest man. He never wore the decoration he was given when made a member of the Légion d'Honneur, and to raise money for the poor he sold the luxurious robes of office he received when he was made a canon. He died in Ars, and was canonized in 1925. The cultus for this saint is now worldwide.

# GASPAR BERTONI

ALTHOUGH GASPAR BERTONI WAS DRIVEN BY POLITICAL PRESSURE TO TURN FROM MISSION WORK TO EDUCATION, THIS CHANGE OF DIRECTION BROUGHT WISDOM AND FULFILMENT.

**KEY FACTS**
*Founder*
DATES: *1777–1853*
BIRTH PLACE: *Verona, Italy*
FEAST DAY: *12 June*

When Gaspar Bertoni was born, revolutionary anti-clericalism held sway in Europe. He came from a legal family in Verona but chose to work as a parish priest after his ordination in 1800. Undeterred when the Napoleonic conquerors held Pope Pius VII prisoner, he abandoned neither his leader nor his faith.

After Napoleon's defeat in 1814, Verona fell under Austrian control and the pope was released. In 1816–17, Gaspar founded a mission that would preach on the Passion of Christ – the suffering of Jesus on the cross. However, the work was jeopardized by hostility from the new regime, and he refocused his attentions on education.

With his brotherhood, Gaspar began teaching in free schools, hoping to inspire boys into a life of service to God. His group became the Congregation of Holy Stigmatics, an educational mission that now works in Europe, Africa, the Americas and Asia. Although he was bedridden for many years Gaspar continued to guide his congregation. He died in Verona and was canonized in 1989.

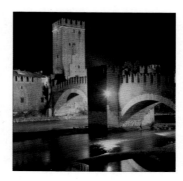

*Above Verona, the city where Gaspar Bertoni was born and died.*

# CATHERINE LABOURÉ

THE "MIRACULOUS MEDAL" OF CATHERINE LABOURÉ INSPIRED ALPHONSE RATISBONNE, AN ALSATIAN JEW, TO CONVERT AND FOUND THE FATHERS AND SISTERS OF SION.

**KEY FACTS**
*Visionary*
DATES: *1806–76*
BIRTH PLACE: *Fain-les-Moutiers, near Dijon, France*
FEAST DAY: *28 November*

Catherine Labouré was a peasant from Fain-les-Moutiers. She cared for her widowed father, worked in Paris as a waitress and then, in 1830, joined the Sisters of Charity at the rue du Bac.

Her superiors thought little of this plain woman who tended the convent hens, but Catherine had extraordinary visions, the most enduring of which was a picture of the Virgin standing on a globe. The vision was accompanied by the words, "Mary conceived without sin, pray for us who have recourse to thee." On the reverse of the picture was an M with a cross and two hearts.

*Above Apparition of the Virgin to St Catherine Labouré 31 July 1830 (Le Cerf, 1835).*

THE MIRACULOUS MEDALS
The Archbishop of Paris was persuaded to sanction medals stamped with these images, and in 1832, 1,500 were minted. After the appearance of a pamphlet describing Catherine's vision, 130,000 further medals were sold. The "Miraculous Medal" was authenticated by canonical decree, and is now distributed across the Catholic world.

Catherine's cultus was strengthened by the incorruptibility of her body after her death in the convent she had called home for 46 years. She was canonized in 1947.

# MADELEINE SOPHIE BARAT

MADELEINE SOPHIE BARAT DEVOTED HER LIFE TO THE SERVICE OF OTHERS, BRINGING A CATHOLIC EDUCATION TO PUPILS ACROSS THE WORLD THROUGH THE SOCIETY OF THE SACRED HEART.

**KEY FACTS**
*Virgin, founder, educational reformer*
DATES: *1779–1865*
BIRTH PLACE: *Joigny, France*
FEAST DAY: *25 May*

From a very early age, Madeleine was placed under the harsh tutelage of her brother, Louis, who was 11 years her senior. She learnt how to deflect his unpleasant manners through patience, charm and diplomacy, traits that were to serve her well throughout her life. Her brother's stubborn, aggressive nature led to his imprisonment for two years when he refused to accept the civil constitution of the clergy.

## SCHOOL TEACHER

Madeleine nursed an ambition to become a lay sister with the Carmelites, but was persuaded by l'Abbé Varin to instead join his new community, the Society of the Sacred Heart, dedicated to teaching Christian children, rich and poor alike. In 1800, she was sent to Amiens, to the Society's first convent school. Two years

later, aged just 23, she was made Superior, and soon afterwards travelled to Grenoble and Poitiers to establish other convent schools.

Her youth made her high position precarious, and while she was away from Amiens, a chaplain and another nun tried to displace her. Madeleine responded with char-

*Left A portrait of Madeleine Sophie Barat (artist and date unknown).*

acteristic tact and patience and, supported by l'Abbé Varin, strengthened her role as Mother Superior, a position she was to hold for 63 years.

## EDUCATIONAL REFORMER

During this time she implemented standards of education across every school of the Sacred Heart. Although these guides were uniform, they were not inflexible, with provision made for regular reviews and adjustments to meet changing needs.

The society became truly international under Madeleine's guidance, with communities established in 12 different countries during her lifetime, including foundations in the United States, orchestrated by her friend Rose Philippine Duchesne. Madeleine personally travelled to found new schools and monitor old ones in France, Switzerland and England. The Society of the Sacred Heart has since become one of the most successful institutes in the Roman Catholic educational system.

Still in office at the age of 85, Madeleine died in Paris. Her incorrupt body lies at Jette in Belgium. She was canonized in 1925.

*Left The Society of the Sacred Heart operates around the world. Here, Sacred Heart nuns wait to board a ship in May 1949, during the civil war in China.*

# ANTONY CLARET

ANTONY WAS A PRIEST OF GREAT INTELLECTUAL TALENT, BUT HE WAS ALSO A MIRACLE WORKER AND A GIFTED TEACHER, WHO REACHED OUT TO ALL BELIEVERS IN HIS SERMONS AND WRITINGS.

**KEY FACTS**
*Founder*
DATES: *1807–70*
BIRTH PLACE: *Sallent, Spain*
PATRON OF: *Weavers, savings banks*
FEAST DAY: *24 October*

Antony was the son of a Spanish weaver, but decided to enter a seminary and was ordained in 1835. He joined the Jesuits in Rome, but ill health caused his return to Spain. He spread the message of Christianity widely and was a keen speaker and a successful and prolific writer, preaching some 10,000 sermons and writing around 200 texts during his lifetime.

In 1849, Antony founded the Missionary Sons of the Immaculate Heart of Mary (the "Claretians"), an order that still flourishes today. The following year, Queen Isabella II requested he serve as the Archbishop of Santiago in Cuba. Antony's reforms angered many, resulting in an attempt on his life.

After seven years in this post, he was recalled to be Isabella's confessor and used his powerful position to fund educational institutes. In 1868, a revolution drove Queen Isabella into exile, and Antony went with her. He died at the Fontfroide monastery near Narbonne, where he had been placed under house arrest.

*Right Antony Claret (artist and date unknown).*

# CLELIA BARBIERI

CLELIA BARBIERI WAS A PIOUS CHILD AND THE YOUNGEST FOUNDER IN THE HISTORY OF THE ROMAN CATHOLIC CHURCH. ALTHOUGH SHE DIED YOUNG, HER COMMUNITY HAS SPREAD TO 35 COUNTRIES.

**KEY FACTS**
*Founder*
DATES: *1847–70*
BIRTH PLACE: *Budrie, near Bologna, Italy*
FEAST DAY: *13 July*

Clelia was born in Budrie, Italy. Her wealthy mother married a servant far below her station and instilled religious values in their children. Their eldest daughter, Clelia, was 11 years old when she was confirmed and had a spiritual experience that made her mourn for her sins and those of all the world.

Clelia joined the Christian Catechism Workers, a mostly male group, and encouraged other girls to follow her example of hard work and religious devotion. In 1868, she founded the Suore Minime dell'Addolorata for her followers. Though she faced public disdain, she persevered in her mission, nursing sick children and teaching the catechism. Despite her youth, the sisters and the children she cared for called her "Mother".

The conditions in which she lived made her vulnerable to tuberculosis and as she lay dying, she told her followers, "I'm leaving, but I'll never abandon you." She was canonized in 1989.

*Left Clelia's order is named after the Mater Dolorosa, the Virgin of the Sorrows (Albert Bouts, c.1495).*

# BERNADETTE OF LOURDES

BERNADETTE HAD VISIONS OF MARY, THE BLESSED VIRGIN, AND HER REMAINS PROVED INCORRUPT, BUT IT WAS HER SINCERITY AND TRUST IN GOD THAT QUALIFIED HER AS A SAINT.

**KEY FACTS**
*Visionary*
DATES: *1844–79*
BIRTH PLACE: *Lourdes, France*
FEAST DAY: *16 April (in parts of France 18 February)*

In the tradition of other saints of devout simplicity, such as Jean-Baptiste Vianney and Joseph of Copertino, Bernadette Soubirous was deeply spiritual and blessed by heavenly visions. And, as with those great men, she bore her role with dignity.

Bernadette was a country girl, the eldest of six children born to an impoverished miller in the Basque region of France. As a child, she was thin and stunted from lack of proper nutrition and suffered from asthma.

### VISIONS OF MARY

When she was 14 years old, Bernadette experienced her first vision at the rock of Massabielle near Lourdes. Over the next six months, the same apparition of a beautiful young woman appeared

*Above Since Bernadette's visions at Lourdes, many ill pilgrims visit the site in the hope that they will be cured.*

*Below The incorrupt body of Bernadette of Lourdes, kept at the convent in Nevers, where she lived for many years.*

to her 18 times. No one else saw or heard the vision, but there were witnesses to her reaction. The vision informed Bernadette that the beautiful woman was Mary of the Immaculate Conception and instructed her to drink from the nearby spring and show penitence.

Church clerics and minor state officials interrogated Bernadette for months. Her answers, simple and unchanging, led some of them to label her stupid, but most were impressed by her sincerity. The resulting publicity frightened Bernadette, but she faced the jokes and cruel jibes, showing no anger. No matter how remorseless the goading became, she never denied her miraculous experience.

In 1866, she joined the Sisters of Notre-Dame of Nevers, and found merciful seclusion from the public. Her health was poor and she spent her remaining years in stoic suffering. Bernadette was canonized in 1933, in recognition of her patience, integrity, simplicity and devout trustfulness.

### A PILGRIMAGE CENTRE

Secluded in the convent, Bernadette was unaware that the site where she had met the Blessed Virgin was being transformed into a pilgrimage centre, or that the basilica built there was consecrated in 1876, three years before her death.

Lourdes has become one of the great pilgrimage centres of the Christian faith, drawing to its miraculous waters those seeking spiritual healing.

# JOSEPH MKASA

JOSEPH MKASA SHOWED GREAT COURAGE AND FAITH WHEN HE DARED TO CONFRONT A TYRANT FEARED FROM ZANZIBAR TO THE CONGO. HE IS NAMED AMONG THE MARTYRS OF UGANDA.

**KEY FACTS**
*Martyr of Uganda*
DATES: *c. 1860–85*
BIRTH PLACE: *Uganda*
FEAST DAY: *3 June*

In 1885 Mwanga, the King of Uganda, ordered the killing of the Anglican missionary bishop, James Hannington, and his companions. Joseph Mkasa, a Roman Catholic convert and adviser to the king, was outraged by the killings, and was determined to do something about it, although he was aware that King Mwanga was a dangerous man.

This had not always been the case. As prince, Mwanga had shown no untoward behaviour or aggression toward Christians, but the moment he became king, he turned into a tyrant and a degenerate man, who treated slaves and servants cruelly, and made sexual advances toward the pages in his court. Mwanga was angered by the Christians because their loyalty to God outweighed that shown to himself, and he resolved to rid his country of Christianity.

## CONFRONTING THE KING

Fearless for his own safety, Joseph Mkasa decided to make a stand and reproached the king for the murder. The bravery displayed by Joseph is even more impressive in the light of contemporary extracts from the diary of Henry Stanley, an American explorer in Africa. Stanley records the infamous reputation of Mwanga, who was feared by the British Foreign Office, the Arab authorities and merchants in East Africa. Even the infamous slave trader Tippu Tib was wary of him. Anyone travelling through Uganda needed military protection against violence from the king's men.

*Above A plaque commemorating some of the Martyrs of Uganda. In 1885 and 1886, a total of 22 Africans were martyred.*

*Below A stained glass window of the boy martyrs in St Andrews Parish Church, Surrey, England.*

On being confronted by Joseph Mkasa, the mad monarch immediately sentenced his adviser to death for being a traitorous convert. Joseph replied simply, "A Christian who gives his life for Christ is not afraid to die." He was publicly beheaded and fierce persecution of both Catholics and Protestants followed.

In time, Mwanga's religious persecution succeeded in uniting Christian and Muslim Ugandans, who put aside their traditional enmity and deposed him in 1889, placing his brother on the throne.

Joseph Mkasa and other named martyrs of Uganda were canonized by Pope Paul VI in 1964.

# CHARLES LWANGA

CHARLES LWANGA, ONE OF THE NAMED MARTYRS OF UGANDA, WAS MURDERED BECAUSE HE PROTECTED THE CHILDREN IN HIS CARE AND REFUSED TO DENY HIS FAITH.

**KEY FACTS**
*Martyr of Uganda*
DATES: *1865–86*
BIRTH PLACE: *Uganda*
FEAST DAY: *3 June*

The tyrant of Uganda, King Mwanga, beheaded the bishop missionary James Hannington and the Ugandan convert Joseph Mkasa, but he did not stop there.

When Mwanga killed a page, Denis Sebuggwawo, for teaching the catechism, Charles Lwanga, who supervised the court pages, voiced his rage. That night, fearing the worst, Lwanga baptized four of the boys in his charge.

In the morning, the King called up Charles Lwanga, 15 pages and numerous other Christians captured by his warriors. He told

*Above The Martyrs Monument at Namugongo in Uganda, which commemorates the martyrdom of Christians on 3 June 1886.*

them to deny their faith but they said they would remain Christians "until death". They were marched to Namugongo, where they were beaten, wrapped in reed mats and burnt alive. Their joyful courage has been likened to that of the early Christians.

Mwanga murdered many more Christians, including Matthias Murumba and Andrew Kagwa. In 1964, 22 of the young men, including Charles Lwanga, were canonized as the Martyrs of Uganda. Their feast day is a public holiday in Uganda.

# MARIE ADOLPHINE DIERKS

MARIE ADOLPHINE DIERKS WAS A HUMBLE DUTCH WOMAN WHO FELT CALLED UPON AND COMPELLED BY GOD TO BECOME A NUN. SHE SAID, "I WANT TO SUFFER FOR THE LORD".

**KEY FACTS**
*Martyr of China*
DATES: *1866–1900*
BIRTH PLACE: *Ossendrecht, Holland*
FEAST DAY: *17 February*

Marie was born in Holland, one of six siblings who lost their mother at an early age and were taken in by poor but kindly neighbours. Marie was dedicated to her studies and her prayers, but soon realized that her adoptive family needed financial help. She worked as a factory hand and as a domestic servant, giving part of her earnings to her family.

However, she felt a strong call to serve God, and in 1893 she joined the Franciscan Missionaries of Mary in Antwerp. With six other nuns, she was sent to the

*Left A colour lithograph depicting the murder of a nun during the Boxer Rebellion in China.*

Shanxi diocese in China. Work at the hospital and orphanage in Shanxi was hard, but Marie served with patience.

She was beheaded, along with her six Christian colleagues, in a crackdown on foreign missionaries during the Boxer Rebellion of 1900. Her name is included in the list of the 120 Blessed Martyrs of China, canonized by Pope John Paul II in 2000.

# JOHN BOSCO

JOHN BOSCO WAS A GREAT TEACHER WHO NEVER PUNISHED HIS
PUPILS BUT, INSTEAD, GUIDED BY A CHILDHOOD VISION, USED THE
"PREVENTIVE" MEASURES OF LOVE, PATIENCE AND FIRMNESS.

**KEY FACTS**
*Founder*
DATES: *1815–88*
BIRTH PLACE: *Piedmont, Italy*
PATRON OF: *Editors, young
people, young workers, apprentices
and youth of Mexico*
FEAST DAY: *31 January*

John Bosco's life was given direction by a dream he had when he was very young. In this dream, he saw a group of young boys who were playing and swearing. To stop their blaspheming he punched them with his fists, but a man intervened, saying "You will have to win these friends of yours not by blows, but by gentleness and love."

## A LIFE OF POVERTY

John was born into a peasant family from Piedmont, Italy, but lost his father when he was only two years old. He was brought up by his mother, and such was their poverty that, when he decided to enter a seminary in 1831, his clothes and shoes were donated by neighbours.

After he was ordained priest in 1841, John became chaplain of a girl's school in Turin. On Sundays, a group of boys who lived on the city streets would come to the school to play and learn their catechism. John quickly realized, with the help of his guide and teacher, Joseph Cafasso, that his life's work lay with these boys.

## LED BY HIS DREAM

Bosco left the school and went to live in shabby rooms in the Valdocco area of Turin, where, with his mother as housekeeper, he housed and educated the abandoned boys of the city. He set up shoemaking, tailoring and printing workshops, where the boys could learn a trade, and gave them lessons in Latin and grammar. Never forgetting his dream, Bosco

*Above A mosaic tile depiction of St John Bosco in Seville, Spain.*

fostered a good relationship with his pupils through recreation, and encouraged picnics, outdoor play and a love of nature and music.

By 1856, he was housing 150 boys and he began to train likeminded people to help him in his work. He called these teachers

"Salesians", after St Francis of Sales. They were approved as a religious order in 1874.

Bosco founded a similar order for women – the Daughters of Our Lady, Help of Christians – in 1872. These orders are now established across the globe, and run seminaries and technical and agricultural colleges.

John Bosco died in 1888, shortly after the completion of his church dedicated to the Sacred Heart in Rome, where he had been able to offer only one mass. About 40,000 mourners visited his body and the people of Turin lined the streets to watch the cortège. He was canonized by Pope Pius XI in 1934.

*Below Part of an engraving from an Italian newspaper showing the canonization of John Bosco in St Peter's in 1934.*

# HOUSES OF GOD

MEDIEVAL CHURCHES WERE DESIGNED TO CAST THE MIND TOWARD
HEAVEN AND INSPIRE AWE. MODERN CHURCHES TEND TO BE MORE
SIMPLE AND INTIMATE TO HELP THE VISITOR FEEL CLOSER TO GOD.

*Above The royal portal on the west front of Notre-Dame Cathedral in Chartres, France (c. 1145).*

As Christianity spread across the Middle East and Europe, so churches were built to provide places of worship for believers. In small towns and villages, these buildings became the centre of community life.

The church was the house of God, and as such, money, time and talent came to be lavished on great cathedrals and grand churches. The faithful entered these wondrous buildings and were filled with awe and reverence. Statues and paintings inside confirmed the reality of the saints, and Christians were convinced that, in these surroundings, their prayers would fly to heaven, where the saints were listening.

## THE GOTHIC STYLE

The medieval period saw the building of churches throughout the Christian world on an unprecedented scale. In the West, the predominant architectural style was Gothic.

The Gothic architects erected structures of great grandeur to express the majesty of God and emphasize man's insignificance. These cathedrals featured huge flying buttresses, pointed arches, rib vaults, and large windows. Enormous doors opened into interiors lit by the mysterious glow of stained glass.

> "I AM THE ETERNAL DOOR: PASS THROUGH ME, FAITHFUL ONES. I AM THE FOUNTAIN OF LIFE: THIRST FOR ME MORE THAN WINE."
>
> ON THE PORTAL OF THE CHURCH OF SANTA CRUZ DE LA SERÓS, SPAIN

Façades were laced with decoration and statues of saints, and to remind the faithful of hell, small devilish gargoyles flew from the buttresses or were carved into pews. One of the finest examples of the Gothic style is the 12th-century Notre-Dame Cathedral in Chartres, France.

The construction of Gothic cathedrals often took centuries to complete, so these buildings frequently incorporate a range of architectural and artistic styles.

*Left The front façade of the Cathedral of St Michel and St Gudule in Brussels, Belgium.*

Construction of the Cathedral of St Michel and St Gudule in Brussels, for example, commenced in the early 13th century but the work was not completed for another 300 years. Cologne Cathedral, which has the largest façade of any church in the world, was begun in 1248 and finished 600 years later. Much of the stained glass in the cathedral is from the 19th century.

## A NEW DIRECTION

When Martin Luther criticized the power and practices of the Roman Catholic Church in 1517, he began a new era for the church in northern Europe, known as the Reformation.

During the Reformation and in its aftermath, exterior carvings and statues, and the splendid interiors, walls hung with paintings, reliquaries gleaming with precious metals and jewels, and even the shrines so carefully constructed for relics were destroyed by Luther's Protestant supporters.

A new and austere style emerged, and this mood prevails in much modern northern European church architecture. Architects of Protestant churches

*Left* The dome of the Hagia Sophia in Istanbul, Turkey. This magnificent Byzantine building was the mother church of the Eastern Christians for 916 years before it was turned into a mosque by the Ottomans in 1453. It is now a museum.

no longer seek to replicate heaven; neither do they wish to inspire awe in visitors. Churches are usually designed to be informal, and space is meant to promote fellowship among believers and stress a sense of community. Altar tables and light fittings are simple, and roof levels may be flattened or given low curves more in sympathy with an earthly landscape.

## SURVIVAL OF DECORATION

Despite the efforts of the reformers, most medieval churches survived the Reformation. Even after the destructive Civil War in England, hundreds of examples are still relatively intact.

Where the Roman Catholic Church survived, or was unaffected by, the Reformation – in Italy, Spain, Poland, and parts of France and Germany – church architecture remained centred upon the glorification of God with beauty.

In the Balkans, Greece and the Middle East, where the Eastern Orthodox Church prevails, many ancient religious buildings can still be found, although some of these became mosques after the Islamic conquest of the East and the rule of the Ottoman Empire from Istanbul (once Constantinople).

*Below* The interior of Cologne Cathedral in Germany.

## STAINED GLASS WINDOWS

The origin of the stained glass window is unknown, but artists were working in this medium by 1100. Coloured sections of glass, cut to shape and held together by black lead strips, formed elaborate designs that depicted biblical stories and lives of the saints. By the 16th century, artists preferred to paint the glass, and by the 18th century, many windows had been removed. Superb examples of medieval glass can still be seen in their original setting, for example at Notre-Dame Cathedral in Chartres, France, and York Minster in England. Many stained glass windows are preserved in the world's great museums.

*Above* A stained glass window at Chartres Cathedral showing St Lubin, Bishop of Chartres in the 6th century (c.1200–10).

# THERESA OF LISIEUX

THERESA, THE "LITTLE FLOWER", WROTE OF HER RELATIONSHIP
WITH GOD WITH AN ARTLESS SIMPLICITY THAT CONVEYED A DEEP
SPIRITUALITY, QUALIFYING HER AS A DOCTOR OF THE CHURCH.

## KEY FACTS
*Virgin, mystic, Doctor
of the Church*
DATES: *1873–1897*
BIRTH PLACE: *Alençon, France*
PATRON OF: *France, missions,
florists and flower growers*
FEAST DAY: *1 October*
EMBLEM: *Flowers*

Theresa of Lisieux lived a very ordinary life. She did not perform great works, found a religious order or convert thousands to Christianity. And yet this young girl, who lived for such a brief time, left a rich spiritual legacy.

### AN EARLY VOCATION
Although she was only four years old when her mother died, Theresa had four older sisters to look after her. The eldest, Pauline, became her surrogate mother, but by the time Theresa was ten, her two eldest sisters had left home to enter the local Carmelite convent in Lisieux.

Theresa begged constantly to join the convent, but she was too young to take such vows. On a pilgrimage to Rome with her father, she knelt for a blessing

*Above Theresa of Lisieux (artist and
date unknown). Aware she was dying,
Theresa wrote that, after her death, she
would "let fall a shower of roses",
meaning that in heaven she would
intercede for her friends.*

from Pope Leo XIII. Knowing that she was forbidden to speak to him, she broke all protocol and begged him to let her be a nun. He supported the decision of the Carmelites, but when Theresa reached the age of 15, the Bishop of Bayeux, impressed by her piety and determination, allowed the prioress to admit her.

In April 1888, the young girl began her life in the enclosed Carmelite convent, where she began to develop her spirituality by reading the Carmelite mystics and following the austere rules of the order. The abbess forbade

*Left A photograph of Theresa of
Lisieux in the garden of the Carmelite
convent in Lisieux in France (c.1890).*

Theresa to fast because she was not physically robust, but she sensed that the young girl was an intuitive thinker, and encouraged her to write. This wise advice allowed Theresa the time and space to produce *The Story of a Soul*, and her many other texts, which include 54 poems, 20 prayers, eight plays and more than 200 letters. In a simple poetic style, these writings describe how every "little life" can be enhanced by faith and reveal her extraordinary relationship with God.

### THE "LITTLE WAY"
The young nun longed to be a saint, but aware that, as a Carmelite, she would not be able to achieve great works, she looked for a new path that would lead her to sanctity. "I knew I was a very little soul who could offer only little things to the good God", she wrote. From this thought grew her "little way" of "the doing of the least actions for love".

A year after she had joined the Carmelites, Theresa's father suffered two strokes that left him weak and dependent. Emotionally disturbed and unhappy, he had a nervous breakdown, and in 1894, died in a lunatic asylum. Her fourth sister, Celine, who had spent her life caring for their father, joined Theresa at the Carmelite convent.

Theresa wanted to follow the example of the apostles and

*Above The Basilica of St Theresa in Lisieux, France, is the saint's major shrine.*

longed for the opportunity to spread the love of Christ in foreign lands. She had always prayed for missionaries – it was a Carmelite discipline to pray for Christian missions abroad – but she also corresponded with the Carmelite nuns in Hanoi, Indo-China (now Vietnam), and they wanted her to join them.

### QUIET SUFFERING
Then, in 1895, Theresa had a curious experience. During the night between Maundy Thursday and

Good Friday, she heard "as it were, a far-off murmur announcing the coming of the Bridegroom". She seemed unaware that she was bleeding from her mouth – a symptom of tuberculosis. With her health broken, her dream of becoming a missionary would never be realized.

For 18 months, Theresa suffered pain and difficulty in breathing. She was eventually confined to the convent infirmary, where she was so ill that she was unable to receive Holy Communion. She died at the age of 24.

Pilgrims still flock to Lisieux to venerate St Theresa, who is known as the "little flower of Jesus" and Theresa-of-the-Child-Jesus, names that reflect her simple, childlike faith. Her book has been translated into 50 languages and has brought inspiration to millions of people. Theresa of Lisieux was canonized in 1925.

*Below St Theresa, from a cycle of Carmelite Life made from mosaic in the Basilica of St Theresa in Lisieux, France (Pierre Gaudin, 1958).*

> "I DESIRE TO BE A SAINT, BUT I KNOW MY WEAKNESS AND SO I ASK YOU, MY GOD, THAT YOU YOURSELF WILL BE MY HOLINESS."
>
> THERESA OF LISIEUX

### GEMMA GALGANI
Born in 1878, Gemma was an orphan, terribly afflicted by tuberculosis of the spine. She resembled Theresa of Lisieux in other ways, too. Hers was a "little life" without office, wealth or public recognition. Faith guided all her actions, only ill health preventing her from entering a convent. Her mysticism was expressed in ecstasies, during which she gave spiritual messages. She had visions of Jesus and stigmata appeared on her body. Heroic in enduring illness and poverty, Gemma died in 1903 and was canonized in 1941.

*Above Lucca in Tuscany, Italy. St Gemma Galgani's relics are housed at the Passionist monastery in the city.*

# RAPHAEL KALINOWSKI

IN HIS ROLE AS A PRIEST, RAPHAEL KALINOWSKI FOSTERED HOPES OF UNITING CHRISTIANS, THROUGH SPIRITUAL GUIDANCE, TO COMBAT THE GROWING POWER OF THE SECULAR STATE.

**KEY FACTS**
*Carmelite*
DATES: *1835–1907*
BIRTH PLACE: *Vilnius, Poland (now Lithuania)*
FEAST DAY: *15 November*

The 19th century in Europe is a story of industrialization, nationalism and secular politics. The life of Raphael Kalinowski reflects the period. Raised a devout Catholic, he became an engineer, working on the new Russian railways. While running a Sunday school at the fortress in Brest-Litovsk where he was a captain, he became increasingly aware of the state persecution of the Church, and of his native Poles.

When the Poles rose against the Russians in 1863, Raphael joined them and was soon taken prisoner. Few survived the forced

march to slave labour in Siberia, but Raphael was sustained by his faith and became spiritual leader to the prisoners. He was released ten years later.

*Left* Polish Insurrectionists of the 1863 Rebellion *(Stanislaus von Chlebowski, 19th century).*

Profoundly changed by his experiences in Siberia, Kalinowski joined the Carmelites, and in 1882, he was ordained priest at the monastery at Czerna, near Cracow, the last Carmelite brotherhood allowed in Poland.

Raphael strove to revive the Carmelites in Poland and to bring religious freedom to his oppressed countrymen. He died in Wadowice and was canonized in 1991.

# MIGUEL CORDERO

MIGUEL CORDERO OF ECUADOR WAS A GIFTED TEACHER, WHO, THROUGH HIS TEACHING AND WRITINGS, SPREAD THE WORD OF JESUS ACROSS HIS COUNTRY.

**KEY FACTS**
*de la Sallist*
DATES: *1854–1910*
BIRTH PLACE: *Cuenca, Ecuador*
FEAST DAY: *9 February*

Miguel Cordero was physically disabled but intellectually precocious. In his thinking, he was a precise theologian, but his actions showed a man concerned with the welfare of his students and fellow priests.

The de la Salle Brothers (the international teaching order founded by St John-Baptist de la Salle) accepted Cordero when he was only 14, and a year later, sent him to Quito in Ecuador. He proved to be an outstanding teacher. At the age of 20, he published a Spanish grammar that became adopted nationwide, and later

*Above Cuenca in Ecuador, birth place of Miguel Cordero. Cordero was the first Ecuadorian to be accepted into the de la Salle teaching order.*

wrote other acclaimed textbooks, and translated a life of John-Baptist de La Salle.

The Ecuadorian government despised the Church, but in spite of the state's efforts to suppress religion, Cordero's fame as a holy teacher and writer spread.

In 1907, he was called to work in Belgium. However, the Belgian climate did not suit him and he was moved to Barcelona. When an anti-clerical revolution erupted in the city, Cordero had to be rescued by gunboat. He died in Premia del Mar, Spain, in 1910, and was canonized in 1984.

# FRANCES CABRINI

A MISSIONARY AMONG ITALIAN IMMIGRANTS IN AMERICA, FRANCES IS KNOWN AS THE "MOTHER OF EMIGRANTS" FOR HER WORK TO KEEP THE FAITH ALIVE AMONG CHRISTIANS FAR FROM HOME.

**KEY FACTS**
*Founder*
DATES: *1850–1917*
BIRTH PLACE: *Sant' Angelo Lodigiano, near Pavia, Italy*
PATRON OF: *Migrants and emigrants*
FEAST DAY: *22 December*

Frances Cabrini was a missionary in the New World, but she did not work among the indigenous people. Instead, she was sent to revive the faith of Italian immigrants in America. Initially, she thought the mission unnecessary, believing all Italians to be as devout as her relatives.

Frances was the youngest of 13 children of northern Italian parents. After qualifying as a teacher, she tried to become a nun but was refused by two orders for health reasons. She was a tiny woman, barely 164cm/5ft tall, but a friendly priest, guessing at her

*Above The body of Frances Cabrini lies in state in the chapel at the Mother Cabrini High School in New York City.*

*Left A statue of St Frances Cabrini in the National Shrine of the Immaculate Conception in Washington, DC.*

inner strength, appealed to his bishop, who invited her to manage a small orphanage in Codogno, Lombardy. She remained there until the house closed.

## THE MISSIONARY SISTERS

The bishop encouraged Frances to start her own missionary congregation. She gathered seven women who had worked with her at Codogno and founded the Missionary Sisters of the Sacred Heart, dedicated to the education of Christian girls.

Frances had always wanted to work in China, but the Archbishop of New York had invited her to set up schools and orphanages for Italian immigrants. When, in 1889, she and six sisters crossed the Atlantic, they found no one had prepared for their arrival, and they had to live in poverty with the immigrants until Frances was able to find a building and open the orphanage.

## SPREAD OF THE MISSION

Success followed, and Frances opened more orphanages and schools in New York. She also founded schools in Managua, the capital of Nicaragua, and in New Orleans. Over the following years, her mission spread to Italy, Costa Rica, Panama, Chile, Brazil, France and England. Her profound faith drove her, and her proudest achievement was in opening the Columbus Hospital in New York.

Before moving to the United States, Frances had never met a Protestant and had difficulty in accepting that they, too, could be Christian. Her views were stern on subjects such as illegitimacy, but her deep love of God and a sense of justice tempered her thinking and ideas.

When her Missionary Sisters of the Sacred Heart were approved in 1907, there were 1,000 members in eight countries, and they served orphans, schools, prisons and hospitals.

Frances died in Chicago in 1917 and, in 1946, was the first American to be canonized.

# TERESA OF LOS ANDES

TERESA WANTED TO DEVOTE HER LIFE COMPLETELY TO JESUS AND "TO LOVE AND SUFFER FOR THE SALVATION OF SOULS". THE SIMPLE FAITH OF THIS YOUNG WOMAN HAS BECOME AN EXAMPLE TO MANY.

**KEY FACTS**
*Virgin, Carmelite*
DATES: *1900–20*
BIRTH PLACE: *Santiago, Chile*
FEAST DAY: *12 April*

The shrine of St Teresa of Los Andes at La Riconda attracts 100,000 pilgrims every year. She is among those pious young women, such as Theresa of Lisieux, whose every thought and action was directed toward God.

## CALLED TO SUFFER
One of six children born in Santiago, Chile, to wealthy, unassuming Christian parents, Teresa was well educated in the sciences, music and the arts. Her parents, who named her Juanita, were pleased by the religious faith of their daughter and the happiness it seemed to bring her.

When she was 14 years old, and suffering a painful bout of appendicitis, Teresa heard the voice of Jesus telling her that her pain was in imitation of his suffering. She had been lively and athletic until then, nicknamed "the Amazon" by her brothers, but after hearing

*Above A statue of St Teresa of Los Andes in Chile. A cultus developed after her death and she remains popular, especially with young women.*

Jesus speak, she made an inner vow of chastity, took to teaching the catechism to deprived children, and read the biographies of Teresa of Avila and of Blessed Elizabeth of the Trinity.

## DEVOTION TO CHRIST
Teresa considered joining the Sacred Heart Sisters, who were an educational order, but was overwhelmed by the need to devote her life to Christ. Her father was reluctant to give his permission when she told him she preferred to join an enclosed order, but he and the family did support her when, at 19, she became a noviciate with the Carmelite nuns.

The Carmelite convent in Los Andes was a rough building that lacked electricity and plumbing. Here, she took the vow of Victimhood, which meant that she was prepared to suffer for the Church and for sinners. Teresa's hours were spent deep in prayer, fasting, learning methods of contemplation, and recording and sharing her spiritual experiences in letters and a diary.

She was not quite 20 years old when she died of typhus at the convent, but her piety was regarded with great respect, and slowly, the power of her "hidden life" of devotion was revealed. A cultus grew around her memory and she was canonized by Pope John Paul II in 1993.

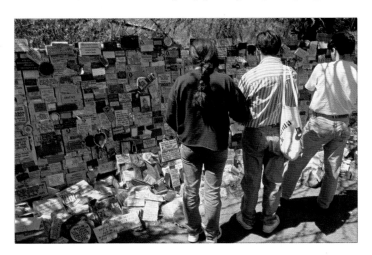

*Left Personal messages for St Teresa of Los Andes cover a wall outside the church dedicated to her in Los Andes, Chile.*

# BERTILLA BOSCARDIN

BERTILLA WAS A SIMPLE PEASANT WOMAN WHO HAD BEEN BADLY TREATED AS A CHILD, BUT HER PATIENCE AND STAUNCH RELIGIOUS FAITH MADE HER A WONDERFUL NURSE.

**KEY FACTS**
*Nun, nurse*
DATES: *1888–1922*
BIRTH PLACE: *near Vicenza, Italy*
FEAST DAY: *20 October*

This saint lived a humble life, but those whom she cared for loved her, and miracles have been attributed to her intercession.

Maria Bertilla Boscardin was a peasant girl who joined the Sisters of St Dorothy in Vicenza in 1904. The other nuns, considering her dim-witted, used her as a kitchen and laundry maid until her profession in 1907, when she was sent to care for children with diphtheria at the hospital in Treviso.

During World War I, Vicenza was bombed, but Bertilla remained calm, intent only on saving her patients. When the hospital was moved away from the front line to Como, the military authorities praised her work. But again, her simplicity was misinterpreted, and she was put to work in the laundry. Bertilla never complained, but in 1919, the Superior-General of the order rescued her and placed her in charge of the children's isolation ward back at Treviso, where she nursed with compassion.

Bertilla died while undergoing surgery. Her family and some of her former patients were present at her canonization in 1961.

*Above Bertilla Boscardin worked as a nurse in Treviso, where she cared for the sick with patience and sympathy.*

# GIUSEPPE MOSCATI

GIUSEPPE MOSCATI BELIEVED HIS SCIENTIFIC KNOWLEDGE AND CARE OF THE SICK WERE A WAY TO REVEAL THE GLORY OF GOD AND CONSIDERED HIS MEDICAL WORK TO BE A "SUBLIME MISSION".

**KEY FACTS**
*Doctor of medicine*
DATES: *1860–1927*
BIRTH PLACE: *Benevento, Italy*
FEAST DAY: *16 November*

Giuseppe Moscati came from a family brave in their faith. His father was a magistrate who had risked his livelihood, when he refused to deny Christianity during the anti-clerical control of Italy during the mid-19th century.

Giuseppe was a top medical student at the University of Naples, where he specialized in biochemistry. After qualifying, he began working with patients afflicted with syphilis at the Hospital for Incurables, Santa Maria del Populo.

Parallel to his hospital duties, Giuseppe conducted medical research and gave free care to the poor. This entailed visiting the swarming slums of Naples, often at night, to tend the sick. His scientific learning was underpinned by his faith, and he treated patients for spiritual as well as medical problems.

In 1911, he was appointed Chair of Physiology at Naples University, but success did not turn him from his prayers or his veneration of Mary, the Blessed Virgin. Neither did he neglect his charity work. Patients, priests and laymen appreciated the spiritual dimension he brought to medicine. He died peacefully in his home and was canonized in 1987.

*Above Pilgrims touch the hand of the Giuseppe Moscati statue at Gesù Nuovo Church in Naples, Italy.*

# THE CULT OF MARY

MARY, THE BLESSED VIRGIN, IS HONOURED WORLDWIDE BY MILLIONS OF FAITHFUL FOR HER PURITY AS WELL AS FOR HER EXTRAORDINARY ROLE AS THE MOTHER OF GOD.

***Above*** *A statue of the crowned Virgin and Child in Siena, Italy.*

Devotion to Mary can be traced as far back as the 4th or 5th centuries AD, but the full doctrine has developed gradually. In the earliest days of the Church, Mary, the Blessed Virgin, was called Christokos, "Mother of Christ", but this caused some wrangling among theologians because it implied that Jesus was not divine. In the 6th century AD, they agreed on Theotokos, "Mother of God", and this more emphatic description of Mary confirmed her strong position in the faith as the mother of Jesus, the Son of God. Even the Protestant Church accepted her unique role as the virgin mother of Christ, but some Protestant sects have recently questioned this.

"GRANT WE BESEECH THEE, O LORD GOD, UNTO US THY SERVANTS, THAT WE MAY REJOICE IN CONTINUAL HEALTH OF MIND AND BODY; AND, BY THE GLORIOUS INTERCESSION OF BLESSED MARY EVER VIRGIN, MAY BE DELIVERED FROM PRESENT SADNESS, AND ENTER INTO THE JOY OF THINE ETERNAL GLADNESS. THROUGH CHRIST OUR LORD. AMEN."

FINAL WORDS OF THE LITANY OF LORETO

in its calendar. The day of the Assumption, 15 August, occasions great celebration as it is considered to be Mary's heavenly birthday.

## THE GREATEST SAINT

Mary has long been perceived as chief among all the saints, mediating with Jesus on behalf of the world. For this reason, the faithful turn to her to resolve their most difficult problems.

In 1587, Pope Sixtus V sealed this view of Mary's role when he approved the Litany of Loreto. In

## AN EXCEPTIONAL WOMAN

Christians who venerate Mary often call her the Immaculate Conception. This refers to the belief that her spirit was conceived free from original sin, untainted by the sins of Adam and Eve in the Garden of Eden. This has led some theologians to refer to her as the "new Eve".

Not only is Mary believed to be immune from original sin, but she was also a virgin when Jesus was born, hence the title given to her, the Blessed Virgin. Because she embodies

purity and perfect motherly love, she has always held a special place in the heart of believers. Augustine of Hippo, when discussing the nature of Mary, said, "After all, how do we know what abundance of grace was granted to her who had the merit to conceive and bring forth him who was unquestionably without sin?"

When Mary had completed her life on earth, it is believed that she was received into heaven as a complete being – body and soul together. This special event is key to both Roman Catholic and Eastern Orthodox belief, but the Anglican Church also includes it

***Left*** *A West African wood carving of Madonna and child (20th century).*

***Right*** *Catholics seek blessings for their child from a statue of Mary in Hyderabad, India.*

*Left An Ethiopian icon triptych depicting the Virgin and child (18th–19th century).*

Catholic homes, schools and institutions display the image of the Blessed Virgin and often create small shrine-like altars in veneration of her. No Catholic church is without a statue to Mary, the Blessed Virgin and the infant Jesus.

In modern times, Mary is firmly lodged in the Christian culture. She is a central figure in literature and popular idiom, and she is patron saint to a number of countries.

The principal Marian shrines attract huge numbers of pilgrims, millions visiting every year the sites of Lourdes in France, Guadalupe in Mexico, Fatima in Portugal, Walsingham in England and the House of Loreto in Italy.

this long prayer, believers call upon God to heed Mary, and the text uses her many titles.

## WORLDWIDE INFLUENCE

The Eastern Orthodox Church has been untouched by debate about Mary's role. There, she has always had a profound significance and many Orthodox icons are devoted to the image of Mary as Mother with her Holy Infant.

In the Western Church, theologians have long debated her role, but since the 15th century, popular religion has developed a deep devotion to Mary. She represents motherhood and family life, one who understands the universal experiences of joy and pain. Those believers suffering tragedy

meditate on the image of Mary with her dying son. The rosary is a set of prayers often recited by Christians who venerate Mary, the Blessed Virgin. A string of beads, also called a rosary, is used as an aide-mémoire for the correct order of the prayers.

*Right The famous La Pietà in St Peter's, Rome (Michelangelo, 1496).*

### SOME TITLES OF MARY

There are numerous titles for Mary, many used in the long prayer, the Litany of Loreto. Here are a few examples:

Advocate of Grace
Champion of God's People
Chosen Daughter of the Father
Gracious Lady
Handmaid of the Lord
Holy Mary
Holy Mother of God
Joy of Israel
Most Honoured of Virgins
Mother of Christ
Mother Mary
Our Lady
Perfect Disciple of Christ
Queen of All Saints
Queen of Apostles and Martyrs
Queen of Confessors and Virgins
Queen of Mercy
Queen of Peace
Splendour of the Church
The Blessed Virgin
The Immaculate Conception

# MARIA FAUSTINA KOWALSKA

MARIA FAUSTINA KOWALSKA WAS A HUMBLE LAY SISTER, BUT HER HEAVENLY VISIONS, HER OBEDIENCE AND HER DEEP DEVOTION TO GOD, RECORDED IN HER DIARIES, BROUGHT HER SAINTHOOD.

**KEY FACTS**
*Visionary and Polish mystic*
DATES: *1905–38*
BIRTH PLACE: *Glogowiec, Poland*
FEAST DAY: *25 August*

Maria Faustina Kowalska offered her own suffering to God to make amends for her sins and the sins of others. Her inspiration came from a miracle described in John's Gospel: after Jesus had healed a man who had been an invalid for 38 years, he said to him, "Sin no more, lest a worse thing come unto thee." The man went away and told others that Jesus had made him well. Maria believed that with faith and virtue, sins would be forgiven, just as the faith of the invalid had banished his disability.

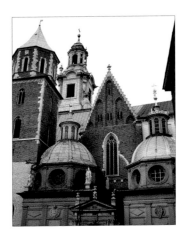

*Above Cracow, Poland, where Maria Faustina Kowalska spent the last few years of her life in contemplation and prayer while she fought off illness.*

## A LIFE GUIDED BY VISIONS

Born in Glogowiec, Poland, Maria was the third of ten children. She was certain that she had a vocation to the religious life, and in 1923,

she had a vision of Christ that strengthened her conviction. In 1925, she joined the Congregation of Our Lady of Mercy in Warsaw as a lay sister.

She did not aim for high office, and nursed no ambition but, in humility and obedience, worked in the garden, the kitchen and as a porter. The compassion and patience she showed toward the poor who visited the convent impressed her fellow nuns.

## DIVINE MERCY

Visions of Jesus were a frequent part of Maria's experience, and in one of these Christ is said to have asked her to keep a diary. In this, she began to record the spiritual guidance the visions brought her, primarily the message of the "Divine Mercy of God". Her diary was later published with the title *Divine Mercy in My Soul: The Diary of St Faustina*.

Her health was delicate, and in 1936 she was moved to a sanatorium in Cracow with suspected tuberculosis. Here, she was given her own cell, and in this privacy she was able to surrender herself to prayer and contemplation. Her last years were spent fighting for breath and in constant pain. She died in Cracow, still a young woman, in 1938, and was canonized by Pope John Paul II in 2000.

*Left The canonization of Maria Faustina Kowalska by Pope John Paul II took place in front of 100,000 pilgrims in 2000.*

# MAXIMILIAN KOLBE

MAXIMILIAN KOLBE MADE THE ULTIMATE SACRIFICE, GIVING UP HIS LIFE FOR THE SAKE OF ANOTHER IN A GERMAN CONCENTRATION CAMP. HE IS KNOWN AS THE "MARTYR OF CHARITY".

**KEY FACTS**
*Martyr*
DATES: *1894–1941*
BIRTH PLACE: *near Lodz, Poland*
FEAST DAY: *14 August*

Maximilian Kolbe was the son of devout, patriotic Polish parents. After Maximilian entered the Franciscan Order in 1910, his parents separated and began living religious lives. His father was hanged by the Russian government in 1914, because he was fighting with the Polish Legion for Polish independence.

In 1912, Maximilian was sent to Cracow, then to Rome, where he studied philosophy, theology, physics and mathematics. After his ordination in Rome in 1919, he founded Franciscan communities dedicated to prayer and serving the poor at Niepokalanow, near Warsaw, and at Nagasaki in Japan. He was keen to revive the faith and started various religious publications in both Poland and Japan to accomplish this. He also took advantage of modern technology by installing a radio station at Niepokalanow.

## HOUSING REFUGEES

When the Germans invaded Poland in 1939, Maximilian closed the Niepokalanow community and sent the priests home, anxious that they should not endanger themselves by joining the resistance. Heedless of his own safety, he and the remaining brothers housed 4,500 Polish refugees, of whom 1,500 were Jewish. Maximilian's various publications continued and included articles critical of the German invaders. In 1941, he and four brothers were arrested and taken to the Nazi concentration camp at Auschwitz in Poland.

**Above** *An undated photograph of Maximilian Kolbe, the Franciscan priest who served, then gave up his life for fellow Poles in World War II.*

## GIVING HIS LIFE

Maximilian had suffered tuberculosis most of his life, so he found his duties at the camp – carrying logs and moving the bodies of dead inmates – particularly hard. He applied himself to giving his fellow sufferers religious comfort, and somehow even managed to smuggle bread and wine inside the walls so that he could offer the Holy Eucharist.

One day, the inmates from Maximilian's hut were lined up and the wardens selected several men to die. This was a reprisal for a successful escape attempt. One of the chosen, a Polish sergeant named Francis Gajowniczek, cried out, "My poor wife! My poor children! What will they do?" Maximilian stepped forward and announced, "I wish to die for that man. I am old; he has a wife and children."

The swap was approved and the condemned men were locked into Cell 18 and left to starve. Maximilian comforted them, sang psalms and prayed in preparation for their deaths. After two weeks, he was the only man still conscious. He was killed by lethal injection in August 1941.

Sergeant Gajowniczek – who himself died at the age of 94 in 1995 – attended the canonization of St Maximilian Kolbe in 1982.

**Below** *Francis Gajowniczek, the man saved by Maximilian Kolbe in 1941, is embraced by Pope John Paul II in St Peter's Square in 1982.*

# EDITH STEIN

EDITH STEIN, A JEWISH CONVERT AND PHILOSOPHER, BECAME A CARMELITE NUN, BELIEVING THAT IT WAS HER VOCATION "TO INTERCEDE TO GOD FOR EVERYONE".

**KEY FACTS**
*Martyr*
DATES: *1891–1942*
BIRTH PLACE: *Breslau, Germany (now Wroclaw, Poland)*
PATRON OF: *France*
FEAST DAY: *9 August*

Edith Stein was brought up in the Jewish faith and studied philosophy at the German universities of Göttingen and Freiburg. During this time, she was profoundly affected by the writings of St Teresa of Ávila. She converted to Catholicism and was baptized in 1922. Edith did not regard her Christianity as a denial of her family's faith but as an expansion of their Jewish beliefs. She continued to attend synagogue with her mother in order to soften the impact that her conversion would have on her devout Jewish family.

## TEACHING AND STUDYING

Although Edith was not at ease in front of a class, she became a German language and literature teacher at a Dominican girls' school. As a woman, academic work in a university was closed to her. She joined the Educational Institute but privately continued her philosophical studies, including a work on the role of women

*Left The Jewish philosopher, photographed aged 39, became a Carmelite nun in 1934. Reading the autobiography of St Teresa of Ávila inspired her to convert.*

in the Christian Church. In 1932, Hitler initiated his anti-Jewish propaganda and Edith wrote, "Christ's Cross is being laid upon the Jewish people...".

In 1933, Edith entered the Carmelite order, where a sympathetic abbess allowed her to con-

tinue writing on religious and scholarly topics. Edith prepared philosophical texts on prayer and the Eternal Being, and began a study of St John of the Cross.

By 1937, those of Jewish origin were no longer safe in Germany and the Carmelites sent her to Holland. The Dutch Church campaigned against Nazi anti-Semitic policies but to no avail.

## AUSCHWITZ

Edith refused to stay hidden in her convent, fearing her presence would harm the other nuns, and said on learning that she would be sent to Auschwitz in 1939, "I am going for my people."

Edith's faith brought her comfort and strength, and she ministered to her fellow prisoners. An insight into how she regarded her fate can be drawn from her own words: "Sufferings endured with the Lord are his sufferings, and bear great fruit in the context of his great work of redemption." Edith Stein was killed, with her sister Rose, in Auschwitz in 1942, and was canonized in 1998.

*Left Edith Stein was captured in the Netherlands during a persecution of Jewish converts. She was sent to Auschwitz death camp, where she was gassed in 1942.*

# JOSEPHINE BAKHITA

JOSEPHINE WAS SO TRAUMATIZED WHEN CAPTURED AND ILL-TREATED BY SLAVE TRADERS THAT SHE FORGOT HER NAME. PROPHETICALLY, HER KIDNAPPERS NAMED HER BAKHITA – "THE FORTUNATE ONE".

**KEY FACTS**
*Convert, nun*
DATES: *1869–1947*
BIRTH PLACE: *Olgossa, Darfur, Sudan*
PATRON OF: *the Sudan*
FEAST DAY: *8 February*

Josephine represents all victims of oppression, and is venerated for her message of forgiveness. For many years a slave, Josephine claimed that, if she were to meet the men who enslaved her, she "would kneel to them to kiss their hands", because without them, she would never have met Jesus.

Born in Darfur, Sudan, Josephine was only nine years old when Arab traders abducted and sold her in Khartoum. She was traded from one unpleasant owner to another until, in 1882,

*Right A convoy of slaves in the Sudan, where Josephine Bakhita herself was traded as a slave while still a child.*

an Italian named Callisto Legnani bought her. He in turn gave her to his friend Augusto Michieli, who took her to Italy.

While he was away on business, Bakhita, as Josephine had been named, and Michieli's daughter stayed at the Canossian convent in Venice, where Josephine became a Christian. On her master's return, she requested permission to stay at the convent, and took her vows there in 1896.

Josephine was moved to the Canossian convent at Schio, Vicenza, where she remained for the rest of her life, apart from three years in Milan spent teaching young sisters to work in Africa. She was known and loved for her gentleness, calming voice, and ever-present smile. She died in Schio, murmuring, "Madonna, Madonna!" Pope John Paul II canonized her in 2000.

# JOHN CALABRIA

ON THE TOMB OF JOHN CALABRIA ARE THE WORDS: "HE SHONE LIKE A LIGHTHOUSE IN THE CHURCH OF GOD. HIS MISSION WAS 'TO PROVE TO THE WORLD THAT DIVINE PROVIDENCE EXISTS'."

**KEY FACTS**
*Founder*
DATES: *1873–1954*
BIRTH PLACE: *Verona, Italy*
FEAST DAY: *4 December*

John Calabria's holiness was recognized beyond the Roman Catholic community. During World War II, he protected persecuted Jews, disguising one woman as a nun to save her. He practised charity to everyone, regardless of faith or creed.

John was born in poverty in Verona, and was educated at the Institute for Poor Children. In 1897, he began to work with orphaned and abandoned boys, starting a "Charitable Institution for assistance to poor, sick people",

which became the Congregation of the Poor Servants, and its sister house, the Poor Women Servants of Divine Providences.

John assured his followers that faith would help them in difficult situations "where there is nothing humanly possible", and he sent them to open hospitals and care homes in Italy and India. His writings and sermons encouraged people to follow God's love without prejudice. John died in San Zeno, Verona in 1954 and was canonized in 1988.

*Left The San Zeno Basilica, the best-known church in Verona, where John Calabria spent his life.*

# KATHARINE DREXEL

KATHARINE DREXEL, MOTIVATED BY A PROFOUND FAITH, USED HER INHERITANCE TO IMPROVE THE SOCIAL AND RELIGIOUS WELFARE OF RACIAL MINORITIES AND DEPRIVED PEOPLES.

Katharine Marie Drexel learnt the Christian virtue of charity from her stepmother, Emma Bouvier, who donated $20,000 a year to the welfare of the poor in Philadelphia. Another influence was Dr James O'Connor, a priest and family friend who campaigned for the just administration of Native Americans.

In 1878, Katharine "came out" in society, but she remained unmoved by the lavish circuit of balls and parties enjoyed by many of her peers. During a trip to Europe, she made a pilgrimage to the home of St Catherine of

*Above A painting of Katharine Drexel (artist and date unknown) shows her with some of the children she gave her life to serve.*

*Below A statue of Katharine Drexel in the National Shrine of the Immaculate Conception in Washington, D.C.*

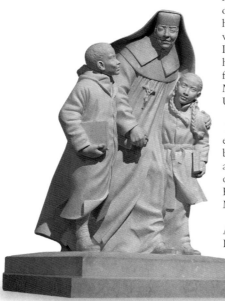

Siena, and later confided to Dr O'Connor that she wished to become a nun.

By 1885, O'Connor, who had recently been appointed Bishop of Omaha, called on Katharine to help him resolve disputes between white and Native Americans in Dakota. On her return, she and her sisters, all wealthy women, founded the Drexel Chair of Moral Theology at Washington University (D.C.).

At an audience with Pope Leo XIII in 1887, she was encouraged by the pope to become a missionary. Taking his advice, and fulfilling her dream of a life dedicated to God, Katharine joined the Sisters of Mary in Pittsburgh.

## AIDING MINORITIES

Katharine was determined to start a community devoted to helping ethnic minorities, and, in 1891, founded the Sisters of the Blessed

Sacrament. In 1894, the order's first school for Native American children, St Catherine Indian School, was built in Santa Fe, New Mexico.

She established schools, missions and hospitals in Boston, Chicago, New Orleans, New York, Texas and Tennessee, and her congregation trained nearly 200 teaching sisters and 80 lay teachers. She also founded the first university for African American students, Xavier University in New Orleans.

Katharine worked until she was disabled by illness (she suffered a severe heart attack in 1935). Thereafter, she continued to pray for, and advise her communities, who all knew her as "First Sister". She died in Philadelphia in 1955 at the age of 97. At her funeral, the pallbearers represented the groups she had helped – Native Americans, African Americans and European Americans.

Although Katharine focused on the welfare of racial minorities, her work extended to all the underprivileged. From the time she founded her order at the age of 33 until the end of her life, Katherine gave away a personal fortune of 20 million US dollars to the work of the Sisters of the Blessed Sacrament.

She also funded many convents, monasteries and chapels. Her congregation, which remains rooted in the welfare and education programmes she instituted, still has an important role within the Church. Katharine Drexel was canonized by Pope John Paul II in 2000.

# FATHER GEORGE PRECA

FATHER GEORGE PRECA LOVED THE GOSPELS, WHICH HE CALLED "THE VOICE OF THE BELOVED". A HUMBLE MAN, HE DEVOTED HIS LIFE TO TEACHING THE DEPRIVED AND UNEDUCATED.

**KEY FACTS**
*Founder*
DATES: *1880–1962*
BIRTH PLACE: *Valletta, Malta*
FEAST DAY: *9 May*

The young George Preca was cured of an illness after prayers of intercession to St Joseph. Throughout his life, George heard heavenly voices and had visions, and these spiritual experiences gave him a powerful sense of his mission on earth. He was inspired, too, by the words of Jesus, "Blessed are the meek, for they shall inherit the earth" (Matthew 5:5).

## MALTESE MISSION

After he was ordained in 1906, George began to seek out ordinary working people, and he set up a mission on the waterfront of Valletta, Malta. In 1907, he founded a community that came to be called the Society of Christian Doctrine. This order of laymen and women pursued mission work throughout Malta, and Father George sent them forth with the hope that "the world would follow the gospel". These missions organized daily sessions of prayer and discussion, and taught children the Catechism.

However, the Church in Malta was displeased with George's inclusion of lay people in the Church hierarchy and his use of female missionaries. They tried to shut down the order, but encountered such uproar from believers and other priests that Father George was eventually reinstated, and the Society of Christian Doctrine was given approval in 1932. During the controversy, Father George cautioned his followers to quell their anger and forgive those who taunted them.

*Above Pope John Paul II prays at the tomb of Father George Preca in Hamrun, Malta, in 2001.*

*Below The cityscape of Valletta, Malta, the birthplace of Father George Preca.*

## A HOLY, HUMBLE MAN

The Maltese admired Father George as a gentle, sympathetic confessor, and as a priest who welcomed the laity into the rituals of the Church. He was regarded as a holy man and saw a vision of the boy Jesus, which, he reported, brought him a sense of great spiritual sweetness. Others claimed he had cured their physical ailments.

The society's reputation spread, and it now has missions in Albania, Australia, Kenya, Peru and Sudan. Pope Pius XII made Father George a Monsignor of the Church, but the honour embarrassed him, and he dropped the title after the pope's death.

Father George Preca died at Santa Venera, Malta, in 1962, and his relics lie in Blata I-Badja. Prayers for his intercession have been known to cure the sick. He was canonized in 2007 by Pope Benedict XVI.

# PADRE PIO

THE HUMBLE CAPUCHIN MONK, NOW BEST KNOWN AS PADRE PIO, MODESTLY TRIED TO HIDE THE MARKS OF HIS STIGMATA, SAYING, "I ONLY WANT TO BE A POOR FRIAR WHO PRAYS".

**KEY FACTS**
*Stigmatist*
DATES: *1887–1968*
BIRTH PLACE: *near Naples, Italy*
FEAST DAY: *23 September*

St Pius of Pietrelcina, better known as Padre Pio, first knew he belonged to God at the age of five. Throughout his childhood, he experienced visions and spoke with Jesus and Mary. He joined the Capuchin Order and was ordained at the friary of San Giovanni Rotondo, Pietrelcina in 1910.

### RECEIVING THE STIGMATA
In 1918, he became "aware that my hands, feet and side were pierced and were dripping with blood". He had received stigmata, but he covered the wounds and tried unsuccessfully to hide them.

Padre Pio may have been awed, even frightened, by this gift of holy marks, but he could not have anticipated the antagonism he met within the Church. When his secret was revealed, other churchmen claimed he was a fake and accused him of sexual licence, but

*Above Padre Pio as depicted on the front of Italian magazine La Domenica del Corriere in 1956.*

*Below A friar bends over the coffin of Padre Pio. During his lifetime Pio was both revered and reviled. The controversy continued after his death in 1968.*

believers crowded the friary, seeking blessings and forgiveness from him. In 1923, the Church placed increasingly severe restrictions on Padre Pio until he was virtually locked away and only allowed to take Mass in private. After Pope Pius XII lifted all these restrictions in 1933, life became easier for Padre Pio, but spiteful attacks from other clergy continued. True to Christ's teachings, Padre Pio remained meek and dedicated, despite slander and injustice.

### MAN OF PRAYER
The Capuchins had built, in the friary grounds, a House for the Relief of Suffering, a place that was a hospital, hospice and retreat directed toward families in need. Pius XII encouraged Padre Pio to pray for the hospital. The saint spent long hours praying and meditating on the Way of the Cross, saying, "In books we seek God, in prayer we meet him."

In 1959, he began regular broadcasts on national radio, his sermons reinforcing his belief that "Prayer is the best weapon we possess, the key that opens the heart of God." His example inspired prayer groups across the world and these continue today.

Padre Pio wore mittens to hide the stigmata on his hands, and remained a humble friar, who spent all his life in his friary and died there, yet more than 100,000 people attended his funeral. A mother claimed a miracle cure of her child's meningitis after prayers to Padre Pio, who was canonized in 2002.

# JOSEMARÍA ESCRIVÁ

THE FOUNDER OF OPUS DEI, JOSEMARÍA ESCRIVÁ, LIVED
CHRISTIAN VIRTUES TO THE HIGHEST DEGREE AND HAD A MISSION
TO FILL EVERYDAY LIVES WITH FAITH AND HOPE.

**KEY FACTS**
*Founder*
DATES: *1902–75*
BIRTH PLACE: *Barbastro, Spain*
FEAST DAY: *26 June*

As a youth, Josemaría Escrivá saw the footprints of a monk in the snow. He took this as a sign to follow the path to God and was ordained in 1925, soon after his father's death. He began a graduate law course in Madrid and supported his mother and siblings by tutoring other students. His personal experiences taught him that there was a path to God through family life, work and social duty.

## OPUS DEI

In 1928, inspired by a religious experience on a retreat, Escrivá founded Opus Dei. This order of laymen lived communally, but their only rule was obedience to their founder. Josemaría taught them how to "sanctify their lives in the midst of the world", and to show how an everyday life can be enriched if it is dedicated to God.

When Spain erupted into civil war, thousands of religious were killed and, despite support from the pro-Church side, Josemaría was forced to flee across the Pyrenees. Some of those martyred have been canonized as individuals, while others are honoured as the Martyrs of the Spanish Civil War.

After the war ended in 1939, Opus Dei grew rapidly, working largely in the world of education, establishing houses in Europe and Latin America. In 1943, Pope Pius XII gave approval for members of Opus Dei to become priests. The order now has 80,000 members, many of whom are lay men and women, in 80 different countries. It owns radio stations and newspapers, which it uses to promote traditional faith and liturgy, to integrate faith into work and social responsibility, and to encourage religious domestic life.

*Above Chapel of St Josemaría Escrivá at the Catedral de la Almudena, Madrid.*

Alongside providing guidance for his order, Josemaría continued to study and to support his mother. When she died, he went to Rome to further his studies, and was made an honorary prelate of the Pontifical Academy of Theology.

Secularists have criticized Opus Dei for blurring the line between religion and politics. Others accuse the order of being secretive and exclusive, but few deny the goodness and spirituality of Josemaría, who died in his office in Rome, and was canonized in 2002 by John Paul II.

*Left Josemaría Escrivá with a group of his followers in Rome in 1971.*

# GAZETTEER OF OTHER SAINTS

ON THE FOLLOWING PAGES ARE BRIEF ACCOUNTS OF SAINTS WHO
HAVE NOT BEEN INCLUDED IN THE MAIN SECTION OF THIS BOOK
BUT WHO NEVERTHELESS DESERVE MENTION.

### CORENTIN
*dates unknown*
Cornish hermit who later became
a bishop in Brittany, where his
cultus revived in the 1600s after he
appeared to a believer in a vision.
**Feast Day: 1 May**

### JULIAN THE HOSPITALLER
*dates unknown*
According to legend, he killed his
parents in a case of mistaken identity, then fled and built a house for
poor people. He revived a dying
man who disappeared into a bright
cloud, which was seen as a sign
that Jesus had forgiven Julian's sins.
**Feast Day: 29 January**

### URITH OF CHITTLEHAMPTON
*dates unknown*
Legend has it that her pagan stepmother arranged her death – by
harvesters wielding scythes – but
that as she fell to the ground, a
spring burst from the earth.
**Feast Day: 8 July**

### ALBAN
*3rd century AD*
Protomartyr of Britain, this Roman
citizen was converted by a priest
whom he hid from persecution and
helped escape. After disguising
himself as the priest, he was arrested and later beheaded.
**Feast Day: 2 August**

### CALLISTUS I
*died AD 222*
Born a slave and served time as a
criminal before his conversion.
He became Bishop of Rome and a

pope, respected for his kind treatment of sinners. It is thought he
died a martyr.
**Feast Day: 14 October**

### PONTIAN AND HIPPOLYTUS
*died c.AD 236*
Hippolytus criticized bishops of
Rome, Zephyrinus and Callistus I.
He was banished to the Sardinian
quarries, where he met Pontian,
a former pope. Both died as
prisoners and were later hailed as
martyrs. Hippolytus' text, *Apostolic
Tradition,* is a record of Christian
worship during the Roman era.
**Feast Day: 13 August**

### APOLLONIA
*died c.AD 249*
This aged deaconess of Alexandria
was persecuted by an anti-Christian
mob, who knocked out all her
teeth. She chose to walk into the
flames rather than deny her faith.
Patron of toothache.
**Feast Day: 9 February**

### BABYLAS
*died c.AD 250*
Antioch's most famous early bishop was martyred along with three
boys whom he had converted. He
is the first martyr whose relics are
recorded as having been translated.
**Feast Day: 24 January**

### LAURENCE
*died AD 258*
Legend claims he was a deacon of
Rome and that he was roasted on
a gridiron. Fra Angelico painted
his life cycle in the Vatican.
**Feast Day: 10 August**

*Above* The Martyrdom of St
Laurence *(altar from Waldburg, c.1520).*

### CRISPIN AND CRISPINIAN
*died c.AD 285*
It would seem these men were of
Roman origin and fled the city to
avoid persecution. Their relics
were moved to Soissons, France,
which became the centre for their
cultus from the 6th century.
**Feast Day: 25 October**

### SEBASTIAN
*died c.AD 300*
Roman martyr sentenced to be
shot to death by arrows. Popular
subject for Renaissance painters.
Patron of archers; one of the
Fourteen Holy Helpers.
**Feast Day: 20 January**

### ERASMUS (ELMO)
*died c.AD 300*
According to legend, this bishop
fled persecution in Syria to hide
as a hermit in Lebanon, but was
discovered, rolled in pitch and set
alight. An angel rescued him.
**Feast Day: 2 June**

## MEN(N)AS
### died c.AD 300

This Roman soldier was converted and martyred in Egypt, where he is still highly venerated. Miracles were attributed to him, and the water inside clay bottles made at his grave was believed to have curative powers.

**Feast Day: 11 November**

## FLORIAN
### died AD 304

A converted Roman army officer, Florian joined persecuted Christians and was tortured, then drowned in the River Enns. His body was recovered and his relics enshrined in St Florian Abbey, Linz.

**Feast Day: 4 May**

## NINO
### died c.AD 340

A slave girl credited with bringing Christianity to Georgia. She was taken to the royal court, where her powers of curing illness in Jesus' name caused the king to ask her to teach his people about Christianity.

**Feast Day: 15 December**

*Above* The martyrdom of Crispin and Crispinian *(French glass painting, 15th century).*

## PAULA
### died AD 404

A young widow of noble Roman birth, Paula settled in Bethlehem, where she built a convent and monastery, helped Jerome with his studies, and gave away her wealth.

**Feast Day: 26 January**

## MOSES THE BLACK
### c.AD 330–c.AD 405

An Ethiopian servant in Egypt who became a criminal. After his conversion, he joined a community of desert monks and was ordained. He was killed by raiding Berbers.

**Feast Day: 28 August**

## HONORATUS OF ARLES
### died AD 429

Born and converted in Rome, he founded a monastic community in Greece with his brother. After the latter's death, he moved to southern France and built another monastery. He died two years after becoming Bishop of Arles.

**Feast Day: 16 January**

## PAULINUS OF NOLA
### died AD 431

Born in Bordeaux, Paulinus trained as a lawyer and poet in Italy. After their baby died, he and his wife found faith, began to give away their wealth, and moved to a large house in Nola, Spain, where they provided shelter for pilgrims and fugitives. Paulinus was ordained Bishop of Nola c.AD 409.

**Feast Day: 22 June**

## CASSIAN
## (JOHN CASSIAN)
### c.AD 360–433

Probably born in Romania, Cassian became a disciple of John Chrysostom in Constantinople. When the latter was exiled, Cassian went to Rome to plead his cause with the pope. He later founded two monasteries in Marseille.

**Feast Day: 23 July**

## DANIEL THE STYLITE
### AD 409–93

Joined an abbey when he was only 12. An admirer of Simeon Stylites, he locked himself in an abandoned temple for nine years, and when Simeon died in AD 459, he built a pillar and lived on it until his death.

**Feast Day: 11 December**

## FLORENCE OF MONT GLONNE
### 5th century

Ordained by Martin of Tours, he lived as a hermit before founding a monastery in Saumur. His cultus lasted for centuries.

**Feast Day: 22 September**

## CLOTILDE
### c.AD 474–545

Married to Frankish King Clovis, a pagan who converted after he asked "Clotilde's God" for victory in battle and his prayer was granted. She later retired to a monastery, but through her northern Europe took its first steps toward Christianity.

**Feast Day: 3 June**

*Above* Clovis and Clotilde *(French stained glass, 19th century).*

## MARCOUL
*died c.AD 558*

Born into a rich family, Marcoul preached in Normandy before becoming a hermit. He had many disciples and founded a monastery. Kings of France used to pray before his shrine.
**Feast Day: 1 May**

## PETROC
*6th century AD*

This Celtic missionary trekked Cornwall, Devon and Brittany, made pilgrimage to Jerusalem and Rome, and was briefly a hermit.
**Feast Day: 4 June**

## VENANTIUS FORTUNATUS
*c.AD 530–610*

An Italian who settled in Poitiers (elected its bishop in AD 600), he became chaplain to a convent. He wrote hymns, verse to the Blessed Virgin, and biographies of saints.
**Feast Day: 14 December**

## FINBAR
*c.AD 560–610*

Irish saint who made a pilgrimage to Rome with Welsh St David. Venerated in Cork as founder of its monastery and for mission work.
**Feast Day: 25 September**

## KENTIGERN
*died AD 612*

Celtic monk and Bishop of Glasgow and Cumbria. Legends abound: one tells that his mother was thrown into the sea and he (her illegitimate son) was born in a coracle.
**Feast Day: 13 January**

## THEODORE OF SYKEON
*died AD 613*

Child of a prostitute mother and circus-artist father, Theodore was ordained a priest at 18. He took a pilgrimage to Jerusalem, then returned to Galatia, where he was an influential preacher. For a while,

he was Bishop of Anastasiopolis, near Ankara, but returned to live as a monk at Sykeon.
**Feast Day: 22 April**

## BRAULIO OF SARAGOSSA
*died AD 650*

Braulio became a monk and joined St Isidore in Seville before returning to his hometown of Saragossa, where he became the city's bishop. He defended converted Jews and fought against Arianism.
**Feast Day: 26 March**

## ELOI
*c.AD 588–660*

His artistry in metalwork made Eloi famous throughout western Europe. He was Bishop of Noyen and counsellor to the queen-regent, Bathilde, a freed slave. Together they forbade the export of slaves from the kingdom.
**Feast Day: 1 December**

## FIACRE
*died c.AD 670*

Irish by birth, Fiacre lived as a hermit most of his life in France. He was known as a gardener and cared for those suffering from venereal diseases. His cultus flourished in France until the 1700s.
**Feast Day: 30 August**

*Below Eloi miraculously replaces the foreleg of a horse in this French tapestry (16th century).*

## AMAND
*c.AD 584–675*

French-born bishop who travelled as a missionary to Flanders and Carinthia, and founded monasteries near Ghent and a convent at Nivelles. His cultus spread through Flanders, Picardy and England.
**Feast Day: 6 February**

## EBBE
*died AD 683*

Ebbe, the daughter of the King of Northumbria, was the first abbess of Coldingham. Despite the convent's lax reputation, she was holy and wise, and was instrumental in releasing St Wilfred from prison.
**Feast Day: 25 August**

## THEODORE OF CANTERBURY
*AD 602–90*

Born a Greek, yet became Archbishop of Canterbury, England. His devout and scholarly leadership brought much-needed unity. His canonization was supported by the Venerable Bede's writings.
**Feast Day: 10 September**

## LAMBERT
*c.AD 635–c.AD 705*

A leading churchman in the Low Countries, where pagans predominated. As Bishop of Liège, he was forced into exile for a time and later died as a martyr in the city.
**Feast Day: 17 September**

## GILES
*died c.AD 710*

Born in Athens, he became a hermit near Nîmes, France. A strong cultus developed after his death, penitents believing his intercession would bring forgiveness.
**Feast Day: 7 September**

## ODILE
*AD 660–720*

Daughter of the Duke of Alsace, Odile was born blind, but her sight was restored at baptism. She became an abbess and founded a nunnery. Her relics were spread across Europe to give those with weak sight access to her power.
**Feast Day: 14 December**

## JOHN OF BEVERLEY
*died AD 721*

A monk in Whitby, then Bishop of Hexham and later of York, he showed patience and kindness to the mentally handicapped. A cultus grew quickly after his death.
**Feast Day: 7 May**

## FRIDESWIDE
*c.AD 680–727*

Fleeing from a seducer, this virgin sought refuge in Oxford, where she became abbess of a monastery. Her shrine in Christ Church, Oxford, still attracts pilgrims.
**Feast Day: 19 October**

## HUBERT
*died AD 727*

A missionary in the Ardennes, he became Bishop of Liège, where he built the cathedral. Many miracles were attributed to him.
**Feast Day: 30 May**

## WILLIBRORD
*AD 658–739*

A Yorkshireman sent by the pope to organize a diocese in Utrecht. He seemed successful in establishing the faith, despite persecution.
**Feast Day: 7 November**

## JOHN DAMASCENE
*c.AD 657–749*

A monk, then a priest, he spent his whole life under Muslim rule, first in Damascus, later at an abbey near Jerusalem. He was declared a Doctor of the Church in 1890.
**Feast Day: 4 December**

## PIRMIN
*died AD 753*

Probably a Spaniard who fled Moorish rulers. He went first to Switzerland, where he rebuilt a monastery at Dissentis and later, as abbot of Riechenau monastery, built up a library. Political unrest forced him to flee to Alsace, where he founded more monasteries.
**Feast Day: 3 November**

## ANDREW OF CRETE
*died AD 766*

Eighth-century Constantinople saw fierce arguments over icons, with Emperor Constantine V torturing and killing his opponents. Andrew (from Crete), who was visiting the city, criticized the emperor for his cruelty and was beaten, scourged, then stabbed to death in the streets.
**Feast Day: 20 October**

*Above* The Miracle of St Walburga *(Peter Paul Rubens, c.1610–11).*

## WALBURGA
*died AD 779*

English-born missionary who became abbess of the monastery in Heidenheim. After her death, it is said that her shrine exuded oil believed to cure ailments. But her name became associated with witchcraft: on Walpurgisnacht in Germany, people dress as spooks, bats and witches.
**Feast Day: 25 February**

## LIOBA
*died AD 782*

Educated in England, she went to Germany as a nun. As abbess of Tauberbischofsheim, she was known for being calm, cheerful and wise.
**Feast Day: 28 September**

## ANSKAR
*AD 801–65*

Born near Amiens, France, Anskar devoted his life to taking the Christian message to pagans from Denmark to Sweden. Christianity was established in Scandinavia 200 years after his death.
**Feast Day: 3 February**

## LUDMILLA
*died AD 921*
Martyr saint and grandmother of Prince (King) Wenceslas.
**Feast Day: 16 September**

## ADALBERT OF PRAGUE
*AD 956–97*
A pioneer in taking Christianity to north-eastern Europe. After being exiled twice, he became a missionary in Poland, Prussia and the Baltics, and was martyred near Königsberg. His relics lie in Prague.
**Feast Day: 23 April**

## ABBO OF FLEURY
*died 1004*
A Benedictine monk, scholar and martyr saint, he visited England, where he wrote a biography of St Edmund and reformed the monastic movement.
**Feast Day: 13 November**

## WILLIGIS
*died 1011*
Priest, politician and missionary in Germany and Scandinavia.
**Feast Day: 23 February**

## VLADIMIR
*AD 955–1015*
Forced to convert on marrying Princess Anne of Constantinople, he is venerated for introducing Christianity to Russia.
**Feast Day: 15 July**

## WILLIAM OF ROSKILDE
*died 1070*
Set up a mission in Denmark, where he became a preacher and Bishop of Roskilde, Zeeland.
**Feast Day: 2 September**

## DOMINIC OF SILOS
*c.1000–73*
A peasant from Navarre, Spain, whose piety, miracles, and liberation of captives taken by the Moors made him a much-loved priest.
**Feast Day: 20 December**

*Above* Vladimir the Saint
*(Ivan Yakovlevich Bilibin, 1925).*

## BERNARD OF MONTJOUX
*c.AD 996–c.1081*
As archdeacon of Aosta Cathedral in the Alps, he cleared mountain passes of robbers and established resthouses for travellers.
**Feast Day: 28 May**

## ROSALIA OF PALERMO
*12th century*
Born into a noble Sicilian family, she chose to live in a cave. Pilgrimages are still made to the church built over her hermitage.
**Feast Day: 4 September**

## BRUNO
*c.1032–1101*
His Carthusian Order set a benign but influential example of spirituality throughout Europe.
**Feast Day: 6 October**

## IVES
*died c.1107*
In 1100, in the village of Slepe, four bodies were found: someone dreamt their unusal insignia belonged to a Persian bishop (Ives), who had lived in England as a hermit. The bodies were translated to Ramsey Abbey, and miracles occurred.
**Feast Day: 24 April**

## ALBERIC
*died 1109*
Co-founder of Cistercian Order, which insisted on poverty and labour for God. By the time of his death, there were nearly 400 Cistercian houses in Europe.
**Feast Day: 26 January**

## ROBERT OF MOLESME
*1027–1110*
Spent most of his life as abbot at Molesme. Co-founder of the Cistercian Order at Citeaux, based on the rule of St Benedict, which grew into an influential worldwide organization.
**Feast Day: 29 April**

## LEOPOLD III
*1075–1136*
Reigned for 40 years as the third Duke of Austria. He reformed existing monasteries and founded new ones, strengthened Austria as a nation and promoted Christianity.
**Feast Day: 15 November**

## WILLIAM OF NORWICH
*died 1144*
When the 12-year-old's body was found in a wood near Norwich, his uncle claimed Jews had tortured and murdered him. A cultus developed, but papal letters directed Norwich to stop the ghastly story, and his shrine was abandoned.
**Feast Day: 26 March**

## MALACHY
*1094–1148*
Archbishop of Armagh who introduced the Cistercian Order into Ireland and was a pioneer in Ireland's early religious reform.
**Feast Day: 3 November**

## UBALDO
### died 1160

As dean (later bishop) of Gubbio Cathedral in Umbria, he persuaded clerics to live a communal life. Patron against rabies.
**Feast Day: 16 May**

## GODRIC
### c.1069–1170

He walked barefoot to Rome before becoming a hermit. His poems set to music are the earliest known in the English language.
**Feast Day: 21 May**

## GILBERT OF SEMPRINGHAM
### c.1083–1189

An English pastor who organized women, then men, into Benedictine communities, where they nursed orphans and lepers.
**Feast Day: 4 February**

## BARTHOLOMEW OF FARNE
### died 1193

A priest and monk until his vision of Christ, after which he went to Farne Island as a hermit. Miracles were attributed to him by visitors.
**Feast Day: 24 June**

## THORLAC OF SKALHOLT
### 1133–93

As bishop of Skalholt, Iceland, Thorlac reformed the priesthood and founded a community. His miracles are recorded, and a cultus flourished until the Reformation.
**Feast Day: 23 December**

## HOMOBONUS
### c.1120–97

Neither priest, king nor martyr, this "good man" of Cremona, Italy, was a tailor and merchant, who cared for the sick, fed the poor and buried the dead. Patron of tailors and clothworkers.
**Feast Day: 13 November**

## WILLIAM OF ROCHESTER
### died 1201

This Scottish fisherman vowed to visit Jerusalem, but was murdered by his travelling companion near Rochester. Miracles are said to have occurred at his burial site.
**Feast Day: 8 June**

## SAVA (SABAS) OF SERBIA
### c.1173–1236

Born a prince, he became a monk. He founded a monastery on Mount Athos, Greece.
**Feast Day: 14 January**

## RAYMUND NONNATUS
### 1204–40

Ordained priest who became a slave in Algiers, hoping to rescue others from this dreadful fate.
**Feast Day: 31 August**

## LUTGARDIS
### 1182–1246

Cistercian nun whose contemplative life caused many to turn to her for spiritual counselling.
**Feast Day: 16 June**

## FERDINAND III
### 1199–1252

Revered King of Castile and Leon who wrested Andalusia from the occupying Moors, bringing it into the Christian world.
**Feast Day: 30 May**

## ROSE OF VITERBO
### c.1235–52

The 12-year-old Rose, dressed as a Franciscan, preached in the streets and loudly supported the pope, despite hostile opposition.
**Feast Day: 4 September**

## ZITA
### 1218–72

A lifelong servant, venerated for her devotion and for her care of the poor and condemned convicts.
**Feast Day: 27 April**

## RAYMUND OF PENNAFORT
### c.1180–1275

He worked in Barcelona and Bologna before becoming confessor to Pope Gregory IX. He codified laws and wrote many texts. In his old age, he tried to convert the Moors who occupied Spain.
**Feast Day: 7 January**

## CELESTINE V
### 1210–96

A devout hermit, he founded the Celestine Order in 1274. He was appointed Pope Celestine V in 1294, but abdicated five months later, the only pope ever to do so.
**Feast Day: 19 May**

## LOUIS OF TOULOUSE
### 1274–97

Held for seven years as hostage after the King of Aragon captured his father, Charles II of Naples. Released in 1295 and ordained a Franciscan in 1297, he was immediately promoted to Bishop of Toulouse, but rejected the trappings of office, living in poverty.
**Feast Day: 19 August**

*Above* Louis of Toulouse *(panel, Simone Martini, 1317).*

## MARGARET OF CORTONA
### c.1247–97

Mistreated by her stepmother, she ran off with a knight and bore him a son. When her lover died, she was destitute and became a Franciscan tertiary, famous for public acts of penance. Miracles were attributed to her, and sinners sought her help.
**Feast Day: 22 February**

## ALEXIS FALCONIERI
### died 1310

Joined a community of hermits as a lay brother. The group (the Seven Founders) funded a mendicant order, the Servants of Mary (Servites). He also helped establish a Servite community in Siena.
**Feast Day: 7 February**

## PEREGRINE LAZIOSI
### died 1345

A Servite, recognized for his piety and dedication to the poor.
**Feast Day: 1 May**

## CATHERINE OF SWEDEN
### 1331–81

Daughter of Bridget of Sweden. After nursing her husband until his death, she joined her mother in the convent of Vadstena, later becoming abbess. She worked hard to obtain approval of the Brigittines (her mother's order), and for the latter's canonization.
**Feast Day: 24 March**

## SERGIUS OF RADONEZH
### 1315–92

From a noble family who fled the Tartars and settled in Radonezh, near Moscow. He and his brother restored the monastery there and Sergius became an important figure in religious and state life.
**Feast Day: 25 September**

*Right Gospel Folios of St Sergius of Radonezh (Russian School, 14th century).*

## HEDWIG
### 1374–99

Daughter of the King of Hungary and Poland, she was used as a political pawn, but eventually married Jagiello, Grand Duke of Lithuania and Ruthenia, and together they set about converting their subjects.
**Feast Day: 17 July**

## VINCENT FERRER
### 1350–1419

Dynamic preacher who converted Jews and Muslims in his native Spain and gained a reputation for miracle cures.
**Feast Day: 5 April**

## FRANCES OF ROME
### 1384–1440

A powerful, religious presence in Rome, she experienced visions and cared for plague victims and war-wounded. Other women joined her and she founded the Oblates of Tor de' Specchi, which still exists.
**Feast Day: 9 March**

## BERNARDINO OF SIENA
### 1380–1444

After nursing plague victims, he became a Franciscan evangelist, attacking greed and the warmongering of Italy's city-states.
**Feast Day: 20 May**

## COLETTE
### 1381–1447

The antipope Bernard XIII made her a Poor Clare in charge of France's Franciscan nuns. She founded 17 new convents.
**Feast Day: 6 March**

## JOHN OF CAPISTRANO
### 1386–1456

A married man and governor of Perugio, he became a Franciscan. A fierce believer, keen to reform, he was appointed inquisitor-general to Vienna in 1451.
**Feast Day: 23 October**

## ANTONINUS OF FLORENCE
### 1389–1459

Dominican friar who founded the convent at San Marco. As archbishop of Florence, he lived in poverty, nursed plague victims and fed the hungry. He wrote important texts and advised papal reforms.
**Feast Day: 10 May**

## CATHERINE DE'VIGRI OF BOLOGNA
### 1413–63

Well-born and highly educated, she refused marriage and joined the Augustinian tertiaries.
**Feast Day: 9 March**

*Above* Stanislaus Kostka
*(artist unknown, 17th century).*

## JOHN OF SAHAGUN
### c.1430–79
He reconciled fighting factions in Salamanca, a town riven by feuds. In 1463, he joined the Austin Friars. Miracles followed his death.
**Feast Day: 12 June**

## CATHERINE OF GENOA
### 1447–1510
After she helped win her husband back to faith, they ran a hospital together in Pammatone. In later life, she wrote about spirituality and experienced visions.
**Feast Day: 15 September**

## JEROME EMILIANI
### 1481–1537
A priest, Jerome founded a small community (the Somaschi), where he built hospitals, orphanages and homes for reformed prostitutes.
**Feast Day: 8 February**

## JUAN DIEGO
### died 1548
Born near Mexico City, he was baptized at age 50. Allegedly received an image of the Blessed Virgin miraculously printed on his cloak, signifying Jesus' rebirth.
**Feast Day: 12 December**

## STANISLAUS KOSTKA
### 1550–68
Refused by local Jesuits, he walked more than 300 miles to Rome. A devout young man who experienced mystical visions.
**Feast Day: 13 November**

## PHILIP OF MOSCOW
### 1507–69
As metropolitan of the Russian Church, he upbraided Ivan the Terrible for his bloodshed and cruelty. He was arrested, held in chains, and eventually martyred.
**Feast Day: 9 January**

## EDMUND CAMPION
### 1540–81
An Anglican, scholar and founder of Trinity College in Ireland, he became a Jesuit in Rome. Arrested and executed on a false conspiracy charge, he is one of the Forty Martyrs of England and Wales.
**Feast Day: 25 October**

## ALEXANDER BRIANT
### c.1556–81
When Catholicism was banned in England, he refused to reveal the hiding place of a family he had persuaded to convert. For this he was cruelly tortured, then executed. He is one of the Forty Martyrs of England and Wales.
**Feast Day: 25 October**

## CHARLES BORROMEO
### 1538–84
Archbishop of Milan and favoured nephew of Pope Pius IV. He instituted Sunday schools and opened seminaries to train priests.
**Feast Day: 4 November**

## MARGARET CLITHEROW
### 1556–86
With her Protestant husband, she hid Catholic priests during a time of persecution. One of the Forty Martyrs of England and Wales.
**Feast Day: 25 October**

*Above* St Charles Borromeo *Fasting (19th-century copy, after Daniele Crespi from 1620).*

## CATHERINE DE'RICCI
### 1522–90
Became a Dominican nun in 1535, later promoted to prioress.
**Feast Day: 2 February**

## ALOYSIUS GONZAGA
### 1568–91
Despite his family's military ambitions for him, he became a Jesuit.
**Feast Day: 21 June**

*Above* St Aloysius Gonzaga in Glory *(Giovanni Battista Tiepolo, c.1726).*

*Above Philip Howard imprisoned in the Tower of London (Henry Barraud, 19th century).*

## PHILIP HOWARD
### 1557–95
Converted to Catholicism from Anglicanism. He would not deny his faith and spent the rest of his life in the Tower. One of the Forty Martyrs of England and Wales.
**Feast Day: 19 October**

## MARY MAGDALENE DE' PAZZI
### 1566–1607
She entered the Carmelite convent in Florence at the age of 17. Her writings reveal a love of the local landscape, as well as her devotion to God.
**Feast Day: 25 May**

## ANDREW AVELLINO
### 1521–1608
After failing in a mission to reform a riotous house of nuns, he joined the Theatines, a new order, revealing his talent as a preacher and sensitivity toward confessors.
**Feast Day: 10 November**

## CAMILLUS OF LELLIS
### 1550–1614
Founded the Servants of the Sick for priests and laymen, opened hospitals around Italy and was the first to send ambulances to a battlefront.
**Feast Day: 14 July**

## JOHN BERCHMANS
### 1599–1621
His youthful piety and theological understanding encouraged a cultus.
**Feast Day: 13 August**

## JOSAPHAT
### 1580–1623
Archbishop of Polotsk in Belarus, and martyr saint. A brisk reformer who sought unity with Rome.
**Feast Day: 12 November**

## JOHN FRANCIS REGIS
### 1597–1640
Jesuit priest who worked exhaustively, preaching, serving the poor and nursing plague victims.
**Feast Day: 2 July**

## JANE FRANCES DE CHANTAL
### 1572–1641
Founded the Visitation Order. By the time she died, 86 convents had been established in Europe.
**Feast Day: 12 December**

## JOSEPH CALASANZ
### 1550–1648
He gave up his office of vicar-general of Andorra to teach slum children in Rome. After his death, his congregation was revived as the Piarists.
**Feast Day: 25 August**

## ANDREW BOBOLA
### 1591–1657
Polish nobleman who devoted his life to God, cared for the suffering and died for his faith.
**Feast Day: 21 May**

## JOHN KEMBLE
### 1599–1679
Jesuit priest and one of the Forty Martyrs of England and Wales.
**Feast Day: 25 October**

## OLIVER PLUNKET
### 1625–81
Jesuit archbishop of Armagh. His charm won the grudging admiration of Irish Protestants, but English overlords dragged him to Newgate, London, tried him for high treason, and executed him.
**Feast Day: 1 July**

## CLAUDE DE LA COLOMBIÈRE
### 1641–82
French Jesuit imprisoned in England as a Catholic. He was saved by Louis XIV of France, but he died soon after.
**Feast Day: 15 February**

## MARGARET MARY ALACOQUE
### 1647–90
Entered the Visitation convent at Paray-le-Monial, where she revived the medieval cult of devotion to the Sacred Heart of Jesus.
**Feast Day: 17 October**

## GREGORIO BARBARIGO
### 1625–97
Priest who founded a seminary, set up printing presses and tried to reconcile Eastern Orthodox and Roman Catholic Churches.
**Feast Day: 18 June**

## JOSEPH ORIOL
### 1650–1702
A popular ascetic priest. It is said he saw the Virgin as he lay dying.
**Feast Day: 23 March**

## JOSEPH TOMASI
### 1649–1713
Much-loved scholar and teacher, known as "the prince of liturgists".
**Feast Day: 1 January**

## FRANCIS DE GIROLAMO
### 1642–1716
A Jesuit who preached in the docks and slums of Naples.
**Feast Day: 11 May**

## JOHN BAPTIST ROSSI
*1698–1764*
Preached to and cared for beggars, prisoners and prostitutes in Rome.
**Feast Day: 23 May**

## JULIE BILLIART
*1751–1816*
Co-founder of the Institute of the Sisters of Notre Dame, dedicated to teaching children.
**Feast Day: 8 April**

## VINCENT STRAMBI
*1745–1824*
Bishop who improved education of priests. Exiled for refusing to take an oath of allegiance to Napoleon.
**Feast Day: 25 September**

## MARCELLIN CHAMPAGNAT
*died 1840*
Born a peasant, he was known for his zeal for education and schools.
**Feast Day: 6 June**

*Above Many missionaries, including Theophane Vénard, were martyred in Vietnam in the 19th century (Indo-Chinese School, 1838).*

## PETER CHANEL
*1803–41*
An early member of the Society of Mary, he was sent as a missionary to the French territory of Futuna, where he was martyred.
**Feast Day: 28 April**

## VINCENT PALLOTTI
*1795–1850*
Founded the Society of Catholic Apostolate and later the Pallotine Missionary Sisters, which encouraged membership of lay men and women. His mission is now found throughout the Catholic world.
**Feast Day: 22 January**

## PHILIPPINE DUCHESNE
*1769–1852*
Born in Grenoble, she established schools for Native American children in Louisiana and Missouri.
**Feast Day: 17 November**

## JOSEPH CAFASSO
*1811–60*
Ministered to young priests, prisoners and condemned men, and established an institute for boys.
**Feast Day: 23 June**

## JOHN NEUMANN
*1811–60*
Bishop of Philadelphia. Supervised the building of 100 churches and 80 schools and wrote several texts.
**Feast Day: 5 January**

## THEOPHANE VÉNARD
*1829–61*
One of the named Martyrs of Vietnam, he was held in a bamboo cage before being beheaded.
**Feast Day: 2 February**

## MARY ROSE MOLAS Y VALLVE
*1815–76*
Founded the Sisters of Our Lady of Consolation to serve the needs of deprived children.
**Feast Day: 11 June**

*Above A woman prays in the Maronite church of St Sharbel in Lebanon.*

## TERESA OF JESUS JORNET Y IBARS
*1843–97*
Founded the Little Sisters of the Poor in 1872. She showed particular sympathy for the elderly.
**Feast Day: 26 August**

## SHARBEL THE MARONITE
*1828–98*
A Lebanese, he joined Our Lady of Mayfug monastery before becoming a hermit. Miracles occurred after his death.
**Feast Day: 24 December**

## MARIA GORETTI
*1890–1902*
A youth tried to rape the 12-year-old Maria. When she fought back, he stabbed her. She died the next day, having forgiven her attacker.
**Feast Day: 6 July**

## LEOPOLD MANDIC
*1866–1942*
Born in Croatia, he was ordained a Capuchin Franciscan and ministered in Padua for 40 years. He showed great compassion as a spiritual adviser and confessor.
**Feast Day: 12 May**

# GLOSSARY

**ABSOLUTION** The power of forgiveness that can be exercised by a priest during the sacrament of penance (confession).

**ANATHEMA** From the Greek word originally meaning an offering to a god, but subsequently coming to mean despised, hated and accursed; excommunicated from or condemned by the Church.

**ANNUNCIATION** A festival celebrated on 25 March to commemorate the announcement by the archangel Gabriel to Mary of Jesus' coming birth.

**ANTICHRIST** From the New Testament, the ultimate enemy of Christ who will oppose Christ's teachings and substitute himself for Christ.

**APOSTASY** A total rejection of the Christian faith by a baptized person.

**APOSTLE** A messenger with the purpose of spreading the Christian message; specifically, the name given by Jesus to 12 of his faithful followers, who were given the task to spread the Word by preaching the gospels.

*Above Pope John Paul II moved a step closer to sainthood when he was beatified after a dossier was presented to the Vatican.*

**APOSTLES' CREED** A 1st-century AD formula of Church teachings established by the first pope, St Peter.

**APOSTOLIC FATHERS** Writers of the Christian faith in the 1st and 2nd centuries AD, thought to have known or been personally influenced by the apostles and their writings.

**ASCENSION** The elevation of Christ to heaven on the 40th day after his Resurrection, celebrated as a feast day that falls 40 days after Easter.

**ASSUMPTION OF MARY** The entrance of the body and soul of Mary to heaven after her death, commemorated on 15 August.

**ATHANASIAN CREED** A formula of Catholic faith, probably drawn up in the 4th or 5th century AD in response to various heretical theories on the nature of Christ.

**BAPTISM** A sacramental rite involving water that cleanses a person of sin; in Catholic doctrine, due to original sin, baptism is a necessary requirement to gain entry into heaven.

**BEATITUDES** The blessings due to followers of Christianity listed by Jesus at the beginning of the Sermon on the Mount, recorded in Matthew (5:3–12) and Luke (23:42).

**BEATIFICATION** A papal declaration of a deceased person as officially "blessed", a stage in the process of canonization.

**CANONIZATION** The process by which a deceased person who has previously been beatified is formally declared a saint.

**CATECHISM** An exposition of the doctrines of Catholicism taught in a catechistic, or question and answer, form.

**COMMUNION** The act of celebrating the Eucharist (thanksgiving) through partaking of bread and wine

*Above St Matthew the Evangelist, shown in this 12th-century Byzantine evangelistary, was one of the four apostles responsible for the gospels.*

that Catholicism states are the true body and blood of Jesus Christ.

**CONFESSION** The sacrament of penance, or admission of sins committed after baptism, to a priest in order to obtain forgiveness.

**COUNTER-REFORMATION** A period of Catholic revival from *c.*1522 to 1648, during which time attempts were made to stem the rise of Protestantism through reforms in the Catholic Church.

**CULT OR CULTUS** A system of beliefs and religious observances surrounding a particular saint.

**DEUTEROCANONICALS** Also known as the Apocrypha, certain Old Testament books and passages that are present in the Catholic Bible but that are not part of the Jewish or Protestant canon.

**DOCTRINE** An authoritative set of beliefs taught by the Church.

**DOGMA** Church doctrine that has been revealed by God and therefore is deemed to be indisputable, belief in which is said by the Catholic Church to be necessary for salvation.

EVANGELIST Someone who aims to convert others to their cause; specifically the authors of the four Gospels, Sts Matthew, Mark, Luke and John.

EXCOMMUNICATION The suspension of a person from the possibility of redemption by revoking their membership of the Church community.

FEAST DAY A fixed or movable holy festival designated for giving special honour to God, members of the Holy Family or saints, often commemorating specific events.

HERESY A belief or set of beliefs at variance with the official or orthodox doctrine of the Church.

INCARNATION The union of the divine and human natures of the Son of God in the person of Jesus Christ.

INDULGENCES The remittance of temporal punishments given to a sinner after the sin has been confessed and absolved, dispensed by the Church.

JUDGEMENT DAY The time at which a final judgement and trial of all mankind will take place after Armageddon, where each person will be rewarded or punished according to his or her merits.

LAST SUPPER The last meal eaten by Jesus before his Crucifixion, where he asked that bread and wine be shared by those at the meal in memory of him, and when he gave his final instructions to his followers.

LIMBO The destination of righteous but unbaptized souls, such as infants who die without baptism or those who died before Christ.

MAGISTERIUM The teaching office or authority of the Catholic Church embodied in the pope and bishops, who are the representatives of the Church.

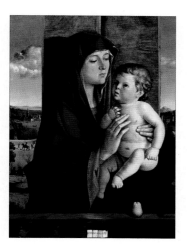

*Above* Some feast days honour the Madonna and child, shown in this 15th-century painting by Giovanni Bellini.

MASS The church service during which Eucharist is celebrated, which is the central act of worship in Catholic liturgy.

MORTAL SIN A deadly sin that revolts against God and deprives the sinner of their right to enter heaven.

NICENE CREED A formulation of Catholic doctrine first released in AD 325 and revised in AD 381, which outlines the nature of Christ in response to the Arian heresy.

ORIGINAL SIN The state of sin that all of humankind are born into as a result of the fall from grace of Adam and Eve, and which is cleansed through baptism.

PURGATORY The temporary destination for those who have died in a state of grace, where they can atone for their sins before they can enter heaven.

REDEMPTION The salvation of humanity through Jesus Christ, who gave his life in return for the expiation of humanity's debt of sin.

REFORMATION A period of religious, social and political unrest from 1517 to 1648, which resulted in the formation of Protestantism.

RESURRECTION The miracle of Christ's return to life three days after his death and burial, followed by his Ascension to heaven.

REVELATION The disclosure by God of himself and his plan to humanity, for example, through private revelation in the form of visions of the Virgin Mary.

SACRAMENT A formal religious ceremony, during which a specific grace is conferred upon those who receive it, such as Communion and confession.

TRANSUBSTANTIATION The process by which Catholics believe that bread and wine become the body and blood of Christ during the celebration of the Eucharist.

TRINITY, THE HOLY The name used to represent the three distinct persons present in the Christian God: the Father, the Son and the Holy Spirit.

VENIAL SIN A pardonable sin that offends against God but does not on its own deprive the sinner of his or her right to enter heaven.

*Above* Limbo is shown in this 14th-century panel from an altarpiece in Santo Sepulchro, a convent in Zaragoza.

# INDEX

*Above* A vintage engraving depicts the ecclesiastical order of the Catholic Church in the 14th century. The Pope is shown at the centre, flanked by cardinals, bishops, priests and laypersons.

***Above** A statue of St Peter holding a key to the gates of Heaven, St Peter's Square, Vatican City.*

*Above Fresco from the San Miniato al Monte (St Minias on the Mountain) Basilica in Florence, Italy, depicting St Mark's famous emblem, the winged lion.*

*Above* Prayer candles are lit and placed before a statue of Jesus or the Blessed Virgin
Mary; they can be long and tapering or tealight candles.

***Above*** *The rite of baptism involves friends or relatives of the child's parents as 'godparents'.*

***Above*** *A stained glass window depicting the sacred heart of Jesus, at St Joseph's Catholic Church in Macon, Georgia, USA.*

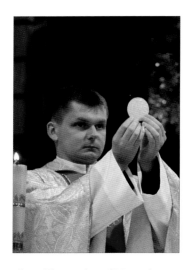

*Above* The central act of Mass is the priest's consecration of wheaten bread and grape wine into Christ.

*Above St Peter's Basilica facade is topped by 13 statues that represent Thaddeus, Matthew, Philip, Thomas, James the Great, John the Baptist, Christ the Redeemer (in the centre), Andrew, John the Evangelist, James the Less, Bartholomew, Simon and Matthias.*

*Above* Many priests still wear a black cassock for daily duties, but some wear a suit with a shirt and a clerical collar.